# How to Design Programs

# How to Design Programs

An Introduction to Programming and Computing

Matthias Felleisen
Robert Bruce Findler
Matthew Flatt
Shriram Krishnamurthi

The MIT Press
Cambridge, Massachusetts
London, England

Library of Congress Cataloging-in-Publication Data

How to design programs: an introduction to programming and
   computing / Matthias Felleisen, Robert Bruce Findler, Matthew Flatt,
   Shriram Krishnamurthi; chapter art by Torrey Butzer
   p.  cm.
Includes index.
ISBN-13: 978-0-262-06218-3 (hc. : alk. paper)
ISBN-10: 0-262-06218-6 (hc. : alk. paper)
1. Computer Programming.   2. Electronic data processing.

QA76.6  .H697  2001
005.1'2—dc21

00-048169

10  9  8

# Contents

# List of Figures

# Preface

*It goes against the grain of modern education to teach children to program. What fun is there in making plans, acquiring discipline in organizing thoughts, devoting attention to detail and learning to be self-critical?*

—Alan Perlis, *Epigrams in Programming*

Many professions require some form of computer programming. Accountants program spreadsheets and word processors; photographers program photo editors; musicians program synthesizers; and professional programmers instruct plain computers. Programming has become a required skill.

Yet programming is more than just a vocational skill. Indeed, *good programming* is a fun activity, a creative outlet, and a way to express abstract ideas in a tangible form. And designing programs teaches a variety of skills that are important in all kinds of professions: critical reading, analytical thinking, creative synthesis, and attention to detail.

We therefore believe that the study of program design deserves the same central role in general education as mathematics and English. Or, put more succinctly,

**everyone should learn how to design programs.**

On one hand, program design teaches the same analytical skills as mathematics. But, unlike mathematics, working with programs is an active approach to learning. Interacting with software provides immediate feedback and thus leads to exploration, experimentation, and self-evaluation. Furthermore, designing programs produces useful and fun things, which vastly increases the sense of accomplishment when compared to drill exercises in mathematics. On the other hand, program design teaches the same analytical reading and writing skills as English. Even the smallest programming tasks are formulated as word problems. Without critical reading skills, a student cannot design programs that match the specification. Conversely, good program design methods force a student to articulate thoughts about programs in proper English.

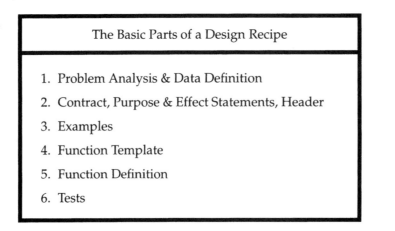

Figure 1: The basic steps of a program design recipe

This book is the first book on programming as the core subject of a liberal arts education. Its main focus is *the design process* that leads from problem statements to well-organized solutions; it deemphasizes the study of programming language details, algorithmic minutiae, and specific application domains. Our desire to focus on the design process requires two radical innovations for introductory courses. The first innovation is a set of *explicit design guidelines*. Existing curricula tend to provide vague and ill-defined suggestions, such as "design from top to bottom" or "make the program structural." We have instead developed design guidelines that lead students from a problem statement to a computational solution in step-by-step fashion with well-defined intermediate products. In the process they learn to read, to analyze, to organize, to experiment, to think in a systematic manner. The second innovation is a radically new programming environment. In the past, texts on programming ignored the role of the programming environment in the learning process; they simply assumed that students had access to a professional environment. This book provides a *programming environment for beginners*. It also grows with the students as they master more and more of the material until it supports a full-fledged language for the whole spectrum of programming tasks: large-scale programming as well as scripting.

Our guidelines are formulated as a number of *program design recipes*.[1] A design recipe guides a beginning programmer through the entire problem-solving process. With design recipes, a beginner almost never again stares at a blank piece of paper or a blank computer screen. Instead, the student will check the design recipe and use the question-and-answer guidelines to make some progress.

We created the design recipes by identifying categories of problems. The identification of a problem category is based on the classes of data that are used to represent the relevant information. Starting from the structure of this class description students derive the programs with a checklist. Figure 1 shows the basic six steps of a design recipe checklist. Each step produces a well-defined intermediate product:

1. the description of the class of problem data;

2. the informal specification of a program's behavior;

3. the illustration of the behavior with examples;

4. the development of a program template or layout;

5. the transformation of the template into a complete definition; and

6. the discovery of errors through testing.

The major difference concerns the relationship of steps 1 and 4.

Design recipes help beginners and teachers alike. Teachers can use the recipes to inspect a beginner's problem-solving skills, to diagnose weaknesses, and to suggest specific remedial steps. After all, each stage of the design recipe yields a well-defined, checkable product. If a beginner is stuck, a teacher can inspect the intermediate products and determine what the problem is. Based on this analysis, the teacher can then provide guidance for a specific step in the recipe, raise appropriate questions, and recommend additional practice exercises.

---

[1] Readers whose experience is exclusively based on programming languages such as C/C++, Basic, and Pascal should read "procedure" or "method" where the preface mentions "program."

## Why Everyone Should Learn to Program

*And as imagination bodies forth
The forms of things to unknown, and the poet's pen
Turns them to shapes, and gives to airy nothing
A local habitation and a name.*

—Shakespeare, *A Midsummer Night's Dream* V(i)

Our claim that everyone programs or should learn to program might appear strange considering that, at first glance, fewer and fewer people seem to program these days. Instead, the majority of people use application packages, which don't seem to require any programming. Even programmers use "program generators," packages that create programs from, say, business rules. So why should anyone learn to program?

The answer consists of two parts. First, it is indeed true that *traditional forms of programming* are useful for just a few people. But, programming *as we the authors understand it* is useful for everyone: the administrative secretary who uses spreadsheets as well as the high-tech programmer. In other words, we have a broader notion of programming in mind than the traditional one. We explain our notion in a moment. Second, we teach our idea of programming with a technology that is based on the principle of minimal intrusion. Hence our notion of programming teaches problem-analysis and problem-solving skills *without* imposing the overhead of traditional programming notations and tools.

To get a better understanding of modern programming, take a closer look at spreadsheets, one of today's popular application packages. A user enters formulas into a spreadsheet. The formulas describe how a cell $A$ depends on another cell $B$. Then, as the user enters a number into $B$, the spreadsheet automatically calculates the contents of cell $A$. For complicated spreadsheets, a cell may depend on many other cells, not just one.

Other application packages require similar activities. Consider word processors and style sheets. A style sheet specifies how to create a (part of a) document from yet-to-be-determined words or sentences. When someone provides specific words and a style sheet, the word processor creates the document by replacing names in the style sheet with specific words. Similarly, someone who conducts a Web search may wish to specify what words to look for, what words should be next to each other, and what words should not occur in the page. In this case, the output depends on the search engine's cache of Web pages and the user's search expression.

Finally, using a program generator in many ways relies on the same skills as those necessary for application packages. A program generator creates a program in a traditional programming language, such as C++ or Java, from high-level descriptions, such as business rules or scientific laws. Such rules typically relate quantities, sales, and inventory records and thus specify computations. The other parts of the program, especially how it interacts with a user and how it stores data in the computer's disk, are generated with little or no human intervention.

All of these activities instruct some computer software to do something for us. Some use scientific notation, some may use stylized English, some use a concrete programming notation. All of them are some form of programming. The essence of these activities boils down to two concepts:

1. relating one quantity to another quantity, and

2. evaluating a relationship by substituting values for names.

Indeed, the two concepts characterize programming at the lowest level, the computer's native language, and in a modern fashionable language such as Java. A program relates its inputs to outputs; and, when a program is used for specific inputs, the evaluation substitutes concrete values for names.

No one can predict what kind of application packages will exist five or ten years from now. But application packages will continue to require some form of programming. To prepare students for these kinds of programming activities, schools can either force them to study algebra, which is the mathematical foundation of programming, or expose them to some form of programming. Using modern programming languages and environments, schools can do the latter, they can do it effectively, and they can make algebra fun.

## Design Recipes

> *Cooking is at once child's play and adult joy. And cooking done with care is an act of love.*
>
> —Craig Claiborne (1920–2000), Food Editor, *New York Times*

Learning to design programs is like learning to play soccer. A player must learn to trap a ball, to dribble with a ball, to pass, and to shoot a ball. Once the player knows those basic skills, the next goals are to learn to play a position, to play certain strategies, to choose among feasible strategies, and, on occasion, to create variations of a strategy because none of the existing strategies fits.

A programmer is also very much like an architect, a composer, or a writer. They are creative people who start with ideas in their heads and blank pieces of paper. They conceive of an idea, form a mental outline, and refine it on paper until their writings reflect their mental image as much as possible. As they bring their ideas to paper, they employ basic drawing, writing, and instrumental skills to express certain style elements of a building, to describe a person's character, or to formulate portions of a melody. They can practice their trade because they have honed their basic skills for a long time and can use them on an instinctive level.

Programmers also form outlines, translate them into first designs, and iteratively refine them until they truly match the initial idea. Indeed, the best programmers edit and rewrite their programs many times until they meet certain aesthetic standards. And just like soccer players, architects, composers, or writers, programmers must practice the basic skills of their trade for a long time before they can be truly creative.

Design recipes are the equivalent of soccer ball handling techniques, writing techniques, techniques of arrangements, and drawing skills. A single design recipe represents a point of the program design space. We have studied this space and have identified many important categories. This book selects the most fundamental and the most practical recipes and presents them in increasing order of difficulty.[2]

About half the design recipes focus on the connection between input data and programs. More specifically, they show how the template of a program is derived from the description of the input data. We call this *data-driven* program design, and it is the most frequently used form of design. Data-driven designs are easy to create, easy to understand, and easy to extend and modify. Other design recipes introduce the notion of *generative recursion, accumulation,* and *history sensitivity*. The first one produces recursive programs that generate new instances of problems as they recur; accumulator-style programs collect data as they process inputs; and history-sensitive programs remember information between successive applications. Last, but not least, we also introduce a design recipe for *abstracting* over programs. Abstracting is the act of generalizing two (or more) similar designs into one and of deriving the original instances from it.

---

[2]Our design recipes were inspired by work with Daniel P. Friedman on structural recursion, with Robert Harper on type theory, and by Michael A. Jackson's design method.

On many occasions, a problem naturally suggests one design recipe. On others, a programmer must choose from among several possibilities; each choice may produce programs with vastly different organizations. Making choices is natural for a creative programmer. But, unless a programmer is thoroughly familiar with the bag of design recipes to choose from and completely understands the consequences of choosing one over the other, the process is necessarily *ad hoc* and leads to whimsical, bad designs. We hope that by mapping out a collection of design recipes, we can help programmers understand what to choose from and how to choose.

Now that we have explained what we mean by "programming" and "program design," the reader can see why and how teaching program design instills thinking skills that are important in a variety of professions. To design a program properly, a student must:

1. analyze a problem statement, typically stated as a word problem;

2. express its essence, abstractly and with examples;

3. formulate statements and comments in a precise language;

4. evaluate and revise these activities in light of checks and tests; and

5. pay attention to details.

All of these are activities that are useful for a businessman, a lawyer, a journalist, a scientist, an engineer, and many others.

While traditional programming requires these skills, too, beginners often don't understand this connection. The problem is that traditional programming languages and traditional forms of programming force students to perform a large amount of book-keeping work and to memorize a large number of language-specific facts. In short, *menial work drowns the teaching of essential skills.* To avoid this problem, teachers must use a programming environment that imposes as little overhead as possible and that accommodates beginners. Because such tools didn't exist when we started, we developed them.

## The Choice of Scheme and DrScheme

*We ascribe beauty to that which is simple,*
*which has no superfluous parts;*
*which exactly answers its end,*
*which stands related to all things,*
*which is the mean of many extremes.*

—Ralph Waldo Emerson, *The Conduct of Life*

We have chosen Scheme as the programming language for this book, and we have designed and implemented DrScheme, a programming environment for the language with special assistance for beginning students. The programming environment is freely available at the book's official Web site.[3]

Still, the book it is not about programming in Scheme. We only use a small number of Scheme constructs in this book. Specifically, we use six constructs (function definition and application, conditional expressions, structure definition, local definitions, and assignments) plus a dozen or so basic functions. This tiny subset of the language is all that is needed to teach the principles of computing and programming. Someone who wishes to use Scheme as a tool will need to read additional material.

The choice of Scheme for beginners is natural. First, the core of Scheme permits programmers to focus on just those two elements of programming that we pointed out at the beginning of the preface: programs as relations between quantities and evaluating programs for specific inputs. Using just this core language, students can develop complete programs *during the first session* with a teacher.

Second, Scheme can easily be arranged as a tower of language levels. This property is crucial for beginners who make simple notational mistakes that generate obscure error messages about advanced features of a language. The result is often a wasteful search and a feeling of frustration on the student's part. To avoid this problem, our programming environment, DrScheme, implements several carefully chosen sublanguages of Scheme. Based on this arrangement, the environment can signal error messages that

---

[3]Scheme has an official definition—the Revised Report on Scheme, edited by Richard Kelsey, William Clinger, and Jonathan Rees—and many implementations. For a copy of the report and for a list of alternative Scheme implementations, visit www.schemers.org on the Web. Note, however, that the language of this book extends that of the report and is tailored to beginners.

are appropriate to a student's level of knowledge. Better still, the layering of languages prevents many basic mistakes. We developed the layers and the protection modes by observing beginners for weeks in Rice's computer lab. As students learn more about programming and the language, the teacher can expose students to richer layers of the language, which allows students to write more interesting and more concise programs.

Third, the DrScheme programming environment offers a truly interactive evaluator. It consists of two windows: a `Definitions` window, where students define programs, and an `Interactions` window, which acts like a pocket calculator. Students can enter expressions into the latter, and DrScheme determines their values. In other words, computation starts with pocket-calculator arithmetic, which they know quite well, and quickly proceeds from there to calculations with structures, lists, and trees—the kinds of data that computer programs really manipulate. Furthermore, an interactive mode of evaluation encourages students to experiment in all kinds of ways and thus stimulates their curiosity.

Finally, the use of an interactive evaluator with a rich data language permits students to focus on problem solving and program design activities. The key improvement is that interactive evaluation renders a discussion of input and output operations (almost) superfluous. This has several consequences. First, input and output operations require memorization. Learning these things is tedious and boring. Conversely, students are better off learning problem-solving skills and using canned input and output support. Second, *good* text-oriented input requires deep programming skills, which are best acquired in a course on computational problem-solving. Teaching bad text-oriented input is a waste of the teachers' and the students' time. Third, modern software employs graphical user interfaces (GUI), which programmers design with editors and "wizards" but not by hand. Again, students are best off learning to design the functions that are connected to rulers, buttons, text fields and so on, rather than memorizing the specific protocols that currently fashionable GUI libraries impose. In short, discussing input and output is a waste of valuable learning time during a first introduction to programming. If students decide to pursue programming in more depth, acquiring the necessary (Scheme) knowledge about input and output procedures is straightforward.

In summary, students can learn the core of Scheme in a couple of hours, yet the language is as powerful as a conventional programming language. As a result, students can focus immediately on the essence of programming, which greatly enhances their general problem-solving skills.

## The Parts of the Book

The book consists of eight parts and seven intermezzos. The parts focus on program design; the intermezzos introduce other topics concerning programming and computing. Figure 2 shows the dependence graph for the pieces of the book. The graph demonstrates that there are several paths through the book and that a partial coverage of the material is feasible.

Parts I through III cover the foundations of data-driven program design. Part IV introduces abstraction in designs. Parts V and VI are about generative recursion and accumulation. For these first six parts, the book uses a completely functional—or algebraic—form of programming. One and the same expression always evaluates to the same result, no matter how often we evaluate it. This property makes it easy to design, and to reason about, programs. To cope with interfaces between programs and the rest of the world, however, we enrich the language with assignment statements and abandon some of our algebraic reasoning. The last two parts show what this means for the design of programs. More precisely, they show how the design recipes of the first six parts apply and why we must be much more careful once assignments are added.

Intermezzos introduce topics that are important for computing and programming in general but not for program design per se. Some introduce the syntax and semantics of our chosen subsets of Scheme on a rigorous basis, a few introduce additional programming constructs. Intermezzo 5 is a discussion of the abstract cost of computing (time, space, energy) and introduces vectors. Intermezzo 6 contrasts two ways of representing numbers and processing them.

The coverage of some intermezzos can be delayed until a specific need arises. This is especially true of the intermezzos on Scheme's syntax and semantics. But, considering the central role of intermezzo 3 in figure 2, it should be covered in a timely fashion.

ITERATIVE REFINEMENT AND ITERATION OF TOPICS: Systematic program design is particularly interesting and important for large projects. The step from small single-function problems to small multifunction projects requires an additional design idea: iterative refinement. The goal is to design the core of a program and to add functionality to this core until the entire set of requirements is met.

Students in a first course can, and must, get their first taste of iterative refinement. Hence, in order to acquaint students with the technique, we

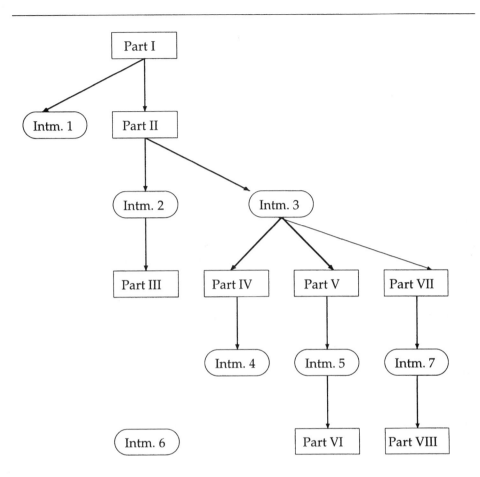

Figure 2: The dependencies among parts and intermezzos

have included extended exercises. Typically, a brief overview sets the stage for a collection of exercises. The exercises gently guide students through some design iterations. In section 16, the idea is spelled out explicitly.

Furthermore, the book revisits certain exercise and example topics time and again. For example, sections 6.6, 7.4, 10.3, 21.4, 41.4, and a few exercises in between the last two sections cover the idea of moving pictures across a canvas. The students thus see the same problem several times, each time with more and more knowledge about how to organize programs.

Adding pieces of functionality to a program demonstrates why programmers must follow a design discipline. Solving the problem again shows students how to choose from alternative design recipes. Finally, on occasion, new knowledge just helps students improve the program organization; in other words, students learn that programs aren't finished after they work for the first time but that, like papers and books, they need editing.

TEACHPACKS: A second aspect of working on projects is that programmers have to work in teams. In an instructional context, this means that one student's program has to fit precisely to someone else's. To simulate what "fitting one's function to someone else's" means, we provide DrScheme teachpacks. Roughly speaking, a teachpack simulates a team partner yet avoids the frustration of working with mistakes in a partner's program component. More technically, the projects almost always consist of a view and a model program component (in the sense of the model-view software architecture). In a typical setting, students design the model component. The teachpacks provide the view components, often in the form of (graphical) user interfaces. Thus they eliminate the tedious, mindless portions of coding. Furthermore, this particular separation of concerns mimics that of real-world projects.

Fitting model components to view components requires students to pay attention to precise specifications of functions. It demonstrates the paramount importance of following a design discipline. It is also a critical skill for programmers and is often underemphasized in beginning courses. In part IV we show how to construct some simple GUIs and how GUI events trigger the application of model functions. The goal is to explain that constructing GUIs is no mystery, but not to spend a lot of time on a topic that requires mostly rote learning and little computational thinking.

SCHEDULE: Each university, college, and school has its own needs and must find an appropriate schedule. At Rice University, we conventionally cover the entire book plus some additional material in a single semester. An instructor at a research university should probably keep up a similar pace. A high school teacher will necessarily pursue a slower pace. Many of the high schools that tested the book covered the first three parts in a semester; some used only the first part to teach algebraic problem solving from a computational perspective; and yet others worked through the entire book in a year. For more information on schedules, visit the book's Web site.

THE BOOK ON THE WEB: The book comes in two versions: a paper copy and a freely accessible on-line version at

```
http://www.htdp.org/
```

The Web site also provides additional material, especially extended exercises of the style mentioned above. At this time, the Web page offers exercises on the visual simulation of ball games and the management of Web site. More exercises will be added.

The two versions of the book come with different kinds of hints. Each is marked with one of the following three icons:

 This marker refers to *DrScheme hints*. The programming environment has been designed with students in mind. The hints suggest how to use DrScheme at the various stages of the learning process.

 This marker refers to *teacher hints*, which suggest strategies on how to present a section, on how to approach an exercise, or on how to supplement some material.

☞ This marker links to *on-line solutions*. Some solutions are freely available; others are accessible to registered teachers only. To find out more about registration, see the book's Web site.

TYPOGRAPHY AND DEFINITIONS: For readability, Scheme programs are typeset using a small number of fonts. *Italic* words refer to program names and variables. Sans Serif items are constants and built-in operations. **Bold-face** words are Scheme keywords.

Definitions come in three varieties. There are those terms that concern the principles of programming and computing. The book lists the first occurrence of such terms with SMALL CAPITAL LETTERS. Other definitions are of a more fleeting nature; they introduce terms that are important for a section, an example, an exercise, or some other small part of the book. The book uses *slanted* words to emphasize such definitions. Finally, the book also defines classes of data. Most data definitions are boxed, and the first occurrence of the defined name is also typeset using *slanted* words.

## Acknowledgments

Four people deserve special thanks: Robert "Corky" Cartwright, who co-developed a predecessor of Rice's introductory course with the first author;

Daniel P. Friedman, for asking the first author to rewrite *The Little LISPer* (also MIT Press) in 1984, because it started this project; John Clements, who designed, implemented, and maintains DrScheme's stepper; and Paul Steckler, who faithfully supported the team with contributions to our suite of programming tools.

The development of the book benefited from many other friends and colleagues who used it in their courses and/or gave detailed comments on early drafts. We are grateful to them for their help and their patience: Ian Barland, John Clements, Bruce Duba, Mike Ernst, Kathi Fisler, Daniel P. Friedman, John Greiner, John Stone, Geraldine Morin, and Valdemar Tamez.

A dozen generations of *Comp 210* students at Rice University used early drafts of the text and contributed improvements in various ways. In addition, numerous attendees of our TeachScheme! workshops used early drafts in their classrooms. Many sent in comments and suggestions. As representative of these we mention the following active contributors: Ms. Barbara Adler, Dr. Stephen Bloch, Mr. Jack Clay, Dr. Richard Clemens, Mr. Kyle Gillette, Ms. Karen Buras, Mr. Marvin Hernandez, Mr. Michael Hunt, Ms. Karen North, Mr. Jamie Raymond, and Mr. Robert Reid. Christopher Felleisen patiently worked through the first few parts of the book with his father and provided direct insight into the views of a young student. Hrvoje Blazevic (Master of LPG/C Harriette), Joe Zachary (University of Utah) and Daniel P. Friedman (Indiana University) discovered numerous typos in the first printing, which we have now fixed. Thank you to everyone.

Finally, Matthias expresses his gratitude to Helga for her many years of patience and for creating a home for an absent-minded husband and father. Robby is grateful to Hsing-Huei Huang for her support and encouragement; without her, he would not have gotten anything done. Matthew thanks Wen Yuan for her constant support and enduring music. Shriram is indebted to Kathi Fisler for support, patience and puns, and for her participation in this project.

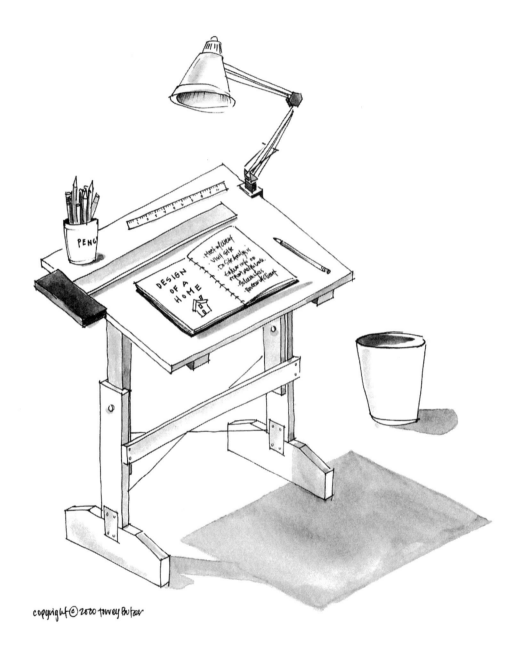

# Processing Simple Forms of Data

# 1   Students, Teachers, and Computers

We learn to compute at a young age. At first we just add and subtract numbers.

> One plus one equals two. Five minus two is three.

As we grow older we learn about additional mathematical operations, like exponentiation and sine, but we also learn to describe rules of computation.

> Given a circle of radius $r$, its circumference is $r$ times two times *pi*. A minimum-wage laborer who works for $N$ hours earns $N$ times 5.35 dollars.

The truth is, our teachers turn us into computers and program us to execute simple computer programs.

So, the secret is out. Computer programs are just very fast students. They can perform millions of additions while we might still be struggling with the first one. But computer programs can do more than just manipulate numbers. They can guide an airplane. They can play games. They can look up a person's phone number. They can print the payroll checks for huge corporations. In short, computers process all kinds of information.

People state information and instructions in English.

> The temperature is $35^{o}C$; convert this temperature into Fahrenheit. It takes this car 35 seconds to accelerate from zero to 100 miles per hour; determine how far the car gets in 20 seconds.

Computers, however, barely understand basic English and certainly can't understand complex instructions expressed in English. Instead we must learn to speak a computer language so that we can communicate information and instructions.

A computer's language of instruction and information is a PROGRAM-
MING LANGUAGE. Information expressed in a programming language is
called DATA. There are many flavors of data. *Numbers* are one class of data.
*Number series* belong to the class of COMPOUND DATA, because each series
is made up of other pieces of smaller pieces of data, namely, numbers. To
contrast the two kinds of data, we also call numbers ATOMIC DATA. Letters
are other examples of atomic data; family trees are compound data.

Data represents information, but the concrete interpretation is up to us.
For example, a number like 37.51 may represent a temperature, a time, or a
distance. A letter like "A" may denote a school grade, a quality symbol for
eggs, or a part of an address.

Like data, instructions, also called OPERATIONS, come in several flavors.
Each class of data comes with a set of PRIMITIVE OPERATIONS. For numbers, we naturally get +, −, ∗, and so on. Programmers compose primitive
operations into PROGRAMS. Thus, we may think of primitive operations as
the words of a foreign language and of programming as forming sentences
in this language.

Some programs are as small as essays. Others are like sets of ency-
clopedias. Writing good essays and books requires careful planning, and
writing good programs does, too. Small or large, a good program cannot
be created by tinkering around. It must be carefully *designed*. Each piece
needs a lot of attention; composing programs into larger units must follow
a well-planned strategy. Designing programs properly must be practiced
from our very first day of programming.

In this book, we will learn to design computer programs, and we will
learn to understand how they function. Becoming and being a programmer
is fun, but it is not easy. The best part of being a programmer is watching
our "products" grow and become successful. It is fun to observe a computer program play a game. It is exciting to see a computer program help
someone. To get to this point, however, we must practice many skills. As
we will find out, programming languages are primitive; especially, their
grammar is restrictive. And unfortunately, computers are stupid. The
smallest grammatical mistake in a program is a fatal stumbling block for
a computer. Worse, once our program is in proper grammatical shape, it
might not perform the computations as intended.

Programming a computer requires patience and concentration. Only attention to minute details will avoid frustrating grammatical mistakes. Only
rigorous planning and adherence to the plan will prevent serious logical
mistakes in our designs. But when we finally master the design of pro-

grams, we will have learned skills that are useful far beyond the realm of programming.

Let's get started!

## 2   Numbers, Expressions, Simple Programs

In the beginning, people thought of computers as number crunchers. And indeed, computers are very good at working with numbers. Since teachers start their first-graders on computing with numbers, we start with numbers, too. Once we know how computers deal with numbers, we can develop simple programs in no time; we just translate common sense into our programming notation. Still, even developing such simple programs requires discipline, and so we introduce the outline of the most fundamental design recipe and the basic programming guideline at the end of this section.

### 2.1   Numbers and Arithmetic

Computing Numbers come in many different flavors: positive and negative integers, fractions (also known as rationals), and reals are the most widely known classes of numbers:

5              −5              2/3              17/3              #i1.4142135623731

The first is an integer, the second one a negative integer, the next two are fractions, and the last one is an inexact representation of a real number.

Like a pocket calculator, the simplest of computers, Scheme permits programmers to add, subtract, multiply, and divide numbers:

(+ 5 5)        (+ −5 5)       (+ 5 −5)       (− 5 5)        (* 3 4)        (/ 8 12)

The first three ask Scheme to perform additions; the last three demand a subtraction, a multiplication, and a division. All arithmetic expressions are parenthesized and mention the operation first; the numbers follow the operation and are separated by spaces.

Stepper      As in arithmetic or algebra, we can nest expressions:

(* (+ 2 2) (/ (* (+ 3 5) (/ 30 10)) 2))

Scheme evaluates these expressions exactly as we do. It first reduces the innermost parenthesized expressions to numbers, then the next layer, and so on:

```
  (* (+ 2 2) (/ (* (+ 3 5) (/ 30 10)) 2))
= (* 4 (/ (* 8 3) 2))
= (* 4 (/ 24 2))
= (* 4 12)
= 48
```

Because every Scheme expression has the shape

> (*operation A ... B*)

there is never any question about which part has to be evaluated first. Whenever $A \ldots B$ are numbers, the expression can be evaluated; otherwise, $A \ldots B$ are evaluated first. Contrast this with

$$3 + 4 \cdot 5\,,$$

which is an expression that we encounter in grade school. Only a substantial amount of practice guarantees that we remember to evaluate the multiplication first and the addition afterwards.[4]

Finally, Scheme not only provides simple arithmetical operations but a whole range of advanced mathematical operations on numbers. Here are five examples:

1. (sqrt $A$) computes $\sqrt{A}$;

2. (expt $A$ $B$) computes $A^B$;

3. (remainder $A$ $B$) computes the remainder of the integer division $A/B$;

4. (log $A$) computes the natural logarithm of $A$; and

5. (sin $A$) computes the sine of $A$ radians.

When in doubt whether a primitive operation exists or how it works, use DrScheme to test whether an operation is available with a simple example.

**A Note on Numbers**: Scheme computes with EXACT integers and rationals as long as we use primitive operations that produce exact results. Thus, it displays the result of (/ 44 14) as 22/7. Unfortunately, Scheme and other

---

[4]Another advantage of Scheme's notation is that we always know where to place an operator or where to find it: to the immediate right of the opening parenthesis. This is important in computing because we need many more operators than just the few numerical operators that we use in arithmetic and algebra.

programming languages compromise as far as real numbers are concerned. For example, since the square root of 2 is not a rational but a real number, Scheme uses an INEXACT NUMBER:

```
(sqrt 2)
= #i1.4142135623731
```

The #i notation warns the programmer that the result is an approximation of the true number. Once an inexact number has become a part of a calculation, the process continues in an approximate manner. To wit:

```
(− #i1.0 #i0.9)
= #i0.09999999999999998
```

but

```
(− #i1000.0 #i999.9)
= #i0.10000000000002274
```

even though we know from mathematics that both differences should be 0.1 and equal. Once numbers are inexact, caution is necessary.

This imprecision is due to the common simplification of writing down numbers like the square root of 2 or $\pi$ as rational numbers. Recall that the decimal representations of these numbers are infinitely long (without repetition). A computer, however, has a finite size, and therefore can only represent a portion of such a number. If we choose to represent these numbers as rationals with a fixed number of digits, the representation is necessarily inexact. Intermezzo 6 will explain how inexact numbers work.

To focus our studies on the important concepts of computing and not on these details, the teaching languages of DrScheme deal as much as possible with numbers as precise numbers. When we write 1.25, DrScheme interprets this number as a precise fraction, not as an inexact number. When DrScheme's `Interactions` window displays a number such as 1.25 or 22/7, it is the result of a computation with precise rationals and fractions. Only numbers prefixed by #i are inexact representations. ∎

## Exercises

**Exercise 2.1.1** Find out whether DrScheme has operations for squaring a number; for computing the sine of an angle; and for determining the maximum of two numbers. ∎

**Exercise 2.1.2** Evaluate (sqrt 4), (sqrt 2), and (sqrt −1) in DrScheme. Then, find out whether DrScheme knows an operation for determining the tangent of an angle. ∎

Programming

## 2.2 Variables and Programs

In algebra we learn to formulate dependencies between quantities using VARIABLE EXPRESSIONS. A variable is a placeholder that stands for an unknown quantity. For example, a disk of radius $r$ has the approximate area[5]

$$3.14 \cdot r^2 \, .$$

In this expression, $r$ stands for any positive number. If we now come across a disk with radius 5, we can determine its area by substituting 5 for $r$ in the above formula and reducing the resulting expression to a number:

$$3.14 \cdot 5^2 = 3.14 \cdot 25 = 78.5 \, .$$

More generally, expressions that contain variables are rules that describe how to compute a number *when* we are given values for the variables.

A program is such a rule. It is a rule that tells us and the computer how to produce data from some other data. Large programs consist of many small programs and combine them in some manner. It is therefore important that programmers name each rule as they write it down. A good name for our sample expression is *area-of-disk*. Using this name, we would express the rule for computing the area of a disk as follows:

(**define** (*area-of-disk r*)
  (∗ 3.14 (∗ *r r*)))

The two lines say that *area-of-disk* is a rule, that it consumes a single INPUT, called $r$, and that the result, or OUTPUT, is going to be (∗ 3.14 (∗ *r r*)) once we know what number $r$ represents.

Programs combine basic operations. In our example, *area-of-disk* uses only one basic operation, multiplication, but **defined** programs may use as many operations as necessary. Once we have defined a program, we may use it as if it were a primitive operation. For each variable listed to the

---

[5]It is common to speak of the area of a circle, but mathematically speaking, the circle is only the disk's outer edge.

right of the program name, we must supply one input. That is, we may write expressions whose operation is *area-of-disk* followed by a number:

(*area-of-disk* 5)

We also say that we APPLY *area-of-disk* to 5.

The application of a **defined** operation is evaluated by copying the expression named *area-of-disk* and by replacing the variable (*r*) with the number we supplied (5):

(*area-of-disk* 5)
= (* 3.14 (* 5 5))
= (* 3.14 25)
= 78.5

Many programs consume more than one input. Say we wish to define a program that computes the area of a ring, that is, a disk with a hole in the center:

The area of the ring is that of the outer disk minus the area of the inner disk, which means that the program requires *two* unknown quantities: the outer and the inner radii. Let us call these unknown numbers *outer* and *inner*. Then the program that computes the area of a ring is defined as follows:

(**define** (*area-of-ring outer inner*)
  (− (*area-of-disk outer*)
     (*area-of-disk inner*)))

The three lines express that *area-of-ring* is a program, that the program accepts two inputs, called *outer* and *inner*, and that the result is going to be the difference between (*area-of-disk outer*) and (*area-of-disk inner*). In other words, we have used both basic Scheme operations and **defined** programs in the definition of *area-of-ring*.

When we wish to use *area-of-ring*, we must supply two inputs:

(*area-of-ring* 5 3)

The expression is evaluated in the same manner as (*area-of-disk* 5). We copy the expression from the definition of the program and replace the variable with the numbers we supplied:

(*area-of-ring* 5 3)

= (− (*area-of-disk* 5)
    (*area-of-disk* 3))

= (− (∗ 3.14 (∗ 5 5))
    (∗ 3.14 (∗ 3 3)))

= . . .

The rest is plain arithmetic.

### Exercises

Teachpacks

**Exercise 2.2.1** Define the program *Fahrenheit→ Celsius*,[6] which consumes a temperature measured in Fahrenheit and produces the Celsius equivalent. Use a chemistry or physics book to look up the conversion formula.

When the function is fully developed, test it using the teachpack **convert.ss**. The teachpack provides three functions: *convert-gui*, *convert-repl*, and *convert-file*. The first creates a graphical user interface. Use it with

(*convert-gui Fahrenheit→ Celsius*)

The expression will create a new window in which users can manipulate a slider and buttons.

The second emulates the Interactions window. Users are asked to enter a Fahrenheit temperature, which the program reads, evaluates, and prints. Use it via

(*convert-repl Fahrenheit→ Celsius*)

The last operation processes entire files. To use it, create a file with those numbers that are to be converted. Separate the numbers with blank spaces or new lines. The function reads the entire file, converts the numbers, and writes the results into a new file. Here is the expression:

(*convert-file* "in.dat" *Fahrenheit→ Celsius* "out.dat")

---

[6]An arrow is keyed in as - followed by >.

This assumes that the name of the newly created file is `in.dat` and that we wish the results to be written to the file `out.dat`. For more information, use DrScheme's Help Desk to look up the teachpack **convert.ss**. ∎

**Exercise 2.2.2** Define the program *dollar→ euro*, which consumes a number of dollars and produces the euro equivalent. Use the currency table in the newspaper to look up the current exchange rate. ∎

**Exercise 2.2.3** Define the program *triangle*. It consumes the length of a triangle's side and its height. The program produces the area of the triangle. Use a geometry book to look up the formula for computing the area of a triangle. ∎

**Exercise 2.2.4** Define the program *convert3*. It consumes three digits, starting with the least significant digit, followed by the next most significant one, and so on. The program produces the corresponding number. For example, the expected value of

(*convert3* 1 2 3)

is 321. Use an algebra book to find out how such a conversion works. ∎

**Exercise 2.2.5** A typical exercise in an algebra book asks the reader to evaluate an expression like

$$\frac{n}{3} + 2$$

for $n = 2$, $n = 5$, and $n = 9$. Using Scheme, we can formulate such an expression as a program and use the program as many times as necessary. Here is the program that corresponds to the above expression:

(**define** (*f* *n*)
  (+ (/ *n* 3) 2))

First determine the result of the expression at $n = 2$, $n = 5$, and $n = 9$ by hand, then with DrScheme's stepper.

Also formulate the following three expressions as programs:

1. $n^2 + 10$

2. $\frac{1}{2} \cdot n^2 + 20$

3. $2 - \frac{1}{n}$

Determine their results for $n = 2$ and $n = 9$ by hand and with DrScheme. ∎

## 2.3   Word Problems

Programmers are rarely handed mathematical expressions to turn into programs. Instead they typically receive informal problem descriptions that often contain irrelevant and sometimes ambiguous information. The programmers' first task is to extract the relevant information and then to formulate appropriate expressions.

Here is a typical example:

> Company XYZ & Co. pays all its employees $12 per hour. A typical employee works between 20 and 65 hours per week. Develop a program that determines the wage of an employee from the number of hours of work.

The last sentence is the first to mention the actual task: to write a program that determines one quantity based on some other quantity. More specifically, the program consumes one quantity, the number of hours of work, and produces another one, the wage in dollars. The first sentence implies how to compute the result, but doesn't state it explicitly. In this particular example, though, this poses no problem. If an employee works $h$ hours, the wage is

$$12 \cdot h \, .$$

Now that we have a rule, we can formulate a Scheme program:

```
(define (wage h)
  (* 12 h))
```

The program is called *wage*; its parameter $h$ stands for the hours an employee works; and its result is (* 12 h), the corresponding wage.

---

## Exercises

**Exercise 2.3.1** Utopia's tax accountants always use programs that compute income taxes even though the tax rate is a solid, never-changing 15%. Define the program *tax*, which determines the tax on the gross pay.

Also define *netpay*. The program determines the net pay of an employee from the number of hours worked. Assume an hourly rate of $12. ∎

**Exercise 2.3.2** The local supermarket needs a program that can compute the value of a bag of coins. Define the program *sum-coins*. It consumes four numbers: the number of pennies, nickels, dimes, and quarters in the bag; it produces the amount of money in the bag. ∎

**Exercise 2.3.3** An old-style movie theater has a simple profit function. Each customer pays $5 per ticket. Every performance costs the theater $20, plus $.50 per attendee. Develop the function *total-profit*. It consumes the number of attendees (of a show) and produces how much income the attendees produce. ∎

## 2.4 Errors

Errors   When we write Scheme programs, we must follow a few carefully designed rules, which are a compromise between a computer's capabilities and human behavior.[7] Fortunately, forming Scheme definitions and expressions is intuitive. Expressions are either ATOMIC, that is, numbers and variables; or they are COMPOUND expressions, in which case they start with "(", followed by an operation, some more expressions, and terminated by ")". Each expression in a compound expression should be preceded by at least one space; line breaks are permissible, and sometimes increase readability.

Definitions have the following schematic shape:

> (**define** (*f x* ... *y*)
>   *an-expression*)

That is, a definition is a sequence of several words and expressions: "(", the word "define", "(", a non-empty sequence of names separated by spaces, ")", an expression, and a closing ")". The embedded sequence of names, *f x* ... *y*, introduces the name of the program and the names of its parameters.

**Syntax Errors:**[8] Not all parenthesized expressions are Scheme expressions. For example, (10) is a parenthesized expression, but Scheme does not accept it as a legal Scheme expression because numbers are not supposed to be included in parentheses. Similarly, a sentence like (10 + 20) is also ill formed; Scheme's rules demand that the operator is mentioned first. Finally, the following two definitions are not well formed:

> (**define** (*P x*)
>   (+ (*x*) 10))

---

[7] This statement is true for any other programming language as well, for example, spreadsheet languages, C, word processor macro. Scheme is simpler than most of these and easy to understand for computers. Unfortunately, to human beings who grow up on infix expressions such as 5 + 4, Scheme prefix expressions such as (+ 5 4) initially appear to be complicated. A bit of practice will quickly eliminate this misconception.

[8] We will find out in section 8 why such errors are called *syntax* errors.

> (**define** ($Q$ $x$)
>   $x$ 10)

The first one contains an extra pair of parentheses around the variable $x$, which is not a compound expression; the second contains two atomic expressions, $x$ and 10, instead of one.

When we click DrScheme's `Execute` button, the programming environment first determines whether the definitions are formed according to Scheme's rules. If some part of the program in the `Definitions` window is ill formed, DrScheme signals a SYNTAX ERROR with an appropriate error message and highlights the offending part. Otherwise it permits the user to evaluate expressions in the `Interactions` window.

Errors

### Exercises

**Exercise 2.4.1** Evaluate the following sentences in DrScheme, one at a time:

> (+ (10) 20)
> (10 + 20)
> (+ +)

Read and understand the error messages. ∎

**Exercise 2.4.2** Enter the following sentences, one by one, into DrScheme's `Definitions` window and click `Execute`:

> (**define** ($f$ 1)
>   (+ $x$ 10))

> (**define** ($g$ $x$)
>   + $x$ 10)

> (**define** $h(x)$
>   (+ $x$ 10))

Read the error messages, fix the offending definition in an appropriate manner, and repeat until all definitions are legal. ∎

**Run-time Errors:** The evaluation of Scheme expressions proceeds according to the intuitive laws of algebra and arithmetic. When we encounter new operations, we will extend these laws, first intuitively and then, in section 8, rigorously. For now, it is more important to understand that not all legal Scheme expressions have a result. One obvious example is (/ 1 0). Similarly, if we define

> (**define** (*f n*)
> (+ (/ *n* 3) 2))

we cannot ask DrScheme to evaluate (*f* 5 8).

When the evaluation of a legal Scheme expression demands a division by zero or similarly nonsensical arithmetic operations, or when a program is applied to the wrong number of inputs, DrScheme stops the evaluation and signals a RUN-TIME ERROR. Typically it prints an explanation in the Interactions window and highlights the faulty expression. The highlighted expression triggered the error signal.

## Exercises

**Exercise 2.4.3** Evaluate the following grammatically legal Scheme expressions in DrScheme's Interactions window:

> (+ 5 (/ 1 0))

> (sin 10 20)

> (*somef* 10)

Read the error messages. ∎

**Exercise 2.4.4** Enter the following grammatically legal Scheme program into the Definitions window and click the Execute button:

> (**define** (*somef x*)
> (sin *x x*))

Then, in the Interactions window, evaluate the expressions:

> (*somef* 10 20)

> (*somef* 10)

and read the error messages. Also observe what DrScheme highlights. ∎

**Logical Errors:** A good programming environment assists the programmer in finding syntax and runtime errors. The exercises in this section illustrate how DrScheme catches syntax and run-time errors. A programmer, however, can also make LOGICAL ERRORS. A logical mistake does not trigger any error messages; instead, the program computes incorrect results. Consider the *wage* program from the preceding section. If the programmer had accidentally defined it as

> (**define** (*wage h*)
>   (+ 12 *h*))

the program would still produce a number every time it is used. Indeed, if we evaluate (*wage* 12/11), we even get the correct result. A programmer can catch such mistakes only by designing programs carefully and systematically.

## 2.5 Designing Programs

Designing
Programs

The preceding sections show that the development of a program requires many steps. We need to determine what's relevant in the problem statement and what we can ignore. We need to understand what the program consumes, what it produces, and how it relates inputs to outputs. We must know, or find out, whether Scheme provides certain basic operations for the data that our program is to process. If not, we might have to develop auxiliary programs that implement these operations. Finally, once we have a program, we must check whether it actually performs the intended computation. This might reveal syntax errors, run-time problems, or even logical errors.

To bring some order to this apparent chaos, it is best to set up and to follow a DESIGN RECIPE, that is, a step-by-step prescription of what we should do and the order[9] in which we should do things. Based on what we have experienced thus far, the development of a program requires at least the following four activities:

**Understanding the Program's Purpose:** The goal of designing a program is to create a mechanism that consumes and produces data. We therefore start every program development by giving the program a meaningful name and by stating what kind of information it consumes and produces. We call this a CONTRACT.

---

[9]As we will see later, the order is not completely fixed. It is possible, and for a number of reasons, desirable to switch the order of some steps in some cases.

```
;; Contract: area-of-ring : number number → number

;; Purpose: to compute the area of a ring whose radius is
;; outer and whose hole has a radius of inner

;; Example: (area-of-ring 5 3) should produce 50.24

;; Definition: [refines the header]
(define (area-of-ring outer inner)
  (− (area-of-disk outer)
     (area-of-disk inner)))

;; Tests:
(area-of-ring 5 3)
;; expected value
50.24
```

Figure 3: The design recipe: A complete example

Here is how we write down a contract for *area-of-ring*, one of our first programs:[10]

> ;; *area-of-ring : number number → number*

The semicolons indicate that this line is a COMMENT. The contract consists of two parts. The first, to the left of the colon, states the program's name. The second, to the right of the colon, specifies what kind of data the program consumes and what it produces; the inputs are separated from the output by an arrow.

Once we have a contract, we can add the HEADER. It restates the program's name and gives each input a distinct name. These names are (algebraic) variables and are referred to as the program's PARAMETERS.[11]

Let's take a look at the contract and header for *area-of-ring*:

> ;; *area-of-ring : number number → number*
> (**define** (*area-of-ring outer inner*) . . . )

---

[10] An arrow is keyed in as - followed by >.

[11] Others also call them FORMAL ARGUMENTS or INPUT VARIABLES.

It says that we will refer to the first input as *outer* and the second one as *inner*.

Finally, using the contract and the parameters, we should formulate a short PURPOSE STATEMENT for the program, that is, a brief comment of *what* the program is to compute. For most of our programs, one or two lines will suffice; as we develop larger and larger programs, we may need to add more information to explain a program's purpose.

Here is the complete starting-point for our running example:

> ;; *area-of-ring : number number → number*
> ;; to compute the area of a ring whose radius is
> ;; *outer* and whose hole has a radius of *inner*
> (**define** (*area-of-ring outer inner*) ... )

**Hints:**  If the problem statement provides a mathematical formula, the number of distinct variables in the formula suggests how many inputs the program consumes.

For other word problems, we must inspect the problem to separate the given facts from what is to be computed.  If a given is a fixed number, it shows up in the program.  If it is an unknown number that is to be fixed by someone else later, it is an input. The question (or the imperative) in the problem statement suggests a name for the program.

**Program Examples:**  To gain a better understanding of what the program should compute, we make up examples of inputs and determine what the output should be. For example, *area-of-ring* should produce 50.24 for the inputs 5 and 3, because it is the difference between the area of the outer disk and the area of the inner disk.

We add examples to the purpose statement:

> ;; *area-of-ring : number number → number*
> ;; to compute the area of a ring whose radius is
> ;; *outer* and whose hole has a radius of *inner*
> ;; example: (*area-of-ring* 5 3) *should produce* 50.24
> (**define** (*area-of-ring outer inner*) ... )

Making up examples—**before we write down the program's body**—helps in many ways. First, it is the only sure way to discover logical errors with testing. If we use the finished program to make up examples, we are tempted to trust the program because it is so much easier to run the program than to predict what it does. Second, examples force us to think through the computational process, which, for the complicated cases we will encounter later, is critical to the development of the function body. Finally, examples illustrate the informal prose of a purpose statement. Future readers of the program, such as teachers, colleagues, or buyers, greatly appreciate illustrations of abstract concepts.

**The Body:** Finally, we must formulate the program's body. That is, **we must replace the "..." in our header with an expression**. The expression computes the answer from the parameters, using Scheme's basic operations and Scheme programs that we already **define**d or intend to **define**.

We can only formulate the program's body if we understand how the program computes the output from the given inputs. If the input-output relationship is given as a mathematical formula, we just translate mathematics into Scheme. If, instead, we are given a word problem, we must craft the expression carefully. To this end, it is helpful to revisit the examples from the second step and to understand *how* we computed the outputs for specific inputs.

In our running example, the computational task was given via an informally stated formula that reused *area-of-disk*, a previously **define**d program. Here is the translation into Scheme:

```
(define (area-of-ring outer inner)
  (- (area-of-disk outer)
     (area-of-disk inner)))
```

**Testing:** After we have completed the program definition, we must still test the program. At a minimum, we should ensure that the program computes the expected outputs for the program examples. To facilitate testing, we may wish to add the examples to the bottom of the Definitions window as if they were equations. Then, when we click the Execute button, they are evaluated, and we see whether the program works properly on them.

Testing cannot show that a program produces the correct outputs for all possible inputs—because there are typically an infinite number of possible inputs. But testing can reveal syntax errors, run-time problems, and logical mistakes.

For faulty outputs, we must pay special attention to our program examples. It is possible that the examples are wrong; that the program contains a logical mistake; or that both the examples and the program are wrong. In either case, we may have to step through the entire program development again.

Figure 3 shows what we get after we have developed the program according to our recipe. Figure 4 summarizes the recipe in tabular form. It should be consulted whenever we design a program.

The design recipe is not a magic bullet for the problems we encounter during the design of a program. It provides some guidance for a process that can often appear to be overwhelming. The most creative and most difficult step in our recipe concerns the design of the program's body. At this point, it relies heavily on our ability to read and understand written material, on our ability to extract mathematical relationships, and on our knowledge of basic facts. None of these skills is specific to the development of computer programs; the knowledge we exploit is specific to the application domain in which we are working. The remainder of the book will show what and how much computing can contribute to this most complicated step.

**Domain Knowledge:**  Formulating the body of a program often requires knowledge about the area, also known as domain, from which the problem is drawn. This form of knowledge is called DOMAIN KNOWLEDGE. It may have to be drawn from simple mathematics, such as arithmetic, from complex mathematics, such as differential equations, or from non-mathematical disciplines: music, biology, civil engineering, art, and so on.

Because programmers cannot know all of the application domains of computing, they must be prepared to understand the language of a variety of application areas so that they can discuss problems with domain experts. The language is often that of mathematics, but in some cases, the programmers must invent a language, especially a data language for the application area. For that reason, it is imperative that programmers have a solid understanding of the full possibilities of computer languages. ∎

| Phase | Goal | Activity |
|---|---|---|
| Contract Purpose and Header | to name the function; to specify its classes of input data and its class of output data; to describe its purpose; to formulate a header | choose a *name* that fits the problem • study the problem for clues on how many unknown "givens" the function consumes • pick one variable per input; if possible, use names that are mentioned for the "givens" in the problem statement • describe what the function should produce using the chosen variables names • formulate the contract and header: <br> ;; *name : number ... → number* <br> ;; to compute ... from *x1* ... <br> (**define** (*name x1 ...*) ...) |
| Examples | to characterize the input-output relationship via examples | search the problem statement for examples • work through the examples • validate the results, if possible • make up examples |
| Body | to define the function | formulate how the function computes its results • develop a Scheme expression that uses Scheme's primitive operations, other functions, and the variables • translate the mathematical expressions in the problem statement, when available |
| Test | to discover mistakes ("typos" and logic) | apply the function to the inputs of the examples • check that the outputs are as predicted |

Figure 4: The design recipe at a glance

## 3   Programs are Function Plus Variable Definitions

In general, a program consists not just of one, but of many definitions. The *area-of-ring* program, for example, consists of two definitions: the one for *area-of-ring* and another one for *area-of-disk*. We refer to both as FUNCTION

DEFINITIONs and, using mathematical terminology in a loose way, say that the program is COMPOSED of several functions. Because the first one, *area-of-ring*, is the function we really wish to use, we refer to it as the MAIN FUNCTION; the second one, *area-of-disk*, is an AUXILIARY FUNCTION.

The use of auxiliary functions makes the design process manageable and renders programs readable. Compare the following two versions of *area-of-ring*:

```
(define (area-of-ring outer inner)        (define (area-of-ring outer inner)
  (- (area-of-disk outer)                   (- (* 3.14 (* outer outer))
     (area-of-disk inner)))                    (* 3.14 (* inner inner))))
```

The definition on the left composes auxiliary functions. Designing it helped us break up the original problem into smaller, more easily solvable problems. Reading it reminds us of our reasoning that the area is the difference between the area of the full disk and the area of the hole. In contrast, the definition on the right requires a reader to reconstruct the idea that the two subexpressions compute the area of two disks. Furthermore, we would have had to produce the right definition in one monolithic block, without benefit of dividing the problem-solving process into smaller steps.

For a small program such as *area-of-ring*, the differences between the two styles are minor. For large programs, however, using auxiliary functions is not an option but a necessity. That is, even if we are asked to write a single program, we should consider breaking it up into several small programs and COMPOSING them as needed. Although we are not yet in a position to develop truly large programs, we can still get a feeling for the idea by developing two versions in parallel.

The first subsection contrasts the two development styles with an example from the business domain. It demonstrates how breaking up a program into several function definitions can greatly increase our confidence in the correctness of the overall program. The second subsection introduces the concept of a variable definition, which is an additional important ingredient for the development of programs. The last subsection proposes some exercises.

## 3.1 Composing Functions

Consider the following problem:

> Imagine the owner of a movie theater who has complete freedom in setting ticket prices. The more he charges, the fewer

the people who can afford tickets. In a recent experiment the owner determined a precise relationship between the price of a ticket and average attendance. At a price of $5.00 per ticket, 120 people attend a performance. Decreasing the price by a dime ($.10) increases attendance by 15. Unfortunately, the increased attendance also comes at an increased cost. Every performance costs the owner $180. Each attendee costs another four cents ($0.04). The owner would like to know the exact relationship between profit and ticket price so that he can determine the price at which he can make the highest profit.

While the task is clear, how to go about it is not. All we can say at this point is that several quantities depend on each other.

When we are confronted with such a situation, it is best to tease out the various dependencies one at a time:

1. *Profit* is the difference between revenue and costs.

2. The *revenue* is exclusively generated by the sale of tickets. It is the product of ticket price and number of attendees.

3. The *costs* consist of two parts: a fixed part ($180) and a variable part that depends on the number of attendees.

4. Finally, the problem statement also specifies how the number of attendees depends on the ticket price.

Let's formulate a function for each of these dependencies; after all, functions compute how quantities depend on each other.

We start with contracts, headers, and purpose statements. Here is the one for *profit*:

```
;; profit : number → number
;; to compute the profit as the difference between revenue and costs
;; at some given ticket-price
(define (profit ticket-price) ...)
```

It depends on the ticket price because both revenue and cost depend on the ticket price. Here are the remaining three:

```
;; revenue : number → number
;; to compute the revenue, given ticket-price
(define (revenue ticket-price) ...)
```

```
;; cost : number → number
;; to compute the costs, given ticket-price
(define (cost ticket-price) ...)

;; attendees : number → number
;; to compute the number of attendees, given ticket-price
(define (attendees ticket-price) ...)
```

Each purpose statement is a rough transliteration of some part of the problem statement.

## Exercises

**Exercise 3.1.1** The next step is to make up examples for each of the functions. Determine how many attendees can afford a show at a ticket price of $3.00, $4.00, and $5.00. Use the examples to formulate a general rule that shows how to compute the number of attendees from the ticket price. Make up more examples if needed. ∎

**Exercise 3.1.2** Use the results of exercise 3.1.1 to determine how much it costs to run a show at $3.00, $4.00, and $5.00. Also determine how much revenue each show produces at those prices. Finally, figure out how much profit the monopolistic movie owner can make with each show. Which is the best price (of these three) for maximizing the profit? ∎

Once we have written down the basic material about our functions and calculated out several examples, we can replace the "..." with Scheme expressions. The left column of figure 5 contains complete definitions of all four functions. The *profit* function computes its result as the difference between the result of *revenue* and *cost*, just as the problem analysis and purpose statement suggest. The computation of both depends on *ticket-price*, which is what the applications say. To compute the revenue, we first compute the number of attendees for the given *ticket-price* and multiply it with *ticket-price*. Similarly, to compute the cost we add the fixed portion of the cost to the variable part, which is the product of the number of attendees and 0.04 (four cents). Finally, the computation of the number of attendees also follows the problem statement. The base attendance at a price of five dollars is 120, and for each 10 cents less than five dollars, 15 more attendees show up.

```
;; How to design a program              ;; How not to design a program
(define (profit ticket-price)           (define (profit price)
   (− (revenue ticket-price)              (− (* (+ 120
      (cost ticket-price)))                        (* (/ 15 .10)
                                                      (− 5.00 price)))
(define (revenue ticket-price)                 price)
   (* (attendees ticket-price) ticket-price))  (+ 180
                                                   (* .04
(define (cost ticket-price)                         (+ 120
   (+ 180                                              (* (/ 15 .10)
      (* .04 (attendees ticket-price))))                  (− 5.00 price)))))))))

(define (attendees ticket-price)
   (+ 120
      (* (/ 15 .10) (− 5.00 ticket-price))))
```

Figure 5: Two ways to express the *profit* program

Instead of developing a function per dependency in the problem statement, we could have tried to express the relationship between the ticket
price and the owner's profit in a single function. The right column in figure 5 shows the most straightforward way of doing so. And indeed, it is
easy to check that the two profit programs in figure 5 produce the same
profit when given the same ticket price. Still, it is also obvious that while
the arrangement on the left conveys the intention behind the program directly, the program on the right is nearly impossible to understand. Worse,
if we are asked to modify some aspect of the program, say, the relationship
between the number of attendees and the price of the ticket, we can do this
for the left column in a small amount of time, but we need to spend a much
longer time for the right one.

Based on our experience, we thus formulate the first and most important guideline of programming:

---

GUIDELINE ON AUXILIARY FUNCTIONS

Formulate auxiliary function definitions for every dependency between quantities mentioned in the problem statement or discovered
with example calculations.

---

Sometimes we will find that some of the required functions are already available as programs for other problems. Indeed, we have already encountered such an example: *area-of-disk*. At other times, we will make a list of functions and develop each one separately. We may then find that some of the functions, such as *attendees*, are useful in several other definitions, leading to a network-like relationship among functions.

## Exercises

**Exercise 3.1.3** Determine the profit that the movie owner makes at $3.00, $4.00, and $5.00 using the program definitions in both columns. Make sure that the results are the same as those predicted in exercise 3.1.2. ∎

**Exercise 3.1.4** After studying the cost structure of a show, the owner discovered several ways of lowering the cost. As a result of his improvements, he no longer has a fixed cost. He now simply pays $1.50 per attendee.

Modify both programs to reflect this change. When the programs are modified, test them again with ticket prices of $3.00, $4.00, and $5.00 and compare the results. ∎

## 3.2   Variable Definitions

Defining Variables

When a number occurs many times in our program(s), we should give it a name using a VARIABLE DEFINITION, which associates a name with a value. One example is 3.14, which we have used in place of $\pi$. Here is how we could give this number a name:

(**define** *PI* 3.14)

Now, every time we refer to *PI*, DrScheme replaces it with 3.14.

Using a name for a constant makes it easier to replace it with a different value. Suppose our program contains the definition for *PI*, and we decide that we need a better approximation of $\pi$ for the entire program. By changing the definition to

(**define** *PI* 3.14159)

the improvement is used everywhere where we use *PI*. If we didn't have a name like *PI* for $\pi$, we would have to find and all instances of 3.14 in the program and replace them with 3.14159.

Let us formulate this observation as our second guideline:

> GUIDELINE ON VARIABLE DEFINITIONS
>
> Give names to frequently used constants and use the names instead of the constants in programs.

Initially, we won't use many variable definitions for constants, because our programs are small. But, as we learn to write larger programs, we will make more use of variable definitions. As we will see, the ability to have a single point of control for changes is important for variable and function definitions.

## Exercises

**Exercise 3.2.1** Provide variable definitions for all constants that appear in the profit program of figure 5 and replace the constants with their names. ∎

## 3.3   Finger Exercises on Composing Functions

Using "..." **Exercise 3.3.1** The United States uses the *English* system of (length) measurements. The rest of the world uses the *metric* system. So, people who travel abroad and companies that trade with foreign partners often need to convert English measurements to metric ones and vice versa.

Here is a table that shows the six major units of length measurements of the English system:[12]

| English | | | metric | |
|---|---|---|---|---|
| 1 **inch** | | | = 2.54 | cm |
| 1 **foot** | = | 12 | in. | |
| 1 **yard** | = | 3 | ft. | |
| 1 **rod** | = | $5\frac{1}{2}$ | yd. | |
| 1 **furlong** | = | 40 | rd. | |
| 1 **mile** | = | 8 | fl. | |

Develop the functions *inches→ cm*, *feet→ inches*, *yards→ feet*, *rods→ yards*, *furlongs→ rods*, and *miles→ furlongs*.

Then develop the functions *feet→ cm*, *yards→ cm*, *rods→ inches*, and *miles→ feet*.

---

[12]See *The World Book Encyclopedia* **1993**, Weights and Measurements.

**Hint:** Reuse functions as much as possible. Use variable definitions to specify constants. ∎

**Exercise 3.3.2** Develop the program *volume-cylinder*. It consumes the radius of a cylinder's base disk and its height; it computes the volume of the cylinder. ∎

**Exercise 3.3.3** Develop *area-cylinder*. The program consumes the radius of the cylinder's base disk and its height. Its result is the surface area of the cylinder. ∎

**Exercise 3.3.4** Develop the function *area-pipe*. It computes the surface area of a pipe, which is an open cylinder. The program consumes three values: the pipe's inner radius, its length, and the thickness of its wall.

Develop two versions: a program that consists of a single definition and a program that consists of several function definitions. Which one evokes more confidence? ∎

**Exercise 3.3.5** Develop the program *height*, which computes the height that a rocket reaches in a given amount of time. If the rocket accelerates at a constant rate $g$, it reaches a speed of $g \cdot t$ in $t$ time units and a height of $1/2 * v * t$ where $v$ is the speed at $t$. ∎

**Exercise 3.3.6** Recall the program *Fahrenheit→ Celsius* from exercise 2.2.1. The program consumes a temperature measured in Fahrenheit and produces the Celsius equivalent.

Develop the program *Celsius→ Fahrenheit*, which consumes a temperature measured in Celsius and produces the Fahrenheit equivalent.

Now consider the function

;; *I : number → number*
;; to convert a Fahrenheit temperature to Celsius and back
(**define** (*I f*)
   (*Celsius→ Fahrenheit* (*Fahrenheit→ Celsius f*)))

Evaluate (*I* 32) by hand and using DrScheme's stepper. What does this suggest about the composition of the two functions? ∎

# 4   Conditional Expressions and Functions

For many problems, computer programs must deal with different situations in different ways. A game program may have to determine whether an object's speed is in some range or whether it is located in some specific area of the screen. For an engine control program, a condition may describe whether or when a valve is to be opened. To deal with conditions, we need to have a way of saying a condition is true or false; we need a new class of values, which, by convention, are called BOOLEAN (or truth) values. This section introduces booleans, expressions that evaluate to Booleans, and expressions that compute values depending on the boolean result of some evaluation.

Boolean
Operations

## 4.1   Booleans and Relations

Consider the following problem statement:

> Company XYZ & Co. pays all its employees $12 per hour. A typical employee works between 20 and 65 hours per week. Develop a program that determines the wage of an employee from the number of hours of work, *if the number is within the proper range.*

The italic words highlight the new part (compared to section 2.3). They imply that the program must deal with its input in one way if it is in the legitimate range, and in a different way if it is not. In short, just as people need to reason about conditions, programs must compute in a conditional manner.

Conditions are nothing new. In mathematics we talk of true and false claims, which are conditions. For example, a number may be equal to, less than, or greater than some other number. If $x$ and $y$ are numbers, we state these three claims about $x$ and $y$ with

1. $x = y$: "$x$ is equal to $y$";

2. $x < y$: "$x$ is strictly less than $y$";

3. $x > y$: "$x$ is strictly greater than $y$".

For any specific pair of (real) numbers, exactly one of these claims holds. If $x = 4$ and $y = 5$, the second claim is a true statement, and the others are false. If $x = 5$ and $y = 4$, however, the third claim is true, and the others are false. In general, a claim is true for some values of the variables and false for others.

In addition to determining whether an atomic claim holds in a given situation, it is sometimes important to determine whether combinations of claims hold. Consider the three claims above, which we can combine in several ways:

1. $x = y$    and    $x < y$    and    $x > y$

2. $x = y$    or    $x < y$    or    $x > y$

3. $x = y$    or    $x < y$ .

The first compound claim is false because no matter what numbers we pick for $x$ and $y$, two of the three claims are false. The second compound claim, however, always holds no matter what numbers we pick for $x$ and $y$. Finally, the third kind of compound claim is the most important of all, because it is true in some cases and false in others. For example, it holds when $x = 4$, $y = 4$ and $x = 4$, $y = 5$, but it is false if $x = 5$ and $y = 3$.

Like mathematics, Scheme has "words" for expressing truth and falsity, for stating atomic claims, for combining claims into compound claims, and for expressing that a claim is true or false. The "word" for true is true and the "word" for false is false. If a claim concerns the relationship between two numbers, it can typically be expressed with a RELATIONAL OPERA-TION, for example, $=$, $<$, and $>$.

Translating the three mathematical claims from above follows our well-known pattern of writing a left parenthesis, followed by the operator, its arguments, and a right parenthesis:

1. $(= x\ y)$: "$x$ is equal to $y$";

2. $(< x\ y)$: "$x$ is strictly less than $y$"; and

3. $(> x\ y)$: "$x$ is strictly greater than $y$".

We will also encounter $<=$ and $>=$ as relational operators.

A Scheme expression that compares numbers has a result just like any other Scheme expression. The result, however, is true or false, not a number. That is, when an atomic Scheme claim about two numbers is true, it evaluates to true. For example,

    $(< 4\ 5)$
= true

Similarly, a false claim evaluates to false:

> (= 4 5)
> = false

Expressing compound conditions in Scheme is equally natural. Suppose we want to combine (= *x y*) and (< *y z*) so that the compound claim holds if both conditions are true. In Scheme we would write

> (**and** (= *x y*) (< *y z*))

to express this relationship. Similarly, if we want to formulate a compound claim that is true if (at least) one of two claim holds, we write

> (**or** (= *x y*) (< *y z*))

Finally, when we write something such as

> (not (= *x y*))

we state that we wish the negation of a claim to be true.[13]

Compound conditions, like atomic conditions, evaluate to true or false. Consider the following compound condition:

> (**and** (= 5 5) (< 5 6))

It consists of two atomic claims: (= 5 5) and (< 5 6). Both evaluate to true, and therefore the evaluation of the **and**-expression continues as follows:

> ...
> = (**and** true true)
> = true

The last step follows because, if both parts of an **and**-expression are true, the entire expression evaluates to true. In contrast, if one of the two claims in an **and**-expression evaluates to false, the **and**-expression evaluates to false:

> (**and** (= 5 5) (< 5 5))
> = (**and** true false)
> = false

The evaluation rules for **or** and not are similarly intuitive.

The next few sections will explain why programming requires formulating conditions and reasoning about them.

---

[13]In truth, the operations **and** and **or** are different from not, which is why they are typeset in different fonts. We ignore this minor difference for now.

## Exercises

**Exercise 4.1.1** What are the results of the following Scheme conditions?

1. **(and** (> 4 3) (<= 10 100))

2. **(or** (> 4 3) (= 10 100))

3. (not (= 2 3)) ∎

**Exercise 4.1.2** What are the results of

1. (> *x* 3)

2. **(and** (> 4 *x*) (> *x* 3))

3. (= (* *x* *x*) *x*)

for (a) *x* = 4, (b) *x* = 2, and (c) *x* = 7/2 ? ∎

## 4.2   Functions that Test Conditions

Testing   Here is a simple function that tests some condition about a number:

```
;; is-5? : number → boolean
;; to determine whether n is equal to 5
(define (is-5? n)
   (= n 5))
```

The function produces true if, and only if, its input is equal to 5. Its contract contains one novel element: the word *boolean*. Just like *number*, *boolean* represents a class of values that is built into Scheme. Unlike *number*, *boolean* consists of just two values: true and false.

Here is a slightly more interesting function with a boolean output:

```
;; is-between-5-6? : number → boolean
;; to determine whether n is between 5 and 6 (exclusive)
(define (is-between-5-6? n)
   (and (< 5 n) (< n 6)))
```

It consumes a number and produces true if the number is between, but does not include, 5 and 6. One good way to understand the function is to say that it describes the following interval on the number line:

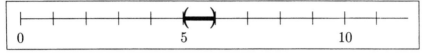

**Interval Boundaries**: An interval boundary marked with "(" or ")" is excluded from the interval; an interval boundary marked with "[" or "]" is included. ∎

The following third function from numbers to boolean values represents the most complicated form of interval:

;; *is-between-5-6-or-over-10? : number → boolean*
;; to determine whether *n* is between 5 and 6 (exclusive)
;; or larger than or equal to 10
(**define** (*is-between-5-6-or-over-10? n*)
  (**or** (*is-between-5-6? n*) (>= *n* 10))))

The function returns true for two portions of the number line:

The left part of the interval is the portion between, but not including, 5 and 6; the right one is the infinite line starting at, and including, 10. Any point on those two portions of the line satisfies the condition expressed in the function *is-between-5-6-or-over-10?*.

All three functions test numeric conditions. To design or to comprehend such functions, we must understand intervals and combinations (also known as unions) of intervals. The following exercises practice this important skill.

## Exercises

**Exercise 4.2.1** Translate the following five intervals on the real line into Scheme functions that accept a number and return true if the number is in the interval and false if it is outside:

1. the interval $(3, 7]$:

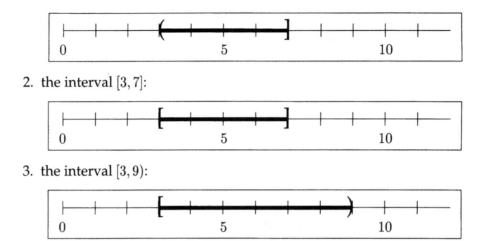

2. the interval $[3, 7]$:

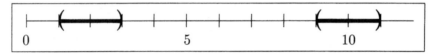

3. the interval $[3, 9)$:

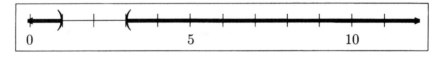

4. the union of $(1, 3)$ and $(9, 11)$:

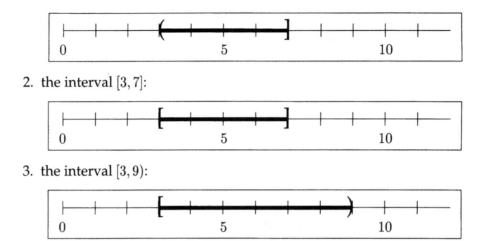

5. and the range of numbers *outside* of $[1, 3]$.

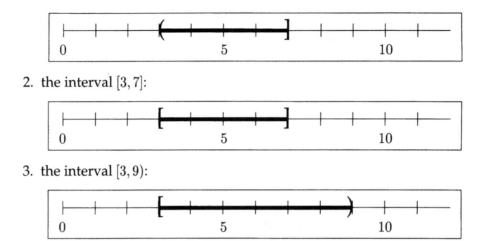

■

**Exercise 4.2.2** Translate the following three Scheme functions into intervals on the line of reals:

    1. (**define** (*in-interval-1? x*)
        (**and** $(< -3\ x)\ (< x\ 0)$)))

    2. (**define** (*in-interval-2? x*)
        (**or** $(< x\ 1)\ (> x\ 2)$)))

    3. (**define** (*in-interval-3? x*)
        (not (**and** $(<= 1\ x)\ (<= x\ 5)$))))

Also formulate contracts and purpose statements for the three functions.
    Evaluate the following expressions by hand:

    1. (*in-interval-1?* $-2$)

2. (*in-interval-2?* −2)

3. (*in-interval-3?* −2)

Show the important steps. Use the pictures to check your results. ∎

**Exercise 4.2.3** Mathematical equations in one variable are claims about an unknown number. For example, the quadratic equation

$$x^2 + 2 \cdot x + 1 = 0$$

is a claim concerning some unknown number $x$. For $x = -1$, the claim holds:

$$x^2 + 2 \cdot x + 1 = (-1)^2 + 2 \cdot (-1) + 1 = 1 - 2 + 1 = 0 \,.$$

For $x = 1$, it doesn't, because

$$x^2 + 2 \cdot x + 1 = (1)^2 + 2 \cdot (1) + 1 = 1 + 2 + 1 = 4 \,,$$

and 4 is *not* equal to 0. A number for which the claim holds is called a *solution* to the equation.

We can use Scheme to formulate equational conditions as a function. If someone then claims to have a solution, we can use the function to test whether the proposed solution is, in fact, a solution. Our running example corresponds to the function

```
;; equation1 : number → boolean
;; to determine whether x is a solution for x² + 2 · x + 1 = 0
(define (equation1 x)
  (= (+ (* x x) (+ (* 2 x) 1)) 0))
```

When we apply *equation1* to some number, we get true or false:

```
(equation1 −1)
= true
```

and

```
(equation1 +1)
= false
```

Translate the following equations into Scheme functions:

1. $4 \cdot n + 2 = 62$

2. $2 \cdot n^2 = 102$

3. $4 \cdot n^2 + 6 \cdot n + 2 = 462$

Determine whether 10, 12, or 14 are solutions of these equations. ∎

Testing

**Exercise 4.2.4** Equations are not only ubiquitous in mathematics, they are also heavily used in programming. We have used equations to state what a function should do with examples, we have used them to evaluate expressions by hand, and we have added them as test cases to the Definitions window. For example, if our goal is to define *Fahrenheit→ Celsius*, we might have added our examples as test cases as follows:

;; test expression:
(*Fahrenheit→ Celsius* 32)
;; expected result:
0

and

;; test expression:
(*Fahrenheit→ Celsius* 212)
;; expected result:
100

After clicking the Execute button we can compare the two numbers. If they are equal, we know our function works.

As our results become more and more complex, comparing values becomes more and more tedious. Using =, we can instead translate these equations into claims:

(= (*Fahrenheit→ Celsius* 32)
    0)

and

(= (*Fahrenheit→ Celsius* 212)
    100)

Now, if all claims evaluate to true, we know that our function works for the specified examples. If we see a false anywhere, something is still wrong.

Reformulate the test cases for exercises 2.2.1, 2.2.2, 2.2.3, and 2.2.4 as claims.

**Testing**: Writing tests as claims is good practice, though we need to know more about equality to develop good automatic tests. To do so, we resume the discussion of equality and testing in section 17.8. ∎

## 4.3 Conditionals and Conditional Functions

Conditionals Some banks pay different levels of interest for saving accounts. The more a customer deposits, the more the bank pays. In such arrangements, the interest rate depends on the *interval* into which the savings amount falls. To assist their bank clerks, banks use interest-rate functions. An interest function consumes the amount that a customer wishes to deposit and responds with the interest that the customer receives for this amount of money.

Our interest rate function must determine which of several conditions holds for the input. We say that the function is a CONDITIONAL FUNCTION, and we formulate the definition of such functions using CONDITIONAL EXPRESSIONS. The general shape of a conditional expression is

(**cond**                                      (**cond**

[*question answer*]                  [*question answer*]

. . .                                  . . .

[*question answer*])      or      [**else** *answer*])

The dots indicate that a **cond**-expression may contain an arbitrary number of **cond**-lines. Each **cond**-line, also called a **cond**-clause, contains two expressions, called CONDITION and ANSWER. A condition is a conditional expression that involves the parameters; the answer is a Scheme expression that computes the result from the parameters and other data if the conditional expression holds.[14]

Conditional expressions are the most complicated form of expressions we have encountered and will encounter. It is therefore easy to make mistakes when we write them down. Compare the following two parenthesized expressions:

(**cond**                                  (**cond**

[(< *n* 10) 5.0]               [(< *n* 10) 30 12]

[(< *n* 20) 5]                 [(> *n* 25) false]

[(< *n* 30) true])             [(> *n* 20) 0])

---

[14]The use of brackets, that is, [ and ], in place of parentheses is optional, but it sets apart the conditional clauses from other expressions and helps people read functions.

The left one is a valid **cond**-expression because each **cond**-line contains two expressions. In contrast, the right one is *not* a valid **cond**-expression. Its first line contains three expressions instead of two.

When Scheme evaluates a **cond**-expression, it determines the value of each condition, one by one. A condition must evaluate to true or false. For the first condition that evaluates to true, Scheme evaluates the corresponding answer, and the value of the answer is the value of the entire **cond**-expression. If the last condition is **else** and all other conditions fail, the answer for the **cond** is the value of the last answer expression.[15]

Here are two simple examples:

```
(cond                           (cond
  [(<= n 1000) .040]              [(<= n 1000) .040]
  [(<= n 5000) .045]              [(<= n 5000) .045]
  [(<= n 10000) .055]            [(<= n 10000) .055]
  [(> n 10000) .060])            [else .060])
```

If we replace $n$ with 20000, the first three conditions evaluate to false in both expressions. For the expression on the left the fourth condition, (> 20000 10000), evaluates to true and therefore the answer is 0.60. For the expression on the right, the **else** clause specifies what the result of the entire expression is. In contrast, if $n$ is 10000, the value is .055 because for both expressions, (<= 10000 1000) and (<= 10000 5000) evaluate to false and (<= 10000 10000) evaluates to true.

---

## Exercises

**Exercise 4.3.1** Decide which of the following two **cond**-expressions is legal:

```
(cond                           (cond
  [(< n 10) 20]                   [(< n 10) 20]
  [(> n 20) 0]                    [(and (> n 20) (<= n 30))]
  [else 1])                       [else 1])
```

Explain why the other one is not. Why is the following illegal?

```
(cond [(< n 10) 20]
  [* 10 n]
  [else 555]) ;            ∎
```

---
[15]If the **cond**-expression has no **else** clause and all conditions evaluate to false, an error is signaled in Beginning Student Scheme.

**Exercise 4.3.2** What is the value of

> **(cond**
>     [(<= *n* 1000) .040]
>     [(<= *n* 5000) .045]
>     [(<= *n* 10000) .055]
>     [(> *n* 10000) .060])

when *n* is (a) 500, (b) 2800, and (c) 15000? ∎

**Exercise 4.3.3** What is the value of

> **(cond**
>     [(<= *n* 1000) (∗ .040 1000)]
>     [(<= *n* 5000) (+ (∗ 1000 .040)
>                        (∗ (− *n* 1000) .045))]
>     [**else** (+ (∗ 1000 .040)
>             (∗ 4000 .045)
>             (∗ (− *n* 10000) .055))])

when *n* is (a) 500, (b) 2800, and (c) 15000? ∎

With the help of **cond**-expressions, we can now define the interest rate function that we mentioned at the beginning of this section. Suppose the bank pays 4% for deposits of up to $1,000 (inclusive), 4.5% for deposits of up to $5,000 (inclusive), and 5% for deposits of more than $5,000. Clearly, the function consumes one number and produces one:

> ;; *interest-rate : number → number*
> ;; to determine the interest rate for the given *amount*
> (**define** (*interest-rate amount*) . . . )

Furthermore, the problem statement provides three examples:

1. (= (*interest-rate* 1000) .040)

2. (= (*interest-rate* 5000) .045)

3. (= (*interest-rate* 8000) .050)

Recall that examples are now formulated as boolean expressions when possible.

The body of the function must be a **cond**-expression that distinguishes the three cases mentioned in the problem statement. Here is a sketch:

> (**cond**
>     [(<= *amount* 1000) ... ]
>     [(<= *amount* 5000) ... ]
>     [(> *amount* 5000) ... ])

Using the examples and the outline of the **cond**-expression, the answers are easy:

> (**define** (*interest-rate amount*)
>     (**cond**
>         [(<= *amount* 1000) 0.040]
>         [(<= *amount* 5000) 0.045]
>         [(> *amount* 5000) 0.050]))

Since we know that the function requires only three cases, we can also replace the last condition with **else**:

> (**define** (*interest-rate amount*)
>     (**cond**
>         [(<= *amount* 1000) 0.040]
>         [(<= *amount* 5000) 0.045]
>         [**else** 0.050]))

When we apply *interest-rate* to an amount, say, 4000, the calculation proceeds as usual. Scheme first copies the body of the function and replaces *amount* by 4000:

> (*interest-rate* 4000)
> = (**cond**
>     [(<= 4000 1000) 0.040]
>     [(<= 4000 5000) 0.045]
>     [**else** 0.050])
> = 0.045

The first condition is false but the second one is true, so the result is 0.045 or 4.5%. The evaluation would proceed in the same manner if we had used the variant of the function with (> *amount* 5000) instead of **else**.

## 4.4  Designing Conditional Functions

Developing conditional functions is more difficult than designing a plain function. The key is to recognize that the problem statement lists cases and to identify the different cases. To emphasize the importance of this idea, we introduce and discuss a design recipe for designing conditional functions. The new recipe introduces a new step, DATA ANALYSIS, which requires a programmer to understand the different situations that the problem statement discusses. It also modifies the Examples and the Body steps of the design recipe in section 2.5:

**Data Analysis and Definition:** After we determine that a problem statement deals with distinct situations, we must identify all of them. The second step is a DATA DEFINITION, an idea that we will explore a lot more.

For numeric functions, a good strategy is to draw a number line and to identify the intervals that correspond to a specific situation. Consider the contract for the *interest-rate* function:

;; *interest-rate : number → number*
;; to determine the interest rate for the given *amount* $>= 0$
(**define** (*interest-rate amount*) ...)

It inputs non-negative numbers and produces answers for three distinct situations:

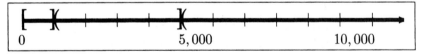

For functions that process booleans, the **cond**-expression must distinguish between exactly two situations: true and false. We will soon encounter other forms of data that require case-based reasoning.

**Function Examples:** Our choice of examples accounts for the distinct situations. At a minimum, we must develop one function example per situation. If we characterized the situations as numeric intervals, the examples should also include all borderline cases.

For our *interest-rate* function, we should use 0, 1000, and 5000 as borderline cases. In addition, we should pick numbers like 500, 2000, and 7000 to test the interiors of the three intervals.

**The Function Body—Conditions:** The function's body must consist of a **cond**-expression that has as many clauses as there are distinct situations. This requirement immediately suggests the following body of our solution:

```
(define (interest-rate amount)
  (cond
    [... ...]
    [... ...]
    [... ...]))
```

Next we must formulate the conditions that characterize each situation. The conditions are claims about the function's parameters, expressed with Scheme's relational operators or with our own functions.

The number line from our example translates into the following three conditions:

1. (and ($<=$ 0 *amount*) ($<=$ *amount* 1000))

2. (and ($<$ 1000 *amount*) ($<=$ *amount* 5000))

3. ($<$ 5000 *amount*)

Adding these conditions to the function produces a better approximation of the final definition:

```
(define (interest-rate amount)
  (cond
    [(and (<= 0 amount) (<= amount 1000)) ...]
    [(and (< 1000 amount) (<= amount 5000)) ...]
    [(> amount 5000) ...]))
```

At this stage, a programmer should check that the chosen conditions distinguish inputs in an appropriate manner. Specifically, if some input belongs to a particular situation and **cond**-line, the preceding conditions should evaluate to false and the condition of the line should evaluate to true.

**The Function Body—Answers:** Finally, it is time to determine what the function should produce for each **cond**-clause. More concretely, we consider each line in the **cond**-expression separately, assuming that the condition holds.

In our example, the results are directly specified by the problem statement. They are 4.0, 4.5, and 5.0. In more complicated examples, we may have to determine an expression for each **cond**-answer following the suggestion of our first design recipe.

**Hint:** If the answers for each **cond**-clause are complex, it is good practice to develop one answer at a time. Assume that the condition evaluates to true, and develop an answer using the parameters, primitives, and other functions. Then apply the function to inputs that force the evaluation of this new answer. It is legitimate to leave "..." in place of the remaining answers.

**Simplification:** When the definition is complete and tested, a programmer might wish to check whether the conditions can be simplified. In our example, we know that *amount* is always greater than or equal to 0, so the first condition could be formulated as

$(<= amount\ 1000)$

Furthermore, we know that **cond**-expressions are evaluated sequentially. That is, by the time the second condition is evaluated the first one must have produced false. Hence we know that the amount is *not* less than or equal to 1000, which makes the left component of the second condition superfluous. The appropriately simplified sketch of *interest-rate* is as follows:

```
(define (interest-rate amount)
  (cond
    [(<= amount 1000) ...]
    [(<= amount 5000) ...]
    [(> amount 5000) ...]))
```

Figure 6 summarizes these suggestions on the design of conditional functions. Read it in conjunction with figure 4 and compare the two rows for "Body." Reread the table when designing a conditional function!

## Exercises

**Exercise 4.4.1** Develop the function *interest*. Like *interest-rate*, it consumes a deposit amount. Instead of the rate, it produces the actual amount of interest that the money earns in a year. The bank pays a flat 4% for deposits of up to $1,000, a flat 4.5% per year for deposits of up to $5,000, and a flat 5% for deposits of more than $5,000. ∎

| Phase | Goal | Activity |
|---|---|---|
| Data Analysis | to determine the distinct situations a function deals with | inspect the problem statement for distinct situations • enumerate all possible situations |
| Examples | to provide an example per situation | choose at least one example per situation • for intervals or enumerations, the examples must include borderline cases |
| Body (1) Conditions | to formulate a conditional expression | write down the skeleton of a **cond** expression, with one clause per situation • formulate one condition per situation, using the parameters • ensure that the conditions distinguish the examples appropriately |
| Body (2) Answers | to formulate the answers for the **cond**-clauses | deal with each **cond**-line *separately* • assume the condition holds and develop a Scheme expression that computes the appropriate answer for this case |

Figure 6: Designing the body of a conditional function
(Use with the recipe in figure 4 (pg. 21))

**Exercise 4.4.2** Develop the function *tax*, which consumes the gross pay and produces the amount of tax owed. For a gross pay of $240 or less, the tax is 0%; for over $240 and $480 or less, the tax rate is 15%; and for any pay over $480, the tax rate is 28%.

Also develop *netpay*. The function determines the net pay of an employee from the number of hours worked. The *net pay* is the gross pay minus the tax. Assume the hourly pay rate is $12.
**Hint:** Remember to develop auxiliary functions when a definition becomes too large or too complex to manage. ∎

**Exercise 4.4.3** Some credit card companies pay back a small portion of the charges a customer makes over a year. One company returns

1. .25% for the first $500 of charges,

2. .50% for the next $1000 (that is, the portion between $500 and $1500),

3. .75% for the next $1000 (that is, the portion between $1500 and $2500),

4. and 1.0% for everything above $2500.

Thus, a customer who charges $400 a year receives $1.00, which is $0.25 \cdot 1/100 \cdot 400$, and one who charges $1,400 a year receives $5.75, which is $1.25 = 0.25 \cdot 1/100 \cdot 500$ for the first $500 and $0.50 \cdot 1/100 \cdot 900 = 4.50$ for the next $900.

Determine by hand the pay-backs for a customer who charged $2000 and one who charged $2600.

Define the function *pay-back*, which consumes a charge amount and computes the corresponding pay-back amount. ∎

**Exercise 4.4.4** An equation is a claim about numbers; a quadratic equation is a special kind of equation. All quadratic equations (in one variable) have the following general shape:

$$a \cdot x^2 + b \cdot x + c = 0 .$$

In a specific equation, $a$, $b$ and $c$ are replaced by numbers, as in

$$2 \cdot x^2 + 4 \cdot x + 2 = 0$$

or

$$1 \cdot x^2 + 0 \cdot x + (-1) = 0 .$$

The variable $x$ represents the unknown.

Depending on the value of $x$, the two sides of the equation evaluate to the same value (see exercise 4.2.3). If the two sides are equal, the claim is true; otherwise it is false. A number that makes the claim true is a *solution*. The first equation has one solution, $-1$, as we can easily check:

$$2 \cdot (-1)^2 + 4 \cdot (-1) + 2 = 2 - 4 + 2 = 0 .$$

The second equation has two solutions: $+1$ and $-1$.

The number of solutions for a quadratic equation depends on the values of $a$, $b$, and $c$. If the coefficient $a$ is 0, we say the equation is *degenerate* and do not consider how many solutions it has. Assuming $a$ is not 0, the equation has

1. two solutions if $b^2 > 4 \cdot a \cdot c$,

2. one solution if $b^2 = 4 \cdot a \cdot c$, and

3. no solution if $b^2 < 4 \cdot a \cdot c$.

To distinguish this case from the degenerate one, we sometimes use the phrase *proper* quadratic equation.

Develop the function *how-many*, which consumes the coefficients $a$, $b$, and $c$ of a proper quadratic equation and determines how many solutions the equation has:

(*how-many* 1 0 −1) = 2
(*how-many* 2 4 2) = 1

Make up additional examples. First determine the number of solutions by hand, then with DrScheme.

How would the function change if we didn't assume the equation was proper? ∎

# 5  Symbolic Information

Symbols, Images

These days computers mostly process symbolic information such as names, words, directions, or images. All modern programming languages support at least one way of representing symbolic information. Scheme supports several ways to express symbolic information: symbols, strings, (keyboard) characters, and images. A *symbol* is a sequence of keyboard characters[16] preceded by a single forward quotation mark:

'the      'dog      'ate      'a      'chocolate      'cat!      'two^3      'and%so%on?

Like a number, a symbol has no inherent meaning. It is up to the function's user to relate symbolic data and real-world information, though the connection is typically obvious in a specific context. For example, 'east will usually refer to the direction where the sun rises, 'professor will be the title of a person teaching and researching at a university.

---

[16]Not all keyboard characters are legal in symbols. For example, a blank space or a comma are illegal.

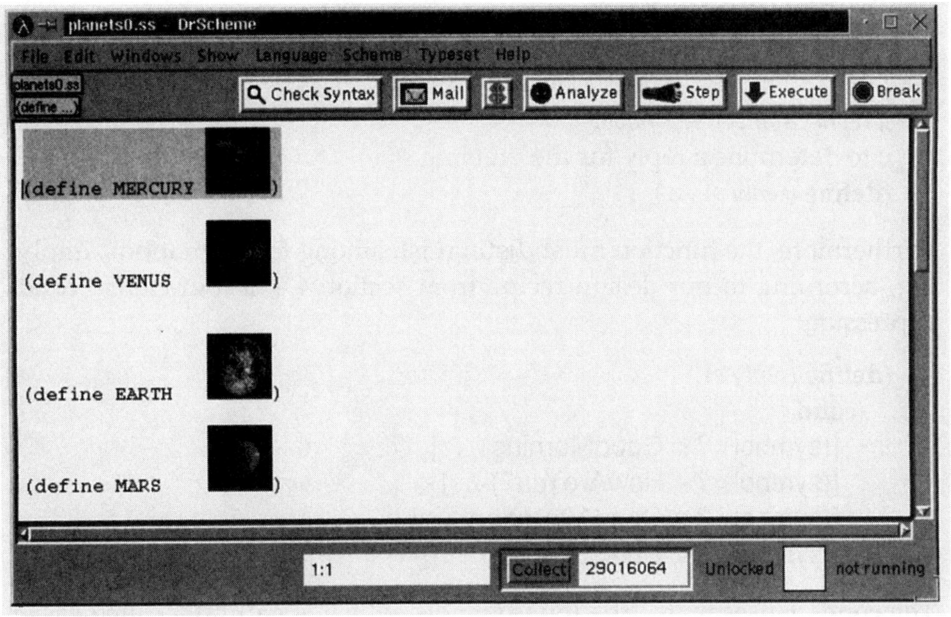

Figure 7: The planets as images in DrScheme

Like numbers, symbols are atomic pieces of data. Their purpose is to represent things such as family and first names, job titles, commands, announcements, and so on. Scheme provides only one basic operation on symbols: symbol=?, a comparison operation. It consumes two symbols and produces true if and only if the two symbols are identical:

(symbol=? 'Hello 'Hello) = true

(symbol=? 'Hello 'Howdy) = false

(symbol=? 'Hello $x$) = true if $x$ stands for 'Hello

(symbol=? 'Hello $x$) = false if $x$ stands for 'Howdy

Symbols were first introduced to computing by researchers in artificial intelligence who wanted to design functions that could have conversations with people. Consider the function *reply*, which replies with some remark to the following greetings: "good morning," "how are you," "good afternoon," and "good evening." Each of those short sentences can be represented as a symbol: 'GoodMorning, 'HowAreYou, 'GoodAfternoon, and 'GoodEvening. Thus, *reply* consumes a symbol and replies with a symbol:

```
;; reply : symbol → symbol
;; to determine a reply for the greeting s
(define (reply s) ...)
```

Furthermore, the function must distinguish among four situations, implying, according to our design recipe from section 4.4, a four-clause **cond**-expression:

```
(define (reply s)
  (cond
    [(symbol=? s 'GoodMorning) ...]
    [(symbol=? s 'HowAreYou?) ...]
    [(symbol=? s 'GoodAfternoon) ...]
    [(symbol=? s 'GoodEvening) ...]))
```

The **cond**-clauses match the four symbols, which is naturally much easier than matching four intervals.

From this function template it is a short step to the final function. Here is one version of *reply*:

```
(define (reply s)
  (cond
    [(symbol=? s 'GoodMorning) 'Hi]
    [(symbol=? s 'HowAreYou?) 'Fine]
    [(symbol=? s 'GoodAfternoon) 'INeedANap]
    [(symbol=? s 'GoodEvening) 'BoyAmITired]))
```

We can think of many different ways of how to replace the "..." in the template with replies. But no matter what we replace them with, the basic template could be defined without concern for the output of the function. We will see in subsequent sections that this focus on the input data is actually the norm and that concern for the output data can be postponed.

**A Note on Strings**: A *string* is a second form of symbolic data. Like a symbol, a string consists of a sequence of keyboard characters, but they are enclosed in string quotes:

"the dog"    "isn't"    "made of"    "chocolate"    "two^3"    "and so on?"

In contrast to symbols, strings are not atomic. They are compound data, which we discuss later in the book. For now, we use strings as if they were fancy symbols; the only operation needed is string=?, which compares two strings the way symbol=? compares two symbols. Otherwise we ignore strings, and when we use them, we act as if they were symbols. ∎

**A Note on Images**: An *image* is a third form of symbolic data, and it is fun to develop functions that process images. Like symbols, images don't have any a priori meaning, but we tend to connect them easily with the intended information.

DrScheme supports images: see figure 7, which shows the beginning of a function that manipulates planet pictures. Images are values like numbers and booleans. They can therefore be used inside of expressions. Most often though, we give images names because they are typically used by several functions. If we don't like the picture, it is then easily replaced with a different one (see section 3.2). ∎

Teachpacks

## 5.1 Finger Exercises with Symbols

**Exercise 5.1.1** Evaluate (*reply* 'HowAreYou?) by hand and with DrScheme's stepper. Formulate a complete set of examples for *reply* as boolean expressions (using symbol=?). ∎

**Exercise 5.1.2** Develop the function *check-guess*. It consumes two numbers, *guess* and *target*. Depending on how *guess* relates to *target*, the function produces one of the following three answers: 'TooSmall, 'Perfect, or 'TooLarge.

The function implements one part of a two-player number guessing game. One player picks a random number between 0 and 99999. The other player's goal is to determine this number, called *target*, with the least number of guesses. To each guess, the first player responds with one of the three responses that *check-guess* implements.

The function *check-guess* and the teachpack **guess.ss** implement the first player. The teachpack picks the random number, pops up a window in which the second player can choose digits, and hands over the *guess* and the *target* to *check-guess*. To play the game, set the teachpack to **guess.ss** using the Language|Set teachpack option. Then evaluate the expression

(*guess-with-gui check-guess*)

after *check-guess* has been thoroughly tested. ∎

**Exercise 5.1.3** Develop the function *check-guess3*. It implements a larger portion of the number guessing game of exercise 5.1.2 than the function *check-guess*. Now the teachpack hands over the *digits* that the user guesses, not the number that they form.

To simplify the problem a little bit, the game works with only three numbers. Thus, *check-guess3* consumes three digits and a number. The first digit is the least significant, the third one is the most significant. The number is called *target* and represents the randomly chosen number. Depending on how *guess*, the number determined by the three digits, relates to *target*, *check-guess3* produces one of the following three answers: 'TooSmall, 'Perfect, or 'TooLarge.

The rest of the game is still implemented by **guess.ss**. To play the game with *check-guess3*, evaluate

   (*guess-with-gui-3 check-guess3*)

after the function has been thoroughly tested.
**Hint:** Remember to develop an auxiliary function per concept. ∎

**Exercise 5.1.4** Develop *what-kind*. The function consumes the coefficients *a*, *b*, and *c* of a quadratic equation. It then determines whether the equation is degenerate and, if not, how many solutions the equation has. The function produces one of four symbols: 'degenerate, 'two, 'one, or 'none.
**Hint:** Compare with exercise 4.4.4. ∎

**Exercise 5.1.5** Develop the function *check-color*. It implements a key portion of a color guessing game. One player picks two colors for two squares; we call those *targets*. The other one tries to guess which color is assigned to which square; they are guesses. The first player's response to a guess is to check the colors and to produce one of the following answers:

1. 'Perfect, if the first target is equal to the first guess and the second target is equal to the second guess;

2. 'OneColorAtCorrectPosition, if the first guess is equal to the first target or the second guess is equal to the second target;

3. 'OneColorOccurs, if either guess is one of the two targets; and

4. 'NothingCorrect, otherwise.

These four answers are the only answers that the first player gives. The second player is to guess the two chosen target colors with as few guesses as possible.

The function *check-color* simulates the first player's checking action. It consumes four colors; for simplicity, we assume that a color is a symbol, say, 'red. The first two arguments to *check-color* are "targets," the latter two are "guesses." The function produces one of the four answers.

When the function is tested, use the teachpack to **master.ss** to play the color-guessing game.[17] The teachpack provides the function *master*. Evaluate (*master check-color*) and choose colors with the mouse. ∎

# 6 Compound Data, Part 1: Structures

The input of a function is seldom a single measurement (number), a single switch position (boolean), or a single name (symbol). Instead, it is almost always a piece of data that represents an object with many properties. Each property is a piece of information. For example, a function may consume a record about a CD; the relevant information might include the artist's name, the CD title, and the price. Similarly, if we are to model the movement of an object across a plane with a function, we must represent the position of the object in the plane, its speed in each direction, and possibly its color. In both cases, we refer to several pieces of information as if they were one: *one* record and *one* point. In short, we COMPOUND several pieces of data into a single piece of data.

Scheme provides many different methods for compounding data. In this section, we deal with *structures*. A structure combines a fixed number of values into a single piece of data. In section 9, we will encounter a method for combining an arbitrarily large number of values into a single piece of data.

## 6.1 Structures

Structures   Suppose we wish to represent the *pixels* (colored dots) on our computer monitors. A pixel is very much like a Cartesian point. It has an $x$ coordinate, which tells us where the pixel is in the horizontal direction, and it has a $y$ coordinate, which tells us where the pixel is located in the downwards

---

[17]MasterMind, the commercial version of this game, is played in a different manner.

vertical direction. Given the two numbers, we can locate a pixel on the monitor, and so can a computer program.

DrScheme's teachpacks represent pixels with *posn* structures. A *posn* structure combines two numbers. That is, a *posn* is a single value that contains two values. We can create a *posn* structure with the operation make-posn, which consumes two numbers and makes a *posn*. For example,

(make-posn 3 4)

(make-posn 8 6)

(make-posn 5 12)

are *posn* structures. Each of these structures has the same status as a number as far as computations are concerned. Both primitive operations and functions can consume and produce structures.

Now consider a function that computes how far some pixel is from the origin. The contract, header, and purpose statement are easy to formulate:

;; *distance-to-0 : posn → number*
;; to compute the distance of *a-posn* to the origin
(**define** (*distance-to-0 a-posn*) ...)

In other words, *distance-to-0* consumes a single value, a *posn* structure, and produces a single value, a number.

We already have some input examples, namely, the three *posn* structures mentioned above. What we need next are examples that relate inputs and outputs. For points with 0 as one of the coordinates, the result is the other coordinate:

(*distance-to-0* (make-posn 0 5))
= 5

and

(*distance-to-0* (make-posn 7 0))
= 7

In general, we know from geometry that the distance from the origin to a position with coordinates $x$ and $y$ is distance

$$\sqrt{x^2 + y^2} \ .$$

Thus,

(*distance-to-0* (make-posn 3 4))
= 5

*(distance-to-0* (make-posn 8 6))
= 10

*(distance-to-0* (make-posn 5 12))
= 13

Once we have examples, we can turn our attention to the definition of the function. The examples imply that the design of *distance-to-0* doesn't need to distinguish between different situations. Still, we are stuck now, because *distance-to-0* has a single parameter that represents the entire pixel but we need the two coordinates to compute the distance. Put differently, we know how to combine two numbers into a *posn* structure using make-posn and we don't know how to extract these numbers from a *posn* structure.

Scheme provides operations for extracting values from structures.[18] For *posn* structures, Scheme supports two such operations: posn-x and posn-y. The former operation extracts the $x$ coordinate; the latter extracts the $y$ coordinate.

To describe how posn-x, posn-y, and make-posn are related, we can use equations that are roughly analogous to the equations that govern addition and subtraction:

(posn-x (make-posn 7 0))
= 7

and

(posn-y (make-posn 7 0))
= 0

The equations only confirm what we already know. But suppose we introduce the following definition:

(**define** *a-posn* (make-posn 7 0))

Then we can use the two operations as follows in the Interactions window:

(posn-x *a-posn*)
= 7

(posn-y *a-posn*)
= 0

---

[18] An alternative terminology is "to access the fields of a record." We prefer to think of structure values as containers from which we can extract other values.

Naturally, we can nest such expressions:

    (* (posn-x *a-posn*) 7)
    = 49

    (+ (posn-y *a-posn*) 13)
    = 13

Now we know enough to complete the definition of *distance-to-0*. We know that the function's *a-posn* parameter is a *posn* structure and that the structure contains two numbers, which we can extract with (posn-x *a-posn*) and (posn-y *a-posn*). Let us add this knowledge to our function outline:

    (**define** (*distance-to-0 a-posn*)
      ... (posn-x *a-posn*) ...
      ... (posn-y *a-posn*) ...)

Using this outline and the examples, the rest is easy:

    (**define** (*distance-to-0 a-posn*)
      (sqrt
        (+ (sqr (posn-x *a-posn*))
           (sqr (posn-y *a-posn*)))))

The function squares (posn-x *a-posn*) and (posn-y *a-posn*), which represent the $x$ and $y$ coordinates, sums up the results, and takes the square root. With DrScheme, we can also quickly check that our new function produces the proper results for our examples.

## Exercises

**Exercise 6.1.1** Evaluate the following expressions:

1. (*distance-to-0* (make-posn 3 4))

2. (*distance-to-0* (make-posn (* 2 3) (* 2 4)))

3. (*distance-to-0* (make-posn 12 (− 6 1)))

by hand. Show all steps. Assume that sqr performs its computation in a single step. Check the results with DrScheme's stepper. ∎

## 6.2 Extended Exercise: Drawing Simple Pictures

Drawing DrScheme provides the graphics teachpack **draw.ss**, which introduces simple graphics operations:

1. *draw-solid-line*, which consumes two *posn* structures, the beginning and the end of the line on the canvas, and a color.

2. *draw-solid-rect*, which consumes four arguments: a *posn* structure for the upper-left corner of the rectangle, a number for the width of the rectangle, another number for its height, and a color.

3. *draw-solid-disk*, which consumes three arguments: a *posn* structure for the center of the disk, a number for the radius of the disk, and a color.

4. *draw-circle*, which consumes three arguments: a *posn* structure for the center of the circle, a number for the radius, and a color.

Each of the operation produces true, if it succeeds in changing the canvas as specified. We refer to the action to the canvas as an EFFECT, but we will ignore studying the precise nature of effects until part VII. Also, if anything goes wrong with the operation, it stops the evaluation with an error.

Each drawing operation also comes with a matching *clear-* operation: *clear-solid-line*, *clear-solid-rect*, *clear-solid-disk*, and *clear-circle*. If these functions are applied to the same arguments as their matching *draw-* function, they clear the corresponding shapes of the canvas.[19]

Drawing operations on computers interpret the screen as follows:

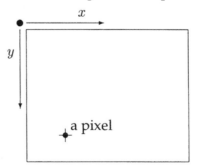

First, the origin of the plane is in the upper-left corner. Second, $y$ coordinates grow in the downwards direction. Understanding the difference

---

[19]For more documentation, see DrScheme's Help Desk.

between this picture and the more conventional Cartesian plane is critical for drawing shapes with programs.

Drawing

## Exercises

**Exercise 6.2.1** Evaluate the following expressions in order:

1. (*start* 300 300), which opens a canvas for future drawing operations;

2. (*draw-solid-line* (make-posn 1 1) (make-posn 5 5) 'red), which draws a red line;

3. (*draw-solid-rect* (make-posn 20 10) 50 200 'blue), which draws a blue rectangle of width 50 parallel to the line; and

4. (*draw-circle* (make-posn 200 10) 50 'red), which draws a red circle of radius 50 and a center point at the upper line of the rectangle.

5. (*draw-solid-disk* (make-posn 200 10) 50 'green), which draws a green disk of radius 50 and a center point at the height of the upper line of the rectangle.

6. (*stop*), which closes the canvas.

Read the documentation for **draw.ss** in DrScheme's HelpDesk. ∎

The definitions and expressions in figure 8 draw a traffic light. The program fragment illustrates the use of global definitions for specifying and computing constants. Here, the constants represent the dimensions of the canvas, which is the outline of the traffic light, and the positions of three light bulbs.

**Exercise 6.2.2** Develop the function *clear-bulb*. It consumes a symbol that denotes one of the possible colors: 'green, 'yellow, or 'red, and it produces true. Its effect is "to turn off" the matching bulb in the traffic light. Specifically, it should clear the disk and display a circle of the matching color instead.

**Choice of Design Recipe**: See section 5 for designing functions that consume one of an enumeration of symbols.

**Testing**: When testing functions that draw shapes into a canvas, we ignore test expressions. Although it is possible to implement appropriate test suites, the problem is beyond the scope of this book.

```
;; dimensions of traffic light
(define WIDTH 50)
(define HEIGHT 160)
(define BULB-RADIUS 20)
(define BULB-DISTANCE 10)

;; the positions of the bulbs
(define X-BULBS (quotient WIDTH 2))
(define Y-RED (+ BULB-DISTANCE BULB-RADIUS))
(define Y-YELLOW (+ Y-RED BULB-DISTANCE (* 2 BULB-RADIUS)))
(define Y-GREEN (+ Y-YELLOW BULB-DISTANCE (* 2 BULB-RADIUS)))

;; draw the light with the red bulb turned on
(start WIDTH HEIGHT)
(draw-solid-disk (make-posn X-BULBS Y-RED) BULB-RADIUS 'red)
(draw-circle (make-posn X-BULBS Y-YELLOW) BULB-RADIUS 'yellow)
(draw-circle (make-posn X-BULBS Y-GREEN) BULB-RADIUS 'green)
```

Figure 8: Drawing a traffic light

**Combining Effects**: The primitive operations for drawing and clearing disks and circles produce true if they successfully complete their task. The natural way to combine the values and the effects of these functions is to use an **and**-expression. In particular, if *exp1* and *exp2* produce effects and we wish to see the effects of *exp2* after those of *exp1*, we write

(**and** *exp1 exp2*)

Later we will study effects in more detail and learn different ways to combine effects. ∎

**Exercise 6.2.3** Develop a function *draw-bulb*. It consumes a symbol that denotes one of the possible colors: 'green, 'yellow, or 'red, and produces true. Its effect is "to turn on" the matching bulb in the traffic light. ∎

**Exercise 6.2.4** Develop the function *switch*. It consumes two symbols, each of which stands for a traffic light color, and produces true. Its effects are to clear the bulb for the first color and then to draw the second bulb. ∎

**Exercise 6.2.5** Here is the function *next*:

*;; next : symbol → symbol*
*;;* to switch a traffic light's current color and to return the next one
(**define** (*next current-color*)
  (**cond**
    [(**and** (symbol=? *current-color* 'red) (*switch* 'red 'green))
    'green]
    [(**and** (symbol=? *current-color* 'yellow) (*switch* 'yellow 'red))
    'red]
    [(**and** (symbol=? *current-color* 'green) (*switch* 'green 'yellow))
    'yellow]))

It consumes the current color of a traffic light (as a symbol) and produces
the next color that the traffic light shows. That is, if the input is 'green, it
produces 'yellow; if it is 'yellow, it produces 'red; and if it is 'red, it produces
'green. Its effect is to switch the traffic light from the input color to the next
color.

Replace the last three lines of the program fragment in figure 8 with
(*draw-bulb* 'red). This creates a traffic light that is red. Then use *next* to
switch the traffic light four times. ∎

## 6.3   Structure Definitions

In the preceding section we explored one particular class of structures: the
*posn* structures. A *posn* structure combines two numbers, and it is useful
to represent pixels. If we wish to represent employee records or points in
three-dimensional space, however, *posn*s are useless. DrScheme therefore
permits programmers to define their own structures so that they can represent all kinds of objects with a fixed number of properties.

Using and
Defining
Structures

    A STRUCTURE DEFINITION is, as the term says, a new form of definition.
Here is DrScheme's definition of *posn*:

(**define-struct** *posn* (*x y*))

When DrScheme evaluates this structure definition, it creates three operations for us, which we can use to create data and to program:

1. make-posn, the CONSTRUCTOR, which creates *posn* structures;

2. posn-x, a SELECTOR, which extracts the $x$ coordinate;

3. posn-y, also a selector, which extracts the $y$ coordinate.

In general, the names of these new operations are created by prefixing the name of the structure with "make-" and by postfixing the name with all the field names. This naming convention appears to be complicated but, with some practice, it is easy to remember.

Now consider the following example:

(**define-struct** *entry* (*name zip phone*))

The structure represents a simplified entry into an address book. Each *entry* combines three values. We also say that each *entry* structure has *three* fields: *name*, *zip*, and *phone*. Because there are three fields, the constructor make-entry consumes three values. For example,

(make-entry 'PeterLee 15270 '606-7771)

creates an *entry* structure with 'PeterLee in the *name*-field, 15270 in the *zip*-field, and '606-7771 in the *phone*-field.

One way to think of a structure is as a box with as many compartments as there are fields:

| *name:* | *zip:* | *phone:* |
|---------|--------|----------|
| 'PeterLee | 15270 | '606-7771 |

The italicized labels name the fields. By putting values in the compartments, we illustrate specific *entry* structures.

The **define-struct** definition of *entry* also introduces new selectors:

entry-name   entry-zip   entry-phone

Here is how we can use the first one:

(entry-name (make-entry 'PeterLee 15270 '606-7771))
= 'PeterLee

If we give the structure a name,

(**define** *phonebook* (make-entry 'PeterLee 15270 '606-7771))

then we can use the selectors in the Interactions window to extract the data from the three fields:

(entry-name *phonebook*)
= 'PeterLee

(entry-zip *phonebook*)
= 15270

(entry-phone *phonebook*)
= '606-7771

Put more graphically, a constructor creates a box with several compartments and puts values in it. A selector reveals the contents of a particular
compartment, but leaves the box alone.

Here is one final example, a structure for representing rock stars:

(**define-struct** *star* (*last first instrument sales*))

It defines the class of *star* structures, each of which has four fields. Accordingly, we get five new primitive operations:

make-star  star-last  star-first  star-instrument  star-sales

The first is for constructing *star* structures; the others are selector operations
for extracting values from a *star* structure.

To create a *star* structure, we apply make-star to three symbols and a
positive integer:

(make-star 'Friedman 'Dan 'ukelele 19004)

(make-star 'Talcott 'Carolyn 'banjo 80000)

(make-star 'Harper 'Robert 'bagpipe 27860)

To select the first name of a star structure called *E*, we use

(star-first *E*)

Other fields are extracted with other selectors.

## Exercises

**Exercise 6.3.1** Consider the following structure definitions:

1. (**define-struct** *movie* (*title producer*))

2. (**define-struct** *boyfriend* (*name hair eyes phone*))

3. (**define-struct** *cheerleader* (*name number*))

4. (**define-struct** *CD* (*artist title price*))

5. (**define-struct** *sweater* (*material size producer*))

What are the names of the constructors and the selectors that each of them adds to Scheme? Draw box representations for each of these structures. ∎

**Exercise 6.3.2** Consider the following structure definition

(**define-struct** *movie* (*title producer*))

and evaluate the following expressions:

1. (movie-title (make-movie 'ThePhantomMenace 'Lucas))

2. (movie-producer (make-movie 'TheEmpireStrikesBack 'Lucas))

Now evaluate the following expressions, assuming $x$ and $y$ stand for arbitrary symbols:

1. (movie-title (make-movie $x$ $y$))

2. (movie-producer (make-movie $x$ $y$))

Formulate equations that state general laws concerning the relationships of movie-title and movie-producer and make-movie. ∎

Functions both consume and produce structures. Suppose we need to record an increase of sales for one of our stars. This act should be recorded in the star's record. To do so, we should have a function that consumes a *star* structure and produces a *star* structure with the same information except for the sales component. Let's assume for now that the function adds 20000 to the star's sales.

First, we write down a basic description of the function, using our contract, header, and purpose format:

;; *increment-sales : star* → *star*
;; to produce a *star* record like *a-star* with 20000 more sales
(**define** (*increment-sales a-star*) ... )

Here is an example of how the function should process *star* structures:

(*increment-sales* (make-star 'Abba 'John 'vocals 12200))

should produce

(make-star 'Abba 'John 'vocals 32200)

---

```
;; increment-sales : star → star
;; to produce a star record like a-star with 20000 more sales
(define (increment-sales a-star)
   (make-star (star-last a-star)
              (star-first a-star)
              (star-instrument a-star)
              (+ (star-sales a-star) 20000)))
```

Figure 9: The complete definition of *increment-sales*

---

The three sample *star* structures from above are also good examples of potential inputs.

The *increment-sales* function must construct a new *star* structure with make-star, but to do so, it must also extract the data in *a-star*. After all, almost all of the data in *a-star* is a part of the *star* structure produced by *increment-sales*. This suggests that the definition of *increment-sales* contains expressions that extract the four fields of *a-star*:

```
(define (increment-sales a-star)
   ... (star-last a-star) ...
   ... (star-first a-star) ...
   ... (star-instrument a-star) ...
   ... (star-sales a-star) ... )
```

As we have seen with the examples, the function adds 20000 to (star-sales *a-star*) and assembles the four pieces of data into a *star* structure with make-star. Figure 9 contains the complete definition.

---

## Exercises

**Exercise 6.3.3** Provide a structure definition that represents an airforce's jet fighters. Assume that a fighter has four essential properties: designation ('f22, 'tornado, or 'mig22), acceleration, top-speed, and range. Then develop the function *within-range*. The function consumes a fighter record and the distance of a target from the (fighter's) base. It determines whether the fighter can reach the intended target. Also develop the function *reduce-range*. The function consumes a fighter record and produces one in which the *range* field is reduced to 80% of the original value. ∎

## 6.4   Data Definitions

Consider the following expression:

(make-posn 'Albert 'Meyer)

It constructs a *posn* structure from two symbols. If we now apply *distance-to-0* to this structure, the computation fails miserably:

(*distance-to-0* (make-posn 'Albert 'Meyer))

= (sqrt
     (+ (sqr (posn-x (make-posn 'Albert 'Meyer)))
        (sqr (posn-y (make-posn 'Albert 'Meyer)))))

= (sqrt
     (+ (sqr 'Albert)
        (sqr (posn-y (make-posn 'Albert 'Meyer)))))

= (sqrt
     (+ (* 'Albert 'Albert)
        (sqr (posn-y (make-posn 'Albert 'Meyer)))))

That is, it requires us to multiply 'Albert with itself. Similarly,

(make-star 'Albert 'Meyer 10000 'electric-organ)

Data
Definitions

does not produce a *star* structure according to our intentions. In particular, the structure is not suitable for processing by *increment-sales*.

   To avoid such problems and to assist with the development of functions, we must add a data definition to each structure definition. A DATA DEFINITION states, in a mixture of English and Scheme, how we intend to use a class of structures and how we construct elements of this class of data. For example, here is a data definition for *posn* structures:

---

A *posn* is a structure:
>            (make-posn *x y*)
where *x* and *y* are numbers.

---

It says that a valid *posn* structure always contains two numbers, and nothing else. Hence, when we use make-posn to create a *posn* structure, we must apply it to two numbers; when a function contains selector expressions for *posn* structures, we may now assume that their result is a number.

The data definition for *star* structures is only slightly more complicated:

> A *star* is a structure:
> (make-star *last first instrument sales*)
> where *last*, *first*, and *instrument* are symbols and *sales* is a number.

This data definition says that valid *star* structures contain symbols in the fields for *last* name, *first* name, and *instrument*, and a number in the *sales* field.

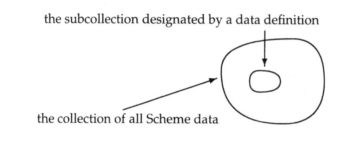

Figure 10: The meaning of data definitions

In general, a data definition identifies a subclass of Scheme's universe of values: see figure 10. As we have seen so far, Scheme's universe contains numbers, symbols, images, strings, chars, booleans, and many different classes of structures. Our functions, however, are intended to work only for a subclass of values. For example, *area-of-disk* consumes only numbers; *reply* from section 5 consumes only symbols. A few subclasses, such as *number*, already have names, because they are useful for all kinds of programming tasks. Others are only interesting in the context of a specific problem. For those cases, a programmer should introduce a data definition.

The most important role of a data definition is that of a covenant between programmers and users. We expect both groups to respect such data definitions, and we expect the programmer to exploit it for the function construction. For example, when the programmer of *distance-to-0* specifies that all *posn*s contain two numbers, a user must always apply *distance-to-0* to a *posn* structure with two numbers. Furthermore, as we will discuss over the next few sections, we expect a programmer to exploit data definitions for function developments. Naturally, a data definition in English and Scheme does not prevent us from abusing make-posn. It is, however, a written statement of intent, and a person who willingly violates or ignores this covenant must face the consequences of ill-behaving computations.[20]

## Exercises

**Exercise 6.4.1** Provide data definitions for the following structure definitions:

1. (**define-struct** *movie* (*title producer*))

2. (**define-struct** *boyfriend* (*name hair eyes phone*))

3. (**define-struct** *cheerleader* (*name number*))

4. (**define-struct** *CD* (*artist title price*))

5. (**define-struct** *sweater* (*material size producer*))

Make appropriate assumptions about what data goes with which field. ∎

**Exercise 6.4.2** Provide a structure definition and a data definition for representing points in time since midnight. A point in time consists of three numbers: hours, minutes, and seconds. ∎

**Exercise 6.4.3** Provide a structure definition and a data definition for representing three-letter *word*s. A word consists of letters, which we represent with the symbols 'a through 'z. ∎

## 6.5 Designing Functions for Compound Data

Sections 6.1 through 6.4 suggest that the design of functions for compound data proceeds in a regular manner. First, a programmer must recognize that structures are needed. We follow the simple rule of using structures whenever the description of some object specifies several pieces of information. If we don't use structures in these cases, we quickly lose track of

---

[20]DrScheme provides an optional tool that permits programmers to check whether users and programmers respect the data definition for a particular structure. To do so, a programmer must state data definitions in a special language. Although checking the adherence to data definitions is important for large programs, an introductory course can avoid this topic.

which data belongs to which object, especially when we write large functions that process massive amounts of data.

Second, a programmer can use the structure and data definitions for the organization of a function. We use the term template when we design functions. As we will see in this and many future sections, the template matches the data definition, and the template is *the* essential step in the careful design of functions.

To emphasize this point, we modify our function design recipe from section 2.5 to accommodate compound data. Most importantly, working with compound data requires adjustments in a few of the basic design steps and two new steps: data analysis and template design:

**Data Analysis and Design:** Before we can develop a function, we must understand how to represent the information in our problem statement within our chosen programming language. To do so, we search the problem statement for descriptions of (relevant) objects and then design a data representation based on the results of our analysis.

Until now we could use Scheme's classes of atomic data (numbers, symbols, images, etc.) to represent information. But they are not enough. If we discover that an object has $N$ properties, we introduce a structure definition with $N$ fields and supply a data definition that specifies what kind of data the fields may contain.

Let us consider functions that process student records at a school. If a student's interesting properties for a school are

1. the first name,
2. the last name, and
3. the name of the home-room teacher,

then we should represent information about a student as a structure:

**(define-struct** *student* (*last first teacher*))

Here is the data definition that specifies the class of student structures as precisely as possible:

A *student* is a structure:
$$(\text{make-student } l\, f\ t)$$
where $l, f$, and $t$ are symbols.

```
;; Data Analysis & Definitions:
(define-struct student (last first teacher))
;; A student is a structure: (make-student l f t) where f, l, and t are symbols.

;; Contract: subst-teacher : student symbol → student

;; Purpose: to create a student structure with a new
;; teacher name if the teacher's name matches 'Fritz

;; Examples:
;; (subst-teacher (make-student 'Find 'Matthew 'Fritz) 'Elise)
;; =
;; (make-student 'Find 'Matthew 'Elise)
;; (subst-teacher (make-student 'Find 'Matthew 'Amanda) 'Elise)
;; =
;; (make-student 'Find 'Matthew 'Amanda)

;; Template:
;; (define (process-student a-student a-teacher)
;; ... (student-last a-student) ...
;; ... (student-first a-student) ...
;; ... (student-teacher a-student) ...)

;; Definition:
(define (subst-teacher a-student a-teacher)
  (cond
    [(symbol=? (student-teacher a-student) 'Fritz)
     (make-student (student-last a-student)
                   (student-first a-student)
                   a-teacher)]
    [else a-student]))

;; Tests:
(subst-teacher (make-student 'Find 'Matthew 'Fritz) 'Elise)
;; expected value:
(make-student 'Find 'Matthew 'Elise)

(subst-teacher (make-student 'Find 'Matthew 'Amanda) 'Elise)
;; expected value:
(make-student 'Find 'Matthew 'Amanda)
```

Figure 11: The design recipe for compound data: A complete example

The corresponding data class contains structures like these:

```
(make-student 'findler 'kathi 'matthias)
(make-student 'fisler 'sean 'matthias)
(make-student 'flatt 'shriram 'matthias)
```

**Contract:** For the formulation of contracts, we can use the names of the atomic classes of data, such as *number* and *symbol*, and those names that we introduced in data definitions, such as *student*.

**Template:** A function that consumes compound data is likely to compute its result from the components of its input. To remind ourselves of the components, we first design a template. For compound data, a TEMPLATE consists of a header and a body that lists all possible selector expressions. Each selector expression is the application of an appropriate selector primitive to a parameter that stands for a structure.

In other words, a template expresses what we know about the inputs, and nothing about the outputs. We can therefore use the same template for all functions that consume the same kind of structure. Also, because a template does not express anything about the purpose of the function, **we can formulate it before or after we have developed examples.**

Consider a function that consumes a *student* structure and a teacher name:

```
;; process-student : student symbol → ???
(define (process-student a-student a-teacher) ...)
```

Then *a-student* is a parameter that stands for a structure and *a-teacher* stands for just a symbol. The template therefore has the following shape:

```
;; process-student : student symbol → ???
(define (process-student a-student a-teacher)
   ... (student-last a-student) ...
   ... (student-first a-student) ...
   ... (student-teacher a-student) ...)
```

The *???* output reminds us that we don't assume anything about the output of the function. We design every function that consumes a *student* structure using this template.

**Examples:** Let us study two examples of functions that consume *student* structures. The first function, *check*, is supposed to return the last name of the student if the teacher's name is equal to *a-teacher* and 'none otherwise:

(*check* (make-student 'Wilson 'Fritz 'Harper) 'Harper)
;; expected value:
'Wilson

(*check* (make-student 'Wilson 'Fritz 'Lee) 'Harper)
;; expected value
'none

The second function, *transfer*, is supposed to produce a student structure that contains the same information as *a-student* except for the teacher field, which should be *a-teacher*:

(*transfer* (make-student 'Wilson 'Fritz 'Harper) 'Lee)
;; expected value:
(make-student 'Wilson 'Fritz 'Lee)

(*transfer* (make-student 'Woops 'Helen 'Flatt) 'Fisler)
;; expected value:
(make-student 'Woops 'Helen 'Fisler)

**Body:** The template provides as many clues for the definition of the function as the examples. As before, the goal of this step is to formulate an expression that computes the answer from the available data using other functions or Scheme's primitive. The template reminds us that the available data are the parameters and the data computed by the selector expressions. To determine what the selectors produce, we read the data definition for the structure.

Let us return to our first example, *check*:

```
(define (check a-student a-teacher)
  (cond
    [(symbol=? (student-teacher a-student) a-teacher)
     (student-last a-student)]
    [else 'none]))
```

This particular function uses two of the three selector expressions from the template. Specifically, it compares the result of the selector expression (student-teacher *a-student*) with *a-teacher* and, if they are equal, produces the result of (student-last *a-student*). Just naming the results of the selector expressions and reading the problem statement makes the definition obvious.

Similarly, the *transfer* function is easy to define using the template and the examples:

```
(define (transfer a-student a-teacher)
  (make-student (student-last a-student)
                (student-first a-student)
                a-teacher))
```

This second function uses the same two selector expressions as the first example, but in a different way. The key observation, however, is that the template reminds us of all the information that we have available. **When we define the function, we must use and combine the available information.**

Figure 12 presents the recipe for compound data in tabular form. In practice, though, a function contains many functions that all work on the same class of input data. It is therefore normal to reuse the template many times, which means that examples are often constructed after the template is set up. Compare it with the design recipes in figures 4 and 6.

## Exercises

**Exercise 6.5.1** Develop templates for functions that consume the following structures:

1. (**define-struct** *movie* (*title producer*))

2. (**define-struct** *boyfriend* (*name hair eyes phone*))

3. (**define-struct** *cheerleader* (*name number*))

4. (**define-struct** *CD* (*artist title price*))

5. (**define-struct** *sweater* (*material size producer*)) . ∎

| Phase | Goal | Activity |
|---|---|---|
| Data Analysis and Design | to formulate a data definition | determine how many pieces of data describe the "interesting" aspects of the objects mentioned in the problem statement • add a structure definition and a data definition (for each class of problem object) |
| Contract Purpose and Header | to name the function; to specify its classes of input data and its class of output data; to describe its purpose; to formulate a header | name the function, the classes of input data, the class of output data, and specify its purpose: ;; *name : in1 in2 ...→ out* ;; *to compute ... from x1 ...* (**define** (*name x1 x2 ...*) ...) |
| Examples | to characterize the input-output relationship via examples | search the problem statement for examples • work through the examples • validate the results, if possible • make up examples |
| Template | to formulate an outline | for those parameters that stand for compound values, annotate the body with selector expressions • if the function is conditional, annotate all appropriate branches |
| Body | to define the function | develop a Scheme expression that uses Scheme's primitive operations, other functions, selector expressions, and the variables |
| Test | to discover mistakes ("typos" and logic) | apply the function to the inputs of the examples • check that the outputs are as predicted |

Figure 12: Designing a function for compound data
(Refines the recipe in figure 4 (pg. 21))

**Exercise 6.5.2** Develop the function *time→ seconds*, which consumes a **time** structure (see exercise 6.4.2) and produces the number of seconds since midnight that the **time** structure represents.

Example:

(*time→ seconds* (make-time 12 30 2))
;; expected value:
45002

Explain the example. ∎

Use **draw.ss**

## 6.6   Extended Exercise: Moving Circles and Rectangles

Implementing a computer game often requires moving a picture across a computer monitor. In figure 13, for example, a simplistic face is moved from the left part of the canvas toward the right border. For simplicity, our pictures consist of many colored circles and rectangles. From section 6.2, we already know, for example, how to draw and erase a circle. Here we learn to translate a circle, that is, to move its representation along some line. In sections 7.4, 10.3, and 21.4 we learn to move entire pictures with compact programs.[21]

Figure 13: A moving face

Following the design recipe, we start with structure and data definitions, then move on to templates, and finally write the necessary functions.

---

[21]This series of sections was inspired by Ms. Karen Buras and her son.

The first sequence of exercises covers circles; the second one is about rectangles.

**A First Note on Iterative Refinement**: This method of developing large programs is our first taste of ITERATIVE REFINEMENT. The basic idea behind iterative refinement is to start with a simple version of the program, that is, a version that deals with the most important part of the problem. In this section, we start with functions that move the most basic shapes: circles and rectangles. Then we refine the program to deal with more and more complex situations. For example, in section 10.3 we learn to deal with pictures that consist of an arbitrary number of circles and rectangles. Once we have a complete program, we edit it so that others can easily read and modify it, too. Section 21.4 covers this aspect of the example.

Refining a program in this manner is the most prevalent method of designing complex programs. Of course, we must know the eventual goal for this method to succeed, and we must always keep it in mind. It is therefore a good idea to write down an action plan, and to reconsider the plan after each refinement step. We will discuss this process again in section 16. ∎

## Exercises

**Exercise 6.6.1** Provide a structure definition and a data definition for representing colored circles. A *circle* is characterized by three pieces of information: its center, its radius, and the color of its perimeter. The first is a *posn* structure, the second a number, and the third a (color) symbol.

Develop the template *fun-for-circle*, which outlines a function that consumes *circle*s. Its result is undetermined. ∎

**Exercise 6.6.2** Use *fun-for-circle* to develop *draw-a-circle*. The function consumes a *circle* structure and draws the corresponding circle on the screen. Use (*start* 300 300) to create the canvas before testing the function. ∎

**Exercise 6.6.3** Use the template *fun-for-circle* to develop *in-circle?*. The function consumes a *circle* structure and a *posn* and determines whether or not the pixel is inside the circle. All pixels whose distance to the center is less or equal to the radius are inside the circle; the others are outside.

Consider the circle in figure 14. The circle's center is (make-posn 6 2), its radius is 1. The pixel labeled *A*, located at (make-posn 6 1.5), is inside the circle. The pixel labeled *B*, located at (make-posn 8 6), is outside. ∎

**Exercise 6.6.4** Use the template *fun-for-circle* to develop *translate-circle*. The function consumes a *circle* structure and a number *delta*. The result is a *circle* whose center is *delta* pixels to the right of the input. **The function has no effect on the canvas.**

**Geometric Translation**: Moving a geometric shape along a straight line is referred to as a *translation*. ∎

**Exercise 6.6.5** Use the template *fun-for-circle* to develop *clear-a-circle*. The function consumes a *circle* structure and clears the corresponding circle on the canvas. ∎

**Exercise 6.6.6** Define the function *draw-and-clear-circle*, which draws a *circle* structure, waits for a short time, and clears it. To implement a waiting period, the teachpack **draw.ss** provides the function *sleep-for-a-while*. It consumes a number and puts the program to sleep for that many seconds; its result is true. For example, (*sleep-for-a-while* 1) waits for one second. ∎

The following function is the key ingredient for moving a circle across a canvas, one step at a time:

```
;; move-circle : number circle → circle
;; to draw and clear a circle, translate it by delta pixels
(define (move-circle delta a-circle)
  (cond
    [(draw-and-clear-circle a-circle) (translate-circle a-circle delta)]
    [else a-circle]))
```

It draws and clears the circle on the canvas and then produces the new *circle* structure so that another draw-and-clear effect displays the circle at a new position:

```
(start 200 100)

(draw-a-circle
  (move-circle 10
    (move-circle 10
      (move-circle 10
        (move-circle 10 ... a circle ...)))))
```

This expression moves the circle four times, by 10 pixels each, and also shows this movement on the canvas. The last *draw-a-circle* is necessary because we wouldn't otherwise see the last move on the screen.

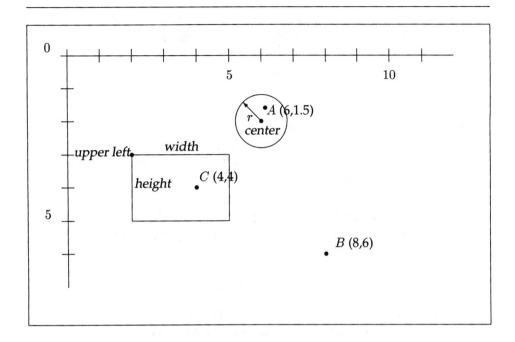

Figure 14: Circles, rectangles, and pixels

**Exercise 6.6.7** Provide a structure definition and a data definition for representing colored rectangles. A *rectangle* is characterized by four pieces of information: its upper-left corner, its width, its height, and its fill color. The first is a *posn* structure, the second and third quantities are plain numbers, and the last one is a color.

Develop the template *fun-for-rect*, which outlines a function that consumes *rectangles*. Its result is undetermined. ∎

**Exercise 6.6.8** Use the template *fun-for-rect* to develop *draw-a-rectangle*. The function consumes a *rectangle* structure and draws the corresponding rectangle on the screen. In contrast to circles, the entire rectangle is painted in the matching color. Remember to use (*start* 300 300) to create the canvas before testing the function. ∎

**Exercise 6.6.9** Use the template *fun-for-rect* to develop *in-rectangle?*. The function consumes a *rectangle* structure and a *posn* and determines whether or not the pixel is inside the rectangle. A pixel is within a rectangle if its horizontal and vertical distances to the upper-left corner are positive and smaller than the width and height of the rectangle, respectively.

Consider the rectangle in figure 14. This rectangle's key parameters are (make-posn 2 3), 3, and 2. The pixel labeled *C* is inside of the rectangle, *B* is outside. ∎

**Exercise 6.6.10** Use the template *fun-for-rect* to develop *translate-rectangle*. The function consumes a *rectangle* structure and a number *delta*. The result is a *rectangle* whose upper-left corner is *delta* pixels to the right of the input. **The function has no effect on the canvas.** ∎

**Exercise 6.6.11** Use the template *fun-for-rect* to develop *clear-a-rectangle*. It consumes a *rectangle* structure and clears the corresponding rectangle on the canvas. ∎

**Exercise 6.6.12** Here is the *move-rectangle* function:

```
;; move-rectangle : number rectangle → rectangle
;; to draw and clear a rectangle, translate it by delta pixels
(define (move-rectangle delta a-rectangle)
  (cond
    [(draw-and-clear-rectangle a-rectangle)
     (translate-rectangle a-rectangle delta)]
    [else a-rectangle]))
```

It draws and clears a rectangle circle on the canvas and then produces a translated version.

Develop *draw-and-clear-rectangle*, which draws a rectangle, sleeps for a while, and then clears the rectangle. Finally, create a rectangle and use the functions of this exercise set to move it four times. ∎

## 6.7   Extended Exercise: Hangman

Use **draw.ss**, **hangman.ss** Hangman is a two-player, word-guessing game. One player thinks of a three-letter[22] word and draws the noose of a gallows (see figure 15); the other player tries to guess the word, one letter at a time. For every wrong

---

[22]In reality, we would want to play the game with words of arbitrary length, but a game based on three-letter words is easier to implement for now. We return to the problem in exercise 17.6.2.

Figure 15: Three stages of the hangman picture

guess, the first player adds another part to the drawing (see figure 15): first the head, then the body, the arms, and the legs. If, however, a guess agrees with one or two letters in the chosen word, the first player reveals the position(s) where this letter occurs. The game is over when the second player guesses the complete word or when the first player has completed the stick figure.

Let's design a program that plays the role of the first player. The program consists of two parts: one for drawing the figure, and another for determining whether a guess occurs in the chosen word and where.

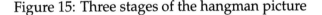

## Exercises

**Exercise 6.7.1** Develop the function *draw-next-part*, which draws the pieces of a hangman figure. The function consumes one of the seven symbols:

'right-leg    'left-leg    'left-arm    'right-arm    'body    'head    'noose

It always returns true and draws the matching part of the figure. See figure 15 for three snapshots of intermediate stages.[23]

---

[23]Thanks to Mr. John Clements for the artistic version of *draw-next-part*.

**Hints:** Add (*start* 200 200) to the top of the definition window. Start with the noose and develop one component at a time. If a component of the stick figure requires more than one drawing operation, combine the operations using an **and**-expression, which evaluates the two expressions and ensure that both results are true. ∎

The second task of the first player is to determine whether a guess is among the letters of the chosen word and, if so, where it occurs. Our recipe requires that, before we design a function for this task, we need to analyze our data and provide data definitions. The key objects of the game are words and letters. A *word* consists of three letters. A *letter* is represented with the symbols 'a through 'z. Using just those letters, however, is not enough because the program also needs to maintain a word that records how much the second player has guessed. The solution is to add one extra "letter" to our alphabet that is distinct from the others; the hangman teachpack uses '_ for this purpose.

## Exercises

**Exercise 6.7.2** Provide a structure definition and a data definition for representing three-letter words. ∎

**Exercise 6.7.3** Develop the function *reveal*. It consumes three arguments:

1. the *chosen* word, which is the word that we have to guess;

2. the *status* word, which shows which portion of the word has been revealed so far; and

3. a letter, which is our current *guess*.

The function produces a new status word, that is, a word that contains ordinary letters and '_. The fields in the new status word are determined by comparing the guess with each pair of letters from the status word and the chosen word:

1. If the guess is equal to the letter in the chosen word, the guess is the corresponding letter in the new status word.

2. Otherwise, the new letter is the corresponding letter from the status word.

Test the function with the following examples:

(*reveal* (make-word 't 'e 'a) (make-word '_ 'e '_) 'u)
;; expected value
(make-word '_ 'e '_)

(*reveal* (make-word 'a 'l 'e) (make-word 'a '_ '_) 'e)
;; expected value:
(make-word 'a '_ 'e)

(*reveal* (make-word 'a 'l 'l) (make-word '_ '_ '_) 'l)
;; expected value
(make-word '_ 'l 'l)

The first one shows what happens when the *guess* does not occur in the word; the second one shows what happens when it does occur; and the last one shows what happens when it occurs twice.

**Hints:** (1) Remember to develop auxiliary functions when a definition becomes too large or too complex to manage.

(2) The function *reveal* consumes two structures and one atomic value (a letter). This suggests that we use the design recipe for compound data (figure 12). For the template, it is best to write down the selector expressions in a two-column format, one column per word. ∎

When the functions *draw-next-part* and *reveal* are properly tested, set teachpack to **hangman.ss** and play the game by evaluating

(*hangman* make-word *reveal* *draw-next-part*)

The *hangman* function chooses a three-letter word randomly and displays a window with a pop-up menu for letters. Choose letters and, when ready, click the Check button to see whether the guess is correct. Comment out the test cases for exercise 6.7.1 so that their drawing effects don't interfere with those of *hangman*.

# 7  The Varieties of Data

The previous section significantly expands our world of data. We must now deal with a universe that contains booleans, symbols, and structures of many kinds. Let's bring some order to this world.

Up to this point, our functions have always processed subclasses of four different kinds of data:[24]

**numbers:** representations of numeric information;

**booleans:** truth and falsity;

**symbols:** representations of symbolic information; and

**structures:** representations of compounds of information.

On occasion, however, a function must process a class of data that includes both numbers and structures or structures of several different kinds. We learn to design such functions in this section. In addition, we learn how to protect functions from bad uses. Here a bad use means that some user can accidentally apply a function for drawing circles to a rectangle. Although we have agreed that such users violate our data definitions, we should nevertheless know how to protect our functions against such uses, when necessary.

## 7.1    Mixing and Distinguishing Data

In the preceding section, we used *posn* structures with exactly two components to represent pixels. If many of the pixels are on the $x$ axis, we can simplify the representation by using plain numbers for those pixels and *posn* structures for the remaining ones.

Figure 16 contains a sample collection of such points. Three of the five points, namely, $C$, $D$, and $E$, are on the $x$ axis. Only two points require two coordinates for an accurate description: $A$ and $B$. Our new idea for representing points permits us to describe this class of points succinctly: (make-posn 6 6) for $A$; (make-posn 1 2) for $B$; and 1, 2, and 3 for $C$, $D$, and $E$, respectively.

If we now wish to define the function *distance-to-0*, which consumes such point representations and produces their distance to the origin, we are confronted with a problem. The function may be applied to a number *or a posn*. Depending on the class to which the input belongs, *distance-to-0* must employ a different method to calculate the distance to the origin. Thus we need to use a **cond**-expression to distinguish the two cases. Unfortunately, we don't have any operations to formulate the appropriate conditions.

---

[24]We have also discussed images and strings, but we ignore these for now.

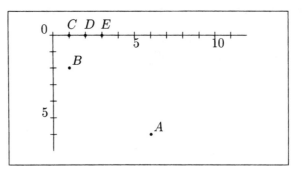

Figure 16: A small collection of points

To accommodate this kind of function, Scheme provides PREDICATES, which are operations that recognize a particular form of data. The predicates for the classes of data we know are:

number?, which consumes an arbitrary value and produces true if the value is a number and false otherwise;

boolean?, which consumes an arbitrary value and produces true if the value is a boolean value and false otherwise;

symbol?, which consumes an arbitrary value and produces true if the value is a symbol and false otherwise;

struct?, which consumes an arbitrary value and produces true if the value is a structure and false otherwise.

For each structure definition, Scheme also introduces a separate predicate so that we can distinguish between distinct classes of structures. Suppose the Definitions window contains the following structure definitions:[25]

(**define-struct** *posn (x y)*)

(**define-struct** *star (last first dob ssn)*)

(**define-struct** *airplane (kind max-speed max-load price)*)

---

[25]The *posn* structure is automatically provided in DrScheme's teaching languages and should never be defined.

Then, Scheme also knows the following three predicates:

posn?, which consumes an arbitrary value and produces true if the value
    is a *posn* structure and false otherwise;

star?, which consumes an arbitrary value and produces true if the value
    is a *star* structure and false otherwise;

airplane?, which consumes an arbitrary value and produces true if the
    value is a *airplane* structure and false otherwise.

Hence a function can distinguish a structure from a number as well as a
*posn* structure from an *airplane* structure.

---

**Exercises**

**Exercise 7.1.1** Evaluate the following expressions by hand:

1. (number? (make-posn 2 3))

2. (number? (+ 12 10))

3. (posn? 23)

4. (posn? (make-posn 23 3))

5. (star? (make-posn 23 3))

Check the answers in DrScheme. ∎

---

Now we can develop *distance-to-0*. Let's start with a data definition:

A *pixel-2* is either

1. a *number*, or

2. a *posn* structure.

Stating the contract, purpose, and header is straightforward:

;; *distance-to-0 : pixel-2 → number*
;; to compute the distance of *a-pixel* to the origin
(**define** (*distance-to-0 a-pixel*) ...)

As mentioned before, the function must distinguish between its two kinds of inputs, which can be accomplished with a **cond**-expression:

```
(define (distance-to-0 a-pixel)
  (cond
    [(number? a-pixel) ... ]
    [(posn? a-pixel) ... ]))
```

The two conditions match the two possible inputs of the new *distance-to-0* function. If the first one holds, the input is a pixel on the $x$ axis. Otherwise the pixel is a *posn* structure. For the second **cond**-line, we also know that the input contains two items: the $x$ and $y$ coordinates. To remind ourselves, we annotate the template with two selector expressions:

```
(define (distance-to-0 a-pixel)
  (cond
    [(number? a-pixel) ... ]
    [(posn? a-pixel) ... (posn-x a-pixel) ... (posn-y a-pixel) ... ]))
```

Completing the function is easy. If the input is a number, it *is* the distance to the origin. If it is a structure, we use the old formula for determining the distance to the origin:

```
(define (distance-to-0 a-pixel)
  (cond
    [(number? a-pixel) a-pixel]
    [(posn? a-pixel) (sqrt
                       (+ (sqr (posn-x a-pixel))
                          (sqr (posn-y a-pixel))))]))
```

Let us consider a second example. Suppose we are to write functions that deal with geometric shapes. One function might have to compute the area covered by a shape, another one the perimeter, and a third could draw the shape. For the sake of simplicity, let's assume that the class of shapes includes only squares and circles and that their description includes their location (a *posn*) and their size (a *number*).

Information about both shapes must be represented with structures, because both have several attributes. Here are the structure definitions:

```
(define-struct square (nw length))
(define-struct circle (center radius))
```

and the matching data definition:

---
A *shape* is either

   1. a circle structure:

                  (make-circle *p s*)

     where *p* is a *posn* and *s* is a number; or

   2. a square structure:

                  (make-square *p s*)

     where *p* is a *posn* and *s* is a number.

---

Together, the two classes make up the class of shapes:

The next step of our design recipe requires that we make up examples. Let's start with input examples:

   1. (make-square (make-posn 20 20) 3),

   2. (make-square (make-posn 2 20) 3), and

   3. (make-circle (make-posn 10 99) 1).

To make up examples of input-output relationships, we need to know the purpose of the function. So suppose we need the function *perimeter*, which computes the *perimeter* of a shape. From geometry, we know that the perimeter of a square is four times its side, and the perimeter of a circle is $\pi$ times the diameter, which is twice the radius.[26] Thus, the perimeter of the above three examples are: 12, 12, and (roughly) 6.28, respectively.

Following the design recipe and the precedent of *distance-to-0*, we start with the following skeleton of the function:

```
;; perimeter : shape → number
;; to compute the perimeter of a-shape
(define (perimeter a-shape)
  (cond
    [(square? a-shape) ... ]
    [(circle? a-shape) ... ]))
```

because the function must first determine to which class *a-shape* belongs.

Furthermore, each possible input is a structure, so we can also add two selector expressions to each **cond**-clause:

---

[26]The perimeter of a circle is also known as *circumference*.

```
;; perimeter : shape → number
;; to compute the perimeter of a-shape
(define (perimeter a-shape)
  (cond
    [(square? a-shape)
     ... (square-nw a-shape) ... (square-length a-shape) ... ]
    [(circle? a-shape)
     ... (circle-center a-shape) ... (circle-radius a-shape) ... ]))
```

The selector expressions remind us of the available data.

Now we are ready to finish the definition. We fill the gaps in the two answers by translating the mathematical formulae into Scheme notation:

```
(define (perimeter a-shape)
  (cond
    [(square? a-shape) (* (square-length a-shape) 4)]
    [(circle? a-shape) (* (* 2 (circle-radius a-shape)) pi)]))
```

Since the position of a shape does not affect its perimeter, the template's selector expressions for *nw* and *center* disappear.

## Exercises

**Exercise 7.1.2** Test *perimeter* with the examples. ∎

**Exercise 7.1.3** Develop the function *area*, which consumes either a circle or a square and computes the area. Is it possible to reuse the template for *perimeter* by changing the name to *area*? ∎

## 7.2 Designing Functions for Mixed Data

The function development in the preceding section suggests some amendments to our design recipe. Specifically, the data analysis step, the template construction step, and the definition of the function's body require adjustments.

**Data Analysis and Design:** When we analyze a problem statement, our first task is to determine whether it mentions distinct classes of data—which we call MIXED DATA and which is also known as the UNION of data classes. In other words, the data analysis must take into account several aspects now. First, we must determine how many distinct classes of objects are mentioned in the problem and what their important attributes are. If there are several different classes of objects, we are mixing data. Second, we must understand whether the various objects have several properties. If an object has several attributes, we use compound data for its representation. As a result, the resulting data definition may have several clauses that enumerate several possibilities. Indeed, we will see that the data analysis may yield a hierarchy of data definitions.

The example of the preceding section deals with two distinct kinds of shapes, each of which has several properties. We captured this idea with the following data definition:

---

A *shape* is either

1. a circle structure:
                (make-circle *p s*)
    where *p* is a *posn* and *s* is a number; or

2. a square structure:
                (make-square *p s*)
    where *p* is a *posn* and *s* is a number.

---

It specifies that every *shape* belongs to one of two subclasses of data.

For a data definition to make sense, it must be possible to formulate conditions that distinguish the various subclasses in a definition. That is, if $x$ stands for a piece of data in the defined class, we must be able to use built-in and user-defined predicates to distinguish the enumerated subclasses from each other. In our running example, the two conditions would be (square? $x$) and (circle? $x$).

**Template:** Recall that the template is a translation of the input data definition into Scheme. Thus, imagine that we have a data definition that enumerates several distinct possibilities. The first step is to write down a **cond**-expression with as many clauses as there are enumerated possibilities in the data definition. The second step is to add a condition to each line. Each condition should hold if the input belongs to the corresponding subclass of data mentioned in the data definition.

Here is the template for our running example:

```
;; f : shape → ???
(define (f a-shape)
  (cond
    [(square? a-shape) ...]
    [(circle? a-shape) ...]))
```

The output specification and the purpose statement are missing to emphasize that a template has no connection to the output or the purpose of a function.

Once we have formulated the template for the conditional, we refine the template further, **cond**-line by **cond**-line. If the purpose of a line is to process atomic information, we are done. If a line processes compound data, we enrich the template with appropriate selector expressions.

Let's illustrate the idea with our running example again:

```
(define (f a-shape)
  (cond
    [(square? a-shape)
     ... (square-nw a-shape) ... (square-length a-shape) ...]
    [(circle? a-shape)
     ... (circle-center a-shape) ... (circle-radius a-shape) ...]))
```

**Body:** Using the conditional template, we split the task into simpler tasks. Specifically, we can focus on each **cond**-line separately, simply considering the question what is the output if we are given this kind of input. All other cases are ignored as we work out one particular clause.

Suppose we want to define a function that computes the perimeter of a shape. Then we start from the template and fill in the gaps:

```
;; perimeter : shape → number
;; to compute the perimeter of a-shape
(define (perimeter a-shape)
  (cond
    [(square? a-shape) (* (square-length a-shape) 4)]
    [(circle? a-shape) (* (* 2 (circle-radius a-shape)) pi)]))
```

Figure 17 summarizes the development of our running example.

The remaining steps of the recipes in figures 4, 6, and 12 should be followed on an as-is basis. Figure 18 summarizes the design recipe, with all steps included.

```
;; Data Definition:
(define-struct circle (center radius))
(define-struct square (nw length))
;; A shape is either
;; 1. a structure: (make-circle p s)
;;    where p is a posn, s a number;
;; 2. a structure: (make-square p s)
;;    where p is a posn, s a number.

;; Contract, Purpose, Header:
;; perimeter : shape → number
;; to compute the perimeter of a-shape

;; Examples: see tests

;; Template:
;; (define (f a-shape)
;;   (cond
;;     [(square? a-shape)
;;      ... (square-nw a-shape) ... (square-length a-shape) ...]
;;     [(circle? a-shape)
;;      ... (circle-center a-shape) ... (circle-radius a-shape) ...]))

;; Definition:
(define (perimeter a-shape)
  (cond
    [(circle? a-shape)
     (* (* 2 (circle-radius a-shape)) pi)]
    [(square? a-shape)
     (* (square-length a-shape) 4)]))

;; Tests: (same as examples)
(= (perimeter (make-square ... 3)) 12)
(= (perimeter (make-circle ... 1)) (* 2 pi))
```

Figure 17: The design recipe for mixed data: A complete example

| Phase | Goal | Activity |
|---|---|---|
| Data Analysis and Design | to formulate a data definition | determine how many distinct classes of "objects" make up the classes of problem data • enumerate the alternatives in a data definition • formulate a data definition for each alternative, if it is a form of compound data |
| Contract Purpose and Header | to name the function; to specify its classes of input data and its class of output data; to describe its purpose; to formulate a header | name the function, the classes of input data, the class of output data, and specify its purpose: <br> *;; name : in1 in2 ... → out* <br> *;; to compute ... from x1 ...* <br> (**define** (*name x1 x2 ...*) ...) |
| Examples | to characterize the input-output relationship via examples | create examples of the input-output relationship • make sure there is at least one example per subclass |
| Template | to formulate an outline | introduce a **cond**-expression with one clause per subclass • formulate a condition for each case, using built-in and predefined predicates |
| Body | to define the function | develop a Scheme expression for each **cond**-line (an answer), assuming that the condition holds |
| Test | to discover mistakes ("typos" and logic) | apply the function to the inputs of the examples • check that the outputs are as predicted |

Figure 18: Designing a function for mixed data
(Refines the recipes in figures 4 (pg. 21) and 12 (pg. 71))

Even a cursory comparative reading of the design recipes in sections 2.5, 4.4, 6.5, and the current one suggests that the data analysis and the template design steps are becoming more and more important. If we do not understand what kind of data a function consumes, we cannot design it and organize it properly. If, however, we do understand the structure of the data definition and organize our template properly, it is easy to modify or to extend a function. For example, if we add new information to the representation of a *circle*, then only those **cond**-clauses related to circles may require changes. Similarly, if we add a new kind of shape to our data definition, say, rectangles, we must add new **cond**-clauses to our functions.

---

### Exercises

**Exercise 7.2.1** Develop structure and data definitions for a collection of zoo animals. The collection includes

**spiders,** whose relevant attributes are the number of remaining legs (we assume that spiders can lose legs in accidents) and the space they need in case of transport;

**elephants,** whose only attributes are the space they need in case of transport;

**monkeys,** whose attributes are intelligence and space needed for transportation.

Then develop a template for functions that consume zoo animals.

Develop the function *fits?*. The function consumes a zoo animal and the volume of a cage. It determines whether the cage is large enough for the animal. ∎

**Exercise 7.2.2** The administrators of metropolitan transportation agencies manage fleets of vehicles. Develop structure and data definitions for a collection of such vehicles. The collection should include at least buses, limos, cars, and subways. Add at least two attributes per class of vehicle.

Then develop a template for functions that consume vehicles. ∎

---

### 7.3  Composing Functions, Revisited

As we analyze a problem statement, we might wish to develop the data representation in stages. This is especially true when the problem statement mentions several different kinds of objects. It is easier to understand several smaller data definitions than one larger one.

Let's return to our shape problem again. Instead of the class of shapes in a single data definition, we could start with two data definitions, one for each basic shape:

> A *circle* is a structure:
>
> (make-circle *p s*)
>
> where *p* is a *posn* and *s* is a number.

> A *square* is a structure:
>
> (make-square *p s*)
>
> where *p* is a *posn* and *s* is a number.

Once we have developed and understood the basic data definitions, possibly by playing with examples and by writing simple functions, we can introduce data definitions that combine them. For example, we can introduce a data definition for a class of shapes that refers to the two above:

> A *shape* is either
>
> 1. a *circle*, or
>
> 2. a *square*.

Now suppose we need a function that consumes *shapes*. First, we form a **cond**-expression with conditions for each part of the data definition:

```
;; f : shape → ???
(define (f a-shape)
  (cond
    [(circle? a-shape) ...]
    [(square? a-shape) ...]))
```

Given our guideline concerning the composition of functions from section 3.1 and given that the data definition refers to two other data definitions, the natural second step is to pass the argument to auxiliary functions:

```
(define (f a-shape)
  (cond
    [(circle? a-shape) (f-for-circle a-shape)]
    [(square? a-shape) (f-for-square a-shape)]))
```

This, in turn, requires that we develop the two auxiliary functions, *f-for-circle* and *f-for-square*, including their templates.

```
;; Data Definition:                      ;; Data Definitions:
(define-struct circle (center radius))   (define-struct circle (center radius))
(define-struct square (nw length))       ;; A circle is a structure:
;; A shape is either                     ;;     (make-circle p s)
;; 1. a structure: (make-circle p s)     ;;  where p is a posn, s a number;
;;   where p is a posn, s a number;
;; 2. a structure: (make-square p s)     (define-struct square (nw length))
;;   where p is a posn, s a number.      ;; A square is a structure:
                                         ;;     (make-square p s)
                                         ;;  where p is a posn, s a number.

                                         ;; A shape is either
                                         ;; 1. a circle, or
                                         ;; 2. a square.
```

```
;; Final Definition:                     ;; Final Definitions:
;; perimeter : shape → number            ;; perimeter : shape → number
;; to compute the perimeter of a-shape   ;; to compute the perimeter of a-shape
(define (perimeter a-shape)              (define (perimeter a-shape)
  (cond                                    (cond
    [(circle? a-shape)                       [(circle? a-shape)
     (* (* 2 (circle-radius a-shape)) pi)]    (perimeter-circle a-shape)]
    [(square? a-shape)                       [(square? a-shape)
     (* (square-length a-shape) 4)]))         (perimeter-square a-shape)]))

                                         ;; perimeter-circle : circle → number
                                         ;; to compute the perimeter of a-circle
                                         (define (perimeter-circle a-circle)
                                           (* (* 2 (circle-radius a-circle)) pi))

                                         ;; perimeter-square : square → number
                                         ;; to compute the perimeter of a-square
                                         (define (perimeter-square a-square)
                                           (* (square-length a-square) 4))
```

Figure 19: Two ways to define *perimeter*

If we follow this suggestion, we arrive at a collection of three functions, one per data definition. The essential points of the program development are summarized in the right column of figure 19. For a comparison, the left column contains the corresponding pieces of the original program development. In each case, we have as many functions as there are data definitions. Furthermore, the references between the functions in the right column directly match the references among the corresponding data definitions. While this symmetry between data definitions and functions may seem trivial now, it becomes more and more important as we study more complex ways of defining data.

## Exercises

**Exercise 7.3.1** Modify the two versions of *perimeter* so that they also process rectangles. For our purposes, the description of a rectangle includes its upper-left corner, its width, and its height. ∎

## 7.4 Extended Exercise: Moving Shapes

In section 6.6, we developed functions for drawing, translating, and clearing circles and rectangles. As we have just seen, we should think of the two classes of data as subclasses of a class of shapes so that we can just draw, translate, and clear shapes.

## Exercises

**Exercise 7.4.1** Provide a data definition for a general class of *shape*s. The class should at least subsume the classes of colored circles and rectangles from section 6.6.

Develop the template *fun-for-shape*, which outlines functions that consume *shape*s. ∎

**Exercise 7.4.2** Use the template *fun-for-shape* to develop *draw-shape*. The function consumes a *shape* and draws it on the canvas. ∎

**Exercise 7.4.3** Use the template *fun-for-shape* to develop *translate-shape*. The function consumes a *shape* and a number *delta*, and produces a shape whose key position is moved by *delta* pixels in the $x$ direction. ∎

**Exercise 7.4.4** Use the template *fun-for-shape* to develop *clear-shape*. The function consumes a *shape*, erases it from the canvas, and returns true. ∎

**Exercise 7.4.5** Develop the function *draw-and-clear-shape*. The function consumes a *shape*, draws it, sleeps for a while, and clears it. If all the effects work out, it produces true. ∎

**Exercise 7.4.6** Develop *move-shape*, which moves a shape across the canvas. The function consumes a number (delta) and a shape. The function should draw-and-clear the shape and return a new shape that has been translated by delta pixels. Use this function several times to move a shape across the canvas. ∎

## 7.5   Input Errors

Recall our first function:

;; *area-of-disk : number → number*
;; to compute the area of a disk with radius *r*
(**define** (*area-of-disk r*)
  (∗ 3.14 (∗ *r r*)))

Clearly, our friends may wish to use this function, especially for some of their geometry homework. Unfortunately, when our friends use this function, they may accidentally apply it to a symbol rather than a number. When that happens, the function stops with a whimsical and uninformative error message:

> (*area-of-disk* 'my-disk)
∗: *expects type* <*number*> *as 1st argument, given:* 'my-disk; ...

Using predicates, we can do better.

To prevent this kind of accident, we should define checked versions of our functions, when we wish to hand them to our friends. In general, a CHECKED FUNCTION inputs an arbitrary Scheme value: a number, a boolean, a symbol, or a structure. For all those values that are in the class of values for which the original function is defined, the checked version applies the latter; for all others, it signals an error. Concretely, *checked-area-of-disk* consumes an arbitrary Scheme value, uses *area-of-disk* to compute the area of the a disk if the input is a number, and stops with an error message otherwise.

Based on the enumeration of Scheme's classes of values, the template for a checked function is as follows:

*;; f : Scheme-value → ???*

```
(define (f v)
  (cond
    [(number? v) ...]
    [(boolean? v) ...]
    [(symbol? v) ...]
    [(struct? v) ...]))
```

Each line corresponds to one possible class of input. If we need to distinguish between the structures, we expand the last line appropriately.

The first clause is the only one where we can use *area-of-disk*. For the others, however, we must signal an error. In Scheme we use the operation error to do so. It consumes a symbol and a string. Here is an example:

```
(error 'checked-area-of-disk "number expected")
```

Hence the full definition of *checked-area-of-disk* is:

```
(define (checked-area-of-disk v)
  (cond
    [(number? v) (area-of-disk v)]
    [(boolean? v) (error 'checked-area-of-disk "number expected")]
    [(symbol? v) (error 'checked-area-of-disk "number expected")]
    [(struct? v) (error 'checked-area-of-disk "number expected")]))
```

Using **else** we can greatly simplify the function:

```
;; checked-area-of-disk : Scheme-value → number
;; to compute the area of a disk with radius v,
;; if v is a number
(define (checked-area-of-disk v)
  (cond
    [(number? v) (area-of-disk v)]
    [else (error 'checked-area-of-disk "number expected")]))
```

Of course, such a simplification may not always be possible and may require a reordering of the **cond**-clauses first.

Writing checked functions and simplifying them is important if we distribute the programs to others. Designing programs that work properly, however, is far more important. The book therefore focuses on the design process for the program proper and deemphasizes writing checked versions.

## Exercises

**Exercise 7.5.1** A checked version of *area-of-disk* can also enforce that the arguments to the function are positive numbers, not just arbitrary numbers. Modify *checked-area-of-disk* in this way. ∎

**Exercise 7.5.2** Develop checked versions of the functions *profit* (figure 5), *is-between-5-6?* (section 4.2), *reply* (section 5), *distance-to-0* (section 6.1), and *perimeter* (in the left column of figure 19). ∎

**Exercise 7.5.3** Take a look at these structure and data definitions:

(**define-struct** *vec* (*x y*))

> A *speed-vector* (*vec*) is a structure:
> (make-vec *x y*)
> where both *x* and *y* are positive numbers.

Develop the function *checked-make-vec*, which should be understood as a checked version of the primitive operation make-vec. It ensures that the arguments to make-vec are positive numbers, and not just arbitrary numbers. In other words, *checked-make-vec* enforces our informal data definition. ∎

# Intermezzo 1: Syntax and Semantics

Thus far we have approached Scheme as if it were a spoken language. Like toddlers, we learned the vocabulary of the language, we acquired an intuitive understanding of its meaning, and we figured out some basic rules of how to compose and not to compose sentences. Truly effective communication, however, in any language—be it natural like English or artificial like Scheme—eventually requires a formal study of its vocabulary, its grammar, and the meaning of sentences.

A programming language is in many ways like a spoken language. It has a vocabulary and a grammar. The vocabulary is the collection of those "basic words" from which we can compose "sentences" in our language. A sentence in a programming language is an expression or a function; the language's grammar dictates how to form complete sentences from words. Programmers use the terminology SYNTAX to refer to the vocabularies and grammars of programming languages.

Not all grammatical sentences are meaningful—neither in English nor in a programming language. For example, the English sentence "the cat is round" is a meaningful sentence, but "the brick is a car" makes no sense, even though it is completely grammatical. To determine whether or not a sentence is meaningful, we must study the MEANING, or SEMANTICS, of words and sentences. For spoken languages, we typically explain the meaning of words with sentences that use simpler words; in the case of a foreign language, we sometimes explain a word with simple sentences in the foreign language or we translate words to a known language. For programming languages, there are also several ways to explain the meaning of individual sentences. In this book, we discuss the meaning of Scheme programs through an extension of the familiar laws of arithmetic and algebra. After all, computation starts with this form of simple mathematics, and we should understand the connection between this mathematics and computing.

The first three sections present the vocabulary, grammar, and meaning of a small, but powerful subset of Scheme. The fourth one resumes our discussion of run-time errors in Scheme, based on our new understanding of its meaning. The remaining three sections revisit **and** and **or** expressions, variable definitions, and structures.

## The Scheme Vocabulary

Scheme's basic vocabulary consists of five categories of words. The five
lines in figure 20 show how computer scientists discuss the vocabulary of
a language.[27] All lines employ the same notation. They enumerate some
simple examples separated by a bar (" | "). Dots indicate that there are
more things of the same kind in some category.

$$\begin{aligned}
\langle var \rangle &= & x \mid \textit{area-of-disk} \mid \textit{perimeter} \mid \ldots \\
\langle con \rangle &= & \text{true} \mid \text{false} \\
& & \text{'a} \mid \text{'doll} \mid \text{'sum} \mid \ldots \\
& & 1 \mid -1 \mid 3/5 \mid 1.22 \mid \ldots \\
\langle prm \rangle &= & + \mid - \mid \ldots
\end{aligned}$$

Figure 20: Beginning Student Scheme: The core vocabulary

The first category is that of variables, which are the names of functions
and values. The second introduces constants: boolean, symbolic, and numeric constants. As indicated before, Scheme has a powerful number system, which is best introduced gradually by examples. The final category is
that of primitive operations, which are those basic functions that Scheme
provides from the very beginning. While it is possible to specify this collection in its entirety, it is best introduced in pieces, as the need arises.

For the classification of Scheme sentences, we also need three *keywords*:
**define**, **cond**, and **else**. These keywords have no meaning. Their role resembles that of punctuation marks, especially that of commas and semicolons, in English writing; they help programmers distinguish one sentence from another. No keyword may be used as a variable.

## The Scheme Grammar

Grammar,
Layout, and Editing

In contrast to many other programming languages, Scheme has a simple
grammar. It is shown in its entirety in figure 21.[28] The grammar defines

---

[27]We use different fonts to distinguish the words of different categories. Constants and
primitive operations are type set in sans serif, variables in *italics*, and keywords in **boldface**.

[28]This grammar describes only that portion of Scheme we have used so far (minus variable and structure definitions), which still covers a large subset of the full language. Scheme
is a bit larger, and we will get to know more of it in the remaining parts of the book.

two categories of sentences: Scheme definitions, ⟨*def*⟩, and expressions, ⟨*exp*⟩. While the grammar does not dictate the use of white space between the items of sentences, we follow the convention to put at least one blank space behind each item unless an item is followed by a right parenthesis ")". Scheme is flexible concerning blank space, and we can replace a single blank space by many spaces, line breaks, and page breaks.

---

$$
\begin{array}{rcl}
\langle def \rangle & = & (\textbf{define} \; (\langle var \rangle \; \langle var \rangle \ldots \langle var \rangle) \; \langle exp \rangle) \\
\langle exp \rangle & = & \langle var \rangle \\
& | & \langle con \rangle \\
& | & (\langle prm \rangle \; \langle exp \rangle \ldots \langle exp \rangle) \\
& | & (\langle var \rangle \; \langle exp \rangle \ldots \langle exp \rangle) \\
& | & (\textbf{cond} \; (\langle exp \rangle \; \langle exp \rangle) \ldots (\langle exp \rangle \; \langle exp \rangle)) \\
& | & (\textbf{cond} \; (\langle exp \rangle \; \langle exp \rangle) \ldots (\textbf{else} \; \langle exp \rangle)) \\
\end{array}
$$

Figure 21: `Beginning Student` Scheme: The core grammar

---

The two grammar definitions describe how to form atomic sentences and compound sentences, which are sentences built from other sentences. For example, a function definition is formed by using "(", followed by the keyword **define**, followed by another "(", followed by a non-empty sequence of variables, followed by ")", followed by an expression, and closed by a right parenthesis ")" that matches the very first one. The keyword **define** distinguishes definitions from expressions.

The category of expressions consists of six alternatives: variables, constants, primitive applications, (function) applications, and two varieties of **cond**itionals. The last four are again composed of other expressions. The keyword **cond** distinguishes conditional expressions from primitive and function applications.

Here are three examples of expressions: 'all, *x*, and (*x x*). The first one belongs to the class of symbols and is therefore an expression. The second is a variable, and every variable is an expression. Finally, the third is a function application, because *x* is a variable.

In contrast, the following parenthesized sentences are not expressions: (*f* **define**), (**cond** *x*), and (). The first one partially matches the shape of a function application but it uses **define** as if it were a variable. The second one fails to be a correct **cond**-expression because it contains a variable as the second item and not a pair of expressions surrounded by parentheses. The last one is just a pair of parentheses, but the grammar requires that every left parenthesis is followed by something other than a right parenthesis.

## Exercises

**Exercise 8.2.1** Why are the sentences
   1. $x$   2. $(= y\, z)$   3. $(= (= y\, z)\, 0)$
syntactically legal expressions?
Explain why the following sentences are illegal expressions:
   1. $(3 + 4)$   2. empty?$(l)$   3. $(x)$ ∎

**Exercise 8.2.2** Why are the sentences
   1. (**define** $(f\, x)\, x$)   2. (**define** $(f\, x)\, y$)   3. (**define** $(f\, x\, y)\, 3$)
syntactically legal definitions?
Explain why the following sentences are illegal definitions:
   1. (**define** $(f\, 'x)\, x$)   2. (**define** $(f\, x\, y\, z)\, (x)$)   3. (**define** $(f)\, 10$) ∎

**Exercise 8.2.3** Distinguish syntactically legal from illegal sentences:
   1. $(x)$   2. $(+ 1\, (\text{not}\, x))$   3. $(+ 1\, 2\, 3)$
Explain why the sentences are legal or illegal. ∎

**Exercise 8.2.4** Distinguish syntactically legal from illegal sentences:
   1. (**define** $(f\, x)\, 'x$)   2. (**define** $(f\, 'x)\, x$)   3. (**define** $(f\, x\, y)\, (+ 'y\, (\text{not}\, x))$)
Explain why the sentences are legal definitions or why they fail to be legal definitions. ∎

**Grammatical Terminology**: The components of compound sentences have names. We have introduced some of these names on an informal basis; for better communication, we introduce all useful ones here. The second component of a definition, that is, the non-empty sequence of variables, is a HEADER. Accordingly, the expression component of a definition is called BODY. The variables that follow the first variable in a header are the PARAMETERS of a function. ∎

People who think of definition as the definition of a mathematical function also use the terminology LEFT-HAND SIDE for a definition's header and RIGHT-HAND SIDE for the body. For the same reason, the first component in an application is called FUNCTION and the remaining components are referred to as ARGUMENTS. Occasionally, we also use ACTUAL ARGUMENTS.

---

(**define** (⟨*function-name*⟩ ⟨*parameter*⟩ ... ⟨*parameter*⟩) ⟨*body*⟩)

(⟨*function*⟩ ⟨*argument*⟩ ... ⟨*argument*⟩)

(**cond** (⟨*question*⟩ ⟨*answer*⟩) ⟨**cond**-*clause*⟩ ...)

Figure 22: Syntactic naming conventions

---

Finally, a **cond**-expression consists of **cond**-lines or **cond**-clauses. Each line consists of two expressions: the QUESTION and the ANSWER. A question is also called a CONDITION.

Figure 22 provides a summary of the conventions.

Stepper

## The Meaning of Scheme

A legal DrScheme program consists of two items: a sequence of function definitions (in the Definitions window) and a sequence of interactions (in the Interactions window). Each interaction is a demand for the evaluation of one Scheme expression, which typically refers to the functions defined in the upper part of DrScheme.

When DrScheme evaluates an expression, it uses nothing but the laws of arithmetic and algebra to convert an expression into a value. In ordinary mathematics courses, values are just numbers. We also include symbols, booleans, and indeed all constants:

$$\langle val \rangle \;=\; \langle con \rangle$$

The collection of values is thus just a subset of the collection of expressions.

Now that we have defined the set of values, it is easy to introduce and to explain the evaluation rules. The rules come in two categories: those that appeal to arithmetic knowledge and those that rely on a small amount of algebra. First, we need an infinite number of rules like those of arithmetic to evaluate applications of primitives:

$(+\ 1\ 1) = 2$
$(-\ 2\ 1) = 1$

But Scheme "arithmetic" is more general than just number crunching. It also includes rules for dealing with boolean values, symbols, and lists like these:

```
(not true) = false
(symbol=? 'a 'b) = false
(symbol=? 'a 'a) = true
```

Second, we need one rule from algebra to understand how the application of a user-defined function advances computation. Suppose the Definitions window contains the definition

**(define** (*f x-1 ... x-n*)
   exp)

and *f, x-1, ..., x-n* are variables and exp is some (legal) expression. Then an application of a function is governed by the law:

(*f v-1 ... v-n*)   =   exp with all *x-1 ... x-n* replaced by *v-1 ... v-n*

where *v-1 ... v-n* is a sequence of values that is as long as *x-1 ... x-n*.

This rule is as general as possible, so it is best to look at a concrete example. Say the definition is

**(define** (*poly x y*)
   (+ (expt 2 *x*) *y*))

Then the application (*poly* 3 5) can be evaluated as follows:

```
   (poly 3 5)
= (+ (expt 2 3) 5))
   ;; This line is (+ (expt 2 x) y) where x was replaced by 3 and y by 5 .
= (+ 8 5)
= 13
```

These last two steps follow from plain arithmetic.

Third and finally, we need some rules that help us determine the value of **cond**-expressions. These rules are algebraic rules but are not a part of the standard algebra curriculum:

**cond_false:** when the first condition is false:

```
(cond              = (cond
 [false ...]           ; The first line disappeared.
 [exp1 exp2]           [exp1 exp2]
  ...)                  ...)
```

then the first **cond**-line disappears;

**cond_true:** when the first condition is true:

```
(cond          = exp
   [true exp]
   ...)
```

the entire **cond**-expressions is replaced by the first answer;

**cond_else:** when the only line left is the **else**-line:

```
(cond          = exp
   [else exp])
```

the **cond**-expressions is replaced by the answer in the **else**-clause.

No other rules are needed to understand **cond**.

Consider the following evaluation:

```
(cond
   [false 1]
   [true (+ 1 1)]
   [else 3])
```

```
= (cond
     [true (+ 1 1)]
     [else 3])
```

$$= (+ 1 \ 1)$$

$$= 2$$

It first eliminates a **cond**-line and then equates the **cond**-expression with (+ 1 1). The rest is plain arithmetic again.

The rules are equations of the form that we use in arithmetic and algebra on a daily basis. Indeed, the same laws apply to this system of equations as to those in mathematics. For example, if $a = b$ and $b = c$, then we also know that $a = c$. A consequence is that as we get better at hand-evaluations, we can skip obvious steps and combine several equational inferences into one. Here is one shorter version of the previous evaluation:

```
(cond
   [false 1]
   [true (+ 1 1)]
   [else 3])
```

= (+ 1 1)

= 2

Even more importantly, we can replace any expression by its equal in every context—just as in algebra. Here is a another **cond**-expression and its evaluation:

(**cond**
    [(= 1 0) 0]
    [**else** (+ 1 1)])
;; The underlined expression is evaluated first.
= (**cond**
    [false 0]
    [**else** (+ 1 1)])
;; Here **cond_false** applies.
= (**cond**
    [**else** (+ 1 1)])
;; Using **cond_else**, we now get an arithmetic expression.
= (+ 1 1)
= 2

For the first step, we evaluated the nested, underlined expression, which is clearly essential here, because no **cond** rule would apply otherwise. Of course, there is nothing unusual about this kind of computing. We have done this many times in algebra and in the first few sections of this book.

## Exercises

**Exercise 8.3.1** Evaluate the following expressions step by step:

1. (+ (* (/ 12 8) 2/3)
      (− 20 (sqrt 4)))

2. (**cond**
      [(= 0 0) false]
      [(> 0 1) (symbol=? 'a 'a)]
      [**else** (= (/ 1 0) 9)])

3. (**cond**
      [(= 2 0) false]
      [(> 2 1) (symbol=? 'a 'a)]
      [**else** (= (/ 1 2) 9)]) ;                    ∎

**Exercise 8.3.2** Suppose the Definitions window contains

*;; f : number number → number*
(**define** *(f x y)*
  *(+ (∗ 3 x) (∗ y y)))*

Show how DrScheme evaluates the following expressions, step by step:

1. *(+ (f 1 2) (f 2 1))*

2. *(f 1 (∗ 2 3))*

3. *(f (f 1 (∗ 2 3)) 19)* ; ∎

---

## Errors

Parenthesized sentences may or may not belong to Scheme, depending on whether or not they are legal according to the grammar in figure 21. If DrScheme verifies that a sentence does not belong to the language dubbed Beginning Student, it signals a SYNTAX ERROR.

The remaining expressions are syntactically legal, but some of those may still pose problems for our evaluation rules. We say that such legal expressions contain LOGICAL ERRORS or RUN-TIME ERRORS. Consider the simplest example: (/ 1 0). We already know from mathematics that

$$\frac{1}{0}$$

does not have a value. Clearly, since Scheme's calculations must be consistent with mathematics, it too must not equate (/ 1 0) with a value.

In general, if an expression is not a value and if the evaluation rules allow no further simplification, we say that an error occurred or that the function raises an error signal. Pragmatically this means that the evaluation stops immediately with an appropriate error message, such as "/: **divide by zero**" for division by zero.

For an example, consider the following evaluation:

  *(+ (∗ 20 2) (/ 1 (− 10 10)))*
= *(+ 40 (/ 1 0))*
= */: divide by zero*

The error eliminates the context $(+ 40 \ldots)$ around $(/\ 1\ 0)$, which represents the remainder of the computation with respect to the division.

To understand how run-time errors are signaled, we must inspect the evaluation rules again. Consider the function

```
;; my-divide : number → number
(define (my-divide n)
  (cond
    [(= n 0) 'inf]
    [else (/ 1 n)]))
```

Now suppose we apply *my-divide* to 0. Then the first step is:

```
(my-divide 0)
```

```
= (cond
    [(= 0 0) 'inf]
    [else (/ 1 0)])
```

It would obviously be wrong to say that the function signals the error "/: divide by zero" now, even though an evaluation of the underlined subexpression would demand it. After all, $(= 0\ 0)$ is true and therefore the application has a proper result:

```
(my-divide 0)
```

```
= (cond
    [(= 0 0) 'inf]
    [else (/ 1 0)])
```

```
= (cond
    [true 'inf]
    [else (/ 1 0)])
```

```
= 'inf
```

Fortunately, our laws of evaluation take care of these situations automatically. We just need to keep in mind when the laws apply. For example, in

```
(+ (* 20 2) (/ 20 2))
```

the addition cannot take place before the multiplication or division. Similarly, the underlined division in

```
(cond
   [(= 0 0) 'inf]
   [else (/ 1 0)])
```

cannot be evaluated until the corresponding line is the first condition in the **cond**-expression.

As a rule of thumb, it is best to keep the following in mind:

> GUIDELINE ON EXPRESSION EVALUATION
>
> Simplify the outermost (and left-most) subexpression that is ready for evaluation.

While this guideline is a simplification, it always explains Scheme's results.

In some cases, programmers also want to define functions that raise errors. Recall the checked version of *area-of-disk* from section 6:

```
;; checked-area-of-disk : Scheme-value → boolean
;; to compute the area of a disk with radius v, if v is a number
(define (checked-area-of-disk v)
   (cond
      [(number? v) (area-of-disk v)]
      [else (error 'checked-area-of-disk "number expected")]))
```

If we were to apply *checked-area-of-disk* to a symbol, we would get the following evaluation:

```
(− (checked-area-of-disk 'a)
   (checked-area-of-disk 10))
```

```
= (− (cond
         [(number? 'a) (area-of-disk 'a)]
         [else (error 'checked-area-of-disk "number expected")])
      (checked-area-of-disk 10))
```

```
= (− (cond
         [false (area-of-disk 'a)]
         [else (error 'checked-area-of-disk "number expected")])
      (checked-area-of-disk 10))
```

```
= (− (error 'checked-area-of-disk "number expected")
   (checked-area-of-disk 10))
```

```
= checked-area-of-disk : number expected
```

In other words, when we evaluate an the error expression, we proceed as if
we had encountered a division by zero.

## Boolean Expressions

Our current definition of the Beginning Student Scheme language omits
two forms of expressions: **and** and **or** expressions. Adding them provides
a case study of how to study new language construct. We must first understand their syntax, then their semantics, and finally their pragmatics.

Here is the revised grammar:

$$\langle exp \rangle \quad = \quad \begin{array}{l} (\textbf{and } \langle exp \rangle \ \langle exp \rangle) \\ | \ (\textbf{or } \langle exp \rangle \ \langle exp \rangle) \end{array}$$

The grammar says that **and** and **or** are keywords, each followed by two
expressions. At first glance, the two look like (primitive or function) applications. To understand why they are not, we must look at the pragmatics
of these expressions first.

Suppose we need to formulate a condition that determines whether the
$n$-th fraction of 1 is $m$:

```
(and (not (= n 0))
     (= (/ 1 n) m))
```

We formulate the condition as an **and** combination of two boolean expressions, because we don't wish to divide by 0 accidentally. Next, assume $n$
becomes 0 during the course of the evaluation. Then the expression becomes

```
(and (not (= 0 0))
     (= (/ 1 0) m))
```

Now, if **and** were an ordinary operation, we would have to evaluate both
subexpressions, which would trigger an error in the second one. For this
reason, **and** is not a primitive operation, but a special expression. In short,
we use **and** and **or** expressions to combine boolean computations that may
have to short-cut an evaluation.

Once we understand how **and** and **or** expressions should be evaluated,
it is easy to formulate matching rules. Better still, we can formulate expressions in our first language that are equivalent to these expressions:

(**and** ⟨*exp-1*⟩ ⟨*exp-2*⟩)
≡
(**cond**
   [⟨*exp-1*⟩ ⟨*exp-2*⟩]
   [**else** false])

and

(**or** ⟨*exp-1*⟩ ⟨*exp-2*⟩)
≡
(**cond**
   [⟨*exp-1*⟩ true]
   [**else** ⟨*exp-2*⟩])

These equivalences simplify what actually takes place in DrScheme but they are a perfectly appropriate model for now.

## Variable Definitions

Programs consist not only of function definitions but also variable definitions, but these weren't included in our first grammar.

Here is the grammar rule for variable definitions:

$$\langle def \rangle \quad = \quad (\textbf{define} \ \langle var \rangle \ \langle exp \rangle)$$

The shape of a variable definition is similar to that of a function definition. It starts with a "(", followed by the keyword **define**, followed by a variable, followed by an expression, and closed by a right parenthesis ")" that matches the very first one. The keyword **define** distinguishes variable definitions from expressions, but not from function definitions. For that, a reader must look at the second component of the definition.

Next we must understand what a variable definition means. A variable definition like

(**define** *RADIUS* 5)

has a plain meaning. It says that wherever we encounter *RADIUS* during an evaluation, we may replace it with 5.

When DrScheme encounters a definition with a proper expression on the right-hand side, it must evaluate that expression immediately. For example, the right-hand side of the definition

(**define** *DIAMETER* (∗ 2 *RADIUS*))

is the expression (∗ 2 *RADIUS*). Its value is 10 because *RADIUS* stands for 5. Hence we can act as if we had written

(**define** *DIAMETER* 10)

In short, when DrScheme encounters a variable definition, it determines the value of the right-hand side. For that step, it uses all those definitions that *precede* the current definition but not those that follow. Once DrScheme has a value for the right-hand side, it remembers that the name on the left-hand side stands for this value. Whenever we evaluate an expression, every occurrence of the **define**d variable is replaced by its value.

---

(**define** *RADIUS* 10)

(**define** *DIAMETER* (∗ 2 *RADIUS*))

;; *area : number → number*
;; to compute the area of a disk with radius *r*
(**define** (*area r*)
  (∗ 3.14 (∗ *r r*)))

(**define** *AREA-OF-RADIUS* (*area RADIUS*))

Figure 23: An example of variable definitions

---

Consider the sequence of definitions in figure 23. As DrScheme steps through this sequence of definitions, it first determines that *RADIUS* stands for 10, *DIAMETER* for 20, and area is the name of a function. Finally, it evaluates (*area RADIUS*) to 314.0 and associates *AREA-OF-RADIUS* with that value.

## Exercises

**Exercise 8.6.1** Make up five examples of variable definitions. Use constants and expressions on the right-hand side. ∎

**Exercise 8.6.2** Evaluate the following sequence of definitions

(**define** *RADIUS* 10)

(**define** *DIAMETER* (∗ 2 *RADIUS*))

(**define** *CIRCUMFERENCE* (∗ 3.14 *DIAMETER*))

by hand. ∎

**Exercise 8.6.3** Evaluate the following sequence of definitions

(**define** *PRICE* 5)

(**define** *SALES-TAX* (∗ .08 *PRICE*))

(**define** *TOTAL* (+ *PRICE SALES-TAX*))

by hand. ∎

## Structure Definitions

We still have to understand the syntax and semantics of one more Scheme construct: **define-struct**. When we define a structure, we really define several primitive operations: a constructor, several selectors, and a predicate. Hence, **define-struct** is by far the most complex Scheme construct we use.

A structure definition is a third form of definition. The keyword **define-struct** distinguishes this form of definition from function and variable definitions. The keyword is followed by a name and a sequence of names enclosed in parentheses:

$$\langle def \rangle = (\textbf{define-struct } \langle var0 \rangle (\langle var\text{-}1 \rangle \ldots \langle var\text{-}n \rangle)) .$$

The names in a **define-struct** definition must be chosen as if they were function names, though none of them is used as a function (or variable) name.

Here is a simple example:

(**define-struct** *point* (*x y z*)) .

Since *point*, *x*, *y*, and *z* are variables and the parentheses are placed according to the grammatical pattern, it is a proper definition of a structure. In contrast, these two parenthesized sentences

(**define-struct** (*point x y z*))

(**define-struct** *point x y z*)

are improper definitions, because **define-struct** is not followed by a single variable name and a sequence of variables in parentheses.

A **define-struct** definition introduces new primitive operations. The names of these operations are formed from those that occur in the definition. Suppose a data structure definition has the following shape:

(**define-struct** *c* (*s-1* ... *s-n*))

Then Scheme introduces the following primitive operations:

1. make-c: a CONSTRUCTOR;

2. c-s-1 ... c-s-n: a series of SELECTORS; and

3. c?: a PREDICATE.

These primitives have the same status as $+$, $-$, or $*$. Before we can understand the rules that govern these new primitives, however, we must return to the definition of values. After all, the purpose of **define-struct** is to introduce a new class of values: structures.

Simply put, the set of values no longer consists of just constants, but also of structures, which compound several values into one. In terms of our grammar of values, we must add one clause per **define-struct**:

$$\langle val \rangle \quad = \quad (\text{make-c } \langle val \rangle ... \langle val \rangle)$$

Let us return to the *points* structures. Since the list of fields contains three names, (make-point *u v w*) is a value if *u, v,* and *w* are values.

Now we are in a position to understand the evaluation rules of the new primitives. If c-s-1 is applied to a *c* structure, it returns the first component of the value. Similarly, the second selector extracts the second component, the third selector the third component, and so on. The relationship between the new data constructor and the selectors is best characterized with *n* equations:

(c-s-1 (make-c *V-1* ... *V-n*)) = *V-1*

$$\vdots$$

(c-s-n (make-c *V-1* ... *V-n*)) = *V-n*

where *V-1* ... *V-n* is a sequence of values that is as long as *s-1* ... *s-n*.

For our running example, we get the equations

(point-x (make-point *V U W*)) = *V*
(point-y (make-point *V U W*)) = *U*
(point-z (make-point *V U W*)) = *W*

In particular, (point-y (make-point 3 4 5)) is equal to 4, and (point-x (make-point (make-point 1 2 3) 4 5)) evaluates to (make-point 1 2 3) because the latter is also a value.

The predicate c? can be applied to any value. It returns true if the value is of kind *c* and false otherwise. We can translate both parts into equations. The first one,

(c? (make-c *V-1* ... *V-n*)) = true ,

relates c? and values constructed with make-c; the second one,

(c? *V*) = false; if *V* is a value not constructed with make-c ,

relates c? to all other values.

Again, the equations are best understood in terms of our example. Here are the general equations:

(point? (make-point *V U W*)) = true
(point? *U*) = false ; if *U* is value, but not a *point* structure.

Thus, (point? (make-point 3 4 5)) is true and (point? 3) is false.

---

## Exercises

**Exercise 8.7.1** Distinguish legal from illegal sentences:

1. (**define-struct** *personnel-record* (*name salary dob ssn*))

2. (**define-struct** *oops* ())

3. (**define-struct** *child* (*dob date* (− *date dob*)))

4. (**define-struct** (*child person*) (*dob date*))

5. (**define-struct** *child* (*parents dob date*))

Explain why the sentences are legal **define-struct** definitions or how they fail to be legal **define-struct** definitions. ∎

**Exercise 8.7.2** Which of the following are values?

1. (make-point 1 2 3)

2. (make-point (make-point 1 2 3) 4 5)

3. (make-point (+ 1 2) 3 4)               ∎

**Exercise 8.7.3** Suppose the Definitions window contains

(**define-struct** *ball* (*x y speed-x speed-y*))

Determine the results of the following expressions:

1. (number? (make-ball 1 2 3 4))

2. (ball-speed-y (make-ball (+ 1 2) (+ 3 3) 2 3))

3. (ball-y (make-ball (+ 1 2) (+ 3 3) 2 3))

Also check how DrScheme deals with the following expressions:

1. (number? (make-ball 1 3 4))

2. (ball-x (make-posn 1 2))

3. (ball-speed-y 5)

Verify your solutions with DrScheme. ∎

$\langle def \rangle$ = (**define** ($\langle var \rangle$ $\langle var \rangle$ ... $\langle var \rangle$) $\langle exp \rangle$)
| (**define** $\langle var \rangle$ $\langle exp \rangle$)
| (**define-struct** $\langle var0 \rangle$ ($\langle var\text{-}1 \rangle$ ... $\langle var\text{-}n \rangle$))
$\langle exp \rangle$ = $\langle var \rangle$
| $\langle con \rangle$
| ($\langle prm \rangle$ $\langle exp \rangle$ ... $\langle exp \rangle$)
| ($\langle var \rangle$ $\langle exp \rangle$ ... $\langle exp \rangle$)
| (**cond** ($\langle exp \rangle$ $\langle exp \rangle$) ... ($\langle exp \rangle$ $\langle exp \rangle$))
| (**cond** ($\langle exp \rangle$ $\langle exp \rangle$) ... (**else** $\langle exp \rangle$))
| (**and** $\langle exp \rangle$ $\langle exp \rangle$)
| (**or** $\langle exp \rangle$ $\langle exp \rangle$)

Figure 24: Beginning Student Scheme: The full grammar

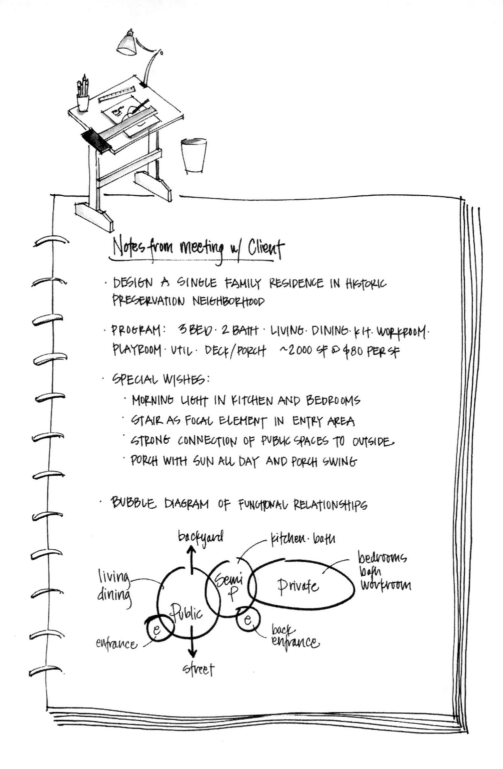

## Notes from meeting w/ Client

- DESIGN A SINGLE FAMILY RESIDENCE IN HISTORIC PRESERVATION NEIGHBORHOOD

- PROGRAM: 3 BED · 2 BATH · LIVING · DINING · KIT · WORKROOM · PLAYROOM · UTIL · DECK/PORCH   ~2000 SF @ $80 PER SF

- SPECIAL WISHES:
  - MORNING LIGHT IN KITCHEN AND BEDROOMS
  - STAIR AS FOCAL ELEMENT IN ENTRY AREA
  - STRONG CONNECTION OF PUBLIC SPACES TO OUTSIDE
  - PORCH WITH SUN ALL DAY AND PORCH SWING

- BUBBLE DIAGRAM OF FUNCTIONAL RELATIONSHIPS

backyard — kitchen · bath — bedrooms bath workroom

living dining — Public — Semi P — Private

entrance — e — e — back entrance

street

# 9    Compound Data, Part 2: Lists

Structures are one way to represent compound information. They are useful when we know how many pieces of data we wish to combine. In many cases, however, we don't know how many things we wish to enumerate, and in that case we form a list. A list can be of arbitrary length, that is, it contains a finite, but undetermined number of pieces of data.

Forming lists is something that all of us do. Before we go grocery shopping, we often write down a list of items that we want to purchase. When we plan out a day in the morning, we write down a list of things to do. During December, many children prepare Christmas wish lists. To plan a party, we list the people we want to invite. In short, arranging information in the form of lists is a ubiquitous part of our life, and we should learn to represent lists as Scheme data. In this section, we first learn to create lists and then move on to developing functions that consume lists.

## 9.1    Lists

When we form a list, we always start out with the empty list. In Scheme,

     empty

represents the empty list. From here, we can construct a longer list with the operation cons. Here is a simple example:

     (cons 'Mercury empty)

In this example, we constructed a list from the empty list and the symbol 'Mercury. Figure 25 presents this list in the same pictorial manner we used for structures. The box for cons has two fields: first and rest. In this specific example the first field contains 'Mercury and the rest field contains empty.

(cons 'Mercury empty)

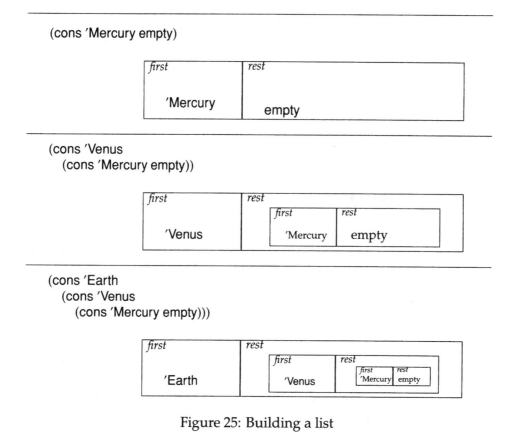

(cons 'Venus
     (cons 'Mercury empty))

(cons 'Earth
     (cons 'Venus
          (cons 'Mercury empty)))

Figure 25: Building a list

Once we have a list with one item on it, we can **construct** lists with two items by using **cons** again:

(cons 'Venus (cons 'Mercury empty))

The middle row of figure 25 shows how we should imagine the second list. It is also a box of two fields, but this time the rest field contains a box. Indeed, it contains the box from the top row of the same figure.

Finally, we construct a list with three items:

(cons 'Earth (cons 'Venus (cons 'Mercury empty)))

The last row of figure 25 illustrates the list with three items. Its rest field contains a box that contains a box again. So, as we create lists we put boxes into boxes into boxes, etc. While this may appear strange at first glance, it is just like a set of Chinese gift boxes or a set of nested drinking cups, which we sometimes get for our early birthdays. The only difference is that Scheme programs can nest lists much deeper than any artist could nest physical boxes.

## Exercises

**Exercise 9.1.1** Create Scheme lists that represent

1. the list of all planets in our solar system;

2. the following meal: steak, pommes-frites, beans, bread, water, juice, brie-cheese, and ice-cream; and

3. the list of basic colors.

Sketch box representations of these lists, similar to those in figure 25. ∎

We can also make lists of numbers. As before, empty is the list without any items. Here is a list with 10 numbers:

```
(cons 0
  (cons 1
    (cons 2
      (cons 3
        (cons 4
          (cons 5
            (cons 6
              (cons 7
                (cons 8
                  (cons 9 empty))))))))))
```

To build it requires 10 list constructions and one empty list.

In general a list does not have to contain values of one kind, but may contain arbitrary values:

```
(cons 'RobbyRound
  (cons 3
    (cons #t
      empty)))
```

Here the first item is a symbol, the second one is a number, and the last one a boolean. We could think of this list as the representation of a personnel record that includes the name of the employee, the number of years spent at the company, and whether the employee has health insurance through the company plan.

Now suppose we are given a list of numbers. One thing we might wish to do is add up the numbers on the list. To make this more concrete, let us assume that we are only interested in lists of three numbers:

---

A *list-of-3-numbers* is

$$(cons\ x\ (cons\ y\ (cons\ z\ empty)))$$

where $x$, $y$, and $z$ are numbers.

---

We write down the contract, purpose, header, and examples as before:

```
;; add-up-3 : list-of-3-numbers → number
;; to add up the three numbers in a-list-of-3-numbers
;; examples and tests:
;; (= (add-up-3 (cons 2 (cons 1 (cons 3 empty)))) 6)
;; (= (add-up-3 (cons 0 (cons 1 (cons 0 empty)))) 1)
(define (add-up-3 a-list-of-3-numbers) ...)
```

To define the body, however, presents a problem. A constructed list is like a structure. Hence we should layout a template with selector expressions next. Unfortunately, we don't know how to select items from a list.

In analogy to structure selectors, Scheme implements operations for extracting the fields from a constructed list: first and rest.[29] The first operation extracts the item that we used to construct a list; the rest operation extracts the list field.

To describe how first, rest, and cons are related, we can use equations that are similar to the equations that govern addition and subtraction and structure creation and field extraction:

$$\frac{(first\ (cons\ 10\ empty))}{= 10}$$

$$\frac{(rest\ (cons\ 10\ empty))}{= empty}$$

$$\frac{(first\ (rest\ (cons\ 10\ (cons\ 22\ empty))))}{= (first\ (cons\ 22\ empty))}$$
$$= 22$$

---

[29]The traditional names are *car* and *cdr*, but we will not use these nonsensical names.

The last one demonstrates how to evaluate nested expressions. The key is to think of (cons *a-value a-list*) as a value. And, as always, we start with the evaluation of the innermost parenthesized expressions that can be reduced, just as in arithmetic. In the above calculations, the expressions that are about to be reduced next are underlined.

Using first and rest we can now write down a template for *add-up-3*:

```
;; add-up-3 : list-of-3-numbers → number
;; to add up the three numbers in a-list-of-3-numbers
(define (add-up-3 a-list-of-3-numbers)
    ... (first a-list-of-3-numbers) ...
    ... (first (rest a-list-of-3-numbers)) ...
    ... (first (rest (rest a-list-of-3-numbers))) ... )
```

The three expressions remind us that the input, called *a-list-of-3-numbers*, contains three components and how to extract them.

## Exercises

**Exercise 9.1.2** Let *l* be the list

```
(cons 10 (cons 20 (cons 5 empty)))
```

What are the values of the following expressions?

1. (rest *l*)

2. (first (rest *l*))

3. (rest (rest *l*))

4. (first (rest (rest *l*)))

5. (rest (rest (rest *l*))) ∎

**Exercise 9.1.3** Finish the development of *add-up-3*, that is, define the body and test the complete function on some examples.

A list of three numbers is one possible representation for 3-dimensional points. The distance of a 3-dimensional point to the origin of the coordinate grid is computed in the same manner as that of 2-dimensional point: by squaring the numbers, adding them up, and taking the square root.

Use the template for *add-up-3* to develop *distance-to-0-for-3*, which computes the distance of a 3-dimensional point to the origin. ∎

---

**Exercise 9.1.4** Provide a data definition for lists of two symbols. Then develop the function *contains-2-doll?*, which consumes a list of two symbols and determines whether one of them is 'doll. ∎

---

**On the Precise Relationship between Cons and Structures:** The discussion of cons, first, and rest suggests that cons creates a structure and first and rest are ordinary selectors:

(**define-struct** *pair* (*left right*))

(**define** (*our-cons a-value a-list*) (make-pair *a-value a-list*))

(**define** (*our-first a-pair*) (pair-left *a-pair*))

(**define** (*our-rest a-pair*) (pair-right *a-pair*))

(**define** (*our-cons? x*) (pair? *x*))

Although these definitions are a good first approximation, they are inaccurate in one important point. DrScheme's version of cons is really a checked version of make-pair. Specifically, the cons operation ensures that the *right* field is always a list, that is, constructed or empty. This suggests the following refinement:

(**define** (*our-cons a-value a-list*)
  (**cond**
    [(empty? *a-list*) (make-pair *any a-list*)]
    [(*our-cons? a-list*) (make-pair *any a-list*)]
    [**else** (error 'our-cons "list as second argument expected")]))

The definitions for *our-first*, *our-rest*, and *our-cons?* remain the same. Finally, we must also promise not to use make-pair directly so that we don't accidentally build a bad list. ∎

## 9.2  Data Definitions for Lists of Arbitrary Length

first, rest  Suppose we wish to represent the inventory of a toy store that sells such things as dolls, make-up sets, clowns, bows, arrows, and soccer balls. To make an inventory, a store owner would start with an empty sheet of paper and slowly write down the names of the toys on the various shelves.

Representing a list of toys in Scheme is straightforward. We can simply use Scheme's symbols for toys and then construct lists from them. Here are a few short samples:

```
empty
(cons 'ball empty)
(cons 'arrow (cons 'ball empty))
(cons 'clown empty)
(cons 'bow (cons 'arrow (cons 'ball empty)))
(cons 'clown (cons 'bow (cons 'arrow (cons 'ball empty))))
```

For a real store, the list will contain many more items, and the list will grow and shrink over time. In any case, we cannot say in advance how many items these inventory lists will contain. Hence, if we wish to develop a function that consumes such lists, we cannot simply say that the input is a list with either one, two, three, or four items. We must be prepared to think about lists of arbitrary length.

In other words, we need a data definition that precisely describes the class of lists that contain an arbitrary number of symbols. Unfortunately, the data definitions we have seen so far can only describe classes of data where each item is of a fixed size, such as a structure with a specific number of components or a list with a specific number of items. So how can we describe a class of lists of arbitrary size?

Looking back we see that all our examples fall into one of two categories. The store owner starts with an empty list and constructs longer and longer lists. The construction proceeds by constructing together a toy and another list of toys. Here is a data definition that reflects this process:

---

A *list-of-symbols* is either

1. the empty list, **empty**, or

2. (**cons** *s los*) where *s* is a symbol and *los* is a list of symbols.

---

This definition is unlike any of the definitions we have seen so far or that we encounter in high school English or mathematics. Those definitions explain a new idea in terms of old, well-understood concepts. In contrast, this definition refers to *itself* in the item labeled 2, which implies that it explains what a list of symbols is in terms of lists of symbols. We call such definitions SELF-REFERENTIAL or RECURSIVE.

At first glance, a definition that explains or specifies something in terms of itself does not seem to make much sense. This first impression, however, is wrong. A recursive definition, such as the one above, makes sense as long as we can construct some elements from it; the definition is correct if we can construct all intended elements.[30]

Let's check whether our specific data definition makes sense and contains all the elements we are interested in. From the first clause we immediately know that empty is a list of symbols. From the second clause we know that we can create larger lists with cons from a symbol and a list of symbols. Thus (cons 'ball empty) is a list of symbols because we just determined that empty is one and we know that 'doll is a symbol. There is nothing special about 'doll. Any other symbol could serve equally well to form a number of one-item lists of symbols:

```
(cons 'make-up-set empty)
(cons 'water-gun empty)
. . .
```

Once we have lists that contain one symbol, we can use the same method to build lists with two items:

```
(cons 'Barbie (cons 'robot empty))
(cons 'make-up-set (cons 'water-gun empty))
(cons 'ball (cons 'arrow empty))
. . .
```

From here, it is easy to see how we can form lists that contain an arbitrary number of symbols. More important still for our problem, all possible inventories are adequately described by our data definition.

---

### Exercises

**Exercise 9.2.1** Show that all the inventory lists discussed at the beginning of this section belong to the class *list-of-symbols*. ∎

**Exercise 9.2.2** Do all lists of two symbols also belong to the class *list-of-symbols*? Provide a concise argument. ∎

---

[30]It is common that a data definition describes a class of data that contains more than the intended elements. This limitation is inherent and is just one of the many symptoms of the limits of computing.

**Exercise 9.2.3** Provide a data definition for the class of list of booleans. The class contains all arbitrarily large lists of booleans. ∎

Unnatural
Recursions

## 9.3 Processing Lists of Arbitrary Length

A real store will want to have a large inventory on-line, that is, put into a computer, so that an employee can quickly determine whether a toy is available or not. For simplicity, assume that we need *contains-doll?*, a function that checks whether the store has a 'doll. Translated into Scheme terminology, the function determines whether 'doll occurs on some list of symbols.

Because we already have a rigorous definition of *contains-doll?*'s input, we turn to the contract, header, and purpose statement:

;; *contains-doll? : list-of-symbols → boolean*
;; to determine whether the symbol 'doll occurs on *a-list-of-symbols*
(**define** (*contains-doll? a-list-of-symbols*) ... )

Following the general design recipe, we next make up some examples that illustrate *contains-doll?* purpose. First, we clearly need to determine the output for the simplest input: empty. Since the list does not contain any symbol, it certainly does not contain 'doll, and the answer should be false:

(boolean=? (*contains-doll?* empty)
        false)

Next, we consider lists with a single item. Here are two examples:

(boolean=? (*contains-doll?* (cons 'ball empty))
        false)

(boolean=? (*contains-doll?* (cons 'doll empty))
        true)

In the first case, the answer is false because the single item on the list is not 'doll; in the second case, the item is 'doll, and the answer is true. Finally, here are two more general examples, with lists of several items:

(boolean=? (*contains-doll?* (cons 'bow (cons 'ax (cons 'ball empty))))
        false)

(boolean=? (*contains-doll?* (cons 'arrow (cons 'doll (cons 'ball empty))))
        true)

Again, the answer in the first case must be false because the list does not contain 'doll, and in the second case it must be true because 'doll is one of the items on the list provided to the function.

The next step is to design a function template that matches the data definition. Since the data definition for lists of symbols has two clauses, the function's body must be a **cond**-expression. The **cond**-expression determines which of the two kinds of lists the function received: the empty list or a constructed list:

(**define** (*contains-doll? a-list-of-symbols*)
  (**cond**
    [(empty? *a-list-of-symbols*) ... ]
    [(cons? *a-list-of-symbols*) ... ]))

Instead of (cons? *a-list-of-symbols*), we can use **else** in the second clause.

We can add one more hint to the template by studying each clause of the **cond**-expression in turn. Specifically, recall that the design recipe suggests annotating each clause with selector expressions if the corresponding class of inputs consists of compounds. In our case, we know that empty does not have compounds, so there are no components. Otherwise the list is constructed from a symbol and another list of symbols, and we remind ourselves of this fact by adding (first *a-list-of-symbols*) and (rest *a-list-of-symbols*) to the template:

(**define** (*contains-doll? a-list-of-symbols*)
  (**cond**
    [(empty? *a-list-of-symbols*) ... ]
    [**else** ... (first *a-list-of-symbols*) ... (rest *a-list-of-symbols*) ... ]))

Now that we have a template based on our design recipes for mixed and compound data, we turn to the definition of the function's body, dealing with each **cond**-clause separately. If (empty? *a-list-of-symbols*) is true, the input is the empty list, in which case the function must produce the result false. In the second case, (cons? *a-list-of-symbols*) is true. The annotations in the template remind us that there is a first symbol and the rest of the list. So let us consider an example that falls into this category:

(cons 'arrow
  (cons ...
      ... empty)))

The function, just like a human being, must clearly compare the first item with 'doll. In this example, the first symbol is 'arrow and not 'doll, so the comparison will yield false. If we had considered some other example instead, say,

```
(cons 'doll
  (cons ...
    ... empty)))
```

the function would determine that the first item on the input is 'doll, and would therefore respond with true. All of this implies that the second line in the **cond**-expression should contain another **cond**-expression:

```
(define (contains-doll? a-list-of-symbols)
  (cond
    [(empty? a-list-of-symbols) false]
    [else (cond
            [(symbol=? (first a-list-of-symbols) 'doll)
             true]
            [else
             ... (rest a-list-of-symbols) ...])]))
```

Furthermore, if the comparison of (first *a-list-of-symbols*) yields true, the function is done and produces true, too.

If the comparison yields false, we are left with another list of symbols: (rest *a-list-of-symbols*). Clearly, we can't know the final answer in this case, because depending on what "..." represents, the function must produce true or false. Put differently, if the first item is not 'doll, we need some way to check whether the rest of the list contains 'doll.

Fortunately, we have just such a function: *contains-doll?*, which according to its purpose statement determines whether a list contains 'doll. The purpose statement implies that if *l* is a list of symbols, (*contains-doll? l*) tells us whether *l* contains the symbol 'doll. Similarly, (*contains-doll?* (rest *l*)) determines whether the rest of *l* contains 'doll. And in the same vein, (*contains-doll?* (rest *a-list-of-symbols*)) determines whether or not 'doll is in (rest *a-list-of-symbols*), which is precisely what we need to know now.

Here is the complete definition of the function:

```
(define (contains-doll? a-list-of-symbols)
  (cond
    [(empty? a-list-of-symbols) false]
    [else (cond
            [(symbol=? (first a-list-of-symbols) 'doll) true]
            [else (contains-doll? (rest a-list-of-symbols))])]))
```

It consumes a list of symbols and determines whether or not it is empty. If it is, the result is false. Otherwise, the list is not empty and the result of the function depends on the first item of the list. If the first item is 'doll, the result is true; if not, the function's result is the result of searching the rest of the input list—whatever it is.

## Exercises

**Exercise 9.3.1** Use DrScheme to test the definition of *contains-doll?* on our examples:

```
empty
(cons 'ball empty)
(cons 'arrow (cons 'doll empty))
(cons 'bow (cons 'arrow (cons 'ball empty)))
```

■

**Exercise 9.3.2** Another way of formulating the second **cond**-clause in the function *contains-doll?* is to understand

(*contains-doll?* (rest *a-list-of-symbols*))

as a condition that evaluates to either true or false, and to combine it appropriately with the condition

(symbol=? (first *a-list-of-symbols*) 'doll)

Reformulate the definition of *contains-doll?* according to this observation. ■

**Exercise 9.3.3** Develop the function *contains?*, which consumes a symbol and a list of symbols and determines whether or not the symbol occurs in the list. ■

## 9.4  Designing Functions for Self-Referential Data Definitions

At first glance, self-referential data definitions seem to be far more complex than those for compound or mixed data. But, as the example in the preceding subsection shows, our design recipes still work. Nevertheless, in this section we discuss a new design recipe that works better for self-referential data definitions. As implied by the preceding section, the new recipe generalizes those for compound and mixed data. The new parts concern the process of discovering when a self-referential data definition is needed, deriving a template, and defining the function body:

**Data Analysis and Design:** If a problem statement discusses compound information of arbitrary size, we need a recursive or self-referential data definition. At this point, we have only seen one such class, *list-of-symbols*, but it is easy to imagine other, yet similar classes of lists. We will get to know many other examples in this and the following part.[31]

For a recursive data definition to be valid, it must satisfy two conditions. First, it must contain at least two clauses. Second, at least one of the clauses must not refer back to the definition. It is good practice to identify the self-references explicitly with arrows from the references in the data definition back to its beginning.

Our running example for this section are functions that consume lists of symbols:

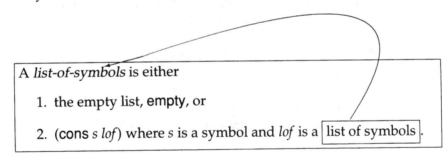

A *list-of-symbols* is either

1. the empty list, empty, or

2. (cons *s lof*) where *s* is a symbol and *lof* is a | list of symbols |.

**Template:** A self-referential data definition specifies a mixed class of data, and one of the clauses should specify a subclass of compound data. Hence the design of the template can proceed according to the recipes in sections 6.5 and 7.2. Specifically, we formulate a **cond**-expression with as many **cond**-clauses as there are clauses in the data definition, match each recognizing condition to the corresponding clause in the data definition, and write down appropriate selector expressions in all **cond**-lines that process compound values.

---

[31]Numbers also seem to be arbitrarily large. For inexact numbers, this is an illusion. For precise integers, this is indeed the case, and we will discuss them later in this part.

In addition, we inspect each selector expression. For each that extracts a value of the same class of data as the input, we draw an arrow back to the function parameter. At the end, we must have as many arrows as we have in the data definition.

Let's return to the running example. The template for a list-processing function contains a **cond**-expression with two clauses and one arrow:

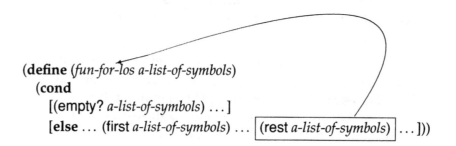

```
(define (fun-for-los a-list-of-symbols)
  (cond
    [(empty? a-list-of-symbols) ... ]
    [else ... (first a-list-of-symbols) ... (rest a-list-of-symbols) ... ]))
```

For simplicity, this book will use a textual alternative to arrows. Instead of drawing an arrow, the templates contain self-applications of the function to the selector expression(s):

```
(define (fun-for-los a-list-of-symbols)
  (cond
    [(empty? a-list-of-symbols) ... ]
    [else ... (first a-list-of-symbols) ...
        ... (fun-for-los (rest a-list-of-symbols)) ... ]))
```

We refer to these self-applications as NATURAL RECURSIONS.

**Body:** For the design of the body we start with those **cond**-lines that do not contain natural recursions. They are called BASE CASES. The corresponding answers are typically easy to formulate or are already given by the examples.

Then we deal with the self-referential cases. We start by reminding ourselves what each of the expressions in the template line computes. For the recursive application we assume that the function already works as specified in our purpose statement. **The rest is then a matter of combining the various values.**

Suppose we wish to define the function *how-many*, which determines how many symbols are on a list of symbols. Assuming we have followed the design recipe, we have the following:

```
;; how-many : list-of-symbols → number
;; to determine how many symbols are on a-list-of-symbols
(define (how-many a-list-of-symbols)
  (cond
    [(empty? a-list-of-symbols) ...]
    [else ... (first a-list-of-symbols) ...
      ... (how-many (rest a-list-of-symbols)) ...]))
```

The answer for the base case is 0 because the empty list contains nothing. The two expressions in the second clause compute the first item and the number of symbols on the (rest *a-list-of-symbols*). To compute how many symbols there are on all of *a-list-of-symbols*, we just need to add 1 to the value of the latter expression:

```
(define (how-many a-list-of-symbols)
  (cond
    [(empty? a-list-of-symbols) 0]
    [else (+ (how-many (rest a-list-of-symbols)) 1)]))
```

**Combining Values:** In many cases, the combination step can be expressed with Scheme's primitives, for example, +, **and**, or cons. If the problem statement suggests that we ask questions about the first item, we may need a nested **cond**-statement. Finally, in some cases, we may have to define auxiliary functions.

Figure 26 summarizes this discussion in the usual format; those design steps that we didn't discuss are performed as before. The following section discusses several examples in detail.

## 9.5 More on Processing Simple Lists

Let us now look at another aspect of inventory management: the cost of an inventory. In addition to a list of the available toys, a store owner should also maintain a list of the cost of each item. The cost list permits the owner to determine how much the current inventory is worth or, given the inventory at the beginning of the year and that of the end of the year, how much profit the store makes.

| Phase | Goal | Activity |
|---|---|---|
| Data Analysis and Design | to formulate a data definition | develop a data definition for mixed data with at least two alternatives • one alternative must not refer to the definition • explicitly identify all self-references in the data definition |
| Contract Purpose and Header | to name the function; to specify its classes of input data and its class of output data; to describe its purpose; to formulate a header | name the function, the classes of input data, the class of output data, and specify its purpose:<br>;; *name* : *in1 in2 ...* → *out*<br>;; to compute ... from *x1* ...<br>(**define** (*name x1 x2 ...*) ...) |
| Examples | to characterize the input-output relationship via examples | create examples of the input-output relationship • make sure there is at least one example per subclass |
| Template | to formulate an outline | develop a **cond**-expression with one clause per alternative • add selector expressions to each clause • annotate the body with *natural recursions* • TEST: the self-references in this template and the data definition match! |
| Body | to define the function | formulate a Scheme expression for each simple **cond**-line • explain for all other **cond**-clauses what each natural recursion computes according to the purpose statement |
| Test | to discover mistakes ("typos" and logic) | apply the function to the inputs of the examples • check that the outputs are as predicted |

Figure 26: Designing a function for self-referential data
(Refines the recipes in figures 4 (pg. 21), 12 (pg. 71), and 18 (pg. 89))

A list of costs is most easily represented as a list. For example:

```
empty
(cons 1.22 empty)
(cons 2.59 empty)
(cons 1.22 (cons 2.59 empty))
(cons 17.05 (cons 1.22 (cons 2.59 empty)))
```

Again, for a real store, we cannot place an arbitrary limit on the size of such a list, and functions that process such cost lists must be prepared to consume lists of arbitrary size.

Suppose the toy store needs a function that computes the value of an inventory from the cost of the individual toys. We call this function *sum*. Before we can define *sum*, we must figure out how to describe all possible lists of numbers that the function may consume. In short, we need a data definition that precisely defines what an arbitrarily large list of numbers is. We can obtain this definition by replacing "symbol" with "number" in the definition of lists of symbols:

---

A *list-of-numbers* is either

1. the empty list, empty, or

2. (cons *n lon*) where *n* is a number and *lon* is a list of numbers.

---

Given that this data definition is self-referential again, we must first confirm that it actually defines some lists and that it defines all those inventories that we wish to represent. All of the examples above are lists of numbers. The first one, empty, is included explicitly. The second and third are constructed by adding the numbers 1.22 and 2.59, respectively, to the empty list. The others are lists of numbers for similar reasons.

As always, we start the development of the function with a contract, header, and purpose statement:

```
;; sum : list-of-numbers → number
;; to compute the sum of the numbers on a-list-of-nums
(define (sum a-list-of-nums) ...)
```

Then we continue with function examples:

```
(= (sum empty)
   0)
```

```
(= (sum (cons 1.00 empty))
   1.0)
```

```
(= (sum (cons 17.05 (cons 1.22 (cons 2.59 empty))))
   20.86)
```

If *sum* is applied to empty, the store has no inventory and the result should be 0. If the input is (cons 1.00 empty), the inventory contains only one toy, and the cost of the toy is the cost of the inventory. Hence the result is 1.00. Finally, for (cons 17.05 (cons 1.22 (cons 2.59 empty))), *sum* should yield

$$17.05 + 1.22 + 2.59 = 20.86 .$$

For the design of *sum*'s template, we follow the design recipe, step by step. First, we add the **cond**-expression:

```
(define (sum a-list-of-nums)
  (cond
    [(empty? a-list-of-nums) ...]
    [(cons? a-list-of-nums) ...]))
```

The second clause indicates with a comment that it deals with constructed lists. Second, we add the appropriate selector expressions for each clause:

```
(define (sum a-list-of-nums)
  (cond
    [(empty? a-list-of-nums) ...]
    [(cons? a-list-of-nums)
     ... (first a-list-of-nums) ... (rest a-list-of-nums) ...]))
```

Finally, we add the natural recursion of *sum* that reflects the self-reference in the data definition:

```
(define (sum a-list-of-nums)
  (cond
    [(empty? a-list-of-nums) ...]
    [else ... (first a-list-of-nums) ... (sum (rest a-list-of-nums)) ...]))
```

The final template reflects almost every aspect of the data definition: the two clauses, the construction in the second clauses, and the self-reference of the second clauses. The only part of the data definition that the function template does not reflect is that the first item of a constructed input is a number.

Now that we have a template, let us define the answers for the **cond**-expression on a clause-by-clause basis. In the first clause, the input is empty, which means that the store has no inventory. We already agreed that in this case the inventory is worth nothing, which means the corresponding answer is 0. In the second clause of the template, we find two expressions:

1. (first *a-list-of-nums*), which extracts the cost of the first toy; and

2. (*sum* (rest *a-list-of-nums*)), which, according to the purpose statement of *sum*, computes the sum of (rest *a-list-of-nums*).

From these two reminders of what the expressions already compute for us, we see that the expression

(+ (first *a-list-of-nums*) (*sum* (rest *a-list-of-nums*)))

computes the answer in the second **cond**-clause.

Here is the complete definition of *sum*:

```
(define (sum a-list-of-nums)
  (cond
    [(empty? a-list-of-nums) 0]
    [else (+ (first a-list-of-nums) (sum (rest a-list-of-nums)))]))
```

A comparison of this definition with the template and the data definition shows that the step from the data definition to the template is the major step in the function development process. Once we have derived the template from a solid understanding of the set of possible inputs, we can focus on the creative part: combining values. For simple examples, this step is easy; for others, it requires rigorous thinking.

We will see in future sections that this relationship between the shape of the data definition and the function is not a coincidence. Defining the class of data that a function consumes always determines to a large extent the shape of the function.

## Exercises

**Exercise 9.5.1** Use DrScheme to test the definition of *sum* on the following sample lists of numbers:

```
empty
(cons 1.00 empty)
(cons 17.05 (cons 1.22 (cons 2.59 empty)))
```

Compare the results with our specifications. Then apply *sum* to the following examples:

```
empty
(cons 2.59 empty)
(cons 1.22 (cons 2.59 empty))
```

First determine what the result *should* be; then use DrScheme to evaluate the expressions. ∎

**Exercise 9.5.2** Develop the function *how-many-symbols*, which consumes a list of symbols and produces the number of items in the list.

Develop the function *how-many-numbers*, which counts how many numbers are in a list of numbers. How do *how-many-symbols* and *how-many-numbers* differ? ∎

**Exercise 9.5.3** Develop the function *dollar-store?*, which consumes a list of prices (numbers) and checks whether all of the prices are below 1.
For example, the following expressions should evaluate to true:

(*dollar-store?* empty)

(not (*dollar-store?* (cons .75 (cons 1.95 (cons .25 empty)))))

(*dollar-store?* (cons .75 (cons .95 (cons .25 empty))))

Generalize the function so that it consumes a list of prices (numbers) and a threshold price (number) and checks that all prices in the list are below the threshold. ∎

**Exercise 9.5.4** Develop the function *check-range1*, which consumes a list of temperature measurements and checks whether all measurements are between $5^\circ C$ and $95^\circ C$.

Generalize the function to *check-range*, which consumes a list of temperature measurements and a legal interval and checks whether all measurements are within the legal interval. ∎

**Exercise 9.5.5** Develop the function *convert*. It consumes a list of digits and produces the corresponding number. The first digit is the least significant, and so on.

Also develop the function *check-guess-for-list*. It implements a general version of the number-guessing game of exercise 5.1.3. The function consumes a list of digits, which represents the player's *guess*, and a number, which represents the randomly chosen and hidden number. Depending on how the *converted* digits relate to *target*, *check-guess-for-list* produces one of the following three answers: 'TooSmall, 'Perfect, or 'TooLarge.

The rest of the game is implemented by **guess.ss**. To play the game, use the teachpack to **guess.ss** and evaluate the expression

(*guess-with-gui-list* 5 *check-guess-for-list*)

*after* the functions have been thoroughly developed. ∎

**Exercise 9.5.6** Develop the function *delta*, which consumes two price lists, that is, lists of numbers. The first represents the inventory at the beginning of a time period, the second one the inventory at the end. The function outputs the difference in value. If the value of the inventory has increased, the result is positive; if the value has decreased, it is negative. ∎

**Exercise 9.5.7** Define the function *average-price*. It consumes a list of toy prices and computes the average price of a toy. The average is the total of all prices divided by the number of toys.

**Iterative Refinement**: First develop a function that works on non-empty lists. Then produce a checked function (see section 7.5) that signals an error when the function is applied to an empty list. ∎

**Exercise 9.5.8** Develop the function *draw-circles*, which consumes a *posn p* and a list of numbers. Each number of the list represents the radius of some circle. The function draws concentric red circles around *p* on a canvas, using the operation *draw-circle*. Its result is true, if it can draw all of them; otherwise an error has occurred and the function does not need to produce a value.

Use the teachpack **draw.ss**; create the canvas with (*start* 300 300). Recall that **draw.ss** provides the structure definition for *posn* (see section 7.1). ∎

## 10  More on Processing Lists

The functions in section 9 consume lists that contain atomic data, especially numbers, symbols, and booleans. But functions must also be able to produce such lists. Furthermore, they must be able to consume and produce lists that contain structures. We discuss these cases in this section, and we continue practicing the use of the design recipe.

## 10.1  Functions that Produce Lists

Recall the function *wage* from section 2.3:

```
;; wage : number → number
;; to compute the total wage (at $12 per hour)
;; of someone who worked for h hours
(define (wage h)
  (* 12 h))
```

The *wage* function consumes the number of hours some employee worked and produces the weekly wage payment. For simplicity, we assume that all employees earn the same hourly rate, namely, $12. A company, however, isn't interested in a function like *wage*, which computes the wage of a single employee. Instead, it wants a function that computes the wages for all of its employees, especially if there are a lot of them.

Call this new function *hours→ wages*. It consumes a list that represents how many hours the employees of the company worked and must produce a list of the weekly wages they earned. We can represent both the input and the output as Scheme lists of numbers. Since we already have a data definition for the inputs and outputs, we can immediately start our function development:

```
;; hours→ wages : list-of-numbers → list-of-numbers
;; to create a list of weekly wages from a list of weekly hours (alon)
(define (hours→ wages alon) ...)
```

Next we need some examples of inputs and the corresponding outputs:

```
empty                           empty
(cons 28 empty)                 (cons 336 empty)
(cons 40 (cons 28 empty))       (cons 480 (cons 336 empty))
```

The outputs are obtained by calculating the wage for each item on the list to the left.

Given that *hours→ wages* consumes the same class of data as, say, the function *sum*, and given that the shape of a function template depends only on the shape of the data definition, we can reuse the *list-of-numbers* template:

```
(define (hours→ wages alon)
  (cond
    [(empty? alon) ...]
    [else ... (first alon) ... (hours→ wages (rest alon)) ...]))
```

Starting with this template, we can turn to the most creative step of function development: the definition of the function body. Following our recipe, we consider each **cond**-line in isolation, starting with the simpler case. First, assume (empty? *alon*) is true, which means that the input is empty. The answer in this case is empty:

```
(define (hours→ wages alon)
  (cond
    [(empty? alon) empty]
    [else ... (first alon) ... (hours→ wages (rest alon)) ...]))
```

Second, assume that *alon* was constructed from a number and a list of numbers. The expressions in the second line remind us of this assumption, and the recipe tells us that we should state explicitly what they compute:

1. (first *alon*) yields the first number on *alon*, which is the first number of hours worked; and

2. (*hours→ wages* (rest *alon*)) reminds us that (rest *alon*) is a list and can be processed by the very function we are defining. According to the purpose statement, the expression computes the list of wages for the rest of the list of hours, and we may assume this relationship in our construction—even though the function is not yet completely defined.

From here it is a short step to the complete function definition. Since we already have the list of wages for all but the first item of *alon*, the function must do two things to produce an output for the *entire* list of hours:

1. Compute the weekly wage for the first number of hours.

2. Construct a list that represents all weekly wages for *alon*, using the first weekly wage and the list of weekly wages for (rest *alon*).

For the first part, we reuse *wage*. For the second, we cons the two pieces of information together into one list:

```
(cons (wage (first alon)) (hours→ wages (rest alon)))
```

```
;; hours→ wages : list-of-numbers → list-of-numbers
;; to create a list of weekly wages from a list of weekly hours (alon)
(define (hours→ wages alon)
  (cond
    [(empty? alon) empty]
    [else (cons (wage (first alon)) (hours→ wages (rest alon)))]))

;; wage : number → number
;; to compute the total wage (at $12 per hour)
;; of someone who worked for h hours
(define (wage h)
  (* 12 h))
```

Figure 27: Computing weekly wages

And with that, we have a complete function. It is shown in figure 27. To finish the design of the function, we must still test it.

## Exercises

**Exercise 10.1.1** How do we have to change the function in figure 27 if we want to give everyone a raise to $14? ∎

**Exercise 10.1.2** No employee could possibly work more than 100 hours per week. To protect the company against fraud, the function should check that no item of the input list of *hours→ wages* exceeds 100. If one of them does, the function should immediately signal the error "too many hours".

How do we have to change the function in figure 27 if we want to perform this basic reality check? ∎

**Exercise 10.1.3** Develop *convertFC*. The function converts a list of Fahrenheit measurements to a list of Celsius measurements. ∎

**Exercise 10.1.4** Develop the function *convert-euro*, which converts a list of U.S. dollar amounts into a list of euro amounts. Assume the exchange rate is 1.22 euro for each dollar.

Generalize *convert-euro* to the function *convert-euro-1*, which consumes an exchange rate and a list of dollar amounts and converts the latter into a list of euro amounts. ∎

**Exercise 10.1.5** Develop the function *eliminate-exp* to eliminate expensive toys. The function consumes a number, called *ua*, and a list of toy prices, called *lotp*, and produces a list of all those prices in *lotp* that are below or equal to *ua*. For example,[32]

(*eliminate-exp* 1.0 (cons 2.95 (cons .95 (cons 1.0 (cons 5 empty)))))
;; expected value:
(cons .95 (cons 1.0 empty))

∎

**Exercise 10.1.6** Develop the function *name-robot*, which consumes a list of toy descriptions (names) and produces an equivalent list of more accurate descriptions. Specifically, it replaces all occurrences of 'robot with 'r2d2 and otherwise retains the toy descriptions in the same order.

Generalize *name-robot* to the function *substitute*. The new function consumes two symbols, called *new* and *old*, and a list of symbols. It produces a new list of symbols by substituting all occurrences of *old* by *new*. For example,

(*substitute* 'Barbie 'doll (cons 'robot (cons 'doll (cons 'dress empty))))
;; expected value:
(cons 'robot (cons 'Barbie (cons 'dress empty)))

∎

**Exercise 10.1.7** Develop the function *recall* to eliminate specific toys from a list. The function consumes the name of a toy, called *ty*, and a list of names, called *lon*, and produces a list of names that contains all components of *lon* with the exception of *ty*. For example,

(*recall* 'robot (cons 'robot (cons 'doll (cons 'dress empty))))
;; expected value:
(cons 'doll (cons 'dress empty))

∎

**Exercise 10.1.8** Develop *quadratic-roots*, which solves quadratic equations: see exercises 4.4.4 and 5.1.4. The function accepts the coefficients $a$, $b$, and $c$. The computations it performs depend on the input:

---

[32]Since we don't know yet how to compare two lists with a function, we use the old style of specifying examples and tests.

1. if $a = 0$, its output is 'degenerate.

2. if $b^2 < 4 \cdot a \cdot c$, the quadratic equation has no solution; *quadratic-roots* produces 'none in this case.

3. if $b^2 = 4 \cdot a \cdot c$, the equation has one solution:

$$\frac{-b}{2 \cdot a};$$

the solution is the answer.

4. if $b^2 > 4 \cdot a \cdot c$, the equation has two solutions:

$$\frac{-b + \sqrt{b^2 - 4 \cdot a \cdot c}}{2 \cdot a}$$

and

$$\frac{-b - \sqrt{b^2 - 4 \cdot a \cdot c}}{2 \cdot a};$$

the result is a list of two numbers: the first solution followed by the second solution.

Test the function with the examples from exercises 4.4.4 and 5.1.4. First decide the answer for each example, then determine it with DrScheme. ∎

**Exercise 10.1.9** The cash registers at many grocery stores talk to customers. The register's computer receives the number of cents that the customer must pay and then builds a list with the following five items:

1. the dollar amount;

2. the symbol 'dollar if the dollar amount is 1 and 'dollars otherwise;

3. the symbol 'and;

4. the cent amount; and

5. the symbol 'cent if the cent amount is 1 and 'cents otherwise.

Develop the function *controller*, which consumes a number and produces a list according to the above description. For example, if the amount is $1.03, then the cash register evaluates (*controller* 103):

```
(controller 103)
;; expected value:
(cons 1 (cons 'dollar (cons 'and (cons 3 (cons 'cents empty)))))
```

**Hint**: Scheme provides the arithmetic operations quotient and remainder, which produce the quotient and remainder of the expression $n/m$ for integers $n$ and $m$, respectively.

Once the controller returns the correct list for amounts whose dollar and cent amounts are between 0 and 20, test the controller with a computer that can speak. Set the teachpack to **sound.ss**, which makes two operations available: *speak-word* and *speak-list*. The first accepts a symbol or a number, the second a list of symbols and numbers. Both pronounce the symbols they consume. Evaluate the following expressions (*speak-word* 1), (*speak-list* (cons 1 (cons 'dollar empty))), and (*speak-list* (cons 'beautiful (cons 'lady empty))) to understand how the operations operate.

**Simple Challenge**: The sound teachpack contains only the sounds for the numbers 0 through 20 and 30, 40, 50, 60, 70, 80, and 90. Because of this restriction, this challenge problem works only on amounts with cents and dollars between 0 to 20. Implement a controller that deals with arbitrary amounts between 0 and 99.99. ∎

## 10.2   Lists that Contain Structures

The representation of an inventory as a list of symbols or a list of prices is naive. A sales clerk in a toy store needs to know not only the name of the toy, but also its price, and possibly other attributes like warehouse availability, delivery time, or even a picture of the item. Similarly, representing the personnel's work week as a list of hours is a bad choice. Even the printing of a paycheck requires more information about the employee than the hours worked per week.

Fortunately, the items of lists do not have to be atomic values. Lists may contain whatever values we want, especially structures. Let's try to make our toy store inventory functions more realistic. We start with the structure and the data definition of a class of inventory records:

(**define-struct** *ir* (*name price*))

---

An *inventory-record* (short: *ir*) is a structure:
(make-ir *s n*)
where *s* is a symbol and *n* is a (positive) number.

---

Most important, we can define a class of lists that represent inventories much more realistically:

---

An *inventory* is either

1. empty or

2. (cons *ir inv*)
where *ir* is an inventory record and *inv* is an inventory.

---

While the shape of the list definition is the same as before, its components are defined in a separate data definition. Since this is our first such data definition, we should make up some examples before we proceed.

The simplest example of an inventory is empty. To create a larger inventory, we must create an inventory record and cons it onto another inventory:

```
(cons (make-ir 'doll 17.95)
  empty)
```

From here, we can create yet a larger inventory listing:

```
(cons (make-ir 'robot 22.05)
  (cons (make-ir 'doll 17.95)
    empty))
```

Now we can adapt our inventory-processing functions. First look at *sum*, the function that consumes an inventory and produces its total value. Here is a restatement of the basic information about the function:

```
;; sum : inventory → number
;; to compute the sum of prices on an-inv
(define (sum an-inv) ...)
```

For our three sample inventories, the function should produce the following results: 0, 17.95, and 40.0.

Since the data definition of inventories is basically that of lists, we can again start from the template for list-processing functions:

```
(define (sum an-inv)
  (cond
    [(empty? an-inv) ...]
    [else ... (first an-inv) ... (sum (rest an-inv)) ...]))
```

Following our recipe, the template only reflects the data definition of the input, not that of its constituents. Therefore the template for *sum* here is indistinguishable from that in section 9.5.

For the definition of the function body, we consider each **cond**-line in isolation. First, if (empty? *an-inv*) is true, *sum* is supposed to produce 0. Hence the answer expression in the first **cond**-line is obviously 0.

---

```
(define (sum an-inv)
  (cond
    [(empty? an-inv) 0]
    [else (+ (ir-price (first an-inv)) (sum (rest an-inv)))]))
```

Figure 28: Computing the value of an inventory

---

Second, if (empty? *an-inv*) is false, in other words, if *sum* is applied to a constructed inventory, the recipe requires us to understand the purpose of two expressions:

1. (first *an-inv*), which extracts the first item of the list; and

2. (*sum* (rest *an-inv*)), which extracts the rest of *an-inv* and then computes its cost with *sum*.

To compute the total cost of the entire input *an-inv* in the second case, we must determine the cost of the first item. The cost of the first item may be obtained via the selector ir-price, which extracts the price from an inventory record. Now we just add the cost of the first item and the cost of the rest of the inventory:

```
(+ (ir-price (first an-inv))
   (sum (rest an-inv)))
```

The complete function definition is contained in figure 28.

---

## Exercises

**Exercise 10.2.1** Adapt the function *contains-doll?* so that it consumes inventories instead of lists of symbols:

```
;; contains-doll? : inventory → boolean
;; to determine whether an-inv contains a record for 'doll
(define (contains-doll? an-inv) ...)
```

Also adapt the function *contains?*, which consumes a symbol and an inventory and determines whether an inventory record with this symbol occurs in the inventory:

*;; contains? : symbol inventory → boolean*
*;;* to determine whether *inventory* contains a record for *asymbol*
(**define** (*contains? asymbol an-inv*) ...)

∎

**Exercise 10.2.2** Provide a data definition and a structure definition for an inventory that includes pictures with each object. Show how to represent the inventory listing in figure 29.[33]

Develop the function *show-picture*. The function consumes a symbol, the name of a toy, and one of the new inventories. It produces the picture of the named toy or **false** if the desired item is not in the inventory. Pictures of toys are available on the Web. ∎

**Exercise 10.2.3** Develop the function *price-of*, which consumes the name of a toy and an inventory and produces the toy's price. ∎

**Exercise 10.2.4** A phone directory combines names with phone numbers. Develop a data definition for phone records and directories. Using this data definition develop the functions

1. *whose-number*, which determines the name that goes with some given phone number and phone directory, and

2. *phone-number*, which determines the phone number that goes with some given name and phone directory.

∎

Suppose a business wishes to separate all those items that sell for a dollar or less from all others. The goal might be to sell these items in a separate department of the store. To perform this split, the business also needs a function that can extract these items from its inventory listing, that is, a function that produces a list of structures.

---

[33]Thanks to Mr. John Clements for drawing these pictures.

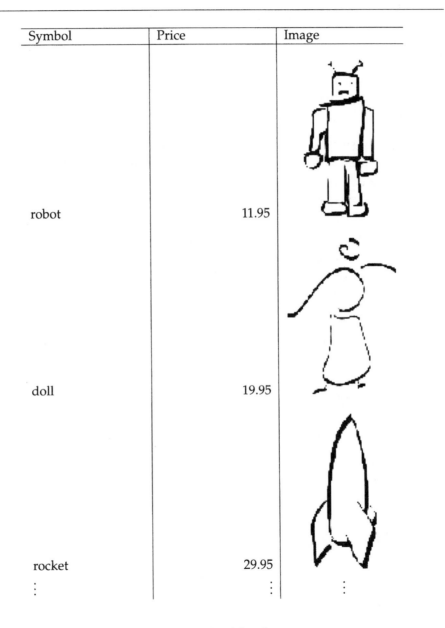

| Symbol | Price | Image |
|--------|-------|-------|
| robot | 11.95 | |
| doll | 19.95 | |
| rocket | 29.95 | |
| ⋮ | ⋮ | ⋮ |

Figure 29: A table of toys

Let us name the function *extract1* because it creates an inventory from all those inventory records whose price item is less than or equal to 1.00. The function consumes an inventory and produces one with items of appropriate prices. Thus the contract for *extract1* is easy to formulate:

```
;; extract1 : inventory → inventory
;; to create an inventory from an-inv for all
;; those items that cost less than $1
(define (extract1 an-inv) ...)
```

We can reuse our old inventory examples to make examples of *extract1*'s input-output relationship. Unfortunately, for these three examples it must produce the empty inventory, because all prices are above one dollar. For a more interesting input-output example, we need an inventory with more variety:

```
(cons (make-ir 'dagger .95)
      (cons (make-ir 'Barbie 17.95)
            (cons (make-ir 'key-chain .55)
                  (cons (make-ir 'robot 22.05)
                        empty))))
```

Out of the four items in this new inventory, two have prices below one dollar. If given to *extract1*, we should get the result

```
(cons (make-ir 'dagger .95)
      (cons (make-ir 'key-chain .55)
            empty))
```

The new listing enumerates the items in the same order as the original, but contains only those items whose prices match our condition.

The contract also implies that the template for *extract1* is identical to that of *sum*, except for a name change:

```
(define (extract1 an-inv)
  (cond
    [(empty? an-inv) ...]
    [else ... (first an-inv) ... (extract1 (rest an-inv)) ...]))
```

As always, the difference in outputs between *sum* and *extract1* does not affect the template derivation.

For the definition of the function body, we again analyze each case separately. First, if (empty? *an-inv*) is true, then the answer is clearly empty, because no item in an empty store costs less than one dollar. Second, if

```
;; extract1 : inventory → inventory
;; to create an inventory from an-inv for all
;; those items that cost less than $1
(define (extract1 an-inv)
  (cond
    [(empty? an-inv) empty]
    [else (cond
            [(<= (ir-price (first an-inv)) 1.00)
             (cons (first an-inv) (extract1 (rest an-inv)))]
            [else (extract1 (rest an-inv))])]))
```

Figure 30: Extracting dollar items from an inventory

the inventory is not empty, we first determine what the expressions in the matching **cond**-clause compute. Since *extract1* is the first recursive function to produce a list of structures, let us look at our interesting example:

```
(cons (make-ir 'dagger .95)
      (cons (make-ir 'Barbie 17.95)
            (cons (make-ir 'key-chain .55)
                  (cons (make-ir 'robot 22.05)
                        empty))))
```

If *an-inv* stands for this inventory,

```
(first an-inv) = (make-ir 'dagger .95)
```

```
(rest an-inv) = (cons (make-ir 'Barbie 17.95)
                      (cons (make-ir 'key-chain .55)
                            (cons (make-ir 'robot 22.05)
                                  empty)))
```

Assuming *extract1* works correctly, we also know that

```
(extract1 (rest an-inv)) = (cons (make-ir 'key-chain .55)
                                 empty)
```

In other words, the recursive application of *extract1* produces the appropriate selection from the rest of *an-inv*, which is a list with a single inventory record.

To produce an appropriate inventory for all of *an-inv*, we must decide what to do with the first item. Its price may be more or less than one dollar, which suggests the following template for the second answer:

```
... (cond
     [(<= (ir-price (first an-inv)) 1.00) ... ]
     [else ... ]) ...
```

If the first item's price is one dollar or less, it must be included in the final output and, according to our example, should be the first item on the output. Translated into Scheme, the output should be a list whose first item is (first *an-inv*) and the rest of which is whatever the recursion produces. If the price is more than one dollar, the item should not be included. That is, the result should be whatever the recursion produces for the rest of *an-inv* and nothing else. The complete definition is displayed in figure 30.

## Exercises

**Exercise 10.2.5** Define the function *extract>1*, which consumes an inventory and creates an inventory from those records whose prices are above one dollar. ∎

**Exercise 10.2.6** Develop a precise data definition for inventory1, which are inventory listings of one-dollar stores. Using the new data definition, the contract for *extract1* can be refined:

```
;; extract1 : inventory → inventory1
(define (extract1 an-inv) ... )
```

Does the refined contract affect the development of the function above? ∎

**Exercise 10.2.7** Develop the function *raise-prices*, which consumes an inventory and produces an inventory in which all prices are raised by 5%. ∎

**Exercise 10.2.8** Adapt the function *recall* from exercise 10.1.7 for the new data definition of inventory. The function consumes the name of a toy *ty* and an inventory and produces an inventory that contains all items of the input with the exception of those labeled *ty*. ∎

**Exercise 10.2.9** Adapt the function *name-robot* from exercise 10.1.6 for the new data definition of inventory. The function consumes an inventory and produces an inventory with more accurate names. Specifically, it replaces all occurrences of 'robot with 'r2d3.

Generalize *name-robot* to the function *substitute*. The new function consumes two symbols, called *new* and *old*, and an inventory. It produces a new inventory by substituting all occurrences of *old* with *new* and leaving all others alone. ∎

## 10.3 Extended Exercise: Moving Pictures

In sections 6.6 and 7.4, we studied how to move individual shapes. A picture, however, isn't just a single shape but a whole collection of them. Considering that we have to draw, translate, and clear pictures, and that we may wish to change a picture or manage several pictures at the same time, it is best to collect all of the parts of a picture into a single piece of data. Because pictures may consist of a varying number of items, a list representation for pictures naturally suggests itself.

### Exercises

**Exercise 10.3.1** Provide a data definition that describes the class of lists of *shape*s. The class of *shape*s was defined in exercise 7.4.1.

Create a sample list that represents the face of figure 10.3.6 and name it *FACE*. Its basic dimensions are gathered in the following table:

| shape | position | size(s) | color |
|---|---|---|---|
| circle | (50,50) | 40 | red |
| rectangle | (30,20) | $5 \times 5$ | blue |
| rectangle | (65,20) | $5 \times 5$ | blue |
| rectangle | (40,75) | $20 \times 10$ | red |
| rectangle | (45,35) | $10 \times 30$ | blue |

The table assumes a canvas of size 300 by 100.

Develop the template *fun-for-losh*, which outlines functions that consume a *list-of-shapes*. ∎

**Exercise 10.3.2** Use the template *fun-for-losh* to develop the function *draw-losh*. It consumes a *list-of-shapes*, draws each item on the list, and returns true. Remember to use (*start n m*) to create the canvas before the function is used. ∎

**Exercise 10.3.3** Use the template *fun-for-losh* to develop *translate-losh*. The function consumes a *list-of-shapes* and a number *delta*. The result is a list of shapes where each of them has been moved by *delta* pixels in the $x$ direction. **The function has no effect on the canvas.** ∎

**Exercise 10.3.4** Use the template *fun-for-losh* to develop *clear-losh*. The function consumes a *list-of-shapes*, erases each item on the list from the canvas, and returns true. ∎

**Exercise 10.3.5** Develop the function *draw-and-clear-picture*. It consumes a *picture*. Its effect is to draw the picture, sleep for a while, and to clear the picture.

**Exercise 10.3.6** Develop the function *move-picture*. It consumes a number (*delta*) and a *picture*. It draws the picture, sleeps for a while, clears the picture and then produces a translated version. The result should be moved by *delta* pixels.

Test the function with expressions like these:

(*start* 500 100)

(*draw-losh*
  (*move-picture* −5
    (*move-picture* 23
      (*move-picture* 10 *FACE*))))

(*stop*)

This moves *FACE* (see exercise 10.3.1) by 10, 23, and −5 pixels in the $x$ direction. ∎

When the function is fully tested, use the teachpack **arrow.ss** and evaluate the expression:

(*start* 500 100)

(*control-left-right FACE* 100 *move-picture draw-losh*)

The last one creates a graphical user interface that permits users to move the shape *FACE* by clicking on arrows. The shape then moves in increments of 100 (right) and −100 (left) pixels. The teachpack also provides arrow controls for other directions. Use them to develop other moving pictures.

# 11   Natural Numbers

The only self-referential data definitions we have seen thus far involved cons and lists of arbitrary length. We needed such data definitions because the classes of lists that we wanted to process were of arbitrary size. Natural numbers are another class of data whose elements are of arbitrary size; after all, there is no limit on how large a natural number can be, and, at least in principle, a function should be able to process them all.

In this section, we study how to describe natural numbers with self-referential data definitions and how to develop functions that process natural numbers in a systematic fashion. Since such functions come in many flavors, we study several different flavors of definitions.

## 11.1   Defining Natural Numbers

People normally introduce natural numbers via enumeration: 0, 1, 2, etc.[34] The abbreviation "etc." at the end says that the series continues in this manner. Mathematicians and mathematics teachers often use dots for the same purpose. For us, however, neither the "etc." nor the dots is good enough, if we wish to design functions on natural numbers systematically. So, the question is what it means to write down "etc.," or put differently, what a complete, self-contained description of the natural numbers is.

The only way to remove the informal "etc." from the enumeration is to describe the collection of numbers with a self-referential description. Here is a first attempt:

> 0 is a natural number.
> If $n$ is a natural number, then one more than $n$ is one, too.

While this description is still not quite rigorous,[35] it is a good starting point for a Scheme-style data description:

| A *natural-number* is either |
|---|
| 1. 0 or |
| 2. (add1 $n$) if $n$ is a natural number. |

---

[34] It is important to start counting at 0 so that we can use the natural numbers for counting the number of items on a list or the members of a family tree.

[35] For that, we need to defer to a course on mathematical sets.

The operation add1 adds 1 to a natural number. Of course, we could use (+ ... 1) but add1 stands out and signals "natural number," as opposed to arbitrary number, to the reader of a data definition and a function.

Although we are familiar with natural numbers from school, it is instructive to construct examples from the data definition. Clearly,

    0

is the first natural number, so

    (add1 0)

is the next one. From here, it is easy to see the pattern:

    (add1 (add1 0))
    (add1 (add1 (add1 0)))
    (add1 (add1 (add1 (add1 0))))

The examples should remind us of the lists construction process. We built lists by starting with empty and by constructing on more items. Now we build natural natural numbers by starting with 0 and by *add*ing on 1. In addition, natural numbers come with century-old abbreviations. For example, (add1 0) is abbreviated as 1, (add1 (add1 0)) as 2, and so on.

A function on natural numbers must extract the number that went into the construction of a positive natural number just like a function on lists must extract the list that went into a constructed list. The operation that performs this "extraction" is called sub1. It satisfies the law

$$(\text{sub1 } (\text{add1 } n)) = n$$

just as the rest operation satisfies the law

$$(\text{rest } (\text{cons } \textit{a-value a-list})) = \textit{a-list}$$

Of course, (− $n$ 1) would also work, but sub1 stands out and signals that the function processes natural numbers.

## 11.2    Processing Natural Numbers of Arbitrary Size

Let us develop the function *hellos*. It consumes a natural number $n$ and produces a list of $n$ copies of 'hello. We can write the contract for this function:

    ;; hellos : **N** → list-of-symbols
    ;; to create a list of n copies of 'hello
    (**define** (hellos n) ...)

And we can make up examples:

> (*hellos* 0)
> ;; expected value:
> empty
>
> (*hellos* 2)
> ;; expected value:
> (cons 'hello (cons 'hello empty))

The design of a template for *hellos* follows the design recipe for self-referential data definitions. We immediately see that *hellos* is a conditional function, that its **cond**-expression has two clauses, and that the first clause must distinguish 0 from other possible inputs:

> (**define** (*hellos* n)
>   (**cond**
>     [(zero? n) ... ]
>     [**else** ... ]))

Furthermore, the data definition says that 0 is an atomic value, and every other natural number is a compound value that "contains" the predecessor to which 1 was added. Hence, if n is not 0, we subtract 1 from n. The result is also a natural number, so according to the design recipe we wrap the expression with (*hellos* ... ):

> (**define** (*hellos* n)
>   (**cond**
>     [(zero? n) ... ]
>     [**else** ... (*hellos* (sub1 n)) ... ]))

Now we have exploited every hint in the data definition and are ready to proceed with the definition.

Assume (zero? n) evaluates to true. Then the answer must be empty, as the examples illustrate. So assume the input is greater than 0. For concreteness, let us say it is 2. According to the suggestion in the template, *hellos* should use (*hellos* 1) to compute a part of the answer. The purpose statement specifies that (*hellos* 1) produces (cons 'hello empty), a list with one 'hello. In general, (*hellos* (sub1 n)) produces a list that contains $n - 1$ occurrences of 'hello. Clearly, to produce a list with n occurrences, we must cons another 'hello onto this list:

```
(define (hellos n)
  (cond
    [(zero? n) empty]
    [else (cons 'hello (hellos (sub1 n)))]))
```

As usual, the final definition is just the template with a few extras.
Let's test *hellos* with some hand-evaluations:

(*hellos* 0)

= (cond
    [(zero? 0) empty]
    [else (cons 'hello (*hellos* (sub1 0)))])

= (cond
    [true empty]
    [else (cons 'hello (*hellos* (sub1 0)))])

= empty

It confirms that *hellos* works properly for the first example.
Here is another example:

(*hellos* 1)

= (cond
    [(zero? 1) empty]
    [else (cons 'hello (*hellos* (sub1 1)))])

= (cond
    [false empty]
    [else (cons 'hello (*hellos* (sub1 1)))])

= (cons 'hello (*hellos* (sub1 1)))

= (cons 'hello (*hellos* 0))

= (cons 'hello empty)

For the last step in the calculation, we can exploit that we already know
that (*hellos* 0) evaluates to empty and replace the (underlined) expression
with its result.

The last hand-evaluation shows that the function works for the second
example:

(*hellos* 2)

= (**cond**
  [(zero? 2) empty]
  [**else** (cons 'hello (*hellos* (sub1 2)))])

= (**cond**
  [false empty]
  [**else** (cons 'hello (*hellos* (sub1 2)))])

= (cons 'hello (*hellos* (sub1 2)))

= (cons 'hello (*hellos* 1))

= (cons 'hello (cons 'hello empty))

We can again exploit what we know about (*hellos* 1), which greatly shortens the hand-evaluation.

## Exercises

**Exercise 11.2.1** Generalize *hellos* to *repeat*, which consumes a natural number *n* and a symbol and produces a list with *n* occurrences of the symbol. ∎

**Exercise 11.2.2** Develop the function *tabulate-f*, which tabulates the values of

```
;; f : number → number
(define (f x)
  (+ (* 3 (* x x))
     (+ (* −6 x)
        −1)))
```

for some natural numbers. Specifically, it consumes a natural number *n* and produces a list of *n* posns. The first one combines *n* with (*f n*), the second one *n-1* with (*f n-1*), etc. ∎

**Exercise 11.2.3** Develop *apply-n*. The function consumes a natural number, *n*. It applies the function *move* from exercise 10.3.6 *n* times to *FACE*, the list of shapes from exercise 10.3.1. Each application should translate the shape by one pixel. The purpose of the function is to simulate a continuously moving shape on a canvas, the last missing piece of the extended exercise 10.3. ∎

**Exercise 11.2.4** Lists may contain lists that contain lists and so on. Here is a data definition that takes this idea to an extreme:

---

A *deep-list* is either

  1. *s* where *s* is some symbol or

  2. (cons *dl* empty), where *dl* is a deep list.

---

Develop the function *depth*, which consumes a deep list and determines how many times cons was used to construct it.

Develop the function *make-deep*, which consumes a symbol *s* and a natural number and produces a deep list containing *s* and constructed with *n* conses. ∎

## 11.3   Extended Exercise: Creating Lists, Testing Functions

We often encounter situations where we would like to create lists of data that involve numbers. For example, we may wish to create large lists of numbers to test a function like *extract1* in section 10.2 on large lists instead of hand-coded small ones. Sometimes we would like to visualize randomly picked data. We can create such functions using recursion on natural numbers and a random number generator.

## Exercises

**Exercise 11.3.1** Scheme provides the operation random. It consumes a natural number *n* greater than 1, and produces a random integer between 0 and *n* − 1:

    ;; random : N → N
    ;; to compute a natural number between 0 and *n-1*
    (**define** (random *n*) ... )

Two successive uses of (random *n*) may produce two distinct results.

Now consider the following definition:

```
;; random-n-m : integer integer → integer
;; ...
;; Assume: n < m
(define (random-n-m n m)
  (+ (random (- m n)) n))
```

Formulate a succinct and precise purpose statement for *random-n-m*. Use a number line with an interval to explain the result of (random *n*). Use a symbolic evaluation to support your explanation. ∎

**Exercise 11.3.2** Develop the function *tie-dyed*. It consumes a natural number and produces a list of that many numbers, each randomly chosen in the range from **20** and **120**. Use *tie-dyed* to apply *draw-circles* from exercise 9.5.8. ∎

**Exercise 11.3.3** Develop the function *create-temps*. It consumes a natural number *n* and two integers, called *low* and *high*. It produces a list of *n* integers that are between *low* and *high*.

Use *create-temps* to test *check-range* from exercise 9.5.4.

Finally, discuss the following questions. Can we simply feed the result of *create-temps* into *check-range* or do we need to know the list that *create-temps* produced? Are there values for *low* and *high* such that we don't need to know the result of *create-temps* and yet we can predict the result of the test? Which function tests which? What does this tell us about testing with automatically generated test data? ∎

**Exercise 11.3.4** Develop the function *create-prices*, which consumes a natural number and produces a list with a corresponding number of prices between $.10 and $10.00 with increments of a dime. Use *create-prices* to test *dollar-store?* from exercise 9.5.3.

**Hint:** How many dimes are there between $.10 and $10.00? ∎

**Exercise 11.3.5** Develop a program that visualizes a student riot. In preparation of a student riot, a small group of students meets to make paint-filled balloons. The typical riot uses 'red only. Then, on the evening of the riot, the students enter a university's progressive theater with the balloons and throw them all over the seats.

The program's only input should be a natural number, which represents the number of balloons thrown. The visualization should use a canvas that contains a black grid and the positions of the balls:

Assume a random distribution of the balls over the theater's seats. Each box in the grid represents a seat. Configure the program so the change of one variable definition changes the number of columns in the grid and a change to another changes the number of rows.

**Hint:** Develop auxiliary functions that draw some given number of lines in the vertical and the horizontal direction. ∎

## 11.4 Alternative Data Definitions for Natural Numbers

Using the above, standard data definition for natural numbers makes it easy to develop all kinds of functions on numbers. Consider, for example, a function that multiplies the first $n$ numbers. Put differently, it consumes a natural number $n$ and multiplies all numbers between 0 (exclusive) and $n$ (inclusive). The function is called factorial and has the mathematical notation $!$. Its contract is easy to formulate:

```
;; ! : N → N
;; to compute n · (n − 1) · . . . · 2 · 1
(define (! n) ...)
```

It consumes a natural number and produces one.

Specifying its input-output relationship is a bit more tricky. We know, of course, what the product of 1, 2, and 3 is, so we should have

```
(= (! 3)
   6)
```

and, similarly,

```
(= (! 10)
   3628800)
```

The real question is what to do with the input 0. According to the informal description of the task, $!$ is supposed to produce the product of all numbers between 0 (exclusive) and $n$ (inclusive), the argument. Since $n$ is 0, this request is rather strange because there are no numbers between 0 (exclusive) and 0 (inclusive). We solve the problem by following mathematical convention and set that (*!* 0) evaluates to 1.

From here, the rest is straightforward. The template for *!* is clearly that of a natural number processing function:

```
(define (! n)
  (cond
    [(zero? n) ... ]
    [else ... (! (sub1 n)) ... ]))
```

The answer in the first **cond**-clause is given: 1. In the second clause, the recursion produces the product of the first $n - 1$ numbers. To get the product of the first $n$ numbers, we just need to multiply the (value of the) recursion by $n$. Figure 31 contains the complete definition of *!*.

## Exercises

**Exercise 11.4.1** Determine the value of (*!* 2) by hand and with DrScheme. Also test *!* with 10, 100, and 1000.

**Note**: The results of these expressions are large numbers, well beyond the native capacities of many other programming languages. ∎

Now suppose we wish to design the function *product-from-20*, which computes the product from 20 (exclusive) to some number $n$ (inclusive) that is greater or equal to 20. We have several choices here. First, we could define a function that computes (*!* $n$) and (*!* 20) and divides the former by the latter. A simple mathematical argument shows that this approach indeed yields the product of all numbers between 20 (exclusive) and $n$ (inclusive):

$$\frac{n \cdot (n-1) \cdot \ldots 21 \cdot 20 \cdot \ldots 1}{20 \cdot \ldots 1} = n \cdot (n-1) \cdot \ldots \cdot 21 \cdot \frac{20 \cdot \ldots 1}{20 \cdot \ldots 1} = n \cdot (n-1) \cdot \ldots \cdot 21 .$$

**Exercise 11.4.2** Use the idea to define *product*, a function that consumes two natural numbers, $n$ and $m$, with $m > n$, and that produces the product of the numbers between $n$ (exclusive) and $m$ (inclusive). ∎

Second, we can follow our design recipe, starting with a precise characterization of the function's input. Obviously, the inputs belong to the natural numbers, but we know more than that. It belongs to the following collection of numbers: 20, 21, 22, .... By now we know how to describe such a set precisely with a data definition:

---

A *natural number [>= 20]* is either

1. 20 or

2. (add1 $n$) if $n$ is a natural number [>= 20].

Notation: In contracts, we use **N** [>= 20] instead of "natural numbers [>= 20]."

---

Using the new data definition, we can formulate a contract for *product-from-20*:

;; *product-from-20:* **N** [>= 20] → **N**
;; to compute $n \cdot (n - 1) \cdot \ldots \cdot 21 \cdot 1$
(**define** (*product-from-20 n-above-20*) ... )

Here is a first example for *product-from-20*'s input-output specification:

(= (*product-from-20* 21)
   21)

Since the function multiplies all numbers between 20 (exclusively) and its input, (*product-from-20* 21) must produce 21, which is the only number in the interval. Similarly,

(= (*product-from-20* 22)
   462)

for the same reason. Finally, we again follow mathematical convention and agree that

(= (*product-from-20* 20)
   1)

The template for *product-from-20* is a straightforward adaptation of the template for *!*, or any natural number-processing function:

(**define** (*product-from-20 n-above-20*)
  (**cond**
    [(= *n-above-20* 20) ... ]
    [**else** ... (*product-from-20* (sub1 *n-above-20*)) ... ]))

The input *n-above-20* is either 20 or larger. If it is 20, it does not have any components according to the data definition. Otherwise, it is the result of adding 1 to a natural number [>= 20], and we can recover this "component" by subtracting 1. The value of this selector expression belongs to the same class of data as the input and is thus a candidate for natural recursion.

Completing the template is equally straightforward. As specified, the result of (*product-from-20* 20) is 1, which determines the answer for the first **cond**-clause. Otherwise, (*product-from-20* (sub1 *n-above-20*)) already produces the product of all the numbers between 20 (exclusive) and *n-above-20* − 1. The only number not included in this range is *n-above-20*. Hence (* *n-above-20* (*product-from-20* (sub1 *n-above-20*))) is the correct answer in the second clause. Figure 31 contains the complete definition of *product-from-20*.

---

### Exercises

**Exercise 11.4.3** Develop *product-from-minus-11*. The function consumes an integer *n* greater or equal to −11 and produces the product of all the integers between −11 (exclusive) and *n* (inclusive). ∎

**Exercise 11.4.4** In exercise 11.2.2, we developed a function that tabulates some mathematical function *f* for an interval of the shape $(0, n]$.

Develop the function *tabulate-f20*, which tabulates the values of *f* for natural numbers greater than 20. Specifically, the function consumes a natural number *n* greater or equal to 20 and produces a list of *posn*s, each of which has the shape (make-posn *n* (*f* *n*)) for some *n* between 20 (exclusive) and *n* (inclusive). ∎

---

A comparison of *!* and *product-from-20* suggests the natural question of how to design a function that multiplies *all* natural numbers in some range. Roughly speaking, *product* is like *product-from-20* except that the limit is not a part of the function definition. Instead, it is another input, which suggests the following contract:

> ;; *product:* **N N** $\rightarrow$ **N**
> ;; to compute $n \cdot (n-1) \cdot \ldots \cdot (limit+1) \cdot 1$
> (**define** (*product limit n*) ...)

The intention is that *product*, like *product-from-20*, computes the product from *limit* (exclusive) to some number *n* (inclusive) that is greater or equal to *limit*.

```
;; ! : N → N
;; to compute n · (n − 1) · . . . · 2 · 1
(define (! n)
  (cond
    [(zero? n) 1]
    [else (* n (! (sub1 n)))]))

;; product-from-20: N [>= 20] → N
;; to compute n · (n − 1) · . . . · 21 · 1
(define (product-from-20 n-above-20)
  (cond
    [(= n-above-20 20) 1]
    [else (* n-above-20 (product-from-20 (sub1 n-above-20)))]))

;; product: N[limit] N[>= limit] → N
;; to compute n · (n − 1) · . . . · (limit + 1) · 1
(define (product limit n)
  (cond
    [(= n limit) 1]
    [else (* n (product limit (sub1 n)))]))
```

Figure 31: Computing factorial, product-from-20, and product

Unfortunately, *product*'s contract, in contrast with *product-from-20*'s, is rather imprecise. In particular, it does not describe the collection of numbers that *product* consumes as the second input. Given its first input, *limit*, we know that the second input belongs to *limit*, (add1 *limit*), (add1 (add1 *limit*)), etc. While it is easy to enumerate the possible second inputs, it also shows that the description of the collection *depends on the first input*—an unusal situation that we have not encountered before.

Still, if we assume limit is some number, the data description for the second input is nearly obvious:

---

Let *limit* be a natural number.   A *natural number [>= limit]* (N[>=*limit*]) is either

1. *limit* or

2. (add1 *n*) if *n* is a natural number [>= *limit*].

---

In other words, the data definition is like that for natural numbers $[>= limit]$ with 20 replaced by a variable *limit*. Of course, in high school, we refer to $\mathbf{N}[>=0]$ as *the* natural numbers, and $\mathbf{N}[>=1]$ as *the* positive integers.

With this new data definition, we specify the contract for *product* as follows:

;; *product:* $\mathbf{N}[limit]$ $\mathbf{N}$ $[>= limit]$ $\rightarrow$ $\mathbf{N}$
;; to compute $n \cdot (n - 1) \cdot \ldots \cdot (limit + 1) \cdot 1$
(**define** (*product limit n*) ...)

That is, we name the first input, a natural number, with the notation [*limit*] and specify the second input using the name for the first one.

The rest of the program development is straightforward. It is basically the same as that for *product-from-20* with 20 replaced by *limit* throughout. The only modification concerns the natural recusion in the function template. Since the function consumes a *limit* and a $\mathbf{N}$ $[>= limit]$, the template must contain an application of *product* to *limit* and (sub1 *n*):

(**define** (*product limit n*)
  (**cond**
    [(= *n limit*) ...]
    [**else** ... (*product limit* (sub1 *n*)) ...]))

Otherwise things remain the same. The full function definition is contained in figure 31.

---

## Exercises

**Exercise 11.4.5** In exercises 11.2.2 and 11.4.4, we developed functions that tabulate *f* from some natural number or natural number $[>= 20]$ down to 0 or 20 (exclusive), respectively.

Develop the function *tabulate-f-lim*, which tabulates the values of *f* in an analogous manner from some natural number *n* down to some other natural number *limit*. ∎

**Exercise 11.4.6** In exercises 11.2.2, 11.4.4, and 11.4.5, we developed functions that tabulate the mathematical function *f* in various ranges. In both cases, the final function produced a list of *posns* that was ordered in *descending* order. That is, an expression like (*tabulate-f* 3) yields the list

```
(cons (make-posn 3 2.4)
  (cons (make-posn 2 3.4)
    (cons (make-posn 1 3.6)
      (cons (make-posn 0 3.0)
        empty))))
```

If we prefer a list of *posns* in *ascending* order, we must look at a different data collection, natural numbers up to a certain point in the chain:

---

A *natural number [<= 20]* (**N**[*<=20*]) is either

1. 20 or

2. (sub1 *n*) if *n* is a natural number [<= 20].

---

Of course, in high school, we refer to **N**[*<=-1*] as *the* negative integers.
Develop the function

;; *tabulate-f-up-to-20 :* **N** [<= 20] → **N**
(**define** (*tabulate-f-up-to-20 n-below-20*) ...)

which tabulates the values of *f* for natural numbers less than 20. Specifically, it consumes a natural number *n* less than or equal to 20 and produces a list of *posns*, each of which has the shape (make-posn *n* (*f* *n*)) for some *n* between 0 and *n* (inclusively). ∎

**Exercise 11.4.7** Develop the function *is-not-divisible-by<=i*. It consumes a natural number [>= 1], *i*, and a natural number *m*, with *i* < *m*. If *m* is not divisible by any number between 1 (exclusive) and *i* (inclusive), the function produces true; otherwise, its output is false.

Use *is-not-divisible-by<=i* to define *prime?*, which consumes a natural number and determines whether or not it is prime. ∎

## 11.5  More on the Nature of Natural Numbers

The natural numbers are a small subset of Scheme's numbers, not all of them. Hence the function template above *cannot* be used for processing arbitrary numbers, in particular, inexact numbers. Still, the template is a good starting point for functions whose definitions involve both natural numbers and other Scheme numbers. To illustrate this point, let us design the function *add-to-pi*, which consumes a natural number $n$ and produces $n + 3.14$ without using +.

Following the design recipe, we start with

*;; add-to-pi : **N** → number*
*;; to compute $n + 3.14$ without using +*
(**define** (*add-to-pi n*) ...)

Another easy step is to determine the output for a few sample inputs:

(= (*add-to-pi* 0) 3.14)
(= (*add-to-pi* 2) 5.14)
(= (*add-to-pi* 6) 9.14)

The difference between *hellos*'s contract (see exercise 11.2.1) and that of *add-to-pi* is the output, but as we have seen this does not affect the template design. We obtain the template for *add-to-pi* by renaming *hellos* appropriately:

(**define** (*add-to-pi n*)
  (**cond**
    [(zero? *n*) ... ]
    [**else** ... (*add-to-pi* (sub1 *n*)) ... ])))

In combination with the examples, the template immediately suggests how to complete the function. If the input is 0, *add-to-pi*'s answer is 3.14. Otherwise, (*add-to-pi* (sub1 *n*)) produces $(-n\ 1) + 3.14$; since the correct answer is 1 more than this value, the answer expression in the second **cond**-line is (add1 (*add-to-pi* (sub1 *n*))). Figure 32 contains the complete function definition.

## Exercises

**Exercise 11.5.1** Define *add*, which consumes two natural numbers, $n$ and $x$, and produces $n + x$ without using Scheme's +. ∎

**Exercise 11.5.2** Develop the function *multiply-by-pi*, which consumes a natural number and multiplies it by 3.14 without using ∗. For example,

(= (*multiply-by-pi* 0) 0)
(= (*multiply-by-pi* 2) 6.28)
(= (*multiply-by-pi* 3) 9.42)

Define *multiply*, which consumes two natural numbers, *n* and *x*, and produces *n* * *x* without using Scheme's *. Eliminate + from this definition, too.

**Hint:** Recall that multiplying *x* by *n* means adding *x* to itself *n* times. ∎

**Exercise 11.5.3** Develop the function *exponent*, which consumes a natural number *n* and a number *x* and computes

$$x^n .$$

Eliminate * from this definition, too.

**Hint:** Recall that exponentiating *x* by *n* means multiplying *x* with itself *n* times. ∎

**Exercise 11.5.4** Deep lists (see exercise 11.2.4) are another representation for natural numbers. Show how to represent 0, 3, and 8.

Develop the function *addDL*, which consumes two deep lists, representing the natural numbers *n* and *m*, and produces a deep list representing *n* + *m*. ∎

---

```
;; add-to-pi : N  →  number
;; to compute n + 3.14 without using +
(define (add-to-pi n)
  (cond
    [(zero? n) 3.14]
    [else (add1 (add-to-pi (sub1 n)))]))
```

Figure 32: Adding a natural number to pi

---

# 12   Composing Functions, Revisited Again

In section 3 we said that programs were collections of function definitions and possibly some variable definitions, too. To guide the division of labor among functions, we also introduced a rough guideline:

Formulate auxiliary function definitions for every dependency between quantities in the problem statement.

So far the guideline has been reasonably effective, but it is now time to take a second look at it and to formulate some additional guidance concerning auxiliary functions.

In the first subsection, we refine our original guideline concerning auxiliary programs. The suggestions mostly put into words the experiences that we made with the exercises. The second and third one illustrate two of the ideas in more depth; the last one is an extended exercise.

## 12.1 Designing Complex Programs

When we develop a program, we may hope to implement it with a single function definition but we should always be prepared to write auxiliary functions. In particular, if the problem statement mentions several dependencies, it is natural to express each of them as a function. Others who read the problem statement and the program can follow our reasoning more easily that way. The movie-theater example in section 3.1 is a good example for this style of development.

Otherwise, we should follow the design recipe and start with a thorough analysis of the input and output data. Using the data analysis we should design a template and attempt to refine the template into a complete function definition. Turning a template into a complete function definition means combining the values of the template's subexpressions into the final answer. As we do so, we might encounter several situations:

1. If the formulation of an answer requires a case analysis of the available values, use a **cond**-expression.

2. If a computation requires knowledge of a particular domain of application, for example, drawing on (computer) canvases, accounting, music, or science, use an auxiliary function.

3. If a computation must process a list, a natural number, or some other piece of data of arbitrary size, use an auxiliary function.

4. If the natural formulation of the function isn't quite what we want, it is most likely a generalization of our target. In this case, the main function is a short definition that defers the computation to the generalized auxiliary program.

The last two criteria are situations that we haven't discussed yet. The following two subsections illustrate them with examples.

After we determine the need for an auxiliary function, we should add a contract, a header, and a purpose statement to a WISH LIST of functions.[36]

| GUIDELINE ON WISH LISTS |
| --- |
| Maintain a list of functions that must be developed to complete a program. Develop each function according to a design recipe. |

Before we put a function on the wish list, we must check whether something like the function already exists or is already on the wish list. Scheme provides many primitive operations and functions, and so do other languages. We should find out as much as possible about our working language, though only when we settle on one. For beginners, a superficial knowledge of a language is fine.

If we follow these guidelines, we interleave the development of one function with that of others. As we finish a function that does not depend on anything on our wish list, we can test it. Once we have tested such basic functions, we can work our way backwards and test other functions until we have finished the wish list. By testing each function rigorously before we test those that depend on it, we greatly reduce the effort of searching for logical mistakes.

## 12.2 Recursive Auxiliary Functions

People need to sort things all the time. Investment advisors sort portfolios by the profit each holding generates. Doctors sort lists of transplant patients. Mail programs sort messages. More generally, sorting lists of values by some criteria is a task that many programs need to perform.

Here we study how to sort a list of numbers not because it is important for many programming tasks, but also because it provides a good case study of the design of auxiliary programs. A sorting function consumes a list and produces one. Indeed, the two lists contain the same numbers, though the output list contains them in a different order. This is the essence of the contract and purpose statement:

*;; sort : list-of-numbers → list-of-numbers*
*;; to create a sorted list of numbers from all the numbers in alon*
(**define** (*sort alon*) ...)

---

[36]The term "wish list" in this context is due to Dr. John Stone.

Here is one example per clause in the data definition:

(*sort* empty)
;; expected value:
empty

(*sort* (cons 1297.04 (cons 20000.00 (cons −505.25 empty)))))
;; expected value:
(cons 20000.00 (cons 1297.04 (cons −505.25 empty))))

The answer for the input empty is empty, because empty contains the same items (none) and in sorted order.

Next we must translate the data definition into a function template. Again, we have dealt with lists of numbers before, so this step is easy:

```
(define (sort alon)
  (cond
    [(empty? alon) ...]
    [else ... (first alon) ... (sort (rest alon)) ...]))
```

Using this template, we can finally turn to the interesting part of the program development. We consider each case of the **cond**-expression separately, starting with the simple case. If *sort*'s input is empty, then the answer is empty, as specified by the example. So let's assume that the input is not empty. That is, let's deal with the second **cond**-clause. It contains two expressions and, following the design recipe, we must understand what they compute:

1. (first *alon*) extracts the first number from the input;

2. (*sort* (rest *alon*)) produces a sorted version of (rest *alon*), according to the purpose statement of the function.

Putting together these two values means inserting the first number into its appropriate spot in the sorted rest of the list.

Let's look at the second example in this context. When *sort* consumes (cons 1297.04 (cons 20000.00 (cons −505.25 empty))), then

1. (first *alon*) evaluates to 1297.04,

2. (rest *alon*) is (cons 20000.00 (cons −505.25 empty)), and

3. (*sort* (rest *alon*)) produces (cons 20000.00 (cons −505.25 empty)).

To produce the desired answer, we must insert 1297.04 between the two numbers of the last list. More generally, the answer in the second **cond**-line must be an expression that inserts (first *alon*) in its proper place into the sorted list (*sort* (rest *alon*)).

Inserting a number into a sorted list isn't a simple task. We may have to search through the entire list before we know what the proper place is. Searching through a list, however, can be done only with a function, because lists are of arbitrary size and processing such values requires recursive functions. Thus we must develop an auxiliary function that consumes the first number and a sorted list and creates a sorted list from both. Let us call this function *insert* and let us formulate a wish-list entry:

```
;; insert : number list-of-numbers → list-of-numbers
;; to create a list of numbers from n and the numbers on alon
;; that is sorted in descending order; alon is already sorted
(define (insert n alon) ... )
```

Using *insert*, it is easy to complete the definition of *sort*:

```
(define (sort alon)
  (cond
    [(empty? alon) empty]
    [else (insert (first alon) (sort (rest alon)))]))
```

The answer in the second line says that in order to produce the final result, *sort* extracts the first item of the non-empty list, computes the sorted version of the rest of the list, and *insert*s the former into the latter at its appropriate place.

Of course, we are not really finished until we have developed *insert*. We already have a contract, a header, and a purpose statement. Next we need to make up function examples. Since the first input of *insert* is atomic, let's make up examples based on the data definition for lists. That is, we first consider what *insert* should produce when given a number and **empty**. According to *insert*'s purpose statement, the output must be a list, it must contain all numbers from the second input, and it must contain the first argument. This suggests the following:

```
(insert 5 empty)
;; expected value:
(cons 5 empty)
```

Instead of 5, we could have used any number.

The second example must use a non-empty list, but then, the idea for *insert* was suggested by just such an example when we studied how *sort* should deal with non-empty lists. Specifically, we said that *sort* had to insert 1297.04 into (cons 20000.00 (cons −505.25 empty)) at its proper place:

(*insert* 1297.04 (cons 20000.00 (cons −505.25 empty)))
;; expected value:
(cons 20000.00 (cons 1297.04 (cons −505.25 empty)))

In contrast to *sort*, the function *insert* consumes *two* inputs. But we know that the first one is a number and atomic. We can therefore focus on the second argument, which is a list of numbers and which suggests that we use the list-processing template one more time:

(**define** (*insert n alon*)
  (**cond**
    [(empty? *alon*) ... ]
    [**else** ... (first *alon*) ... (*insert n* (rest *alon*)) ... ]))

The only difference between this template and the one for *sort* is that this one needs to take into account the additional argument *n*.

To fill the gaps in the template of *insert*, we again proceed on a case-by-case basis. The first case concerns the empty list. According to the purpose statement, *insert* must now construct a list with one number: *n*. Hence the answer in the first case is (cons *n* empty).

The second case is more complicated than that. When *alon* is not empty,

1. (first *alon*) is the first number on *alon*, and

2. (*insert n* (rest *alon*)) produces a sorted list consisting of *n* and all numbers on (rest *alon*).

The problem is how to combine these pieces of data to get the answer. Let us consider an example:

(*insert* 7 (cons 6 (cons 5 (cons 4 empty))))

Here *n* is 7 and larger than any of the numbers in the second input. Hence it suffices if we just cons 7 onto (cons 6 (cons 5 (cons 4 empty))). In contrast, when the application is something like

(*insert* 3 (cons 6 (cons 2 (cons 1 (cons −1 empty)))))

*n* must indeed be inserted into the rest of the list. More concretely,

1. (first *alon*) is 6

2. (*insert n* (rest *alon*)) is (cons 3 (cons 2 (cons 1 (cons −1 empty)))).

By adding 6 onto this last list with cons, we get the desired answer.

Here is how we generalize from these examples. The problem requires a further case distinction. If *n* is larger than (or equal to) (first *alon*), all the items in *alon* are smaller than *n*; after all, *alon* is already sorted. The result is (cons *n alon*) for this case. If, however, *n* is smaller than (first *alon*), then we have not yet found the proper place to insert *n* into *alon*. We do know that the first item of the result must be the (first *alon*) and that *n* must be inserted into (rest *alon*). The final result in this case is

(cons (first *alon*) (*insert n* (rest *alon*)))

because this list contains *n* and all items of *alon* in sorted order—which is what we need.

The translation of this discussion into Scheme requires the formulation of a conditional expression that distinguishes between the two possible cases:

```
(cond
    [(>= n (first alon)) ... ]
    [(<  n (first alon)) ... ])
```

From here, we just need to put the proper answer expressions into the two **cond**-clauses. Figure 33 contains the complete definitions of *insert* and *sort*.

**Terminology**: This particular program for sorting is known as INSERTION SORT in the programming literature. ∎

---

## Exercises

**Exercise 12.2.1** Develop a program that sorts lists of mail messages by date. Mail structures are defined as follows:

(**define-struct** *mail* (*from date message*))

---

A *mail-message* is a structure:

(make-mail *name n s*)

where *name* is a string, *n* is a number, and *s* is a string.

---

Also develop a program that sorts lists of mail messages by name. To compare two strings alphabetically, use the string<? primitive. ∎

```
;; sort : list-of-numbers → list-of-numbers (sorted)
;; to create a list of numbers with the same numbers as
;; alon sorted in descending order
(define (sort alon)
  (cond
    [(empty? alon) empty]
    [(cons? alon) (insert (first alon) (sort (rest alon)))]))

;; insert : number list-of-numbers (sorted) → list-of-numbers (sorted)
;; to create a list of numbers from n and the numbers on
;; alon that is sorted in descending order; alon is sorted
(define (insert n alon)
  (cond
    [(empty? alon) (cons n empty)]
    [else (cond
            [(>= n (first alon)) (cons n alon)]
            [(< n (first alon)) (cons (first alon) (insert n (rest alon)))])]))
```

Figure 33: Sorting lists of numbers

**Exercise 12.2.2** Here is the function *search*:

```
;; search : number list-of-numbers → boolean
(define (search n alon)
  (cond
    [(empty? alon) false]
    [else (or (= (first alon) n) (search n (rest alon)))]))
```

It determines whether some number occurs in a list of numbers. The function may have to traverse the entire list to find out that the number of interest isn't contained in the list.

Develop the function *search-sorted*, which determines whether a number occurs in a sorted list of numbers. The function must take advantage of the fact that the list is sorted.

**Terminology**: The function *search-sorted* conducts a LINEAR SEARCH. ∎

## 12.3   Generalizing Problems, Generalizing Functions

Consider the problem of drawing a *polygon*, that is, a geometric shape with an arbitrary number of corners.[37] A natural representation for a polygon is a list of *posn* structures:

---

A *list-of-posns* is either

1.  the empty list, **empty**, or

2.  (**cons** *p lop*) where *p* is a *posn* structure and *lop* is a list of posns.

---

Each *posn* represents one corner of the polygon. For example,

```
(cons (make-posn 10 10)
  (cons (make-posn 60 60)
    (cons (make-posn 10 60)
      empty)))
```

represents a triangle. The question is what **empty** means as a polygon. The answer is that **empty** does not represent a polygon and therefore shouldn't be included in the class of polygon representations. A polygon should always have at least one corner, and the lists that represent polygons should always contain at least one *posn*. This suggest the following data definition:

---

A *polygon* is either

1.  (**cons** *p* **empty**) where *p* is a *posn*, or

2.  (**cons** *p lop*) where *p* is a *posn* structure and *lop* is a polygon.

---

In short, a discussion of how the chosen set of data (lists of *posns*) represents the intended information (geometric polygons) reveals that our choice was inadequate. Revising the data definition brings us closer to our intentions and makes it easier to design the program.

Because our drawing primitives always produce **true** (if anything), it is natural to suggest the following contract and purpose statement:

```
;; draw-polygon : polygon → true
;; to draw the polygon specified by a-poly
(define (draw-polygon a-poly) ...)
```

---

[37]Mr. Paul C. Fisher inspired this section.

In other words, the function draws the lines between the corners and, if all primitive drawing steps work out, it produces true. For example, the above list of *posn*s should produce a triangle.

Although the data definition is not just a variant on our well-worn list theme, the template is close to that of a list-processing function:

```
;; draw-polygon : polygon → true
;; to draw the polygon specified by a-poly
(define (draw-polygon a-poly)
  (cond
    [(empty? (rest a-poly)) ... (first a-poly) ... ]
    [else ... (first a-poly) ...
          ... (second a-poly) ...
          ... (draw-polygon (rest a-poly)) ... ]))
```

Given that both clauses in the data definition use cons, the first condition must inspect the rest of the list, which is empty for the first case and non-empty for the second one. Furthermore, in the first clause, we can add (first *a-poly*); and in the second case, we not only have the first item on the list but the second one, too. After all, polygons generated according to the second clause consist of at least two *posn*s.

Now we can replace the "..." in the template to obtain a complete function definition. For the first clause, the answer must be true, because we don't have two *posn*s that we could connect to form a line. For the second clause, we have two *posn*s, we can draw a line between them, and we know that (*draw-polygon* (rest *a-poly*)) draws all the remaining lines. Put differently, we can write

```
(draw-solid-line (first a-poly) (second a-poly))
```

in the second clause because we know that *a-poly* has a second item. Both (*draw-solid-line* ...) and (*draw-poly* ...) produce true if everything goes fine. By combining the two expressions with **and**, *draw-poly* draws all lines.

Here is the complete function definition:

```
(define (draw-polygon a-poly)
  (cond
    [(empty? (rest a-poly)) true]
    [else (and (draw-solid-line (first a-poly) (second a-poly))
               (draw-polygon (rest a-poly)))]))
```

Unfortunately, testing it with our triangle example immediately reveals a flaw. Instead of drawing a polygon with three sides, the function draws only an open curve, connecting all the corners but not closing the curve:

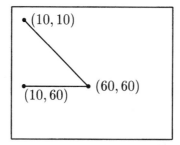

Mathematically put, we have defined a more general function than the one we wanted. The function we defined should be called "connect-the-dots" and not *draw-polygon*.

To get from the more general function to what we want, we need to figure out some way to connect the last dot to the first one. There are several ways to accomplish this goal, but all of them mean that we define the main function in terms of the function we just defined or something like it. In other words, we define one auxiliary function in terms of a more general one.

One way to define the new function is to add the first position of a polygon to the end and to have this new list drawn. A symmetric method is to pick the last one and add it to the front of the polygon. A third alternative is to modify the above version of *draw-polygon* so that it connects the last *posn* to the first one. Here we discuss the second alternative; the exercises cover the other two.

To add the last item of *a-poly* at the beginning, we need something like

(cons (*last a-poly*) *a-poly*)

where *last* is some auxiliary function that extracts the last item from a non-empty list. Indeed, this expression is the definition of *draw-polygon* assuming we define *last*: see figure 34.

Formulating the wish list entry for *last* is straightforward:

;; *last : polygon → posn*
;; to extract the last *posn* on *a-poly*
(**define** (*last a-poly*) ... )

And, because *last* consumes a polygon, we can reuse the template from above:

```
(define (last a-poly)
  (cond
    [(empty? (rest a-poly)) ... (first a-poly) ... ]
    [else ... (first a-poly) ...
         ... (second a-poly) ...
         ... (last (rest a-poly)) ... ]))
```

Turning the template into a complete function is a short step. If the list is empty except for one item, this item is the desired result. If (rest *a-poly*) is not empty, (*last* (rest *a-poly*)) determines the last item of *a-poly*. The complete definition of *last* is displayed at the bottom of figure 34.

```
;; draw-polygon : polygon → true
;; to draw the polygon specified by a-poly
(define (draw-polygon a-poly)
  (connect-dots (cons (last a-poly) a-poly)))


;; connect-dots : polygon → true
;; to draw connections between the dots of a-poly
(define (connect-dots a-poly)
  (cond
    [(empty? (rest a-poly)) true]
    [else (and (draw-solid-line (first a-poly) (second a-poly) RED)
               (connect-dots (rest a-poly)))]))


;; last : polygon → posn
;; to extract the last posn on a-poly
(define (last a-poly)
  (cond
    [(empty? (rest a-poly)) (first a-poly)]
    [else (last (rest a-poly))]))
```

Figure 34: Drawing a polygon

In summary, the development of *draw-polygon* naturally led us to consider a more general problem: connecting a list of dots. We solved the original problem by defining a function that uses (a variant of) the more general function. As we will see again and again, generalizing the purpose of a function is often the best method to simplify the problem.

## Exercises

**Exercise 12.3.1** Modify *draw-polygon* so that it adds the first item of *a-poly* to its end. This requires a different auxiliary function: *add-at-end*. ∎

**Exercise 12.3.2** Modify *connect-dots* so that it consumes an additional *posn* structure to which the last *posn* is connected.

Then modify *draw-polygon* to use this new version of *connect-dots*.

**Accumulator:** The new version of *connect-dots* is a simple instance of an accumulator-style function. In part VI we will discuss an entire class of such problems. ∎

## 12.4   Extended Exercise: Rearranging Words

Newspapers often contain exercises that ask readers to find all possible words made up from some letters. One way to play this game is to form all possible arrangements of the letters in a systematic manner and to see which arrangements are dictionary words. Suppose the letters "a," "d," "e," and "r" are given. There are twenty-four possible arrangements of these letters:

| ader | eadr | erad | drea | ared |
|------|------|------|------|------|
| daer | edar | erda | arde | raed |
| dear | edra | adre | rade | read |
| dera | aerd | dare | rdae | reda |
| aedr | eard | drae | rdea |      |

The three legitimate words in this list are "read," "dear," and "dare."

The systematic enumeration of all possible arrangements is clearly a task for a computer program. It consumes a word and produces a list of the word's letter-by-letter rearrangements.

One representation of a word is a list of symbols. Each item in the input represents a letter: 'a, 'b, …, 'z. Here is the data definition for words:

---

A *word* is either

1. empty, or

2. (cons *a w*) where *a* is a symbol ('a, 'b, …, 'z) and *w* is a word.

---

## Exercises

**Exercise 12.4.1** Formulate the data definition for lists of words. Systematically make up examples of words and lists of words. ∎

Let us call the function *arrangements*.[38] Its template is that of a list-processing function:

```
;; arrangements : word → list-of-words
;; to create a list of all rearrangements of the letters in a-word
(define (arrangements a-word)
  (cond
    [(empty? a-word) ... ]
    [else ... (first a-word) ... (arrangements (rest a-word)) ... ]))
```

Given the contract, the supporting data definitions, and the examples, we can now look at each **cond**-line in the template:

1. If the input is empty, there is only one possible rearrangement of the input: the empty word. Hence the result is (cons empty empty), the list that contains the empty list as the only item.

2. Otherwise there is a first letter in the word, and (first *a-word*) is that letter and the recursion produces the list of all possible rearrangements for the rest of the word. For example, if the list is

   (cons 'd (cons 'e (cons 'r empty)))

   then the recursion is (*arrangements* (cons 'e (cons 'r empty))). It will produce the result

   (cons (cons 'e (cons 'r empty))
     (cons (cons 'r (cons 'e empty))
       empty))

   To obtain all possible rearrangements for the entire list, we must now insert the first item, 'd in our case, into all of these words between all possible letters and at the beginning and end.

---

[38] The mathematical term is *permutation*.

The task of inserting a letter into many different words requires processing an arbitrarily large list. So, we need another function, call it *insert-everywhere/in-all-words*, to complete the definition of *arrangements*:

```
(define (arrangements a-word)
  (cond
    [(empty? a-word) (cons empty empty)]
    [else (insert-everywhere/in-all-words (first a-word)
            (arrangements (rest a-word)))]))
```

**Exercise 12.4.2** Develop the function *insert-everywhere/in-all-words*. It consumes a symbol and a list of words. The result is a list of words like its second argument, but with the first argument inserted between all letters and at the beginning and the end of all words of the second argument.
**Hint:** Reconsider the example from above. We stopped and decided that we needed to insert 'd into the words (cons 'e (cons 'r empty)) and (cons 'r (cons 'e empty)). The following is therefore a natural candidate:

```
(insert-everywhere/in-all-words 'd
  (cons (cons 'e (cons 'r empty))
    (cons (cons 'r (cons 'e empty))
      empty)))
```

for the "function examples" step. Keep in mind that the second input corresponds to the sequence of (partial) words "er" and "re".

Also, use the Scheme operation **append**, which consumes two lists and produces the concatenation of the two lists. For example:

```
  (append (list 'a 'b 'c) (list 'd 'e))
= (list 'a 'b 'c 'd 'e)
```

We will discuss the development of functions such as **append** in section 17. ∎

# Intermezzo 2: List Abbreviations

Using cons to create lists is cumbersome if a list contains many items. Fortunately, Scheme provides the list operation, which consumes an arbitrary number of values and creates a list. Here is Scheme's extended syntax:

$\langle prm \rangle = $ list

The extended collection of values is

$\langle val \rangle = $ (list $\langle val \rangle \ldots \langle val \rangle$)

A simpler way to understand list expressions is to think of them as abbreviations. Specifically, every expression of the shape

(list *exp-1 ... exp-n*)

stands for a series of $n$ cons expressions:

(cons *exp-1* (cons ... (cons *exp-n* empty)))

Recall that empty is not an item of the list here, but the rest of the list. Here are three examples:

(list 1 2)
= (cons 1 (cons 2 empty))

(list 'Houston 'Dallas 'SanAntonio)
= (cons 'Houston (cons 'Dallas (cons 'SanAntonio empty)))

(list false true false false)
= (cons false (cons true (cons false (cons false empty))))

They introduce lists with two, three, and four items, respectively.

Of course, we can apply list not only to values but also to expressions:

(list (+ 0 1) (+ 1 1))
= (list 1 2)

Before the list is constructed, the expressions must be evaluated. If during the evaluation of an expression an error occurs, the list is never formed:

(list (/ 1 0) (+ 1 1))
= /: *divide by zero*

In short, list behaves just like any other primitive operation.

The use of list greatly simplifies the notation for lists with many items and lists that contains lists or structures. Here is an example:

(list 0 1 2 3 4 5 6 7 8 9)

This list contains 10 items and its formation with cons and empty would require 10 uses of cons and one instance of empty. Similarly, the list

```
(list (list 'bob 0 'a)
      (list 'carl 1 'a)
      (list 'dana 2 'b)
      (list 'erik 3 'c)
      (list 'frank 4 'a)
      (list 'grant 5 'b)
      (list 'hank 6 'c)
      (list 'ian 8 'a)
      (list 'john 7 'd)
      (list 'karel 9 'e))
```

requires 11 uses of list in contrast to 40 of cons and 11 of empty.

## Exercises

**Exercise 13.0.3** Use cons and empty to construct the equivalent of the following lists:

1. (list 0 1 2 3 4 5)

2. (list (list 'adam 0) (list 'eve 1) (list 'louisXIV 2))

3. (list 1 (list 1 2) (list 1 2 3)).

∎

**Exercise 13.0.4** Use list to construct the equivalent of the following lists:

1. (cons 'a (cons 'b (cons 'c (cons 'd (cons 'e empty)))))

2. (cons (cons 1 (cons 2 empty)) empty)

3. (cons 'a (cons (cons 1 empty) (cons false empty))).

4. (cons (cons 1 (cons 2 empty)) (cons (cons 2 (cons 3 empty)) empty))

Start by determining how many items each list and each nested list contains. ∎

**Exercise 13.0.5** On rare occasions, we encounter lists formed with cons and list. Reformulate the following lists using cons and empty exclusively:

1. (cons 'a (list 0 false))

2. (list (cons 1 (cons 13 empty)))

3. (list empty empty (cons 1 empty))

4. (cons 'a (cons (list 1) (list false empty))).

Then formulate the lists using list. ∎

**Exercise 13.0.6** Determine the values of the following expressions:

1. (list (symbol=? 'a 'b) (symbol=? 'c 'c) false)

2. (list (+ 10 20) (* 10 20) (/ 10 20))

3. (list 'dana 'jane 'mary 'laura)

∎

**Exercise 13.0.7** Determine the values of

(first (list 1 2 3))

(rest (list 1 2 3))

∎

The use of list makes it significantly easier to evaluate expressions involving lists. Here are the recursive steps from an example from section 9.5:

```
(sum (list (make-ir 'robot 22.05) (make-ir 'doll 17.95)))
= (+ (ir-price (first (list (make-ir 'robot 22.05) (make-ir 'doll 17.95))))
     (sum (rest (list (make-ir 'robot 22.05) (make-ir 'doll 17.95)))))
= (+ (ir-price (make-ir 'robot 22.05))
     (sum (list (make-ir 'doll 17.95))))
```

At this place, we use one of the equations governing the new primitive operations for the first time:

= (+ 22.05
    (*sum* (list (make-ir 'doll 17.95))))
= (+ 22.05
    (+ (ir-price (first (list (make-ir 'doll 17.95))))
       (*sum* (rest (list (make-ir 'doll 17.95))))))
= (+ 22.05
    (+ (ir-price (make-ir 'doll 17.95))
       (*sum* empty)))
= (+ 22.05 (+ 17.95 (*sum* empty)))
= (+ 22.05 (+ 17.95 0))

Since the laws of first and rest carry over to list values in a natural manner, an evaluation using list does not need to expand list into uses of cons and empty.

Following an old programming language convention,[39] we may abbreviate lists and symbols even further. If a list is formulated with list, we can simply agree to drop list and that each opening parenthesis stands for itself and the word list. For example,

'(1 2 3)

abbreviates

(list 1 2 3)

or

(cons 1 (cons 2 (cons 3 empty))) .

Similarly,

'((1 2) (3 4) (5 6))

stands for

(list (list 1 2) (list 3 4) (list 5 6)),

which can be further expanded into cons and empty expressions.

If we drop quotes in front of symbols, writing lists of symbols is a breeze:

'(a b c)

---

[39]The convention is due to LISP, an early but highly advanced programming language designed in 1958. Scheme inherited many ideas from LISP, but it is a different language.

This short-hand is an abbreviation for

(list 'a 'b 'c)

And, more impressively,

'(<html>
  (<title> My First Web Page)
  (<body> Oh!))

stands for

(list '<html>
  (list '<title> 'My 'First 'Web 'Page)
  (list '<body> 'Oh!)) .

## Exercises

**Exercise 13.0.8** Restore list and quotes where necessary:

1.
   '(1 a 2 b 3 c)

2.
   '((alan 1000)
     (barb 2000)
     (carl 1500)
     (dawn 2300))

3.
   '((My First Paper)
     (Sean Fisler)
     (Section 1
        (Subsection 1 Life is difficult)
        (Subsection 2 But learning things makes it interesting))
     (Section 2
        Conclusion? What conclusion?))

∎

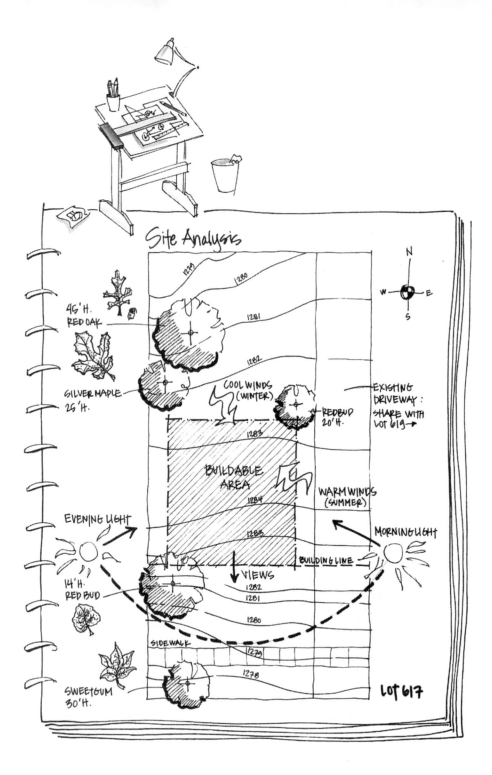

Site Analysis

N
W E
S

45' H.
RED OAK

SILVER MAPLE
25' H.

COOL WINDS
(WINTER)

REDBUD
20' H.

EXISTING
DRIVEWAY:
SHARE WITH
LOT 619 →

1279
1280
1281
1282
1283

BUILDABLE
AREA

WARM WINDS
(SUMMER)

1284
1285

EVENING LIGHT

MORNING LIGHT

BUILDING LINE

VIEWS

14' H.
RED BUD

1282
1281
1280

SIDEWALK
1279
1278

SWEETGUM
30' H.

LOT 617

# III  More on Processing Arbitrarily Large Data

## 14  More Self-referential Data Definitions

Lists and natural numbers are two classes of data whose description requires self-referential data definitions. Both data definitions consist of two clauses; both have a single self-reference. Many interesting classes of data, however, require more complex definitions than that. Indeed, there is no end to the variations. It is therefore necessary to learn how to formulate data definitions on our own, starting with informal descriptions of information. Once we have those, we can just follow a slightly modified design recipe for self-referential data definitions.

### 14.1  Structures in Structures

Medical researchers rely on family trees to do research on hereditary diseases. They may, for example, search a family tree for a certain eye color. Computers can help with these tasks, so it is natural to design representations of family trees and functions for processing them.

One way to maintain a family tree of a family is to add a node to the tree every time a child is born. From the node, we can draw connections to the node for the father and the one for the mother, which tells us how the people in the tree are related. For those people in the tree whose parents are unknown, we do not draw any connections. The result is a so-called *ancestor family tree* because, given any node in the tree, we can find the ancestors of that person if we follow the arrows but not the descendants.

As we record a family tree, we may also want to record certain pieces of information. The birth date, birth weight, the color of the eyes, and the color of the hair are the pieces of information that we care about. Others record different information.

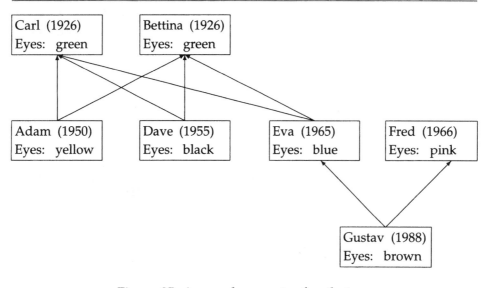

Figure 35: A sample ancestor family tree

See figure 35 for a drawing of an ancestor family tree. Adam is the child of Bettina and Carl; he has yellow eyes and was born in 1950. Similarly, Gustav is the child of Eva and Fred, has brown eyes, and was born in 1988. To represent a child in a family tree is to combine several pieces of information: information about the father, the mother, the name, the birth date, and eye color. This suggests that we define a new structure:

(**define-struct** *child* (*father mother name date eyes*))

The five fields of *child* structures record the required information, which suggests the following data definition:

A *child* is a structure:
$$\text{(make-child } f \ m \ na \ da \ ec)$$
where *f* and *m* are *child* structures; *na* and *ec* are symbols; and *da* is a number.

While this data definition is simple, it is unfortunately also useless. The definition refers to itself but, because it doesn't have any clauses, there is no way to create a *child* structure. If we tried to create a *child* structure, we would have to write

```
(make-child
  (make-child
    (make-child
      (make-child
        . . .
      )))
    . . . . . . . . . . . . )
```

without end. It is for this reason that we demand that all self-referential data definitions consist of several clauses (for now) and that at least one of them does not refer to the data definition.

Let's postpone the data definition for a moment and study instead how we can use *child* structures to represent family trees. Suppose we are about to add a child to an existing family tree, and furthermore suppose that we already have representations for the parents. Then we can just construct a new *child* structure. For example, for Adam we could create the following *child* structure:

(make-child *Carl Bettina* 'Adam 1950 'yellow)

assuming *Carl* and *Bettina* stand for representations of Adam's parents.

The problem is that we don't always know a person's parents. In the family depicted in figure 35, we don't know Bettina's parents. Yet, even if we don't know a person's father or mother, we must still use some Scheme value for the two fields in a *child* structure. We could use all kinds of values to signal a lack of information (5, false, or 'none); here, we use empty. For example, to construct a *child* structure for Bettina, we do the following:

(make-child empty empty 'Bettina 1926 'green)

Of course, if only one of the two parents is missing, we fill just that field with empty.

Our analysis suggests that a *child* node has the following data definition:

A *child node* is (make-child *f m na da ec*) where

1. *f* and *m* are either
   (a) empty or
   (b) *child* nodes;
2. *na* and *ec* are symbols;
3. *da* is a number.

This definition is special in two regards. First, it is a self-referential data definition involving structures. Second, the data definition mentions two alternatives for the first and second component. This violates our conventions concerning the shape of data definitions.

We can avoid this problem by defining the collection of nodes in a family tree instead:

---

A *family-tree-node* (short: *ftn*) is either

1. empty; or

2. (make-child *f m na da ec*)
   where *f* and *m* are *ftn*s, *na*
   and *ec* are symbols, and *da* is a number.

---

This new definition satisfies our conventions. It consists of two clauses. One of the clauses is self-referential, the other is not.

In contrast to previous data definitions involving structures, the definition of *ftn* is not a plain explanation of what kind of data can show up in which field. Instead, it is multi-clausal and self-referential. Considering that this is the first such data definition, let us carefully translate the example from figure 35 and thus reassure ourselves that the new class of data can represent the information of interest.

The information for Carl is easy to translate into a *ftn*:

```
(make-child empty empty 'Carl 1926 'green)
```

Bettina and Fred are represented with similar nodes. Accordingly, the node for Adam is created with

```
(make-child (make-child empty empty 'Carl 1926 'green)
            (make-child empty empty 'Bettina 1926 'green)
            'Adam
            1950
            'yellow)
```

As the examples show, a simple-minded, node-by-node transliteration of figure 35 requires numerous repetitions of data. For example, if we constructed the *child* structure for Dave like the one for Adam, we would get

```
(make-child (make-child empty empty 'Carl 1926 'green)
            (make-child empty empty 'Bettina 1926 'green)
            'Dave
            1955
            'black)
```

Hence it is a good idea to introduce a variable definition per node and to use the variable thereafter. To make things easy, we use *Carl* to stand for the *child* structure that describes Carl, and so on. The complete transliteration of the family tree into Scheme can be found in figure 36.

---

```
;; Oldest Generation:
(define Carl (make-child empty empty 'Carl 1926 'green))
(define Bettina (make-child empty empty 'Bettina 1926 'green))

;; Middle Generation:
(define Adam (make-child Carl Bettina 'Adam 1950 'yellow))
(define Dave (make-child Carl Bettina 'Dave 1955 'black))
(define Eva (make-child Carl Bettina 'Eva 1965 'blue))
(define Fred (make-child empty empty 'Fred 1966 'pink))

;; Youngest Generation:
(define Gustav (make-child Fred Eva 'Gustav 1988 'brown))
```

Figure 36: A Scheme representation of the sample family tree

---

The structure definitions in figure 36 naturally correspond to an image of deeply nested boxes. Each box has five compartments. The first two contain boxes again, which in turn contain boxes in their first two compartments, and so on. Thus, if we were to draw the structure definitions for the family tree using nested boxes, we would quickly be overwhelmed by the details of the picture. Furthermore, the picture would copy certain portions of the tree just like our attempt to use make-child without variable definitions. For these reasons, it is better to imagine the structures as boxes and arrows, as originally drawn in figure 35. In general, a programmer must flexibly switch back and forth between both of these graphical illustrations. For extracting values from structures, the boxes-in-boxes image works best; for finding our way around large collections of interconnected structures, the boxes-and-arrows image works better.

Equipped with a firm understanding of the family tree representation, we can turn to the design of functions that consume family trees. Let us first look at a generic function of this kind:

```
;; fun-for-ftn : ftn → ???
(define (fun-for-ftn a-ftree) ...)
```

After all, we should be able to construct the template without considering the purpose of a function.

Since the data definition for *ftn*s contains two clauses, the template must consist of a **cond**-expression with two clauses. The first deals with empty, the second with *child* structures:

```
;; fun-for-ftn : ftn → ???
(define (fun-for-ftn a-ftree)
  (cond
    [(empty? a-ftree) ... ]
    [else ; (child? a-ftree)
      ... ]))
```

Furthermore, for the first clause, the input is atomic so there is nothing further to be done. For the second clause, though, the input contains five pieces of information: two other family tree nodes, the person's name, birth date, and eye color:

```
;; fun-for-ftn : ftn → ???
(define (fun-for-ftn a-ftree)
  (cond
    [(empty? a-ftree) ... ]
    [else
      ... (fun-for-ftn (child-father a-ftree)) ...
      ... (fun-for-ftn (child-mother a-ftree)) ...
      ... (child-name a-ftree) ...
      ... (child-date a-ftree) ...
      ... (child-eyes a-ftree) ... ]))
```

We also apply *fun-for-ftn* to the *father* and *mother* fields because of the self-references in the second clause of the data definition.

Let us now turn to a concrete example: *blue-eyed-ancestor?*, the function that determines whether anyone in some given family tree has blue eyes:

```
;; blue-eyed-ancestor? : ftn → boolean
;; to determine whether a-ftree contains a child
;; structure with 'blue in the eyes field
(define (blue-eyed-ancestor? a-ftree) ...)
```

Following our recipe, we first develop some examples. Consider the family tree node for Carl. He does not have blue eyes, and because he doesn't have any (known) ancestors in our family tree, the family tree represented by this node does not contain a person with blue eyes. In short,

(*blue-eyed-ancestor? Carl*)

evaluates to false. In contrast, the family tree represented by *Gustav* contains a node for Eva who does have blue eyes. Hence

(*blue-eyed-ancestor? Gustav*)

evaluates to true.

The function template is like that of *fun-for-ftn*, except that we use the name *blue-eyed-ancestor?*. As always, we use the template to guide the function design. First we assume that (empty? *a-ftree*) holds. In that case, the family tree is empty, and nobody has blue eyes. Hence the answer must be false.

The second clause of the template contains several expressions, which we must interpret:

1. (*blue-eyed-ancestor?* (child-father *a-ftree*)), which determines whether someone in the father's *ftn* has blue eyes;

2. (*blue-eyed-ancestor?* (child-mother *a-ftree*)), which determines whether someone in the mother's *ftn* has blue eyes;

3. (child-name *a-ftree*), which extracts the *child*'s name;

4. (child-date *a-ftree*), which extracts the *child*'s date of birth; and

5. (child-eyes *a-ftree*), which extracts the *child*'s eye color.

It is now up to us to use these values properly. Clearly, if the *child* structure contains 'blue in the *eyes* field, the function's answer is true. Otherwise, the function produces true if there is a blue-eyed person in either the father's or the mother's family tree. The rest of the data is useless.

Our discussion suggests that we formulate a conditional expression and that the first condition is

(symbol=? (child-eyes *a-ftree*) 'blue)

The two recursions are the other two conditions. If either one produces true, the function produces true. The **else**-clause produces false.

In summary, the answer in the second clause is the expression:

```
(cond
  [(symbol=? (child-eyes a-ftree) 'blue) true]
  [(blue-eyed-ancestor? (child-father a-ftree)) true]
  [(blue-eyed-ancestor? (child-mother a-ftree)) true]
  [else false])
```

The first definition in figure 37 pulls everything together. The second definition shows how to formulate this **cond**-expression as an equivalent **or**-expression, testing one condition after the next, until one of them is true or all of them have evaluated to false.

```
;; blue-eyed-ancestor? : ftn → boolean
;; to determine whether a-ftree contains a child
;; structure with 'blue in the eyes field
;; version 1: using a nested cond-expression
(define (blue-eyed-ancestor? a-ftree)
  (cond
    [(empty? a-ftree) false]
    [else (cond
            [(symbol=? (child-eyes a-ftree) 'blue) true]
            [(blue-eyed-ancestor? (child-father a-ftree)) true]
            [(blue-eyed-ancestor? (child-mother a-ftree)) true]
            [else false])]))
```

```
;; blue-eyed-ancestor? : ftn → boolean
;; to determine whether a-ftree contains a child
;; structure with 'blue in the eyes field
;; version 2: using an or-expression
(define (blue-eyed-ancestor? a-ftree)
  (cond
    [(empty? a-ftree) false]
    [else (or (symbol=? (child-eyes a-ftree) 'blue)
              (or (blue-eyed-ancestor? (child-father a-ftree))
                  (blue-eyed-ancestor? (child-mother a-ftree))))]))
```

Figure 37: Two functions for finding a blue-eyed ancestor

The function *blue-eyed-ancestor?* is unusual in that it uses the recursions as conditions in a **cond**-expressions. To understand how this works, let us evaluate an application of *blue-eyed-ancestor?* to *Carl* by hand:

```
(blue-eyed-ancestor? Carl)
= (blue-eyed-ancestor? (make-child empty empty 'Carl 1926 'green))
= (cond
    [(empty? (make-child empty empty 'Carl 1926 'green)) false]
    [else
      (cond
        [(symbol=?
           (child-eyes (make-child empty empty 'Carl 1926 'green))
           'blue)
         true]
        [(blue-eyed-ancestor?
           (child-father (make-child empty empty 'Carl 1926 'green)))
         true]
        [(blue-eyed-ancestor?
           (child-mother (make-child empty empty 'Carl 1926 'green)))
         true]
        [else false])])
= (cond
    [(symbol=? 'green 'blue) true]
    [(blue-eyed-ancestor? empty) true]
    [(blue-eyed-ancestor? empty) true]
    [else false])
= (cond
    [false true]
    [false true]
    [false true]
    [else false])
= false
```

The evaluation confirms that *blue-eyed-ancestor?* works properly for *Carl*, and it also illustrates how the function works.

---

## Exercises

**Exercise 14.1.1** The second definition of *blue-eyed-ancestor?* in figure 37 uses an **or**-expression instead of a nested conditional. Use a hand-evaluation to show that this definition produces the same output for the inputs empty and *Carl*. ∎

**Exercise 14.1.2** Confirm that

(*blue-eyed-ancestor?* empty)

evaluates to false with a hand-evaluation.

Evaluate (*blue-eyed-ancestor? Gustav*) by hand and with DrScheme. For the hand-evaluation, skip those steps in the evaluation that concern extractions, comparisons, and conditions involving empty?. Also reuse established equations where possible, especially the one above. ∎

**Exercise 14.1.3** Develop *count-persons*. The function consumes a family tree node and produces the number of people in the corresponding family tree. ∎

**Exercise 14.1.4** Develop the function *average-age*. It consumes a family tree node and the current year. It produces the average age of all people in the family tree. ∎

**Exercise 14.1.5** Develop the function *eye-colors*, which consumes a family tree node and produces a list of all eye colors in the tree. An eye color may occur more than once in the list.
**Hint:** Use the Scheme operation append, which consumes two lists and produces the concatenation of the two lists. For example:

```
    (append (list 'a 'b 'c) (list 'd 'e))
= (list 'a 'b 'c 'd 'e)
```

We discuss the development of functions like append in section 17. ∎

**Exercise 14.1.6** Suppose we need the function *proper-blue-eyed-ancestor?*. It is like *blue-eyed-ancestor?* but responds with true only when some proper ancestor, not the given one, has blue eyes.

The contract for this new function is the same as for the old one:
;; *proper-blue-eyed-ancestor?* : *ftn* → *boolean*
;; to determine whether *a-ftree* has a blue-eyed ancestor
(**define** (*proper-blue-eyed-ancestor? a-ftree*) ...)

The results differ slightly.

To appreciate the difference, we need to look at Eva, who is blue-eyed, but does not have a blue-eyed ancestor. Hence

(*blue-eyed-ancestor? Eva*)

is true but

> (*proper-blue-eyed-ancestor? Eva*)

is false. After all *Eva* is not a proper ancestor of herself.

Suppose a friend sees the purpose statement and comes up with this solution:

```
(define (proper-blue-eyed-ancestor? a-ftree)
  (cond
    [(empty? a-ftree) false]
    [else (or (proper-blue-eyed-ancestor? (child-father a-ftree))
              (proper-blue-eyed-ancestor? (child-mother a-ftree)))]))
```

What would be the result of (*proper-blue-eyed-ancestor? A*) for *any ftn A*? Fix the friend's solution. ∎

## 14.2 Extended Exercise: Binary Search Trees

Programmers often work with trees, though rarely with family trees. A particularly well-known form of tree is the binary search tree. Many applications employ binary search trees to store and to retrieve information.

To be concrete, we discuss binary trees that manage information about people. In this context, a binary tree is similar to a family tree but instead of *child* structures it contains *node*s:

> (**define-struct** *node* (*ssn name left right*))

Here we have decided to record the social security number, the name, and two other trees. The latter are like the parent fields of family trees, though the relationship between a *node* and its *left* and *right* trees is not based on family relationships.

The corresponding data definition is just like the one for family trees:

---

A *binary-tree* (short: *BT*) is either

1. false; or

2. (make-node *soc pn lft rgt*)
   where *soc* is a number, *pn* is a symbol, and *lft* and *rgt* are *BT*s.

---

The choice of false to indicate lack of information is arbitrary. We could have chosen empty again, but false is an equally good and equally frequent choice that we should become familiar with.

Here are two binary trees:

```
(make-node                    (make-node
  15                            15
  'd                            'd
  false                         (make-node 87 'h false false)
  (make-node 24 'i false false))  false)
```

Figure 38 shows how we should think about such trees. The trees are drawn upside down, that is, with the root at the top and the crown of the tree at the bottom. Each circle corresponds to a node, labeled with the *ssn* field of a corresponding *node* structure. The trees omit false.

---

## Exercises

**Exercise 14.2.1** Draw the two trees above in the manner of figure 38. Then develop *contains-bt*. The function consumes a number and a *BT* and determines whether the number occurs in the tree. ∎

**Exercise 14.2.2** Develop *search-bt*. The function consumes a number *n* and a *BT*. If the tree contains a *node* structure whose *soc* field is *n*, the function produces the value of the *pn* field in that node. Otherwise, the function produces false.
**Hint:** Use *contains-bt*. Or, use boolean? to find out whether *search-bt* was successfully used on a subtree. We will discuss this second technique, called backtracking, in the intermezzo at the end of this part. ∎

---

Both trees in figure 38 are binary trees but they differ in a significant way. If we read the numbers in the two trees from left to right we obtain two sequences:

| Tree A: | 10 | 15 | 24 | 29 | 63 | 77 | 89 | 95 | 99 |
|---------|----|----|----|----|----|----|----|----|----|
| Tree B: | 87 | 15 | 24 | 29 | 63 | 33 | 89 | 95 | 99 |

The sequence for tree A is sorted in ascending order, the one for B is not.

A binary tree that has an ordered sequence of information is a BINARY SEARCH TREE. Every binary search tree is a binary tree, but not every binary

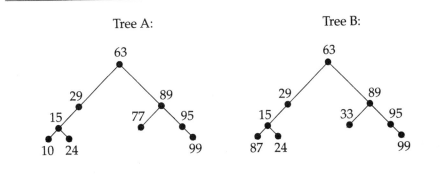

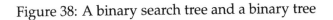

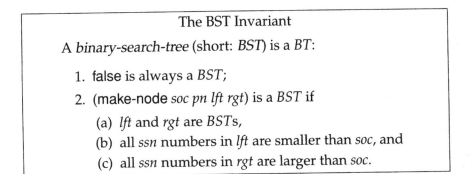

Figure 38: A binary search tree and a binary tree

tree is a binary search tree. We say that the class of binary search trees is a PROPER SUBCLASS of that of binary trees, that is, a class that does not contain all binary trees. More concretely, we formulate a condition—or data invariant—that distinguishes a binary search tree from a binary tree:

> ### The BST Invariant
>
> A *binary-search-tree* (short: *BST*) is a *BT*:
>
> 1. false is always a *BST*;
> 2. (make-node *soc pn lft rgt*) is a *BST* if
>    (a) *lft* and *rgt* are *BSTs*,
>    (b) all *ssn* numbers in *lft* are smaller than *soc*, and
>    (c) all *ssn* numbers in *rgt* are larger than *soc*.

The second and third conditions are different from what we have seen in previous data definitions. They place an additional and unusual burden on the construction *BSTs*. We must inspect all numbers in these trees and ensure that they are smaller (or larger) than *soc*.

**Exercises**

**Exercise 14.2.3** Develop the function *inorder*. It consumes a binary tree and produces a list of all the *ssn* numbers in the tree. The list contains the numbers in the left-to-right order we have used above.

**Hint:** Use the Scheme operation append, which concatenates lists:

(append (list 1 2 3) (list 4) (list 5 6 7))

evaluates to

(list 1 2 3 4 5 6 7)

What does *inorder* produce for a binary search tree? ∎

Looking for a specific *node* in a *BST* takes fewer steps than looking for the same *node* in a *BT*. To find out whether a *BT* contains a node with a specific *ssn* field, a function may have to look at *every* *node* of the tree. In contrast, to inspect a binary search tree requires far fewer inspections than that. Suppose we are given the *BST*:

(make-node 66 'a *L R*)

If we are looking for **66**, we have found it. Now suppose we are looking for **63**. Given the above *node*, we can focus the search on *L* because *all nodes* with *ssn*s smaller than **66** are in *L*. Similarly, if we were to look for **99**, we would ignore *L* and focus on *R* because *all nodes* with *ssn*s larger than **66** are in *R*.

**Exercises**

**Exercise 14.2.4** Develop *search-bst*. The function consumes a number *n* and a *BST*. If the tree contains a *node* structure whose *soc* field is *n*, the function produces the value of the *pn* field in that node. Otherwise, the function produces false. The function organization must exploit the BST Invariant so that the function performs as few comparisons as necessary. Compare searching in binary search trees with searching in sorted lists (exercise 12.2.2). ∎

Building a binary tree is easy; building a binary search tree is a complicated, error-prone affair. To create a *BT* we combine two *BT*s, an *ssn* number and a *name* with make-node. The result is, by definition, a *BT*. To create a *BST*, this procedure fails because the result would typically not be a *BST*. For example, if one tree contains 3 and 5, and the other one contains 2 and 6, there is no way to join these two *BST*s into a single binary search tree.

We can overcome this problem in (at least) two ways. First, given a list of numbers and symbols, we can determine by hand what the corresponding *BST* should look like and then use make-node to build it. Second, we can write a function that builds a *BST* from the list, one *node* after another.

## Exercises

**Exercise 14.2.5** Develop the function *create-bst*. It consumes a *BST B*, a number *N*, and a symbol *S*. It produces a *BST* that is just like *B* and that in place of one false subtree contains the *node* structure

(make-node *N S* false false)

Test the function with (*create-bst* false 66 'a); this should create a single *node*. Then show that the following holds:

(*create-bst* (*create-bst* false 66 'a) 53 'b)
= (make-node 66
      'a
      (make-node 53 'b false false)
      false)

Finally, create tree A from figure 38 using *create-bst*. ∎

**Exercise 14.2.6** Develop the function *create-bst-from-list*. It consumes a list of numbers and names; it produces a *BST* by repeatedly applying *create-bst*.

The data definition for a list of numbers and names is as follows:

A *list-of-number/name* is either

1. empty or

2. (cons (list *ssn nom*) *lonn*)
   where *ssn* is a number, *nom* a symbol,
   and *lonn* is a *list-of-number/name*.

Consider the following examples:

| (**define** *sample* | (**define** *sample* |
|---|---|
| '((99 o) | (list (list 99 'o) |
| (77 l) | (list 77 'l) |
| (24 i) | (list 24 'i) |
| (10 h) | (list 10 'h) |
| (95 g) | (list 95 'g) |
| (15 d) | (list 15 'd) |
| (89 c) | (list 89 'c) |
| (29 b) | (list 29 'b) |
| (63 a))) | (list 63 'a))) |

They are equivalent, although the left one is defined with the quote abbreviation, the right one using list. The left tree in figure 38 is the result of using *create-bst-from-list* on this list. ∎

## 14.3   Lists in Lists

The World Wide Web, or just "the Web," has become the most interesting part of the Internet, a global network of computers. Roughly speaking, the Web is a collection of Web pages. Each Web page is a sequence of words, pictures, movies, audio messages, and many more things. Most important, Web pages also contain links to other Web pages.

A Web browser enables people to view Web pages. It presents a Web page as a sequence of words, images, and so on. Some of the words on a page may be underlined. Clicking on underlined words leads to a new Web page. Most modern browsers also provide a Web page composer. These are tools that help people create collections of Web pages. A composer can, among other things, search for words or replace one word with another. In short, Web pages are things that we should be able to represent on computers, and there are many functions that process Web pages.

To simplify our problem, we consider only Web pages of words and nested Web pages. One way of understanding such a page is as a sequence of words and Web pages. This informal description suggests a natural representation of Web pages as lists of symbols, which represent words, and Web pages, which represent nested Web pages. After all, we have emphasized before that a list may contain different kinds of things. Still, when we spell out this idea as a data definition, we get something rather unusual:

---

A *Web-page* (short: *WP*) is either

1. empty;

2. (cons *s wp*)
   where *s* is a symbol and *wp* is a Web page; or

3. (cons *ewp wp*)
   where both *ewp* and *wp* are Web pages.

---

This data definition differs from that of a list of symbols in that it has three clauses instead of two and that it has three self-references instead of one. Of these self-references, the one at the beginning of a constructed list is the most unusual. We refer to such Web pages as *immediately embedded* Web pages.

Because the data definition is unusual, we construct some examples of Web pages before we continue. Here is a plain page:

```
'(The TeachScheme! Project aims to improve the
  problem-solving and organization skills of high
  school students. It provides software and lecture
  notes as well as exercises and solutions for teachers.)
```

It contains nothing but words. Here is a complex page:

```
'(The TeachScheme Web Page
  Here you can find:
  (LectureNotes for Teachers)
  (Guidance for (DrScheme: a Scheme programming environment))
  (Exercise Sets)
  (Solutions for Exercises)
  For further information: write to scheme@cs)
```

The immediately embedded pages start with parentheses and the symbols 'LectureNotes, 'Guidance, 'Exercises, and 'Solutions. The second embedded Web page contains another embedded page, which starts with the word 'DrScheme. We say this page is *embedded* with respect to the entire page.

Let's develop the function *size*, which consumes a Web page and produces the number of words that it and all of its embedded pages contain:

```
;; size : WP → number
;; to count the number of symbols that occur in a-wp
(define (size a-wp) ...)
```

The two Web pages above suggest two good examples, but they are too complex. Here are three examples, one per subclass of data:

```
(= (size empty)
   0)

(= (size (cons 'One empty))
   1)

(= (size (cons (cons 'One empty) empty))
   1)
```

The first two examples are obvious. The third one deserves a short explanation. It is a Web page that contains one immediately embedded Web page, and nothing else. The embedded Web page is the one of the second example, and it contains the one and only symbol of the third example.

To develop the template for *size*, let's carefully step through the design recipe. The shape of the data definition suggests that we need three **cond**-clauses: one for the empty page, one for a page that starts with a symbol, and one for a page that starts with an embedded Web page. While the first condition is the familiar test for empty, the second and third need closer inspection because both clauses in the data definition use cons, and a simple cons? won't distinguish between the two forms of data.

If the page is not empty, it is certainly constructed, and the distinguishing feature is the first item on the list. In other words, the second condition must use a predicate that tests the first item on *a-wp*:

```
;; size : WP → number
;; to count the number of symbols that occur in a-wp
(define (size a-wp)
  (cond
    [(empty? a-wp) ... ]
    [(symbol? (first a-wp)) ... (first a-wp) ... (size (rest a-wp)) ... ]
    [else ... (size (first a-wp)) ... (size (rest a-wp)) ... ]))
```

The rest of the template is as usual. The second and third **cond** clauses contain selector expressions for the first item and the rest of the list. Because (rest *a-wp*) is always a Web page and because (first *a-wp*) is one in the third case, we also add a recursive call to size for these selector expressions.

Using the examples and the template, we are ready to design *size*: see figure 39. The differences between the definition and the template are minimal, which shows again how much of a function we can design by merely thinking systematically about the data definition for its inputs.

---

```
;; size : WP → number
;; to count the number of symbols that occur in a-wp
(define (size a-wp)
  (cond
    [(empty? a-wp) 0]
    [(symbol? (first a-wp)) (+ 1 (size (rest a-wp)))]
    [else (+ (size (first a-wp)) (size (rest a-wp)))]))
```

Figure 39: The definition of *size* for Web pages

---

## Exercises

**Exercise 14.3.1** Briefly explain how to define *size* using its template and the examples. Test *size* using the examples from above.

**Exercise 14.3.2** Develop the function *occurs1*. The function consumes a Web page and a symbol. It produces the number of times the symbol occurs in the Web page, ignoring the nested Web pages.

Develop the function *occurs2*. It is like *occurs1*, but counts *all* occurrences of the symbol, including in embedded Web pages. ∎

**Exercise 14.3.3** Develop the function *replace*. The function consumes two symbols, *new* and *old*, and a Web page, *a-wp*. It produces a page that is structurally identical to *a-wp* but with all occurrences of *old* replaced by *new*. ∎

**Exercise 14.3.4** People do not like deep Web trees because they require too many page switches to reach useful information. For that reason a Web page designer may also want to measure the depth of a page. A page containing only symbols has depth 0. A page with an immediately embedded page has the depth of the embedded page plus 1. If a page has several immediately embedded Web pages, its depth is the maximum of the depths of embedded Web pages plus 1. Develop *depth*, which consumes a Web page and computes its depth. ∎

## 14.4   Extended Exercise: Evaluating Scheme

DrScheme is itself a program that consists of several parts. One function checks whether the definitions and expressions we wrote down are grammatical Scheme expressions. Another one evaluates Scheme expressions. With what we have learned in this section, we can now develop simple versions of these functions.

Our first task is to agree on a data representation for Scheme programs. In other words, we must figure out how to represent a Scheme expression as a piece of Scheme data. This sounds unusual, but it is not difficult. Suppose we just want to represent numbers, variables, additions, and multiplications for a start. Clearly, numbers can stand for numbers and symbols for variables. Additions and multiplications, however, call for a class of compound data because they consist of an operator and two subexpressions.

A straightforward way to represent additions and multiplications is to use two structures: one for additions and another one for multiplications. Here are the structure definitions:

(**define-struct** *add* (*left right*))
(**define-struct** *mul* (*left right*))

Each structure has two components. One represents the left expression and the other one the right expression of the operation.

Let's look at some examples:

| Scheme expression | representation of Scheme expression |
|---|---|
| 3 | 3 |
| *x* | 'x |
| (* 3 10) | (make-mul 3 10) |
| (+ (* 3 3) (* 4 4)) | (make-add (make-mul 3 3) (make-mul 4 4)) |
| (+ (* *x x*) (* *y y*)) | (make-add (make-mul 'x 'x) (make-mul 'y 'y)) |
| (* 1/2 (* 3 3)) | (make-mul 1/2 (make-mul 3 3)) |

These examples cover all cases: numbers, variables, simple expressions, and nested expressions.

---

### Exercises

**Exercise 14.4.1** Provide a data definition for the representation of Scheme expressions. Then translate the following expressions into representations:

  1. (+ 10 −10)

2. $(+ (* 20 \ 3) \ 33)$

3. $(* 3.14 \ (* \ r \ r))$

4. $(+ (* 9/5 \ c) \ 32)$

5. $(+ (* 3.14 \ (* \ o \ o)) \ (* 3.14 \ (* \ i \ i)))$ ∎

A Scheme evaluator is a function that consumes a representation of a Scheme expression and produces its value. For example, the expression 3 has the value 3, $(+ 3 \ 5)$ has the value 8, $(+ (* 3 \ 3) \ (* 4 \ 4))$ has the value 25, etc. Since we are ignoring definitions for now, an expression that contains a variable, for example, $(+ 3 \ x)$, does not have a value; after all, we do not know what the variable stands for. In other words, our Scheme evaluator should be applied only to representations of expressions that do not contain variables. We say such expressions are *numeric*.

**Exercise 14.4.2** Develop the function *numeric?*, which consumes (the representation of) a Scheme expression and determines whether it is numeric. ∎

**Exercise 14.4.3** Provide a data definition for numeric expressions. Develop the function *evaluate-expression*. The function consumes (the representation of) a numeric Scheme expression and computes its value. When the function is tested, modify it so it consumes all kinds of Scheme expressions; the revised version raises an error when it encounters a variable. ∎

**Exercise 14.4.4** When people evaluate an application $(f \ a)$ they substitute $a$ for $f$'s parameter in $f$'s body. More generally, when people evaluate expressions with variables, they substitute the variables with values.

Develop the function *subst*. The function consumes (the representation of) a variable $(V)$, a number $(N)$, and (the representation of) a Scheme expression. It produces a structurally equivalent expression in which all occurrences of $V$ are substituted by $N$. ∎

# 15 Mutually Referential Data Definitions

In the preceding section, we developed data representations of family trees, Web pages, and Scheme expressions. Developing functions for these data definitions was based on one and the same design recipe. If we wish to develop more realistic representations of Web pages or Scheme expressions, or if we wish to study descendant family trees rather than ancestor trees, we must learn to describe classes of data that are interrelated. That is, we must formulate several data definitions at once where the data definitions not only refer to themselves, but also refer to other data definitions.

## 15.1   Lists of Structures, Lists in Structures

When we build a family tree retroactively, we often start from the child's perspective and proceed from there to parents, grandparents, etc. As we construct the tree, we write down who is whose child rather than who is whose parents. We build a *descendant family tree*.

Drawing a descendant tree proceeds just like drawing an ancestor tree, except that all arrows are reversed. Figure 40 represents the same family as that of figure 35, but drawn from the descendant perspective.

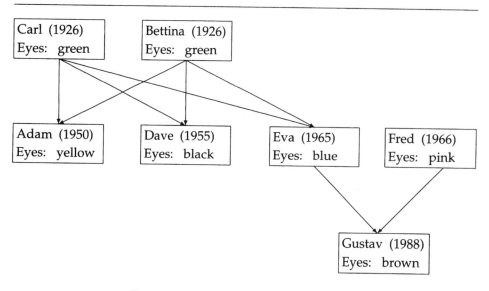

Figure 40: A descendant family tree

Representing these new kinds of family trees and their nodes in a computer requires a different class of data than do the ancestor family trees. This time a node must include information about the children instead of the two parents. Here is a structure definition:

**(define-struct** *parent* (*children name date eyes*)**)**

The last three fields in a parent structure contain the same basic information as a corresponding child structure, but the contents of the first one poses an interesting question. Since a parent may have an arbitrary number of children, the *children* field must contain an undetermined number of nodes, each of which represents one child.

The natural choice is to insist that the *children* field always stands for a list of *parent* structures. The list represents the children; if a person doesn't have children, the list is empty. This decision suggests the following data definition:

A *parent* is a structure:

$$\text{(make-parent } loc \ n \ d \ e)$$

where *loc* is a list of children, *n* and *e* are symbols, and *d* is a number.

Unfortunately, this data definition violates our criteria concerning definitions. In particular, it mentions the name of a collection that is not yet defined: list of children.

Since it is impossible to define the class of parents without knowing what a list of children is, let's start from the latter:

A *list of children* is either

1. empty or

2. (cons *p loc*) where *p* is a parent and *loc* is a list of children.

This second definition looks standard, but it suffers from the same problem as the one for *parents*. The unknown class it refers to is that of the class of parents, which cannot be defined without a definition for the list of children, and so on.

The conclusion is that the two data definitions refer to each other and are only meaningful if introduced *together*:

---

A *parent* is a structure:
$$\text{(make-parent } loc \ n \ d \ e)$$
where *loc* is a list of children, *n* and *e* are symbols, and *d* is a number.

A *list-of-children* is either

1. empty or

2. (cons *p loc*) where *p* is a parent and *loc* is a list of children.

---

When two (or more) data definitions refer to each other, they are said to be MUTUALLY RECURSIVE or MUTUALLY REFERENTIAL.

Now we can translate the family tree of figure 40 into our Scheme data language. Before we can create a *parent* structure, of course, we must first define all of the nodes that represent children. And, just as in section 14.1, the best way to do this is to name a *parent* structure before we reuse it in a list of children. Here is an example:

(**define** *Gustav* (make-parent empty 'Gustav 1988 'brown))

(make-parent (list *Gustav*) 'Fred 1950 'yellow)

To create a *parent* structure for Fred, we first define one for Gustav so that we can form (list *Gustav*), the list of children for Fred.

Figure 41 contains the complete Scheme representation for our descendant tree. To avoid repetitions, it also includes definitions for lists of children. Compare the definitions with figure 36 (see page 193), which represents the same family as an ancestor tree.

---

```
;; Youngest Generation:
(define Gustav (make-parent empty 'Gustav 1988 'brown))

(define Fred&Eva (list Gustav))

;; Middle Generation:
(define Adam (make-parent empty 'Adam 1950 'yellow))
(define Dave (make-parent empty 'Dave 1955 'black))
(define Eva (make-parent Fred&Eva 'Eva 1965 'blue))
(define Fred (make-parent Fred&Eva 'Fred 1966 'pink))

(define Carl&Bettina (list Adam Dave Eva))

;; Oldest Generation:
(define Carl (make-parent Carl&Bettina 'Carl 1926 'green))
(define Bettina (make-parent Carl&Bettina 'Bettina 1926 'green))
```

Figure 41: A Scheme representation of the descendant family tree

---

Let us now study the development of *blue-eyed-descendant?*, the natural companion of *blue-eyed-ancestor?*. It consumes a *parent* structure and determines whether it or any of its descendants has blue eyes:

```
;; blue-eyed-descendant? : parent → boolean
;; to determine whether a-parent or any of its descendants (children,
;; grandchildren, and so on) have 'blue in the eyes field
(define (blue-eyed-descendant? a-parent) ...)
```

Here are three simple examples, formulated as tests:

```
(boolean=? (blue-eyed-descendant? Gustav) false)
(boolean=? (blue-eyed-descendant? Eva) true)
(boolean=? (blue-eyed-descendant? Bettina) true)
```

A glance at figure 40 explains the answers in each case.

According to our rules, the template for *blue-eyed-descendant?* is simple. Since its input is a plain class of structures, the template contains nothing but selector expressions for the fields in the structure:

```
(define (blue-eyed-descendant? a-parent)
  ... (parent-children a-parent) ...
  ... (parent-name a-parent) ...
  ... (parent-date a-parent) ...
  ... (parent-eyes a-parent) ... )
```

The structure definition for *parent* specifies four fields so there are four expressions.

The expressions in the template remind us that the eye color of the parent is available and can be checked. Hence we add a **cond**-expression that compares (parent-eyes *a-parent*) to 'blue:

```
(define (blue-eyed-descendant? a-parent)
  (cond
    [(symbol=? (parent-eyes a-parent) 'blue) true]
    [else
      ... (parent-children a-parent) ...
      ... (parent-name a-parent) ...
      ... (parent-date a-parent) ...]))
```

The answer is true if the condition holds. The **else** clause contains the remaining expressions. The *name* and *date* field have nothing to do with the eye color of a person, so we can ignore them. This leaves us with

```
(parent-children a-parent)
```

an expression that extracts the list of children from the *parent* structure.

If the eye color of some *parent* structure is not 'blue, we must clearly search the list of children for a blue-eyed descendant. Following our guidelines for complex functions, we add the function to our wish list and continue from there. The function that we want to put on a wish list consumes a list of children and checks whether any of these or their grandchildren has blue eyes. Here are the contract, header, and purpose statement:

;; *blue-eyed-children? : list-of-children* → *boolean*
;; to determine whether any of the structures on *aloc* is blue-eyed
;; or has any blue-eyed descendant
(**define** (*blue-eyed-children? aloc*) ... )

Using *blue-eyed-children?* we can complete the definition of *blue-eyed-descendant?*:

(**define** (*blue-eyed-descendant? a-parent*)
  (**cond**
    [(symbol=? (parent-eyes *a-parent*) 'blue) true]
    [**else** (*blue-eyed-children?* (parent-children *a-parent*))]))

That is, if *a-parent* doesn't have blue eyes, we just look through the list of its children.

Before we can test *blue-eyed-descendant?*, we must define the function on our wish list. To make up examples and tests for *blue-eyed-children?*, we use the list-of-children definitions in figure 41:

(not (*blue-eyed-children?* (list *Gustav*)))

(*blue-eyed-children?* (list *Adam Dave Eva*))

Gustav doesn't have blue eyes and doesn't have any recorded descendants. Hence, *blue-eyed-children?* produces false for (list *Gustav*). In contrast, *Eva* has blue eyes, and therefore *blue-eyed-children?* produces true for the second list of children.

Since the input for *blue-eyed-children?* is a list, the template is the standard pattern:

(**define** (*blue-eyed-children? aloc*)
  (**cond**
    [(empty? *aloc*) ... ]
    [**else**
      ... (first *aloc*) ...
      ... (*blue-eyed-children?* (rest *aloc*)) ... ]))

Next we consider the two cases. If *blue-eyed-children?*'s input is empty, the answer is false. Otherwise we have two expressions:

1. (first *aloc*), which extracts the first item, a *parent* structure, from the list; and

2. (*blue-eyed-children?* (rest *aloc*)), which determines whether any of the structures on *aloc* is blue-eyed or has any blue-eyed descendant.

Fortunately we already have a function that determines whether a *parent* structure or any of its descendants has blue eyes: *blue-eyed-descendant?*. This suggests that we check whether

    (*blue-eyed-descendant?* (first *aloc*))

holds and, if so, *blue-eyed-children?* can produce true. If not, the second expression determines whether we have more luck with the rest of the list.

    Figure 42 contains the complete definitions for both functions: *blue-eyed-descendant?* and *blue-eyed-children?*. Unlike any other group of functions, these two functions refer to each other. They are MUTUALLY RECURSIVE. Not surprisingly, the mutual references in the definitions match the mutual references in data definitions. The figure also contains a pair of alternative definitions that use **or** instead of nested **cond**-expressions.

## Exercises

**Exercise 15.1.1** Evaluate (*blue-eyed-descendant?* Eva) by hand. Then evaluate (*blue-eyed-descendant?* Bettina). ∎

**Exercise 15.1.2** .Develop the function *how-far-removed*. It determines how far a blue-eyed descendant, if one exists, is removed from the given parent. If the given *parent* has blue eyes, the distance is 0; if *eyes* is not blue but some of the structure's children's eyes are, the distance is 1; and so on. If no descendant of the given *parent* has blue eyes, the function returns false when it is applied to the corresponding family tree. ∎

**Exercise 15.1.3** Develop the function *count-descendants*, which consumes a parent and produces the number of descendants, including the parent.

    Develop the function *count-proper-descendants*, which consumes a parent and produces the number of proper descendants, that is, all nodes in the family tree, not counting the parent. ∎

```
;; blue-eyed-descendant? : parent → boolean
;; to determine whether a-parent any of the descendants (children,
;; grandchildren, and so on) have 'blue in the eyes field
(define (blue-eyed-descendant? a-parent)
  (cond
    [(symbol=? (parent-eyes a-parent) 'blue) true]
    [else (blue-eyed-children? (parent-children a-parent))]))

;; blue-eyed-children? : list-of-children → boolean
;; to determine whether any of the structures in aloc is blue-eyed
;; or has any blue-eyed descendant
(define (blue-eyed-children? aloc)
  (cond
    [(empty? aloc) false]
    [else
      (cond
        [(blue-eyed-descendant? (first aloc)) true]
        [else (blue-eyed-children? (rest aloc))])]))
```

```
;; blue-eyed-descendant? : parent → boolean
;; to determine whether a-parent any of the descendants (children,
;; grandchildren, and so on) have 'blue in the eyes field
(define (blue-eyed-descendant? a-parent)
  (or (symbol=? (parent-eyes a-parent) 'blue)
      (blue-eyed-children? (parent-children a-parent))))

;; blue-eyed-children? : list-of-children → boolean
;; to determine whether any of the structures in aloc is blue-eyed
;; or has any blue-eyed descendant
(define (blue-eyed-children? aloc)
  (cond
    [(empty? aloc) false]
    [else (or (blue-eyed-descendant? (first aloc))
              (blue-eyed-children? (rest aloc)))]))
```

Figure 42: Two programs for finding a blue-eyed descendant

**Exercise 15.1.4** Develop the function *eye-colors*, which consumes a parent and produces a list of all eye colors in the tree. An eye color may occur more than once in the list.

**Hint:** Use the Scheme operation append, which consumes two lists and produces the concatenation of the two lists. ∎

## 15.2 Designing Functions for Mutually Referential Definitions

The recipe for designing functions on mutually referential data definitions generalizes that for self-referential data. Indeed, it offers only two pieces of additional advice. First, we must create *several* templates simultaneously, one for each data definition. Second, we must annotate templates with self-references and CROSS-REFERENCES, that is, references among different templates. Here is a more detailed explanation of the differences:

**The data analysis and design:** If a problem mentions a number of different classes of information (of arbitrary size), we need a group of data definitions that are self-referential and that refer to each other. In these groups, we identify the self-references and the cross-references between two data definitions.

In the above example, we needed two interrelated definitions:

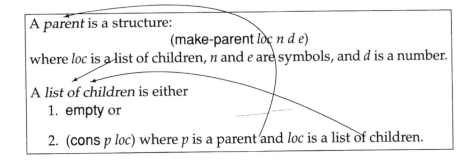

A *parent* is a structure:
            (make-parent *loc n d e*)
where *loc* is a list of children, *n* and *e* are symbols, and *d* is a number.

A *list of children* is either
    1. empty or
    2. (cons *p loc*) where *p* is a parent and *loc* is a list of children.

The first one concerns parents and another one for list of children. The first (unconditionally) defines a parent in terms of symbols, numbers, and a list of children, that is, it contains a cross-reference to the second definition. This second definition is a conditional definition. Its first clause is simple; its second clause references both the definition for *parent*s and *list-of-children*.

**Contract, Purpose, Header:** To process interrelated classes of data, we typically need as many functions as there are class definitions. Hence, we must formulate as many contracts, purpose statements, and headers in parallel as there are data definitions.

**Templates:** The templates are created in parallel, following the advice concerning compound data, mixed data, and self-referential data. Finally, we must determine for each selector expression in each template whether it corresponds to a cross-reference to some definition. If so, we annotate it in the same way we annotate cross-references.

Here are the templates for our running example:

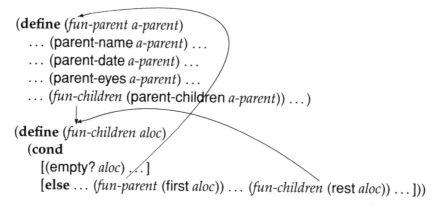

```
(define (fun-parent a-parent)
  ... (parent-name a-parent) ...
  ... (parent-date a-parent) ...
  ... (parent-eyes a-parent) ...
  ... (fun-children (parent-children a-parent)) ...)

(define (fun-children aloc)
  (cond
    [(empty? aloc) ... ]
    [else ... (fun-parent (first aloc)) ... (fun-children (rest aloc)) ... ]))
```

The *fun-parent* template is unconditional because the data definition for *parent*s does not contain any clauses. It contains a cross-reference to the second template: to process the *children* field of a *parent* structure. By the same rules, *fun-children* is conditional. The second **cond**-clause contains one self-reference, for the rest of the list, and one cross-reference for the first item of the list, which is a *parent* structure.

A comparison of the data definitions and the templates shows how analogous the two are. To emphasize the similarity in self-references and cross-references, the data definitions and templates have been annotated with arrows. It is easy to see how corresponding arrows have the same origin and destination in the two pictures.

**The body:** As we proceed to create the final definitions, we start with a template or a **cond**-clause that does not contain self-references to the template and cross-references to other templates. The results are typically easy to formulate for such templates or **cond**-clauses.

The rest of this step proceeds as before. When we deal with other clauses or functions, we remind ourselves what each expression in the template computes, assuming that *all* functions already work as specified in the contracts. Then we decide how to combine these pieces of data into a final answer. As we do that, we must not forget the guidelines concerning the composition of complex functions (sections 7.3 and 12).

Figure 43 summarizes the extended design recipe.

| Phase | Goal | Activity |
|---|---|---|
| Data Analysis and Design | to formulate a group of related data definitions | develop a group of mutually recursive data definitions • at least one definition or one alternative in a definition must refer to basic data • *explicitly identify all references among the data definitions* |
| Template | to formulate a group of function outlines | develop *as many templates as there are data definitions* simultaneously • develop each templates according to the rules for compound and/or mixed data definitions as appropriate • annotate the templates with recursions and cross-applications to match the (cross-)references in the data definitions |
| Body | to define a group of functions | formulate a Scheme expression for each template, and for each **cond**-clause in a template • explain what each expression in each template computes • use additional auxiliary functions where necessary |

Figure 43: Designing groups of functions for groups of data definitions
the essential steps; for others see figures 4 (pg. 21), 12 (pg. 71), and 18 (pg. 89)

## 15.3   Extended Exercise: More on Web Pages

With mutually referential data definitions we can represent Web pages in a more accurate manner than in section 14.3. Here is the basic structure definition:

(**define-struct** *wp* (*header body*))

The two fields contain the two essential pieces of data in a Web page: a *header* and a *body*. The data definition specifies that a body is a list of words and Web pages:

---

A *Web-page* (short: *WP*) is a structure:
(make-wp *h p*)
where *h* is a symbol and *p* is a (Web) document.

A *(Web) document* is either

1. empty,

2. (cons *s p*)
   where *s* is a symbol and *p* is a document, or

3. (cons *w p*)
   where *w* is a Web page and *p* is a document.

---

## Exercises

**Exercise 15.3.1** Develop the function *size*, which consumes a Web page and produces the number of symbols (words) it contains. ∎

**Exercise 15.3.2** Develop the function *wp-to-file*. The function consumes a Web page and produces a list of symbols. The list contains all the words in a body and all the headers of embedded Web pages. The bodies of immediately embedded Web pages are ignored. ∎

**Exercise 15.3.3** Develop the function *occurs*. It consumes a symbol and a Web page and determines whether the former occurs anywhere in the latter, including the embedded Web pages. ∎

**Exercise 15.3.4** Develop the program *find*. The function consumes a Web page and a symbol. It produces false, if the symbol does not occur in the body of the page or its embedded Web pages. If the symbol occurs at least once, it produces a list of the headers that are encountered on the way to the symbol.

**Hint:** Define an auxiliary like *find* that produces only true when a Web page contains the desired word. Use it to define *find*. Alternatively, use boolean? to determine whether a natural recursion of *find* produced a list or a boolean. Then compute the result again. We will discuss this second technique, called backtracking, in the intermezzo at the end of this part. ∎

# 16   Development through Iterative Refinement

When we develop real functions, we are often confronted with the task of designing a data representation for complicated forms of information. The best strategy to approach this task is apply a well-known scientific technique: ITERATIVE REFINEMENT. A scientist's problem is to represent a part of the real world using mathematics. The result of the effort is called a MODEL. The scientist then tests the model in many ways, in particular by predicting certain properties of events. If the model truly captured the essential elements of the real world, the prediction will be accurate; otherwise, there will be discrepancies between the predictions and the actual outcomes. For example, a physicist may start by representing a jet plane as a point and by predicting its movement in a straight line using Newton's equations. Later, if there is a need to understand the plane's friction, the physicist may add certain aspects of the jet plane's contour to the model. In general, a scientist refines a model and retests its usefulness until it is sufficiently accurate.

A programmer or a computing scientist should proceed like a scientist. Since the representation of data plays a central role in the work of a programmer, the key is to find an accurate data representation of the real-world information. The best way to get there in complicated situations is to develop the representation in an iterative manner, starting with the essential elements and adding more attributes when the current model is fully understood.

In this book, we have encountered iterative refinement in many of our extended exercises. For example, the exercise on moving pictures started with simple circles and rectangles; later on we developed programs for moving entire lists of shapes. Similarly, we first introduced Web pages as a list of words and embedded Web pages; in section 15.3 we refined the representation of embedded Web pages. For all of these exercises, however, the refinement was built into the presentation.

This section illustrates iterative refinement as a principle of program development. The goal is to model a file system. A file system is that part of the computer that remembers programs and data when the computer is turned off. We first discuss files in more detail and then iteratively develop three data representations. The last part of the section suggests some programming exercises for the final model. We will use iterative refinement again in later sections.

## 16.1  Data Analysis

When we turn a computer off, it should remember the functions and the data we worked on. Otherwise we have to reenter everything when we turn it on again. Things that a computer is to remember for a long time are put into *files*. A file is a sequence of small pieces of data. For our purposes, a file resembles a list; we ignore why and how a computer stores a file in a permanent manner.

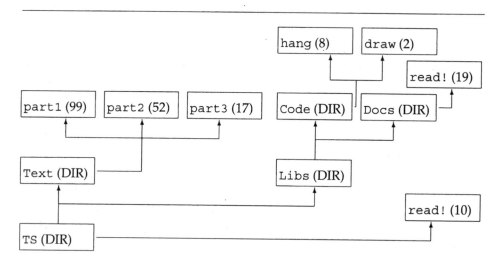

Figure 44: A sample directory tree

It is more important to us that, on most computer systems, the collection of files is organized in *directories*.[40] Roughly speaking, a directory contains some files and some more directories. The latter are called subdirectories and may contain yet more subdirectories and files, and so on. The entire collection is collectively called a *file system* or a *directory tree*.

Figure 44 contains a graphical sketch of a small directory tree.[41] The tree's *root directory* is TS. It contains one file, called read!, and two subdirectories, called Text and Libs. The first subdirectory, Text, contains only three files; the latter, Libs, contains only two subdirectories, each of which contains at least one file. Each box has one of two annotations. A directory is annotated with DIR, and a file is annotated with a number, which signifies the file's size. Altogether TS contains seven files and consists of five (sub)directories.

## Exercises

**Exercise 16.1.1** How many times does a file name read! occur in the directory tree TS? What is the total size of all the files in the tree? How deep is the tree (how many levels does it contain)? ∎

## 16.2   Defining Data Classes and Refining Them

Let's develop a data representation for file systems using the method of iterative refinement. The first decision we need to make is what to focus on and what to ignore.

Consider the directory tree in figure 44 and let's imagine how it is created. When a user first creates a directory, it is empty. As time goes by, the user adds files and directories. In general, a user refers to files by names but thinks of directories as containers of other things.

**Model 1**: Our thought experiment suggests that our first and most primitive model should focus on files as atomic entities, say, a symbol that represents a file's name, and on the directories' nature as containers. More concretely, we should think of a directory as just a list that contains files and directories.

---

[40]On some computers, a directory is called a *folder*.

[41]The picture explains why computer scientists call such directories trees.

All of this suggests the following two data definitions:

---

A *file* is a symbol.

---

A *directory* (short: *dir*) is either

1. empty;

2. (cons *f d*) where *f* is a *file* and *d* is a *dir*; or

3. (cons *d1 d2*) where *d1* and *d2* are *dir*s.

---

The first data definition says that files are represented by their names. The second one captures how a directory is gradually constructed by adding files and directories.

A closer look at the second data definition shows that the class of directories is the class of Web pages of section 14.3. Hence we can reuse the template for Web-page processing functions to process directory trees. If we were to write a function that consumes a directory (tree) and counts how many files are contained, it would be identical to a function that counts the number of words in a Web tree.

**Exercises**

**Exercise 16.2.1** Translate the file system in figure 44 into a Scheme representation according to model 1. ∎

**Exercise 16.2.2** Develop the function *how-many*, which consumes a *dir* and produces the number of files in the *dir* tree. ∎

**Model 2**: While the first data definition is familiar to us and easy to use, it obscures the nature of directories. In particular, it hides the fact that a directory is not just a collection of files and directories but has several interesting attributes. To model directories in a more faithful manner, we must introduce a structure that collects all relevant properties of a directory. Here is a minimal structure definition:

(**define-struct** *dir* (*name content*))

It suggests that a directory has a name and a content; other attributes can now be added as needed.

The intention of the new definition is that a directory has two attributes: a name, which is a symbol, and a content, which is a list of files and directories. This, in turn, suggests the following data definitions:

---

A *directory* (short: *dir*) is a structure:
$$(\text{make-dir } n \ c)$$
where $n$ is a symbol and $c$ is a list of files and directories.

A *list-of-files-and-directories* (short: *LOFD*) is either

1. empty;

2. (cons $f$ $d$) where $f$ is a file and $d$ is a *LOFD*; or

3. (cons $d1$ $d2$) where $d1$ is a *dir* and $d2$ is a *LOFD*.

---

Since the data definition for *dir* refers to the definition for *LOFDs*, and the definition for *LOFDs* refers back to that of *dirs*, the two are mutually recursive definitions and must be introduced together.

Roughly speaking, the two definitions are related like those of *parent* and *list-of-children* in section 15.1. This, in turn, means that the design recipe for programming from section 15.2 directly applies to *dirs* and *LOFDs*. More concretely, to design a function that processes *dirs*, we must develop templates for *dir*-processing functions and *LOFD*-processing functions **in parallel**.

---

### Exercises

**Exercise 16.2.3** Show how to model a directory with two more attributes: a size and a systems attribute. The former measures how much space the directory itself (as opposed to its files and subdirectories) consumes; the latter specifies whether the directory is recognized by the operating system. ∎

**Exercise 16.2.4** Translate the file system in figure 44 into a Scheme representation according to model 2. ∎

**Exercise 16.2.5** Develop the function *how-many*, which consumes a *dir* according to model 2 and produces the number of files in the *dir* tree. ∎

**Model 3**: The second data definition refined the first one with the introduction of attributes for directories. Files also have attributes. To model those, we proceed just as above. First, we define a structure for files:

(**define-struct** *file* (*name size content*))

Second, we provide a data definition:

---

A *file* is a structure:

(make-file *n s x*)

where *n* is a symbol, *s* is a number, and *x* is some Scheme value.

---

For now, we think of the *content* field of a file as set to empty. Later, we will discuss how to get access to the data in a file.

Finally, let's split the *content* field of *dir*s into two pieces: one for a list of files and one for a list of subdirectories. The data definition for a list of files is straightforward and relies on nothing but the definition for *file*s:

---

A *list-of-files* is either

1. empty, or

2. (cons *s lof*) where *s* is a *file* and *lof* is a list of files.

---

In contrast, the data definitions for *dir*s and its list of subdirectories still refer to each other and must therefore be introduced together. Of course, we first need a structure definition for *dir*s that has a field for files and another one for subdirectories:

(**define-struct** *dir* (*name dirs files*))

Here are the data definitions:

---

A *dir* is a structure:

(make-dir *n ds fs*)

where *n* is a symbol, *ds* is a list of directories, and *fs* is a list of files.

A *list-of-directories* is either

1. empty or

2. (cons *s lod*) where *s* is a *dir* and *lod* is a list of directories.

---

This third model (or data representation) of a directory hierarchy captures the nature of a file system as a user typically perceives it. With two structure definitions and four data definitions, it is, however, far more complicated than the first model. But, by starting with a the simple representation of the first model and refining it step by step, we have gained a good understanding of how to work with this complex web of classes. It is now our job to use the design recipe from section 15.2 for developing functions on this set of data definitions. Otherwise, we cannot hope to understand our functions at all.

## 16.3   Refining Functions and Programs

The goal of the following sequence of exercises is to develop several common utility functions for directory and file systems, using our third and most refined model. Even though these functions process Scheme-based representations of files and directories, they give us a good idea how such real-world programs work.

---

**Exercises**

**Exercise 16.3.1** Translate the file system in figure 44 into a Scheme representation. Remember to use empty for the content of the files. ∎
     To make the exercise more realistic, DrScheme supports the teachpack **dir.ss**. It introduces the two necessary structure definitions and a function to create representations of directories according to our third model:

> ;; *create-dir : string → dir*
> ;; to create a representation of the directory that *a-path* specifies:
> ;; 1. Windows: (*create-dir* "c:\\windows")
> ;; 2. Mac: (*create-dir* "My Disk:")
> ;; 3. Unix: (*create-dir* "/home/scheme/")
> (**define** (*create-dir a-path*) ... )

Use the function to create some small and large examples based on the directories in a real computer. **Warning**: For large directory trees, DrScheme may need a lot of time to build a representation. Use *create-dir* on small directory trees first. Do **not** define your own *dir* structures.

**Exercise 16.3.2** Develop the function *how-many*, which consumes a *dir* (according to model 3) and produces the number of files in the *dir* tree. Test the function on the directories created in exercise 16.3.1. Why are we confident that the function produces correct results? ∎

**Exercise 16.3.3** Develop the function *du-dir*. The function consumes a directory and computes the total size of all the files in the entire directory tree. This function approximates a true disk-usage meter in that it assumes that directories don't require storage.

Refine the function to compute approximate sizes for subdirectories. Let's assume that storing a file and a directory in a *dir* structure costs 1 storage unit. ∎

**Exercise 16.3.4** Develop the function *find?*, which consumes a *dir* and a file name and determines whether or not a file with this name occurs in the directory tree.

**Challenge**: Develop the function *find*. It consumes a directory *d* and a file name *f*. If (*find? d f*) is true, it produces a path to the file; otherwise it produces false. A path is a list of directory names. The first one is that of the given directory; the last one is that of the subdirectory whose *files* list contains *f*. For example:

```
(find TS 'part3)
;; expected value:
(list 'TS 'Text)
```

```
(find TS 'read!)
;; expected value:
(list 'TS)
```

assuming *TS* is **defin**ed to be the directory in figure 44.

Which read! file in figure 44 should *find* discover? Generalize the function to return a list of paths if the file name occurs more than once. Each path should lead to a different occurrence, and there should be a path for each occurrence. ∎

# 17   Processing Two Complex Pieces of Data

On occasion, a function consumes two arguments that belong to classes with non-trivial data definitions. In some cases, one of the arguments should be treated as if it were atomic; a precisely formulated purpose statement typically clarifies this. In other cases, the two arguments must be processed in lockstep. Finally, in a few rare cases, the function must take into account all possible cases and process the arguments accordingly. This section illustrates the three cases with examples and provides an augmented design recipe for the last one. The last section discusses the equality of compound data and its relationship to testing; it is essential for automating test suites for functions.

## 17.1   Processing Two Lists Simultaneously: Case 1

Consider the following contract, purpose statement, and header:

> ;; *replace-eol-with : list-of-numbers list-of-numbers* → *list-of-numbers*
> ;; to construct a new list by replacing empty in alon1 with alon2
> (**define** (*replace-eol-with alon1 alon2*) ...)

The contract says that the function consumes two lists, which we haven't seen in the past. Let's see how the design recipe works in this case.

First, we make up examples. Suppose the first input is empty. Then *replace-eol-with* should produce the second argument, no matter what it is:

> (*replace-eol-with* empty $L$)
> = $L$

In this equation, $L$ stands for an arbitrary list of numbers. Now suppose the first argument is not empty. Then the purpose statement requires that we replace empty at the end of *alon1* with *alon2*:

> (*replace-eol-with* (cons 1 empty) $L$)
> ;; expected value:
> (cons 1 $L$)

> (*replace-eol-with* (cons 2 (cons 1 empty)) $L$)
> ;; expected value:
> (cons 2 (cons 1 $L$))

> (*replace-eol-with* (cons 2 (cons 11 (cons 1 empty))) $L$)
> ;; expected value:
> (cons 2 (cons 11 (cons 1 $L$)))

Again, $L$ stands for any list of numbers in these examples.

The examples suggest that it doesn't matter what the second argument is—as long as it is a list; otherwise, it doesn't even make sense to replace

---

```
;; replace-eol-with : list-of-numbers list-of-numbers → list-of-numbers
;; to construct a new list by replacing empty in alon1 with alon2
(define (replace-eol-with alon1 alon2)
  (cond
    ((empty? alon1) alon2)
    (else (cons (first alon1) (replace-eol-with (rest alon1) alon2)))))
```

Figure 45: The complete definition of *replace-eol-with*

---

empty with the second argument. This implies that the template should be
that of a list-processing function with respect to the first argument:

```
(define (replace-eol-with alon1 alon2)
  (cond
    ((empty? alon1) ...)
    (else ... (first alon1) ... (replace-eol-with (rest alon1) alon2) ... )))
```

The second argument is treated as it were an atomic piece of data.

Let's fill the gaps in the template, following the design recipe and using
our examples. If *alon1* is empty, *replace-eol-with* produces *alon2* according
to our examples. For the second **cond**-clause, when *alon1* is not empty, we
must proceed by inspecting the available expressions:

1. (first *alon1*) evaluates to the first item on the list, and

2. (*replace-eol-with* (rest *alon1*) *alon2*) replaces empty in (rest *alon1*) with
   *alon2*.

To gain a better understanding of what this means, consider one of the
examples:

```
(replace-eol-with (cons 2 (cons 11 (cons 1 empty))) L)
;; expected value:
(cons 2 (cons 11 (cons 1 L)))
```

Here (first *alon1*) is 2, (rest *alon1*) is (cons 11 (cons 1 empty)), and (*replace-
eol-with* (rest *alon1*) *alon2*) is (cons 11 (cons 1 *alon2*)). We can combine 2 and
the latter with cons and can thus obtain the desired result. More generally,

```
(cons (first alon1) (replace-eol-with (rest alon1) alon2))
```

is the answer in the second **cond**-clause. Figure 45 contains the complete
definition.

## Exercises

**Exercise 17.1.1** In several exercises, we have used the Scheme operation append, which consumes three lists and juxtaposes their items:

```
(append (list 'a) (list 'b 'c) (list 'd 'e 'f))
;; expected value:
(list 'a 'b 'c 'd 'e 'f)
```

Use *replace-eol-with* to define *our-append*, which acts just like Scheme's append. ∎

**Exercise 17.1.2** Develop *cross*. The function consumes a list of symbols and a list of numbers and produces all possible pairs of symbols and numbers. Example:

```
(cross '(a b c) '(1 2))
;; expected value:
(list (list 'a 1) (list 'a 2) (list 'b 1) (list 'b 2) (list 'c 1) (list 'c 2))
```

∎

## 17.2   Processing Two Lists Simultaneously: Case 2

In section 10.1, we developed the function *hours→ wages* for the computation of weekly wages. It consumed a list of numbers—hours worked per week—and produced a list of weekly wages. We had based the function on the simplifying assumption that all employees received the same pay rate. Even a small company, however, employs people at different rate levels. Typically, the company's accountant also maintains two collections of information: a permanent one that, among other things, includes an employee's personal pay-rate, and a temporary one that records how much time an employee has worked during the past week.

The revised problem statement means that the function should consume *two* lists. To simplify the problem, let us assume that the lists are just lists of numbers, pay rates and weekly hours. Then here is the problem statement:

*;; hours→ wages : list-of-numbers list-of-numbers → list-of-numbers*
*;; to construct a new list by multiplying the corresponding items on*
*;; alon1* and *alon2*
*;;* ASSUMPTION: the two lists are of equal length
(**define** (*hours→ wages alon1 alon2*) ...)

We can think of *alon1* as the list of pay-rates and of *alon2* as the list of hours worked per week. To get the list of weekly wages, we must multiply the corresponding numbers in the two input lists.

Let's look at some examples:

(*hours→ wages* empty empty)
;; expected value:
empty

(*hours→ wages* (cons 5.65 empty) (cons 40 empty))
;; expected value:
(cons 226.0 empty)

(*hours→ wages* (cons 5.65 (cons 8.75 empty))
                   (cons 40.0 (cons 30.0 empty))))
;; expected value:
(cons 226.0 (cons 262.5 empty))

For all three examples the function is applied to two lists of equal length. As stated in the addendum to the purpose statement, the function assumes this and, indeed, using the function makes no sense if the condition is violated.

The condition on the inputs can also be exploited for the development of the template. Put more concretely, the condition says that (empty? *alon1*) is true if, and only if, (empty? *alon2*) is true; and furthermore, (cons? *alon1*) is true if, and only if, (cons? *alon2*) is true. In other words, the condition simplifies the design of the template's **cond**-structure, because it says the template is similar to that of a plain list-processing function:

(**define** (*hours→ wages alon1 alon2*)
  (**cond**
    ((empty? *alon1*) ...)
    (**else** ... )))

In the first **cond**-clause, both *alon1* and *alon2* are empty. Hence no selector expressions are needed. In the second clause, both *alon1* and *alon2* are constructed lists, which means we need four selector expressions:

```
(define (hours→ wages alon1 alon2)
  (cond
    ((empty? alon1) ...)
    (else
      ... (first alon1) ... (first alon2) ...
      ... (rest alon1) ... (rest alon2) ... )))
```

Finally, because the last two are lists of equal length, they make up a natural candidate for the natural recursion of *hours→ wages*:

```
(define (hours→ wages alon1 alon2)
  (cond
    ((empty? alon1) ...)
    (else
      ... (first alon1) ... (first alon2) ...
      ... (hours→ wages (rest alon1) (rest alon2)) ... )))
```

The only unusual aspect of this template is that the recursive application consists of two expressions, both selector expressions for the two arguments. But, as we have seen, the idea is easily explicable owing to the assumption that *alon1* and *alon2* are of equal length.

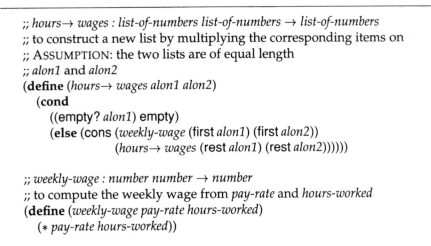

```
;; hours→ wages : list-of-numbers list-of-numbers → list-of-numbers
;; to construct a new list by multiplying the corresponding items on
;; ASSUMPTION: the two lists are of equal length
;; alon1 and alon2
(define (hours→ wages alon1 alon2)
  (cond
    ((empty? alon1) empty)
    (else (cons (weekly-wage (first alon1) (first alon2))
                (hours→ wages (rest alon1) (rest alon2))))))

;; weekly-wage : number number → number
;; to compute the weekly wage from pay-rate and hours-worked
(define (weekly-wage pay-rate hours-worked)
  (* pay-rate hours-worked))
```

Figure 46: The complete definition of *hours→wage*

To define the function from here, we follow the design recipe. The first example implies that the answer for the first **cond**-clause is empty. In the second one, we have three values available:

1. (first *alon1*) evaluates to the first item on the list of pay-rates;

2. (first *alon2*) evaluates to the first item on the list of hours worked; and

3. (*hours→ wages* (rest *alon1*) (rest *alon2*)) computes the list of weekly wages for the remainders of *alon1* and *alon2*.

We merely need to combine these values to get the final answer. More specifically, given the purpose statement, we must compute the weekly wage for the first employee and construct a list from that wage and the rest of the wages. This suggests the following answer for the second **cond**-clause:

```
(cons (weekly-wage (first alon1) (first alon2))
      (hours→ wages (rest alon1) (rest alon2)))
```

The auxiliary function *weekly-wage* consumes the two first items and computes the weekly wage. Figure 46 contains the complete definitions.

## Exercises

**Exercise 17.2.1** In the real world, *hours→ wages* consumes lists of employee structures and lists of work structures. An employee structure contains an employee's name, social security number, and pay rate. A work structure contains an employee's name and the number of hours worked in a week. The result is a list of structures that contain the name of the employee and the weekly wage.

Modify the function in figure 46 so that it works on these classes of data. Provide the necessary structure definitions and data definitions. Use the design recipe to guide the modification process. ∎

**Exercise 17.2.2** Develop the function *zip*, which combines a list of names and a list phone numbers into a list of phone records. Assuming the following structure definition:

(**define-struct** *phone-record* (*name number*)) ,

a phone record is constructed with (make-phone-record *s n*) where *s* is a symbol and *n* is a number. Assume the lists are of equal length. Simplify the definition, if possible. ∎

## 17.3    Processing Two Lists Simultaneously: Case 3

Here is a third problem statement, given as in the form of a function contract, purpose statement, and header:

> ;; *list-pick : list-of-symbols* **N**[>= 1] → *symbol*
> ;; to determine the *n*th symbol from *alos*, counting from 1;
> ;; signals an error if there is no *n*th item
> (**define** (*list-pick alos n*) ... )

That is, the problem is to develop a function that consumes a natural number and a list of symbols. Both belong to classes with complex data definitions, though, unlike for the previous two problems, the classes are distinct. Figure 47 recalls the two definitions.

---

**The data definitions:**

A *natural number [>= 1]* (**N**[>= 1]) is either

1.  1 or

2.  (**add1** *n*) if *n* is a **N**[>= 1].

A *list-of-symbols* is either

1.  the empty list, **empty**, or

2.  (**cons** *s lof*) where *s* is a symbol and *lof* is a list of symbols.

Figure 47: Data definitions for *list-pick*

---

Because the problem is non-standard, we should ensure that our examples cover all important cases. We usually accomplish this goal by picking one item per clause in the definition and choosing elements from basic forms of data on a random basis. In this example, this procedure implies that we pick at least two elements from *list-of-symbols* and two from **N**[>= 1]. Let's choose **empty** and (**cons** 'a **empty**) for the former, and 1 and 3 for the latter. But two choices per argument means four examples total; after all, there is no immediately obvious connection between the two arguments and no restriction in the contract:

(*list-pick* empty 1)
;; expected behavior:
(error 'list-pick "...")

(*list-pick* (cons 'a empty) 1)
;; expected value:
'a

(*list-pick* empty 3)
;; expected behavior:
(error 'list-pick "...")

(*list-pick* (cons 'a empty) 3)
;; expected behavior:
(error 'list-pick "...")

Only one of the four results is a symbol; in the other cases, we see an error, indicating that the list doesn't contain enough items.

The discussion on examples indicates that there are indeed four possible, independent cases that we must consider for the design of the function. We can discover the four cases by arranging the necessary conditions in a table format:

|            | (empty? *alos*) | (cons? *alos*) |
|------------|-----------------|----------------|
| (= *n* 1)  |                 |                |
| (> *n* 1)  |                 |                |

The horizontal dimension of the table lists those questions that *list-pick* must ask about the list argument; the vertical dimension lists the questions about the natural number. Furthermore, the partitioning of the table yields four squares. Each square represents the case when both the condition on the horizontal and the one on the vertical are true. We can express this fact with **and**-expressions in the squares:

|            | (empty? *alos*)                  | (cons? *alos*)                  |
|------------|----------------------------------|---------------------------------|
| (= *n* 1)  | (**and** (= *n* 1) (empty? *alos*)) | (**and** (= *n* 1) (cons? *alos*)) |
| (> *n* 1)  | (**and** (> *n* 1) (empty? *alos*)) | (**and** (> *n* 1) (cons? *alos*)) |

It is straightforward to check that for any given pair of arguments exactly one of the four composite claims must evaluate to true.

Using our cases analysis, we can now design the first part of the template, the conditional expression:

(**define** (*list-pick alos n*)
  (**cond**
    [(**and** (= *n* 1) (empty? *alos*)) ... ]
    [(**and** (> *n* 1) (empty? *alos*)) ... ]
    [(**and** (= *n* 1) (cons? *alos*)) ... ]
    [(**and** (> *n* 1) (cons? *alos*)) ... ]))

The **cond**-expression asks all four questions, thus distinguishing all possibilities. Next we must add selector expressions to each **cond**-clause if possible:

(**define** (*list-pick alos n*)
  (**cond**
    [(**and** (= *n* 1) (empty? *alos*))
     ... ]
    [(**and** (> *n* 1) (empty? *alos*))
     ... (sub1 *n*) ... ]
    [(**and** (= *n* 1) (cons? *alos*))
     ... (first *alos*) ... (rest *alos*)... ]
    [(**and** (> *n* 1) (cons? *alos*))
     ... (sub1 *n*) ... (first *alos*) ... (rest *alos*) ... ]))

For *n*, a natural number, the template contains at most one selector expression, which determines the predecessor of *n*. For *alos*, it might contain two. In those cases where either (= *n* 1) or (empty? *alos*) holds, one of the two arguments is atomic and there is no need for a corresponding selector expression.

The final step of the template construction demands that we annotate the template with recursions where the results of selector expressions belong to the same class as the inputs. In the template for *list-pick*, this makes sense only in the last **cond**-clause, which contains both a selector expression for **N**[>= 1] and one for *list-of-symbols*. All other clauses contain at most one relevant selector expression. It is, however, unclear how to form the natural recursions. If we disregard the purpose of the function, and the template construction step asks us to do just that, there are three possible recursions:

1. (*list-pick* (rest *alos*) (sub1 *n*))

2. (*list-pick alos* (sub1 *n*))

3. (*list-pick* (rest *alos*) *n*)

Since we cannot know which one matters or whether all three matter, we move on to the next development stage.

---

```
;; list-pick : list-of-symbols N[>= 1] → symbol
;; to determine the nth symbol from alos, counting from 1;
;; signals an error if there is no nth item
(define (list-pick alos n)
  (cond
    [(and (= n 1) (empty? alos)) (error 'list-pick "list too short")]
    [(and (> n 1) (empty? alos)) (error 'list-pick "list too short")]
    [(and (= n 1) (cons? alos)) (first alos)]
    [(and (> n 1) (cons? alos)) (list-pick (rest alos) (sub1 n))]]))
```

Figure 48: The complete definition of *list-pick*

---

Following the design recipe, let us analyze each **cond**-clause in the template and decide what a proper answer is:

1. If (**and** (= *n* 1) (empty? *alos*)) holds, *list-pick* was asked to pick the first item from an empty list, which is impossible. The answer must be an application of error.

2. If (**and** (> *n* 1) (empty? *alos*)) holds, *list-pick* was again asked to pick an item from an empty list. The answer is also an error.

3. If (**and** (= *n* 1) (cons? *alos*)) holds, *list-pick* is supposed to produce the first item from some list. The selector expression (first *alos*) reminds us how to get this item. It is the answer.

4. For the final clause, if (**and** (> *n* 1) (cons? *alos*)) holds, we must analyze what the selector expressions compute:

   (a) (first *alos*) selects the first item from the list of symbols;

   (b) (rest *alos*) is the rest of the list; and

   (c) (sub1 *n*) is one less that the original given list index.

Let us consider an example to illustrate the meaning of these expressions. Suppose *list-pick* is applied to (cons 'a (cons 'b empty)) and 2:

$$(\textit{list-pick} \ (\text{cons } 'a \ (\text{cons } 'b \ \text{empty})) \ 2)$$

The answer must be 'b, (first *alos*) is 'a, and (sub1 *n*) is 1. Here is what the three natural recursions would compute with these values:

(a) (*list-pick* (cons 'b empty) 1) produces 'b, the desired answer;

(b) (*list-pick* (cons 'a (cons 'b empty)) 1) evaluates to 'a, which is a symbol, but the the wrong answer for the original problem; and

(c) (*list-pick* (cons 'b empty) 2) signals an error because the index is larger than the length of the list.

This suggests that we use (*list-pick* (rest *alos*) (sub1 *n*)) as the answer in the last **cond**-clause. But, example-based reasoning is often treacherous, so we should try to understand why the expression works in general.

Recall that, according to the purpose statement,

$$(\textit{list-pick} \ (\text{rest } \textit{alos}) \ (\text{sub1 } n))$$

picks the $(n-1)$st item from (rest *alos*). In other words, for the second application, we have decreased the index by 1, shortened the list by *one* item, and now look for an item. Clearly, the second application always produces the same answer as the first one, assuming *alos* and *n* are "compound" values. Hence our choice for the last clause is truly justified.

## Exercises

**Exercise 17.3.1** Develop *list-pick0*, which picks items from a list like *list-pick* but starts counting at 0.
Examples:

```
(symbol=? (list-pick0 (list 'a 'b 'c 'd) 3)
          'd)
```

```
(list-pick0 (list 'a 'b 'c 'd) 4)
;; expected behavior:
(error 'list-pick0 "the list is too short")
```

## 17.4   Function Simplification

The *list-pick* function in figure 48 is more complicated than necessary. Both the first and the second **cond**-clause produce the same answer: an error. In other words, if either

    (**and** ($=$ *n* 1) (empty? *alos*))

or

    (**and** ($>$ *n* 1) (empty? *alos*))

evaluates to **true**, the answer is an error. We can translate this observation into a simpler **cond**-expression:

```
(define (list-pick alos n)
  (cond
    [(or (and (= n 1) (empty? alos))
         (and (> n 1) (empty? alos))) (error 'list-pick "list too short")]
    [(and (= n 1) (cons? alos)) (first alos)]
    [(and (> n 1) (cons? alos)) (list-pick (rest alos) (sub1 n))]))
```

The new expression is a direct transliteration of our English observation.

    To simplify this function even more, we need to get acquainted with an algebraic law concerning booleans:

```
  (or (and condition1 a-condition)
      (and condition2 a-condition))
= (and (or condition1 condition2)
       a-condition)
```

The law is called de Morgan's law of distributivity. Applying it to our function yields the following:

```
(define (list-pick n alos)
  (cond
    [(and (or (= n 1) (> n 1))
          (empty? alos)) (error 'list-pick "list too short")]
    [(and (= n 1) (cons? alos)) (first alos)]
    [(and (> n 1) (cons? alos)) (list-pick (rest alos) (sub1 n))]))
```

Now consider the first part of the condition: (**or** ($=$ *n* 1) ($>$ *n* 1)). Because *n* belongs to **N**[$>=$ 1], the condition is always true. But, if we replace it with **true** we get

```
(and true
     (empty? alos))
```

which is clearly equivalent to (empty? *alos*). In other words, the function can be written as

    (**define** (*list-pick alos n*)
      (**cond**
        [(empty? *alos*) (error 'list-pick "list too short")]
        [(**and** (= *n* 1) (cons? *alos*)) (first *alos*)]
        [(**and** (> *n* 1) (cons? *alos*)) (*list-pick* (rest *alos*) (sub1 *n*))]))

which is already significantly simpler than that in figure 48.

Still, we can do even better than that. The first condition in the latest version of *list-pick* filters out all those cases when *alos* is empty. Hence (cons? *alos*) in the next two clauses is always going to evaluate to true. If we replace the condition with true and simplify the **and**-expressions, we get the simplest possible version of *list-pick*, which is displayed in figure 49. While this last function is simpler than the original, it is important to understand that we designed both the original and the simplified version in a systematic manner and that we can therefore trust both. If we try to find the simple versions directly, we sooner or later fail to consider a case and produce flawed functions.

---

;; *list-pick : list-of-symbols* **N**[>= 1] → *symbol*
;; to determine the *n*th symbol from *alos*, counting from 1;
;; signals an error if there is no *n*th item
(**define** (*list-pick alos n*)
    (**cond**
      [(empty? *alos*) (error 'list-pick "list too short")]
      [(= *n* 1) (first *alos*)]
      [(> *n* 1) (*list-pick* (rest *alos*) (sub1 *n*))]))

Figure 49: The simplified definition of *list-pick*

---

## Exercises

**Exercise 17.4.1** Develop the function *replace-eol-with* following the strategy of section 17.2. Then simplify it systematically. ∎

**Exercise 17.4.2** Simplify the function *list-pick0* from exercise 17.3.1 or explain why it can't be simplified. ∎

## 17.5   Designing Functions that Consume Two Complex Inputs

On occasion, we will encounter problems that require functions on two complex classes of inputs. The most interesting situation occurs when both inputs are of unknown size. As we have seen in the first three subsections, we may have to deal with such functions in three different ways.

The proper approach to this problem is to follow the general design recipe. In particular, we must conduct a data analysis and we must define the relevant classes of data. Then we can state the contract and the purpose of the function, which, in turn, puts us in a position where we can think ahead. Before we continue from this point, we should decide which one of the following three situations we are facing:

1. In some cases, one of the parameters plays a dominant role. Conversely, we can think of one of the parameters as an atomic piece of data as far as the function is concerned.

2. In some other cases, the two parameters are synchronized. They must range over the same class of values, and they must have the same structure. For example, if we are given two lists, they must have the same length. If we are given two Web pages, they must have the same length, and where one of them contains an embedded page, the other one does, too. If we decide that the two parameters have this equal status and must be processed in a synchronized manner, then we can pick one of them and organize the function around it.

3. Finally, in some rare cases, there may not be any obvious connection between the two parameters. In this case, we must analyze all possible cases before we pick examples and design the template.

For the first two cases, we use an existing design recipe. The last case deserves some special consideration.

After we have decided that a function falls into the third category but before we develop examples and the function template, we develop a two-dimensional table. Here is the table for *list-pick* again:

|   |          | alos |  |
|---|----------|----------------|----------------|
|   |          | (empty? *alos*) | (cons? *alos*) |
| n | $(= n\ 1)$ | | |
|   | $(> n\ 1)$ | | |

Along the horizontal direction we enumerate the conditions that recognize the subclasses for the first parameter, and along the vertical direction we enumerate the conditions for the second parameter.

The table guides the development of both the set of function examples and the function template. As far as the examples are concerned, they must cover all possible cases. That is, there must be at least one example for each cell in the table.

As far as the template is concerned, it must have one **cond**-clause per cell. Each **cond**-clause, in turn, must contain all feasible selector expressions for both parameters. If one of the parameters is atomic, there is no need for a selector expression. Finally, instead of a single natural recursion, we might have several. For *list-pick*, we discovered three cases. In general, all possible combinations of selector expressions are candidates for a natural recursion. Because we can't know which ones are necessary and which ones aren't, we write them all down and pick the proper ones for the actual function definition.

In summary, the design of multi-parameter functions is just a variation on the old design-recipe theme. The key idea is to translate the data definitions into a table that shows all feasible and interesting combinations. The development of function examples and the template exploit the table as much as possible. Filling in the gaps in the template takes practice, just like anything else.

## 17.6 Exercises on Processing Two Complex Inputs

**Exercise 17.6.1** Develop the function *merge*. It consumes two lists of numbers, sorted in ascending order. It produces a single sorted list of numbers that contains all the numbers on both inputs lists (and nothing else). A number occurs in the output as many times as it occurs on the two input lists together.
Examples:

    (merge (list 1 3 5 7 9) (list 0 2 4 6 8))
    ;; expected value:
    (list 0 1 2 3 4 5 6 7 8 9)

    (merge (list 1 8 8 11 12) (list 2 3 4 8 13 14))
    ;; expected value:
    (list 1 2 3 4 8 8 8 11 12 13 14) ;

**Exercise 17.6.2** The goal of this exercise is to develop a version of the Hangman game of section 6.7 for words of arbitrary length.

Provide a data definition for representing words of arbitrary length with lists. A *letter* is represented with the symbols 'a through 'z plus '_.

Develop the function *reveal-list*. It consumes three arguments:

1. the *chosen* word, which is the word that we have to guess;

2. the *status* word, which states how much of the word we have guessed so far; and

3. a letter, which is our current *guess*.

It produces a new status word, that is, a word that contains ordinary letters and '_. The fields in the new status word are determined by comparing the guess with each pair of letters from the status word and the chosen word:

1. If the guess is equal to the letter in the chosen word, the guess is the corresponding letter in the new status word.

2. Otherwise, the new letter is the corresponding letter from the status word.

Test the function with the following examples:

1. (*reveal-list* (list 't 'e 'a) (list '_ 'e '_) 'u)

2. (*reveal-list* (list 'a 'l 'e) (list 'a '_ '_) 'e)

3. (*reveal-list* (list 'a 'l 'l) (list '_ '_ '_) 'l)

First determine what the result should be.

Use the teachpack **hangman.ss** and the functions *draw-next-part* (from exercise 6.7.1) and *reveal-list* to play the Hangman game. Evaluate the following expression:

(*hangman-list reveal-list draw-next-part*)

The function *hangman-list* chooses a word randomly and pops up a window with a choice menu for letters. Choose letters and, when ready, click on the Check button to see whether your guess is correct. Enjoy! ◖

**Exercise 17.6.3** In a factory, employees punch time cards as they arrive in the morning and leave in the evening. In the modern age of electronic punch cards, a punch card contains an employee number and the number of hours worked. Also, employee records always contain the name of the employee, an employee number, and a pay rate.

Develop the function *hours→ wages2*. The function consumes a list of employee records and a list of (electronic) punch cards. It computes the weekly wage for each employee by matching the employee record with a punch card based on employee numbers. If a pair is missing or if a pair's employee numbers are mismatched, the function stops with an appropriate error message. Assume that there is at most one card per employee and employee number.

**Hint:** An accountant would sort the two lists by employee number first. ■

**Exercise 17.6.4** A *linear combination* is the sum of many linear terms, that is, products of variables and numbers. The latter are called coefficients in this context. Here are some examples:

$$5 \cdot x$$
$$5 \cdot x \quad +17 \cdot y$$
$$5 \cdot x \quad +17 \cdot y + 3 \cdot z$$

In all three examples, the coefficient of $x$ is 5, that of $y$ is 17, and the one for $z$ is 3.

If we are given values for variables, we can determine the value of a polynomial. For example, if $x = 10$, the value of $5 \cdot x$ is 50; if $x = 10$ and $y = 1$, the value of $5 \cdot x + 17 \cdot y$ is 67; and if $x = 10$, $y = 1$, and $z = 2$, the value of $5 \cdot x + 17 \cdot y + 3 \cdot z$ is 73.

In the past, we would have developed functions to compute the values of linear combinations for specific values. An alternative representation is a list of its coefficients. The above combinations would be represented as:

```
(list 5)
(list 5 17)
(list 5 17 3)
```

This representation assumes that we always agree on using variables in a fixed order.

Develop the function *value*. It consumes the representation of a polynomial and a list of numbers. The lists are of equal length. It produces the value of the polynomial for these values. ■

**Exercise 17.6.5** Louise, Jane, Laura, Dana, and Mary are sisters who would like to save money and work spent on Christmas gifts. So they decide to hold a lottery that assigns to each one of them a single gift recipient. Since Jane is a computer programmer, they ask her to write a program that performs the lottery in an impartial manner. Of course, the program must not assign any of the sisters to herself.

Here is the definition of *gift-pick*. It consumes a list of distinct names (symbols) and randomly picks one of those arrangements of the list that do not agree with the original list at any position:

;; *gift-pick: list-of-names* → *list-of-names*
;; to pick a "random" non-identity arrangement of *names*
(**define** (*gift-pick names*)
  (*random-pick*
    (*non-same names* (*arrangements names*))))

Recall that *arrangements* (see exercise 12.4.2) consumes a list of symbols and produces the list of all rearrangements of the items in the list.

Develop the auxiliary functions

1. *random-pick : list-of-list-of-names* → *list-of-names*, which consumes a list of items and randomly picks one of them as the result;

2. *non-same : list-of-names list-of-list-of-names* → *list-of-list-of-names*, which consumes a list of names $L$ and a list of arrangements and produces the list of those that do not agree with $L$ at any position.

   Two permutations agree at some position if we can extract the same name from both lists by applying first and the same number of rest operations to both. For example, (list 'a 'b 'c) and (list 'c 'a 'b) do not agree, but (list 'a 'b 'c) and (list 'c 'b 'a) agree at the second position. We can prove that by applying rest followed by first to both lists.

Follow the appropriate recipe in each case carefully.
**Hint:** Recall that (random $n$) picks a random number between 0 and $n-1$ (compare with exercise 11.3.1). ∎

**Exercise 17.6.6** Develop the function *DNAprefix*. The function takes two arguments, both lists of symbols (only 'a, 'c, 'g, and 't occur in DNA, but we can safely ignore this issue here). The first list is called a *pattern*, the second one a *search-string*. The function returns true if the pattern is a prefix of the search-string. In all other cases, the function returns false.

Examples:

   (*DNAprefix* (list 'a 't) (list 'a 't 'c))

   (not (*DNAprefix* (list 'a 't) (list 'a)))

   (*DNAprefix* (list 'a 't) (list 'a 't))

   (not (*DNAprefix* (list 'a 'c 'g 't) (list 'a 'g)))

   (not (*DNAprefix* (list 'a 'a 'c 'c) (list 'a 'c)))

Simplify *DNAprefix*, if possible.

   Modify *DNAprefix* so that it returns the first item beyond the pattern in the search-string if the pattern is a proper prefix of the search-string. If the lists do not match or if the pattern is no shorter than the search-string, the modified function should still return false. Similarly, if the lists are equally long and match, the result is still true.

Examples:

   (symbol=? (*DNAprefix* (list 'a 't) (list 'a 't 'c))
             'c)

   (not (*DNAprefix* (list 'a 't) (list 'a)))

   (*DNAprefix* (list 'a 't) (list 'a 't))

Can this variant of *DNAprefix* be simplified? If so, do it. If not, explain. ∎

## 17.7   Extended Exercise: Evaluating Scheme, Part 2

The goal of this section is to extend the evaluator of section 14.4 so that it can cope with function applications and function definitions. In other words, the new evaluator simulates what happens in DrScheme when we enter an expression in the Interactions window after clicking Execute. To make things simple, we assume that all functions in the Definitions window consume one argument.

---

## Exercises

**Exercise 17.7.1** Extend the data definition of exercise 14.4.1 so that we can represent the application of a user-defined function to an expression such as (*f* (+ 1 1)) or (* 3 (*g* 2)). The application should be represented as a structure with two fields. The first field contains the name of the function, the second one the representation of the argument expression. ∎

A full-fledged evaluator can also deal with function definitions.

**Exercise 17.7.2** Provide a structure definition and a data definition for definitions. Recall that a function definition has three essential attributes:

1. the function's name,

2. the parameter name, and

3. the function's body.

This suggests the introduction of a structure with three fields. The first two contain symbols, the last one a representation of the function's body, which is an expression.
Translate the following definitions into Scheme values:

1. (**define** (*f x*) (+ 3 *x*))

2. (**define** (*g x*) (* 3 *x*))

3. (**define** (*h u*) (*f* (* 2 *u*)))

4. (**define** (*i v*) (+ (* *v v*) (* *v v*)))

5. (**define** (*k w*) (* (*h w*) (*i w*)))

Make up more examples and translate them, too. ∎

**Exercise 17.7.3** Develop *evaluate-with-one-def*. The function consumes (the representation of) a Scheme expression and (the representation of) a single function definition, *P*.
The remaining expressions from exercise 14.4.1 are evaluated as before. For (the representation of) a variable, the function signals an error. For an application of the function *P*, *evaluate-with-one-def*

1. evaluates the argument;

2. substitutes the value of the argument for the function parameter in the function's body; and

3. evaluates the new expression via recursion. Here is a sketch:[42]

$$(\textit{evaluate-with-one-def } (\textit{subst} \ldots \ldots \ldots)$$
$$\textit{a-fun-def})$$

For all other function applications, *evaluate-with-one-def* signals an error. ∎

**Exercise 17.7.4** Develop the function *evaluate-with-defs*. The function consumes (the representation of) a Scheme expression and a list of (representations of) function definitions, *defs*. The function produces the number that DrScheme would produce if we were to evaluate the actual Scheme expression in the `Interactions` window and if the `Definitions` window contained the actual definitions.

The remaining expressions from exercise 14.4.1 are evaluated as before. For an application of the function *P*, *evaluate-with-defs*

1. evaluates the argument;

2. looks up the definition of *P* in *defs*;

3. substitutes the value of the argument for the function parameter in the function's body; and

4. evaluates the new expression via recursion.

Like DrScheme, *evaluate-with-defs* signals an error for a function application whose function name is not on the list and for (the representation of) a variable. ∎

## 17.8 Equality and Testing

Many of the functions we designed produce lists. When we test these functions, we must compare their results with the predicted value, both of which are lists. Comparing lists by hand is tedious and error-prone.

---

[42]We discuss this form of recursion in detail in part V.

Let's develop a function that consumes two lists of numbers and determines whether they are equal:

;; *list=? : list-of-numbers list-of-numbers → boolean*
;; to determine whether *a-list* and *another-list*
;; contain the same numbers in the same order
(**define** (*list=? a-list another-list*) ... )

The purpose statement refines our general claim and reminds us that, for example, shoppers may consider two lists equal if they contain the same items, regardless of the order, but programmers are more specific and include the order in the comparison. The contract and the purpose statement also show that *list=?* is a function that processes two complex values, and indeed, it is an interesting case study.

Comparing two lists means looking at each item in both lists. This rules out designing *list=?* along the lines of *replace-eol-with* in section 17.1. At first glance, there is also no connection between the two lists, which suggests that we should use the modified design recipe.

Let's start with the table:

|                          | (empty? *a-list*) | (cons? *a-list*) |
|--------------------------|-------------------|------------------|
| (empty? *another-list*)  |                   |                  |
| (cons? *another-list*)   |                   |                  |

It has four cells, which implies that we need (at least) four tests and four **cond**-clauses in the template.

Here are five tests:

(*list=?* empty empty)

(not
  (*list=?* empty (cons 1 empty)))

(not
  (*list=?* (cons 1 empty) empty))

(*list=?* (cons 1 (cons 2 (cons 3 empty)))
          (cons 1 (cons 2 (cons 3 empty))))

(not
  (*list=?* (cons 1 (cons 2 (cons 3 empty)))
            (cons 1 (cons 3 empty))))

The second and third show that *list=?* must deal with its arguments in a symmetric fashion. The last two show how *list=?* can produce true and false.

Three of the template's four **cond**-clauses contain selector expressions and one contains natural recursions:

```
(define (list=? a-list another-list)
  (cond
    [(and (empty? a-list) (empty? another-list)) ... ]
    [(and (cons? a-list) (empty? another-list))
     ... (first a-list) ... (rest a-list) ... ]
    [(and (empty? a-list) (cons? another-list))
     ... (first another-list) ... (rest another-list) ... ]
    [(and (cons? a-list) (cons? another-list))
     ... (first a-list) ... (first another-list) ...
     ... (list=? (rest a-list) (rest another-list)) ...
     ... (list=? a-list (rest another-list)) ...
     ... (list=? (rest a-list) another-list) ... ]))
```

There are three natural recursions in the fourth clause because we can pair the two selector expressions and we can pair each parameter with one selector expression.

From the template to the complete definition is only a small step. Two lists can contain the same items only if they are both empty or constructed. This immediately implies true as the answer for the first *clause* and false for the next two. In the last clause, we have two numbers, the first of both lists, and three natural recursions. We must compare the two numbers. Furthermore, *(list=? (rest a-list) (rest another-list))* computes whether the rest of the two lists are equal. The two lists are equal if, and only if, both conditions hold, which means we must combine them with an **and**:

```
(define (list=? a-list another-list)
  (cond
    [(and (empty? a-list) (empty? another-list)) true]
    [(and (cons? a-list) (empty? another-list)) false]
    [(and (empty? a-list) (cons? another-list)) false]
    [(and (cons? a-list) (cons? another-list))
     (and (= (first a-list) (first another-list))
          (list=? (rest a-list) (rest another-list)))]))
```

The other two natural recursions play no role.

Let us now take a second look at the connection between the two parameters. The first development suggests that the second parameter must have the same shape as the first one, if the two lists are to be equal. Put differently, we could develop the function based on the structure of the first parameter and check structure of the other one as needed.

The first parameter is a list of numbers, so we can reuse the template for list-processing functions:

```
(define (list=? a-list another-list)
  (cond
    [(empty? a-list) ... ]
    [(cons? a-list)
     ... (first a-list) ... (first another-list) ...
     ... (list=? (rest a-list) (rest another-list)) ... ]))
```

The only difference is that the second clause processes the second parameter in the same way as the first one. This mimics the development of *hours→ wages* in section 17.2.

Filling the gaps in this template is more difficult than for the first development of *list=?*. If *a-list* is empty, the answer depends on *another-list*. As the examples show, the answer is true if, and only if, *another-list* is also empty. Translated into Scheme this means that the answer in the first **cond**-clause is (empty? *another-list*).

If *a-list* is not empty, the template suggests that we compute the answer from

1. (first *a-list*), the first number of *a-list*;

2. (first *another-list*), the first number on *another-list*; and

3. (*list=?* (rest *a-list*) (rest *another-list*)), which determines whether the rest of the two lists are equal.

Given the purpose of the function and the examples, we now simply compare (first *a-list*) and (first *another-list*) and combine the result with the natural recursion in an **and**-expression:

```
(and (= (first a-list) (first another-list))
     (list=? (rest a-list) (rest another-list)))
```

While this step appears to be simple and straightforward, the result is an improper definition. The purpose of spelling out the conditions in a **cond**-expression is to ensure that all selector expressions are appropriate.

Nothing in the specification of *list=?*, however, suggests that *another-list* is constructed if *a-list* is constructed.

We can overcome this problem with an additional condition:

```
(define (list=? a-list another-list)
  (cond
    [(empty? a-list) (empty? another-list)]
    [(cons? a-list)
     (and (cons? another-list)
          (and (= (first a-list) (first another-list))
               (list=? (rest a-list) (rest another-list))))]))
```

The additional condition is (cons? *another-list*), which means that *list=?* produces false if (cons? *a-list*) is true and (cons? *another-list*) is empty. As the examples show, this is the desired outcome.

In summary, *list=?* shows that, on occasion, we can use more than one design recipe to develop a function. The outcomes are different, though closely related; indeed, we could prove that the two always produce the same results for the same inputs. Also, the second development benefited from the first one.

## Exercises

**Exercise 17.8.1** Test both versions of *list=?*. ∎

**Exercise 17.8.2** Simplify the first version of *list=?*. That is, merge neighboring **cond**-clauses with the same result by combining their conditions in an **or**-expression; switch **cond**-clauses as needed; and use **else** in the last clause of the final version. ∎

**Exercise 17.8.3** Develop *sym-list=?*. The function determines whether two lists of symbols are equal. ∎

**Exercise 17.8.4** Develop *contains-same-numbers*. The function determines whether two lists of numbers contain the same numbers, regardless of the ordering. Thus, for example,

(*contains-same-numbers* (list 1 2 3) (list 3 2 1))

evaluates to true. ∎

**Exercise 17.8.5** The class of numbers, symbols, and booleans are sometimes called atoms:[43]

---

An *atom* is either

1. a number

2. a boolean

3. a symbol

---

Develop the function *list-equal?*, which consumes two lists of atoms and determines whether they are equal. ∎

---

A comparison between the two versions of *list=?* suggests that the second one is easier to understand than the first. It says that two compound values are equal if the second is made from the same constructor and the components are equal. In general, this idea is a good guide for the development of other equality functions.

Let's look at an equality function for simple Web pages to confirm this conjecture:

```
;; web=? : web-page web-page → boolean
;; to determine whether a-wp and another-wp have the same tree shape
;; and contain the same symbols in the same order
(define (web=? a-wp another-wp) ...)
```

Recall the data definition for simple Web pages:

---

A *Web-page* (short: *WP*) is either

1. empty;

2. (cons *s wp*)
   where *s* is a symbol and *wp* is a Web page; or

3. (cons *ewp wp*)
   where both *ewp* and *wp* are Web pages.

---

[43]Some people also include empty and keyboard characters (*chars*).

The data definition has three clauses, which means that if we were to develop *web=?* with the modified design recipe, we would need to study nine cases. By using the insight gained from the development of *list=?* instead, we can start from the plain template for Web sites:

```
(define (web=? a-wp another-wp)
  (cond
    [(empty? a-wp) ...]
    [(symbol? (first a-wp))
     ... (first a-wp) ... (first another-wp) ...
     ... (web=? (rest a-wp) (rest another-wp)) ...]
    [else
     ... (web=? (first a-wp) (first another-wp)) ...
     ... (web=? (rest a-wp) (rest another-wp)) ...]))
```

In the second **cond**-clause, we follow the example of *hours→ wages* and *list=?* again. That is, we say that *another-wp* must have the same shape as *a-wp* if it is to be equal and process the two pages in an analogous manner. The reasoning for the third clause is similar.

As we refine this template into a full definition now, we must again add conditions on *another-wp* to ensure that the selector expressions are justified:

```
(define (web=? a-wp another-wp)
  (cond
    [(empty? a-wp) (empty? another-wp)]
    [(symbol? (first a-wp))
     (and (and (cons? another-wp) (symbol? (first another-wp)))
          (and (symbol=? (first a-wp) (first another-wp))
               (web=? (rest a-wp) (rest another-wp))))]
    [else
     (and (and (cons? another-wp) (list? (first another-wp)))
          (and (web=? (first a-wp) (first another-wp))
               (web=? (rest a-wp) (rest another-wp))))]))
```

In particular, we must ensure in the second and third clause that *another-wp* is a **constructed** list and that the first item is a symbol or a list, respectively. Otherwise the function is analogous to *list=?* and works in the same way.

### Exercises

**Exercise 17.8.6** Draw the table based on the data definition for simple Web pages. Develop (at least) one example for each of the nine cases. Test *web=?* with these examples. ∎

**Exercise 17.8.7** Develop the function *posn=?*, which consumes two binary *posn* structures and determines whether they are equal. ∎

**Exercise 17.8.8** Develop the function *tree=?*, which consumes two binary trees and determines whether they are equal. ∎

**Exercise 17.8.9** Consider the following two, mutually recursive data definitions:

---

A *Slist* is either

   1. empty

   2. (cons *s sl*) where *s* is a *Sexpr* and *sl* is a *Slist*.

A *Sexpr* is either

   1. a number

   2. a boolean

   3. a symbol

   4. a *Slist*

---

Develop the function *Slist=?*, which consumes two *Slist*s and determines whether they are equal. Like lists of numbers, two *Slist*s are equal if they contain the same item at analogous positions. ∎

---

Now that we have explored the idea of equality of values, we can return to the original motivation of the section: testing functions. Suppose we wish to test *hours→ wages* from section 17.2:

(*hours→ wages* (cons 5.65 (cons 8.75 empty))
         (cons 40 (cons 30 empty)))
= (cons 226.0 (cons 262.5 empty))

If we just type in the application into `Interactions` window or add it to the bottom of the `Definitions` window, we must compare the result and the predicted value by inspection. For short lists, like the ones above, this is feasible; for long lists, deep Web pages, or other large compound data, manual inspection is error-prone.

Using equality functions like *list=?*, we can greatly reduce the need for manual inspection of test results. In our running example, we can add the expression

(*list=?*
    (*hours→ wages* (cons 5.65 (cons 8.75 empty))
           (cons 40 (cons 30 empty)))
   (cons 226.0 (cons 262.5 empty)))

to the bottom of the `Definitions` window. When we click the `Execute` button now, we just need to make sure that all test cases produce true as their results are displayed in the `Interactions` window.

---

;; *test-hours→ wages : list-of-numbers list-of-numbers list-of-numbers → test-result*
;; to test *hours→ wages*
(**define** (*test-hours→ wages a-list another-list expected-result*)
   (**cond**
     [(*list=?* (*hours→ wages a-list another-list*) *expected-result*)
     true]
     [**else**
     (list "bad test result:" *a-list another-list expected-result*)]))

Figure 50: A test function

---

Indeed, we can go even further. We can write a test function like the one in figure 50. The class of *test-results* consists of the value true and lists of four items: the string "bad test result:" followed by three lists. Using this new auxiliary function, we can test *hours→ wages* as follows:

(*test-hours→ wages*
   (cons 5.65 (cons 8.75 empty))
   (cons 40 (cons 30 empty))
   (cons 226.0 (cons 262.5 empty)))

If something goes wrong with the test, the four-item list will stand out and specify precisely which test case failed.

**Testing with equal?:**   The designers of Scheme anticipated the need of a general equality procedure and provide:

```
;; equal? : any-value any-value → boolean
;; to determine whether two values are structurally equivalent
;; and contain the same atomic values in analogous positions
```

When equal? is applied to two lists, it compares them in the same manner as *list=?*; when it encounters a pair of structures, it compares their corresponding fields, if they are the same kind of structures; and when it consumes a pair of atomic values, it compares them with =, symbol=?, or boolean=?, whatever is appropriate.

---

GUIDELINE ON TESTING

Use equal? for testing (when comparisons of values are necessary).

---

**Unordered Lists**:   On some occasions, we use lists even though the ordering of the items doesn't play a role. For those cases, it is important to have functions such as *contains-same-numbers* (see exercise 17.8.4) if we wish to determine whether the result of some function application contains the proper items. ∎

---

### Exercises

**Exercise 17.8.10** Define a test function for *replace-eol-with* from section 17.1 using equal? and formulate the examples as test cases using this function. ∎

**Exercise 17.8.11** Define the function *test-list-pick*, which manages test cases for the *list-pick* function from section 17.3. Formulate the examples from the section as test cases using *test-list-pick*. ∎

**Exercise 17.8.12** Define *test-interpret*, which tests *interpret-with-defs* from exercise 17.7.4, using equal?. Reformulate the test cases using this function. ∎

# Intermezzo 3: Local Definitions and Lexical Scope

Programs do not just consist of single definitions. In many cases, a program requires the definition of auxiliary functions or of functions with mutual references. Indeed, as we become more experienced, we write programs that consist of numerous auxiliary functions. If we are not careful, these large collections of functions overwhelm us. As the size of our functions grows, we need to organize them so that we (and other readers) can quickly identify the relationships between parts.

This section introduces **local**, a simple construct for organizing collections of functions. With **local**, a programmer can group function definitions that belong together so that readers immediately recognize the connection between the functions. Finally, the introduction of **local** also forces us to discuss the concept of variable binding. While the variable and function definitions of Beginning Student Scheme already introduce bindings into a program, a good understanding of **local** definitions is possible only with a thorough familiarity of this concept.

## Organizing Programs with local

A **local**-expression groups together an arbitrarily long sequence of definitions similar to those found in the Definitions window. Following our established rules, we first introduce the syntax and then the semantics and pragmatics of **local**-expressions.

### Syntax of local

A **local**-expression is just another kind of expression:

$$\langle exp \rangle \quad = \quad (\textbf{local}\ (\langle def\text{-}1\rangle \ldots \langle def\text{-}n\rangle)\ \langle exp \rangle)$$

As usual, $\langle def\text{-}1\rangle \ldots \langle def\text{-}n\rangle$ is an arbitrarily long sequence of definitions (see figure 51) and $\langle exp \rangle$ is an arbitrary expression. In other words, a **local**-expression consists of the keyword **local**, followed by a sequence of definitions grouped with ( and ), followed by an expression.

The keyword **local** distinguishes this new class of expressions from other expressions, just as **cond** distinguishes conditional expressions from applications. The parenthesized sequence that follows **local** is referred to as the LOCAL DEFINITION .The definitions are called the LOCALLY DEFINED variables, functions, or structures. All those in the Definitions window

$$\langle def \rangle \quad = \quad \textbf{(define } ((\langle var \rangle\ \langle var \rangle \ldots \langle var \rangle)\ \langle exp \rangle)$$
$$| \quad \textbf{(define } \langle var \rangle\ \langle exp \rangle)$$
$$| \quad \textbf{(define-struct } \langle var \rangle\ (\langle var \rangle \ldots \langle var \rangle))$$

Figure 51: Scheme definitions

are called TOP-LEVEL DEFINITIONS. Each name may occur at most once on the left-hand side, be it in a variable definition or a function definition. The expression in each definition is called the RIGHT-HAND SIDE expression. The expression that follows the definitions is the BODY.

Let us take a look at an example:

```
(local ((define (f x) (+ x 5))
        (define (g alon)
          (cond
            [(empty? alon) empty]
            [else (cons (f (first alon)) (g (rest alon)))])))
  (g (list 1 2 3)))
```

The locally defined functions are *f* and *g*. The right-hand side of the first function definition is (+ *x* 5); the second one is

```
(cond
  [(empty? alon) empty]
  [else (cons (f (first alon)) (g (rest alon)))])
```

Finally, the body of the **local**-expression is (*g* (list 1 2 3)).

## Exercises

**Exercise 18.1.1** Circle the locally defined variables and functions in red, the right-hand sides in green, and the body of the following **local**-expression in blue:

1. **(local ((define** *x* (* *y* 3)))
   (* *x* *x*))

2. **(local ((define** (*odd an*)
              **(cond**
                [(zero? *an*) false]
                [**else** (*even* (sub1 *an*))])]))
           **(define** (*even an*)
              **(cond**
                [(zero? *an*) true]
                [**else** (*odd* (sub1 *an*))])])))
        (*even a-nat-num*))


3. **(local ((define** (*f x*) (*g x* (+ *x* 1)))
              **(define** (*g x y*) (*f* (+ *x y*))))
        (+ (*f* 10) (*g* 10 20)))

∎


**Exercise 18.1.2** The following phrases are *not* syntactically legal:

1. **(local ((define** *x* 10)
              (*y* (+ *x x*)))
     *y*)


2. **(local ((define** (*f x*) (+ (* *x x*) (* 3 *x*) 15))
              **(define** *x* 100)
              **(define** *f@100* (*f x*)))
        *f@100 x*)


3. **(local ((define** (*f x*) (+ (* *x x*) (* 3 *x*) 14))
              **(define** *x* 100)
              **(define** *f* (*f x*)))
        *f*)


Explain why! ∎

**Exercise 18.1.3** Determine which of the following definitions or expressions are legal and which ones are not:

1. (**define** *A-CONSTANT*
     (not
         (**local** ((**define** (*odd an*)
                     (**cond**
                         [(= *an* 0) false]
                         [**else** (*even* (− *an* 1))]))
                  (**define** (*even an*)
                     (**cond**
                         [(= *an* 0) true]
                         [**else** (*odd* (− *an* 1))]))))
             (*even a-nat-num*))))

2. (+ (**local** ((**define** (*f x*) (+ (∗ *x x*) (∗ 3 *x*) 15))
             (**define** *x* 100)
             (**define** *f@100* (*f x*)))
         *f@100*)
     1000)

3. (**local** ((**define** *CONST* 100)
         (**define** *f x* (+ *x CONST*)))
     (**define** (*g x y z*) (*f* (+ *x* (∗ *y z*)))))

Explain why each expression is legal or illegal. ∎

## Semantics of local

The purpose of a **local**-expression is to define a variable, a function, or a structure for the evaluation of the body expression. Outside of the **local**-expression the definitions have no effect. Consider the following expression:

   (**local** ((**define** (*f x*) *exp-1*)) exp)

It defines the function *f* during the evaluation of exp. The result of exp is the result of the entire **local**-expression. Similarly,

   (**local** ((**define** *PI* 3)) exp)

temporarily lets the variable *PI* stand for 3 during the evaluation of exp.
    We can describe the evaluation of **local**-expressions with a single rule, but the rule is extremely complex. More specifically, the rule requires two

steps in a hand-evaluation. First, we must systematically replace all locally defined variables, functions, and structures so that the names do not over-lap with those used in the `Definitions` window. Second, we move the entire sequence of definitions to the top level and proceed as if we had just created a new function.

Here is the evaluation rule, stated symbolically:

> *def-1* ... *def-n*
> $E[(\textbf{local} ((\textbf{define} (f\text{-}1\ x)\ exp\text{-}1) \ldots (\textbf{define} (f\text{-}n\ x)\ exp\text{-}n))\ \textsf{exp})]$
>
> =
>
> *def-1* ... *def-n* $(\textbf{define} (f\text{-}1'\ x)\ exp\text{-}1') \ldots (\textbf{define} (f\text{-}n'\ x)\ exp\text{-}n')$
> $E[\textsf{exp}']$

For simplicity, the **local**-expression in this rule defines only one-argument functions, but it is straightforward to generalize from here. As usual, the sequence *def-1* ... *def-n* represents top-level definitions.

The unusual part of the rule is the notation $E[\textsf{exp}]$. It represents an ex-pression $\textsf{exp}$ and its context $E$. More specifically, $\textsf{exp}$ is the next expression that must be evaluated; $E$ is called its EVALUATION CONTEXT.

For example, the expression

> $(+\ (\textbf{local} ((\textbf{define} (f\ x)\ 10))\ (f\ 13))\ 5)$

is an addition. Before we can compute its result, we must evaluate the two subexpressions to numbers. Since the first subexpression is not a number, we focus on it:

> $(\textbf{local} ((\textbf{define} (f\ x)\ 10))\ (f\ 13))$

This **local**-expression must and can be evaluated, so

> $\textsf{exp} = (\textbf{local} ((\textbf{define} (f\ x)\ 10))\ (f\ 13))$
> $E = (+ \ldots 5)$

On the right-hand side of the rule for **local**, we can see several primed names and expressions. The primed names $f\text{-}1', \ldots, f\text{-}n'$ are new function names, distinct from all other names in top-level definitions; the primes on the expressions $exp\text{-}1', \ldots, exp\text{-}n'$ indicate that these expressions are struc-turally identical to $exp\text{-}1, \ldots, exp\text{-}n$ but contain $f\text{-}1'$ instead of $f\text{-}1$, etc.

The evaluation rule for **local**-expressions is the most complex rule that we have encountered so far, and indeed, it is the most complex rule that we will ever encounter. Each of the two steps is important and serves a distinct purpose. Their purpose is best illustrated by a series of simple examples.

The first part of the rule eliminates name clashes between names that are already defined in the top-level environment and those that will be inserted there. Consider the following example:

(**define** *y* 10)
(+ *y*
   (**local** ((**define** *y* 10)
         (**define** *z* (+ *y y*)))
    *z*))

The expression introduces a local definition for *y*, adds *y* to itself to get *z*, and returns the value of *z*.

The informal description of **local** says that the result should be 30. Let's verify this with our rule. If we simply added the definitions in **local** to the top level, the two definitions for *y* would clash. The renaming step prevents this clash and clarifies which of the *y*'s belong together:

= (**define** *y* 10)
  (+ *y* (**local** ((**define** *y1* 10) (**define** *z1* (+ *y1 y1*))) *z1*))

= (**define** *y* 10)
  (**define** *y1* 10)
  (**define** *z1* (+ *y1 y1*))
  (+ *y z1*)

= (**define** *y* 10)
  (**define** *y1* 10)
  (**define** *z1* 20)
  (+ 10 *z1*)

= (**define** *y* 10)
  (**define** *y1* 10)
  (**define** *z1* 20)
  (+ 10 *z1*)

= (**define** *y* 10)
  (**define** *y1* 10)
  (**define** *z1* 20)
  (+ 10 20)

As expected, the result is 30.

Since **local**-expressions may occur inside of function bodies, renaming is important if such functions are applied more than once. The following second example illustrates this point:

```
(define (D x y)
  (local ((define x2 (* x x))
          (define y2 (* y y)))
    (sqrt (+ x2 y2))))
(+ (D 0 1) (D 3 4))
```

The function *D* computes the square root of the sum of the squares of its arguments. Hence the result of (+ (*D* 0 1) (*D* 3 4)) should be 6.

As *D* computes its answer, it introduces two local variables: *x2* and *y2*. Since *D* is applied twice, a modified version of its body is evaluated twice and therefore its local definitions must be added to the top-level twice. The renaming step ensures that no matter how often we lift such definitions, they never interfere with each other. Here is how this works:

```
= (define (D x y)
    (local ((define x2 (* x x))
            (define y2 (* y y)))
      (sqrt (+ x2 y2))))
  (+ (local ((define x2 (* 0 0))
             (define y2 (* 1 1)))
       (sqrt (+ x2 y2)))
     (D 3 4))
```

The expression (*D* 0 1) is evaluated according to the regular rules. Now we rename and lift the **local** definitions:

```
= (define (D x y)
    (local ((define x2 (* x x))
            (define y2 (* y y)))
      (sqrt (+ x2 y2))))
  (define x21 (* 0 0))
  (define y21 (* 1 1))
  (+ (sqrt (+ x21 y21))
     (D 3 4))
```

From here, the evaluation proceeds according to the standard rules until we encounter a second nested **local**-expression in the expression that we are evaluating:

```
  = (define (D x y)
      (local ((define x2 (* x x))
              (define y2 (* y y)))
        (sqrt (+ x2 y2))))
    (define x21 0)
    (define y21 1)
    (+ 1 (local ((define x2 (* 3 3))
                 (define y2 (* 4 4)))
           (sqrt (+ x2 y2))))

  = (define (D x y)
      (local ((define x2 (* x x))
              (define y2 (* y y)))
        (sqrt (+ x2 y2))))
    (define x21 0)
    (define y21 1)
    (define x22 9)
    (define y22 16)
    (+ 1 (sqrt (+ x22 y22)))
```

By renaming *x2* and *y2* again, we avoided clashes. From here, the evaluation of the expression is straightforward:

```
    (+ 1 (sqrt (+ x22 y22)))
  = (+ 1 (sqrt (+ 9 y22)))
  = (+ 1 (sqrt (+ 9 16)))
  = (+ 1 (sqrt 25))
  = (+ 1 5)
  = 6
```

The result is 6, as expected.[44]

---

## Exercises

**Exercise 18.1.4** Since **local** definitions are added to the Definitions window during an evaluation, we might wish to try to see their values by just typing in the variables into the Interactions window. Is this possible? Why or why not? ∎

---

[44] As we evaluate expressions in this manner, our list of definitions grows longer and longer. Fortunately, DrScheme knows how to manage such growing lists. Indeed, it occasionally throws out definitions that will never be used again.

**Exercise 18.1.5** Evaluate the following expressions by hand:

1. (**local** ((**define** (*x y*) (* 3 *y*)))
   (* (*x* 2) 5))

2. (**local** ((**define** (*f c*) (+ (* 9/5 *c*) 32)))
   (− (*f* 0) (*f* 10)))

3. (**local** ((**define** (*odd? n*)
            (**cond**
              [(zero? *n*) false]
              [**else** (*even?* (sub1 *n*))]))
          (**define** (*even? n*)
            (**cond**
              [(zero? *n*) true]
              [**else** (*odd?* (sub1 *n*))]))))
   (*even?* 1))

4. (+ (**local** ((**define** (*f x*) (*g* (+ *x* 1) 22))
           (**define** (*g x y*) (+ *x y*)))
      (*f* 10))
   555)

5. (**define** (*h n*)
     (**cond**
       [(= *n* 0) empty]
       [**else** (**local** ((**define** *r* (* *n n*)))
              (cons *r* (*h* (− *n* 1))))]))
   (*h* 2)

The evaluations should show all **local**-reductions. ∎

## Pragmatics of local, Part 1

The most important use of **local**-expressions is to ENCAPSULATE a collection of functions that serve one purpose. Consider for an example the definitions for our sort function from section 12.2:

```
;; sort : list-of-numbers → list-of-numbers
(define (sort alon)
  (cond
    [(empty? alon) empty]
    [(cons? alon) (insert (first alon) (sort (rest alon)))]))

;; insert : number list-of-numbers (sorted) → list-of-numbers
(define (insert an alon)
  (cond
    [(empty? alon) (list an)]
    [else (cond
            [(> an (first alon)) (cons an alon)]
            [else (cons (first alon) (insert an (rest alon)))])]))
```

The first definition defines *sort* per se, and the second one defines an auxiliary function that inserts a number into a sorted list of numbers. The first one uses the second one to construct the result from a natural recursion, a sorted version of the rest of the list, and the first item.

The two functions together form the program that sorts a list of numbers. To indicate this intimate relationship between the functions, we can, and should, use a **local**-expression. Specifically, we define a program *sort* that immediately introduces the two functions as auxiliary definitions:

```
;; sort : list-of-numbers → list-of-numbers
(define (sort alon)
  (local ((define (sort alon)
            (cond
              [(empty? alon) empty]
              [(cons? alon) (insert (first alon)
                                    (sort (rest alon)))]))
          (define (insert an alon)
            (cond
              [(empty? alon) (list an)]
              [else (cond
                      [(> an (first alon)) (cons an alon)]
                      [else (cons (first alon)
                                  (insert an (rest alon)))])])))
    (sort alon)))
```

Here the body of **local**-expressions simply passes on the argument to the locally defined function *sort*.

> GUIDELINE ON THE USE OF LOCAL
>
> Develop a function following the design recipes. If the function requires the use of auxiliary definitions, group them in a **local**-expression and put the **local**-expression into a new function definition. The body of the **local** should apply the main function to the arguments of the newly defined function.

## Exercises

**Exercise 18.1.6** Evaluate (*sort* (list 2 1 3)) by hand until the locally defined *sort* function is used. Do the same for (**equal?** (*sort* (list 1)) (*sort* (list 2))). ∎

**Exercise 18.1.7** Use a **local** expression to organize the functions for moving pictures from section 10.3. ∎

**Exercise 18.1.8** Use a **local** expression to organize the functions for drawing a polygon in figure 34. ∎

**Exercise 18.1.9** Use a **local** expression to organize the functions for rearranging words from section 12.4. ∎

**Exercise 18.1.10** Use a **local** expression to organize the functions for finding blue-eyed descendants from section 15.1. ∎

### Pragmatics of local, Part 2

Suppose we need a function that produces the last occurrence of some item in a list. To be precise, assume we have lists of records of rock stars. For simplicity, each star is represented as a pair of values:

(**define-struct** *star* (*name instrument*))

> A *star* (record) is a structure:
>
> (make-star *s t*)
>
> where *s* and *t* are symbols.

Here is an example:

```
(define alos
  (list (make-star 'Chris 'saxophone)
        (make-star 'Robby 'trumpet)
        (make-star 'Matt 'violin)
        (make-star 'Wen 'guitar)
        (make-star 'Matt 'radio)))
```

This list contains two occurrences of 'Matt. So, if we wanted to determine the instrument that goes with the last occurrence of 'Matt, we would want 'radio. For 'Wen, on the other hand, our function would produce 'guitar. Of course, looking for the instrument of 'Kate should yield false to indicate that there is no record for 'Kate.

Let's write down a contract, a purpose statement, and a header:

;; *last-occurrence : symbol list-of-star → star* **or** false
;; to find the last star record in *alostars* that contains *s* in *name* field
(**define** (*last-occurrence s alostars*) ... )

The contract is unusual because it mentions two classes of data to the right of the arrow: *star* and false. Although we haven't seen this kind of contract before, its meaning is obvious. The function may produce a *star* or false.

We have already developed some examples, so we can move directly to the template stage of our design recipe:

```
(define (last-occurrence s alostars)
  (cond
    [(empty? alostars) ...]
    [else ... (first alostars) ... (last-occurrence s (rest alostars)) ... ]))
```

The real problem with this function, of course, shows up only when we want to fill in the gaps in this template. The answer in the first case is false, per specification. How to form the answer in the second case is far from clear. Here is what we have:

1. (first *alostars*) is the first *star* record on the given list. If its name field is equal to *s*, it may or may not be the final result. It all depends on the records in the rest of the list.

2. (*last-occurrence s* (rest *alostars*)) evaluates to one of two things: a *star* record with *s* as the name field or false. In the first case, the *star* record is the result; in the second case, the result is either false or the first *record*.

The second point implies that we need to use the result of the natural recursion twice, first to check whether it is a *star* or a *boolean*, and second, to use it as the answer if it is a *star*.

The dual-use of the natural recursion is best expressed with a **local**-expression:

```
(define (last-occurrence s alostars)
  (cond
    [(empty? alostars) false]
    [else (local ((define r (last-occurrence s (rest alostars))))
            (cond
              [(star? r) r]
              ...))]))
```

The nested **local**-expression gives a name to the result of the natural recursion. The **cond**-expression uses it twice. We could eliminate the **local**-expression by replacing *r* with the right-hand side:

```
(define (last-occurrence s alostars)
  (cond
    [(empty? alostars) false]
    [else (cond
            [(star? (last-occurrence s (rest alostars)))
             (last-occurrence s (rest alostars))]
            ...)]))
```

But even a superficial glance shows that reading a natural recursion twice is difficult. The version with **local** is superior.

From the partially refined template it is only a short step to the full definition:

```
;; last-occurrence : symbol list-of-star → star or false
;; to find the last star record in alostars that contains s in name field
(define (last-occurrence s alostars)
  (cond
    [(empty? alostars) false]
    [else (local ((define r (last-occurrence s (rest alostars))))
            (cond
              [(star? r) r]
              [(symbol=? (star-name (first alostars)) s) (first alostars)]
              [else false]))]))
```

The second clause in the nested **cond**-expression compares the first record's *name* field with *s* if *r* is not a *star* record. In that case, there is no record with the matching name in the rest of the list, and, if the first record is the appropriate one, it is the result. Otherwise, the entire list does not contain the name we're looking for and the result is **false**.

## Exercises

**Exercise 18.1.11** Evaluate the following test by hand:

```
(last-occurrence 'Matt
  (list (make-star 'Matt 'violin)
        (make-star 'Matt 'radio)))
```

How many **local**-expressions are lifted? ∎

**Exercise 18.1.12** Consider the following function definition:

```
;; maxi : non-empty-lon → number
;; to determine the largest number on alon
(define (maxi alon)
  (cond
    [(empty? (rest alon)) (first alon)]
    [else (cond
            [(> (first alon) (maxi (rest alon))) (first alon)]
            [else (maxi (rest alon))])]))
```

Both clauses in the nested **cond**-expression compute (*maxi* (**rest** *an-inv*)), which is therefore a natural candidate for a **local**-expression. Test both versions of *maxi* with

```
(list 1 2 3 4 5 6 7 8 9 10 11 12 13 14 15 16 17 18 19 20)
```

Explain the effect. ∎

**Exercise 18.1.13** Develop the function *to-blue-eyed-ancestor*. The function consumes a family tree (*ftn*) (see section 14.1) and produces a list that explains how to get to a blue-eyed ancestor. If there is no blue-eyed ancestor, the function produces **false**.

The function's contract, purpose statement, and header are as follows:

```
;; to-blue-eyed-ancestor : ftn → path or false
;; to compute the path from a-ftn tree to a blue-eyed ancestor
(define (to-blue-eyed-ancestor a-ftn) ...)
```

A path is a list of 'father and 'mother, which we call a direction. Here are the two data definitions:

---

A *direction* is either

1. the symbol 'father or

2. the symbol 'mother

---

A *path* is either

1. empty or

2. (cons *s los*) where *s* is a direction and *los* is a path.

---

The empty path indicates that *a-ftn* has 'blue in the *eyes* field. If the first item is 'mother, we may search in the mother's family tree for a blue-eyed ancestor using the rest of the path. Similarly, we search in the father's family tree if the first item is 'father and use the rest of the path for further directions.

Examples:

1. (*to-blue-eyed-ancestor Gustav*) produces (list 'mother) for the family tree in figure 35;

2. (*to-blue-eyed-ancestor Adam*) produces false in the same setting; and

3. if we added (**define** *Hal* (make-child *Gustav Eva* 'Gustav 1988 'hazel)) then (*to-blue-eyed-ancestor Hal*) would yield (list 'father 'mother).

Build test cases from these examples. Formulate them as boolean expressions, using the strategy of section 17.8. ∎

**Backtracking**: The functions *last-occurrence* and *to-blue-eyed-ancestor* produce two kinds of results: one to indicate a successful search and another one to indicate a failure. Both are recursive. If a natural recursion fails to find the desired result, each tries to compute a result in a different manner. Indeed, *to-blue-eyed-ancestor* may use another natural recursion.

This strategy of computing an answer is a simple form of BACKTRACK-ING. In the world of data that we have dealt with so far, backtracking is simple and just a device to save computing steps. It is always possible to write two separate recursive functions that accomplish the same purpose as one of the backtracking functions here.

We will take an even closer look at backtracking in section 28. Also, we will discuss counting computing steps in intermezzo 5. ∎

**Exercise 18.1.14** Discuss the function *find* from exercise 15.3.4 in terms of backtracking. ∎

### Pragmatics of local, Part 3

Consider the following function definition:

```
;; mult10 : list-of-digits → list-of-numbers
;; to create a list of numbers by multiplying each digit on alod
;; by (expt 10 p) where p is the number of digits that follow
(define (mult10 alod)
  (cond
    [(empty? alod) 0]
    [else (cons (* (expt 10 (length (rest alod))) (first alod))
                (mult10 (rest alod)))]))
```

Here is a test:

```
(equal? (mult10 (list 1 2 3)) (list 100 20 3))
```

Clearly, the function could be used to convert a list of digits into a number.

A small problem with the definition of *mult10* is the computation of the first item of the result in the second clause. It is a large expression and doesn't quite correspond to the purpose statement. By using a **local**-expression in the second clause, we can introduce names for some intermediate values in the computation of the answer:

```
;; mult10 : list-of-digits → list-of-numbers
;; to create a list of numbers by multiplying each digit on alod
;; by (expt 10 p) where p is the number of digits that follow
(define (mult10 alon)
  (cond
    [(empty? alon) empty]
    [else (local ((define a-digit (first alon))
                  (define p (length (rest alon))))
            ;; ───────────────────────────
            (cons (* (expt 10 p) a-digit) (mult10 (rest alon))))]))
```

The use of names helps us understand the expression when we read the definition again because we can study one **local**-definition at a time.

The use of **local** for such cases is most appropriate when a value is computed twice as, for example, the expression (rest *alon*) in *mult10*. By introducing names for repeated expressions, we might also avoid some (small) effort on DrScheme's side:

```
(define (mult10 alon)
  (cond
    [(empty? alon) empty]
    [else (local ((define a-digit (first alon))
                  (define the-rest (rest alon))
                  (define p (length the-rest)))
            ;; ─────────────────────────────────────
            (cons (* (expt 10 p) a-digit) (mult10 the-rest)))]))
```

For the programs that we have developed, this third usage of **local** is hardly ever useful. An auxiliary function is almost always better. We will, however, encounter many different styles of functions in the remaining parts of the book and with them the opportunity, and sometimes the necessity, to use **local**-expressions like the one for *mult10*.

## Exercises

**Exercise 18.1.15** Consider the following function definition:

```
;; extract1 : inventory → inventory
;; to create an inventory from an-inv for all
;; those items that cost less than $1
(define (extract1 an-inv)
  (cond
    [(empty? an-inv) empty]
    [else (cond
            [(<= (ir-price (first an-inv)) 1.00)
             (cons (first an-inv) (extract1 (rest an-inv)))]
            [else (extract1 (rest an-inv))])]))
```

Both clauses in the nested **cond**-expression extract the first item from *an-inv* and both compute (*extract1* (rest *an-inv*)).

Introduce a **local**-expression for these expressions. ∎

## Lexical Scope and Block Structure

The introduction of **local** requires some additional terminology concerning the syntax of Scheme and the structure of functions. Specifically, we need words to discuss the usage of names for variables, functions, and structures. For a simple example, consider the following two definitions:

>   (**define** ($f$ $\underline{x}$) (+ (* $\underline{x}$ $\underline{x}$) 25))

>   (**define** ($g$ $x$) (* 12 (expt $x$ 5)))

Clearly, the underlined occurrences of $x$ in $f$ are completely unrelated to the occurrences of $x$ in $g$. As mentioned before, if we systematically replaced the underlined occurrences with $y$, the function would still compute the exact same numbers. In short, the underlined occurrences of $x$ mean something only in the definition of $f$ and nowhere else.

At the same time, the first occurrence of $x$ is different from the others. When we apply $f$ to a number $n$, this occurrence completely disappears; in contrast, the others are replaced with $n$. To distinguish these two forms of variable occurrences, we call the one to the right of the function name BINDING occurrence of $x$ and those in the body the BOUND occurrences of $x$. We also say that the binding occurrence of $x$ binds all occurrences of $x$ in the body of $f$, and from the discussion above, the body of $f$ is clearly the only textual region of the function where the underlined binding occurrence of $x$ can bind other occurrences. The name of this region is $x$'s LEXICAL SCOPE. We also say that the definitions of $f$ and $g$ (or other definitions in the `Definitions` window) have GLOBAL SCOPE. On occasion, people also use the word FREE OCCURRENCE.

The description of an application of $f$ to a number $n$ suggests the following pictorial representation of the definition:

>   (**define** ($f$ $x$) (+ (* $x$ $x$) 25))

The bullet over the first occurrence indicates that it is a binding occurrence. The arrow that originates from the bullet suggests the flow of values. That is, when the value of a binding occurrence becomes known, the bound occurrences receive their values from there. Put differently, when we know which is the binding occurrence of a variable, we know where the value will come from during an evaluation.

Along similar lines, the scope of a variable also dictates where we can rename it. If we wish to rename a parameter, say, from $x$ to $y$, we search for all bound occurrences in the scope of the parameter and replace them with $y$. For example, if the function definition is the one from above:

**(define** ($f$ $x$) (+ (∗ $x$ $x$) 25))

renaming $x$ to $y$ affects two bound occurrences:

**(define** ($f$ $y$) (+ (∗ $y$ $y$) 25))

No other occurrences of $x$ outside of the definitions need to be changed.

Obviously function definitions also introduce a binding occurrence for the function name. If a definition introduces a function named $f$, the scope of $f$ is the entire sequence of definitions:

**(define** ($e$ $z$) ($f$ (∗ $z$ $z$)))

**(define** ($f$ $x$) (+ (∗ $x$ $x$) 25))

**(define** ($g$ $y$) (+ ($f$ (+ $y$ 1)) ($f$ (− $y$ 1))))

That is, the scope of $f$ includes all definitions above and below the definition of $f$.

## Exercises

**Exercise 18.2.1** Here is a simple Scheme program:

```
(define (p1 x y)
  (+ (* x y)
     (+ (* 2 x)
        (+ (* 2 y) 22))))

(define (p2 x)
  (+ (* 55 x) (+ x 11)))

(define (p3 x)
  (+ (p1 x 0)
     (+ (p1 x 1) (p2 x))))
```

Draw arrows from *p1*'s *x* parameter to all its bound occurrences. Draw
arrows from *p1* to all bound occurrences of *p1*.

Copy the function and rename the parameter *x* of *p1* to *a* and the parameter *x* of *p3* to *b*.

Check the results with DrScheme's Check Syntax button. ∎

In contrast to top-level function definitions, the scope of the definitions
in a **local** are limited. Specifically, the scope of local definitions *is* the **local**-
expression. Consider the definition of an auxiliary function *f* in a **local**-exp-
ression. It binds all occurrences within the **local**-expression but none that
occur outside:

$$\ldots\,(f \ldots)\,\ldots$$

$$(\textbf{local}\,(\,(\textbf{define}\,(e\,z)\,(f\,(*\,z\,z)))$$

$$(\textbf{define}\,(f\,x)\,(+\,(*\,x\,x)\,25))$$

$$(\textbf{define}\,(g\,y)\,(+\,(f\,(+\,y\,1))\,(f\,(-\,y\,1)))$$

$$\ldots\,(f \ldots)\,\ldots)$$

$$\ldots\,(f \ldots)\,\ldots$$

The two occurrences outside of **local** are not bound by the local definition
of *f*.

As always, the parameters of a function definition, local or not, is only
bound in the function's body and nowhere else:

$$(\textbf{local}\,(\,(\textbf{define}\,(f\,x)\,(+\,(*\,x\,x)\,25))$$

$$\ldots\,x\,\ldots)$$

Since the scope of a function name or a function parameter is a textual
region, people often draw a box to indicate some scope. More precisely, for
parameters a box is drawn around the body of a function:

$$(\textbf{define}\,(f\,x)$$

$$\boxed{(+\,(*\,2\,x)\,10)}\,)$$

In the case of a local definition, the box is drawn aorund the entire **local**-expression:

(**define** (*h z*)
    (**local** ((**define** (*f x*) (+ (* *x x*) 55))
             (**define** (*g y*) (+ (*f y*) 10)))
     (*f z*)) )

In this example, the box describes the scope of the definitions of *f* and *g*.

Using a box for a scope, we can also easily understand what it means to reuse the name of function inside a **local**-expression:

(**define** (*a-function y*)
    (**local** ((**define** (*f x y*) (+ (* *x y*) (+ *x y*)))
            (**define** (*g z*)
               (**local** ((**define** (*f x*) (+ (* *x x*) 55))
                      (**define** (*g y*) (+ (*f y*) 10)))
               (*f z*)) )
            (**define** (*h x*) (*f x* (*g x*)))))
     (*h y*)) )

The inner box describes the scope of the inner definition of *f*; the outer box is the scope of the outer definition of *f*. Accordingly, all occurrences of *f* in the inner box refer to the inner **local**; all those in the outer box refer to the definition in the outer **local**. In other words, the scope of the outer definition of *f* has a hole: the inner box, which is the scope of the inner definition of *f*.

Holes can also occur in the scope of a parameter definition. Here is an example:

(**define** (*f x*)
    (**local** ((**define** (*g x*) (+ *x* (* *x* 2)) ))
     (*g x*)) )

In this function, the parameter *x* is used twice: for the function *f* and for *g*. The scope of the latter is nested in the scope of the former and is thus a hole for the scope of the outer use of *x*.

In general, if the same name occurs more than once in a function, the boxes that describe the corresponding scopes never overlap. In some cases the boxes are nested within each other, which gives rise to holes. Still, the picture is always that of a hierarchy of smaller and smaller nested boxes.

**Exercises**

**Exercise 18.2.2** Here is a simple Scheme function:

```
;; sort : list-of-numbers → list-of-numbers
(define (sort alon)
  (local ((define (sort alon)
            (cond
              [(empty? alon) empty]
              [(cons? alon) (insert (first alon) (sort (rest alon)))]))
          (define (insert an alon)
            (cond
              [(empty? alon) (list an)]
              [else (cond
                      [(> an (first alon)) (cons an alon)]
                      [else (cons (first alon) (insert an (rest alon)))])])))
    (sort alon)))
```

Draw a box around the scope of each binding occurrence of *sort* and *alon*. Then draw arrows from each occurrence of *sort* to the matching binding occurrence. ∎

**Exercise 18.2.3** Recall that each occurrence of a variable receives its value from the corresponding binding occurrence. Consider the following definition:

```
(define x (cons 1 x))
```

Where is the underlined occurrence of *x* bound? Since the definition is a variable definition and not a function definition, we need to evaluate the right-hand side if we wish to work with this function. What is the value of the right-hand side according to our rules? ∎

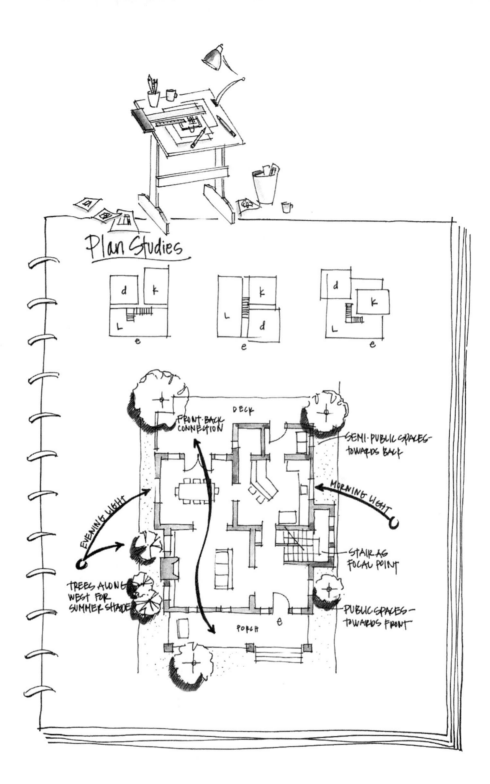

## Plan Studies

d k
L
e

k
L
d
e

d
k
L
e

DECK

FRONT·BACK CONNECTION

SEMI·PUBLIC SPACES TOWARDS BACK

EVENING LIGHT

MORNING LIGHT

STAIR AS FOCAL POINT

TREES ALONG WEST FOR SUMMER SHADE

PUBLIC SPACES TOWARDS FRONT

PORCH
e

## 19   Similarities in Definitions

Many of our data definitions and function definitions look alike. For example, the definition for a list of symbols differs from that of a list of numbers in only two regards: the name of the class of data and the words "symbol" and "number." Similarly, a function that looks for a specific symbol in a list of symbols is nearly indistinguishable from one that looks for a specific number in a list of numbers.

Repetitions are the source of many programming mistakes. Therefore good programmers try to avoid repetitions as much as possible. As we develop a set of functions, especially functions derived from the same template, we soon learn to spot similarities. It is then time to revise the functions so as to eliminate the repetitions as much as possible. Put differently, a set of functions is just like an essay or a memo or a novel or some other piece of writing: the first draft is just a  draft. Unless we edit the essay several times, it does not express our ideas clearly and concisely. It is a pain for others to read it. Because functions are read by many other people and because real functions are modified after reading, we must learn to "edit" functions.

The elimination of repetitions is the most important step in the (program) editing process. In this section, we discuss similarities in function definitions and in data definitions and how to avoid them. Our means of avoiding similarities are specific to Scheme and functional programming languages; still, other languages, in particular object-oriented ones, support similar mechanisms for factoring out similarities—or (code) patterns as they are somtimes called.

## 19.1 Similarities in Functions

The use of our design recipes entirely determines a function's template—
or basic organization—from the data definition for the input. Indeed, the
template is an alternative method of expressing what we know about the
input data. Not surprisingly, functions that consume the same kind of data
look alike.

---

```
;; contains-doll? : los → boolean          ;; contains-car? : los → boolean
;; to determine whether alos contains      ;; to determine whether alos contains
;; the symbol 'doll                        ;; the symbol 'car
(define (contains-doll? alos)              (define (contains-car? alos)
  (cond                                      (cond
    [(empty? alos) false]                      [(empty? alos) false]
    [else                                      [else
     (cond                                      (cond
       [(symbol=? (first alos) 'doll )            [(symbol=? (first alos) 'car )
        true]                                      true]
       [else                                      [else
        (contains-doll? (rest alos))])])])        (contains-car? (rest alos))])])])
```

Figure 52: Two similar functions

---

Take a look at the two functions in figure 52, which consume lists of
symbols (names of toys) and look for specific toys. The function on the
left looks for 'doll, the one on the right for 'car in a list of symbols (los). The
two functions are nearly indistinguishable. Each consumes lists of symbols;
each function body consists of a **cond**-expressions with two clauses. Each
produces false if the input is empty; each uses a second, nested **cond**-exp-
ression to determine whether the first item is the desired item. The only
difference is the symbol that is used in the comparison of the nested **cond**-
expression: *contains-doll?* uses 'doll and *contains-car?* uses 'car, of course. To
highlight the differences, the two symbols are boxed.

Good programmers are too lazy to define several closely related functions. Instead they define a single function that can look for both a 'doll and
a 'car in a list of toys. This more general function consumes an additional
piece of data, the symbol that we are looking for, but is otherwise like the
two original functions:

```
;; contains? : symbol los → boolean
;; to determine whether alos contains the symbol s
(define (contains? s alos)
  (cond
    [(empty? alos) false]
    [else (cond
            [(symbol=? (first alos) ⌐s⌐)
             true]
            [else
             (contains? s (rest alos))])])])
```

We can now look for 'doll by applying *contains?* to 'doll and a list of symbols. But *contains?* works for any other symbol, too. Defining the single version has solved many related problems at once.

The process of combining two related functions into a single definition is called FUNCTIONAL ABSTRACTION. Defining abstract versions of functions is highly beneficial. The first benefit is that a single function can perform many different tasks. In our first example, *contains?* can search for many different symbols instead of just one concrete symbol.[45]

---

```
;; below : lon number → lon              ;; above : lon number → lon
;; to construct a list of those numbers  ;; to construct a list of those numbers
;; on alon that are below t              ;; on alon that are above t
(define (below alon t)                   (define (above alon t)
  (cond                                    (cond
    [(empty? alon) empty]                    [(empty? alon) empty]
    [else                                    [else
     (cond                                    (cond
       [(⌐<⌐ (first alon) t)                    [(⌐>⌐ (first alon) t)
        (cons (first alon)                       (cons (first alon)
          (below (rest alon) t))]                  (above (rest alon) t))]
       [else                                    [else
        (below (rest alon) t)])])])            (above (rest alon) t)])])])
```

Figure 53: Two more similar functions

---

[45]Computing borrows the term "abstract" from mathematics. A mathematician refers to "6" as an abstract number because it only represents all different ways of naming six things. In contrast, "6 inches" or "6 eggs" are concrete instances of "6" because they express a measurement and a count.

In the case of *contains-doll?* and *contains-car?*, abstraction is uninteresting. There are, however, more interesting cases: see figure 53. The function on the left consumes a list of numbers and a threshold and produces a list of all those numbers that are below the threshold; the one on the right produces all those that are above a threshold.

The difference between the two functions is the comparison operator. The left uses <, the right one >. Following the first example, we abstract over the two functions with an additional parameter that stands for the concrete relational operator in *below* and *above*:

```
(define (filter1 rel-op alon t)
  (cond
    [(empty? alon) empty]
    [else (cond
            [( rel-op (first alon) t)
             (cons (first alon)
                   (filter1 rel-op (rest alon) t))]
            [else
             (filter1 rel-op (rest alon) t)])]))
```

To apply this new function, we must supply three arguments: a relational operator $R$ that compares two numbers, a list $L$ of numbers, and a number $N$. The function then extracts all those items $i$ in $L$ for which $(R\ i\ N)$ evaluates to true. Since we do not know how to write down contracts for functions like *filter1*, we omit the contract for now. We will discuss the problem of contracts in section 20.2 below.

Let us see how *filter1* works with an example. Clearly, as long as the input list is empty, the result is empty, too, no matter what the other arguments are:

```
(filter1 < empty 5)
= empty
```

So next we look at a slightly more complicated case:

```
(filter1 < (cons 4 empty) 5)
```

The result should be (cons 4 empty) because the only item of this list is 4 and (< 4 5) is true.

The first step of the evaluation is based on the rule of application:

```
(filter1 < (cons 4 empty) 5)
```

```
= (cond
    [(empty? (cons 4 empty)) empty]
    [else (cond
             [(< (first (cons 4 empty)) 5)
              (cons (first (cons 4 empty))
                    (filter1 < (rest (cons 4 empty)) 5))]
             [else (filter1 < (rest (cons 4 empty)) 5)])])])
```

That is, it is the body of *filter1* with all occurrences of *rel-op* replaced by $<$, t replaced by 5, and *alon* replaced by (cons 4 empty).

The rest of the evaluation is straightforward:

```
(cond
  [(empty? (cons 4 empty)) empty]
  [else (cond
           [(< (first (cons 4 empty)) 5)
            (cons (first (cons 4 empty))
                  (filter1 < (rest (cons 4 empty)) 5))]
           [else (filter1 < (rest (cons 4 empty)) 5)])])
```

```
= (cond
    [(< (first (cons 4 empty)) 5)
     (cons (first (cons 4 empty))
           (filter1 < (rest (cons 4 empty)) 5))]
    [else (filter1 < (rest (cons 4 empty)) 5)])
```

```
= (cond
    [(< 4 5) (cons (first (cons 4 empty))
                   (filter1 < (rest (cons 4 empty)) 5))]
    [else (filter1 < (rest (cons 4 empty)) 5)])
```

```
= (cond
    [true (cons (first (cons 4 empty))
                (filter1 < (rest (cons 4 empty)) 5))]
    [else (filter1 < (rest (cons 4 empty)) 5)])
```

```
= (cons 4 (filter1 < (rest (cons 4 empty)) 5))
= (cons 4 (filter1 < empty 5))
= (cons 4 empty)
```

The last step is the equation we discussed as our first case.

Our final example is an application of *filter1* to a list of two items:

    (*filter1* < (cons 6 (cons 4 empty)) 5)
= (*filter1* < (cons 4 empty) 5)
= (cons 4 (*filter1* < empty 5))
= (cons 4 empty)

The only new step is the first one. It says that *filter1* determines that the first item on the list is not less than the threshold, and that it therefore is not added to the result of the natural recursion.

## Exercises

**Exercise 19.1.1** Verify the equation

    (*filter1* < (cons 6 (cons 4 empty)) 5)
= (*filter1* < (cons 4 empty) 5)

with a hand-evaluation that shows every step. ∎

**Exercise 19.1.2** Evaluate the expression

    (*filter1* > (cons 8 (cons 6 (cons 4 empty))) 5)

by hand. Show only the essential steps. ∎

The calculations show that (*filter1* < *alon t*) computes the same result as (*below alon t*), which is what we expected. Similar reasoning shows that (*filter1* > *alon t*) produces the same output as (*above alon t*). So suppose we define the following:

```
;; below1 : lon number → lon          ;; above1 : lon number → lon
(define (below1 alon t)               (define (above1 alon t)
  (filter1 < alon t))                   (filter1 > alon t))
```

Clearly, *below1* produces the same results as *below* when given the same inputs, and *above1* is related to *above* in the same manner. In short, we have defined *below* and *above* as one-liners using *filter1*.

Better yet: once we have an abstract function like *filter1*, we can put it to other uses, too. Here are three of them:

1. (*filter1* = *alon t*): This expression extracts all those numbers in *alon* that are equal to *t*.

2. (*filter1* <= *alon t*): This one produces the list of numbers in *alon* that are less than or equal to *t*.

3. (*filter1* >= *alon t*): This last expression computes the list of numbers that are greater than or equal to the threshold.

In general, *filter1*'s first argument need not even be one of Scheme's predefined operations; it can be any function that consumes two numbers and produces a boolean value. Consider the following example:

*;; squared>? : number number → boolean*
(**define** (*squared>? x c*)
  (> (* *x x*) *c*))

The function produces true whenever the area of a square with side $x$ is larger than some threshold $c$, that is, the function tests whether the claim $x^2 > c$ holds. We now apply *filter1* to this function and a list of numbers:

(*filter1 squared>?* (list 1 2 3 4 5) 10)

This particular application extracts those numbers in (list 1 2 3 4 5) whose square is larger than 10.

Here is the beginning of a simple hand-evaluation:

```
  (filter1 squared>? (list 1 2 3 4 5) 10)
= (cond
    [(empty? (list 1 2 3 4 5)) empty]
    [else (cond
            [(squared>? (first (list 1 2 3 4 5)) 10)
             (cons (first (list 1 2 3 4 5))
               (filter1 squared>? (rest (list 1 2 3 4 5)) 10))]
            [else
             (filter1 squared>? (rest (list 1 2 3 4 5)) 10)])])
```

That is, we apply our standard law of application and calculate otherwise as usual:

```
= (cond
    [(squared>? 1 10)
     (cons (first (list 1 2 3 4 5))
       (filter1 squared>? (rest (list 1 2 3 4 5)) 10))]
    [else
     (filter1 squared>? (rest (list 1 2 3 4 5)) 10)])
```

```
= (cond
    [false
     (cons (first (list 1 2 3 4 5))
        (filter1 squared>? (rest (list 1 2 3 4 5)) 10))]
    [else
     (filter1 squared>? (rest (list 1 2 3 4 5)) 10)])
```

The last step consists of several steps concerning *squared>?*, which we can
skip at this point:

```
= (filter1 squared>? (list 2 3 4 5) 10)
= (filter1 squared>? (list 3 4 5) 10)
= (filter1 squared>? (list 4 5) 10)
```

We leave the remainder of the evaluation to the exercises.

## Exercises

**Exercise 19.1.3** Show that

```
    (filter1 squared>? (list 4 5) 10)
= (cons 4 (filter1 squared>? (list 5) 10))
```

with a hand-evaluation. Act as if *squared>?* were primitive. ∎

**Exercise 19.1.4** The use of *squared>?* also suggests that the following function will work, too:

```
;; squared10? : number number → boolean
(define (squared10? x c)
  (> (sqr x) 10))
```

In other words, the relational function that *filter1* uses may ignore its second
argument. After all, we already know it and it stays the same throughout
the evaluation of (*filter1 squared>? alon t*).

This, in turn, implies another simplification of the function:

```
(define (filter predicate alon)
  (cond
    [(empty? alon) empty]
    [else (cond
            [(predicate (first alon))
             (cons (first alon)
                (filter predicate (rest alon)))]
            [else
             (filter predicate (rest alon))])]))
```

The function filter consumes only a relational function, called *predicate*, and a list of numbers. Every item *i* on the list is checked with *predicate*. If (*predicate i*) holds, *i* is included in the output; if not, *i* does not appear in the result.

Show how to use filter to define functions that are equivalent to *below* and *above*. Test the definitions. ∎

So far we have seen that abstracted function definitions are more flexible and more widely usable than specialized definitions. A second, and in practice equally important, advantage of abstracted definitions is that we can change a single definition to fix and improve many different uses. Consider the two variants of *filter1* in figure 54. The first variant flattens the nested **cond**-expression, something that an experienced programmer may wish to do. The second variant uses a **local**-expression that makes the nested **cond**-expression more readable.

```
(define (filter1 rel-op alon t)          (define (filter1 rel-op alon t)
  (cond                                     (cond
    [(empty? alon) empty]                     [(empty? alon) empty]
    [(rel-op (first alon) t)                  [else
     (cons (first alon)                        (local ((define first-item (first alon))
       (filter1 rel-op (rest alon) t))]                (define rest-filtered
    [else                                             (filter1 rel-op (rest alon) t)))
     (filter1 rel-op (rest alon) t)]))          (cond
                                                 [(rel-op first-item t)
                                                  (cons first-item rest-filtered)]
                                                 [else
                                                  rest-filtered]))])))
```

Figure 54: Two modifications of *filter1*

Although both of these changes are trivial, the key is that all uses of *filter1*, including those to define the functions *below1* and *above1*, benefit from this change. Similarly, if the modification had fixed a logical mistake, all uses of the function would be improved. Finally, it is even possible to add new tasks to abstracted functions, for example, a mechanism for counting how many elements are filtered. In that case all uses of the function would benefit from the new functionality. We will encounter this form of improvement later.

## Exercises

**Exercise 19.1.5** Abstract the following two functions into a single function:

```
;; mini : nelon → number          ;; maxi : nelon → number
;; to determine the smallest number  ;; to determine the largest number
;; on alon                          ;; on alon
(define (mini alon)                 (define (maxi alon)
  (cond                               (cond
    [(empty? (rest alon)) (first alon)]   [(empty? (rest alon)) (first alon)]
    [else (cond                           [else (cond
            [(< (first alon)                      [(> (first alon)
                (mini (rest alon)))                   (maxi (rest alon)))
             (first alon)]                         (first alon)]
            [else                                 [else
             (mini (rest alon))])])))              (maxi (rest alon))])])))
```

Both consume non-empty lists of numbers and produce a single number. The left one produces the smallest number in the list, the right one the largest.

Define *mini1* and *maxi1* in terms of the abstracted function. Test each of them with the following three lists:

1. (list 3 7 6 2 9 8)

2. (list 20 19 18 17 16 15 14 13 12 11 10 9 8 7 6 5 4 3 2 1)

3. (list 1 2 3 4 5 6 7 8 9 10 11 12 13 14 15 16 17 18 19 20)

Why are they slow on the long lists?

Improve the abstracted function. First, introduce a local name for the result of the natural recursion. Then introduce a local, auxiliary function that picks the "interesting" one of two numbers. Test *mini1* and *maxi1* with the same inputs again. ∎

**Exercise 19.1.6** Recall the definition of *sort*, which consumes a list of numbers and produces a sorted version:

```
;; sort : list-of-numbers → list-of-numbers
;; to construct a list with all items from alon in descending order
(define (sort alon)
  (local ((define (sort alon)
            (cond
              [(empty? alon) empty]
              [else (insert (first alon) (sort (rest alon)))]))
          (define (insert an alon)
            (cond
              [(empty? alon) (list an)]
              [else (cond
                      [(> an (first alon)) (cons an alon)]
                      [else (cons (first alon) (insert an (rest alon)))])])))
    (sort alon)))
```

Define an abstract version of *sort* that consumes the comparison operation in addition to the list of numbers. Use the abstract version to sort (list 2 3 1 5 4) in ascending and descending order. ∎

## 19.2 Similarities in Data Definitions

Inspect the following two data definitions:

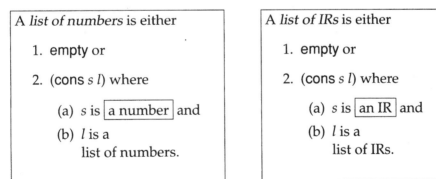

| A *list of numbers* is either | A *list of IRs* is either |
|---|---|
| 1. empty or | 1. empty or |
| 2. (cons *s l*) where | 2. (cons *s l*) where |
|    (a) *s* is [a number] and |    (a) *s* is [an IR] and |
|    (b) *l* is a list of numbers. |    (b) *l* is a list of IRs. |

Both define a class of lists. The one on the left is the data definition for lists of numbers; the one on the right describes lists of inventory records, which we represent with structures. The necessary structure and data definitions follow:

(**define-struct** *ir* (*name price*))

> An *IR* is a structure:
> $$\text{(make-ir } n \ p)$$
> where *n* is a symbol and *p* is a number.

Given the similarity between the data definitions, functions that consume elements of these classes are similar, too. Take a look at the illustrative example in figure 55. The function on the left is the function *below*, which filters numbers from a list of numbers. The one on the right is *below-ir*, which extracts those inventory records from a list whose prices are below a certain threshold. Except for the name of the function, which is arbitrary, the two definitions differ in only one point: the relational operator.

---

```
;; below : number lon → lon          ;; below-ir : number loIR → loIR
;; to construct a list of those numbers   ;; to construct a list of those records
;; on alon that are below t          ;; on aloir that contain a price below t
(define (below alon t)               (define (below aloir t)
  (cond                                (cond
    [(empty? alon) empty]                [(empty? aloir) empty]
    [else (cond                          [else (cond
            [( < (first alon) t)                 [( <ir (first aloir) t)
             (cons (first alon)                   (cons (first aloir)
               (below (rest alon) t))]              (below-ir (rest aloir) t))]
            [else                                [else
             (below (rest alon) t)])]))           (below-ir (rest aloir) t)])]))

                                     ;; <ir : IR number → boolean
                                     (define (<ir ir p)
                                       (< (ir-price ir) p))
```

Figure 55: Marking the differences in similar functions

---

If we abstract the two functions, we obviously obtain *filter1*. Conversely, we can define *below-ir* in terms of *filter1*:

```
(define (below-ir1 aloir t)
  (filter1 <ir aloir t))
```

It should not surprise us to discover yet another use for *filter1*—after all, we already argued that abstraction promotes the reuse of functions for different purposes. Here we see that *filter1* not only filters lists of numbers but lists of arbitrary things—as long as we can define a function that compares these arbitrary things with numbers.

Indeed, all we need is a function that compares items on the list with the items we pass to *filter1* as the second argument. Here is a function that extracts all items with the same label from a list of inventory records:

```
;; find : loIR symbol → boolean
;; to determine whether aloir contains a record for t
(define (find aloir t)
  (cons? (filter1 eq-ir? aloir t)))
```

```
;; eq-ir? : IR symbol → boolean
;; to compare ir's name and p
(define (eq-ir? ir p)
  (symbol=? (ir-name ir) p))
```

This new relational operator compares the name in an inventory record with some other symbol.

**Exercises**

**Exercise 19.2.1** Determine the values of

1. (*below-ir1* 10 (list (make-ir 'doll 8) (make-ir 'robot 12)))

2. (*find* 'doll (list (make-ir 'doll 8) (make-ir 'robot 12) (make-ir 'doll 13)))

by hand and with DrScheme. Show only those lines that introduce new applications of *filter1* to values. ∎

In short, *filter1* uniformly works on many shapes of input data. The word "uniformly" means that if *filter1* is applied to a list of X, its result is also a list of X—no matter what kind of Scheme data X is. Such functions are called POLYMORPHIC[46] or GENERIC functions.

Of course, *filter1* is not the only function that can process arbitrary lists. There are many other functions that process lists independently of what they contain. Here are two functions that determine the length of lists of numbers and *IRs*:

---

[46]The word "poly" means "many" and "morphic" means shape.

*;; length-lon : lon → number*    *;; length-ir : loIR → number*
(**define** (*length-lon alon*)     (**define** (*length-ir alon*)
  (**cond**                    (**cond**
    [(empty? *alon*) empty]            [(empty? *alon*) empty]
    [**else**                       [**else**
      (+ (*length-lon* (rest *alon*)) 1)]))              (+ (*length-ir* (rest *alon*)) 1)]))

The two functions differ only in their names. If we had chosen the same
name, say, length, the two definitions would be identical.

To write precise contracts for functions such as length, we need data
definitions with parameters. We call these PARAMETRIC DATA DEFINITIONS
and agree that they do not specify everything about a class of data. Instead
they use variables to say that any form of Scheme data can be used in a certain place. Roughly speaking, a parametric data definition abstracts from a
reference to a particular collection of data in the same manner as a function
abstracts from a particular value.

Here is a parametric definition of lists of *ITEM*s:

---

A *list of ITEM* is either

  1. empty or

  2. (cons *s l*) where

    (a) *s* is an ITEM and
    (b) *l* is a list of ITEM.

---

The token *ITEM* is a TYPE VARIABLE that stands for any arbitrary collection
of Scheme data: symbols, numbers, booleans, *IRs*, etc. By replacing *ITEM*
with one of these names, we get a concrete instance of this abstract data
definition for lists of symbols, numbers, booleans, *IRs*, etc. To make the
language of contracts more concise, we introduce an additional abbreviation:

  (**listof** *ITEM*)

We use (**listof** *ITEM*) as the name of abstract data definitions such as the
above. Then we can use (**listof** *symbol*) for the class of all lists of symbols,
(**listof** *number*) for the class of all lists of numbers, (**listof** (**listof** *number*))
for the class of all lists of lists of numbers, etc.

In contracts we use (**listof** X) to say that a function works on all lists:

```
;; length : (listof X) → number
;; to compute the length of a list
(define (length alon)
  (cond
    [(empty? alon) empty]
    [else (+ (length (rest alon)) 1)]))
```

The X is just a variable, a name that stands for some class of data. If we now apply length to an element of, say, (**listof** *symbol*) or (**listof** *IR*), we get a number.

The function length is an example of simple polymorphism. It works on all classes of lists. While there are other useful examples of simple polymorphic functions, the more common cases require that we define functions like *filter1*, which consume a parametric form of data and functions that work on this data. This combination is extremely powerful and greatly facilitates the construction and maintenance of software systems. To understand it better, we will next discuss a revision of Scheme's grammar and new ways to write contracts.

## Exercises

**Exercise 19.2.2** Show how to use the abstracted version of *sort* from exercise 19.1.6 to sort a list of *IR*s in ascending and descending order. ∎

**Exercise 19.2.3** Here is a structure definition for pairs

(**define-struct** *pair* (*left right*))

and its parametric data definition:

A (*pair X Y*) is a structure:
(make-pair *l r*)
where *l* is an X and *r* is a Y.

Using this abstract data definition, we can describe many different forms of pairs:

1. (*pair number number*), which is the class of pairs that combine two numbers;

2. (*pair symbol number*), which is the class of pairs that combine a number with a symbol; and

3. (*pair symbol symbol*), which is the class of pairs that combine two symbols.

Still, in all of these examples, each pair contains two values that are accessible via **pair-left** and **pair-right**.

By combining the abstract data definition for lists and pairs we can describe lists of parametric pairs with a single line:

$$(\textbf{listof } (pair \ X \ Y)) \ .$$

Some concrete examples of this abstract class of data are:

1. (**listof** (*pair number number*)), the list of pairs of numbers;

2. (**listof** (*pair symbol number*)), the list of pairs of symbols and numbers;

3. (**listof** (*pair symbol symbol*)), the list of pairs of symbols.

Make an example for each of these classes.

Develop the function *lefts*, which consumes a list of (*pair X Y*) and produces a corresponding list of *X*'s; that is, it extracts the *left* part of each item in its input. ∎

**Exercise 19.2.4** Here is a parametric data definition of non-empty lists:

---

A *(non-empty-listof ITEM)* is either

1. (**cons** *s* empty), or

2. (**cons** *s l*) where *l* is a *(non-empty-listof ITEM)*

and *s* is always an *ITEM*.

---

Develop the function *last*, which consumes a *(non-empty-listof ITEM)* and produces the last *ITEM* in that list.

**Hint:** Replace *ITEM* with a fixed class of data to develop an initial draft of *last*. When finished, replace the class with *ITEM* throughout the function development. ∎

# 20  Functions are Values

The functions of section 19 stretch our understanding of evaluation. It is easy to understand how functions consume numbers and symbols; cosuming structures and lists is a bit more complicated, but still within our grasp; but functions consuming functions is a strange idea. As a matter of fact, the functions of section 19 violate the Scheme grammar of section 8.

In this section, we discuss how to adjust Scheme's grammar and evaluation rules so that we can understand the role of functions as data or values. Without a good understanding of these ideas, we cannot hope to abstract functions. Once we understand these ideas, we can turn to the problem of writing contracts for such functions. Finally, the last part of the section introduces functions that produce functions, another powerful abstraction technique.

## 20.1  Syntax and Semantics

The abstract functions of section 19 violate Scheme's basic grammar in two ways. First, the names of functions and primitive operations are used as arguments in applications. An argument, though, is an expression, and the class of expressions does not contain primitive operations and function names. It does contain variables, but we agreed that they are only those variables mentioned in variable definitions and as function parameters. Second, parameters are used as if they were functions, that is, the first position of applications. But the grammar of section 8 allows only the names of functions and primitive operations in this place.

Spelling out the problem suggests the necessary changes. First, we should include the names of functions and primitive operations in the definition of $\langle exp \rangle$. Second, the first position in an application should allow things other than function names and primitive operations; at a minimum, it must allow variables that play the role of function parameters. In anticipation of other uses of functions, we agree on allowing expressions in that position.

Here is a summary of the three changes:

$$\langle exp \rangle \quad = \quad \begin{aligned} &\langle var \rangle \\ | \ &\langle prm \rangle \\ | \ &(\langle exp \rangle \ \langle exp \rangle \ldots \langle exp \rangle) \end{aligned}$$

Figure 56 displays the entire Scheme grammar, with all the extensions we

$$\langle def \rangle \quad = \quad (\textbf{define } (\langle var \rangle \langle var \rangle \ldots \langle var \rangle) \langle exp \rangle)$$
$$| \quad (\textbf{define } \langle var \rangle \langle exp \rangle)$$
$$| \quad (\textbf{define-struct } \langle var \rangle (\langle var \rangle \langle var \rangle \ldots \langle var \rangle))$$
$$\langle exp \rangle \quad = \quad \langle var \rangle$$
$$| \quad \langle boo \rangle$$
$$| \quad \langle sym \rangle$$
$$| \quad \langle prm \rangle$$
$$| \quad \textsf{empty}$$
$$| \quad (\langle exp \rangle \langle exp \rangle \ldots \langle exp \rangle)$$
$$| \quad (\textbf{cond } (\langle exp \rangle \langle exp \rangle) \ldots (\langle exp \rangle \langle exp \rangle))$$
$$| \quad (\textbf{cond } (\langle exp \rangle \langle exp \rangle) \ldots (\textbf{else } \langle exp \rangle))$$
$$| \quad (\textbf{local } (\langle def \rangle \ldots \langle def \rangle) \langle exp \rangle)$$

$$\langle var \rangle \quad = \quad x \mid \textit{area-of-disk} \mid \textit{circumference} \mid \ldots$$
$$\langle boo \rangle \quad = \quad \textsf{true} \mid \textsf{false}$$
$$\langle sym \rangle \quad = \quad \textsf{'a} \mid \textsf{'doll} \mid \textsf{'sum} \mid \ldots$$
$$\langle num \rangle \quad = \quad 1 \mid -1 \mid 3/5 \mid 1.22 \mid \ldots$$
$$\langle prm \rangle \quad = \quad + \mid - \mid \textsf{cons} \mid \textsf{first} \mid \textsf{rest} \mid \ldots$$

Figure 56: `Intermediate Student` Scheme: The grammar

have encountered so far. It shows that the accommodation of abstract functions does not lengthen the grammar, but makes it simpler.

The same is true of the evaluation rules. Indeed, they don't change at all. What changes is the set of values. To accommodate functions as arguments of functions, the simplest change is to say that the set of values includes the names of functions and primitive operations:

$$\langle val \rangle \quad = \quad \langle boo \rangle \mid \langle sym \rangle \mid \langle num \rangle \mid \textsf{empty} \mid \langle lst \rangle$$
$$| \quad \langle var \rangle \text{ (names of \textbf{define}d functions)}$$
$$| \quad \langle prm \rangle$$
$$\langle lst \rangle \quad = \quad \textsf{empty} \mid (\textsf{cons } \langle val \rangle \langle lst \rangle)$$

Put differently, if we now wish to decide whether we can apply the substitution rule for functions, we must still ensure that all arguments are values, but we must recognize that function names and primitive operations count as values, too.

**Exercises**

**Exercise 20.1.1** Assume the `Definitions` window in DrScheme contains
(**define** (*f x*) *x*). Identify the values among the following expressions:

1. (cons *f* empty)

2. (*f f*)

3. (cons *f* (cons 10 (cons (*f* 10) empty)))

Explain why they are values and why the remaining expressions are not
values. ∎

**Exercise 20.1.2** Argue why the following sentences are legal definitions:

1. (**define** (*f x*) (*x* 10))

2. (**define** (*f x*) *f*)

3. (**define** (*f x y*) (*x* 'a *y* 'b))

∎

**Exercise 20.1.3** Develop *a-function=?*. The function determines whether
two functions from numbers to numbers produce the same results for 1.2,
3, and −5.7.

Can we hope to define *function=?*, which determines whether two functions (from numbers to numbers) are equal? ∎

## 20.2 Contracts for Abstract and Polymorphic Functions

When we first abstracted *below* and *above* into *filter1*, we did not formulate
a contract. Unlike the functions we had defined before, *filter1* consumed a
type of values that we never before used as data: primitive operations and
other functions. Still, we eventually agreed in plain English writing that
*filter1*'s first argument, *rel-op*, would always be a function that consumes
two numbers and produces a boolean value.

If, in the past, we had been asked to write a contract for *rel-op*, we would
have written

;; *rel-op : number number → boolean*

Considering that functions and primitive operations are values, this contract says that an arrow symbol, →, describes a class of values: functions and primitive operations. The names on the left of → specify what each value in the class of functions must be applied to; the name on the right says what each value is going to produce if it is applied to proper values. In general, we say that

   $(A \ B \rightarrow C)$

means the class of all functions and primitives that consume an element in $A$ and an element in $B$ and produce an element in $C$. Or more succinctly, they are functions "from $A$ and $B$ to $C$."

The arrow notation is like the (**listof** ...) notation from the previous section. Both specify a class of data via a combination of other classes. For **listof**, we used data definitions to agree on what they mean. Others can follow the example and introduce their own abbreviations based on data definitions. For arrows, we just made an agreement, and it stays with us for good.

Using the arrow notation, we can formulate a first contract and a proper purpose statement for *filter1*:

   ;; *filter1 : (number number → boolean) lon number → lon*
   ;; to construct the list of those numbers *n* on *alon* for which
   ;; (*rel-op n t*) evaluates to true
   (**define** (*filter1 rel-op alon t*) ...)

The unusual part of the contract is that it specifies the class to which the first argument must belong not with a name introduced by a data definition but with a direct data definition, using the arrow notation. More concretely, it specifies that the first argument must be a function or a primitive operation and, as discussed, what kind of arguments it consumes and what kind of value it produces.

---

## Exercises

**Exercise 20.2.1** Explain the following classes of functions:

1. (*number → boolean*),

2. (*boolean symbol → boolean*),

3. (*number number number → number*),

4. (*number* → (**listof** *number*)), and

5. ((**listof** *number*) → *boolean*). ∎

**Exercise 20.2.2** Formulate contracts for the following functions:

1. *sort*, which consumes a list of numbers and a function that consumes two numbers and produces a boolean; *sort* produces a list of numbers.

2. map, which consumes a function from numbers to numbers and a list of numbers; it also produces a list of numbers.

3. *project*, which consumes a list of lists of symbols and a function from lists of symbols to symbols; it produces a list of symbols. ∎

The second version of *filter1* was the result of abstracting *below* and *below-ir*. Its definition did not differ from the first version, but the process of abstracting from *below-ir* clarified that *filter1* could be applied to all kinds of lists, not just lists of numbers.

To describe all kinds of lists, we use (**listof** *X*). Here is a first attempt at a contract for *filter1*:

;; *filter1* : ... (**listof** *X*) *number* → (**listof** *X*)

The key to using *filter1* with different classes of lists is to use a comparison function that can compare the items on the list with the second argument, which is a number. That is, the first argument is a function in the class

(*X number* → *boolean*)

which means it consumes an element of *X* and a number, and produces a boolean. Put together, we get the following contract for *filter1*:

;; *filter1* : (*X number* → *boolean*) (**listof** *X*) *number* → (**listof** *X*)

As in our contract for length, *X* here stands for an arbitrary collection of Scheme data. We can replace it with anything, as long as all three occurrences are replaced by the same thing. Hence, by using *X* in the description of the first parameter, the second parameter, and the result, we specify that *rel-op* consumes elements of class *X*, that the second argument is a list of *X*s, and that the result of *filter1* is also a list of *X*s.

When we wish to apply *filter1*, we must check that the arguments make sense. Suppose we wish to evaluate

(*filter1* < (list 3 8 10) 2)

Before we do that, we should confirm that *filter1* can indeed consume $<$ and (list 3 8 10), given its contract. A quick check shows that $<$ makes sense because it belongs to the class

(*number number* $\rightarrow$ *boolean*)

and (list 3 8 10) makes sense because it belongs to

(**listof** *number*)

The two classes are identical to the first two argument parts of *filter1*'s contract if $X$ is replaced by *number*. More generally, to ensure that arguments make sense, we must find replacements of the variables in contracts so that the functions contract and the classes of the arguments match.

For a second example, consider

(*filter1* $<_{ir}$ *LOIR* 10)

Here, we must replace $X$ with *IR*, because $<_{ir}$ has the contract

(*IR number* $\rightarrow$ *boolean*)

and *LOIR* belongs to (**listof** *IR*). Again, the application is legitimate because all the arguments belong to the required collections of data.

Let us look at one more example: the use of *filter1* to extract all toys with the same name from a list of inventory records:

```
;; find : (listof IR) symbol → (listof IR)
(define (find aloir t)
  (filter1 eq-ir? aloir t))
```

```
;; eq-ir? : IR symbol → boolean
(define (eq-ir? ir p)
  (symbol=? (ir-name ir) p))
```

It is straightforward to check with examples that the function works properly. Our task here is to understand how this agrees with *filter1*'s contract. The obvious problem is that the "threshold" argument is a symbol, not a number. The use of *filter1* is therefore in conflict with its current contract. To overcome this deficiency, we must introduce another variable, say, *TH* for thresholds, that stands for some collection of data:

```
;; filter1 : (X TH → boolean) (listof X) TH → (listof X)
```

Now we can replace $X$ with the name of one data collection and *TH* with that of a second one or possibly the same. In particular, the application

(*filter1* eq-ir? *LOIR* 'doll)

works because a replacement of *X* by *IR* and *TH* by symbol in *filter1*'s contract shows that the arguments are legitimate.

## Exercises

**Exercise 20.2.3** Use *filter1* to develop a function that consumes a list of symbols and extracts all those that are not equal to 'car. Give *filter1*'s corresponding contract. ∎

**Exercise 20.2.4** Formulate general contracts for the following functions:

1. *sort*, which consumes a list and a function that consumes two items from the list and produces a boolean; it produces a list of numbers.

2. map, which consumes a function from list items to *Xs* and a list; it produces a list of *Xs*.

3. *project*, which consumes a list of lists and a function from lists to *Xs*; it produces a list of *Xs*.

Compare with exercise 20.2.2. ∎

**Contracts and Types**: In summary, the contracts for functions are made up of types. A TYPE is either

1. a basic type, such as number, symbol, boolean, or empty;

2. a defined type, such as *inventory-record*, *list-of-numbers*, or *family-tree*;

3. a function type, such as ($number \rightarrow number$) or ($boolean \rightarrow symbol$);

4. a parametric type, which is either a defined type or a function type with type variables.

When we wish to use a function with a parametric type, we must first find a replacement for all the variables in the function's contract so that we know the arguments belong to proper classes. If this cannot be done, we must either revise the contract or question our decision to reuse this function. ∎

# 21  Designing Abstractions from Examples

When we first learn to add, we use concrete examples. Later on, we study how to add two arbitrary numbers; that is, we form an abstraction of the addition operation. Much later still, we learn to formulate abstractions directly as expressions: expressions that compute the wage of some employee, expressions that convert temperatures, or expressions that determine the area of a geometric shape. In short, we initially go from concrete examples to abstraction, but eventually we learn to form abstractions directly without thinking (much) about concrete instances.

In this section, we discuss a design recipe for creating abstractions from concrete examples. Later, in sections 21.5 and 22 we study additional approaches to function abstraction.

## 21.1  Abstracting from Examples

Forming abstractions from examples is easy. As we have seen in section 19, we start from two concrete function definitions, compare them, mark the differences, and abstract. Let us formulate these steps as a recipe:

**The comparison:** When we find two function definitions that are almost the same except at a few places and for their names, we compare them and mark the differences with boxes. If the boxes contain only values, we can abstract.

> **Warning: Abstracting over Non-values**: The recipe requires a substantial modification for non-values. ∎

Here is a pair of similar function definitions:

```
;; convertCF : lon → lon              ;; names : loIR → los
(define (convertCF alon)              (define (names aloIR)
  (cond                                 (cond
    [(empty? alon) empty]                 [(empty? aloIR) empty]
    [else                                 [else
      (cons ( C→F  (first alon))            (cons ( IR-name  (first aloIR))
        (convertCF (rest alon)))]))          (names (rest aloIR)))]))
```

The two functions apply a function to each item in a list. They differ in only one aspect: what they apply to each item on the list. The two boxes emphasize the difference. Each contains a functional value, so we can abstract.

**The abstraction:** Next we replace the contents of corresponding pairs of boxes with new names and add these names to the parameter list. For example, if there are three pairs of boxes, we need three new names. The two definitions must now be the same, except for the function name. To obtain the abstraction, we systematically replace the function names with one new name.

For our running example, we obtain the following pair of functions:

```
(define (convertCF f alon)          (define (names f aloIR)
  (cond                               (cond
    [(empty? alon) empty]               [(empty? aloIR) empty]
    [else                               [else
      (cons ( f (first alon))             (cons ( f (first aloIR))
        (convertCF f (rest alon)))])        (names f (rest aloIR)))])
```

We have replaced the boxed names with *f* and added *f* as a parameter. Now we replace *convertCF* and *names* with a new name and thus obtain the abstract function:

```
(define (map f lon)
  (cond
    [(empty? lon) empty]
    [else (cons (f (first lon))
            (map f (rest lon)))]))
```

We use the name map for the result in our running example, because it is the traditional name in programming languages for this specific function.

**The test:** Now we must validate that the new function is a correct abstraction of the original concrete functions. The very definition of abstraction suggests that we define the original functions in terms of the abstract one and test the new versions with the original examples.

In most cases, defining the original function based on the abstract one is straightforward. Suppose the abstract function is called *f-abstract*, and furthermore suppose that one original function is called *f-original* and consumes one argument. If *f-original* differs from the other concrete function in the use of one value, say, *boxed-value*, then we define the following function:

> (**define** (*f-from-abstract x*)
>     (*f-abstract boxed-value x*))

For every proper value *V*, (*f-from-abstract V*) now produces the same answer as (*f-original V*).

Let us return to our example. Here are the two new definitions:

| | |
|---|---|
| ;; *convertCF-from-map : lon → lon*<br>(**define** (*convertCF-from-map alon*)<br>    (map *C→ F alon*)) | ;; *names-from-map : loIR → los*<br>(**define** (*names-from-map aloIR*)<br>    (map *IR-name aloIR*)) |

To ensure that these two definitions are equivalent to the old one and, indirectly, that map is a correct abstraction, we now apply these two functions to the examples that we specified for the development of *convertCF* and *names*.

**The contract:** To make the abstraction truly useful, we must also formulate a contract. If the boxed values in stage 2 of our recipe are functions, a contract requires the use of arrow types. Furthermore, to obtain a widely usable contract, we may have to develop or use parametric data definitions and formulate a parametric type.

A case in point is the contract for map. On one hand, if we view map as an abstraction of *convertCF*, the contract could be construed as

> ;; map : (*number → number*) (**listof** *number*) → (**listof** *number*)

On the other hand, if we view map as an abstraction of *names*, the contract could be construed as

> ;; map : (*IR → symbol*) (**listof** *IR*) → (**listof** *symbol*)

But the first contract would be useless in the second case, and vice versa. To accommodate both cases, we must understand what map does and then fix a contract.

By looking at the definition, we can see that map applies its first argument, a function, to every item on the second argument, a list. This implies that the function must consume the class of data that the list contains. That is, we know *f* has the contract

> ;;*f* : *X* → *???*

if *lon* contains Xs. Furthermore, map creates a list from the results of applying *f* to each item. Thus, if *f* produces Ys, then map produces a list of Ys. Translated into our language of contracts we get this:

;; map : $(X \to Y)$ (**listof** $X$) $\to$ (**listof** $Y$)

This contract says that map can produce a list of Ys from a list of Xs and a function from $X$ to $Y$—no matter for what collection of $X$ and $Y$ stand.

Once we have abstracted two (or more) functions, we should check whether there are other uses for the abstract function. In many cases, an abstract function is useful in a much broader array of contexts than we first anticipate and makes functions easier to read, understand, and maintain. For example, we can now use map every time we need a function to produce a new list by processing all items on an existing list. If that function is a primitive operation or a function we have defined, we don't even write a function. Instead, we simply write an expression that performs the task. Unfortunately, there is no recipe that guides this discovery process. We must practice it and develop an eye for matching abstract functions to situations.

## Exercises

**Exercise 21.1.1** Define *tabulate*, which is the abstraction of the following two functions:

```
;; tabulate-sin : number → lon          ;; tabulate-sqrt : number → lon
;; to tabulate sin between n             ;; to tabulate sqrt between n
;; and 0 (inclusive) in a list           ;; and 0 (inclusive) in a list
(define (tabulate-sin n)                 (define (tabulate-sqrt n)
  (cond                                    (cond
    [(= n 0) (list (sin 0))]                 [(= n 0) (list (sqrt 0))]
    [else                                    [else
      (cons (sin n)                            (cons (sqrt n)
        (tabulate-sin (sub1 n)))]))              (tabulate-sqrt (sub1 n)))]))
```

Be sure to define the two functions in terms of *tabulate*. Also use *tabulate* to define a tabulation function for sqr and tan. What would be a good, general contract? ∎

**Exercise 21.1.2** Define *fold*, which is the abstraction of the following two functions:

```
;; sum : (listof number) → number          ;; product : (listof number) → number
;; to compute the sum of                   ;; to compute the product of
;; the numbers on alon                     ;; the numbers on alon
(define (sum alon)                         (define (product alon)
  (cond                                      (cond
    [(empty? alon) 0]                          [(empty? alon) 1]
    [else (+ (first alon)                      [else (* (first alon)
             (sum (rest alon)))]))                    (product (rest alon)))]))
```

Don't forget to test *fold*.

After *fold* is defined and tested, use it to define append, which juxtaposes the items of two lists or, equivalently, replaces empty at the end of the first list with the second list:

```
(equal? (append (list 1 2 3) (list 4 5 6 7 8))
        (list 1 2 3 4 5 6 7 8))
```

Finally, define map using *fold*.

Compare the four examples to formulate a contract. ∎

**Exercise 21.1.3** Define *natural-f*, which is the abstraction of the following two functions:

```
;; copy : N X → (listof X)                 ;; n-adder : N number → number
;; to create a list that contains          ;; to add n to x using
;; obj n times                             ;; (+ 1 ...) only
(define (copy n obj)                       (define (n-adder n x)
  (cond                                      (cond
    [(zero? n) empty]                          [(zero? n) x]
    [else (cons obj                            [else (+ 1
             (copy (sub1 n) obj))]))                  (n-adder (sub1 n) x))]))
```

Don't forget to test *natural-f*. Also use *natural-f* to define *n-multiplier*, which consumes $n$ and $x$ and produces $n$ times $x$ with additions only. Use the examples to formulate a contract.

**Hint:** The two function differ more than, say, the functions *sum* and *product* in exercise 21.1.2. In particular, the base case in one instance is a argument of the function, where in the other it is just a constant value. ∎

**Formulating General Contracts**: To increase the usefulness of an abstract function, we must formulate a contract that describes its applicability in the most general terms possible. In principle, abstracting contracts follows the same recipe that we use for abstracting functions. We compare and contrast the old contracts; then we replace the differences with variables. But the process is complicated and requires a lot of practice.

Let us start with our running example: *convertCF* and *names*:

$$(\textbf{listof } number) \quad \rightarrow \quad (\textbf{listof } number)$$

$$(\textbf{listof } IR) \quad \rightarrow \quad (\textbf{listof } symbol)$$

Comparing the two contracts shows that they differ in two places. To the left of $\rightarrow$ , we have *number* and *IR*; to the right, it is *number* versus *symbol*.

Consider the second stage of our abstraction recipe. The most natural contracts are as follows:

$$(number \rightarrow number) \quad (\textbf{listof } number) \quad \rightarrow \quad (\textbf{listof } number)$$

$$(IR \rightarrow symbol) \quad (\textbf{listof } IR) \quad \rightarrow \quad (\textbf{listof } symbol)$$

These new contracts suggest a pattern. Specifically, they suggest that the first argument, a function, consumes the items on the second argument, a list, and furthermore, that the results produced by these applications make up the output. The second contract is particularly telling. If we replace *IR* and *symbol* with variables, we get an abstract contract, and it is indeed a contract for map:

$$\mathsf{map} : (X \rightarrow Y) \, (\textbf{listof } X) \rightarrow (\textbf{listof } Y)$$

It is straightforward to check that by replacing $X$ with *number* and $Y$ with *number*, we get the first of the intermediate contracts.

Here is a second pair of examples:

$$number \quad (\textbf{listof } number) \quad \rightarrow \quad (\textbf{listof } number)$$

$$number \quad (\textbf{listof } IR) \quad \rightarrow \quad (\textbf{listof } IR)$$

They are the contracts for *below* and *below-ir*. The contracts differ in two places: the lists consumed and produced. As usual, the functions of the second stage consume an additional argument:

$$(number \; number \rightarrow boolean) \quad number \quad (\textbf{listof } number) \quad \rightarrow \quad (\textbf{listof } number)$$

$$(number \; IR \rightarrow boolean) \quad number \quad (\textbf{listof } IR) \quad \rightarrow \quad (\textbf{listof } IR)$$

The new argument is a function, which in the first case consumes a number, and in the second case an *IR*.

A comparison of the two contracts suggests that *number* and *IR* occupy related positions and that we should replace them with a variable. Doing so makes the two contracts equal:

$$(\textit{number } X \rightarrow \textit{boolean}) \quad \textit{number} \quad (\textbf{listof } X) \quad \rightarrow \quad (\textbf{listof } X)$$

$$(\textit{number } X \rightarrow \textit{boolean}) \quad \textit{number} \quad (\textbf{listof } X) \quad \rightarrow \quad (\textbf{listof } X)$$

A closer inspection of *filter1*'s definition shows that we can also replace *number* with *Y* because the second argument is always just the first argument of *filter1*'s first argument.

Here is the new contract:

$$\textit{filter1} : (Y\ X \rightarrow \textit{boolean})\ Y\ (\textbf{listof } X) \rightarrow (\textbf{listof } X)$$

The result of the first argument must be *boolean*, because it is used as a condition. Hence we have found the most general contract possible.

The two examples illustrate how to find general contracts. We compare the contracts of the examples from which we create abstractions. By replacing specific, distinct classes in corresponding positions, one at a time, we make the contract gradually more general. To ensure that our generalized contract works, we check that the contract describes the specific instances of the abstracted function properly. ∎

## 21.2 Finger Exercises with Abstract List Functions

Scheme provides a number of abstract functions for processing lists. Figure 57 collects the specification of the most important ones. Using these functions greatly simplifies many programming tasks and helps readers understand programs quickly. The following exercises provide an opportunity to get acquainted with these functions.

---

**Exercises**

**Exercise 21.2.1** Use build-list

  1. to create the lists (list 0 ... 3) and (list 1 ... 4);

  2. to create the list (list .1 .01 .001 .0001);

```
;; build-list : N (N → X) → (listof X)
;; to construct (list (f 0) ... (f (− n 1)))
(define (build-list n f) ...)


;; filter : (X → boolean) (listof X) → (listof X)
;; to construct a list from all those items on alox for which p holds
(define (filter p alox) ...)


;; quick-sort : (X X → boolean) (listof X) → (listof X)
;; to construct a list from all items on alox in an order according to cmp
(define (quick-sort cmp alox) ...)


;; map : (X → Y) (listof X) → (listof Y)
;; to construct a list by applying f to each item on alox
;; that is, (map f (list x-1 ... x-n)) = (list (f x-1) ... (f x-n))
(define (map f alox) ...)


;; andmap : (X → boolean) (listof X) → boolean
;; to determine whether p holds for every item on alox
;; that is, (andmap p (list x-1 ... x-n)) = (and (p x-1) (and ... (p x-n)))
(define (andmap p alox) ...)


;; ormap : (X → boolean) (listof X) → boolean
;; to determine whether p holds for at least one item on alox
;; that is, (ormap p (list x-1 ... x-n)) = (or (p x-1) (or ... (p x-n)))
(define (ormap p alox) ...)


;; foldr : (X Y → Y) Y (listof X) → Y
;; (foldr f base (list x-1 ... x-n)) = (f x-1 ... (f x-n base))
(define (foldr f base alox) ...)


;; foldl : (X Y → Y) Y (listof X) → Y
;; (foldl f base (list x-1 ... x-n)) = (f x-n ... (f x-1 base))
(define (foldl f base alox) ...)


;; assf : (X → boolean) (listof (list X Y)) → (list X Y) or false
;; to find the first item on alop for whose first item p? holds
(define (assf p? alop) ...)
```

Figure 57: Scheme's built-in abstract functions for list-processing

3. to define *evens*, which consumes a natural number *n* and creates the list of the first *n* even numbers;

4. to define *tabulate* from exercise 21.1.1; and

5. to define *diagonal*, which consumes a natural number *n* and creates a list of lists of 0 and 1.
Example:

```
(equal? (diagonal 3)
        (list
             (list 1 0 0)
             (list 0 1 0)
             (list 0 0 1)))
```

Use local if function definitions require auxiliary functions. ∎

**Exercise 21.2.2** Use map to define the following functions:

1. *convert-euro*, which converts a list of U.S. dollar amounts into a list of euro amounts based on an exchange rate of 1.22 euro for each dollar;

2. *convertFC*, which converts a list of Fahrenheit measurements to a list of Celsius measurements;

3. *move-all*, which consumes a list of *posn* structures and translates each by adding 3 to the $x$-component. ∎

**Exercise 21.2.3** Here is the version of filter that DrScheme provides:

```
;; filter : (X → boolean) (listof X) → (listof X)
;; to construct a list of X from all those items on alon
;; for which predicate? holds
(define (filter predicate? alon)
  (cond
    [(empty? alon) empty]
    [else (cond
            [(predicate? (first alon))
             (cons (first alon) (filter predicate? (rest alon)))]
            [else (filter predicate? (rest alon))])]))
```

Use filter to define the following functions:

1. *eliminate-exp*, which consumes a number, *ua*, and a list of toy structures (containing name and price) and produces a list of all those descriptions whose price is below *ua*;

2. *recall*, which consumes the name of a toy, called *ty*, and a list of names, called *lon*, and produces a list of names that contains all components of *lon* with the exception of *ty*;

3. *selection*, which consumes two lists of names and selects all those from the second one that are also on the first. ∎

---

## 21.3 Abstraction and a Single Point of Control

Just like editing papers, abstracting programs has many advantages. Creating an abstraction often simplifies other definitions. The process of abstracting may uncover problems with existing functions. But, the single most important advantage of abstraction is that it creates a SINGLE POINT OF CONTROL for the functionality in a program. In other words, it (as much as possible) puts in one place the definitions related to some specific task.

Putting the definitions for a specific task in one place makes it easier to maintain a program. Roughly put, program maintenance means fixing the program so that it functions properly in previously untested cases; extending the program so that it can deal with new or unforeseen situations; or changing the representation of some information as data (for example, calendar dates). With everything in one place, fixing an error means fixing it in one function, not four or five similar versions. Extending a function's capabilities means fixing one function, not its related copies. And changing a data representation means changing a general data-traversal function, not all those that came from the same template. Translated into a guideline, this becomes:

> GUIDELINE ON CREATING ABSTRACTIONS
> Form an abstraction instead of copying and modifying a piece of a program.

Experience teaches us that maintaining software is expensive. Programmers can reduce the maintenance cost by organizing programs correctly. The first principle of function organization is to match the function's structure to the structure of its input data. If every programmer follows this rule, it is easy to modify and extend functions when the set of possible input data changes. The second principle is to introduce proper abstractions. Every abstracted function creates a single point of control for at least two different functions, often for several more. After we have abstracted, we often find more uses of the new function.

Our design recipe for abstracting functions is the most basic tool to create abstractions. To use it requires practice. As we practice, we expand our capabilities for building and using abstractions. The best programmers are those who actively edit their programs to build new abstractions so that they collect things related to a task at a single point. Here we use functional abstraction to study this practice. While not all languages provide the freedom to abstract functions as easily as Scheme, modern languages often support similar concepts and practicing in powerful languages such as Scheme is the best possible preparation.[47]

## 21.4   Extended Exercise: Moving Pictures, Again

In sections 6.6, 7.4, and 10.3, we studied the problem of moving pictures across a canvas. The problem had two parts: moving individual shapes and moving a picture, which is a list of shapes. For the first part, we need functions to draw, clear, and translate a shape. For the second part, we need functions that draw all shapes on a list, that clear all shapes on a list, and that translate all shapes on a list. Even the most cursory look at the functions shows many repetitions. The following exercises aim to eliminate these repetitions via manual abstraction and Scheme's built-in operations.

---

**Exercises**

**Exercise 21.4.1** Abstract the functions *draw-a-circle* and *clear-a-circle* into a single function *process-circle*.

Define *translate-circle* using *process-circle*. **Hint:** If a primitive function doesn't quite fit an abstraction, we have to define auxiliary functions. For now, use **define** to do so. Intermezzo 4 introduces a handy and important short-hand for that purpose. ∎

---

[47] A currently popular method of abstraction is INHERITANCE in class-based object-oriented programming languages. Inheritance is quite similar to functional abstraction, though it emphasizes those aspects that change over those that stay the same.

**Exercise 21.4.2** Abstract the functions *draw-a-rectangle* and *clear-a-rectangle* into a single function *process-rectangle*.

Define *translate-rectangle* using *process-rectangle*. ∎

**Exercise 21.4.3** Abstract the functions *draw-shape* and *clear-shape* into a single function *process-shape*. Compare the function with the template *fun-for-shape*.

Define *translate-shape* using *process-shape*. ∎

**Exercise 21.4.4** Use Scheme's map and andmap to define *draw-losh, clear-losh,* and *translate-losh.* ∎

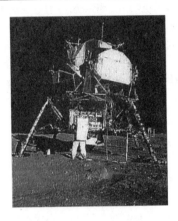

Figure 58: The Apollo 11 lunar lander
NASA: National Space Science Data Center

**Exercise 21.4.5** Modify the functions of exercises 21.4.3 and 21.4.4 so that pictures move up and down on a canvas.

Modify all definitions so that a shape can also be a line; a line has a start position, an end position, and a color.

Define *LUNAR*, a list that sketches a lunar lander picture (see figure 58). The list should consist of rectangles, circles, and lines.

Develop the program *lunar-lander*. It places LUNAR at the top of a canvas and then uses the modified functions to move the lander up or down.

Use the teachpack **arrow.ss** to give users control over how fast and when the lunar lander should move:

> (*start* 500 100)
> (*draw LUNAR*)
> (*control-up-down LUNAR* 10 *move-lander draw-losh*)

If time permits, modify the function so that a player can move the lander up, down, left or right. Use *controller* from **arrow.ss** to control the movements in all directions. ∎

---

## 21.5   Note: Designing Abstractions from Templates

At the very beginning of this part of the book, we discussed how we design sets of functions from the same template. More specifically, when we design a set of functions that all consume the same kind of data, we reuse the same template over and over again. It is therefore not surprising that the function definitions look similar and that we will abstract them later.

Indeed, we could abstract from the templates directly. While this topic is highly advanced and still a subject of research in the area of programming languages, we can discuss it with a short example. Consider the template for lists:

> (**define** (*fun-for-l l*)
>   (**cond**
>     [(empty? *l*) ...]
>     [**else** ... (first *l*) ... (*fun-for-l* (rest *l*)) ...]))

It contains two gaps, one in each clause. When we define a list-processing function, we fill these gaps. In the first clause, we typically place a plain value. For the second one, we combine (first *l*) and (*f* (rest *l*)) where *f* is the recursive function.

We can abstract over this programming task with the following function:

> ;; *reduce* : $X (X \ Y \rightarrow Y)$ (**listof** $Y$) $\rightarrow Y$
> (**define** (*reduce base combine l*)
>   (**cond**
>     [(empty? *l*) *base*]
>     [**else** (*combine* (first *l*)
>              (*reduce base combine* (rest *l*)))]))

It consumes two extra arguments: *base*, which is the value for the base case, and *combine*, which is a function that performs the value combination for the second clause.

Using *reduce* we can define many plain list-processing functions as well as almost all the functions of figure 57. Here are two of them:

;; *sum* : (**listof** *number*) → *number*          ;; *product* : (**listof** *number*) → *number*
(**define** (*sum l*) (*reduce* 0 + *l*))          (**define** (*product l*) (*reduce* 1 * *l*))

For *sum*, the base case always produces 0; adding the first item and the result of the natural recursion combines the values of the second clause. Analogous reasoning explains *product*.

To define *sort*, we need to define an auxiliary function first:

;; *sort* : (**listof** *number*) → (**listof** *number*)
(**define** (*sort l*)
  (**local** ((**define** (*insert an alon*)
            (**cond**
              [(empty? *alon*) (list *an*)]
              [**else** (**cond**
                      [(> *an* (first *alon*)) (cons *an alon*)]
                      [**else** (cons (first *alon*) (*insert an* (rest *alon*)))])])))
    (*reduce* empty *insert l*)))

Other list-processing functions can be defined in a similar manner.

# 22   Designing Abstractions with First-Class Functions

We have seen that functions can consume functions and how important that is for creating single points of control in a function. But functions not only can consume functions, they can also produce them. More precisely, expressions in the new Scheme can evaluate to functions. Because the body of a function definition is also an expression, a function can produce a function. In this section, we first discuss this surprising idea and then show how it is useful for abstracting functions and in other contexts.

## 22.1   Functions that Produce Functions

While the idea of producing a function may seem strange at first, it is extremely useful. Before we can discuss the usefulness of the idea, though, we must explore how a function can produce a function. Here are three examples:

```
(define (f x) first)
(define (g x) f)
(define (h x)
  (cond
    ((empty? x) f)
    ((cons? x) g)))
```

The body of $f$ is first, a primitive operation, so applying $f$ to any argument always evaluates to first. Similarly, the body of $g$ is $f$, so applying $g$ to any argument always evaluates to $f$. Finally, depending on what kind of list we supply as an argument to $h$, it produces $f$ or $g$.

None of these examples is useful but each illustrates the basic idea. In the first two cases, the body of the function definition is a function. In the last case, it evaluates to a function. The examples are useless because the results do not contain or refer to the argument. For a function $f$ to produce a function that contains one of $f$'s arguments, $f$ must define a function and return it as the result. That is, $f$'s body must be a **local**-expression.

Recall that **local**-expressions group definitions and ask DrScheme to evaluate a single expression in the context of these definitions. They can occur wherever an expression can occur, which means the following definition is legal:

```
(define (add x)
  (local ((define (x-adder y) (+ x y)))
    x-adder))
```

The function *add* consumes a number; after all, $x$ is added to $y$. It then defines the function *x-adder* with a **local**-expression. The body of the **local**-expression is *x-adder*, which means the result of *add* is *x-adder*.

To understand *add* better, let us look at how an application of *add* to some number evaluates:

```
  (define f (add 5))
= (define f (local ((define (x-adder y) (+ 5 y)))
               x-adder))
= (define f (local ((define (x-adder5 y) (+ 5 y)))
               x-adder5))
= (define (x-adder5 y) (+ 5 y))
  (define f x-adder5)
```

The last step adds the function *x-adder5* to the collection of our definitions; the evaluation continues with the body of the **local**-expression, *x-adder5*, which is the name of a function and thus a value. Now *f* is defined and we can use it:

$$(f\ 10)$$
$$= (x\text{-}adder5\ 10)$$
$$= (+\ 5\ 10)$$
$$= 15$$

That is, *f* stands for *x-adder5*, a function, which adds 5 to its argument.

Using this example, we can write *add*'s contract and a purpose statement:

```
;; add : number → (number → number)
;; to create a function that adds x to its input
(define (add x)
   (local ((define (x-adder y) (+ x y)))
      x-adder))
```

The most interesting property of *add* is that its result "remembers" the value of *x*. For example, every time we use *f*, it uses 5, the value of *x*, when *add* was used to define *f*. This form of "memory" is the key to our simple recipe for defining abstract functions, which we discuss in the next section.

## 22.2 Designing Abstractions with Functions-as-Values

The combination of **local**-expressions and functions-as-values simplifies our recipe for creating abstract functions. Consider our very first example in figure 53 again. If we replace the contents of the boxes with *rel-op*, we get a function that has a free variable. To avoid this, we can either add *rel-op* to the parameters or we can wrap the definition in a **local** and prefix it with a function that consumes *rel-op*. Figure 59 shows what happnes when we use this idea with filter. If we also make the **local**ly defined function the result of the function, we have defined an abstraction of the two original functions.

Put differently, we follow the example of *add* in the preceding section. Like *add*, *filter2* consumes an argument, defines a function, and returns this function as a result. The result remembers the *rel-op* argument for good as the following evaluation shows:

$$(filter2\ <)$$

```
(define (filter2 rel-op)
  (local ((define (abs-fun alon t)
            (cond
              [(empty? alon) empty]
              [else
                (cond
                  [( rel-op (first alon) t)
                   (cons (first alon)
                     (abs-fun (rest alon) t))]
                  [else
                    (abs-fun (rest alon) t)])])))
    abs-fun))
```

Figure 59: Abstracting with **local**

```
= (local ((define (abs-fun alon t)
            (cond
              [(empty? alon) empty]
              [else
                (cond
                  [(< (first alon) t)
                   (cons (first alon)
                     (abs-fun (rest alon) t))]
                  [else
                    (abs-fun (rest alon) t)])])))
    abs-fun)
```

```
= (define (below3 alon t)
    (cond
      [(empty? alon) empty]
      [else
        (cond
          [(< (first alon) t)
           (cons (first alon)
             (below3 (rest alon) t))]
          [else
            (below3 (rest alon) t)])]))
  below3
```

Remember that as we lift a **local** definition to the top-level definitions, we also rename the function in case the same **local** is evaluated again. Here we choose the name *below3* to indicate what the function does. And indeed, a comparison between *below* and *below3* reveals that the only difference is the name of the function.

From the calculation, it follows that we can give the result of (*filter2* <) a name and use it as if it were *below*. More succinctly,

> (**define** *below2* (*filter2* <))

is equivalent to

> (**define** (*below3 alon t*)
>   (**cond**
>     [(empty? *alon*) empty]
>     [**else**
>       (**cond**
>         [(< (first *alon*) *t*)
>          (cons (first *alon*)
>            (*below3* (rest *alon*) *t*))]
>         [**else**
>          (*below3* (rest *alon*) *t*)])])))

> (**define** *below2 below3*)

which means *below2* is just another name for *below3* and which directly proves that our abstract function correctly implements *below*.

The example suggests a variant of the abstraction recipe from section 21:

**The comparison:** The new recipe still requires us to compare and to mark the differences.

**The abstraction:** The new step concerns the way we define the abstract function. We place one of the functions into a **local**-expression and use the name of the function as the body of the **local**:

> (**local** ((**define** (*concrete-fun x y z*)
>     ... $\boxed{op1}$ ... $\boxed{op2}$ ...))
>   *concrete-fun*)

From that, we can create the abstract function by listing the names in the boxes as parameters:

```
(define (abs-fun op1 op2)
  (local ((define (concrete-fun x y z)
           ... op1 ... op2 ...))
    concrete-fun))
```

If *op1* or *op2* is a special symbol, say <, we name it something that is more meaningful in the new context.

**The test:** To test the abstract function, we define the concrete functions again, as before. Consider the example of *below* and *above*. Obtaining *below* and *above* as instances of *filter2* is now straightforward:

(**define** *below2* (*filter2* <))

(**define** *above2* (*filter2* >))

We simply apply *filter2* to the contents of the box in the respective concrete function and that application produces the old function.

**The contract:** The contract of an abstract function contains two arrows. After all, the function produces a function, and to describe this relationship the type to the right of the first arrow must contain another arrow.

Here is the contract for *filter2*:

$$;; filter2 : (X\ Y \rightarrow boolean) \rightarrow ((\textbf{listof}\ X)\ Y \rightarrow (\textbf{listof}\ X))$$

It consumes a comparison function and produces a concrete filter-style function.

The generalization of the contract works as before.

Given our experience with the first design recipe, the second one is only a question of practice.

## Exercises

**Exercise 22.2.1** Define an abstraction of the functions *convertCF* and *names* from section 21.1 using the new recipe for abstraction. ∎

**Exercise 22.2.2** Define an abstract version of *sort* (see exercise 19.1.6) using the new recipe for abstraction. ∎

**Exercise 22.2.3** Define *fold* using the new recipe for abstraction. Recall that *fold* abstracts the following pair of functions:

```
;; sum : (listof number) → number          ;; product : (listof number) → number
;; to compute the sum of alon              ;; to compute the product of alon
(define (sum alon)                         (define (product alon)
  (cond                                      (cond
    [(empty? alon) 0]                          [(empty? alon) 1]
    [else (+ (first alon)                      [else (* (first alon)
             (sum (rest alon)))]))                     (product (rest alon)))]))
```

∎

## 22.3  A First Look at Graphical User Interfaces

Functions as first-class values play a central role in the design of graphical user interfaces. The term "interface" refers to the boundary between the program and a user. As long as we are the only users, we can apply functions to data in DrScheme's Interactions window. If we want others to use our programs, though, we must provide a way to interact with the program that does not require any programming knowledge. The interaction between a program and a casual user is the USER INTERFACE.

A GRAPHICAL USER INTERFACE (GUI) is the most convenient interface for casual users. A GUI is a window that contains GUI items. Some of these items permit users to enter text; others are included so that users can apply a specific function; and yet others exist to display a function's results. Examples include *buttons*, which the user can click with the mouse and which trigger a function application; *choice menus*, from which the user can choose one of a collection of values; *text fields*, into which the user can type arbitrary text; and *message fields*, into which a program can draw text.

Take a look at the simple GUI in figure 60. The left-most picture shows its initial state. In that state, the GUI contains a text field labeled "Name" and a message field labeled "Number" plus a "LookUp" button. In the second picture, the user has entered the name "Sean" but hasn't yet clicked

Figure 60: A simple GUI for looking up a phone number

the "LookUp" button.[48] Finally, the right-most picture shows how the GUI displays the phone number of "Sean" after the user clicks the "LookUp" button.

The core of the program is a function that looks up a phone number for a name in a list. We wrote several versions of this function in part II but always used it with DrScheme's Interactions window. Using the GUI of figure 60, people who know nothing about Scheme can now use our function, too.

To build a graphical user interface, we build structures[49] that correspond to the GUI items and hand them over to a GUI manager. The latter constructs the visible window from these items. Some of the structures' fields describe the visual properties of the GUI's elements, such as the label of a button, the initial content of a message field, or the available choices on a menu. Other fields stand for functions. They are called CALL-BACK FUNCTIONS because the GUI manager calls—or applies—these functions when the user manipulates the corresponding GUI element. Upon application, a call-back function obtains strings and (natural) numbers from the elements of the GUI and then applies the function proper. This last step computes answers, which the call-back function can place into GUI elements just like graphics functions draw shapes on a canvas.

The ideal program consists of two completely separate components: the MODEL, which is the kind of program we are learning to design, and a VIEW, which is the GUI program that manages the display of information and the user's mouse and keyboard manipulations. The bridge between the two is the CONTROL expression. Figure 61 graphically illustrates the or-

---

[48]The program has also cleared the result field to avoid any misunderstanding. Similarly, the user could also just hit the enter key instead of clicking the button. We ignore such subtleties here.

[49]More precisely, we construct an object, but we do not need to understand the distinction between a structure and an object here.

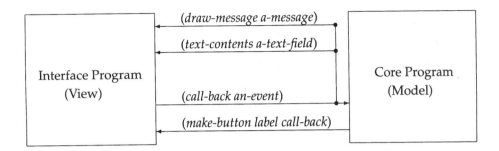

Figure 61: The model-view arrangement

ganization, known as the MODEL-VIEW-CONTROL architecture. The lowest arrow indicates how a program makes up a button along with a call-back function. The left-to-right arrow depicts the mouse-click event and how it triggers an application of the call-back function. It, in turn, uses other GUI functions to obtain user input before it applies a core function or to display results of the core function.

The separation of the program into two parts means that the definitions for the model contain no references to the view, and that the definitions for the view contain no references to the data or the functionality of the model. The organization principle evolved over two decades from many good and bad experiences. It has the advantage that, with an adaptation of just the bridge expression, we can use one and the same program with different GUIs and vice versa. Furthermore, the construction of views requires different tools than does the construction of models. Constructing views is a labor-intensive effort and involves graphical design, but fortunately, it is often possible to generate large portions automatically. The construction of models, in contrast, will always demand a serious program design effort.

Here we study the simplified GUI world of the teachpack **gui.ss**. Figure 62 specifies the operations that the teachpack provides.[50] The GUI manager is represented by the function *create-window*. Its contract and purpose statement are instructive. They explain that we create a window from a list. The function arranges these lists in a corresponding number of rows on the visible window. Each row is specified as a list of *gui-items*. The data definition for *gui-items* in figure 62 shows that there are four kinds:

---

[50]The *gui-items* aren't really structures, which explains the font of the operations' names.

A *gui-item* is either

1. (*make-button string* (X → true))

2. (*make-text string*)

3. (*make-choices* (**listof** *string*)) or

4. (*make-message string*).

---

;; *create-window :* (**listof** (**listof** *gui-item*)) → true
;; to add gui-items to the window and to show the window
;; each list of gui-items defines one row of gui items in the window

;; *hide-window :* → true
;; to hide the window

;; *make-button : string* (*event%* → true) → *gui-item*
;; to create a button with label and call-back function

;; *make-message : string* → *gui-item*
;; to create an item that displays a message

;; *draw-message : gui-item*[*message%*] *string* → true
;; to display a message in a message item
;; it erases the current message

;; *make-text : string* → *gui-item*
;; to create an item (with label) that allows users to enter text

;; *text-contents : gui-item*[*text%*] → *string*
;; to determine the contents of a text field

;; *make-choice :* (**listof** *string*) → *gui-item*
;; to create a choice menu that permits users to choose from some
;; string alternatives

;; *get-choice : gui-item*[*choice%*] → *num*
;; to determine which choice is currently selected in a choice-item
;; the result is the 0-based index in the choice menu

Figure 62: The **gui.ss** operations

**text fields,** which are created with (*make-text a-string*) and allow users to enter arbitrary text into an area in the window;

**buttons,** which are created with (*make-button a-string a-function*) and allow users to apply a function with the click of a mouse button;

**choice menus,** which are created with (*make-choice a-list-of-strings*) and allow users to pick a choice from a specified set of choices; and

**message fields,** which are created with (*make-message a-string*) and enable the model to inform users of results.

The function that goes with a button is a function of one argument: an event. For most uses, we can ignore the event; it is simply a token that signals the user's click action.

How all this works is best illustrated with examples. Our first example is a canonical GUI program:

(*create-window* (list (list (*make-button* "Close" *hide-window*))))

It creates a window with a single button and equips it with the simplest of all call-backs: *hide-window*, the function that hides the window. When the user clicks the button labeled "Close", the window disappears.

The second sample GUI copies what the user enters into a text field to a message field. We first create a text field and a message field:

(**define** *a-text-field*
  (*make-text* "Enter Text:"))

(**define** *a-message*
  (*make-message* "'Hello World' is a silly program."))

Now we can refer to these fields in a call-back function:

```
;; echo-message : X → true
;; to extract the contents of a-text-field and to draw it into a-message
(define (echo-message e)
  (draw-message a-message (text-contents a-text-field)))
```

The definition of the call-back function is based on our (domain) knowledge about the *gui-item*s. Specifically, the function *echo-message* obtains the current contents of the text field with *text-contents* as a string, and it draws this string into the message field with the *draw-message* function. To put everything together, we create a window with two rows:

```
(create-window
  (list (list a-text-field a-message)
        (list (make-button "Copy Now" echo-message))))
```

The first row contains the text and the message field; the second one contains a button with the label "Copy Now" whose call-back function is *echo-message*. The user can now enter text into the text field, click the button, and see the text appear in the message field of the window.

The purpose of the third and last example is to create a window with a choice menu, a message field, and a button. Clicking the button puts the current choice into the message field. As before, we start by defining the input and output *gui-items*:

```
(define THE-CHOICES
  (list "green" "red" "yellow"))

(define a-choice
  (make-choice THE-CHOICES))

(define a-message
  (make-message (first THE-CHOICES)))
```

Because the list of choices is used more than once in the program, it is specified in a separate variable definition.

As before, the call-back function for the button interacts with *a-choice* and *a-message*:

```
;; echo-choice : X → true
;; to determine the current choice of a-choice and
;; to draw the corresponding string into a-message
(define (echo-choice e)
  (draw-message a-message
                (list-ref THE-CHOICES
                          (choice-index a-choice))))
```

Specifically, the call-back function finds the 0-based index of the user's current choice with *choice-index*, uses Scheme's list-ref function to extract the corresponding string from *THE-CHOICES*, and then draws the result into the message field of the window. To create the window, we arrange *a-choice* and *a-message* in one row and the button in a row below:

```
(create-window
  (list (list a-choice a-message)
        (list (make-button "Confirm Choice" echo-choice))))
```

```
;; Model:
;; build-number : (listof digit) → number
;; to translate a list of digits into a number
;; example: (build-number (list 1 2 3)) = 123
(define (build-number x) ...)


;; ————————————————————————————————————————


;; View:
;; the ten digits as strings
(define DIGITS
    (build-list 10 number→ string))

;; a list of three digit choice menus
(define digit-choosers
    (local ((define (builder i) (make-choice DIGITS)))
      (build-list 3 builder)))

;; a message field for saying hello and displaying the number
(define a-msg
    (make-message "Welcome"))


;; ————————————————————————————————————————


;; Controller:
;; check-call-back : X → true
;; to get the current choices of digits, convert them to a number,
;; and to draw this number as a string into the message field
(define (check-call-back b)
    (draw-message a-msg
                  (number→ string
                    (build-number
                      (map choice-index digit-choosers)))))

(create-window
  (list
    (append digit-choosers (list a-msg))
    (list (make-button "Check Guess" check-call-back))))
```

Figure 63: A GUI for echoing digits as numbers

Now that we have examined some basic GUI programs, we can study a program with full-fledged core and GUI components. Take a look at the definitions in figure 63. The program's purpose is to echo the values of several digit choice menus as a number into some message field. The model consists of the *build-number* function, which converts a list of (three) digits into a number. We have developed several such functions, so the figure mentions only what it does. The GUI component of the program sets up three choice menus, a message field, and a button. The control part consists of a single call-back function, which is attached to the single button in the window. It determines the (list of) current choice indices, hands them over to *build-number*, and draws the result as a string into the message field.

Let's study the organization of the call-back functions in more detail. It composes three kinds of functions:

1. The innermost function determines the current state of the *gui-item*s. This is the user's input. With the given functions, we can determine the string that the user entered into either a text field or the 0-based index of a choice menu.

2. This user input is consumed by the main function of the model. The call-back function may convert the user's string into some other data, say, a symbol or a number.

3. The result of the model function, in turn, is drawn into a message field, possibly after converting it to a string first.

The control component of a program is also responsible for the visual composition of the window. The teachpack provides only one function for this purpose: *create-window*. Standard GUI toolboxes provide many more functions, though all of these toolboxes differ from each other and are changing rapidly.

## Exercises

**Exercise 22.3.1** Modify the program of figure 63 so that it implements the number-guessing game from exercises 5.1.2, 5.1.3, and 9.5.5. Make sure that the number of digits that the player must guess can be changed by editing a single definition in the program.

**Hint:** Recall that exercise 11.3.1 introduces a function that generates random numbers. ∎

**Exercise 22.3.2** Develop a program for looking up phone numbers. The program's GUI should consist of a text field, a message field, and a button. The text field permits users to enter names. The message field should display the number that the model finds or the message "name not found", if the model produces false.

Generalize the program so that a user can also enter a phone number (as a sequence of digits containing no other characters).

**Hints:** (1) Scheme provides the function *string→ symbol* for converting a string to a symbol. (2) It also provides the function string→ number, which converts a string to a number if possible. If the function consumes a string that doesn't represent a number, it produces false:

(string→ number "6670004")
= 6670004

(string→ number "667-0004")
= false

The generalization demonstrates how one and the same GUI can use two distinct models.

**Real-world GUIs:** The graphical user interface in figure 60 was not constructed from the items provided by the teachpack. GUIs constructed with the teachpack's *gui-item*s are primitive. They are sufficient, however, to study the basic principles of GUI programming. The design of real-world GUIs involves graphics designers and tools that generate GUI programs (rather than making them by hand). ∎

**Exercise 22.3.3** Develop *pad→ gui*. The function consumes a title (string) and a *gui-table*. It turns the table into a list of lists of *gui-item*s that *create-window* can consume. Here is the data definition for *gui-table*s:

---

A *cell* is either

  1. a number,

  2. a symbol.

---

A *gui-table* is a (**listof** (**listof** *cell*)) .

Here are two examples of gui-tables:

|  |  |
|---|---|
| (**define** *pad* | (**define** *pad2* |
| '((1 2 3) | '((1 2 3 +) |
| (4 5 6) | (4 5 6 −) |
| (7 8 9) | (7 8 9 *) |
| (\# 0 *))) | (0 = \. /))) |

The table on the left lays out a virtual phone pad, the right one a calculator pad.

The function *pad→ gui* should turn each cell into a button. The resulting list should be prefixed with two messages. The first one displays the title and never changes. The second one displays the latest button that the user clicked. The two examples above should produce the following two GUIs:

**Hint:** The second message header requires a short string, for example, "N", as the initial value. ∎

# 23   Mathematical Examples

Applying mathematics to real-world problems requires programs that implement mathematical functions. In many cases, the programs also employ functions that consume and produce functions. Mathematics is therefore a great starting point for practicing programming with functions and, more generally, for creating abstract functions.

The first subsection covers sequences and series, a key element of mathematics. The second section discusses integration, which relies heavily on series. Finally, the third section introduces function differentiation.

## 23.1   Sequences and Series

In pre-algebra and algebra, we encounter *sequences* (also known as progressions) of numbers. Here are three examples:

1. $0, 2, 4, 6, 8$;

2. $1, 3, 5, 7, 9$;

3. $5, 10, 15, 20, 25$.

The first two enumerate the first five even and odd natural numbers, respectively; the last one lists the first five positive integers, evenly divisible by 5. Sequences can also be infinite:

1. $0, 2, 4, 6, 8, \ldots$;

2. $1, 3, 5, 7, 9, \ldots$;

3. $5, 10, 15, 20, 25, \ldots$

Following mathematical tradition, infinite sequences end in "$\ldots$" and the reader must determine how to find more of the terms in the sequence.

One way to understand sequences of numbers, especially infinite ones, is to match them up with an enumeration of the natural numbers. For example, the even and odd (natural) numbers match up like this:

| index | 0 | 1 | 2 | 3 | 4 | 5 | 6 | 7 | 8 | 9 | $\ldots$ |
|---|---|---|---|---|---|---|---|---|---|---|---|
| evens | 0 | 2 | 4 | 6 | 8 | 10 | 12 | 14 | 16 | 18 | $\ldots$ |
| odds | 1 | 3 | 5 | 7 | 9 | 11 | 13 | 15 | 17 | 19 | $\ldots$ |

It is easy to see from this table that every even number is $2 \cdot i$ for its index $i$ and that an odd number is $2 \cdot i + 1$.

Both statements can be translated into simple Scheme functions:

```
;; make-even : N → N[even]          ;; make-odd : N → N[odd]
;; to compute the i-th even number  ;; to compute the i-th odd number
(define (make-even i)               (define (make-odd i)
  (* 2 i))                            (+ (* 2 i) 1))
```

In short, functions from natural numbers to numbers are representations of infinite sequences.

A mathematical *series* is the sum of a sequence. The three finite sequences have the sums 20, 25, and 75, respectively. In the case of infinite sequences it is often interesting to consider a finite portion, staring with the first one.[51]  For example, adding the first 10 even numbers yields 90, and adding the first 10 odd numbers yields 100. Computing a series is clearly a job for a computer.  Here are functions that add up the first $n$ odd or even numbers, respectively, using *make-even* and *make-odd* to compute the required numbers:

```
;; series-even : N → number          ;; series-odd : N → number
;; to sum up the first               ;; to sum up the first
;; n even numbers                    ;; n odd numbers
(define (series-even n)              (define (series-odd n)
  (cond                                (cond
    [(= n 0) (make-even n)]             [(= n 0) (make-odd n)]
    [else (+ (make-even n)              [else (+ (make-odd n)
             (series-even (− n 1)))])))          (series-odd (− n 1)))])))
```

The two functions are natural candidates for abstraction and here is the result of following our basic abstraction recipe:

```
;; series : N (N → number) → number
;; to sum up the first n numbers in the sequence a-term,
(define (series n a-term)
  (cond
    [(= n 0) (a-term n)]
    [else (+ (a-term n)
             (series (− n 1) a-term))]))
```

The first argument specifies where the addition starts.  The second argument of *series* is a function that maps a natural number to the corresponding term in the series. To test *series*, we apply it to *make-even* and *make-odd*:

```
;; series-even1 : N → number          ;; series-odd1 : N → number
(define (series-even1 n)              (define (series-odd1 n)
  (series n make-even))                 (series n make-odd))
```

---

[51]In some cases, an infinite sequence may also have a sum. Specifically, adding up more and more of the terms of a sequence produces numbers that are closer and closer to some number, which we call the sum. For example, the sum of the sequence

$$1, \frac{1}{2}, \frac{1}{4}, \frac{1}{8}, \dots$$

is 2. In contrast, the sequence

$$1, \frac{1}{2}, \frac{1}{3}, \frac{1}{4}, \dots$$

does not have a sum.

For over a century, mathematicians have used the Greek symbol $\Sigma$ to communicate about series. The two series above would be expressed as

$$\sum_{i=0}^{i=n} make\text{-}even(i) \qquad \sum_{i=0}^{i=n} make\text{-}odd(i)$$

A true (lazy) mathematician would also replace *make-even* and *make-odd* by their definitions, that is, $2 \cdot i$ and $2 \cdot i + 1$, but we refrain from doing so to emphasize the analogy to our (well-organized) functions.

## Exercises

**Exercise 23.1.1** Use **local** to create *series-local* from *series-even* and *series-odd*. Show with a hand-evaluation that (*series-local make-even*) is equivalent to *series-even*. ∎

## 23.2 Arithmetic Sequences and Series

In an arithmetic sequence

$$a_0, a_1, a_2, a_3, \ldots, a_n, a_{n+1}, \ldots$$

each successor term $a_{n+1}$ is the result of adding a fixed constant to $a_n$. Here is a concrete example, matched up with the natural numbers:

| index | 0 | 1 | 2 | 3 | 4 | ... |
|---|---|---|---|---|---|---|
| arithmetic sequence | 8 | 13 | 18 | 23 | ... | |

Here the starting point is 3 and the constant is 5. From these two facts, called *starting point* and *summand*, respectively, all other terms in the sequence can be determined.

## Exercises

**Exercise 23.2.1** Develop the recursive function *a-fives*, which consumes a natural number and recursively determines the corresponding term in the above series. ∎

**Exercise 23.2.2** Develop the non-recursive function *a-fives-closed*. It consumes a natural number and determines the corresponding term in the above series. A non-recursive function is sometimes called a *closed form*. ∎

**Exercise 23.2.3** Use *series* to determine the sum of the *a-fives* sequence for the bounds 3, 7, and 88. Can an infinite arithmetic series have a sum? ∎

**Exercise 23.2.4** Develop the function *seq-a-fives*, which consumes a natural number $n$ and creates the sequence of the first $n$ terms according to *a-fives* or *a-fives-closed*. **Hint:** Use build-list. ∎

**Exercise 23.2.5** Develop *arithmetic-series*. The function consumes two numbers: *start* and *s*. Its result is a function that represents the arithmetic series whose starting point is *start* and whose summand is *s*. For example, (*arithmetic-series* 3 5) yields *a-fives* (or *a-fives-closed*). Similarly, (*arithmetic-series* 0 2) produces a function that represents the series of even numbers. ∎

## 23.3 Geometric Sequences and Series

In a geometric sequence

$$g_0, g_1, g_2, g_3, \ldots, g_n, g_{n+1}, \ldots$$

each succesor term $g_{n+1}$ is the result of multiplying a fixed constant with $g_n$. Here is a concrete example, matched up with the natural numbers:

| *index* | 0 | 1 | 2 | 3 | 4 | ... |
|---|---|---|---|---|---|---|
| geometric sequence | 3 | 15 | 75 | 375 | 1875 | ... |

Here the starting point is 3 and the constant is 5. From these, called *starting point* and *factor*, respectively, every other term in the sequence is determined.

## Exercises

**Exercise 23.3.1** Develop the recursive function *g-fives*, which consumes a natural number and recursively determines the corresponding term in the above geometric sequence. ∎

**Exercise 23.3.2** Develop the non-recursive function *g-fives-closed*. It consumes a natural number and determines the corresponding term in the above series. ∎

**Exercise 23.3.3** Develop the function *seq-g-fives*, which consumes a natural number $n$ and creates the sequence of the first $n$ terms according to *g-fives* or *g-fives-closed*. **Hint:** Use build-list. ∎

**Exercise 23.3.4** Develop *geometric-series*. The function consumes two numbers: *start* and *s*. Its result is a function that represents the geometric series whose starting point is *start* and whose factor is *s*. For example, (*geometric-series* 3 5) yields *g-fives* (or *g-fives-closed*). ∎

**Exercise 23.3.5** Use *series* to determine the sum of the *g-fives* sequence for the bounds 3, 7, and 88. Use *series* to determine the sum of (*geometric-series* 1 .1) for the bounds 3, 7, 88. Can an infinite geometric series have a sum? ∎

## Taylor Series

Mathematical constants like $\pi$ and $e$ or functions like sin, cos, log are difficult to compute. Since these functions are important for many daily engineering applications, mathematicians have spent a lot of time and energy looking for better ways to compute these functions. One method is to replace a function with its Taylor series, which is, roughly speaking, an infinitely long polynomial.

A *Taylor series* is the sum of a sequence of terms. In contrast to arithmetic or geometric sequences, the terms of a Taylor series depend on two unknowns: some variable $x$ and the position $i$ in the sequence. Here is the Taylor series for the exponential function:

$$e^x = 1 + \frac{x}{1!} + \frac{x^2}{2!} + \frac{x^3}{3!} + \cdots$$

That is, if we wish to compute $e^x$ for any specific $x$, we replace $x$ with the number and determine the value of the series. In other words, for a specific value of $x$, say, 1, the Taylor series becomes an ordinary series, that is, a sum of some sequence of numbers:

$$e^1 = 1 + \frac{1}{1!} + \frac{1^2}{2!} + \frac{1^3}{3!} + \cdots$$

While this series is the sum of an infinitely long sequence, it actually is a number, and it often suffices to add just the first few terms to have an idea what the number is.

The key to computing a Taylor series is to formulate each term in the underlying sequence as a function of $x$ and its position $i$. In our running example, the Taylor sequence for the exponential function has the shape

$$\frac{x^i}{i!}.$$

Assuming a fixed $x$, here is an equivalent Scheme definition:

```
;; e-taylor : N → number
(define (e-taylor i)
  (/ (expt x i) (! i)))

;; ! : N → number
(define (! n)
  (cond
    [(= n 0) 1]
    [else (* n (! (sub1 n)))]))
```

The first function computes the term; the second computes the factorial of a natural number. To compute the value of $e^x$, we now just need to ask for (*series* 10 *e-taylor*), assuming we want the first 10 items of the sequence included.

Putting everything together, we can define a function that computes the $x$th power of $e$. Since the function requires two auxiliaries, we use a **local**:

```
(define (e-power x)
  (local ((define (e-taylor i)
            (/ (expt x i) (! i)))
          (define (! n)
            (cond
              [(= n 0) 1]
              [else (* n (! (sub1 n)))])))
    (series 10 e-taylor)))
```

## Exercises

**Exercise 23.3.6** Replace 10 by 3 in the definition of *e-power* and evaluate (*e-power* 1) by hand. Show only those lines that contain new applications of *e-taylor* to a number.

The results of *e-power* are fractions with large numerators and denominators. In contrast, Scheme's built-in exp function produces an inexact number. We can turn exact fractions into inexact numbers with the following function:

;; exact→ inexact : *number* [*exact*] → *number* [*inexact*]

Test the function and add it to *e-power*'s body. Then compare the results of exp and *e-power*. Increase the number of items in the series until the difference between the results is small. ∎

**Exercise 23.3.7** Develop the function *ln*, which computes the Taylor series for the natural logarithm. The mathematical definition of the series is

$$ln(x) = 2 \cdot [(\frac{x-1}{x+1}) + \frac{1}{3} \cdot (\frac{x-1}{x+1})^3 + \frac{1}{5} \cdot (\frac{x-1}{x+1})^5 \ldots]$$

This Taylor series has a value for all $x$ that are greater than 0.

DrScheme also provides log, a primitive for computing the natural logarithm. Compare the results for *ln* and log. Then use exact→ inexact (see exercise 23.3.6) to get results that are easier to compare. ∎

**Exercise 23.3.8** Develop the function *my-sin*, which computes the Taylor series for sin, one of the trigonometric functions. The Taylor series is defined as follows:

$$sin(x) = \frac{x}{1!} - \frac{x^3}{3!} + \frac{x^5}{5!} - \frac{x^7}{7!} \ldots$$

It is defined for all $x$.

**Hint:** The sign of a term is positive if the index is even and negative otherwise. Mathematicians compute $(-1)^i$ to determine the sign; programmers can use **cond** instead. ∎

**Exercise 23.3.9** Mathematicians have used series to determine the value of $\pi$ for many centuries. Here is the first such sequence, discovered by Gregory (1638–1675):

$$\pi = 4 \cdot [1 - \frac{1}{3} + \frac{1}{5} - \frac{1}{7} \ldots] .$$

Define the function *greg*, which maps a natural number to the corresponding term in this sequence. Then use *series* to determine approximations of the value of $\pi$.

**Note on $\pi$:** The approximation improves as we increase the number of items in the series. Unfortunately, it is not practical to compute $\pi$ with this definition. ∎

## 23.4   The Area Under a Function

Consider the function graph in figure 64. Suppose we wish to know the area between the $x$ axis, the fat lines labeled $a$ and $b$, and the graph. Determining the area under the graph of a function for some specific interval is called *integrating a function*. Since engineers had to solve this kind of problem before computers were available, mathematicians have studied it extensively. For a small class of functions, it is indeed possible to determine the area exactly. For the other cases, mathematicians have developed several methods to determine close estimates. Since these methods involve lots of mechanical calculations, they are natural candidates for computer functions.

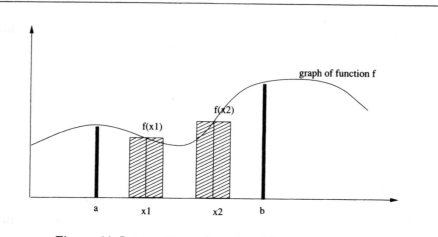

Figure 64: Integrating a function $f$ between $a$ and $b$

A general integration function must consume three inputs: $a$, $b$, and the function $f$. The fourth part, the $x$ axis, is implied. This suggests the following contract:

*;; integrate : (number $\rightarrow$ number) number number $\rightarrow$ number*
*;; to compute the area under the graph of $f$ between $a$ and $b$*
(**define** (*integrate f a b*) ...)

Kepler suggested one simple integration method. It consists of three steps:

1.  divide the interval into two parts: $[a, \frac{a+b}{2}]$ and $[\frac{a+b}{2}, b]$;

2. compute the area of each *trapezoid*; and

3. add the two areas to get an estimate at the integral.

## Exercises

**Exercise 23.4.1** Develop the function *integrate-kepler*. It computes the area under some the graph of some function $f$ between *left* and *right* using Kepler's rule. ∎

Another simple method is to think of the area as a sequence of many small rectangles. Each rectangle is as tall as the function graph in, say, the middle of the rectangle. Figure 64 shows two examples. By adding up the area of the rectangles, we get a good estimate at the area under the graph. The more rectangles we consider, the closer the estimate is to the actual area.

Let us agree that $R$ stands for the number of rectangles that we wish to consider. To determine how large these rectangles are, we need to figure out how large their sides are. The length of the side on the $x$ axis is the length of the interval divided by the number of rectangles:

$$width = \frac{(b-a)}{R} .$$

For the height of the rectangle, we need to determine its midpoint and then the value of $f$ at the midpoint. The first midpoint is clearly at $a$ plus half of the width of the rectangle, that is, if

$$step = \frac{width}{2} ,$$

the area is

$$W \cdot f(a + S) ,$$

where $W$ stands for *width* and $S$ for *step* from now on.

To get from the rectangle starting at $a$ to the next one on the right, we must add the width of one rectangle. That is, the next midpoint (called $x_1$ in figure 64) is at

$$a + W + S ,$$

the third one at

$$a + 2 \cdot W + S \,,$$

and so on. The following table explains the three sequences that are involved in the usual manner:

| index | 0 | 1 | 2 | ... |
|---|---|---|---|---|
| $M$ | $a + S$ | $a + 1 \cdot W + S$ | $a + 2 \cdot W + S$ | ... |
| $f$ at $M$ | $f(a + S)$ | $f(a + 1 \cdot W + S)$ | $f(a + 2 \cdot W + S)$ | ... |
| area | $W \cdot f(a + S)$ | $W \cdot f(a + 1 \cdot W + S)$ | $W \cdot f(a + 2 \cdot W + S)$ | ... |

In the second row, $M$ stands for midpoint. The first rectangle has index 0, the last one $R - 1$.

Using this sequence of rectangles, we can now determine the area under the graph as a series:

$$\sum_{i=0}^{i=R-1} \textit{area-of-rectangle}\,(i) \,.$$

---

**Exercises**

**Exercise 23.4.2** Develop the function *integrate*. It computes the area under some the graph of some function $f$ between *left* and *right* using the rectangle-series method.

Use test cases for $f$, $a$, and $b$ for which one can determine the area exactly and easily by hand, for example, (**define** (*id x*) *x*). Compare the results with those of *integrate* from exercise 23.4.1.

Make $R$ a top-level constant:

```
;; R : number of rectangles to approximate integral
(define R ...)
```

Test *integrate* on sin and increase $R$ gradually from 10 to 10000. What happens to the result? ∎

---

## 23.5   The Slope of a Function

Let us take another look at the function graph in figure 64.   For many problems, we need to be able to draw a line that has the same slope as some curve at a certain point. Indeed, computing the slope is often the true goal. In economics problems, the slope is the growth rate of a company if the curve represents the income over time. In a physics problem, the curve could represent the velocity of some object; its slope, at any point, is then the current acceleration of the object.

Determining the slope of some function $f$ at some point $x$ is to *differentiate* the function. The differential operator (also called a functional) returns a function $f'$ (pronounced "f prime"). It tells us for any $x$ what the slope of $f$ is at that point. Computing $f'$ is complicated, so it is again a good task for a computer program. The program consumes some function $f$ and produces $f'$.

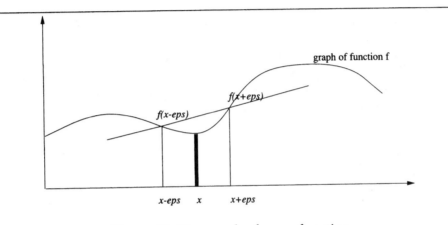

Figure 65: The graph of some function

To design a "differentiator" we must study how we could construct lines that have the same slope as a curve. In principle, such a line touches the curve at just that point. But suppose we relax this constraint for a moment and look at straight lines that intersect the curve close to the point of interest. We pick two points that are equally far away from $x$, say, $x - \epsilon$ and $x + \epsilon$; the constant $\epsilon$, pronounced epsilon, represents some small distance. Using the two corresponding points on the curve, we can determine a straight line that has the proper slope.

The situation is sketched in figure 65. If the point of interest has coordinate $x$, the two points are $(x, f(x - \epsilon))$ and $(x, f(x + \epsilon))$. Hence the slope of the line is

$$\frac{f(x + \epsilon) - f(x - \epsilon)}{2 \cdot \epsilon} .$$

That is, the difference between the height of the right point and the left point divided by their horizontal distance. Determining the line from the slope and one of the points or even from two points is an exercise.

## Exercises

**Exercise 23.5.1** The equation for a line is

$$y(x) = a \cdot x + b.$$

By now, it is straightforward to translate this equation into Scheme:

```
(define (y x)
  (+ (* a x) b))
```

To obtain a concrete line we must replace *a* and *b* with numbers.

The teachpack **graphing.ss** provides one operation for drawing lines: *graph-line*. The operation consumes a line like *y* and a color, say, 'red. Use *graph-line* to draw the graphs of the following lines:

1. $y_1(x) = x + 4$

2. $y_2(x) = 4 - x$

3. $y_3(x) = x + 10$

4. $y_4(x) = 10 - x$

5. $y_5(x) = 12$

∎

**Exercise 23.5.2** It is a standard mathematical exercise to develop the equation for a line from a point on the line and its slope. Look up the method in your mathematics book. Then develop the function *line-from-point+slope*, which implements the method. The function consumes a *posn* (the point) and a number (the slope). It produces a function that represents the line in the spirit of exercise 23.5.1.

Testing a function-producing function like *line-from-point+slope* can be done in two ways. Suppose we apply the function to $(0, 4)$ and 1. The result should be line $y_1$ from exercise 23.5.1. To check this, we can either apply the result of

(*line-from-point+slope* (make-posn 0 4) 1)

to some numbers, or we can draw the result using the operations in **graphing.ss**. In the first case, we must use $y_1$ to compare outputs; in the second case we can draw the result in one color and the hand-constructed line in a different one and observe the effect. ∎

Once we have an intersecting line through $(x, f(x - \epsilon))$ and $(x, f(x + \epsilon))$, we can also get a line with the proper slope. By decreasing $\epsilon$ until it is (almost) indistinguishable from 0, the two intersection points move closer and closer until they are one, namely, $(x, f(x))$, the point for which we wish to know the slope.[52]

## Exercises

**Exercise 23.5.3** Use the operation *graph-fun* in the teachpack **graphing.ss** to draw the mathematical function

$$y(x) = x^2 - 4 \cdot x + 7 .$$

The operation works just like *draw-line* (see exercise 23.5.1.)

Suppose we wish to determine the slope at $x = 2$. Pick an $\epsilon > 0$ and determine the slope of the line that goes through $(x, f(x - \epsilon))$ and $(x, f(x + \epsilon))$ with the above formula. Compute the line with *line-from-point+slope* from exercise 23.5.2 and use *draw-line* to draw it into the same coordinate system as $y$. Repeat the process with $\epsilon/2$ and then with $\epsilon/4$. ∎

If our goal is to define the differential operator as a Scheme function, we can approximate it by setting $\epsilon$ to a small number and by translating the mathematical formula into a Scheme expression:

```
;; d/dx : (num → num) → (num → num)
;; to compute the derivative function of f numerically
(define (d/dx f)
  (local ((define (fprime x)
            (/ (- (f (+ x ε)) (f (- x ε)))
               (* 2 ε)))
          (define ε ... ))
    fprime))
```

---

[52]The process of decreasing $\epsilon$ to 0 is a convergence (or limit) process. It does not always succeed, that is, for some function graphs, the process does not end properly. We ignore those cases, but they are common and require special attention.

Note that *d/dx* consumes and produces functions—just like the differential operator in mathematics.

As mentioned in the introduction to this section, the differential operator computes the function $f'$ from some function $f$. The former computes the slope of $f$ for any $x$. For straight lines, the slope is always known. Hence a function that represents a straight line is an ideal test case for *d/dx*. Let us consider

    (**define** (*a-line x*)
      (+ (* 3 *x*) 1))

The evaluation of (*d/dx a-line*) proceeds as follows:

    (*d/dx a-line*)

= (**local** ((**define** (*fprime x*)
          (/ (− (*a-line* (+ *x* ε)) (*a-line* (− *x* ε)))
          (* 2 ε)))
       (**define** ε ...))
   *fprime*)

= (**define** (*fprime x*)
    (/ (− (*a-line* (+ *x* ε)) (*a-line* (− *x* ε)))
    (* 2 ε)))
  (**define** ε ...)
  *fprime*

Now, if we think of (+ *x* ε) and (− *x* ε) as numbers, we can evaluate the application of *a-line* in the definition of *fprime*:[53]

    (**define** (*fprime x*)
      (/ (− (+ (* 3 (+ *x* ε)) 1) (+ (* 3 (− *x* ε)) 1))
      (* 2 ε)))

= (**define** (*fprime x*)
    (/ (− (* 3 (+ *x* ε)) (* 3 (− *x* ε)))
    (* 2 ε)))

= (**define** (*fprime x*)
    (/ (* 3 (− (+ *x* ε) (− *x* ε)))
    (* 2 ε)))

---

[53]If *x* is a number, then adding or subtracting ε yields a number. If, by accident, we apply *fprime* to something else, both expressions signal an error. It is therefore acceptable to act as if the expressions were values. In general, this is not true.

```
= (define (fprime x)
     (/ (* 3 (* 2 ε))
        (* 2 ε)))
```

```
= (define (fprime x)
     3)
```

In other words, the result of (d/dx a-line) always returns 3, which is the slope of *a-line*. In short, we not only got a close approximation because ε is small, we actually got the correct answer. In general, however, the answer will depend on ε and will not be precise.

## Exercises

**Exercise 23.5.4** Pick a small ε and use *d/dx* to compute the slope of

$$y(x) = x^2 - 4 \cdot x + 7$$

at $x = 2$. How does the result compare with your calculation in exercise 23.5.3? ∎

**Exercise 23.5.5** Develop the function *line-from-two-points*. It consumes two points *p1* and *p2*. Its result is a Scheme function that represents the line through *p1* and *p2*.
Question: Are there any situations for which this function may fail to compute a function? If so, refine the definition to produce a proper error message in this case. ∎

**Exercise 23.5.6** Compute the slope of the following function

```
(define (f x)
   (+ (* 1/60 (* x x x))
      (* -1/10 (* x x))
      5))
```

at $x = 4$. Set ε to 2, 1, .5. Try the same for some other value of *x*. ∎

# Intermezzo 4: Defining Functions on the Fly

Many uses of abstract functions require the definition of auxiliary functions. Consider *filter1*, which consumes a filtering function, a list, and a filtering item. In the previous section alone, we encountered three uses of *filter1* with three different auxiliary functions: *squared?*, $<_{ir}$, and *eq-ir?*.

Since these auxiliary functions are only used as arguments to *filter1*, we should employ the program organization guidelines from the preceding intermezzo (18). That is, we should use a **local**-expression to indicate that the application of *filter1* and the auxiliary function definition belong together. Here is one possible arrangement for the *filter1-eq-ir?* combination:

```
;; find : list-of-IRs symbol → boolean
(define (find aloir t)
  (local ((define (eq-ir? ir p)
            (symbol=? (ir-name ir) p)))
    (filter1 eq-ir? aloir t)))
```

An alternative arrangement places the **local**-expression where the function is needed:

```
;; find : list-of-IRs symbol → boolean
(define (find aloir t)
  (filter1 (local ((define (eq-ir? ir p)
                     (symbol=? (ir-name ir) p)))
             eq-ir?)
           aloir t))
```

This alternative is feasible because the names of functions—like *eq-ir?*—are now legitimate expressions and can play the role of **local**'s body. Thus the **local**-expression introduces a function definition and returns the function as its result.

Because good programmers use abstract functions and organize their programs in a tidy manner, it is not surprising that Scheme provides a short-hand for this particular, frequent use of **local**. The short-hand is called a **lambda**-expression and greatly facilitates the introduction of functions like *eq-ir?*, *squared?*, or $<_{ir}$. The following two subsections introduce the syntax and semantics of **lambda**-expressions. The last subsection discusses its pragmatics.

**Syntax of lambda**

A **lambda**-expression is just a new form of expression:

$$\langle exp \rangle \quad = \quad (\textbf{lambda } (\langle var \rangle \ldots \langle var \rangle) \, \langle exp \rangle)$$

Its distinguishing characteristic is the keyword **lambda**. It is followed by
a sequence of variables, enclosed in a pair of parentheses. The last component is an expression.

Here are three useful examples:

1. **(lambda** $(x\ c)$ $(>(*\ x\ x)\ c))$
2. **(lambda** $(ir\ p)$ $(<($ir-price $ir)\ p))$
3. **(lambda** $(ir\ p)$ $(\textsf{symbol}{=}?\ ($ir-name $ir)\ p))$

They correspond to *squared?*, $<_{ir}$, and *eq-ir?*, respectively, the three motivating examples discussed above.

A **lambda**-expression defines an anonymous function, that is, a function without a name. The sequence of variables behind **lambda** are the
function's parameters; the third component is the function's body.

**Scope and Semantics of lambda**

As discussed in the introduction, a **lambda**-expression is just a short-hand
for a **local**-expression. In general, we can think of

$$(\textbf{lambda } (x\text{-}1 \ldots x\text{-}n)\ \textsf{exp})$$

as

$$(\textbf{local } ((\textbf{define } (a\text{-}new\text{-}name\ x\text{-}1 \ldots x\text{-}n)\ \textsf{exp}))$$
$$a\text{-}new\text{-}name)$$

The name of the function, *a-new-name*, may not occur in exp.

The short-hand explanation suggests that

$$(\textbf{lambda } (x\text{-}1 \ldots x\text{-}n)\ \textsf{exp})$$

introduces $x\text{-}1 \ldots x\text{-}n$ as binding occurrences and that the scope of parameters is exp. Of course, if exp contains further binding constructs (say, a
nested **local**-expression), then the scope of the variables may have a hole.

Similarly, the explanation implies basic facts that govern the evaluation
of **lambda**-expressions:

1. A **lambda**-expression is a value because functions are values.

2. The application of **lambda**-expressions to values proceeds according to our usual laws of function application, assuming we expand the short-hand first.

Here is a sample use of **lambda**:

```
(filter1 (lambda (ir p) (< (ir-price ir) p))
         (list (make-ir 'doll 10))
         8)
```

The application of *filter1* consumes the **lambda**-expression, a (short) list of inventory records, and a threshold. Given our suggestion, the evaluation can be understood by an expansion of the **lambda**-expression into a corresponding **local**-expression:

```
    ...
= (filter1 (local ((define (<ir ir p) (< (ir-price ir) p))) <ir)
         (list (make-ir 'doll 10))
         8)
= (filter1 <ir
         (list (make-ir 'doll 10))
         8)
```

For the last step, the local definition of $<_{ir}$ is lifted and added to the top-level definitions. From here, the evaluation proceeds as in section 19.2.

While it is natural to think of **lambda** as a short-hand, the last two points also suggest a way of understanding **lambda**-expressions directly. In particular, we can adapt the law of application to **lambda**-expressions:

```
((lambda (x-1 ... x-n) exp)      = exp
 val-1 ... val-n)                   with all occurrences of x-1 ... x-n
                                    replaced by val-1 ... val-n
```

That is, the application of a **lambda**-expression proceeds just like that of an ordinary function. We replace the parameters of the function with the actual argument values and compute the value of the function body.

Let us reconsider the above example in this light:

```
(filter1 (lambda (ir p) (< (ir-price ir) p))
         (list (make-ir 'doll 10))
         8)
```

As usual, this application is replaced by the body of *filter1* with all parameters replaced by their values. This step places a **lambda**-expression into the function position of an application:

```
= (cond
    [((lambda (ir p) (< (ir-price ir) p))
      (make-ir 'doll 10) 8)
     (cons (first (list (make-ir 'doll 10)))
       (filter1 (lambda (ir p) (< (ir-price ir) p))
                (rest (list (make-ir 'doll 10)))
                8))]
    [else
      (filter1 (lambda (ir p) (< (ir-price ir) p))
               (rest (list (make-ir 'doll 10)))
               8)])

= (cond
    [(< (ir-price (make-ir 'doll 10)) 8)
     (cons (first (list (make-ir 'doll 10)))
       (filter1 (lambda (ir p) (< (ir-price ir) p))
                (rest (list (make-ir 'doll 10)))
                8))]
    [else
      (filter1 (lambda (ir p) (< (ir-price ir) p))
               (rest (list (make-ir 'doll 10)))
               8)])

= ...
```

From here, the evaluation proceeds as usual. Still, even this short-hand evaluation shows that, while using **lambda**-expressions in programs is convenient, replacing it with a named function (often) simplifies calculations.

## Exercises

**Exercise 24.0.7** Decide which of the following phrases are legal **lambda**-expressions:

1. **(lambda** (x y) (x y y))

2. **(lambda** () 10)

3. **(lambda** (*x*) *x*)

4. **(lambda** (*x y*) *x*)

5. **(lambda** *x* 10)

Explain why they are legal or illegal. ∎

**Exercise 24.0.8** Draw arrows from the underlined occurrences of *x* to their binding occurrences in each of the following three **lambda**-expressions:

1.
   **(lambda** (*x y*)
     (+ <u>*x*</u> (* *x y*)))

2.
   **(lambda** (*x y*)
     (+ <u>*x*</u>
        **(local** ((**define** *x* (* *y y*)))
          (+ (* 3 <u>*x*</u>)
             (/ 1 *x*)))))

3.
   **(lambda** (*x y*)
     (+ <u>*x*</u>
        ((**lambda** (*x*)
           (+ (* 3 <u>*x*</u>)
              (/ 1 *x*)))
         (* *y y*))))

Also draw a box for the corresponding scope of each underlined *x* and holes in the scope where necessary. ∎

**Exercise 24.0.9** Evaluate the following expressions by hand:

1.
   ((**lambda** (*x y*)
      (+ <u>*x*</u> (* *x y*)))
    1 2)

2.
   ((**lambda** (*x y*)
      (+ <u>*x*</u>
         **(local** ((**define** *x* (* *y y*)))
           (+ (* 3 <u>*x*</u>)
              (/ 1 *x*)))))
    1 2)

3.
```
((lambda (x y)
   (+ x
      ((lambda (x)
         (+ (* 3 x)
            (/ 1 x)))
       (* y y))))
 1 2)
```

∎

## Pragmatics of lambda

The guideline for using **lambda**-expressions is straightforward:

> GUIDELINE ON LAMBDA EXPRESSIONS
>
> Use **lambda**-expressions when a function is not recursive and is only needed once in an argument position.

If we were to apply the guideline to the programs in the preceding sections, we would quickly see how much **lambda** simplifies the use of abstracted functions. For that reason, Scheme offers many abstracted functions in its libraries. In future sections, we will encounter many more examples where **lambda**-expressions are convenient.

# Sections

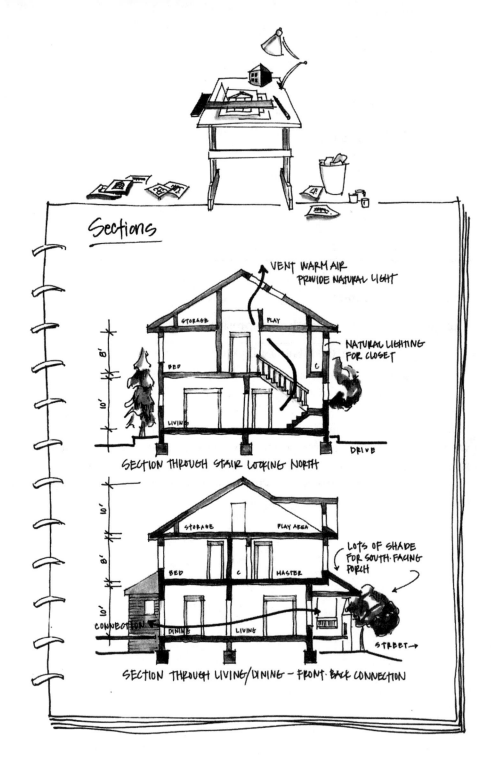

VENT WARM AIR
PROVIDE NATURAL LIGHT

STORAGE    PLAY

NATURAL LIGHTING
FOR CLOSET

8'

BED

C

10'

LIVING

DRIVE

SECTION THROUGH STAIR LOOKING NORTH

10'

STORAGE         PLAY AREA

8'

BED        C     MASTER

LOTS OF SHADE
FOR SOUTH-FACING
PORCH

10'

CONNECTION   DINING     LIVING

STREET →

SECTION THROUGH LIVING/DINING — FRONT-BACK CONNECTION

## 25   A New Form of Recursion

The functions we have developed so far fall into two broad categories. On one hand, we have the category of functions that encapsulate domain knowledge. On the other hand, we have functions that consume structured data. These functions typically decompose their arguments into their immediate structural components and then process those components. If one of the immediate components belongs to the same class of data as the input, the function is recursive. For that reason, we refer to these functions as (STRUCTURALLY) RECURSIVE FUNCTIONS. In some cases, however, we also need functions based on a different form of recursion, namely, generative recursion. The study of this form of recursion is as old as mathematics and is often called the study of ALGORITHMS.

The inputs of an algorithm represent a problem. Except for rare occasions, the problem is an instance of a large class of problems and the algorithm works for all of these problems. In general, an algorithm partitions a problem into other, smaller problems and solves those. For example, an algorithm for planning a vacation trip requires arrangements for a trip from our home to a nearby airport, a flight to an airport near our vacation spot, and a trip from that airport to our vacation hotel. The entire problem is solved by combining the solutions for these problems.

Designing an algorithm distinguishes two kinds of problems: those that are TRIVIALLY SOLVABLE[54] and those that are not. If a given problem is trivially solvable, an algorithm produces the matching solution. For example, the problem of getting from our home to a nearby airport might be trivially solvable. We can drive there, take a cab, or ask a friend to drop us off. If not, the algorithm generates a new problem and solves those new prob-

---

[54]For this part of the book, *trivial* is a technical term. It will be explained in section 26.

lems. A multistage trip is an example of a problem that is non-trivial and can be solved by generating new, smaller problems. In a computational setting one of the smaller problems often belongs to the same class of problems as the original one, and it is for this reason that we call the approach GENERATIVE RECURSION.

In this part of the book, we study the design of algorithms, that is, functions based on generative recursion. From the description of the idea, we know that this process is much more of an ad hoc activity than the data-driven design of structurally recursive functions. Indeed, it is almost better to call it inventing an algorithm than designing one. Inventing an algorithm requires a new insight—a "eureka." Sometimes very little insight is required. For example, solving a "problem" might just require the enumeration of a series of numbers. At other times, however, it may rely on a mathematical theorem concerning numbers. Or, it may exploit a series of mathematical results on systems of equations. To acquire a good understanding of the design process, it is necessary to study examples and to develop a sense for the various classes of examples. In practice, new complex algorithms are often developed by mathematicians and mathematical computer scientists; programmers, though, must throughly understand the underlying ideas so that they can invent the simple algorithms on their own and communicate with scientists about the others.

The two subsections illustrate two vastly different algorithms. The first one is an example of something programmers invent on a daily basis. The second one describes a fast sorting algorithm, one of the first applications of generative recursion in computing.

**Terminology**: Mathematical computer scientists often do not distinguish between structural recursion and generative recursion and refer to both kinds of functions as algorithms. Instead they use the terminology of RECURSIVE and ITERATIVE methods. The latter refers to a subclass of function definitions whose recursive function applications are in a particular position in the definition. We will strictly adhere to the terminology of algorithm and generative recursion when we work with this class of functions because this classification matches our thinking of design recipes better than the purely syntactic classification of applied mathematicians. ∎

## 25.1 Modeling a Ball on a Table

Let's consider the simple-looking problem of modeling the moves of a ball across a table. Assume the ball rolls at a constant speed until it drops off the table. We can model the table with a canvas of some fixed width and height. The ball is a disk that moves across the canvas, which we express with drawing the disk, waiting, and clearing it, until it is out of bounds.

---

```
;; TeachPack: draw.ss

(define-struct ball (x y delta-x delta-y))
;; A ball is a structure:
;; (make-ball number number number number)

;; draw-and-clear : a-ball → true
;; draw, sleep, clear a disk from the canvas
;; structural design, Scheme knowledge
(define (draw-and-clear a-ball)
  (and
    (draw-solid-disk (make-posn (ball-x a-ball) (ball-y a-ball)) 5 'red)
    (sleep-for-a-while DELAY)
    (clear-solid-disk (make-posn (ball-x a-ball) (ball-y a-ball)) 5 'red)))

;; move-ball : ball → ball
;; to create a new ball, modeling a move by a-ball
;; structural design, physics knowledge
(define (move-ball a-ball)
  (make-ball (+ (ball-x a-ball) (ball-delta-x a-ball))
             (+ (ball-y a-ball) (ball-delta-y a-ball))
             (ball-delta-x a-ball)
             (ball-delta-y a-ball)))

;; Dimension of canvas
(define WIDTH 100)
(define HEIGHT 100)
(define DELAY .1)
```

Figure 66: Auxiliaries for *move-until-out*

---

Figure 66 collects the function, structure, data, and variable definitions that model the ball:

1. A ball is a structure with four fields: the current position and the velocity in each direction. That is, the first two numbers in a *ball* structure are the current position on the canvas, and the next two numbers describe how far the ball moves in the two directions per step.

2. The function *move-ball* models the physical movement of the ball. It consumes a ball and creates a new one, modeling one step.

3. The function *draw-and-clear* draws the ball at its current position, then waits for a short time, and clears it again.

The variable definitions specify the dimensions of the canvas and the delay time.

To move the ball a few times we can write

(**define** *the-ball* (make-ball 10 20 −5 +17))

(**and**
 (*draw-and-clear the-ball*)
 (**and**
  (*draw-and-clear* (*move-ball the-ball*))
  ...))

though this gets tedious after a while. We should instead develop a function that moves the ball until it is out of bounds.

The easy part is to define *out-of-bounds?*, a function that determines whether a given ball is still visible on the canvas:

```
;; out-of-bounds? : a-ball → boolean
;; to determine whether a-ball is outside of the bounds
;; domain knowledge, geometry
(define (out-of-bounds? a-ball)
  (not
   (and
    (<= 0 (ball-x a-ball) WIDTH)
    (<= 0 (ball-y a-ball) HEIGHT)))))
```

We have defined numerous functions like *out-of-bounds?* in the first few sections of the book.

In contrast, writing a function that draws the ball on the canvas until it is out of bounds belongs to a group of programs that we haven't encountered thus far. Let's start with the basics of the function:

```
;; move-until-out : a-ball → true
;; to model the movement of a ball until it goes out of bounds
(define (move-until-out a-ball) ...)
```

Because the function consumes a ball and draws its movement on a canvas, it produces **true** like all other functions that draw onto a canvas. Designing it with the recipe for structures makes no sense, however. After all, it is already clear how to *draw-and-clear* the ball and how to move it, too. What is needed instead is a case distinction that checks whether the ball is out of bounds or not.

Let us refine the function header with an appropriate **cond**-expression:

(**define** (*move-until-out a-ball*)
  (**cond**
    [(*out-of-bounds? a-ball*) ...]
    [**else** ...]))

We have already defined the function *out-of-bounds?* because it was clear from the problem description that "being out of bounds" was a separate concept.

If the ball consumed by *move-until-out* is outside of the canvas's boundaries, the function can produce true, following the contract. If the ball is still inside the boundaries, two things must happen. First, the ball must be drawn and cleared from the canvas. Second, the ball must be moved, and then we must do things all over again. This implies that after moving the ball, we apply *move-until-out* again, which means the function is recursive:

;; *move-until-out* : *a-ball* → true
;; to model the movement of a ball until it goes out of bounds
(**define** (*move-until-out a-ball*)
  (**cond**
    [(*out-of-bounds? a-ball*) true]
    [**else** (**and** (*draw-and-clear a-ball*)
          (*move-until-out* (*move-ball a-ball*)))]))

Both (*draw-and-clear a-ball*) and (*move-until-out* (*move-ball a-ball*)) produce true, and both expressions must be evaluated. So we combine them with an **and**-expression.

We can now test the function as follows:

(*start WIDTH HEIGHT*)
(*move-until-out* (make-ball 10 20 −5 +17))
(*stop*)

This creates a canvas of proper size and a ball that moves left and down.

A close look at the function definition reveals two peculiarities. First, although the function is recursive, its body consists of a **cond**-expression whose conditions have nothing to do with the input data. Second, the recursive application in the body does not consume a part of the input. Instead, *move-until-out* generates an entirely new and different *ball* structure, which represents the original ball after one step, and uses it for the recursion. Clearly, none of our design recipes could possibly produce such a definition. We have encountered a new way of programming.

## Exercises

**Exercise 25.1.1** What happens if we place the following three expressions

(*start WIDTH HEIGHT*)
(*move-until-out* (make-ball 10 20 0 0))
(*stop*)

at the bottom of the `Definitions` window and click `Execute`? Does the second expression ever produce a value so that the third expression is evaluated and the canvas disappears? Could this happen with any of the functions designed according to our old recipes? ∎

**Exercise 25.1.2** Develop *move-balls*. The function consumes a list of balls and moves each one until all of them have moved out of bounds.
**Hint:** It is best to write this function using `filter`, `andmap`, and similar abstract functions from part IV. ∎

## 25.2  Sorting Quickly

Hoare's quicksort algorithm is the classic example of generative recursion in computing. Like *sort* in section 12.2, *qsort* is a function that consumes a list of numbers and produces a version that contains the same numbers in ascending order. The difference between the two functions is that *sort* is based on structural recursion and *qsort* is based on generative recursion.

The underlying idea of the generative step is a time-honored strategy: divide and conquer. That is, we divide the non-trivial instances of the problem into two smaller, related problems, solve those smaller problems, and combine their solutions into a solution for the original problem. In the case of *qsort*, the intermediate goal is to divide the list of numbers into two lists: one that contains all the items that are strictly smaller than the first item, and another one with all those items that are strictly larger than the first item. Then the two smaller lists are sorted using the same procedure. Once the two lists are sorted, we simply juxtapose the pieces. Owing to its special role, the first item on the list is often called the *pivot item*.

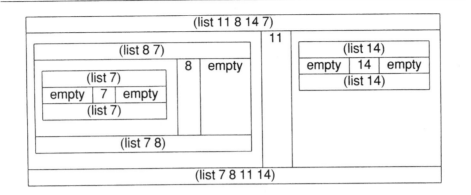

Figure 67: A tabular illustration of *quick-sort*

To develop a better understanding of the process, let's walk through one step of the evaluation by hand. Suppose the input is

(list 11 8 14 7)

The pivot item is 11. Partitioning the list into items larger and smaller than 11 produces two lists:

(list 8 7)

and

(list 14)

The second one is already sorted in ascending order; sorting the first one produces (list 7 8). This leaves us with three pieces from the original list:

1. (list 7 8), the sorted version of the list with the smaller numbers;

2. 11; and

3. (list 14), the sorted version of the list with the larger numbers.

To produce a sorted version of the original list, we concatenate the three pieces, which yields the desired result: (list 7 8 11 14).

 Our illustration leaves open how *qsort* knows when to stop. Since it is a function based on generative recursion, the general answer is that it stops when the sorting problem has become trivial. Clearly, **empty** is one trivial input for *qsort*, because the only sorted version of it is empty. For now, this answer suffices; we will return to this question in the next section.

Figure 67 provides a tabular overview of the entire sorting process for (list 11 8 14 7). Each box has three compartments:

| list to be sorted | | |
|---|---|---|
| sort process for partition with items *smaller* than pivot | pivot item | sort process for partition with items *larger* than pivot |
| sorted list | | |

The top compartment shows the list that we wish to sort, and the bottom-most contains the result. The three columns in the middle display the sorting process for the two partitions and the pivot item.

**Exercises**

**Exercise 25.2.1** Simulate all *qsort* steps for (list 11 9 2 18 12 14 4 1). ∎

Now that we have a good understanding of the generative step, we can translate the process description into Scheme. The description suggests that *qsort* distinguishes two cases. If the input is empty, it produces empty. Otherwise, it performs a generative recursion. This case-split suggests a **cond**-expression:

```
;; quick-sort : (listof number) → (listof number)
;; to create a list of numbers with the same numbers as
;; alon sorted in ascending order
(define (quick-sort alon)
  (cond
    [(empty? alon) empty]
    [else ... ]))
```

The answer for the first case is given. For the second case, when *qsort*'s input is non-empty, the algorithm uses the first item to partition the rest of the list into two sublists: a list with all items smaller than the pivot item and another one with those larger than the pivot item.

Since the rest of the list is of unknown size, we leave the task of partitioning the list to two auxiliary functions: *smaller-items* and *larger-items*.

They process the list and filter out those items that are smaller and larger, respectively, than the first one. Hence each auxiliary function accepts two arguments, namely, a list of numbers and a number. Developing these functions is, of course, an exercise in structural recursion; their definitions are shown in figure 68.

```
;; quick-sort : (listof number) → (listof number)
;; to create a list of numbers with the same numbers as
;; alon sorted in ascending order
(define (quick-sort alon)
  (cond
    [(empty? alon) empty]
    [else (append
            (quick-sort (smaller-items alon (first alon)))
            (list (first alon))
            (quick-sort (larger-items alon (first alon))))]))

;; larger-items : (listof number) number → (listof number)
;; to create a list with all those numbers on alon
;; that are larger than threshold
(define (larger-items alon threshold)
  (cond
    [(empty? alon) empty]
    [else (if (> (first alon) threshold)
            (cons (first alon) (larger-items (rest alon) threshold))
            (larger-items (rest alon) threshold))]))

;; smaller-items : (listof number) number → (listof number)
;; to create a list with all those numbers on alon
;; that are smaller than threshold
(define (smaller-items alon threshold)
  (cond
    [(empty? alon) empty]
    [else (if (< (first alon) threshold)
            (cons (first alon) (smaller-items (rest alon) threshold))
            (smaller-items (rest alon) threshold))]))
```

Figure 68: The quick-sort algorithm

Each sublist is sorted separately, using *quick-sort*. This implies the use of recursion and, more specifically, the following two expressions:

1. (*quick-sort* (*smaller-items alon* (first *alon*))), which sorts the list of items smaller than the pivot; and

2. (*quick-sort* (*larger-items alon* (first *alon*))), which sorts the list of items larger than the pivot.

Once we get the sorted versions of the two lists, we need a function that combines the two lists and the pivot item. Scheme's **append** function accomplishes this:

(**append** (*quick-sort* (*smaller-items alon* (first *alon*))))
         (list (first *alon*))
         (*quick-sort* (*larger-items alon* (first *alon*)))))

Clearly, all items in list 1 are smaller than the pivot and the pivot is smaller than all items in list 2, so the result is a sorted list. Figure 68 contains the full function. It includes the definition of *quick-sort*, *smaller-items*, and *larger-items*.

Let's take a look at the beginning of a sample hand evaluation:

```
  (quick-sort (list 11 8 14 7))
= (append (quick-sort (list 8 7))
          (list 11)
          (quick-sort (list 14)))


= (append (append (quick-sort (list 7))
                  (list 8)
                  (quick-sort empty))
          (list 11)
          (quick-sort (list 14)))


= (append (append (append (quick-sort empty)
                          (list 7)
                          (quick-sort empty))
                  (list 8)
                  (quick-sort empty))
          (list 11)
          (quick-sort (list 14)))
```

```
= (append (append (append empty
                          (list 7)
                          empty)
                  (list 8)
                  empty)
          (list 11)
          (quick-sort (list 14)))

= (append (append (list 7)
                  (list 8)
                  empty)
          (list 11)
          (quick-sort (list 14)))

= ...
```

The calculation shows the essential steps of the sorting process, that is, the partitioning steps, the recursive sorting steps, and the concatenation of the three parts. From this calculation, we can see that *quick-sort* implements the process illustrated in figure 67.

## Exercises

**Exercise 25.2.2** Complete the above hand-evaluation.

The hand-evaluation of (*quick-sort* (list 11 8 14 7)) suggests an additional trivial case for *quick-sort*. Every time *quick-sort* consumes a list of one item, it produces the very same list. After all, the sorted version of a list of one item is the list itself.

Modify the definition of *quick-sort* to take advantage of this observation.

Hand-evaluate the same example again. How many steps does the extended algorithm save? ∎

**Exercise 25.2.3** While *quick-sort* quickly reduces the size of the problem in many cases, it is inappropriately slow for small problems. Hence people often use *quick-sort* to reduce the size of the problem and switch to a different sort function when the list is small enough.

Develop a version of *quick-sort* that uses *sort* from section 12.2 if the length of the input is below some threshold. ∎

**Exercise 25.2.4** If the input to *quick-sort* contains the same number several times, the algorithm returns a list that is strictly shorter than the input. Why? Fix the problem so that the output is as long as the input. ∎

**Exercise 25.2.5** Use the filter function to define *smaller-items* and *larger-items* as one-liners. ∎

**Exercise 25.2.6** Develop a variant of *quick-sort* that uses only one comparison function, say, $<$. Its partitioning step divides the given list *alon* into a list that contains the items of *alon* smaller than (first *alon*) and another one with those that are not smaller.

Use **local** to combine the functions into a single function. Then abstract the new version to consume a list and a comparison function:

    ;; general-quick-sort : (X X → bool) (list X) → (list X)
    (define (general-quick-sort a-predicate a-list) ...)

∎

# 26   Designing Algorithms

At first glance, the algorithms *move-until-out* and *quick-sort* have little in common. One processes structures; the other processes lists. One creates a new structure for the generative step; the other splits up a list into three pieces and recurs on two of them. In short, a comparison of the two examples of generative recursion suggests that the design of algorithms is an ad hoc activity and that it is impossible to come up with a general design recipe. A closer look, however, suggests a different picture.

First, even though we speak of algorithms as processes that solve problems, they are still functions that consume and produce data. In other words, we still choose data to represent a problem, and we must definitely understand the nature of our data if we wish to understand the process. Second, we describe the processes in terms of data, for example, "creating a new structure" or "partitioning a list of numbers." Third, we always distinguish between input data for which it is trivial to produce a solution and those for which it is not. Fourth, the generation of problems is the key to the design of algorithms. Although the idea of how to generate a new problem might be independent of a data representation, it must certainly be implemented for whatever form of representation we choose for our problem. Finally, once the generated problems have been solved, the solutions must be combined with other values.

Let us examine the six general stages of our structural design recipe in light of our discussion:

**Data analysis and design:** The choice of a data representation for a problem often affects our thinking about the process. Sometimes the description of a process dictates a particular choice of representation. On other occasions, it is possible and worthwhile to explore alternatives. In any case, we must analyze and define our data collections.

**Contract, purpose, header:** We also need a contract, a definition header, and a purpose statement. Since the generative step has no connection to the structure of the data definition, the purpose statement should not only specify **what** the function does but should also include a comment that explains in general terms **how** it works.

**Function examples:** In our previous design recipes, the function examples merely specified which output the function should produce for some given input. For algorithms, examples should illustrate **how** the algorithm proceeds for some given input. This helps us to design, and readers to understand, the algorithm. For functions such as *move-until-out* the process is trivial and doesn't need more than a few words. For others, including, *quick-sort*, the process relies on a non-trivial idea for its generative step, and its explanation requires a good example such as the one in figure 67.

**Template:** Our discussion suggests a general template for algorithms:

```
(define (generative-recursive-fun problem)
  (cond
    [(trivially-solvable? problem)
     (determine-solution problem)]
    [else
     (combine-solutions
       ... problem ...
       (generative-recursive-fun (generate-problem-1 problem))
       ⋮
       (generative-recursive-fun (generate-problem-n problem)))]))
```

**Definition:** Of course, this template is only a suggestive blueprint, not a definitive shape. Each function in the template is to remind us that we need to think about the following four questions:

1. What is a trivially solvable problem?

2. What is a corresponding solution?

3. How do we generate new problems that are more easily solvable than the original problem? Is there one new problem that we generate or are there several?

4. Is the solution of the given problem the same as the solution of (one of) the new problems? Or, do we need to combine the solutions to create a solution for the original problem? And, if so, do we need anything from the original problem data?

To define the algorithm, we must express the answers to these four questions in terms of our chosen data representation.

**Test:** Once we have a complete function, we must also test it. As before, the goal of testing is to discover bugs and to eliminate them. Remember that testing cannot validate that the function works correctly for all possible inputs. Also remember that it is best to formulate tests as boolean-valued expressions that automatically compare the expected value with the computed value (see section 17.8).

---

**Exercises**

**Exercise 26.0.7** Formulate informal answers to the four key questions for the problem of modeling a ball's movement across a canvas until it is out of bounds. ∎

**Exercise 26.0.8** Formulate informal answers to the four key questions for the *quick-sort* problem. How many instances of *generate-problem* are there? ∎

---

## 26.1 Termination

Unfortunately, the standard recipe is not good enough for the design of algorithms. Up to now, a function has always produced an output for any legitimate input. That is, the evaluation has always stopped. After all, by the nature of our recipe, each natural recursion consumes an immediate piece of the input, not the input itself. Because data is constructed in a hierarchical manner, this means that the input shrinks at every stage. Hence the function sooner or later consumes an atomic piece of data and stops.

With functions based on generative recursion, this is no longer true. The internal recursions don't consume an immediate component of the input but some new piece of data, which is generated from the input. As exercise 25.1.1 shows, this step may produce the input over and over again and thus prevent the evaluation from ever producing a result. We say that the program LOOPS or is in an INFINITE LOOP.

In addition, even the slightest mistake in translating the process description into a function definition may cause an infinite loop. The problem is most easily understood with an example. Consider the following definition of *smaller-items*, one of the two "problem generators" for *quick-sort*:

```
;; smaller-items : (listof number) number → (listof number)
;; to create a list with all those numbers on alon
;; that are smaller than or equal to threshold
(define (smaller-items alon threshold)
  (cond
    [(empty? alon) empty]
    [else (if (<= (first alon) threshold)
              (cons (first alon) (smaller-items (rest alon) threshold))
              (smaller-items (rest alon) threshold))]))
```

Instead of < it employs <= to compare numbers. As a result, this function produces (list 5) when applied to (list 5) and 5.

Worse, if the *quick-sort* function from figure 68 is combined with this new version of *smaller-items*, it doesn't produce any output for (list 5):

```
  (quick-sort (list 5))
= (append (quick-sort (smaller-items 5 (list 5)))
          (list 5)
          (quick-sort (larger-items 5 (list 5))))
= (append (quick-sort (list 5))
          (list 5)
          (quick-sort (larger-items 5 (list 5))))
```

The first recursive use demands that *quick-sort* solve the problem of sorting (list 5)—but that is the exact problem that we started with. Since this is a circular evaluation, (*quick-sort* (list 5)) never produces a result. More generally, there is no guarantee that the size of the input for a recursive call brings us closer to a solution than the original input.

The lesson from this example is that the design of algorithms requires one more step in our design recipe: a TERMINATION ARGUMENT, which

| Phase | Goal | Activity |
|---|---|---|
| Examples | to characterize the input-output relationship and the computational process via examples | create and show examples of trivially solvable problems • create and show examples that require recursive processing • illustrate how to work through the examples |
| Body | to define an algorithm | formulate tests for trivially solvable problems • formulate answers for the trivial cases • determine how to generate new problems from the given problem, possibly using auxiliary functions • determine how to combine the solutions of these problems into a solution for the given problem |
| ⋮ | ⋮ | ⋮ |
| Termin. | to argue that the algorithm terminates for all possible inputs | show that the inputs to the recursive applications are smaller than the given input |

Figure 69: Designing algorithms

explains why the process produces an output for every input and how the function implements this idea; or a warning, which explains when the process may not terminate. For *quick-sort*, the argument might look like this:

> At each step, *quick-sort* partitions the list into two sublists using *smaller-items* and *larger-items*. Each function produces a list that is smaller than the input (the second argument), even if the threshold (the first argument) is an item on the list. Hence each recursive application of *quick-sort* consumes a strictly shorter list than the given one. Eventually, *quick-sort* receives and returns empty.

Without such an argument an algorithm must be considered incomplete.

A good termination argument may on occasion also reveal additional termination cases. For example, (*smaller-items* N (list N)) and (*larger-items*

*N* (list *N*)) always produce empty for any *N*. Therefore we know that *quick-sort*'s answer for (list *N*) is (list *N*).[55] To add this knowledge to *quick-sort*, we simply add a **cond**-clause:

(**define** (*quick-sort alon*)
　(**cond**
　　[(empty? *alon*) empty]
　　[(empty? (rest *alon*)) *alon*]
　　[**else** (append
　　　　　(*quick-sort* (*smaller-items alon* (first *alon*)))
　　　　　(list (first *alon*))
　　　　　(*quick-sort* (*larger-items alon* (first *alon*))))]))

The condition (empty? (rest *alon*)) is one way to ask whether *alon* contains one item.

Figure 69 summarizes the suggestions on the design of algorithms. The dots indicate that the design of an algorithm requires a new step: the termination argument. Read the table in conjunction with those of the preceding chapters.

## Exercises

**Exercise 26.1.1** Define the function *tabulate-div*, which accepts a number *n* and tabulates the list of all of its divisors, starting with 1 and ending in *n*. A number *d* is a divisior of a number *n* if the remainder of dividing *n* by *d* is 0, that is, (= (remainder *n d*) 0) is true. The smallest divisor of any number is 1; the largest one is the number itself. ∎

**Exercise 26.1.2** Develop the function *merge-sort*, which sorts a list of numbers in ascending order, using the following two auxiliary functions:

1. The first one, *make-singles*, constructs a list of one-item lists from the given list of numbers. For example,

　　　(equal? (*make-singles* (list 2 5 9 3))
　　　　　(list (list 2) (list 5) (list 9) (list 3)))

2. The second one, *merge-all-neighbors*, merges pairs of neighboring lists. More specifically, it consumes a list of lists (of numbers) and merges neighbors. For example,

---

[55]Of course, we could have just argued that the sorted version of a one-item list is the list, which is the basis of exercise 25.2.2.

(equal? (*merge-all-neighbors* (list (list 2) (list 5) (list 9) (list 3)))
        (list (list 2 5) (list 3 9)))

(equal? (*merge-all-neighbors* (list (list 2 5) (list 3 9)))
        (list (list 2 3 5 9)))

In general, this function yields a list that is approximately half as long as the input. Why is the output not always half as long as the input?

Make sure to develop the functions independently.

The function *merge-sort* first uses *make-singles* to create a list of single lists; then it relies on *merge-all-neighbors* to shorten the list of lists until it contains a single list. The latter is the result. ∎

## 26.2  Structural versus Generative Recursion

The template for algorithms is so general that it even covers functions based on structural recursion. Consider the version with one termination clause and one generation step:

```
(define (generative-recursive-fun problem)
  (cond
    [(trivially-solvable? problem)
     (determine-solution problem)]
    [else
      (combine-solutions
        problem
        (generative-recursive-fun (generate-problem problem)))]))
```

If we replace *trivially-solvable?* with empty? and *generate-problem* with rest, the outline *is* a template for a list-processing function:

```
(define (generative-recursive-fun problem)
  (cond
    [(empty? problem) (determine-solution problem)]
    [else
      (combine-solutions
        problem
        (generative-recursive-fun (rest problem)))]))
```

**Exercises**

**Exercise 26.2.1** Define *determine-solution* and *combine-solutions* so that the function *generative-recursive-fun* computes the length of its input. ∎

This discussion raises the question of whether there is a difference between between functions based on structural recursion and those based on generative recursion. The answer is "it depends." Of course, we could say that all functions using structural recursion are just special cases of generative recursion. This "everything is equal" attitude, however, is of no help if we wish to understand the process of designing functions. It confuses two classes of functions that are designed with different approaches and that have different consequences. One relies on a systematic data analysis and not much more; the other requires a deep, often mathematical, insight into the problem-solving process itself. One leads programmers to naturally terminating functions; the other requires a termination argument.

A simple inspection of a function's definition quickly shows whether a function uses structural or generative recursion. All self-applications of a structurally recursive function always receive an immediate component of the current input for further processing. For example, for a **constructed** list, the immediate components are the **first** item and the **rest** of the list. Hence, if a function consumes a plain list and its recursive use does not consume the rest of the list, its definition is not structural but generative. Or, put positively, properly recursive algorithms consume newly generated input, which may or may not contain components of the input. In any case, the new piece of data represents a different problem than the given one, but still a problem of the same general class of problems.

## 26.3  Making Choices

A user cannot distinguish *sort* and *quick-sort*. Both consume a list of numbers; both produce a list that consists of the same numbers arranged in ascending order. To an observer, the functions are completely equivalent.[56] This raises the question of which of the two a programmer should provide. More generally, if we can develop a function using structural recursion and an equivalent one using generative recursion, what should we do?

---

[56]The concept of observably equivalent functions and expressions plays a central role in the study of programming languages and their meaning.

To understand this choice better, let's discuss another classical example of generative recursion from mathematics: the problem of finding the greatest common divisor of two positive natural numbers.[57] All such numbers have at least one divisor in common: 1. On occasion, this is also the only common divisor. For example, 2 and 3 have only 1 as common divisor because 2 and 3, respectively, are the only other divisors. Then again, 6 and 25 are both numbers with several divisors:

1. 6 is evenly divisible by 1, 2, 3, and 6;

2. 25 is evenly divisible by 1, 5, and 25.

Still, the greatest common divisior of 25 and 6 is 1. In contrast, 18 and 24 have many common divisors:

1. 18 is evenly divisible by 1, 2, 3, 6, 9, and 18;

2. 24 is evenly divisible by 1, 2, 3, 4, 6, 8, 12, and 24.

The greatest common divisor is 6.

Following the design recipe, we start with a contract, a purpose statement, and a header:

```
;; gcd : N[>= 1] N[>= 1] → N
;; to find the greatest common divisior of n and m
(define (gcd n m)
   ...)
```

The contract specifies the precise inputs: natural numbers that are greater or equal to 1 (not 0).

Now we need to make a decision whether we want to pursue a design based on structural or on generative recursion. Since the answer is by no means obvious, we develop both. For the structural version, we must consider which input the function should process: $n$, $m$, or both. A moment's consideration suggests that what we really need is a function that starts with the smaller of the two and outputs the first number smaller or equal to this input that evenly divides both $n$ and $m$.

We use **local** to define an appropriate auxiliary function: see figure 70. The conditions "evenly divisible" have been encoded as (= (remainder $n$ $i$) 0) and (= (remainder $m$ $i$) 0). The two ensure that $i$ divides $n$ and $m$ without

---

[57]The material on the greatest common divisor was suggested by John Stone.

```
;; gcd-structural : N[>= 1] N[>= 1] → N
;; to find the greatest common divisior of n and m
;; structural recursion using data definition of N[>= 1]
(define (gcd-structural n m)
  (local ((define (first-divisior-<= i)
            (cond
              [(= i 1) 1]
              [else (cond
                      [(and (= (remainder n i) 0)
                            (= (remainder m i) 0))
                       i]
                      [else (first-divisior-<= (- i 1))])])))
    (first-divisior-<= (min m n))))
```

Figure 70: Finding the greatest common divisor via structural recursion

a remainder. Testing *gcd-structural* with the examples shows that it finds the expected answers.

Although the design of *gcd-structural* is rather straightforward, it is also naive. It simply tests for every number whether it divides both $n$ and $m$ evenly and returns the first such number. For small natural numbers, this process works just fine. Consider the following example, however:

(*gcd-structural* 101135853 45014640)

The result is 177 and to get there *gcd-structural* had to compare 101135676, that is, 101135853 − 177, numbers. This is a large effort and even reasonably fast computers spend several minutes on this task.

## Exercises

**Exercise 26.3.1** Enter the definition of *gcd-structural* into the Definitions window and evaluate (**time** (*gcd-structural* 101135853 45014640)) in the Interactions window.

**Hint:** After testing *gcd-structural* conduct the performance tests in the Full Scheme language (without debugging), which evaluates expressions faster than the lower language levels but with less protection. Add (*require-library* "core.ss") to the top of the Definitions window. Have some reading handy! ∎

Since mathematicians recognized the inefficiency of the "structural algorithm" a long time ago, they studied the problem of finding divisiors in more depth. The essential insight is that for two natural numbers *larger* and *smaller*, their greatest common divisor is equal to the greatest common divisior of *smaller* and the remainder of *larger* divided into *smaller*. Here is how we can put this insight into equational form:

(gcd *larger smaller*)
= (gcd *smaller* (remainder *larger smaller*))

Since (remainder *larger smaller*) is smaller than both *larger* and *smaller*, the right-hand side use of gcd consumes *smaller* first.

Here is how this insight applies to our small example:

1. The given numbers are 18 and 24.

2. According to the mathematicians' insight, they have the same greatest common divisor as 18 and 6.

3. And these two have the same greatest common divisor as 6 and 0.

And here we seem stuck because 0 is nothing expected. But, 0 can be evenly divided by every number, so we have found our answer: 6.

Working through the example not only explains the idea but also suggests how to discover the case with a trivial solution. When the smaller of the two numbers is 0, the result is the larger number. Putting everything together, we get the following definition:

```
;; gcd-generative : N[>= 1] N[>=1] → N
;; to find the greatest common divisior of n and m
;; generative recursion: (gcd n m) = (gcd n (remainder m n)) if (<= m n)
(define (gcd-generative n m)
  (local ((define (clever-gcd larger smaller)
            (cond
              [(= smaller 0) larger]
              [else (clever-gcd smaller (remainder larger smaller))])))
    (clever-gcd (max m n) (min m n))))
```

The **local** definition introduces the workhorse of the function: *clever-gcd*, a function based on generative recursion. Its first line discovers the trivially solvable case by comparing *smaller* to 0 and produces the matching solution. The generative step uses *smaller* as the new first argument and (remainder *larger smaller*) as the new second argument to *clever-gcd*, exploiting the above equation.

If we now use *gcd-generative* with our complex example from above:

(*gcd-generative* 101135853 45014640)

we see that the response is nearly instantaneous. A hand-evaluation shows that *clever-gcd* recurs only nine times before it produces the solution: 177. In short, generative recursion has helped find us a much faster solution to our problem.

---

## Exercises

**Exercise 26.3.2** Formulate informal answers to the four key questions for *gcd-generative*. ∎

**Exercise 26.3.3** Define *gcd-generative* and evaluate

(**time** (*gcd-generative* 101135853 45014640))

in the `Interactions` window.
 Evaluate (*clever-gcd* 101135853 45014640) by hand. Show only those lines that introduce a new recursive call to *clever-gcd*. ∎

**Exercise 26.3.4** Formulate a termination argument for *gcd-generative*. ∎

---

Considering the above example, it is tempting to develop functions using generative recursion. After all, they produce answers faster! This judgment is too rash for three reasons. First, even a well-designed algorithm isn't always faster than an equivalent structurally recursive function. For example, *quick-sort* wins only for large lists; for small ones, the standard *sort* function is faster. Worse, a badly designed algorithm can wreak havoc on the performance of a program. Second, it is typically easier to design a function using the recipe for structural recursion. Conversely, designing an algorithm requires an idea of how to generate new, smaller problems, a step that often requires deep mathematical insight. Finally, people who read functions can easily understand structurally recursive functions, even without much documentation. To understand an algorithm, the generative step must be well explained, and even with a good explanation, it may still be difficult to grasp the idea.
 Experience shows that most functions in a program employ structural recursion; only a few exploit generative recursion. When we encounter a

situation where a design could use either the recipe for structural or generative recursion, the best approach is often to start with a structural version. If it turns out to be too slow, the alternative design using generative recursion should be explored. If it is chosen, it is important to document the problem generation with good examples and to give a good termination argument.

## Exercises

**Exercise 26.3.5** Evaluate

(*quick-sort* (list 10 6 8 9 14 12 3 11 14 16 2))

by hand. Show only those lines that introduce a new recursive call to *quick-sort*. How many recursive applications of *quick-sort* are required? How many recursive applications of **append**? Suggest a general rule for a list of length $N$.

Evaluate

(*quick-sort* (list 1 2 3 4 5 6 7 8 9 10 11 12 13 14))

by hand. How many recursive applications of *quick-sort* are required? How many recursive applications of **append**? Does this contradict the first part of the exercise? ∎

**Exercise 26.3.6** Add *sort* and *quick-sort* to the Definitionswindow. Test the functions and then explore how fast each works on various lists. The experiment should confirm the claim that the plain *sort* function wins (in many comparisons) over *quick-sort* for short lists and vice versa. Determine the cross-over point. Then build a *sort-quick-sort* function that behaves like *quick-sort* for large lists and switches over to the plain *sort* function for lists below the cross-over point.

**Hints:** (1) Use the ideas of exercise 26.3.5 to create test cases. (2) Develop *create-tests*, a function that creates large test cases randomly. Then evaluate

    (**define** *test-case* (*create-tests* 10000))
    (*collect-garbage*)
    (**time** (*sort test-case*))
    (*collect-garbage*)
    (**time** (*quick-sort test-case*))

The uses of *collect-garbage* helps DrScheme deal with large lists. ∎

# 27   Variations on a Theme

As we have seen in the previous two sections, the design of an algorithm usually starts with an informal description of a mechanism. The kernel of this description is about how to create a problem that is more easily solvable than the given one and whose solution contributes to the solution of the given problem. Coming up with such ideas requires studying many different examples. This section presents several illustrative examples of the design recipe for generative recursion. Some are directly drawn from mathematics, which is the source of many ideas for general problem-solving processes; others come from computational contexts. The important point is to understand the generative ideas behind the algorithms so that they can be applied in other contexts.

The first example is a graphical illustration of our principle: the Sierpinski triangle. The second one concerns "parsing," that is, the process of dissecting sequences of symbols. The third one explains the divide-and-conquer principle with a simple mathematical example: finding the root of a function. Many mathematical processes exploit this idea, and it is important to understand the idea for applied mathematics. In the fourth section, we discuss yet another way of finding a root, this time based on Newton's method. The last section is an extended exercise; it introduces Gaussian elimination, the first step in solving a system of equations.

## 27.1   Fractals

Fractals play an important role in computational geometry. Flake (*The Computational Beauty of Nature*, The MIT Press, 1998) says that "geometry can be extended to account for objects with a fractional dimension. Such objects, known as *fractals*, come very close to capturing the richness and variety of forms found in nature. Fractals possess structural self-similarity on multiple ... scales, meaning that a piece of a fractal will often look like the whole."

Figure 71 displays an example of a fractal, widely known as the Sierpinski triangle. The basic shape is an (equilateral) triangle, as shown in the left-most picture. In the right-most example we see that the triangle is repated many times and in many sizes inside of the outermost triangle. The picture in the middle is a snapshot from the middle of the drawing process.

The middle picture also suggests what the generative step might look like. Given the three endpoints of a triangle, we draw the triangle and then

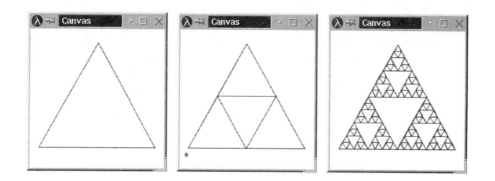

Figure 71: The Sierpinski triangle

compute the midpoint of each side. If we were to connect these midpoints
to each other, we would divide the given triangle into four triangles. The
middle picture illustrates this idea. The Sierpinski triangle is the result of
repeating the process for the three outer triangles and leaving the inner one
alone.

A function that draws this nest of triangles must mirror this process. Its
input data must represent the triangle that we start with. The process stops
when the input data specifies a triangle that is too small to be drawn. Since
all of our drawing functions produce true when they are done, we agree
that our Sierpinski function should also produce true.

If the given triangle is still large enough, the function must draw the
triangle and possibly some nested ones. The trick is to translate the partitioning of the triangle into Scheme. Let us summarize our discussion with
a skeletal Scheme definition:

```
;; sierpinski : posn posn posn → true
;; to draw a Sierpinski triangle down at a, b, and c,
;; assuming it is large enough
(define (sierpinski a b c)
  (cond
    [(too-small? a b c) true]
    [else ... (draw-triangle a b c) ... ]))
```

The function consumes three *posn* structures and returns true when it is
done. The **cond**-expression reflects the general outline of an algorithm. It

is our task to define *too-small?*, the function that determines whether the problem is trivially solvable, and *draw-triangle*. In addition, we must still add a Scheme expression that formulates the partitioning of the triangle.

The partitioning step requires the function to determine the three midpoints between the three end-points. Let us call these new mid-points *a-b*, *b-c*, and *c-a*. Together with the given endpoints, *a*, *b*, and *c*, they determine four triangles: *a*, *a-b*, *c-a*; *b*, *a-b*, *b-c*; *c*, *c-a*, *b-c*; *a-b*, *b-c*, *c-a*. Thus, if we wanted to create the Sierpinski triangle for, say, the first listed triangle, we would use (*sierpinski a a-b c-a*).

Since each midpoint is used twice, we use a **local**-expression to translate the generative step into Scheme. The **local**-expression introduces the three new midpoints. Its body contains three recursive applications of *sierpinski* and the *draw-triangle* application mentioned earlier. To combine the solutions of the three problems, we use an **and**-expression, which ensures that all three recursions must succeed. Figure 72 collects all the relevant definitions, including two small functions based on domain knowledge from geometry.

Since *sierpinski* is based on generative recursion, collecting the code and testing it is not the last step. We must also consider why the algorithm terminates for any given legal input. The inputs of *sierpinski* are three positions. The algorithm terminates if the corresponding triangle is too small. But, each recursive step subdivides the triangle so that the sum of its sides is only half of the given triangle. Hence the size of the triangles indeed decreases and *sierpinski* is bound to produce true.

## Exercises

**Exercise 27.1.1** Develop the functions

1. ;; *draw-triangle : posn posn posn* → true

2. ;; *too-small? : posn posn posn* → *bool*

to complete the definitions in figure 72.

Use the teachpack **draw.ss** to test the code. For a first test of the complete function, use the following definitions:

```
(define A (make-posn 200 0))
(define B (make-posn 27 300))
(define C (make-posn 373 300)
```

```
;; sierpinski : posn posn posn → true
;; to draw a Sierpinski triangle down at a, b, and c,
;; assuming it is large enough
(define (sierpinski a b c)
  (cond
    [(too-small? a b c) true]
    [else
      (local ((define a-b (mid-point a b))
              (define b-c (mid-point b c))
              (define c-a (mid-point a c)))
        (and
          (draw-triangle a b c)
          (sierpinski a a-b c-a)
          (sierpinski b a-b b-c)
          (sierpinski c c-a b-c)))]))

;; mid-point : posn posn → posn
;; to compute the mid-point between a-posn and b-posn
(define (mid-point a-posn b-posn)
  (make-posn
    (mid (posn-x a-posn) (posn-x b-posn))
    (mid (posn-y a-posn) (posn-y b-posn))))

;; mid : number number → number
;; to compute the average of x and y
(define (mid x y)
  (/ (+ x y) 2))
```

Figure 72: The Sierpinski algorithm

Create a canvas with (*start* 400 400). Experiment with other end points and canvas dimensions. ∎

**Exercise 27.1.2** The process of drawing a Sierpinski triangle usually starts from an equilateral shape. To compute the endpoints of an equilateral Sierpinski triangle, we can pick a large circle and three points on the circle that are 120 degrees apart. For example, they could be at 0, 120, 240:

(**define** *CENTER* (make-posn 200 200))

(**define** *RADIUS* 200)

```
;; cicrcl-pt : number → posn
;; to compute a position on the circle with CENTER
;; and RADIUS as defined above
(define (circle-pt factor) ... )


(define A (circle-pt 120/360))
(define B (circle-pt 240/360))
(define C (circle-pt 360/360))
```

Develop the function *circle-pt*.
**Hints:** Recall that DrScheme's sin and cos compute the sine and cosine in terms of radians, not degrees. Also keep in mind that on-screen positions grow downwards not upwards. ∎

**Exercise 27.1.3** Rewrite the function in figure 72 to use structures for the representation of triangles. Then apply the new function to a list of triangles and observe the effect. ∎

**Exercise 27.1.4** Take a look at the following two pictures:

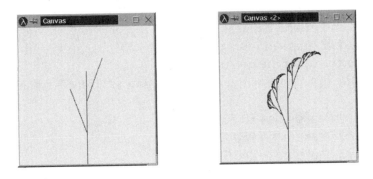

The left one is the basic step for the generation of the "Savannah" tree on the right. It is analogous to the middle picture on page 382. Develop a function that draws trees like the one in the right picture.
**Hint:** Think of the problem as drawing a straight line, given its starting point and an angle in, say, radians. Then, the generative step divides a single straight line into three pieces and uses the two intermediate points as new starting points for straight lines. The angle changes at each step in a regular manner. ∎

**Exercise 27.1.5** In mathematics and computer graphics, people must often connect some given points with a smooth curve. One popular method for this purpose is due to Bezier.[58] Here is a sequence of pictures that illustrate the idea:

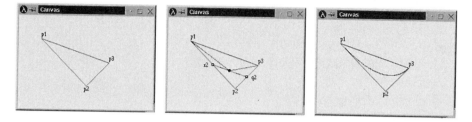

For simplicity, we start with three points: *p1*, *p2*, and *p3*. The goal is to draw a smooth curve from *p1* to *p3*, viewed from *p2*. The original triangle is shown on the left; the desired curve appears on the right.

To draw the curve from a given triangle, we proceed as follows. If the triangle is small enough, draw it. It appears as a large point. If not, generate two smaller triangles as illustrated in the center picture. The outermost points, *p1* and *p3*, remain the respective outermost points. The replacements for the point in the middle are *r2* and *q2*, which are the midpoints between *p1* and *p2* and between *p2* and *p3*, respectively. The midpoint between *r2* and *q2* (marked with •) is the new left-most and right-most endpoint, respectively, for the two new triangles.

To test the function, use the teachpack **draw.ss**. Here is some good test data:

> (**define** *p1* (make-posn 50 50))
> (**define** *p2* (make-posn 150 150))
> (**define** *p3* (make-posn 250 100))

Use (*start* 300 200) to create the canvas. Experiment with other positions. ∎

## 27.2   From Files to Lines, from Lists to Lists of Lists

In section 16, we discussed the organization of computer files, which is one way to equip a computer with permanent memory. We did not discuss the nature of files per se. Roughly put, we can think of a *file* as a list of symbols:

---

[58]Ms. Geraldine Morin suggested this exercise.

> A *file* is either
>
> 1. empty, or
>
> 2. (cons $s$ $f$) where $s$ is a symbol and $f$ is a file.

A fully faithful representation of files should include only symbols that correspond to characters, but for our purposes we may ignore this distinction.

Following a tradition that predates computers,[59] one symbol is almost always treated differently: 'NL. The symbol stands for *newline* and separates two lines from each other. That is, 'NL indicates the end of one line and the beginning of another. In most cases, it is therefore better to think of files as data with more structure. In particular, a file could be represented as a list of lines, where each line is a list of symbols.

For example, the file

```
(list 'how 'are 'you 'NL
      'doing '? 'NL
      'any 'progress '?)
```

should be processed as a list of three lines:

```
(list (list 'how 'are 'you)
      (list 'doing '?)
      (list 'any 'progress '?))
```

Similarly, the file

```
(list 'a 'b 'c 'NL
      'd 'e 'NL
      'f 'g 'h 'NL)
```

is also represented as a list of three lines, because, by convention, an empty line at the end is ignored:

```
(list (list 'a 'b 'c)
      (list 'd 'e)
      (list 'f 'g 'h))
```

---

[59]The tradition of breaking a file into lines is due to the use of punch cards with early mechanical computers, dating back to the 1890 census. It is meaningless for file storage in modern computing. Unfortunately, this historical accident continues to affect the development of computing and software technology in a negative manner.

**Exercises**

**Exercise 27.2.1** Determine what the list-of-lines representation for empty, (list 'NL), and (list 'NL 'NL) should be. Why are these examples important test cases?

**Hint:** Keep in mind that an empty line at the end is ignored. ∎

Here are the contract, purpose statement, and header:

```
;; file→ list-of-lines : file → (listof (listof symbols))
;; to convert a file into a list of lines
(define (file→ list-of-lines afile) ...)
```

Describing the process of separating a file into a list of lines is easy. The problem is trivially solvable if the file is empty; in that case, the file doesn't contain a line. Otherwise, the file contains at least one symbol and thus at least one line. This line must be separated from the rest of the file, and then the rest of the file must be translated into a list of lines.

Let us sketch this process description in Scheme:

```
(define (file→ list-of-lines afile)
  (cond
    [(empty? afile) ...]
    [else
      ... (first-line afile) ...
      ... (file→ list-of-lines (remove-first-line afile)) ...]))
```

Because the separation of the first line from the rest of the file requires a scan of an arbitrarily long list of symbols, we add two auxiliary functions to our wish list: *first-line*, which collects all symbols up to, but excluding, the first occurrence of 'NL or the end of the list; and *remove-first-line*, which removes all those symbols and produces the remainder of *afile*.

From here, we can fill the gaps easily. In *file→ list-of-lines*, the answer in the first clause must be empty because an empty file does not contain any lines. The answer in the second clause must cons the value of (*first-line afile*) onto the value (*file→ list-of-lines (remove-first-line afile)*), because the first expression computes the first line and the second one computes the rest of the lines. Finally, the auxiliary functions process their inputs in a structurally recursive manner; their development is a straightforward

```
;; file→ list-of-lines : file → (listof (listof symbol))
;; to convert a file into a list of lines
(define (file→ list-of-lines afile)
  (cond
    [(empty? afile) empty]
    [else
      (cons (first-line afile)
            (file→ list-of-lines (remove-first-line afile)))]))

;; first-line : file → (listof symbol)
;; to compute the prefix of afile up to the first occurrence of NEWLINE
(define (first-line afile)
  (cond
    [(empty? afile) empty]
    [else (cond
            [(symbol=? (first afile) NEWLINE) empty]
            [else (cons (first afile) (first-line (rest afile)))])]))

;; remove-first-line : file → (listof symbol)
;; to compute the suffix of afile behind the first occurrence of NEWLINE
(define (remove-first-line afile)
  (cond
    [(empty? afile) empty]
    [else (cond
            [(symbol=? (first afile) NEWLINE) (rest afile)]
            [else (remove-first-line (rest afile))])]))

(define NEWLINE 'NL)
```

Figure 73: Translating a file into a list of lines

exercise. Figure 73 collects the three function definitions and a variable definition for *NEWLINE*.

Let us take a look at the process of turning the first file from above into a list of lines:

(file→ *list-of-lines* (list 'a 'b 'c 'NL 'd 'e 'NL 'f 'g 'h 'NL))

= (cons (list 'a 'b 'c) (file→ *list-of-lines* (list 'd 'e 'NL 'f 'g 'h 'NL)))

```
= (cons (list 'a 'b 'c)
        (cons (list 'd 'e)
              (file→ list-of-lines (list 'f 'g 'h 'NL))))
= (cons (list 'a 'b 'c)
        (cons (list 'd 'e)
              (cons (list 'f 'g 'h)
                    (file→ list-of-lines empty))))
= (cons (list 'a 'b 'c)
        (cons (list 'd 'e)
              (cons (list 'f 'g 'h)
                    empty)))
= (list (list 'a 'b 'c)
        (list 'd 'e)
        (list 'f 'g 'h))
```

From this evaluation we can easily tell that the argument of the recursive application of *file→ list-of-lines* is almost never the rest of the given file. That is, it is basically never an immediate component of the given file but always a proper suffix. The only exception occurs when 'NL occurs twice in a row.

Finally, the evaluation and the definition of *file→ list-of-lines* show that its generative recursion is simple. Every recursive application consumes a list that is shorter than the given one. Hence the recursive process eventually stops because the function consumes empty.

## Exercises

**Exercise 27.2.2** Organize the program in figure 73 using **local**.

Abstract the functions *first-line* and *remove-first-line*. Then organize the resulting program using a **local** again. ∎

**Exercise 27.2.3** Design *file→ list-of-checks*. The function consumes a file of numbers and outputs a list of restaurant records.

A *file of numbers* is either

1. empty, or

2. (cons *N F*) where *N* is a number and *F* is a file, or

3. (cons 'NL *F*), where *F* is a file.

The output of *file→ list-of-checks* is a list of restaurant structures with two fields:

(**define-struct** *rr* (*table costs*))

They are: a table number and a list of amounts charged to that table. Example:

```
(equal? (file→ list-of-checks
              (list 1 2.30 4.00 12.50 13.50 'NL
                    2 4.00 18.00 'NL
                    4 2.30 12.50))
        (list (make-rr 1 (list 2.30 4.00 12.50 13.50))
              (make-rr 2 (list 4.00 18.00))
              (make-rr 4 (list 2.30 12.50)))))
```

∎

**Exercise 27.2.4** Develop the function *create-matrix*. It consumes a number $n$ and a list of $n^2$ numbers. It produces a list of $n$ lists of $n$ numbers. Example:

```
(equal? (create-matrix 2 (list 1 2 3 4))
        (list (list 1 2)
              (list 3 4)))
```

∎

## 27.3  Binary Search

Applied mathematicians model the real-world with non-linear equations and then try to solve them. Here is a simplistic example:

> Given a perfect cube that encloses 27m$^3$. What area do its six walls cover?

We know from geometry that if the length of a cube's side is $x$, the enclosed space is $x^3$. Hence we need to know the possible values of $x$ such that

$$x^3 = 27 \ .$$

Once we have solved the equation, the covered area is $6 \cdot x^2$.

In general, we are given a function $f$ from numbers to numbers, and want to know some number $r$ such that

$$f(r) = 0 .$$

The value $r$ is called the *root* of $f$. In our above example, $f(x) = x^3 - 27$, and the value $r$ is the length of the side of the cube.[60]

For the past few centuries, mathematicians have developed many methods for finding the root of different types of functions. In this section, we study a solution that is based on the **Intermediate Value Theorem**, an early result of mathematical analysis. The resulting algorithm is a primary example of generative recursion based on a deep mathematical theorem. It has been adapted to other uses and has become known as the binary search algorithm in computer science.

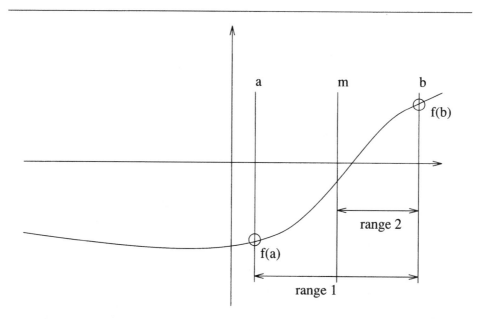

Figure 74: A numeric function $f$ with root in interval $[a, b]$ (stage 1)

The Intermediate Value Theorem says that a continuous function $f$ has a root in an interval $[a, b]$ if the signs of $f(a)$ and $f(b)$ differ. By *continuous*

---

[60]If the equation is originally presented as $g(x) = h(x)$, we set $f(x) = g(x) - h(x)$ to transform the equation into the standard form.

we mean a function that doesn't "jump," that doesn't have gaps, and that always continues in a "smooth" fashion. The theorem is best illustrated with the graph of a function. The function $f$ in figure 74 is below the $x$ axis at $a$ and above the $x$-axis at $b$. It is a continuous function, which we can tell from the uninterrupted, smooth line. And indeed, the function intersects the $x$ axis somewhere between $a$ and $b$.

Now take a look at the midpoint between $a$ and $b$:

$$m = \frac{a + b}{2} .$$

It partitions the interval $[a, b]$ into two smaller, equally large intervals. We can now compute the value of $f$ at $m$ and see whether it is below or above 0. Here $f(m) < 0$, so according to the Intermediate Value Theorem, the root is in the right interval: $[m, b]$. Our picture confirms this because the root is in the right half of the interval, labeled "range 2" in figure 74.

The abstract description of the Intermediate Value Theorem and the illustrative example describe a process for finding a root. Specifically, we use the halving step as many times as necessary to determine a tolerably small range in which $f$ must have a root. Let us now translate this description into a Scheme algorithm, which we call *find-root*.

To begin with, we must agree on the exact task of *find-root*. It consumes a function, let's call it $f$, for which we need to find a root. In addition, it must consume the boundaries of the interval in which we expect to find a root. For simplicity, let's say that *find-root* consumes two numbers: *left* and *right*. But these parameters can't be just any two numbers. For our algorithm to work we must assume that

```
(or (<= (f left) 0 (f right))
    (<= (f right) 0 (f left)))
```

holds. This assumption expresses the condition of the Intermediate Value Theorem that the function must have different signs for *left* and *right*.

According to the informal process description, the task of *find-root* is to find an interval that contains a root and that is tolerably small. The size of the given interval is (− *right left*). For the moment, we assume that the tolerance is defined as a top-level variable *TOLERANCE*. Given that, *find-root* can produce one of the two boundaries of the interval because we know what its size is; let's pick the left one.

Here is a translation of our discussion into a contract, a purpose statement, and a header, including the assumption on the parameters:

;; *find-root : (number → number) number number → number*
;; to determine *R* such that *f* has a root in [*R*,(+ *R TOLERANCE*)]
;;
;; ASSUMPTION: (**or** (<= (*f left*) 0 (*f right*)) (<= (*f right*) 0 (*f left*)))
(**define** (*find-root f left right*) ...)

At this stage, we should develop an example of how the function works. We have already seen one; the following exercise develops a second one.

---

## Exercises

**Exercise 27.3.1** Consider the following function definition:

;; *poly : number → number*
(**define** (*poly x*)
  (* (− *x* 2) (− *x* 4)))

It defines a binomial for which we can determine its roots by hand—they are 2 and 4. But it is also a non-trivial input for *find-root*, so that it makes sense to use it as an example.

Mimic the root-finding process based on the Intermediate Value Theorem for *poly*, starting with the interval 3 and 6. Tabulate the information as follows:

| #step | left | (*f left*) | right | (*f right*) | mid | (*f mid*) |
|-------|------|------------|-------|-------------|-----|-----------|
| $n = 1$ | 3 | -1 | 6.00 | 8.00 | 4.5 | 1.25 |
| $n = 2$ | 3 | -1 | 4.25 | 1.25 | ? | ? |

Find an interval of size .5 (or less) in which *poly* contains a root. ∎

---

Next we turn our attention to the definition of *find-root*. We start from *generative-recursive-fun* and ask the four relevant questions:

1. We need a condition that describes when the problem is solved and a matching answer. This is straightforward. The problem is solved if the distance from *left* to *right* is smaller than or equal to *TOLERANCE*:

   (<= (− *right left*) *TOLERANCE*)

The matching result is *left*.

2. We must formulate an expression that generates new problems for *find-root*. According to our informal process description, this step requires determining the midpoint and choosing the next interval. The midpoint is used several times, so we use a **local**-expression to introduce it:

> (**local** ((**define** *mid* (/ (+ *left right*) 2)))
>   ...)

Choosing an interval is more complicated than that.

Consider the Intermediate Value Theorem again. It says that a given interval is an interesting candidate if the function values at the boundaries have different signs. For the function's purpose statement, we expressed this constraint using

> (**or** (<= (*f left*) 0 (*f right*)) (<= (*f right*) 0 (*f left*)))

Accordingly, the interval between *left* and *mid* is the next candidate if

> (**or** (<= (*f left*) 0 (*f mid*)) (<= (*f mid*) 0 (*f left*)))

And, the interval between *mid* and *right* is it, if

> (**or** (<= (*f mid*) 0 (*f right*)) (<= (*f right*) 0 (*f mid*)))

In short, the body of the **local**-expression must be a conditional:

> (**local** ((**define** *mid* (/ (+ *left right*) 2)))
>   (**cond**
>     [(**or** (<= (*f left*) 0 (*f mid*)) (<= (*f mid*) 0 (*f left*)))
>      (*find-root left mid*)]
>     [(**or** (<= (*f mid*) 0 (*f right*)) (<= (*f right*) 0 (*f mid*)))
>      (*find-root mid right*)]))

In both clauses, we use *find-root* to continue the search.

The completed function is displayed in figure 75. The following exercises suggest some tests and a termination argument.

```
;; find-root : (number → number) number number → number
;; to determine a number R such that f has a
;; root between R and (+ R TOLERANCE)
;;
;; ASSUMPTION: f is continuous and monotonic
(define (find-root f left right)
  (cond
    [(<= (- right left) TOLERANCE) left]
    [else
      (local ((define mid (/ (+ left right) 2)))
        (cond
          [(<= (f mid) 0 (f right))
           (find-root mid right)]
          [else
           (find-root left mid)]))]))
```

Figure 75: The root-finding algorithm *find-root*

## Exercises

**Exercise 27.3.2** Use *poly* from 27.3.1 to test *find-root*. Experiment with different values for *TOLERANCE*. Use the strategy of section 17.8 to formulate the tests as boolean-valued expressions. ∎

**Exercise 27.3.3** Suppose the original arguments of *find-root* describe an interval of size $S1$. How large is the distance between *left* and *right* for the first recursive call to *find-root*? The second one? And the third? After how many evaluation steps is the distance between *left* and *right* smaller than or equal to *TOLERANCE*? How does the answer to this question show that *find-root* produces an answer for all inputs that satisfy the assumption? ∎

**Exercise 27.3.4** For every midpoint *m*, except for the last one, the function *find-root* needs to determine the value of (*f m*) twice. Validate this claim for one example with a hand-evaluation.

Since the evaluation of (*f m*) may be time-consuming, programmers often implement a variant of *find-root* that avoids this recomputation. Modify *find-root* in figure 75 so that it does not need to recompute the value of (*f mid*).

**Hint:** Define a help function *find-root-aux* that takes two extra arguments: the values (*f left*) and (*f right*). ∎

**Exercise 27.3.5** A *table* is a function that consumes natural numbers between 0 and *VL* (exclusive) and produces numbers:

```
;; g : N → num
;; ASSUMPTION: i is between 0 and VL
(define (g i)
  (cond
    [(= i 0) −10]
    [(= i 1) ...]
    ...
    [(= i (− VL 1)) ...]
    [else (error 'g "is defined only between 0 and VL (exclusive)")]))
```

The number *VL* is called the *table's length*. The *root of a table* is the number in the table that is closest to 0. Even if we can't read the definition of a table, we can find its root with a search function.

Develop the function *find-root-linear*, which consumes a table, the table's length, and finds the root of the table. Use structural induction on natural numbers. This kind of root-finding process is often called a LINEAR SEARCH.

A table *t* is sorted in ascending order if (*t* 0) is less then (*t* 1), (*t* 1) is less than (*t* 2), and so on. If a table is monotonic, we can determine the root using binary search. Specifically, we can use binary search to find an interval of size 1 such that either the left or the right boundary is the root's index. Develop *find-root-discrete*, which consumes a table and its length, and finds the table's root.

**Hints:** (1) The interval boundary arguments for *find-root-discrete* must always be natural numbers. Consider how this affects the midpoint computation. (2) Also contemplate how the first hint affects the discovery of trivially solvable problem instances. (3) Does the termination argument from exercise 27.3.3 apply?

If the tabulating function is defined on all natural numbers between 0 and 1024, and if its root is at 0, how many recursive applications are needed with *find-root-discrete* and *find-root-lin* to determine a root interval? ∎

**Exercise 27.3.6** We mentioned in section 23.4 that mathematicians are interested not only about the roots of functions, but also in the area that a function encloses between two points. Mathematically put, we are interested in *integrating* functions over some interval. Take another look at the

graph in figure 64 on page 342. Recall that the area of interest is that enclosed by the bold vertical lines at $a$ and $b$, the $x$ axis, and the graph of the
function.

In section 23.4, we learned to approximate the area by computing and
adding up the area of rectangles like the two above. Using the divide-
and-conquer strategy, we can also design a function that computes the area
based on generative recursion. Roughly speaking, we split the interval into
two pieces, compute the area of each piece, and add the two areas together.

**Step 1**: Develop the algorithm *integrate-dc*, which integrates a function $f$
between the boundaries *left* and *right* via the divide-and-conquer strategy
employed in *find-root*. Use rectangle approximations when an interval has
become small enough.

Although the area of a rectangle is easy to compute, a rectangle is often
a bad approximation of the area under a function graph. A better geometric
shape is the trapezoid limited by $a$, $(f\ a)$, $b$, and $(f\ b)$. Its area is:

$$(right - left) \cdot \frac{f(right) + f(left)}{2} \ .$$

**Step 2**: Modify *integrate-dc* so that it uses trapezoids instead of rectangles.

The plain divide-and-conquer approach is wasteful. Consider that a
function graph is level in one part and rapidly changes in another. For
the level part it is pointless to keep splitting the interval. We could just
compute the trapezoid over $a$ and $b$ instead of the two halves.

To discover when $f$ is level, we can change the algorithm as follows. Instead of just testing how large the interval is, the new algorithm computes
the area of three trapezoids: the given one, and the two halves. Suppose
the difference between the two is less than

$$TOLERANCE \cdot (right - left) \ .$$

This area represents a small rectangle, of height *TOLERANCE*, and represents the error margin of our computation. In other words, the algorithm
determines whether $f$ changes enough to affect the error margin, and if not,
it stops. Otherwise, it continues with the divide-and-conquer approach.

**Step 3**: Develop *integrate-adaptive*, which integrates a function $f$ between
*left* and *right* according to the suggested method. Do not discuss the termination of *integrate-adaptive*.

**Adaptive Integration**: The algorithm is called "adaptive integration" because it automatically adapts its strategy. For those parts of $f$ that are level, it performs just a few calculations; for the other parts, it inspects very small intervals so that the error margin is also decreased accordingly. ∎

## 27.4 Newton's Method

Newton invented another method for finding the root of a function. Newton's method exploits the idea of an approximation. To search a root of some function $f$, we start with a guess, say, $r1$. Then we study the tangent of $f$ at $r1$, that is, the line that goes through the Cartesian point $(r1, f(r1))$ and has the same slope as $f$. This tangent is a linear approximation of $f$ and it has a root that is in many cases closer to the root of $f$ than our original guess. Hence, by repeating this process sufficiently often, we can find an $r$ for which $(f\ r)$ is close to 0.

To translate this process description into Scheme, we follow the familiar process. The function—let's call it *newton* in honor of its inventor—consumes a function $f$ and a number $r0$, the current guess. If $(f\ r0)$ is close to 0, the problem is solved. Of course, close to 0 could be mean $(f\ r0)$ is a small positive number or a small negative number. Hence we translate this idea into

$(<=$ (abs $(f\ r0))$ *TOLERANCE*$)$

That is, we determine whether the absolute value is small. The answer in this case is $r0$.

The generative step of the algorithm consists of finding the root of the tangent of $f$ at $r0$. It generates a new guess. By applying *newton* to this new guess, we resume the process with what we hope is a better guess:

```
;; newton : (number → number) number → number
;; to find a number r such that (< (abs (f r)) TOLERANCE)
(define (newton f r0)
  (cond
    [(<= (abs (f r0)) TOLERANCE) r0]
    [else (newton f (find-root-tangent f r0))]))
```

Since finding the root of a tangent is domain knowledge, we define a separate function for this purpose:

```
;; find-root-tangent : (number → number) number → number
;; to find the root of the tagent of f at r0
(define (find-root-tangent f r0)
  (local ((define fprime (d/dx f)))
    (− r0
       (/ (f r0)
          (fprime r0)))))
```

The function first computes $(d/dx\ f)$, that is, the derivative of $f$ at $r0$ (see section 23.5) at $r0$. The body of the **local**-expression computes the root from the current guess, $(f\ r0)$, and the slope of $f$ at $r0$.[61]

The most interesting aspect of *newton* is that, unlike all other functions we have discussed, it does **not** always terminate. Consider the following function:

```
;; f : number → number
(define (f x)
  (− (* x x) x 1.8))
```

A simple hand-calculation shows that its derivative is

```
;; fprime : number → number
(define (fprime x)
  (− (* 2 x) 1))
```

If we were to use 1/2 as the initial guess, we would have to find the root of a tangent with slope 0, that is, a tangent that is parallel to the $x$ axis. Of course, such a tangent doesn't have a root. As a result, *find-root-of-tangent* cannot find a tangent and *newton* won't find a root.

---

[61]The tangent of a function $f$ at $r_i$ is the linear function

$$
\begin{aligned}
t(x) &= f'(r0) \cdot (x - r0) + f(r0) \\
     &= f'(r0) \cdot x + [f(r0) - f'(r0) \cdot r0]
\end{aligned}
$$

The function $f'$ is the derivative of $f$, and $f'(r0)$ is the slope of $f$ at $r0$. Furthermore, the root of a linear function is the intersection of a straight line with the $x$ axis. In general, if the line's equation is

$$
y(x) = a \cdot x + b
$$

then its root is $-b/a$. In our case, the root of $f$'s tangent is

$$
r - \frac{f(r0)}{f'(r0)} .
$$

**Exercises**

**Exercise 27.4.1** Test *newton* with $f$. Use the initial guesses 1, 2, and 3. Also use *find-root* from the preceding section to find a root.

Use a hand-evaluation to determine how quickly *newton* finds a value close to the root (if it finds one). Compare *newton*'s behavior with *find-root*'s behavior.

Employ the strategy of section 17.8 to formulate the tests as boolean-valued expressions. ∎

## 27.5 Extended Exercise: Gaussian Elimination

Mathematicians not only search for solutions of equations in one variable; they also study whole systems of linear equations. Here is a sample system of equations in three variables, $x$, $y$, and $z$:

$$\begin{array}{rrrrrrr} 2 \cdot x & + & 2 \cdot y & + & 3 \cdot z & = & 10 \\ 2 \cdot x & + & 5 \cdot y & + & 12 \cdot z & = & 31 \\ 4 \cdot x & + & 1 \cdot y & - & 2 \cdot z & = & 1 \end{array} \qquad (\dagger)$$

A solution to a system of equations is a series of numbers, one per variable, such that if we replace the variable with its corresponding number, the two sides of each equation evaluate to the same number. In our running example, the solution is $x = 1$, $y = 1$, and $z = 2$, as we can easily check:

$$\begin{array}{rrrrrrr} 2 \cdot 1 & + & 2 \cdot 1 & + & 3 \cdot 2 & = & 10 \\ 2 \cdot 1 & + & 5 \cdot 1 & + & 12 \cdot 2 & = & 31 \\ 4 \cdot 1 & + & 1 \cdot 1 & - & 2 \cdot 2 & = & 1 \end{array}$$

The first equation now reads as $10 = 10$, the second one as $31 = 31$, and the last one as $1 = 1$.

One of the most famous methods for finding a solution is called Gaussian elimination. It consists of two steps. The first step is to transform the system of equations into a system of different shape but with the same solution. The second step is to find solutions to one equation at a time. Here we focus on the first step because it is another interesting instance of generative recursion.

The first step of the Gaussian elimination algorithm is called "triangulation" because the result is a system of equations in the shape of a triangle.

In contrast, the original system is typically a rectangle. To understand this terminology, take a look at this representation of the original system:

```
(list  (list  2  2    3   10)
       (list  2  5   12   31)
       (list  4  1   -2    1)  )
```

This representation captures the essence of the system, namely, the numeric coefficients of the variables and the right-hand sides. The names of the variables don't play any role.

The generative step in the triangulation phase is to subtract the first row (list) of numbers from all the other rows. Subtracting one row from another means subtracting the corresponding items in the two rows. With our running example, this step would yield

```
(list  (list  2  2    3   10)
       (list  0  3    9   21)
       (list  4  1   -2    1)  )
```

when we subtract the first row from the second.

The goal of these subtractions is to put a 0 into the first column of all but the first row. To achieve this for the last row, we subtract the first row twice from the second one:

```
(list  (list  2    2    3    10)
       (list  0    3    9    21)
       (list  0   -3   -8   -19)  )
```

Put differently, we first multiply each item in the first row with 2 and then subtract the result from the last row. It is easy to check that the solutions for the original system of equations and for this new one are identical.

## Exercises

**Exercise 27.5.1** Check that the following system of equations

$$
\begin{array}{rrrrrrr}
2 \cdot x & + & 2 \cdot y & + & 3 \cdot z & = & 10 \\
          &   & 3 \cdot y & + & 9 \cdot z & = & 21 \\
          & - & 3 \cdot y & - & 8 \cdot z & = & -19
\end{array} \qquad (\ddagger)
$$

has the same solution as the one labeled with $(\dagger)$. ∎

**Exercise 27.5.2** Develop *subtract*. The function consumes two lists of numbers of equal length. It subtracts the first from the second, item by item, as many times as necessary to obtain 0 in the first position. The result is the rest of this list. ∎

Following convention, we drop the leading 0's from the last two equations:

```
(list (list  2   2   3    10)
      (list       3   9    21)
      (list      -3  -8  -19)  )
```

If, in addition, we use the same process for the remainder of the system to generate shorter rows, the final representation has a triangular shape.

Let us study this idea with our running example. For the moment we ignore the first row and focus on the rest of the equations:

```
(list (list    3    9    21)
      (list   -3   -8  -19)  )
```

By subtracting the first row now -1 times from the second one, we get

```
(list (list  3   9   21)
      (list      1    2)  )
```

after dropping the leading 0. The remainder of this system is a single equation, which cannot be simplified any further.

Here is the result of adding this last system to the first equation:

```
(list (list  2  2  3  10)
      (list     3  9  21)        (*)
      (list        1   2)           )
```

As promised, the shape of this system of equations is (roughly) a triangle, and as we can easily check, it has the same solution as the original system.

## Exercises

**Exercise 27.5.3** Check that the following system of equations

$$
\begin{aligned}
2 \cdot x \; + \; 2 \cdot y \; + \; 3 \cdot z \; &= \; 10 \\
3 \cdot y \; + \; 9 \cdot z \; &= \; 21 \qquad (*) \\
1 \cdot z \; &= \; 2
\end{aligned}
$$

has the same solution as the one labeled with (†). ∎

**Exercise 27.5.4** Develop the algorithm *triangulate*, which consumes a rectangular representation of a system of equations and produces a triangular version according the Gaussian algorithm. ∎

Unfortunately, the current version of the triangulation algorithm occasionally fails to produce the solution. Consider the following (representation of a) system of equations:

```
(list  (list  2    3    3   8)
       (list  2    3   -2   3)
       (list  4   -2    2   4)  )
```

Its solution is $x = 1$, $y = 1$, and $z = 1$.

The first step is to subtract the first row from the second and to subtract it twice from the last one, which yields the following matrix:

```
(list  (list  2    3    3     8)
       (list        0   -5    -5)
       (list       -8   -4   -12)  )
```

Next our algorithm would focus on the rest of the matrix:

```
(list  (list    0   -5    -5)
       (list   -8   -4   -12)  )
```

but the first item of this matrix is 0. Since we cannot divide by 0, we are stuck.

To overcome this problem, we need to use another piece of knowledge from our problem domain, namely, that we can switch equations around without changing the solution. Of course, as we switch rows, we must make sure that the first item of the row to be moved is not 0. Here we can simply swap the two rows:

```
(list  (list  -8   -4   -12)
       (list    0   -5    -5)  )
```

From here we may continue as before, subtracting the first equation from the remaining ones a sufficient number of times. The final triangular matrix is:

```
(list  (list  2    3    3     8)
       (list       -8   -4   -12)
       (list            -5    -5)  )
```

It is easy to check that this system of equations still has the solution $x = 1$, $y = 1$, and $z = 1$.

## Exercises

**Exercise 27.5.5** Revise the algorithm *triangulate* from exercise 27.5.4 so that it switches rows when the first item of the matrix is 0.

**Hint:** DrScheme provides the function *remove*. It consumes an item $I$ and a list $L$ and produces a list like $L$ but with the first occurrence of $I$ removed. For example,

```
(equal? (remove (list 0 1) (list (list 2 1) (list 0 1)))
        (list (list 2 1)))
```

∎

**Exercise 27.5.6** Some systems of equations don't have a solution. Consider the following system as an example:

$$
\begin{array}{ccccccc}
2 \cdot x & + & 2 \cdot y & + & 2 \cdot z & = & 6 \\
2 \cdot x & + & 2 \cdot y & + & 4 \cdot z & = & 8 \\
2 \cdot x & + & 2 \cdot y & + & 1 \cdot z & = & 2
\end{array}
$$

Try to produce a triangular system by hand and with *triangulate*. What happens? Modify the function so that it signals an error if it encounters this situation. ∎

**Exercise 27.5.7** After we obtain a triangular system of equations such as $(*)$ on page 403 (or exercise 27.5.3), we can solve the equations. In our specific example, the last equation says that $z$ is 2. Equipped with this knowledge, we can eliminate $z$ from the second equation through a substitution:

$$3 \cdot y + 9 \cdot 2 = 21 \ .$$

Determine the value for $y$. Then repeat the substitution step for $y$ and $z$ in the first equation and find the value for $x$.

Develop the function *solve*, which consumes triangular systems of equations and produces a solution. A triangular system of equations has the shape

$$
\begin{array}{llll}
(\text{list} & (\text{list} & a_{11} & \cdots \quad \cdots \quad b_1) \\
& (\text{list} & & a_{21} \quad \cdots \quad b_2) \\
& (\text{list} & & \vdots \quad \vdots \quad \vdots) \\
& (\text{list} & & a_{nn} \quad b_n) \quad )
\end{array}
$$

where $a_{ij}$ and $b_i$ are numbers. That is, it is a list of lists and each of the lists is one item shorter than the preceding one. A solution is a list of numbers. The last number on the list is

$$\frac{b_n}{a_{nn}} \; .$$

**Hint:** Developing *solve* requires a solution for the following problem. Suppose we are given a row:

(list 3 9 21)

and a list of numbers that solve the remainder of the system:

(list 2).

In the world of equations, these two pieces of data represent the following knowledge:

$$3 \cdot x + 9 \cdot y = 21$$

and

$$y = 2 \, ,$$

which in turn means we must solve the following equation:

$$3 \cdot x + 9 \cdot 2 = 21 \, .$$

Develop the function *evaluate*, which evaluates the rest of the left-hand side of an equation and subtracts the right-hand side from this sum. Equivalently, *evaluate* consumes (list 9 21) and (list 2) and produces $-3$, that is, $9 \cdot 2 - 21$. Now use *evaluate* for the intermediate step in *solve*. ∎

# 28 Algorithms that Backtrack

Solving problems does not always proceed on a direct route to the goal. Sometimes we make progress by pursuing one approach only to discover that we are stuck because we took a wrong turn. In those cases, we backtrack in our exploration and take a different turn at some branch, in the hope that it leads us to a solution. Algorithms can proceed like that. In the first subsection, we deal with an algorithm that can help us traverse a graph, which is of course the situation we just discussed. The second subsection is an extended exercise that uses backtracking in the context of chess.

## 28.1 Traversing Graphs

On occasion, we need to navigate through a maze of one-way streets. Or, we may wish to draw a graph of whom we consider a friend, whom they consider a friend, and so on. Or, we need to plan a route through a network of pipelines. Or, we ask the Internet to find some way to send a message from one place to another.

All these situations share a common element: a *directed graph*.

Specifically, there is always some collection of *nodes* and a collection of *edges*. The edges represent one-way connections between the nodes. Consider figure 76. The black bullets are the nodes; the arrows between them are the one-way connections. The sample graph consists of seven nodes and nine edges.

Now suppose we wish to plan routes in the graph of figure 76. For example, if we plan to go from C to D, the route is simple: it consists of the origination node C and the destination node D. In contrast, if we wish to travel from E to D, we have two choices:

1. We either travel from E to F and then to D.

2. Or, we travel from E to C and then to D.

For some nodes, however, it is impossible to connect them. In particular, it is impossible in our sample graph to move from C to G by following the arrows.

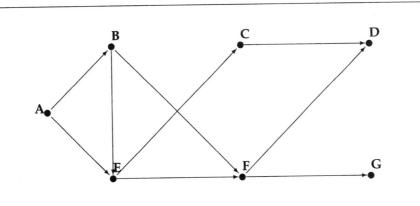

Figure 76: A directed graph

In the real world, graphs have more than just seven nodes and many more edges. Hence it is natural to develop functions that plan routes in graphs. Following the general design recipe, we start with a data analysis. Here is a compact representation of the graph in figure 76 using lists:

```
(define Graph
  '((A (B E))
    (B (E F))
    (C (D))
    (D ())
    (E (C F))
    (F (D G))
    (G ()))))
```

The list contains one list per node. Each of these lists starts with the name of a node followed by the list of its *neighbors*. For example, the second list represents node B with its two outgoing edges to E and F.

**Exercises**

**Exercise 28.1.1** Translate the above definition into proper list form using list and proper symbols.

The data definition for node is straightforward:

A *node* is a symbol.

Formulate a data definition for graphs with arbitrarily many nodes and edges. The data definition must specify a class of data that contains *Graph*. ∎

Based on the data definitions for *node* and *graph*, we can now produce the first draft of a contract for *find-route*, the function that searches a route in a graph:

```
;; find-route : node node graph → (listof node)
;; to create a path from origination to destination in G
(define (find-route origination destination G) ...)
```

What this header leaves open is the exact shape of the result. It implies that the result is a list of nodes, but it does not say exactly which nodes the list contains. To understand this aspect, we must study some examples.

Consider the first problem mentioned above. Here is an expression that formulates the problem in Scheme:

```
(find-route 'C 'D Graph)
```

A route from 'C to 'D consists of just two nodes: the origination and the destination node. Hence, we should expect the answer (list 'C 'D). Of course, one might argue that since both the origination node and the destination node are known, the result should be empty. Here we choose the first alternative since it is more natural, but it requires only a minor change of the final function definition to produce the latter.

Now consider our second problem, going from 'E to 'D, which is more representative of the kinds of problems we might encounter. One natural idea is to inspect all of the neighbors of 'E and to find a route from one of them to 'D. In our sample graph, 'E has two neighbors: 'C and 'F. Suppose for a moment that we didn't know the route yet. In that case, we could again inspect all of the neighbors of 'C and find a route from those to our goal. Of course, 'C has a single neighbor and it is 'D. Putting together the results of all stages shows that the final result is (list 'E 'C 'D).

Our final example poses a new problem. Suppose *find-route* is given the arguments 'C, 'G, and *Graph*. In this case, we know from inspecting figure 76 that there is no connecting route. To signal the lack of a route, *find-route* should produce a value that cannot be mistaken for a route. One good choice is false, a value that isn't a list and naturally denotes the failure of a function to compute a proper result.

This new agreement requires another change in our contract:

;; *find-route : node node graph* → (**listof** *node*) **or** false
;; to create a path from *origination* to *destination* in *G*
;; if there is no path, the function produces false
(**define** (*find-route origination destination G*) ... )

Our next step is to understand the four essential pieces of the function: the "trivial problem" condition, a matching solution, the generation of a new problem, and the combination step. The discussion of the three examples suggests answers. First, if the *origination* argument of *find-route* is equal to its *destination*, the problem is trivial; the matching answer is (list *destination*). Second, if the arguments are different, we must inspect all neighbors of *origination* in *graph* and determine whether there is a route from one of those to *destination*.

Since a node can have an arbitrary number of neighbors, this task is too complex for a single primitive. We need an auxiliary function. The task of the auxiliary function is to consume a list of nodes and to determine for each one of them whether there is a route to the destination node in the given graph. Put differently, the function is a list-oriented version of *find-*

*route.* Let us call this function *find-route/list*. Here is a translation of this informal description into a contract, header, and purpose statement:

```
;; find-route/list : (listof node) node graph → (listof node) or false
;; to create a path from some node on lo-originations to destination
;; if there is no path, the function produces false
(define (find-route/list lo-originations destination G) ...)
```

Now we can write a first draft of *find-route* as follows:

```
(define (find-route origination destination G)
  (cond
    [(symbol=? origination destination) (list destination)]
    [else ... (find-route/list (neighbors origination G) destination G) ...]))
```

The function *neighbors* generates a whole list of problems: the problems of finding routes from the neighbors of *origination* to *destination*. Its definition is a straightforward exercise in structural processing.

## Exercises

**Exercise 28.1.2** Develop the function *neighbors*. It consumes a node *n* and a graph *g* (see exercise 28.1.1) and produces the list of neighbors of *n* in *g*. ∎

Next we need to consider what *find-route/list* produces. If it finds a route from any of the neighbors, it produces a route from that neighbor to the final destination. But, if none of the neighbors is connected to the destination, the function produces false. Clearly, *find-route*'s answer depends on what *find-route/list* produces. Hence we should distinguish the answers with a **cond**-expression:

```
(define (find-route origination destination G)
  (cond
    [(symbol=? origination destination) (list destination)]
    [else (local ((define possible-route
                    (find-route/list (neighbors origination G)
                                     destination G)))
            (cond
              [(boolean? route) ...]
              [else ; (cons? route)
               ...]))]))
```

The two cases reflect the two kinds of answers we might receive: a boolean or a list. If *find-route/list* produces false, it failed to find a route from *origination*'s neighbors, and it is therefore impossible to reach *destination* at all. The answer in this case must therefore be false. In contrast, if *find-route/list* produces a list, the answer must be route from *origination* to *destination*. Since *possible-route* starts with one of *origination*'s neighbors, it suffices to add *origination* to the front of *possible-route*.

---

```
;; find-route : node node graph → (listof node) or false
;; to create a path from origination to destination in G
;; if there is no path, the function produces false
(define (find-route origination destination G)
  (cond
    [(symbol=? origination destination) (list destination)]
    [else (local ((define possible-route
                    (find-route/list (neighbors origination G) destination G)))
            (cond
              [(boolean? possible-route) false]
              [else (cons origination possible-route)]))]))

;; find-route/list : (listof node) node graph → (listof node) or false
;; to create a path from some node on lo-Os to D
;; if there is no path, the function produces false
(define (find-route/list lo-Os D G)
  (cond
    [(empty? lo-Os) false]
    [else (local ((define possible-route (find-route (first lo-Os) D G)))
            (cond
              [(boolean? possible-route) (find-route/list (rest lo-Os) D G)]
              [else possible-route]))]))
```

Figure 77: Finding a route in a graph

---

Figure 77 contains the complete definition of *find-route*. It also contains a definition of *find-route/list*, which processes its first argument via structural recursion. For each node in the list, *find-route/list* uses *find-route* to check for a route. If *find-route* indeed produces a route, that route is the answer. Otherwise, if *find-route* fails and produces false, the function recurs. In other words, it backtracks its current choice of a starting position, (first lo-Os), and instead tries the next one in the list. For that reason, *find-route* is often called a BACKTRACKING ALGORITHM.

**Backtracking in the Structural World**:  Intermezzo 3 discusses backtracking in the structural world. A particularly good example is exercise 18.1.13, which concerns a backtracking function for family trees. The function first searches one branch of a family tree for a blue-eyed ancestor and, if this search produces false, it searches the other half of the tree. Since graphs generalize trees, comparing the two functions is an instructive exercise. ∎

Last, but not least, we need to understand whether the function produces an answer in all situations. The second one, *find-route/list*, is structurally recursive and therefore always produces some value, assuming *find-route* always does. For *find-route* the answer is far from obvious. For example, when given the graph in figure 76 and two nodes in the graph, *find-route* always produces some answer. For other graphs, however, it does not always terminate.

---

## Exercises

**Exercise 28.1.3** Test *find-route*.  Use it to find a route from A to G in the graph of figure 76. Ensure that it produces false when asked to find a route from C to G. ∎

**Exercise 28.1.4** Develop the function *test-on-all-nodes*, which consumes a graph *g* and tests *find-route* on all pairs of nodes in *g*. Test the function on *Graph*. ∎

---

Consider the graph in figure 78. It differs radically from the graph in figure 76 in that it is possible to start a route in a node and to return to the same node. Specifically, it is possible to move from B to E to C and back to B. And indeed, if applied *find-route* to 'B, 'D, and a representation of the graph, it fails to stop. Here is the hand-evaluation:

```
    (find-route 'B 'D Cyclic-graph)
=   ... (find-route 'B 'D Cyclic-graph) ...
=   ... (find-route/list (list 'E 'F) 'D Cyclic-graph) ...
=   ... (find-route 'E 'D Cyclic-graph) ...
=   ... (find-route/list (list 'C 'F) 'D Cyclic-graph) ...
=   ... (find-route 'C 'D Cyclic-graph) ...
=   ... (find-route/list (list 'B 'D) 'D Cyclic-graph) ...
=   ... (find-route 'B 'D Cyclic-graph) ...
=   ...
```

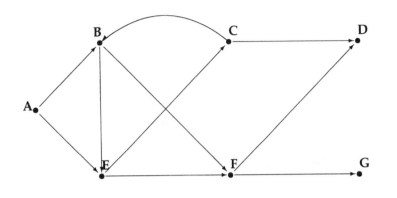

Figure 78: A directed graph with cycle

where *Cyclic-Graph* stands for a Scheme representation of the graph in figure 78. The hand-evaluation shows that after seven applications of *find-route* and *find-route/list* the computer must evaluate the exact same expression from which we started. Since the same input produces the same output and the same behavior for functions, we know that the function loops forever and does not produce a value.

In summary, if some given graph is cycle-free, *find-route* produces some output for any given inputs. After all, every route can only contain a finite number of nodes, and the number of routes is finite, too. The function therefore either exhaustively inspects all solutions starting from some given node or finds a route from the origination to the destination node. If, however, a graph contains a cycle, that is, a route from some node back to itself, *find-route* may not produce a result for some inputs. In the next part, we will study a programming technique that helps us finds routes even in the presence of cycles in a graph.

## Exercises

**Exercise 28.1.5** Test *find-route* on 'B, 'C, and the graph in figure 78. Use the ideas of section 17.8 to formulate the tests as boolean-valued expression. ∎

**Exercise 28.1.6** Organize the *find-route* program as a single function definition. Remove parameters from the locally defined functions. ∎

## 28.2   Extended Exercise: Checking (on) Queens

A famous problem in the game of chess concerns the placement of queens
on a board. For our purposes, a chessboard is a "square" of, say, eight-by-
eight or three-by-three tiles. The queen is a game piece that can move in
a horizontal, vertical, or diagonal direction arbitrarily far. We say that a
queen *threatens* a tile if it is on the tile or can move to it. Figure 79 shows
an example. The solid disk represents a queen in the second column and
sixth row. The solid lines radiating from the disk go through all those tiles
that are threatened by the queen.

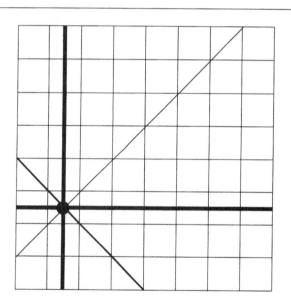

Figure 79: A chessboard with a single queen

The queen-placement problem is to place eight queens on a chessboard
of eight-by-eight tiles such that the queens on the board don't threaten each
other. In computing, we generalize the problem of course and ask whether
we can place *n* queens on some board of arbitrary size *m* by *m*.

Even a cursory glance at the problem suggests that we need a data representation of boards and some basic functions on boards before we can
even think of designing a program that solves the problem. Let's start with
some basic data and function definitions.

## Exercises

**Exercise 28.2.1** Develop a data definition for chessboards.
**Hint:** Use lists. Represent tiles with true and false. A value of true should indicate that a position is available for the placement of a queen; false should indicate that a position is occupied by, or threatened by, a queen. ∎

Next we need a function for creating a board and another one for checking on a specific tile. Following the examples of lists, let's define *build-board* and *board-ref*.

## Exercises

**Exercise 28.2.2** Develop the following two functions on chessboards:

;; *build-board* : $N$ ($N$ $N$ → *boolean*) → *board*
;; to create a board of size $n$ x $n$,
;; fill each position with indices $i$ and $j$ with ($f$ $i$ $j$)
(**define** (*build-board* $n$ $f$) ...)

;; *board-ref* : *board* $N$ $N$ → *boolean*
;; to access a position with indices $i, j$ on a-board
(**define** (*board-ref* *a-board* $i$ $j$) ...)

Test them rigorously! Use the ideas of section 17.8 to formulate the tests as boolean-valued expressions. ∎

In addition to these generic functions on a chessboard representation, we also need at least one function that captures the concept of a "threat" as mentioned in the problem statement.

## Exercises

**Exercise 28.2.3** Develop the function *threatened?*, which computes whether a queen can reach a position on the board from some given position. That is, the function consumes two positions, given as *posn* structures, and produces true if a queen on the first position can threaten the second position.

**Hint:** The exercise translate the chess problem of "threatening queens" into the mathematical problem of determining whether in some given grid, two positions are on the same vertical, horizontal, or diagonal line. Keep in mind that each position belongs to two diagonals and that the slope of a diagonal is either $+1$ or $-1$. ∎

Once we have data definitions and functions for the "language of chessboards," we can turn our attention to the main task: the algorithm for placing a number of queens on some given board.

## Exercises

**Exercise 28.2.4** Develop *placement*. The function consumes a natural number and a board and tries to place that many queens on the board. If the queens can be placed, the function produces an appropriate board. If not, it produces false. ∎

# Intermezzo 5: The Cost of Computing and Vectors

In section 26.3 we discussed the differences between a structurally recursive program and an equivalent, generative version. The comparison revealed that the generative one is much faster than the structural version. We used both informal arguments, using the number of recursive calls, and measurements, using **time** expressions (exercises 26.3.1 and 26.3.3), to support our conclusion.

While timing the application of a program to specific arguments can help us understand a program's behavior in one situation, it is not a fully convincing argument. After all, applying the same program to some other inputs may require a radically different amount of time. In short, timing programs for specific inputs has the same status as testing programs for specific examples. Just as testing may reveal bugs, timing may reveal anomalies concerning the execution behavior for specific inputs. It does not provide a firm foundation for general statements about the behavior of a program.

This intermezzo introduces a tool for making general statements about the time that programs take to compute a result. The first subsection motivates the tool and illustrates it with several examples, though on an informal basis. The second one provides a rigorous definition. The last one uses the tool to motivate an additional class of Scheme data and some of its basic operations.

## Concrete Time, Abstract Time

Let's study the behavior of *how-many*, a function that we understand well:

```
(define (how-many a-list)
  (cond
    [(empty? a-list) 0]
    [else (+ (how-many (rest a-list)) 1)]))
```

It consumes a list and computes how many items the list contains.

Here is a sample evaluation:

(*how-many* (list 'a 'b 'c))

= (+ (*how-many* (list 'b 'c)) 1)

= (+ (+ (*how-many* (list 'c)) 1) 1)

$= (+ \ (+ \ (+ \ (\textit{how-many} \ \mathsf{empty}) \ 1) \ 1) \ 1)$

$= 3$

It consists of only those steps that are natural recursions. The steps in between are always the same. For example, to get from the original application to the first natural recursion, we go through the following steps:

$(\textit{how-many} \ (\mathsf{list} \ \mathsf{'a} \ \mathsf{'b} \ \mathsf{'c}))$

$= (\textbf{cond}$
   $\quad [(\mathsf{empty?} \ (\mathsf{list} \ \mathsf{'a} \ \mathsf{'b} \ \mathsf{'c})) \ 0]$
   $\quad [\textbf{else} \ (+ \ (\textit{how-many} \ (\mathsf{rest} \ (\mathsf{list} \ \mathsf{'a} \ \mathsf{'b} \ \mathsf{'c}))) \ 1)])$

$= (\textbf{cond}$
   $\quad [\mathsf{false} \ 0]$
   $\quad [\textbf{else} \ (+ \ (\textit{how-many} \ (\mathsf{rest} \ (\mathsf{list} \ \mathsf{'a} \ \mathsf{'b} \ \mathsf{'c}))) \ 1)])$

$= (\textbf{cond}$
   $\quad [\textbf{else} \ (+ \ (\textit{how-many} \ (\mathsf{rest} \ (\mathsf{list} \ \mathsf{'a} \ \mathsf{'b} \ \mathsf{'c}))) \ 1)])$

$= (+ \ (\textit{how-many} \ (\mathsf{rest} \ (\mathsf{list} \ \mathsf{'a} \ \mathsf{'b} \ \mathsf{'c}))) \ 1)$

The steps between the remaing natural recursions differ only as far as the substitution for *a-list* is concerned.

If we apply *how-many* to a shorter list, we need fewer natural recursion steps:

$(\textit{how-many} \ (\mathsf{list} \ \mathsf{'e}))$
$= (+ \ (\textit{how-many} \ \mathsf{empty}) \ 1)$
$= 1$

If we apply *how-many* to a longer list, we need more natural recursion steps. The number of steps between natural recursions remains the same.

The example suggests that, not surprisingly, the number of evaluation steps depends on the size of the input. More importantly, though, it also implies that the number of natural recrusions is a good measure of the size of an evaluation sequence. After all, we can reconstruct the actual number of steps from this measure and the function definition. For this reason, programmers have come to express the ABSTRACT RUNNING TIME of a program as a relationship between the size of the input and the number of recursion steps in an evaluation.[62]

---

[62]We speak of an abstract running time because the measure ignores the details of how much time primitive steps take and how much time the overall evaluation takes.

In our first example, the size of the input is simply the size of the list. More specifically, if the list contains one item, the evaluation requires one natural recursion. For two items, we recur twice. For a list with $N$ items, the evaluation requires $N$ steps.

Not all functions have such a uniform measure for their abstract running time. Take a look at our first recursive function:

(**define** (*contains-doll? a-list-of-symbols*)
  (**cond**
     [(empty? *a-list-of-symbols*) false]
     [**else** (**cond**
           [(symbol=? (first *a-list-of-symbols*) 'doll) true]
           [**else** (*contains-doll?* (rest *a-list-of-symbols*))])])]))

If we evaluate

  (*contains-doll?* (list 'doll 'robot 'ball 'game-boy 'pokemon))

the application requires no natural recursion step. In contrast, for the expression

  (*contains-doll?* (list 'robot 'ball 'game-boy 'pokemon 'doll))

the evaluation requires as many natural recursion steps as there are items in the list. Put differently, in the best case, the function can find the answer immediately; in the worst case, the function must search the entire input list.

Programmers cannot assume that inputs are always of the best posisble shape; and they must hope that the inputs are not of the worst possible shape. Instead, they must analyze how much time their functions take on the average. For example, *contains-doll?* may—on the average—find 'doll somewhere in the middle of the list. Thus, we could say that if the input contains $N$ items, the abstract running time of *contains-doll?* is (roughly)

$$\frac{N}{2}$$

—that is, it naturally recurs half as often as the number of items on the input. Because we already measure the running time of a function in an abstract manner, we can ignore the division by 2. More precisely, we assume that each basic step takes $K$ units of time. If, instead, we use $K/2$ as the constant, we can calculate

$$K \cdot \frac{N}{2} = \frac{K}{2} \cdot N$$

which shows that we can ignore other constant factors. To indicate that we are hiding such constants we say that *contains-doll?* takes "on the order of $N$ steps" to find 'doll in a list of $N$ items.

Now consider our standard sorting function from figure 33. Here is a hand-evaluation for a small input:

> (*sort* (list 3 1 2))

> = (*insert* 3 (*sort* (list 1 2)))

> = (*insert* 3 (*insert* 1 (*sort* (list 2))))

> = (*insert* 3 (*insert* 1 (*insert* 2 (*sort* empty))))

> = (*insert* 3 (*insert* 1 (*insert* 2 empty)))

> = (*insert* 3 (*insert* 1 (list 2)))

> = (*insert* 3 (cons 2 (*insert* 1 empty)))

> = (*insert* 3 (list 2 1))

> = (*insert* 3 (list 2 1))

> = (list 3 2 1)

The evaluation is more complicated than those for *how-many* or *contains-doll?*. It also consists of two phases. During the first one, the natural recursions for *sort* set up as many applications of *insert* as there are items in the list. During the second phase, each application of *insert* traverses a list of 1, 2, 3, ... up to the number of items in the original list (minus one).

Inserting an item is similar to finding an item, so it is not surprising that *insert* behaves like *contains-doll?*. More specifically, the applications of *insert* to a list of $N$ items may trigger $N$ natural recursions or none. On the average, we assume it requires $N/2$, which means on the order of $N$. Because there are $N$ applications of *insert*, we have an average of on the order of $N^2$ natural recursions of *insert*.

In summary, if $l$ contains $N$ items, evaluating (*sort* $l$) always requires $N$ natural recursions of *sort* and on the order of $N^2$ natural recursions of *insert*. Taken together, we get

$$N^2 + N$$

steps, but we will see in exercise 29.2.1 that this is equivalent to saying that insertion sort requires on the order of $N^2$ steps.

Our final example is the function *maxi*:

```
;; maxi : ne-list-of-numbers → number
;; to determine the maximum of a non-empty list of numbers
(define (maxi alon)
  (cond
    [(empty? (rest alon)) (first alon)]
    [else (cond
            [(> (maxi (rest alon)) (first alon)) (maxi (rest alon))]
            [else (first alon)])]))
```

In exercise 18.1.12, we investigated its behavior and the behavior of an observationally equivalent function that uses **local**. Here we study its abstract running time rather than just observe some concrete running time.

Let's start with a small example: (*maxi* (list 0 1 2 3)). We know that the result is 3. Here is the first important step of a hand-evaluation:

```
(maxi (list 0 1 2 3))
= (cond
    [(> (maxi (list 1 2 3)) 0) (maxi (list 1 2 3))]
    [else 0])
```

From here, we must evaluate the left of the two underlined natural recursions. Because the result is 3 and the condition is thus true, we must evaluate the second underlined natural recursion as well.

Focusing on just the natural recursion we see that its hand-evaluation begins with similar steps:

```
(maxi (list 1 2 3))
= (cond
    [(> (maxi (list 2 3)) 1) (maxi (list 2 3))]
    [else 1])
```

Again, (*maxi* (list 2 3)) is evaluated twice because it produces the maximum. Finally, even determining the maximum of (*maxi* (list 2 3)) requires two natural recursions:

```
(maxi (list 2 3))
= (cond
    [(> (maxi (list 3)) 2) (maxi (list 3))]
    [else 2])
```

To summarize, *maxi* requires two natural recursions for each application. The following table counts the instances for our example:

| original expression | requires 2 evaluations of |
|---|---|
| (*maxi* (list 0 1 2 3)) | (*maxi* (list 1 2 3)) |
| (*maxi* (list 1 2 3)) | (*maxi* (list 2 3)) |
| (*maxi* (list 2 3)) | (*maxi* (list 3)) |

Altogether the hand-evaluation requires eight natural recursions for a list of four items. If we add 4 (or a larger number) at the end of the list, we need to double the number of natural recursions. Thus, in general we need on the order of

$$2^N$$

recursions for a list of $N$ numbers when the last number is the maximum.[63]

While the scenario we considered is the worst possible case, the analysis of *maxi*'s abstract running time explains the phenomenon we studied in exercise 18.1.12. It also explains why a version of *maxi* that uses a **local-**expression to name the result of the natural recursion is faster:

```
;; maxi2 : ne-list-of-numbers → number
;; to determine the maximum of a list of numbers
(define (maxi2 alon)
  (cond
    [(empty? (rest alon)) (first alon)]
    [else (local ((define max-of-rest (maxi2 (rest alon))))
            (cond
              [(> max-of-rest (first alon)) max-of-rest]
              [else (first alon)])]))
```

Instead of recomputing the maximum of the rest of the list, this version just refers to the variable twice when the variable stands for the maximum of the rest of the list.

---

## Exercises

---

[63]More precisely, the evaluation consists of $2^{N-1}$ steps, but

$$2^{N-1} = \frac{1}{2} \cdot 2^N ,$$

which shows that we ignore a (small) constant when we say on the order of $2^N$.

**Exercise 29.1.1** A number tree is either a number or a pair of number trees. Develop the function *sum-tree*, which determines the sum of the numbers in a tree. How should we measure the size of a tree? What is its abstract running time? ∎

**Exercise 29.1.2** Hand-evaluate (*maxi2* (list 0 1 2 3)) in a manner similar to our evaluation of (*maxi* (list 0 1 2 3)). What is the abstract running time of *maxi2*? ∎

## The Definition of "on the Order of"

It is time to introduce a rigorous description of the phrase "on the order of" and to explain why it is acceptable to ignore some constants. Any serious programmer must be thoroughly familiar with this notion. It is the most fundamental method for analyzing and comparing the behavior of programs. This intermezzo provides a first glimpse at the idea; a second course on computing usually provides some more in-depth considerations.

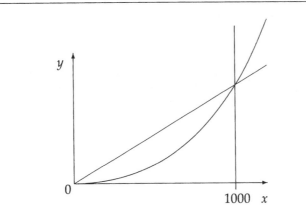

Figure 80: A comparison of two running time expressions

Let's consider a sample "order of" claim with concrete examples before we agree on a definition. Recall that a function $F$ may require on the order of $N$ steps and a function $G$ $N^2$ steps, even though both compute the same results for the same inputs. Now suppose the basic time constants are 1000 for $F$ and 1 for $G$. One way to compare the two claims is to tabulate the abstract running time:

| $N$ | 1 | 10 | 50 | 100 | 500 | 1000 |
|---|---|---|---|---|---|---|
| $F(1000 \cdot N)$ | 1000 | 10000 | 50000 | 100000 | 500000 | 1000000 |
| $G(N \cdot N)$ | 1 | 100 | 2500 | 10000 | 250000 | 1000000 |

At first glance the table seems to say that $G$'s performance is better than $F$'s, because for inputs of the same size ($N$), $G$'s running time is always smaller than $F$'s. But a closer look reveals that as the inputs get larger, $G$'s advantage decreases. Indeed, for an input of size 1000, the two functions need the same number of steps, and thereafter $G$ is always slower than $F$. Figure 80 compares the graphs of the two expressions. It shows that the linear graph for $1000 \cdot N$ dominates the curve of $N \cdot N$ for some finite number of points but thereafter it is below the curve.

The concrete example recalls two important facts about our informal discussion of abstract running time. First, our abstract description is always a claim about the relationship between two quantities: the size of the input and the number of natural recursions evaluated. More precisely, the relationship is a (mathematical) function that maps an abstract size measure of the input to an abstract measure of the running time. Second, when we compare "on the order of" properties of functions, such as

$$N, \ N^2, \ \text{or} \ 2^N,$$

we really mean to compare the corresponding functions that consume $N$ and produce the above results. In short, a statement concerning the order of things compares two functions on natural numbers (**N**).

The comparison of functions on **N** is difficult because they are infinite. If a function $f$ produces larger outputs than some other function $g$ for all natural numbers, then $f$ is clearly larger than $g$. But what if this comparison fails for just a few inputs? Or for 1,000 such as the one illustrated in figure 80? Because we would still like to make approximate judgments, programmers and scientists adapt the mathematical notion of comparing functions up to some factor and some finite number of exceptions.

> ORDER-OF (BIG-O): Given a function $g$ on the natural numbers, $O(g)$ (pronounced: "big-O of $g$") is a class of functions on natural numbers. A function $f$ is in $O(g)$ if there exist numbers $c$ and *bigEnough* such that for all $n \geq$ *bigEnough*, it is true that

$$f(n) \leq c \cdot g(n).$$

Recall the performance of F and G above. For the first, we assumed that it consumed time according to the following function

$$f(N) = 1000 \cdot N \, ;$$

the performance of second one obeyed the function g:

$$g(N) = N^2 \, .$$

Using the definition of big-O, we can say that f is $O(g)$, because for all $n \geq 1000$,

$$f(n) \leq 1 \cdot g(n) \, ,$$

which means $bigEnough = 1000$ and $c = 1$.

More important, the definition of big-O provides us with a shorthand for stating claims about a function's running time. For example, from now on, we say *how-many*'s running time is $O(N)$. Keep in mind that N is the standard abbreviation of the (mathematical) function $g(N) = N$. Similarly, we can say that, in the worst case, *sort*'s running time is $O(N^2)$ and *max*'s is $O(2^N)$.

Finally, the definition of big-O explains why we don't have to pay attention to specific constants in our comparsions of abstract running time. Consider *max* and *max2*. We know that *max*'s worst-case running time is in $O(2^N)$, *max2*'s is in $O(N)$. Say, we need the maximum of a list with 10 numbers. Assuming *max* and *max2* roughly consume the same amount of time per basic step, *max* will need $2^{10} = 1024$ steps and *max2* will need 10 steps, which means *max2* will be faster. Now even if *max2*'s basic step requires twice as much time as *max*'s basic step, *max2* is still around 50 times faster. Futhermore, if we double the size of the input list, *max*'s apparent disadvantage totally disappears. In general, the larger the input is, the less relevant are the specific constants.

## Exercises

**Exercise 29.2.1** In the first subsection, we stated that the function $f(n) = n^2 + n$ belongs to the class $O(n^2)$. Determine the pair of numbers c and *bigEnough* that verify this claim. ∎

**Exercise 29.2.2** Consider the functions $f(n) = 2^n$ and $g(n) = 1000 \cdot n$. Show that g belongs to $O(f)$, which means that f is abstractly speaking more (or at least equally) expensive than g. If the input size is guaranteed to be between 3 and 12, which function is better? ∎

**Exercise 29.2.3** Compare $f(n) = n \log n$ and $g(n) = n^2$. Does $f$ belong to $O(g)$ and/or $g$ to $O(f)$? ∎

## A First Look at Vectors

Until now we have paid little attention to how much time it takes to retrieve data from structures or lists. Now that we have a tool for stating general judgments, let's take a close look at this basic computation step. Recall the last problem of the preceding part: finding a route in a graph. The program *find-route* requires two auxiliaries: *find-route/list* and *neighbors*. We paid a lot of attention to *find-route/list* and none to *neighbors*. Indeed, developing *neighbors* was just an exercise (see 28.1.2), because looking up a value in a list is by now a routine programming task.

Here is a possible definition for *neighbors*:

```
;; neighbors : node graph → (listof node)
;; to lookup the node in graph
(define (neighbors node graph)
  (cond
    [(empty? graph) (error 'neighbors "can't happen")]
    [else (cond
            [(symbol=? (first (first graph)) node) (second (first graph))]
            [else (neighbors node (rest graph))])]))
```

The function is similar to *contains-doll?* and has roughly the same behavior. More concretely, *neighbors* is $O(N)$ when we assume that *graph* is a list of $N$ nodes.

Considering that *neighbors* is used at every stage of the evaluation of *find-route*, *neighbors* is possibly a bottleneck. As a matter of fact, if the route we are looking for involves $N$ nodes (the maximum), *neighbors* is applied $N$ times, so the algorithm requires $O(N^2)$ steps in *neighbors*.

In contrast to lists, structures deal with value extractions as a constant time operation. At first glance this observation seems to suggest that we use structures as representations of graphs. A closer look, however, shows that this idea doesn't work easily. The graph algorithm works best if we are able to work with the names of nodes and access a node's neighbors based on the name. A name could be a symbol or the node's number in the graph. In general, what we really wish to have in a programming language is a class of compound values size with constant lookup time, based on "keys."

Because the problem is so common, Scheme and most other languages offer at least one built-in solution.

Here we study the class of *vectors*. A vector is a well-defined mathematical class of data with specific basic operations. For our purposes, it suffices to know how to construct them, how to extract values, and how to recognize them:

1. The operation vector is like list. It consumes an arbitrary number of values and creates a compound value from them: a vector. For example, (vector *V-0* ... *V-n*) creates a vector from *V-0* through *V-n*.

2. DrScheme also provides a vector analogue to build-list. It is called build-vector. Here is how it works:

   (build-vector $N$ $f$) = (vector ($f$ 0) ... ($f$ ($-$ $N$ 1)))

   That is, build-vector consumes a natural number $N$ and a function $f$ on natural numbers. It then builds a vector of $N$ items by applying $f$ to $0, \ldots, N\text{-}1$.

3. The operation vector-ref extracts a value from a vector in constant time, that is, for $i$ between 0 and $n$ (inclusive):

   (vector-ref (vector *V-0* ... *V-n*) $i$) = *V-i*

   In short, extracting values from a vector is $O(1)$.

   If vector-ref is applied to a vector and a natural number that is smaller than 0 or larger than $n$, vector-ref signals an error.

4. The operation vector-length produces the number of items in a vector:

   (vector-length (vector *V-0* ... *V-n*)) = ($+$ $n$ 1)

5. The operation vector? is the vector-predicate:

   (vector? (vector *V-0* ... *V-n*)) = true
   (vector? $U$) = false

   if $U$ is a value that isn't created with vector.

We can think of vectors as functions on a small, finite range of natural numbers. Their range is the full class of Scheme values. We can also think of them as tables that associate a small, finite range of natural numbers with Scheme values. Using vectors we can represent graphs like those in figures 76 and 78 if we use numbers as names. For example:

| A | B | C | D | E | F | G |
|---|---|---|---|---|---|---|
| 0 | 1 | 2 | 3 | 4 | 5 | 6 |

Using this translation, we can also produce a vector-based representation of the graph in figure 76:

```
(define Graph-as-list          (define Graph-as-vector
  '((A (B E))                    (vector (list 1 4)
    (B (E F))                            (list 4 5)
    (C (D))                              (list 3)
    (D ())                               empty
    (E (C F))                            (list 2 5)
    (F (D G))                            (list 3 6)
    (G ())))                             empty))
```

The definition on the left is the original list-based representation; the one on the right is a vector representation. The vector's $i$-th field contains the list of neighbors of the $i$-th node.

The data definitions for *node* and *graph* change in the expected manner. Let's assume that $N$ is the number of nodes in the given graph:

> A *node* is an natural number between $0$ and $N - 1$.

> A *graph* is a vector of *nodes*: (**vectorof** (**listof** *node*)).

The notation (**vectorof** $X$) is similar to (**listof** $X$). It denotes a vector that contains items from some undetermined class of data $X$.

Now we can redefine *neighbors*:

```
;; neighbors : node graph → (listof node)
;; to lookup the node in graph
(define (neighbors node graph)
  (vector-ref graph node))
```

As a result, looking up the neighbors of a node becomes a constant-time operation, and we can truly ignore it when we study the abstract running time of *find-route*.

## Exercises

**Exercise 29.3.1** Test the new *neighbors* function. Use the strategy of section 17.8 to formulate the tests as boolean expressions. ∎

**Exercise 29.3.2** Adapt the rest of the *find-route* program to the new vector representation. Adapt the tests from exercises 28.1.3 through 28.1.5 to check the new program.

Measure how much time the two *find-route* programs consume to compute a route from node A to node E in the graph of figure 76. Recall that (**time** *expr*) measures how long it takes to evaluate *expr*. It is good practice to evaluate *expr*, say, 1000 times when we measure time. This produces more accurate measurements. ∎

**Exercise 29.3.3** Translate the cyclic graph from figure 78 into our vector representation of graphs. ∎

Before we can truly program with vectors, we must understand the data definition. The situation is comparable to that when we first encountered lists. We know that **vector**, like **cons**, is provided by Scheme, but we don't have a data definition that directs our program development efforts.

So, let us take a look at vectors. Roughly speaking, **vector** is like **cons**. The **cons** primitive constructs lists, the **vector** primitive creates vectors. Since programming with lists usually means programming with the selectors **first** and **rest**, programming with vectors must mean programming with **vector-ref**. Unlike **first** and **rest**, however, **vector-ref** requires manipulating the vector and an index into a vector. This suggests that programming with vectors really means thinking about indices, which are natural numbers.

Let's look at some simple examples to confirm this abstract judgment. Here is the first one:

```
;; vector-sum-for-3 : (vector number number number) → number
(define (vector-sum-for-3 v)
  (+ (vector-ref v 0)
     (vector-ref v 1)
     (vector-ref v 2)))
```

The function *vector-sum-for-3* consumes vectors of three numbers and produces their sum. It uses vector-ref to extract the three numbers and adds them up. What varies in the three selector expressions is the index; the vector remains the same.

Consider a second, more interesting example: *vector-sum*, a generalization of *vector-sum-for-3*. It consumes an arbitrarily large vector of numbers and produces the sum of the numbers:

```
;; vector-sum : (vectorof number) → number
;; to sum up the numbers in v
(define (vector-sum v) ...)
```

Here are some examples:

```
(= (vector-sum (vector −1 3/4 1/4))
   0)
```

```
(= (vector-sum (vector .1 .1 .1 .1 .1 .1 .1 .1 .1 .1))
   1)
```

```
(= (vector-sum (vector))
   0)
```

The last example suggests that we want a reasonable answer even if the vector is empty. As with empty, we use 0 as the answer in this case.

The problem is that the one natural number associated with $v$, its length, is not an argument of *vector-sum*. The length of $v$ is of course just an indication of how many items in $v$ are to be processed, which in turn refers to legal indices of $v$. This reasoning forces us to develop an auxiliary function that consumes the vector and a natural number:

```
;; vector-sum-aux : (vectorof number) N → number
;; to sum up the numbers in v relative to i
(define (vector-sum-aux v i) ...)
```

The natural choice for the initial value of $i$ is the length of $v$, which suggests the following completion of *vector-sum*:

```
(define (vector-sum v)
  (vector-sum-aux v (vector-length v)))
```

Based on this definition, we can also adapt the examples for *vector-sum* to *vector-sum-aux*:

```
(= (vector-sum-aux (vector −1 3/4 1/4) 3)
   0)
```

```
(= (vector-sum-aux (vector .1 .1 .1 .1 .1 .1 .1 .1 .1 .1) 10)
   1)
```

```
(= (vector-sum-aux (vector) 0)
   0)
```

Unfortunately, this doesn't clarify the role of the second argument. To do that, we need to proceed to the next stage of the design process: template development.

When we develop templates for functions of two arguments, we must first decide which of the arguments must be processed, that is, which of the two will vary in the course of a computation. The *vector-sum-for-3* example suggests that it is the second argument in this case. Because this argument belongs to the class of natural numbers, we follow the design recipe for those:

```
(define (vector-sum-aux v i)
  (cond
    [(zero? i) ...]
    [else ... (vector-sum-aux v (sub1 i)) ...]))
```

Although we considered *i* to be the length of the vector initially, the template suggests that we should consider it the number of items of *v* that *vector-sum-aux* must consider and thus as an index into *v*.

The elaboration of *i*'s use naturally leads to a better purpose statement for *vector-sum-aux*:

```
;; vector-sum-aux : (vectorof number) N → number
;; to sum up the numbers in v with index in [0, i)
(define (vector-sum-aux v i)
  (cond
    [(zero? i) ...]
    [else ... (vector-sum-aux v (sub1 i)) ...]))
```

Excluding *i* is natural because it is initially (vector-length *v*) and thus not an index.

To transform the template into a complete function definition, we consider each clause of the **cond**:

1. If *i* is 0, there are no further items to be considered because there are no vector fields between 0 and *i* with *i* excluded. Therefore the result is 0.

```
;; vector-sum : (vectorof number) → number
;; to compute the sum of the numbers in v
(define (vector-sum v)
  (vector-sum-aux v (vector-length v)))

;; vector-sum-aux : (vectorof number) N → number
;; to sum the numbers in v with index in [0, i)
(define (vector-sum-aux v i)
  (cond
    [(zero? i) 0]
    [else (+ (vector-ref v (sub1 i))
             (vector-sum-aux v (sub1 i)))]))
```

Figure 81: Summing up the numbers in a vector (version 1)

```
;; lr-vector-sum : (vectorof number) → number
;; to sum up the numbers in v
(define (lr-vector-sum v)
  (vector-sum-aux v 0))

;; vector-sum : (vectorof number) → number
;; to sum up the numbers in v with index in [i, (vector-length v))
(define (vector-sum-aux v i)
  (cond
    [(= i (vector-length v)) 0]
    [else (+ (vector-ref v i) (vector-sum-aux v (add1 i)))]))
```

Figure 82: Summing up the numbers in a vector (version 2)

2. Otherwise, (*vector-sum-aux* $v$ (sub1 $i$)) computes the sum of the numbers in $v$ between 0 and (sub1 $i$) [exclusive]. This leaves out the vector field with index (sub1 $i$), which according to the purpose statement must be included. By adding (vector-ref $v$ (sub1 $i$)), we get the desired result:

$$(+ \text{ (vector-ref } v \text{ (sub1 } i)) \text{ (}vector\text{-}sum\text{-}aux \text{ } v \text{ (sub1 } i)))$$

See figure 81 for the complete program.

If we were to evaluate one of the examples for *vector-sum-aux* by hand, we would see that it extracts the numbers from the vector in a right to left order as *i* decreases to 0. A natural question is whether we can invert this order. In other words: is there a function that extracts the numbers in a left to right order?

The answer is to develop a function that processes the class of natural numbers below (vector-length *v*) and to start at the first feasible index: 0. Developing this function is just another instance of the design recipe for variants of natural numbers from section 11.4. The new function definition is shown in figure 82. The new auxiliary function now consumes 0 and counts up to (vector-length *v*). A hand-evaluation of

> (*lr-vector-sum* (vector 0 1 2 3))

shows that *vector-sum-aux* indeed extracts the items from *v* from left to right.

The definition of *lr-vector-sum* shows why we need to study alternative definitions of classes of natural numbers. Sometimes it is necessary to count down to 0. But at other times it is equally useful, and natural, to count from 0 up to some other number.

The two functions also show how important it is to reason about intervals. The auxiliary vector-processing functions process intervals of the given vector. A good purpose statement specifies the exact interval that the function works on. Indeed, once we understand the exact interval specification, formulating the full function is relatively straightforward. We will see the importance of this point when we return to the study of vector-processing functions in the last section.

## Exercises

**Exercise 29.3.4** Evaluate (*vector-sum-aux* (vector −1 3/4 1/4) 3) by hand. Show the major steps only. Check the evaluation with DrScheme's stepper. In what order does the function add up the numbers of the vector?

Use a **local**-expression to define a single function *vector-sum*. Then remove the vector argument from the inner function definition. Why can we do that? ∎

**Exercise 29.3.5** Evaluate (*lr-vector-sum* (vector −1 3/4 1/4)) by hand. Show the major steps only. Check the evaluation with DrScheme's stepper. In what order does the function add up the numbers of the vector?

Use a **local**-expression to define a single function *lr-vector-sum*. Then remove those arguments from the inner function definition that remain the same during an evaluation. Also introduce definitions for those expressions that always evaluate to the same value during the evaluation. Why is this useful? ∎

**Exercise 29.3.6** The list-based analogue of *vector-sum* is *list-sum*:

```
;; list-sum : (listof number) → number
;; to compute the sum of the numbers on alon
(define (list-sum alon)
  (list-sum-aux alon (length alon)))
```

```
;; list-sum-aux : N (listof number) → number
;; to compute the sum of the first L numbers on alon
(define (list-sum-aux L alon)
  (cond
    [(zero? L) 0]
    [else (+ (list-ref alon (sub1 L)) (list-sum-aux (sub1 L) alon))]))
```

Instead of using the structural definition of the list, the developer of this program used the size of the list—a natural number—as the guiding element in the design process.

The resulting definition uses Scheme's list-ref function to access each item on the list. Looking up an item in a list with list-ref is an $O(N)$ operation for lists of $N$ items. Determine the abstract running time of *sum* (from section 9.5), *vector-sum-aux* and *list-sum-aux*. What does this suggest about program development? ∎

**Exercise 29.3.7** Develop the function *norm*, which consumes a vector of numbers and produces the square root of the sum of the squares of its numbers. Another name for *norm* is *distance-to-0*, because the result is the distance of a vector to the origin, when we interpret the vector as a point. ∎

**Exercise 29.3.8** Develop the function *vector-contains-doll?*. It consumes a vector of symbols and determines whether the vector contains the symbol 'doll. If so, it produces the index of 'doll's field; otherwise, it produces false.

Determine the abstract running time of *vector-contains-doll?* and compare with that of *contains-doll?*, which we discussed in the preceding subsection.

Now discuss the following problem. Suppose we are to represent a collection of symbols. The only interesting problem concerning the collection is to determine whether it contains some given symbol. Which data representation is preferable for the collection: lists or vectors? Why? ∎

**Exercise 29.3.9** Develop the function *binary-contains?*. It consumes a sorted vector of numbers and a key, which is also a number. The goal is to determine the index of the key, if it occurs in the vector, or false. Use the binary-search algorithm from section 27.3.

Determine the abstract running time of *binary-contains?* and compare with that of *contains?*, the function that searches for a key in a vector in the linear fashion of *vector-contains-doll?*.

Suppose we are to represent a collection of numbers. The only interesting problem concerning the collection is to determine whether it contains some given number. Which data representation is preferable for the collection: lists or vectors? Why? ∎

**Exercise 29.3.10** Develop the function *vector-count*. It consumes a vector *v* of symbols and a symbol *s*. Its result is the number of *s* that occur in *v*.

Determine the abstract running time of *vector-count* and compare with that of *count*, which counts how many times *s* occurs in a list of symbols.

Suppose we are to represent a collection of symbols. The only interesting problem concerning the collection is to determine how many times it contains some given symbol. Which data representation is preferable for the collection: lists or vectors? Why? What do exercises 29.3.8, 29.3.9, and this exercise suggest? ∎

While accessing the items of a vector is one kind of programming problem, constructing vectors is an entirely different problem. When we know the number of items in a vector, we can construct it using vector. When we we wish to write programs that work on a large class of vectors independent of their size, however, we need build-vector.

Consider the following simple example. Suppose we represent the velocity of an object with a vector. For example, (vector 1 2) represents the velocity of an object on a plane that moves 1 unit to the right and 2 down in each time unit. For comparison, (vector −1 2 1) is the veloicity of an object in space; it moves −6 units in the *x* direction in 6 time units, 12 units in the *y* direction in 6 time units, and 6 units in the *z* direction in 6 time units. We call (vector −6 12 6) the *displacement* of the object in 6 time units.

Let's develop a function that computes the displacement for an object with some velocity *v* in *t* time units:

;; displacement : (**vectorof** *number*) *number* → (**vectorof** *number*)
;; to compute the displacement of *v* and *t*
(**define** (*displacement v t*) ...)

Computing the displacement is straightforward for some examples:

```
(equal? (displacement (vector 1 2) 3)
        (vector 3 6))

(equal? (displacement (vector −1 2 1) 6)
        (vector −6 12 6))

(equal? (displacement (vector −1 −2) 2)
        (vector −2 −4))
```

We just multiply each component of the object with the number, which yields a new vector.

The examples' meaning for our programming problem is that *displacement* must construct a vector of the same length as $v$ and must use the items in $v$ to compute those of the new vectors. Here is how we build a vector of the same how-many as some given vector $v$:

```
(build-vector (vector-length v) ... )
```

Now we need to replace ... with a function that computes the 0-th, 1-st, and so on items of the new vector:

```
;; new-item : N → number
;; to compute the contents of the new vector at the i-th position
(define (new-item index) ... )
```

Following our discussion, we multiply (vector-ref $v$ $i$) with $t$ and that's all.

Take a look at the complete definition:

```
;; displacement : (vectorof number) number → (vectorof number)
;; to compute the displacement of v and t
(define (displacement v t)
   (local ((define (new-item i) (* (vector-ref v i) t)))
      (build-vector (vector-length v) new-item)))
```

The locally defined function is not recursive. We can thus replace it with a plain **lambda**-expression:

```
;; displacement : (vectorof number) number → (vectorof number)
;; to compute the displacement of v and t
(define (displacement v t)
   (build-vector (vector-length v) (lambda (i) (* (vector-ref v i) t))))
```

Mathematicians call this function *scalar product*. They have also studied many other operations on vectors, and in Scheme we can develop those in a natural manner.

## Exercises

**Exercise 29.3.11** Develop the function *id-vector*, which consumes a natural number and produces a vector of that many 1's. ∎

**Exercise 29.3.12** Develop the functions *vector+* and *vector−*, which compute the pointwise sum and differences of two vectors. That is, each consumes two vectors and produces a vector by manipulating corresponding programs. Assume the given vectors are of the same length. Also develop the functions *checked-vector+* and *checked-vector−*. ∎

**Exercise 29.3.13** Develop the function *distance*, which consumes two vectors and computes their distance. Think of the distance of two vectors as the length of the line between them. ∎

**Exercise 29.3.14** Develop a vector representation for chessboards of size $n \times n$ for $n$ in **N**. Then develop the following two functions on chessboards:

```
;; build-board : N (N N → boolean) → board
;; to create a board of size n x n,
;; fill each position with indices i and j with (f i j)
(define (build-board n f) ...)
```

```
;; board-ref : board N N → boolean
;; to access a position with indices i, j on a-board
(define (board-ref a-board i j) ...)
```

Can we now run the program of section 28.2 using vectors instead of lists? Inspect the solution of exercises 28.2.3 and 28.2.4. ∎

**Exercise 29.3.15** A matrix is a chessboard of numbers. Use the chessboard representation of exercise 29.3.14 to represent the matrix

$$\begin{vmatrix} 1 & 0 & -1 \\ 2 & 0 & 9 \\ 1 & 1 & 1 \end{vmatrix}$$

Using *build-board*, develop the function *transpose*, which creates a mirror image of the matrix along its diagonal from the upper-left corner to the lower-right one. For example, the given matrix turns into

$$
\begin{vmatrix}
1 & 2 & 1 \\
0 & 0 & 1 \\
-1 & 9 & 1
\end{vmatrix}
$$

More generally, the item at $(i, j)$ becomes the item at $(j, i)$. ∎

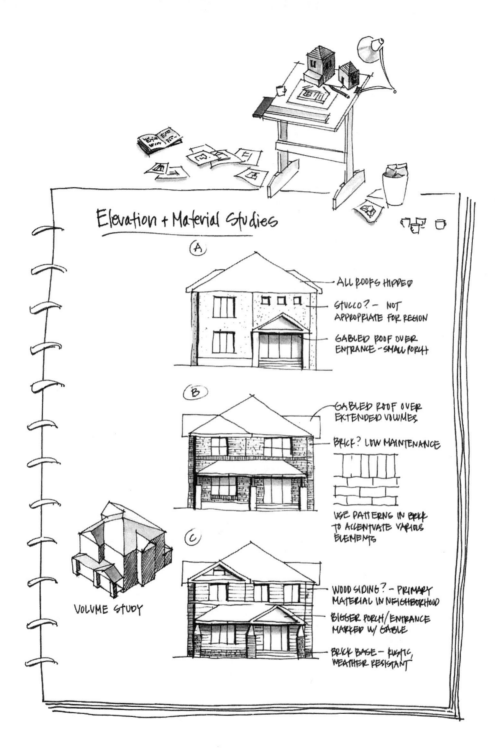

Elevation + Material Studies

(A)

- ALL ROOFS HIPPED
- STUCCO? - NOT APPROPRIATE FOR REGION
- GABLED ROOF OVER ENTRANCE - SMALL PORCH

(B)

- GABLED ROOF OVER EXTENDED VOLUMES
- BRICK? LOW MAINTENANCE
- USE PATTERNS IN BRICK TO ACCENTUATE VARIOUS ELEMENTS

VOLUME STUDY

(C)

- WOOD SIDING? - PRIMARY MATERIAL IN NEIGHBORHOOD
- BIGGER PORCH/ENTRANCE MARKED W/ GABLE
- BRICK BASE - RUSTIC, WEATHER RESISTANT

## 30   The Loss of Knowledge

When we design recursive functions, we don't think about the context of their use. Whether they are applied for the first time or whether they are called for the hundredth time in a recursive manner doesn't matter. They are to work according to their purpose statement, and that's all we need to know as we design the bodies of the functions.

Although this principle of context-independence greatly facilitates the development of functions, it also causes occasional problems. In this section, we illustrate the most important problem with two examples. Both concern the loss of knowledge that occurs during a recursive evaluation. The first subsection shows how this loss makes a structurally recursive function more complicated and less efficient than necessary; the second one shows how the loss of knowledge causes a fatal flaw in an algorithm.

### 30.1   A Problem with Structural Processing

Suppose we are given the relative distances between a series of points, starting at the origin, and suppose we are to compute the absolute distances from the origin. For example, we might be given a line such as this:

Each number specifies the distance between two dots. What we need is the following picture, where each dot is annotated with the distance to the left-most dot:

0        50       90            160   190   220

```
;; relative-2-absolute : (listof number) → (listof number)
;; to convert a list of relative distances to a list of absolute distances
;; the first item on the list represents the distance to the origin
(define (relative-2-absolute alon)
  (cond
    [(empty? alon) empty]
    [else (cons (first alon)
                (add-to-each (first alon) (relative-2-absolute (rest alon))))]))

;; add-to-each : number (listof number) → (listof number)
;; to add n to each number on alon
(define (add-to-each n alon)
  (cond
    [(empty? alon) empty]
    [else (cons (+ (first alon) n) (add-to-each n (rest alon)))]))
```

Figure 83: Converting relative distances to absolute distances

Developing a program that performs this calculation is at this point an exercise in structural function design. Figure 83 contains the complete Scheme program. When the given list is not empty, the natural recursion computes the absolute distance of the remainder of the dots to the first item on (rest *alon*). Because the first item is not the actual origin and has a distance of (first *alon*) to the origin, we must add (first *alon*) to each and every item on the result of the recursive application. This second step, adding a number to each item on a list of numbers, requires an auxiliary function.

While the development of the program is straightforward, using it on larger and larger lists reveals a problem. Consider the evaluation of the following definition:[64]

(**define** x (*relative-2-absolute* (list 0 ... N)))

As we increase N, the time needed grows even faster:[65]

---

[64]The most convenient way to construct this list is to evaluate (build-list (add1 N) identity).

[65]The time of evaluation will differ from computer to computer. These measurements were conducted on a Pentium 166Mhz running Linux. Measuring timings is also difficult. At a minimum, each evaluation should be repeated several times, and the time reported should be the average of those measurements.

| $N$ | time of evaluation |
|-----|-----|
| 100 | 220 |
| 200 | 880 |
| 300 | 2050 |
| 400 | 5090 |
| 500 | 7410 |
| 600 | 10420 |
| 700 | 14070 |
| 800 | 18530 |

Instead of doubling as we go from 100 to 200 items, the time quadruples. This is also the approximate relationship for going from 200 to 400, 300 to 600, and so on.

## Exercises

**Exercise 30.1.1** Reformulate *add-to-each* using map and **lambda**. ∎

**Exercise 30.1.2** Determine the abstract running time of *relative-2-absolute*. **Hint:** Evaluate the expression

   (*relative-2-absolute* (list 0 ... N))

by hand. Start by replacing $N$ with 1, 2, and 3. How many natural recursions of *relative-2-absolute* and *add-to-each* are required each time? ∎

Considering the simplicity of the problem, the amount of "work" that the two functions perform is surprising. If we were to convert the same list by hand, we would tally up the total distance and just add it to the relative distances as we take another step along the line.

Let's attempt to design a second version of the function that is closer to our hand method. The new function is still a list-processing function, so we start from the appropriate template:

```
(define (rel-2-abs alon)
  (cond
    [(empty? alon) ... ]
    [else ... (first alon) ... (rel-2-abs (rest alon)) ... ]))
```

Now imagine an "evaluation" of (*rel-2-abs* (list 3 2 7)):

   (*rel-2-abs* (list 3 2 7))

```
= (cons ... 3 ...
    (convert (list 2 7)))

= (cons ... 3 ...
    (cons ... 2 ...
      (convert (list 7))))

= (cons ... 3 ...
    (cons ... 2 ...
      (cons ... 7 ...
        (convert empty))))
```

The first item of the result list should obviously be 3, and it is easy to construct this list. But, the second one should be (+ 3 2), yet the second instance of *rel-2-abs* has no way of "knowing" that the first item of the original list is 3. The "knowledge" is lost.

Put differently, the problem is that recursive functions are independent of their context. A function processes the list *L* in (cons *N L*) in the exact same manner as *L* in (cons *K L*). Indeed, it would also process *L* in that manner if it were given *L* by itself. While this property makes structurally recursive functions easy to design, it also means that solutions are, on occasion, more complicated than necessary, and this complication may affect the performance of the function.

To make up for the loss of "knowledge," we equip the function with an additional parameter: *accu-dist*. The new parameter represents the accumulated distance, which is the tally that we keep when we convert a list of relative distances to a list of absolute distances. Its initial value must be 0. As the function processes the numbers on the list, it must add them to the tally.

Here is the revised definition:

```
(define (rel-2-abs alon accu-dist)
  (cond
    [(empty? alon) empty]
    [else (cons (+ (first alon) accu-dist)
                (rel-2-abs (rest alon) (+ (first alon) accu-dist)))]))
```

The recursive application consumes the rest of the list and the new absolute distance of the current point to the origin. Although this means that two arguments are changing simultaneously, the change in the second one strictly depends on the first argument. The function is still a plain list-processing procedure.

Evaluating our running example with *rel-2-abs* shows how much the use of an accumulator simplifies the conversion process:

= (*rel-2-abs* (list 3 2 7) 0)
= (cons 3 (*rel-2-abs* (list 2 7) 3))
= (cons 3 (cons 5 (*rel-2-abs* (list 7) 5)))
= (cons 3 (cons 5 (cons 12 (*rel-2-abs* empty 12))))
= (cons 3 (cons 5 (cons 12 empty)))

Each item in the list is processed once. When *rel-2-abs* reaches the end of the argument list, the result is completely determined and no further work is needed. In general, the function performs on the order of $N$ natural recursion steps for a list with $N$ items.

One minor problem with the new definition is that the function consumes two arguments and is thus not equivalent to *relative-2-absolute*, a function of one argument. Worse, someone might accidentally misuse *rel-2-abs* by applying it to a list of numbers and a number that isn't 0. We can solve both problems with a function definition that contains *rel-2-abs* in a **local** definition: see figure 84. Now, *relative-2-absolute* and *relative-2-absolute2* are indistinguishable.

```
;; relative-2-absolute2 : (listof number) → (listof number)
;; to convert a list of relative distances to a list of absolute distances
;; the first item on the list represents the distance to the origin
(define (relative-2-absolute2 alon)
  (local ((define (rel-2-abs alon accu-dist)
            (cond
              [(empty? alon) empty]
              [else (cons (+ (first alon) accu-dist)
                          (rel-2-abs (rest alon) (+ (first alon) accu-dist)))])))
    (rel-2-abs alon 0)))
```

Figure 84: Converting relative distances with an accumulator

## 30.2 A Problem with Generative Recursion

Let us revisit the problem of finding a path in a graph from section 28. Recall that we are given a collection of nodes and connections between nodes, and that we need to determine whether there is a route from a node labeled *orig* to one called *dest*. Here we study the slightly simpler version of the problem of *simple graphs* where each node has exactly one (one-directional) connection to another node.

Consider the example in figure 85. There are six nodes: A through F, and six connections. To get from A to E, we go through B, C, and E. It is impossible, though, to reach F from A or from any other node (besides F itself).

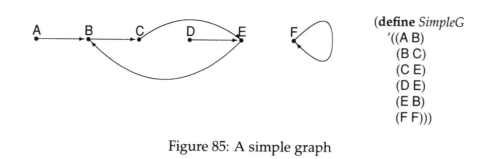

```
(define SimpleG
   '((A B)
     (B C)
     (C E)
     (D E)
     (E B)
     (F F)))
```

Figure 85: A simple graph

The right part of figure 85 contains a Scheme definition that represents the graph. Each node is represented by a list of two symbols. The first symbol is the label of the node; the second one is the reachable node. Here are the relevant data definitions:

> A *node* is a symbol.

> A *pair* is a list of two *node*s:
> $$(cons\ S\ (cons\ T\ empty))$$
> where $S$, $T$ are symbols.

> A *simple-graph* is a list of *pairs*:
> **(listof** *pair***)**.

They are straightforward translations of our informal descriptions.

Finding a route in a graph is a problem of generative recursion.

We have data definitions, we have (informal) examples, and the header material is standard:

```
;; route-exists? : node node simple-graph → boolean
;; to determine whether there is a route from orig to dest in sg
(define (route-exists? orig dest sg) ...)
```

What we need are answers to the four basic questions of the recipe for generative recursion:

**What is a trivially solvable problem?** The problem is trivial if the nodes *orig* and *dest* are the same.

**What is a corresponding solution?** Easy: true.

**How do we generate new problems?** If *orig* is not the same as *dest*, there is only one thing we can do, namely, go to the node to which *orig* is connected and determine whether a route exists between it and *dest*.

**How do we relate the solutions?** There is no need to do anything after we find the solution to the new problem. If *orig*'s neighbor is connected to *dest*, then so is *orig*.

From here we just need to express these answers in Scheme, and we get an algorithm. Figure 86 contains the complete function, including a function for looking up the neighbor of a node in a simple graph.

---

```
;; route-exists? : node node simple-graph → boolean
;; to determine whether there is a route from orig to dest in sg
(define (route-exists? orig dest sg)
  (cond
    [(symbol=? orig dest) true]
    [else (route-exists? (neighbor orig sg) dest sg)]))

;; neighbor : node simple-graph → node
;; to determine the node that is connected to a-node in sg
(define (neighbor a-node sg)
  (cond
    [(empty? sg) (error "neighbor: impossible")]
    [else (cond
            [(symbol=? (first (first sg)) a-node)
             (second (first sg))]
            [else (neighbor a-node (rest sg))])]))
```

Figure 86: Finding a route in a simple graph (version 1)

---

Even a casual look at the function suggests that we have a problem. Although the function is supposed to produce false if there is no route from *orig* to *dest*, the function definition doesn't contain false anywhere. Conversely, we need to ask what the function actually does when there is no route between two nodes.

Take another look at figure 85. In this simple graph there is no route from C to D. The connection that leaves C passes right by D and instead goes to E. So let's look at how *route-exists?* deals with the inputs 'C and 'D for *SimpleG*:

> (*route-exists?* 'C 'D '((A B) (B C) (C E) (D E) (E B) (F F)))
> = (*route-exists?* 'E 'D '((A B) (B C) (C E) (D E) (E B) (F F)))
> = (*route-exists?* 'B 'D '((A B) (B C) (C E) (D E) (E B) (F F)))
> = (*route-exists?* 'C 'D '((A B) (B C) (C E) (D E) (E B) (F F)))

The hand-evaluation confirms that as the function recurs, it calls itself with the exact same arguments again and again. In other words, the evaluation never stops.

Our problem with *route-exists?* is again a loss of "knowledge," similar to that of *relative-2-absolute* in the preceding section. Like *relative-2-absolute*, *route-exists?* was developed according to the recipe and is independent of its context. That is, it doesn't "know" whether some application is the first or the hundredth of a recursive chain. In the case of *route-exists?* this means, in particular, that the function doesn't "know" whether a previous application in the current chain of recursions received the exact same arguments.

The solution follows the pattern of the preceding section. We add a parameter, which we call *accu-seen* and which represents the accumulated list of origination nodes that the function has encountered, starting with the original application. Its initial value must be empty. As the function checks on a specific *orig* and moves to its neighbors, *orig* is added to *accu-seen*.

Here is a first revision of *route-exists?*, dubbed *route-exists-accu?*:

```
;; route-exists-accu? : node node simple-graph (listof node) → boolean
;; to determine whether there is a route from orig to dest in sg,
;; assuming the nodes in accu-seen have already been inspected
;; and failed to deliver a solution
(define (route-exists-accu? orig dest sg accu-seen)
  (cond
    [(symbol=? orig dest) true]
    [else (route-exists-accu? (neighbor orig sg) dest sg
                              (cons orig accu-seen))]))
```

The addition of the new parameter alone does not solve our problem, but, as the following hand-evaluation shows, provides the foundation for one:

$\quad$ (*route-exists-accu?* 'C 'D '((A B) (B C) (C E) (D E) (E B) (F F)) empty)

$=$ (*route-exists-accu?* 'E 'D '((A B) (B C) (C E) (D E) (E B) (F F)) '(C))

$=$ (*route-exists-accu?* 'B 'D '((A B) (B C) (C E) (D E) (E B) (F F)) '(E C))

$=$ (*route-exists-accu?* 'C 'D '((A B) (B C) (C E) (D E) (E B) (F F))

$\qquad\qquad\qquad$ '(B E C))

In contrast to the original function, the revised function no longer calls itself with the exact same arguments. While the three arguments proper are again the same for the third recursive application, the accumulator argument is different from that of the first application. Instead of empty, it is now '(B E C). The new value represents the fact that during the search of a route from 'C to 'D, the function has inspected 'B, 'E, and 'C as starting points.

All we need to do at this point is exploit the accumulated knowledge in the function definition. Specifically, we determine whether the given *orig* is already an item on *accu-seen*. If so, the problem is trivially solvable with false. Figure 87 contains the definition of *route-exists2?*, which is the revision of *route-exists?*. The definition refers to *contains*, our first recursive function (see part II), which determines whether a specific symbol is on a list of symbols.

---

```
;; route-exists2? : node node simple-graph → boolean
;; to determine whether there is a route from orig to dest in sg
(define (route-exists2? orig dest sg)
  (local ((define (re-accu? orig dest sg accu-seen)
            (cond
              [(symbol=? orig dest) true]
              [(contains orig accu-seen) false]
              [else (re-accu? (neighbor orig sg) dest sg (cons orig accu-seen))])))
    (re-accu? orig dest sg empty)))
```

Figure 87: Finding a route in a simple graph (version 2)

---

The definition of *route-exists2?* also eliminates the two minor problems with the first revision. By **local**izing the definition of the accumulating function, we can ensure that the first call to *re-accu?* always uses empty as the initial value for *accu-seen*. And, *route-exists2?* satisfies the exact same contract and purpose statement as *route-exists?*.

Still, there is a significant difference between *route-exists2?* and *relative-to-absolute2*. Whereas the latter was equivalent to the original function, *route-exists2?* is an improvement over the *route-exists?* function. After all, it corrects a fundamental flaw in *route-exists?*, which completely failed to find an answer for some inputs.

## Exercises

**Exercise 30.2.1** Complete the definition in figure 87 and test it with the running example. Use the strategy of section 17.8 to formulate the tests as boolean-valued expressions.

Check with a hand-evaluation that this function computes the proper result for 'A, 'C, and *SimpleG*. ∎

**Exercise 30.2.2** Edit the function in figure 87 so that the locally defined function consumes only those arguments that change during an evaluation. ∎

**Exercise 30.2.3** Develop a vector-based representation of simple graphs. Adapt the function in figure 87 so that it works on a vector-based representation of simple graphs. ∎

**Exercise 30.2.4** Modify the definitions of *find-route* and *find-route/list* in figure 77 so that they produce false, even if they encounter the same starting point twice. ∎

# 31   Designing Accumulator-Style Functions

Section 30 illustrated with two examples the need for accumulating extra knowledge. In some cases, the accumulation makes it easier to understand a function; in others it is necessary for the function to work properly. In both cases, however, we first chose one of the available design recipes, inspected the function, and then revised or fixed it. Put more generally, adding an ACCUMULATOR, that is, a parameter that accumulates knowledge, is something that we add to a function after we have designed a function, not before.

The keys to the development of an accumulator-style function are:

1. to recognize that the function benefits from, or needs, an accumulator;

2. to understand what the accumulator represents.

The first two subsections address these two questions. Because the second one is a difficult topic, the third subsection illustrates how to formulate precise claims about accumulators. More concretely, in this section, we transform several standard recursive functions into functions that use auxiliary functions with accumulators.

## 31.1  Recognizing the Need for an Accumulator

Recognizing the need for accumulators is not an easy task. We have seen two reasons, and they are the most prevalent reasons for adding accumulator parameters. In either case, it is critical that we first built a complete function *based on a design recipe*. Then we study the function and look for one of the following characteristics:

1. If the function is structurally recursive and if the result of a recursive application is processed by an auxiliary, recursive function, then we should consider the use of an accumulator parameter.

Take the function *invert* as an example:

```
;; invert : (listof X) → (listof X)
;; to construct the reverse of alox
;; structural recursion
(define (invert alox)
  (cond
    [(empty? alox) empty]
    [else (make-last-item (first alox) (invert (rest alox)))]))


;; make-last-item : X (listof X) → (listof X)
;; to add an-x to the end of alox
;; structural recursion
(define (make-last-item an-x alox)
  (cond
    [(empty? alox) (list an-x)]
    [else (cons (first alox) (make-last-item an-x (rest alox)))]))
```

The result of the recursive application produces the reverse of the rest of the list. It is processed by *make-last-item*, which adds the first item to the reverse of the rest and thus creates the reverse of the entire list. This second, auxiliary function is also recursive. We have thus identified a potential candidate. It is now time to study some hand-evaluations, as we did in section 30.1, to see whether an accumulator helps.

2. If we are dealing with a function based on generative recursion, we are faced with a much more difficult task. Our goal must be to understand whether the algorithm can fail to produce a result for inputs for which we expect a result. If so, adding a parameter that accumulates knowledge may help. Because these situations are complex, we postpone the discussion of an example until section 32.2.

These two situations are by no means the only ones; they are just the most common ones. To sharpen our perception, we will discuss an additional array of possibilities in the following section.

## 31.2   Accumulator-Style Functions

When we have decided that an accumulator-style function is necessary, we introduce it in two steps:

**Setting-up an accumulator:** First, we must understand what knowledge the accumulator needs to remember about the parameters proper and then how it is to remember it. For example, for the conversion of relative distances to absolute distances, it suffices to accumulate the total distance encountered so far. For the routing problem, we needed the accumulator to remember every node inspected so far. Thus the first accumulator was just a number, the second one a list of nodes.

The best way to discuss the accumulation process is to introduce a template of the accumulator-style function via a **local** definition and to name the parameters of the function proper differently from those of the auxiliary function.

Let's take a look at the *invert* example:

```
;; invert : (listof X) → (listof X)
;; to construct the reverse of alox
(define (invert alox0)
  (local (;; accumulator ...
           (define (rev alox accumulator)
             (cond
               [(empty? alox) ...]
               [else
                 ... (rev (rest alox) ... (first alox) ... accumulator )
                 ... ])))
    (rev alox0 ...)))
```

Here we have a definition of *invert* with an auxiliary function *rev* in template form. This auxiliary template has one parameter in addition to those of *invert*: the accumulating parameter. The box in the recursive application indicates that we need an expression that maintains the accumulation process and that this process depends on the current value of *accumulator* and (first *alox*), the value *rev* is about to forget.

Clearly, *invert* cannot forget anything, because it only reverses the order of items on the list. Hence we might just wish to accumulate all items that *rev* encounters. This means

1. that *accumulator* stands for a list, and
2. that it stands for all those items in *alox0* that precede the *alox* argument of *rev*.

For the second part of the analysis, it is critical that we can distinguish the original argument, *alox0*, from the current one, *alox*.

Now that we know the rough purpose of the accumulator, let's consider what the first value should be and what we should do for the recursion. When we apply *rev* in the body of the **local**-expression, it receives *alox0*, which means that it hasn't encountered any of its items. The initial value for *accumulator* is empty. When *rev* recurs, it has just encountered one extra item: (first *alox*). To remember it, we can cons it onto the current value of accumulator.

Here is the enhanced definition:

```
;; invert : (listof X) → (listof X)
;; to construct the reverse of alox
(define (invert alox0)
    (local (;; accumulator is the reversed list of all those items
            ;; on alox0 that precede alox
            (define (rev alox accumulator)
              (cond
                [(empty? alox) ... ]
                [else
                    ... (rev (rest alox) (cons (first alox) accumulator))
                    ... ])))
        (rev alox0 empty)))
```

A close inspection reveals that *accumulator* is not just the items on *alox0* that precede but a list of these items in reverse order.

**Exploiting an accumulator:** Once we have decided what knowledge the accumulator maintains and how it is maintained, we can move to the question of how to exploit this knowledge for our function.

In the case of *invert*, the answer is almost obvious. If *accumulator* is the list of all items on *alox0* that precede *alox* in reverse order, then, if *alox* is empty, *accumulator* stands for the reverse of *alox0*. Put differently: if *alox* is empty, *rev*'s answer is *accumulator*, and that is the answer we want in both cases:

```
;; invert : (listof X) → (listof X)
;; to construct the reverse of alox
(define (invert alox0)
    (local (;; accumulator is the reversed list of all those items
            ;; on alox0 that precede alox
            (define (rev alox accumulator)
              (cond
                [(empty? alox) accumulator]
                [else
                    (rev (rest alox) (cons (first alox) accumulator))])))
        (rev alox0 empty)))
```

The key step of this development is the precise description of the role of *accumulator*. In general, an ACCUMULATOR INVARIANT describes a relationship between the argument proper of the function, the current argument of the auxiliary function, and the accumulator that must always hold when an accumulator-style function is used.

## 31.3 Transforming Functions into Accumulator-Style

The most complex part of the design recipe is the requirement to formulate an accumulator invariant. Without that we cannot produce functioning accumulator-style functions. Because formulating invariants is clearly an art that deserves a lot of practice, we practice it in this section with three small, well-understood structural functions that do not need an accumulator. The section concludes with a group of exercises concerning this step.

For the first example, consider the function *sum*:

*;; sum :* (**listof** *number*) → *number*
*;;* to compute the sum of the numbers on *alon*
*;;* structural recursion
(**define** (*sum alon*)
  (**cond**
    [(empty? *alon*) 0]
    [**else** (+ (first *alon*) (*sum* (rest *alon*)))]))

Here is the first step toward an accumulator version:

*;; sum :* (**listof** *number*) → *number*
*;;* to compute the sum of the numbers on *alon0*
(**define** (*sum alon0*)
  (**local** (*;; accumulator* ...
          (**define** (*sum-a alon accumulator*)
            (**cond**
              [(empty? *alon*) ... ]
              [**else**
               ... (*sum-a* (rest *alon*) $\boxed{... (\text{first } alon) ... accumulator}$ )
               ... ])))
    (*sum-a alon0* ...)))

As suggested by our first step, we have put the template for *sum-a* into a **local** definition, added an accumulator parameter, and renamed *sum*'s parameter.

Our goal is to develop an accumulator invariant for *sum*. To do so, we must consider how *sum* proceeds and what the goal of the process is. Like *rev*, *sum-a* processes the numbers on the list one by one. The goal is to add up these numbers. This suggests that *accumulator* represents the sum of the numbers seen so far:

```
...
  (local (;; accumulator is the sum of the numbers that preceded
          ;; those in alon on alon0
          (define (sum-a alon accumulator)
           (cond
              [(empty? alon) ... ]
              [else
                 ... (sum-a (rest alon) (+ (first alon) accumulator))
                 ... ])))
    (sum-a alon0 0)))
```

When we apply *sum-a* we must use 0 as the value of *accumulator*, because it hasn't processed any of the numbers on *alon* yet. For the second clause, we must add (first *alon*) to *accumulator* so that the invariant holds again for the function application.

Given a precise invariant, the rest is straightforward again. If *alon* is empty, *sum-a* returns *accumulator* because it represents the sum of all numbers on *alon* now. Figure 88 contains the final definition of the accumulator-style version of *sum*.

Let's compare how the original definition of *sum* and the accumulator-style definition produce an answer for the same input:

```
  (sum (list 10.23 4.50 5.27))                    (sum (list 10.23 4.50 5.27))
= (+ 10.23 (sum (list 4.50 5.27)))            = (sum-a (list 10.23 4.50 5.27) 0)
= (+ 10.23 (+ 4.50 (sum (list 5.27))))        = (sum-a (list 4.50 5.27) 10.23)
= (+ 10.23 (+ 4.50 (+ 5.27 (sum empty))))     = (sum-a (list 5.27) 14.73)
= (+ 10.23 (+ 4.50 (+ 5.27 0)))               = (sum-a empty 20.0)
= (+ 10.23 (+ 4.50 5.27))                     = 20.0
= (+ 10.23 9.77)
= 20.0
```

On the left side, we see how the plain recursive function descends the list of numbers all the way to the end and sets up addition operations on the way. On the right side, we see how the accumulator-style version adds up the numbers as it goes. Furthermore, we see that for each application of *sum-a* the invariant holds with respect to the application of *sum*. When *sum-a* is finally applied to empty, the accumulator is the final result, and *sum-a* returns it.

```
;; sum : (listof number) → number
;; to compute the sum of the numbers on alon0
(define (sum alon0)
    (local (;; accumulator is the sum of the numbers that preceded
            ;; those in alon on alon0
            (define (sum-a alon accumulator)
              (cond
                [(empty? alon) accumulator]
                [else (sum-a (rest alon) (+ (first alon) accumulator))])))
      (sum-a alon0 0)))
```

```
;; ! : N → N
;; to compute n · (n − 1) · . . . · 2 · 1
(define (! n0)
    (local (;; accumulator is the product of all natural numbers in [n0, n)
            (define (!-a n accumulator)
              (cond
                [(zero? n) accumulator]
                [else (!-a (sub1 n) (* n accumulator))])))
      (!-a n0 1)))
```

Figure 88: Some simple accumulator-style functions

## Exercises

**Exercise 31.3.1** A second difference between the two functions concerns the order of addition. While the original version of *sum* adds up the numbers from right to left, the accumulator-style version adds them up from left to right. For exact numbers, this difference has no effect on the final result. For inexact numbers, the difference is significant.

Consider the following definition:

```
(define (g-series n)
    (cond
      [(zero? n) empty]
      [else (cons (expt −0.99 n) (g-series (sub1 n)))]))
```

Applying *g-series* to a natural number produces the beginning of a decreasing geometric series (see section 23.1).

Depending on which function we use to sum up the items of this list, we get vastly different results. Evaluate the expression

(*sum* (*g-series* #i1000))

with both the original version of *sum* as well as its accumulator-style version. Then evaluate

(∗ 10e15 (*sum* (*g-series* #i1000)))

which proves that, depending on the context, the difference can be arbitrarily large. ∎

For the second example, we return to the factorial function from part II:

```
;; ! : N → N
;; to compute n · (n − 1) · . . . · 2 · 1
;; structural recursion
(define (! n)
  (cond
    [(zero? n) 1]
    [else (∗ n (! (sub1 n)))]))
```

While *relative-2-absolute* and *invert* processed lists, the factorial function works on natural numbers. Its template is that for **N**-processing functions.

We proceed as before by creating a **local** definition of *!*:

```
;; ! : N → N
;; to compute n · (n − 1) · . . . · 2 · 1
(define (! n0)
  (local (;; accumulator . . .
          (define (!-a n accumulator)
            (cond
              [(zero? n) . . . ]
              [else
                . . . (!-a (sub1 n) |. . . n . . . accumulator|) . . . ])))
    (!-a n0 . . . )))
```

This sketch suggests that if *!* is applied to the natural number $n$, *!-a* processes $n$, then $n − 1$, $n − 2$, and so on until it reaches 0. Since the goal is to multiply these numbers, the accumulator should be the product of all those numbers that *!-a* has encountered:

...

  (**local** (;; *accumulator* is the product of all natural numbers between
     ;; *n0* (inclusive) and *n* (exclusive)
    (**define** (*!-a n accumulator*)
     (**cond**
      [(zero? *n*) ...]
      [**else**
       ... (*!-a* (sub1 *n*) (∗ *n accumulator*)) ...])))
  (*!-a n0* 1)))

To make the invariant true at the beginning, we must use 1 for the accumulator. When *!-a* recurs, we must multiply the current value of the accumulator with *n* to reestablish the invariant.

From the purpose statement for the accumulator of *!-a*, we can see that if *n* is 0, the accumulator is the product of *n*, ..., 1. That is, it is the desired result. So, like *sum*, *!-a* returns *accumulator* in the first case and simply recurs in the second one. Figure 88 contains the complete definition.

It is instructive to compare hand-evaluations for the two versions of *!*:

$$
\begin{array}{ll}
(!\ 3) & (!\ 3) \\
= (\ast\ 3\ (!\ 2)) & = (!\text{-}a\ 3\ 1) \\
= (\ast\ 3\ (\ast\ 2\ (!\ 1))) & = (!\text{-}a\ 2\ 3) \\
= (\ast\ 3\ (\ast\ 2\ (\ast\ 1\ (!\ 0)))) & = (!\text{-}a\ 1\ 6) \\
= (\ast\ 3\ (\ast\ 2\ (\ast\ 1\ 1))) & = (!\text{-}a\ 0\ 6) \\
= (\ast\ 3\ (\ast\ 2\ 1)) & = 6 \\
= (\ast\ 3\ 2) & \\
= 6 &
\end{array}
$$

The left column shows how the original version works, the right one how the accumulator-style function proceeds. Both traverse the natural number until they reach 0, but while the original version only schedules multiplications, the new one multiplies the numbers as they are processed. In addition, the right column illustrates how the new factorial function maintains the accumulator invariant. For each application, the accumulator is the product of 3 to *n* where *n* is the first argument to *!-a*.

## Exercises

**Exercise 31.3.2** Like *sum*, *!* performs the primitive computation steps (multiplication) in reverse order. Surprisingly, this affects the performance of the function in a negative manner.

Use DrScheme's **time**-facility to determine how long the two variants need to evaluate (*!* 20) 1000 times.

**Hint:** (1) Develop the function

;; *many* : **N** (**N** → **N**) → true
;; to evaluate (*f* 20) *n* times
(**define** (*many n f*) ...)

(2) Evaluating (**time** *an-expression*) determines how much time the evaluation of *an-expression* takes. ∎

For the last example, we study a function on simplified binary trees. The example illustrates that accumulator-style programming is not just for data definitions with a single self-reference. Indeed, it is as common for complicated data definitions as it is for lists and natural numbers.

Here is the structure definition for stripped-down binary trees:

(**define-struct** *node* (*left right*))

and here is its companion data definition:

> A *binary-tree* (short: *tree*) is either
>
> 1. empty
>
> 2. (make-node *tl tr*) where *tl, tr* are *trees*.

These trees contain no information, and all of them end in empty. Still, there are many different trees as figure 89 shows. The table indicates how to think of each tree as a graphical element, that is, of empty as a plain dot and make-node as a dot that combines two trees.

Using the graphical representation of binary trees we can easily determine properties of trees. For example, we can count how many nodes it contains, how many emptys there are, or how high it is. Let's look at the function *height*, which consumes a tree and determines how high it is:

;; *height* : *tree* → *number*
;; to measure the height of *abt0*
;; structural recursion
(**define** (*height abt*)
  (**cond**
    [(empty? *abt*) 0]
    [**else** (+ (*max* (*height* (node-left *abt*)) (*height* (node-right *abt*))) 1)]))

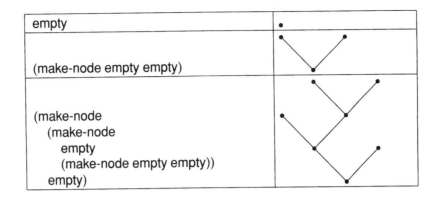

| empty | |
| --- | --- |
| (make-node empty empty) | |
| (make-node <br>   (make-node <br>     empty <br>     (make-node empty empty)) <br>   empty) | |

Figure 89: Some stripped-down binary trees

Like the data definition, this function definition has two self-references.

To transform this function into an accumulator-style function, we follow the standard path. We begin with putting an appropriate template into a **local** definition:

```
;; height : tree → number
;; to measure the height of abt0
(define (height abt0)
  (local (;; accumulator ...
          (define (height-a abt accumulator)
            (cond
              [(empty? abt) ... ]
              [else
               ... (height-a (node-left abt)
                             ... (node-right abt) ... accumulator ) ...
               ... (height-a (node-right abt)
                             ... (node-left abt) ... accumulator ) ... ])))
    (height abt0 ...)))
```

The problem, as always, is to determine what knowledge the accumulator should represent.

An obvious choice is that *accumulator* should be a number. More specifically, *accumulator* should represent the number of *node*s that *height-a* has processed so far. Initially, it has seen 0 nodes; as it descends the tree, it must increase the accumulator as it processes a *node*:

...

```
(local (;; accumulator represents how many nodes height-a
        ;; has encountered on its way to abt from abt0
        (define (height-a abt accumulator)
          (cond
            [(empty? abt) ... ]
            [else
              ... (height-a (node-left abt) (+ accumulator 1)) ...
              ... (height-a (node-right abt) (+ accumulator 1)) ... ])))
  (height abt0 0))
```

That is, the accumulator invariant is that *accumulator* counts how many steps *height-a* has taken on a particular path into the tree *abt*.

The result in the base case is *accumulator* again; after all it represents the height or length of the particular path. But, in contrast to the first two examples, it is not the final result. In the second **cond**-clause, the new function has two heights to deal with. Given that we are interested in the larger one, we use Scheme's *max* operation to select it.

---

```
;; height : tree → number
;; to measure the height of abt0
(define (height abt0)
  (local (;; accumulator represents how many nodes height-a
          ;; has encountered on its way to abt from abt0
          (define (height-a abt accumulator)
            (cond
              [(empty? abt) accumulator]
              [else (max (height-a (node-left abt) (+ accumulator 1))
                         (height-a (node-right abt) (+ accumulator 1)))])))
    (height-a abt0 0)))
```

Figure 90: The accumulator-style version of *height*

---

Figure 90 contains the complete definition for *height*. Our final step is to check out a hand-evaluation of the new function. We use the most complex example from the above table:

```
(height (make-node
          (make-node empty
                     (make-node empty empty))
          empty))
```

= (*height-a* (make-node
    (make-node empty
        (make-node empty empty))
    empty)
  0)

= (*max* (*height-a*
   (make-node empty
       (make-node empty empty))
   1)
  (*height-a* empty 1))

= (*max* (*max*
   (*height-a* empty 2)
   (*height-a* (make-node empty empty) 2))
  (*height-a* empty 1))

= (*max* (*max*
   (*height-a* empty 2)
   (*max* (*height-a* empty 3) (*height-a* empty 3)))
  (*height-a* empty 1))

= (*max* (*max*
   2
   (*max* 3 3))
  1)

= 3

It shows how *height-a* increments the accumulator at each step and that the accumulator at the top of a path represents the number of lines traversed. The hand-evaluation also shows that the results of the various branches are combined at each branching point.

## Exercises

**Exercise 31.3.3** Develop an accumulator-style version of *product*, the function that computes the product of a list of numbers. Show the stage that explains what the accumulator represents. ∎

**Exercise 31.3.4** Develop an accumulator-style version of *how-many*, which is the function that determines the number of items on a list. Show the stage that explains what the accumulator represents. ∎

**Exercise 31.3.5** Develop an accumulator-style version of *add-to-pi*, the function that adds a natural number to *pi* without using + (see section 11.5). Show the stage that explains what the accumulator represents.

Generalize the function so that it adds two numbers, the first one a natural number, without using +. ∎

**Exercise 31.3.6** Develop the function *make-palindrome*, which accepts a nonempty list and constructs a palindrome by mirroring the list around the last item. Thus, if we were to represent the word "abc" and apply *make-palindrome*, we would get back the representation of "abcba". ∎

**Exercise 31.3.7** Develop *to10*. It consumes a list of digits and produces the corresponding number. The first item on the list is the most significant digit.
Examples:

```
(= (to10 (list 1 0 2))
   102)
```

```
(= (to10 (list 2 1))
   21)
```

Now generalize the function so that it consumes a base *b* and a list of *b*-digits. The conversion produces the decimal (10-based) value of the list. The base is between 2 and 10. A *b*-digit is a number between 0 and $b - 1$.
Examples:

```
(= (to10-general 10 (list 1 0 2))
   102)
```

```
(= (to10-general 08 (list 1 0 2))
   66)
```

**Hint:** In the first example, the result is determined by

$$1 \cdot 10^2 + 0 \cdot 10^1 + 2 \cdot 10^0 = ((1 \cdot 10 + 0) \cdot 10) + 2 \,;$$

the second one is

$$1 \cdot 8^2 + 0 \cdot 8^1 + 2 \cdot 8^0 = ((1 \cdot 8) + 0) \cdot 8) + 2 \,.$$

That is, the exponent represents the number of digits that follow. ∎

**Exercise 31.3.8** Develop the function *is-prime?*, which consumes a natural number and returns **true** if it is prime and **false** otherwise. A number $n$ is prime if it is not divisible by any number between 2 and $n - 1$.
**Hints:** (1) The design recipe for **N[>=1]** suggests the following template:

```
;; is-prime? : N[>=1] → boolean
;; to determine whether n is a prime number
(define (is-prime? n)
  (cond
    [(= n 1) ...]
    [else ... (is-prime? (sub1 n)) ... ]))
```

From this outline, we can immediately conclude that the function forgets $n$, its initial argument as it recurs. Since $n$ is definitely needed to determine whether $n$ is divisible by 2 ... $n - 1$, this suggests that we design an accumulator-style local function that remembers $n$ as it recurs. ∎

---

**Pitfalls:**  People who encounter accumulator-style programming for the first time often get the impression that they are always faster or easier to understand (design) than their recursive counterparts. Both parts are plain wrong. While it is impossible to deal with the full scope of the mistake, let us take a look at a small counterexample.

Consider the following table:

| plain factorial | accumulator-style factorial |
| --- | --- |
| 5.760 | 5.970 |
| 5.780 | 5.940 |
| 5.800 | 5.980 |
| 5.820 | 5.970 |
| 5.870 | 6.690 |
| 5.806 | 6.110 |

It represents the results for exercise 31.3.2. Specifically, the left column shows the number of seconds for 1000 evaluations of (! 20) with the plain factorial function; the right column shows what the same experiment yields when we use the factorial function with an accumulator parameter. The last row shows the averages for the two columns. The table shows that the performance of the accumulator-style version of factorial is always worse than that of the original factorial function. ∎

# 32   More Uses of Accumulation

This section presents three extended exercises that require the whole range of skills: design by recipe, including generative recursion, and the addition of accumulators for various purposes.

## 32.1   Extended Exercise: Accumulators on Trees

---

(**define-struct** *child* (*father mother name date eyes*))

```
A node in a family tree (short: ftn) is either

  1. empty, or

  2. (make-child f m na da ec) where f and m are ftns, na and ec are sym-
     bols, and da is a number.
```

;; *all-blue-eyed-ancestors : ftn* → (**listof** *symbol*)
;; to construct a list of all blue-eyed ancestors in *a-ftree*
(**define** (*all-blue-eyed-ancestors a-ftree*)
  (**cond**
    [(empty? *a-ftree*) empty]
    [**else** (**local** ((**define** *in-parents*
               (append (*all-blue-eyed-ancestors* (child-father *a-ftree*))
                    (*all-blue-eyed-ancestors* (child-mother *a-ftree*)))))
        (**cond**
          [(symbol=? (child-eyes *a-ftree*) 'blue)
          (cons (child-name *a-ftree*) *in-parents*)]
        [**else** *in-parents*]))]))

Figure 91: Collecting family trees with *blue-eyed-ancestor?*

---

Figure 91 recalls the structure and data definitions of family trees from section 14.1 where we developed the function *blue-eyed-ancestor?*, which determined whether an ancestor family tree contained a blue-eyed family member. In contrast, *all-blue-eyed-ancestors*, the function in figure 91, collects the names of all blue-eyed family in a given family tree.

The function's structure is that of a tree-processing function. It has two cases: one for the empty tree and another one for a *child* node. The latter clause contains two self-references: one per parent. These recursive applications collect the names of all blue-eyed ancestors from the father's and the mother's family tree; append combines the two lists into one.

The append function is a structurally recursive function. Here it processes the two lists that the natural recursions of *all-blue-eyed-ancestors* produce. According to section 17.1, this observation suggests that the function is a natural candidate for a transformation into accumulator-style.

Let's get started:

```
;; all-blue-eyed-ancestors : ftn → (listof symbol)
;; to construct a list of all blue-eyed ancestors in a-ftree
(define (all-blue-eyed-ancestors a-ftree0)
  (local (;; accumulator ...
          (define (all-a a-ftree accumulator)
            (cond
              [(empty? a-ftree) ... ]
              [else
               (local ((define in-parents
                         (all-a ... (child-father a-ftree) ...
                                ... accumulator ...)
                         (all-a ... (child-mother a-ftree) ...
                                ... accumulator ...)))
                 (cond
                   [(symbol=? (child-eyes a-ftree) 'blue)
                    (cons (child-name a-ftree) in-parents)]
                   [else in-parents]))])))
    (all-a a-ftree0 ... )))
```

Our next goal is the formulation of an accumulator invariant. The general purpose of the accumulator is to remember knowledge about *a-ftree0* that *all-a* loses as it traverses the tree. A look at the definition in figure 91 shows two recursive applications. The first one processes (child-father *a-ftree*), which means this application of *all-blue-eyed-ancestors* loses knowledge about the mother of *a-ftree*. Conversely, the second recursive application has no knowledge of the father of *a-ftree* as it processes the mother's family tree.

At this point, we have two choices:

1. The accumulator could represent all blue-eyed ancestors encountered so far, including those in the mother's family tree, as it descends into the father's tree.

2. The alternative is to have the accumulator stand for the lost items in the tree. That is, as *all-a* processes the father's family tree, it remembers the mother's tree in the accumulator (and everything else it hasn't seen before).

Let's explore both possibilities, starting with the first.

Initially, *all-a* has not seen any of the nodes in the family tree, so *accumulator* is empty. As *all-a* is about to traverse the father's family tree, we must create a list that represents all blue-eyed ancestors in the tree that we are about to forget, which is the mother's tree. This suggests the following accumulator invariant formulation:

```
;; accumulator is the list of blue-eyed ancestors
;; encountered on the mother-side trees of the path in
;; a-ftree0 to a-ftree
```

To maintain the invariant for the natural recursion, we must collect the ancestors on the mother's side of the tree. Since the purpose of *all-a* is to collect those ancestors, we use the expression

(*all-a* (child-mother *a-ftree*) *accumulator*)

to compute the new accumulator for the application of *all-a* to (child-father *a-ftree*). Putting everything together for the second **cond**-clause yields this:

```
(local ((define in-parents
          (all-a (child-father a-ftree)
            (all-a (child-mother a-ftree)
              accumulator))))
  (cond
    [(symbol=? (child-eyes a-ftree) 'blue)
     (cons (child-name a-ftree) in-parents)]
    [else in-parents]))
```

This leaves us with the answer in the first **cond**-clause. Since *accumulator* represents all blue-eyed ancestors encountered so far, it is the result. Figure 92 contains the complete definition.

---

```
;; all-blue-eyed-ancestors : ftn → (listof symbol)
;; to construct a list of all blue-eyed ancestors in a-ftree
(define (all-blue-eyed-ancestors a-ftree)
   (local (;; accumulator is the list of blue-eyed ancestors
           ;; encountered on the mother-side trees of the path in
           ;; a-ftree0 to a-ftree
           (define (all-a a-ftree accumulator)
             (cond
               [(empty? a-ftree) accumulator]
               [else
                (local ((define in-parents
                          (all-a (child-father a-ftree)
                                 (all-a (child-mother a-ftree) accumulator))))
                  (cond
                    [(symbol=? (child-eyes a-ftree) 'blue)
                     (cons (child-name a-ftree) in-parents)]
                    [else in-parents]))])))
     (all-a a-ftree empty)))
```

Figure 92: Collecting blue-eyed ancestors, accumulator-style (version 1)

---

For the second version, we want the accumulator to represent a list of all of the family trees that haven't been processed yet. Because of the different intention, let us call the accumulator parameter *todo*:

```
;; todo is the list of family trees
;; encountered but not processed
```

Like the accumulator-style *invert*, *all-a* initializes *todo* to empty. It updates it by extending the list for the natural recursion:

```
(local ((define in-parents
          (all-a (child-father a-ftree)
                 (cons (child-mother a-ftree) todo))))
   (cond
     [(symbol=? (child-eyes a-ftree) 'blue)
      (cons (child-name a-ftree) in-parents)]
     [else in-parents]))
```

The problem now is that when *all-a* is applied to the empty tree, *todo* does not represent the result but what is left to do for *all-a*. To visit all those family trees, *all-a* must be applied to them, one at a time. Of course, if *todo* is empty, there is nothing left to do; the result is empty. If *todo* is a list, we pick the first tree on the list as the next one to be processed:

```
(cond
  [(empty? todo) empty]
  [else (all-a (first todo) (rest todo))])
```

The rest of the list is what is now left to do.

---

```
;; all-blue-eyed-ancestors : ftn → (listof symbol)
;; to construct a list of all blue-eyed ancestors in a-ftree
(define (all-blue-eyed-ancestors a-ftree0)
  (local (;; todo is the list of family trees encountered but not processed
          (define (all-a a-ftree todo)
            (cond
              [(empty? a-ftree)
               (cond
                 [(empty? todo) empty]
                 [else (all-a (first todo) (rest todo))])]
              [else
               (local ((define in-parents
                         (all-a (child-father a-ftree)
                                (cons (child-mother a-ftree) todo))))
                 (cond
                   [(symbol=? (child-eyes a-ftree) 'blue)
                    (cons (child-name a-ftree) in-parents)]
                   [else in-parents]))])))
    (all-a a-ftree0 empty)))
```

Figure 93: Collecting blue-eyed ancestors, accumulator-style (version 2)

---

Figure 93 contains the complete definition for this second accumulator-style variant of *all-blue-eyed-ancestors*. The auxiliary definition is the most unusual recursive function definition we have seen. It contains a recursive application of *all-a* in both the first and the second **cond**-clause. That is, the function definition does not match the data definition for family trees, the primary inputs. While a function like that can be the result of a careful chain of development steps, starting from a working function developed with a design recipe, it should never be a starting point.

The use of accumulators is also fairly common in programs that process representations of programs. We encountered these forms of data in section 14.4, and like family trees, they have complicated data definitions. In intermezzo 3, we also discussed some concepts concerning variables and their mutual association, though without processing these concepts. The following exercises introduce simple functions that work with the scope of parameters, binding occurrences of variables, and other notions.

## Exercises

**Exercise 32.1.1** Develop a data representation for the following tiny subset of Scheme expressions:

$$\langle exp \rangle \;=\; \langle var \rangle \;\mid\; (\textbf{lambda}\,(\langle var \rangle)\,\langle exp \rangle) \;\mid\; (\langle exp \rangle\,\langle exp \rangle)$$

The subset contains only three kinds of expressions: variables, functions of one argument, and function applications.
Examples:

1. **(lambda** (*x*) *y*)

2. **((lambda** (*x*) *x*)
   **(lambda** (*x*) *x*))

3. **(((lambda** (*y*)
   **(lambda** (*x*)
   *y*))
   **(lambda** (*z*) *z*))
   **(lambda** (*w*) *w*))

Represent variables as symbols. Call the class of data *Lam*.

Recall that **lambda**-expressions are functions without names. Thus they bind their parameter in the body. In other words, the scope of a **lambda**-expression's parameter is the body. Explain the scope of each binding occurrence in the above examples. Draw arrows from all bound occurrences to the binding occurrences.

If a variable occurs in an expression but has no corresponding binding occurrence, the occurrence is said to be free. Make up an expression in which *x* occurs both free and bound. ∎

**Exercise 32.1.2** Develop the function

;; *free-or-bound : Lam → Lam*
;; to replace each non-binding occurrence of a variable in *a-lam*
;; with 'free or 'bound, depending on whether the
;; occurrence is bound or not.
(**define** (*free-or-bound a-lam*) ... )

where *Lam* is the class of expression representations from exercise 32.1.1. ∎

**Exercise 32.1.3** Develop the function

;; *unique-binding : Lam → Lam*
;; to replace variables names of binding occurrences and their bound
;; counterparts so that no name is used twice in a binding occurrence
(**define** (*unique-binding a-lam*) ... )

where *Lam* is the class of expression representations from exercise 32.1.1.
**Hint:** The function gensym creates a new and unique symbol from a given
symbol. The result is guaranteed to be distinct from all other symbols in
the program, including those previously generated with gensym.

Use the technique of this section to improve the function. **Hint:** The
accumulator relates old parameter names to new parameter names. ∎

## 32.2   Extended Exercise: Missionaries and Cannibals

On occasion, accumulators are a part of a piece of compound data because
a function manages many pieces of data (in the same class) at the same
time. The following story poses just such a problem:

> Once upon a time, three cannibals were guiding three mission-
> aries through a jungle. They were on their way to the nearest
> mission station. After some time, they arrived at a wide river,
> filled with deadly snakes and fish. There was no way to cross
> the river without a boat. Fortunately, they found a row boat
> with two oars after a short search. Unfortunately, the boat was
> too small to carry all of them. It could barely carry two people
> at a time. Worse, because of the river's width there was no way
> to bring the boat back other than to row it back.
>
> Since the missionaries could not trust the cannibals they had to
> figure out a plan to get all six of them safely across the river. The

problem was that these cannibals would kill and eat missionaries as soon as there were more cannibals than missionaries at some place. Thus our missionary-programmer had to devise a plan that guaranteed that there were never any missionaries in the minority at either side of the river. The cannibals, however, can be trusted to cooperate otherwise. Specifically, they won't abandon any potential food, just as the missionaries won't abandon any potential converts.

Luckily one of the missionaries had taken a Scheme course and knew how to solve this problem.

While we can solve the problem by hand, solving it with a Scheme function is more fun and more general. If the same story comes up again with different numbers of cannibals and missionaries or different boat sizes, we can use the same function to solve the problem again.

As with every problem, we begin by laying out how to represent the problem in our data language and then study how to represent certain actions in the real world in our programming language. Here are two basic constants concerning the data representation:

(**define** *MC* 3)
(**define** *BOAT-CAPACITY* 2)

Formulate the function in terms of these constants.

---

## Exercises

**Exercise 32.2.1** Provide a data representation for the states of a river crossing. A state should record the number of missionaries and cannibals on each side of the river and the location of the boat. Here is a graphical representation of the states:

The two lines represent the river, the black and white dots the missionaries and cannibals, the black rectangle the boat. Determine the initial and final state of the game. ∎

**Exercise 32.2.2** Develop a data representation for boat loads. Define *BOAT-LOADS*, the list of all possible boat loads.

Develop the function *make-BOAT-LOADS*, which consumes the boat's
maximal capacity and constructs the list of possible boat loads. ∎

One way to deal with search problems in a systematic manner is to generate all possible successor states for the states we have reached so far, to
filter out the interesting ones, and to start the search over from those. A
successor state is reached by using a feasible transition, for example, an
enabled move in a game, a boat trip, etc.

Here is a graphical illustration of the situation for our problem:

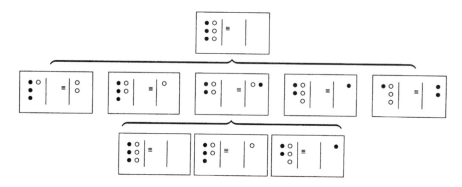

The initial state in the top row has five possible successor states, one per feasible boat load. They are shown in the second row. Two of these successor
states are illegal, because one side contains more cannibals than missionaries. One of the legal ones is the state in which one missionary and cannibal
reached the right side of the river; it has three successor states in turn. The
following exercises deal with generating the successor states and filtering
out the interesting ones.

## Exercises

**Testing:** Formulate all tests as boolean-valued expressions that produce
true if the expected value is the computed one, and false if not. ∎

**Exercise 32.2.3** Develop a function that consumes a state and returns a list
of all possible successor states, that is, all those states that are reachable
with one boat trip from one side of the river to the other.

Develop a generalized version that consumes a list of states, and returns
a list of states reachable with one crossing. ∎

**Exercise 32.2.4** Develop a function that determines whether a given state is legal. A state is legal if it contains the proper number of missionaries and cannibals and if the missionaries on each side of the river are safe.

Develop a generalized function that consumes a list of states and returns the sublist of legal states. ∎

**Exercise 32.2.5** Develop a function that consumes a state and determines if it is final.

Develop a generalized version that consumes a list of states and returns the sublist of final states. ∎

The functions we have developed can generate the successor states of a list of states and can detect whether any of the states reached so far are legal. Now we can develop a function that determines whether we can transport the missionaries and cannibals across the river.

## Exercises

**Exercise 32.2.6** Develop *mc-solvable?*, which consumes a list of states and generates the list of all successor states until it has found a final state. The function should simply produce true when it finds a final state. ∎

**Exercise 32.2.7** Develop *mc-solution*. The function is an adaptation of *mc-solvable?* that not only produces true when it finds a solution but a list of river crossings if a given missionary-and-cannibal problem is solvable.
**Hint:** Modify the state representations so that they accumulate the list of crossings that got the group to this particular state. For the initial state, this is just the empty list; for a final state, it is the desired solution. ∎

**Exercise 32.2.8** A series of boat trips may bring the group of missionaries and cannibals back to the initial state (or some other previous state). The series may include two, four, or more boat trips. In short, the "game" contains cycles. Make up an example.

The function *mc-solution* generates all those states reachable with, say, seven boat trips before it generates all those states reachable with eight crossings. Therefore we do not have to worry about cycles in solution attempts. Why?

Modify the solution so that a state reached via a cycle is also illegal.

**Note**: This shows how the accumulator inside the state representation has two uses. ∎

---

## 32.3   Extended Exercise: Board Solitaire

Peg Solitaire is a board game for individuals. The board comes in various shapes. Here is the simplest one:

```
        ◉
       ◉ ◉
      ◉ ○ ◉
     ◉ ◉ ◉ ◉
```

The circle without a black dot represents an unoccupied hole; the other circles are holes containing little pegs.

The goal of the game is to eliminate the pegs one by one, until only one peg is left. A player can eliminate a peg if one of the neighboring holes is unoccupied and if there is a peg in the hole in the opposite direction. In that case, the second peg can jump over the first one and the first one is eliminated. Consider the following configuration:

```
   2 → ◉
       ◉ ◉
 1 → ◉ ◉ ○
     ◉ ◉ ◉ ◉
```

Here the pegs labeled 1 and 2 could jump. If the player decides to move the peg labeled 2, the next configuration is

```
        ○
       ◉ ○
      ◉ ◉ ◉
     ◉ ◉ ◉ ◉
```

Some configurations are dead-ends. For a simple example, consider the first board configuration. Its hole is in the middle of the board. Hence no peg can jump, because there are no two pegs in a row, column, or diagonal such that one can jump over the other into the hole. A player who discovers a dead-end configuration must stop or backtrack by undoing moves and trying alternatives.

## Exercises

**Exercise 32.3.1** Develop a representation for triangular Solitaire boards.

Develop a data representation for peg moves. Pegs can move along a row, a column, and a diagonal.

**Hints:** (1) There are at least four rows, because it is impossible to play the game with three or fewer. Still, develop the data definition independently of such constraints. (2) Translate our examples from above into the chosen data representations. ∎

**Exercise 32.3.2** Develop a function that, given a board and the board position of a peg, determines whether or not the peg can jump. We call such a peg *enabled*.

Develop a function that, given a board and the board position of an enabled peg, creates a board that represents the next configuration. ∎

**Exercise 32.3.3** Develop the function *solitaire*, which solves a Solitaire problem for different sizes of the equilateral triangle. The function should consume a board. It produces **false**, if the given problem is not solvable. Otherwise, it should produce a list of moves that specifies in what order the pegs must be moved to solve the given Solitaire problem.

Formulate the tests for all functions as boolean-valued expressions. ∎

# Intermezzo 6: The Nature of Inexact Numbers

Computers represent and process information in chunks of a fixed size. Because computers were first used for numerical calculations, early computer engineers developed a representation for numbers in terms of fixed-size chunks. Programming languages must mediate the gap between these fixed-size representations and the true mathematics. Because using the hardware representation for numbers makes a program's calculations as efficient as possible, most designers and implementors of programming languages adopted the hardware-based choice.

This intermezzo explains the fixed-size representation for numbers and its consequences in some detail. The first subsection introduces a concrete fixed-size representation for numbers, discusses what it implies for the representation of numbers, and shows how to calculate with such numbers. The second and third section illustrate the two most fundamental problems of fixed-size number arithmetic: overflow and underflow, respectively.

## Fixed-size Number Arithmetic

Suppose we can use four digits to represent numbers. If we represent natural numbers, the representable range is $0 \ldots 9999$. Alternatively we could represent 10,000 fractions between 0 and 1 with that many digits. In either case, this is a rather small range of numbers and not useful for most scientific or business computations.

We can represent a larger range of numbers if we use a different notation for numbers instead. In science, for example, we encounter so-called scientific notation, which represents numbers as two parts:

1. a MANTISSA, which is a base number, and

2. an EXPONENT, which is used to determine a 10-based factor.

For pure scientific notation, the base is between 0 and 9. We relax this constraint and just write numbers as

$$m \cdot 10^e$$

where $m$ is the mantissa and $e$ the exponent. For example, one representation of 1200 with this scheme is

$$120 \cdot 10^1 \,;$$

another one is

$$12 \cdot 10^2 \, .$$

In general, a number has several equivalents in mantissa-exponent representation.

We can also use negative exponents, which add fractions at the cost of one extra piece of data: the sign of the exponent. For example,

$$1 \cdot 10^{-2}$$

stands for

$$\frac{1}{100} \, .$$

As before, the fraction has several representations in the new notation.

To use a form of mantissa-exponent notation for our problem, we must decide how many digits we wish to use for the representation of the mantissa and how many for the exponent. Here we use two for each and a sign for the exponent; other choices are possible. Given this decision, we can still represent 0 as

$$0 \cdot 10^0 \, .$$

The maximal number we can represent is

$$99 \cdot 10^{99} \, ,$$

which is 99 followed by 99 0's. If we use negative exponents in addition to positive ones, we can also represent

$$01 \cdot 10^{-99} \, ,$$

which is a small number close to 0. Thus we can now represent a vastly larger range of numbers with four digits and a sign than before. But this improvement comes with its own problems.

To understand the problems, it is best to agree on a fixed representation schema and to experiment with the number representations. Let's represent a fixed-size number with a structure that has three fields:

(**define-struct** *inex* (*mantissa sign exponent*))

The first and last field contain the mantissa and exponent of the number, the *sign* field is +1 or −1 and represents the sign of the exponent. This sign field enables us to represent numbers between 0 and 1.

```
;; create-inex : N N N → inex
;; to make an instance of inex after checking the appropriateness
;; of the arguments
(define (create-inex m s e)
  (cond
    [(and (<= 0 m 99) (<= 0 e 99) (or (= s +1) (= s −1)))
     (make-inex m s e)]
    [else
     (error 'make-inex "(<= 0 m 99), +1 or -1, (<= 0 e 99) expected")]))

;; inex→ number : inex → number
;; to convert an inex into its numeric equivalent
(define (inex→ number an-inex)
  (* (inex-mantissa an-inex)
     (expt 10 (* (inex-sign an-inex) (inex-exponent an-inex)))))
```

Figure 94: Functions for inexact representations

Here is the data definition:

> An *inex* is a structure:
>
> (make-inex *m s e*)
>
> where *m* and *e* are natural numbers in [0,99] and *s* is +1 or −1.

Because the conditions on the fields of an *inex* structure are so stringent, we use the function *create-inex* to create these structures. Figure 94 contains the function definition for *create-inex*, which is a generalized constructor, that is, a checked constructor (see section 7.5). The figure also defines the function *inex→ number*, which turns *inex*s into numbers according to the principles of our new notation.

Let's translate the above example, 1200, into our Scheme representation:

(*create-inex* 12 +1 2)

The alternative representation, $120 \cdot 10^1$, is illegal in our Scheme world, however. If we evaluate

(*create-inex* 120 +1 1)

we get an error message because the arguments don't satisfy the stated data contract. For other numbers, though, we can find two *inex* equivalents. One example is 0.0000000000000000005, which we can express as

(*create-inex* 50 −1 20)

and

(*create-inex* 5 −1 19)

Confirm the equivalence of these two representations with *inex→ number*.
The range of *inex* numbers is vast:

(**define** *MAX-POSITIVE* (make-inex 99 +1 99))
(**define** *MIN-POSITIVE* (make-inex 1 −1 99))

That is, we can represent large numbers that consist of up to 101 digits in the standard decimal notation; we can also represent small positive fractions smaller than 1 down to the fraction 1 over 10 . . . 0 with 99 zeros. The appearances, however, are deceiving. Not all real numbers in the range between 0 and *MAX-POSITIVE* can be translated into an *inex* structure. In particular, any positive number less than

$$10^{-99}$$

has no equivalent *inex* structure. Similarly, the *inex* representation has gaps in the middle. For example, the successor of

(*create-inex* 12 +1 2)

is

(*create-inex* 13 +1 2)

The first *inex* structure corresponds to 1200, the second one to 1300. Numbers in the middle, such as 1240 or 1260, can only be represented as one or the other. The standard choice is to round the number to the closest representable equivalent. In short, we must approximate such mathematical numbers as we translate into a chosen representation.

Finally, we must also consider arithmetic operations on *inex* structures. Adding two *inex* representations with the same exponent means adding the two mantissas:

(*inex+* (*create-inex* 1 +1 0)
        (*create-inex* 2 +1 0))
= (*create-inex* 3 +1 0)

Translated into mathematical notation, we have

$$\begin{array}{r} 1 \cdot 10^0 \\ + \quad 2 \cdot 10^0 \\ \hline 3 \cdot 10^0 \end{array}$$

When the addition of two mantissas yields too many digits, we may have to find a suitable representation. Consider the example of adding

$$55 \cdot 10^0$$

to itself. Mathematically we get

$$110 \cdot 10^0 ,$$

but we can't just translate this number naively into our chosen representation because $110 > 99$. The proper corrective action is to represent the result as

$$11 \cdot 10^1 .$$

Or, translated into Scheme, we must ensure that *inex+* computes as follows:

> (*inex+* (*create-inex* 55 +1 0)
>     (*create-inex* 55 +1 0))
> = (*create-inex* 11 +1 1)

More generally, if the mantissa of the result is too large, we must divide it by 10 and increase the exponent by one.

Sometimes the result contains more mantissa digits than we can represent. In those cases, *inex+* must round to the closest equivalent in the *inex* world. For example:

> (*inex+* (*create-inex* 56 +1 0)
>     (*create-inex* 56 +1 0))
> = (*create-inex* 11 +1 1)

This corresponds to the precise calculation:

$$56 \cdot 10^0 + 56 \cdot 10^0 = (56 + 56) \cdot 10^0 = 112 \cdot 10^0$$

Because the result has too many mantissa digits, the integer division of the result mantissa by 10 produces an approximate result:

$$11 \cdot 10^1 .$$

This is an example of the many approximations that make INEXACT ARITH-METIC inexact.

We can also multiply numbers represented as *inex* structures. Recall that

$$(a \cdot 10^n) \cdot (b \cdot 10^m)$$
$$= (a \cdot b) \cdot 10^n \cdot 10^m$$
$$= (a \cdot b) \cdot 10^{(n+m)}$$

Thus we get:

$$2 \cdot 10^{+4} * 8 \cdot 10^{+10} = 16 \cdot 10^{+14}$$

or, in Scheme notation:

```
(inex* (create-inex 2 +1 4)
       (create-inex 8 +1 10))
= (make-inex 16 +1 14)
```

As with addition, things are not always straightforward. When the result has too many significant digits in the mantissa, *inex\** has to increase the exponent:

```
(inex* (create-inex 20 −1 1)
       (create-inex  5 +1 4))
= (create-inex 10 +1 4)
```

In the process, *inex\** will introduce an approximation if the true mantissa doesn't have an exact equivalent in the class of *inex* structures:

```
(inex* (create-inex 27 −1 1)
       (create-inex  7 +1 4))
= (create-inex 19 +1 4)
```

---

## Exercises

**Exercise 33.1.1** Develop the function *inex+*, which adds *inex* representations that have the same exponent. The function must be able to deal with examples that increase the exponent. Furthermore, it must signal its own error if the result is out of range for *inex* representations.

**Challenge:** Extend *inex+* so that it can deal with inputs whose exponents differ by 1:

```
(equal? (inex+ (create-inex 1 +1 0) (create-inex 1 −1 1))
        (create-inex 11 −1 1))
```

Do not attempt to deal with larger classes of inputs than that without reading the following subsection. ∎

**Exercise 33.1.2** Develop the function *inex∗*, which multiplies *inex* representations. The function must be able to deal with examples that increase the exponent. Furthermore, it must signal its own error if the result is out of range for *inex* representations. ∎

**Exercise 33.1.3** The section illustrated how an inexact representation system for real numbers has gaps. For example, 1240 was represented as (*create-inex* 12 +1 2) by rounding off the last significant digit of the mantissa. The problem is, round-off errors can accumulate.

Develop the function *add*, which adds up *n* copies of #i1/185. What is the result for (*add* 185)? What should it be? What happens if we multiply the result of the second expression with a large number?

Develop the function *sub*, which counts how often 1/185 can be subtracted from the argument until the argument is 0. How often should the evaluation recur before (*sub* 1) and (*sub* #i1.) is evaluated? What happens in the second case? Why? ∎

### Overflow

While the use of scientific notation expands the range of numbers we can represent with fixed-size chunks of data, it still doesn't cover arbitrarily large numbers. Some numbers are just too big to fit into a fixed-size number representation. For example,

$$99 \cdot 10^{500}$$

can't be represented, because the exponent 500 won't fit into two digits, and the mantissa is as large as it can be.

Numbers that are too large for our representation schema can arise during a computation. For example, two numbers that we can represent can add up to a number that we cannot represent:

(*inex+* (*create-inex* 50 +1 99)
      (*create-inex* 50 +1 99))
= (*create-inex* 100 +1 99)

which violates the data contract, or

$$(inex+ \; (create\text{-}inex \; 50 \; +1 \; 99)$$
$$(create\text{-}inex \; 50 \; +1 \; 99))$$
$$= (create\text{-}inex \; 10 \; +1 \; 100)$$

which also breaks the contract for *inex* structures. When the result of *inex* arithmetic produces numbers that are too large to be represented, we say (arithmetic) OVERFLOW occurred.

When overflow occurs, some language implementations signal an error and stop the computation. Others designate some symbol, called infinity, for all numbers that are too large. Arithmetic operations are aware of infinity and propagate it.

**Negative Numbers**: If our *inex* structures had a sign field for the mantissa, then two negative numbers can add up to one that is so negative that it can't be represented either. This is also called overflow, though to emphasize the distinction people sometimes say overflow in the negative direction. ∎

## Exercises

**Exercise 33.2.1** DrScheme's inexact number system uses an infinity value to deal with overflow. Determine the integer $n$ such that (expt #i10. $n$) is still an inexact Scheme number and (expt #i10. (+ $n$ 1)) is approximated with infinity. **Hint:** Use a function to compute $n$. ∎

## Underflow

At the opposite end of the spectrum, we have already seen small numbers that cannot be represented with *inex* structures. For example, $10^{-500}$ is not 0, but it's smaller than the smallest non-zero number we can represent. An arithemtic UNDERFLOW arises when we multiply two small numbers and the result is too small to fit into our class of *inex* structures:

$$(inex* \; (create\text{-}inex \; 1 \; -1 \; 10)$$
$$(create\text{-}inex \; 1 \; -1 \; 99))$$
$$= (create\text{-}inex \; 1 \; -1 \; 109)$$

which causes an error.

When underflow occurs, some language implementations signal an error; others use 0 to approximate the result. An approximation with 0 for

underflow is qualitatively different from our ealier kinds of approximations. In approximating 1250 with (*create-inex* 12 +1 2), we approximated
by dropping significant digits from the mantissa, but we were left with a
non-zero mantissa. The result is within 10% of the number we wanted to
represent. Approximating on underflow, however, means dropping the entire mantissa. The result is not within a predictable precentage range of the
true result.

## Exercises

**Exercise 33.3.1** DrScheme's inexact number system uses #i0 to approximate underflow. Determine the smallest integer $n$ such that (expt #i10. $n$)
is still an inexact Scheme number and (expt #i10. $(- n\ 1)$) is approximated
with 0. **Hint:** Use a function to compute $n$. ∎

## DrScheme's Numbers

Most programming languages support only inexact number representations (and arithmetic) for both integers and reals. Scheme, in contrast,
supports both exact and inexact numbers and arithmetic. Of course, the
base of the representation is 2, not 10, because Scheme uses the underlying
computer's on-off machinery.

As the note on page 6 explained, DrScheme's teaching levels interpret
all numbers in our programs as exact rationals, unless they are prefixed
with #i. Some numeric operations, though, produce inexact numbers. Plain
Scheme, which is called Full Scheme in DrScheme, interprets all numbers
with a dot as inexact numbers;[66] it also prints inexact reals with just a dot,
implying that all such numbers are inexact and possibly distant from the
actual result.

Scheme programmers can thus choose to use exact arithmetic or inexact arithmetic as necessary. For example, numbers in financial statements
should always be interpreted as exact numbers; arithmetical operations on
such numbers should be as precise as possible. For some problems, however, we may not wish to spend the extra time to produce exact results. Scientific computations are a primary example. In such cases, we may wish
switch to inexact numbers and arithmetic.

---

[66]We can force Full Scheme to interpret numbers with a dot as exact by prefixing the
numbers with #e.

**Numerical Analysis**: When we use inexact numbers and arithmetic, it is natural to ask how much the program's results differs from the true results. Over the past few decades, the study of this complex question has evolved into an advanced topic, called numerical analysis. The discipline has become a subject of its own right in applied mathematics or in computer science departments. ∎

## Exercises

**Exercise 33.4.1** Evaluate

(expt 1.001 1e−12)

in Full Scheme (any variant) and in Intermediate Student Scheme. Explain the observations. ∎

**Exercise 33.4.2** Develop the function *my-expt*, which raises one number to the power of some integer. Using this function, conduct the following experiment. Add

(**define** *inex* (+ 1 #i1e−12))
(**define** *exac* (+ 1 1e−12))

to the Definitions window. What is (*my-expt inex* 30)? How about (*my-expt exac* 30)? Which answer is more useful? ∎

**Exercise 33.4.3** When we add two inexact numbers of vastly different orders of magnitude, we may get the larger one back as the result. For example, if we are using only 15 significant digits, then we run into problems when adding numbers which vary by more than a factor of $10^{16}$:

$$1.0 \cdot 10^{16} + 1 = 1.00000000000000001 \cdot 10^{16},$$

but if the number system supports only 15 digits, the closest answer is $10^{16}$. At first glance, this doesn't look too bad. After all, being wrong by one part in $10^{16}$ (ten million billion) is close enough to the accurate result. Unfortunately, this kind of problem can add up to huge problems.

Consider the following list of inexact numbers:

```
(define JANUS
  (list #i31
        #i2e+34
        #i-1.2345678901235e+80
        #i2749
        #i-2939234
        #i-2e+33
        #i3.2e+270
        #i17
        #i-2.4e+270
        #i4.2344294738446e+170
        #i1
        #i-8e+269
        #i0
        #i99))
```

Determine the values (*sum JANUS*) and (*sum* (reverse *JANUS*)). Explain the difference. Can we trust computers? ∎

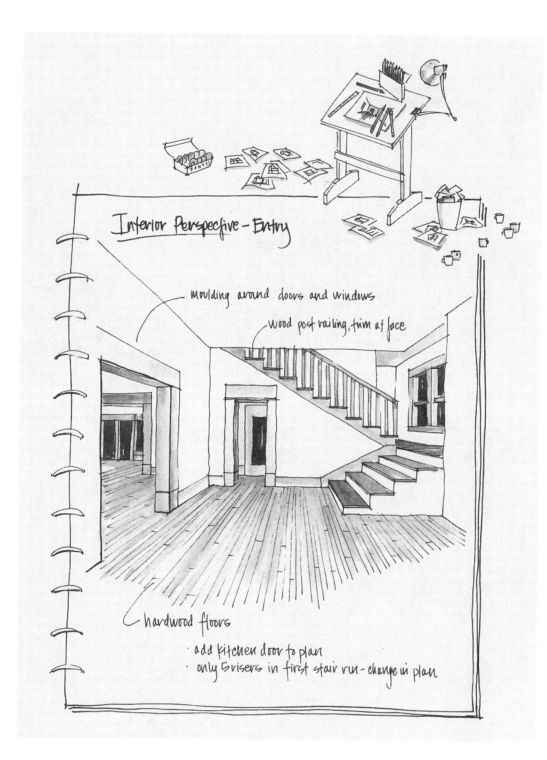

Interior Perspective - Entry

· moulding around doors and windows

· wood post railing, trim at face

Chardwood floors

· add kitchen door to plan
· only 5 risers in first stair run - change in plan

# VII  Changing the State of Variables

Advanced Student

## 34  Memory for Functions

No matter how often we use a function with one and the same argument, we always get the same result. Even an accumulator-style function produces the same result every time we apply it to the same argument, as long as the accumulator argument is also the same. Functions simply do not have any memory about their past uses.

Many programs, though, must remember something about their past uses. Recall that a program typically consists of several functions. In the past we have always assumed that there is one main function and that all others are auxiliary and invisible to the user. In some cases, however, a user may expect more than one service from a program, and each service is best implemented as a function. When a program provides more than one function as a service to the user, it is common that, for sheer convenince or possibly because we add a graphical user interface, the functions must have memory.

Because this point is difficult to grasp in the abstract, we study some examples. The first one concerns a program for managing telephone numbers in an address book. The standard address book software provides at least two services:

1. a service for looking up the phone number of some person; and

2. a service for adding a name and a phone number to the address book.

Based on our guidelines, the program provides two functions to the user. The user can apply those functions in DrScheme's Interactions window to appropriate data. Or, we can develop a graphical user interface with text fields and buttons so that the user doesn't need to know anything about programming. Figure 95 displays such an interface.

Figure 95: A phonebook GUI

The two services roughly correspond to two functions:

*;; lookup : list-of-symbol-number-pairs symbol* → *number* **or** false
*;; to lookup the number associated with* *name* in *pb*
*;; if it doesn't find* *name, the function produces* false
(**define** (*lookup pb name*) ...)

*;; add-to-address-book : symbol number* → *void*
*;; to add* *name* and *number* to *address-book*
(**define** (*add-to-address-book name number*) ...)

(**define** *ADDRESS-BOOK*
    (list (list 'Adam 1)
          (list 'Eve 2)))

We also introduce a variable definition for maintaing a list of name-number associations.

The first function is a variant of our very first recursive function. A user applies it to a list of name-number associations, such as *ADDRESS-BOOK*, and a name. It produces a number, if the name is on the list, or false otherwise. The second function is radically different from what we have seen. The user would apply it to a name and a number; any future lookup of that name would then produce that number.

Let's imagine an interaction in DrScheme:

> (*lookup ADDRESS-BOOK* 'Adam)
1
> (*lookup ADDRESS-BOOK* 'Dawn)
false
> (*add-to-address-book* 'Dawn 4)
> (*lookup ADDRESS-BOOK* 'Dawn)
4

The first two confirm that 'Adam has the phone number 1 and that we don't have a phone number for 'Dawn. The third one adds the phone number 4 for 'Dawn to *ADDRESS-BOOK*. And the last interaction shows that the very same use of *lookup* as before now produces the expected phone number.

In the past, the only way we could have achieved this same effect is by editing the definition of *ADDRESS-BOOK*. But, we do not wish users to edit our programs. Indeed, they shouldn't even have access to our programs. We are therefore forced to provide an interface with a function that permits such changes. We could go even further and implement the graphical interface of figure 95. A dialogue equivalent to the above interaction would proceed as follows:

1. Type Adam into the text field, click the Lookup button, and "1" appears in the lower text field.

2. Enter Dawn into the text field, click the Lookup button, and some message concerning a missing number appears in the lower text field.

3. Replace the message with "4" and click the Add button.

4. Erase the "4" from the lower text field, click the Lookup and the "4" shows up again.

In short, providing a convenient interface to a user forces us to develop a program whose functions know about each other's usage history.

Figure 96: The three stages of a traffic light canvas and its GUI

The second example, a traffic light simulation, illustrates how a single function may need to have some memory. Recall the function *next* from exercise 6.2.5. It consumes the current color of a traffic light and, with the help of *clear-bulb* and *draw-bulb*, switches the state of the traffic light on a canvas to the next traffic color. The result is the next color.

A user who wishes to switch the traffic light four times in a row must enter

(*next* (*next* (*next* (*next* 'red))))

into the Interactions window. An even more convenient user interface, however, would provide a button that the user can click.

Providing a button means providing a call-back function that somehow knows about the current state of the traffic light and changes it. Let's call this function *next*, too, but let's assume that it consumes no arguments. Here is an imaginary interaction using this function:

> (*next*)
> (*next*)
> (*next*)

Every time we apply *next* to no arguments, it produces the invisible value and simulates the switch of state in the traffic light on the canvas. In other words, the canvas cycles through the three states depicted in figure 96. Equivalently, we can have a user click the "NEXT" button three times, which would apply the next function and have the same visual effect. To accomplish this effect, the use of *next* must affect its own future uses.

The final example concerns the *hangman* game, which is also the subject of section 6.7. The game program requires us to develop three functions: make-word, *reveal*, and *draw-next-part*. We start the game by evaluating

(*hangman* make-word *reveal draw-next-part*)

which picks a word, creates the graphical user interface of the lower half of figure 97, and draws the left-most picture in the sequence of the upper half of the figure. The player can then choose a letter from the choice menu in the GUI and click on the "Check" button to determine whether the letter occurs in the word. If so, the *hangman* function reveals where the letter occurs; if not, it uses our *draw-next-part* function to draw the next stage in the hangman picture. The more bad guesses the player makes, the more of the stick figure appears in the picture (see top-half of figure 97).

Our description suggests that the *hangman* function in the teachpack employs a callback function for the "Check" button. Let's call this function *check*. It consumes the letter and produces true if the check reveals new knowledge:

> (*check* 'b)
true

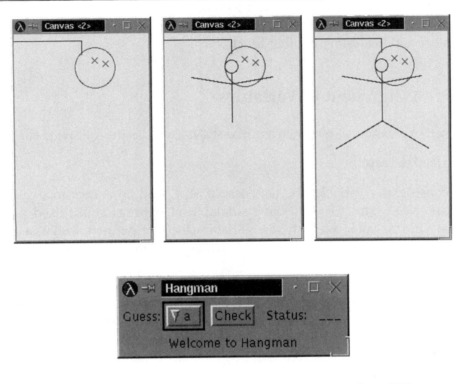

Figure 97: Three stages in the hangman game and its GUI

If not, because the letter has already been guessed, the function produces false to indicate that the player didn't gain new knowledge:

> (*check* 'b)
false

In this case, *check* also employs *draw-next-part* to draw another part of the hangman figure. Of course, to accomplish this, *hangman* and *check* must have some memory about how often the "Check" button was used and how often it was used with a negative result.

With our current knowledge of Scheme, we cannot formulate functions such as *add-to-address-book*, *next*, or *check*. To fill this gap in our knowledge, the next section introduces **set!**[67] expressions. This new form of expression permits functions to change the value that a **define**d variable represents.

---

[67]This keyword is pronounced set-bang.

Using this new construct, we can formulate Scheme functions that have memory. That is, we can define functions that know something about their history and the history of other functions.

# 35   Assignment to Variables

A **set!**-expression, also known as an ASSIGNMENT, has the following shape:

   (**set!** *var* exp)

It consists of a variable, the LEFT-HAND SIDE, and an expression, called RIGHT-HAND SIDE. The left-hand side of a **set!**-expression is a fixed variable. In this book, we only use variables that are **define**d, either at the top-level or in a **local**-expression. A **set!**-expression may occur wherever an expression is legal.

   The value of a **set!**-expression is always the same and is moreover invisible. It is therefore irrelevant. What matters about a **set!**-expression, instead, is the effect of its evaluation. Specifically, for the first step of the evaluation of a **set!**-expression, we determine the value of exp. Let's say this value is $V$. For the second step, we change the definition of *var* to

   (**define** *var* $V$)

The EFFECT of this second step is that from this point on, all references to *var* in an evaluation replace *var* by $V$.[68] Its former value is lost.

   Understanding the true nature of assignments is difficult. We therefore first consider a simple though useless example.

## 35.1   Simple Assignments at Work

Consider the following definition and expression:

   (**define** *x* 3)

   (**local** ((**define** *z* (**set!** *x* (+ *x* 2))))
     *x*)

---

[68]We have already encountered several kinds of effects: drawing to a canvas, changing the text field in a GUI, the creating of files by teachpacks, and so on. These effects aren't as complex as those of **set!** because they don't affect the program proper.

The definition says that $x$ stands for 3. The **local**-expression introduces a definition for $z$. Its body is $x$ so, in the past, the value of this **local**-expression would have been 3 (if anything). Now, with **set!** in the language, this is no longer true. To understand what happens, we must rewrite the program step by step until we have a final answer.

The first step in the evaluation lifts the **local** definition:

(**define** $x$ 3)

(**define** $z$ (**set!** $x$ (+ $x$ 2)))

$x$

Next we must determine the value of (**set!** $x$ (+ $x$ 2)). According to the general explanation of **set!**, this requires the evaluation of the right-hand side of the assignment:

(**define** $x$ 3)

(**define** $z$ (**set!** $x$ 5))

$x$

That value is 5 because the current value of $x$ is 3.

Finally, the general explanation says that the effect of the **set!** expression is to change the value that the left-hand side variable represents. In our example this means that from now on, $x$ is no longer 3 but 5. The best way to express this change is to modify the definition of $x$ for the next step:

(**define** $x$ 5)

(**define** $z$ (void))

$x$

The value of **set!** is (void), the invisible value. By replacing the **set!**-expression with the invisible value, we indicate that its evaluation is finished.

At this point, it is easy to see that the result is 5. The first definition says that $x$ currently represents 5, and the last expression is $x$. Hence the value of the function evaluation is 5.

### Exercises

**Exercise 35.1.1** Consider the following:

1. **(set!** *x* 5)

   **(define** *x* 3)

2. **(set!** (+ *x* 1) 5)

   **(define** *x* 3)
   **(define** *y* 7)
   **(define** *z* false)

3. **(set!** (*z x y*) 5)

Which ones are syntactically legal programs? Which ones are illegal? ∎

**Exercise 35.1.2** Evaluate the following program:

**(define** *x* 1)
**(define** *y* 1)

**(local** ((**define** *u* (**set!** *x* (+ *x* 1)))
        (**define** *v* (**set!** *y* (− *y* 1)))))
   (* *x y*))

If **set!** were not a part of the language, what could we say about the result of the **local**-expression? That is, consider the skeleton

**(define** *x* 1)
**(define** *y* 1)

**(local** ((**define** *u* ...)
        (**define** *v* ...))
   (* *x y*))

where the right-hand sides of the definitions have been removed. What would this expression have produced before the introduction of **set!**-expressions? ∎

## 35.2  Sequencing Expression Evaluations

The hand-evaluation shows that the **local** definition for *z* serves to evaluate a **set!**-expression and "to throw away" its value. After all, a **set!**'s true purpose is to change a definition and not to generate a value. Because this situation is quite common, Scheme also provides the **begin**-expression:

(**begin** *exp-1*
    . . .
    *exp-n*
    exp)

A **begin**-expression consists of the keyword **begin** followed by a sequence of $n + 1$ expressions. The evaluation determines the values of all expressions, in order, and then throws away the first $n$. The value of the last expression is the value of the entire **begin**-expression. In general, the first $n$ subexpressions in a **begin**-expression change some definitions; only the last one has an interesting value.

We can now rewrite our first sample program with **set!** into a short expression:

(**define** *x* 3)

(**begin** (**set!** *x* (+ *x* 2))
    *x*)

The use of **begin** not only simplifies the program, it also suggests a straight-line ordering of the evaluation.

The hand-evaluation also shows that the evaluation of **set!**-expression introduces additional timing constraints. More concretely, the above evaluation consists of two parts: the one before and the one after the assignment exerted its effect on the state of the definitions. Before we introduced assignments, we could replace a variable by its value or a function application by the function's body whenever we wished. Now, we must wait until we truly need the value of a variable before we perform the substitution. After all, definitions may change.

While some partial ordering is always a part of computation, the timing constraints of **set!** are new. By altering a definition, an assignment "destroys" the current value. Unless the programmer carefully plans the arrangement of assignments, such an action may be fatal. The exercises illustrate the problem in more detail.

## Exercises

**Exercise 35.2.1** Evaluate the following program by hand:

```
(define x 1)
(define y 1)

(begin (set! x (+ x 1))
       (set! y (− y 1))
       (* x y))
```

How many time periods can we distinguish in this hand-evaluation?
Compare this with the evaluation of

```
(define a 5)
```

```
(* (+ a 1) (− a 1)))
```

Does the nesting imply an ordering among our calculations? Does the order of addition and subtraction matter? ∎

**Exercise 35.2.2** Evaluate the following program by hand:

```
(define x 3)
(define y 5)

(begin (set! x y)
       (set! y x)
       (list x y))
```

How many time periods can we distinguish in this hand-evaluation?
Now evaluate the following:

```
(define x 3)
(define y 5)

(local ((define z x))
  (begin (set! x y)
         (set! y z)
         (list x y)))
```

Is it true that the definition of $x$ contains the initial value of $y$ and $y$ contains the initial value of $x$ after the two **set!**-expressions are evaluated, no matter what the initial values are?

Discuss what the two examples teach us about time and "destruction of values" in definitions. ∎

**Exercise 35.2.3** Evaluate the following program by hand:

```
(define x 3)
(define y 5)

(begin
  (set! x y)
  (set! y (+ y 2))
  (set! x 3)
  (list x y))
```

How many time intervals must we distinguish in this hand-evaluation? ∎

## 35.3 Assignments and Functions

An assignment can also occur in a function body:

```
(define x 3)

(define y 5)

(define (swap-x-y x0 y0)
  (begin
    (set! x y0)
    (set! y x0)))

(swap-x-y x y)
```

Here the function *swap-x-y* consumes two values and performs two **set!**s.

Let us see how the evaluation works. Because (*swap-x-y x y*) is a function application, we need to evaluate the arguments, which are plain variables here. So we replace the variables with their (current) values:

```
(define x 3)

(define y 5)
```

```
(define (swap-x-y x0 y0)
  (begin
    (set! x y0)
    (set! y x0)))
```

```
(swap-x-y 3 5)
```

From here we proceed with the usual substitution rule for application:

```
(define x 3)
```

```
(define y 5)
```

```
(define (swap-x-y x0 y0)
  (begin
    (set! x y0)
    (set! y x0)))
```

```
(begin
  (set! x 5)
  (set! y 3))
```

That is, the application is now replaced by an assignment of *x* to the current value of *y* and of *y* to the current value of *x*.

The next two steps are also the last ones and thus they accomplish what the name of the function suggests:

```
(define x 5)
```

```
(define y 3)
```

```
(define (swap-x-y x0 y0)
  (begin
    (set! x y0)
    (set! y x0)))
```

```
(void)
```

The value of the application is invisible because the last expression evaluated was a **set!**-expression.

In summary, functions with **set!** have results and effects. The result may be invisible.

## Exercises

**Exercise 35.3.1** Consider the following function definition:

```
(define (f x y)
  (begin
    (set! x y)
    y))
```

Is it syntactically legal or illegal? ∎

**Exercise 35.3.2** Evaluate the following program by hand:

```
(define x 3)

(define (increase-x)
  (begin
    (set! x (+ x 1))
    x))

(increase-x)
(increase-x)
(increase-x)
```

What is the result? What is *increase-x*'s effect? ∎

**Exercise 35.3.3** Evaluate the following program by hand:

```
(define x 0)

(define (switch-x)
  (begin
    (set! x (- x 1))
    x))

(switch-x)
(switch-x)
(switch-x)
```

What is the result? What is *switch-x*'s effect? ∎

**Exercise 35.3.4** Evaluate the following program by hand:

(**define** *x* 0)

(**define** *y* 1)

(**define** (*change-to-3 z*)
  (**begin**
    (**set!** *y* 3)
    *z*))

(*change-to-3 x*)

What is the effect of *change-to-3*? What is its result? ∎

## 35.4  A First Useful Example

Let's take a look at the definitions in figure 98. The function *add-to-address-book* consumes a symbol and a number. The former represents a name, the latter a phone number. Its body contains a **set!**-expression for *address-book*, a variable **define**d at top-level. The function *lookup* consumes an address book and a name; its result is the matching phone number or false, if the name is not in *address-book*.

Using *lookup*, we can study the effect of the **set!** expression in *add-to-address-book*. Suppose we evaluate (*lookup* 'Adam *address-book*) with the given definitions:

    (*lookup* 'Adam *address-book*)
= (*lookup* 'Adam empty)
= (**cond**
    [(empty? empty) false]
    [**else** ... ])
= false

Because *address-book* is empty, we get false, and the calculation is straight-forward.

Now let's evaluate the following in the Interactions window:

(**begin** (*add-to-address-book* 'Adam 1)
      (*add-to-address-book* 'Eve 2)
      (*add-to-address-book* 'Chris 6145384))

(**define** *address-book* empty)

;; *add-to-address-book : symbol number* → *void*
(**define** (*add-to-address-book name phone*)
  (**set!** *address-book* (cons (list *name phone*) *address-book*)))

;; *lookup : symbol* (**listof** (list *symbol number*)) → *number* **or** false
;; to lookup the phone number for *name* in *ab*
(**define** (*lookup name ab*)
  (**cond**
    [(empty? *ab*) false]
    [**else** (**cond**
       [(symbol=? (first (first *ab*)) *name*)
       (second (first *ab*))]
      [**else** (*lookup name* (rest *ab*))])])))

Figure 98: The basic address-book program

The first subexpression is a plain function application. So, the first step relies on the usual law of substitution:[69]

(**define** *address-book* empty)

(**begin** (**set!** *address-book* (cons (list 'Adam 1) *address-book*))
    (*add-to-address-book* 'Eve 2)
    (*add-to-address-book* 'Chris 6145384))

The next expression to be evaluated is the **set!**-expression that is nested in the **begin**-expressions, in particular its right-hand side. The first argument to cons is a value, but the second one is still a variable whose current value is empty. With this, we can see what happens next:

(**define** *address-book* empty)

(**begin** (**set!** *address-book* (cons (list 'Adam 1) empty))
    (*add-to-address-book* 'Eve 2)
    (*add-to-address-book* 'Chris 6145384))

---

[69]Because the calculation does not affect the function definitions, we do not include them in the calculation here. This convention saves space and time, but it should be used carefully.

At this point we are ready to evaluate the **set!**-expression. Specifically, we change the definition of *address-book* so that the variable now stands for (cons (list 'Adam 1) empty):

```
(define address-book
  (cons (list 'Adam 1)
    empty))
```

```
(begin (void)
       (add-to-address-book 'Eve 2)
       (add-to-address-book 'Chris 6145384))
```

The **begin**-expression throws away the invisible value.

Evaluating the remaining applications of *add-to-address-book* yields

```
(define address-book
  (list (list 'Chris 6145384)
        (list 'Eve 2)
        (list 'Adam 1)))
```

```
(void)
```

In short, the three applications turn *address-book* into a list of three pairs.

If we now evaluate (*lookup* 'Adam *address-book*) in the Interactions window again, we get 1:

```
    (lookup 'Adam address-book)
  = (lookup 'Adam (list (list 'Chris 6145384)
                        (list 'Eve 2)
                        (list 'Adam 1))
  = ...
  = 1
```

The comparison of this evaluation and the one at the beginning of the section shows how **set!** changes the meaning of *address-book* over time and how the two functions, *add-to-address-book* and *lookup*, implement the services that we discussed in section 34. The exercises show how useful this collaboration of two functions is in the context of a graphical user interface.

## Exercises

**Exercise 35.4.1** The software for managing address books permits users to remove entries. Develop the function

*;; remove : symbol → void*
(**define** (*remove name*) ... )

which changes *address-book* so that all future *lookup*s for *name* yield false. ∎

**Exercise 35.4.2** The teachpack **phone-book.ss** implements a graphical user interface based on the model-view pattern discussed in section 22.3. Figure 95 shows what the graphical user interface offers:

1. a text-field for entering a name;

2. a text-field for displaying the search result and for entering a phone number;

3. a button for looking up the phone number for a name;

4. a button for adding a name and a phone number; and

5. a button for removing the phone number for a name.

Use the teachpack's *connect* function to create a GUI for the functions in this section and in exercise 35.4.1. The function has the following contract, purpose, and header:

*;; model-T = (button% control-event% → true)*
*;; connect : model-T model-T model-T → true*
(**define** (*connect lookup-cb change-cb remove-cb*) ... )

That is, it consumes three model functions and wires them up with the GUI. The names of the parameters specify which call-back function goes with which button.

A model function may obtain the contents of the name field with (*name-control*) and the contents of the number field with (*number-field*). ∎

## 36 Designing Functions with Memory

Section 34 motivated the idea of functions with memory; section 35 explained how variable definitions and **set!** together can achieve the effect of memory. It is now time to discuss the design of programs with memory.

Designing functions with memory requires three important steps:

1. We must determine that a program requires memory.

2. We must identify the data that goes into the memory.

3. We must understand which of the services are supposed to modify the memory and which are to use the memory.

The need for the first step is obvious. Once we know that a program requires memory, we must conduct a data analysis for the program's memory. That is, we must figure out what kind of data the program puts into memory and retrieves from there. Finally, we must carefully design those functions for the program that change the memory. The others are those that use the variables (without modification); they are typically designed with one of the recipes we have already discussed.

## 36.1 The Need for Memory

Programs need memory because we want them to work with users who know little or nothing about programming. Even if we wanted users to employ DrScheme's Interactions window, we would organize our programs so that each service corresponds to a function and the functions collaborate through memory. With graphical user interfaces, we are almost forced to think of programs as a collection of collaborating functions attached to various widgets in a window. Finally, even programs that work in physical devices such as elevators or VCRs are forced to interact with the device in some fixed way, and that often includes keeping around information about the history of device-program interactions. In short, the interface between the program and the rest of the world dictates whether a program needs memory and what kind of memory it needs.

Fortunately it is relatively easy to recognize when programs need memory. As discussed already, there are two situations. The first involves programs that provide more than one service to users. Each service corresponds to a function. A user may apply these functions in DrScheme's Interactions window, or they may be applied in response to some user action in a graphical user interface. The second involves a program that provides a single service and is implemented with a single user-level function. But the program may have to produce different answers when it is applied to the same arguments.

Let us take a look at some concrete examples for each situation. Software for managing an address book is a classical example of the first kind. In sections 34 and 35, we saw how one function adds entries to the address book and another looks them up. Clearly, the use of the "addition service" affects future uses of the "lookup service" and therefore requires memory. Indeed, the memory in this case corresponds to a natural physical object: the address book that people used to keep before there were electronic notebooks.

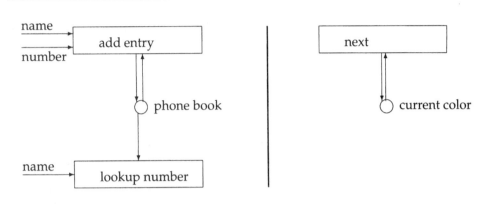

Figure 99: Organizational charts for programs with memory

Next, consider a warehouse with a clerk that registers the items that people deliver and pick up. Every time someone delivers an item, the clerk enters it into a ledger; an inquiry for a specific item triggers a search in the ledger; when someone picks up an item, the clerk removes it from the ledger. If we were to provide a function for managing the ledger, the program would have to offer three services: one for entering items, one for searching in the ledger, and one for removing entries from the ledger. Of course, we can't remove something that isn't in the warehouse, so the program must ensure that the two services interact properly. The memory in this program will be similar to the ledgers that warehouse clerks use (or used), that is, a physical object.

The second class of memory need also has classical examples. The traffic light simulation mentioned in section 34 is one of them. Recall that the description of the program *next* says that every time it is applied, it redraws the picture on a canvas according to the common traffic rules. Because two evaluations of (*next*) in a row produce two different effects, this program needs memory.

For another example, take a look at the Scheme function random. It consumes a natural number $n \geq 1$ and produces a number between 0 and $n - 1$. If we evaluate (random 10) twice in a row, we may or may not obtain the same digit. Again, to achieve this effect, the implementor of random needed to equip the function with some memory.

In general, as we analyze a problem statement, we should draw organization charts. Figure 99 contains sample charts for the phone-book and the traffic-light programs. They represent each service that the program is to support with a rectangular box. Arrows going into the box indicate what kind of data a service consumes; outgoing arrows specify the output. Memory is represented with circles. An arrow from a circle to a box means that the service uses the memory as an input; an arrow to a circle means that the service changes the memory. The two charts show that services commonly use memory and change it.

## 36.2 Memory and State Variables

Memory is implemented with variable definitions. The memory-using programs we have seen use a single variable to represent the memory of a function. In principle, a single variable is enough to implement all memory needs, but this is usually inconvenient. Typically, the memory analysis suggests how many variables we need and which services need which variables. When memory changes, the corresponding variables assume a new value or, put differently, the state of the variable declaration changes and reflects the memory change over time. We therefore refer to variables that implement memory as STATE VARIABLES.

Every service in a program corresponds to a function that may employ auxiliary functions. A service that changes the memory of a program is implemented with a function that uses **set!** on some of the state variables. To understand how a function should change a state variable, we need to know what kind of values the variable may represent and what its purpose is. In other words, we must develop a contract and a purpose statement for state variables in the same manner in which we develop contracts and purpose statements for function definitions.

Let us take a look at the address-book and the traffic-light examples. The first one has one state variable: *address-book*. It is intended to represent a list of entries, where each entry is a list of two items: a name and a number. To document that *address-book* may represent only such lists, we add a contract as follows:

;; *address-book* : (**listof** (list *symbol number*))
;; to keep track of pairs of names and phone numbers
(**define** *address-book* empty)

By the definition of (**listof** *X*), it is permissible to use empty as the initial value of *address-book*.

From the contract for the state variable, we can conclude that the following assignment is nonsensical:

(**set!** *address-book* 5)

It sets *address-book* to 5, which is not a list. The expression therefore violates the state variable's contract. But

(**set!** *address-book* empty)

is proper, because it sets *address-book* back to its initial value. Here is a third assignment:

(**set!** *address-book* (cons (list 'Adam 1) *address-book*))

It helps us gain some understanding of how functions can change the value of *address-book* in a useful manner. Because *address-book* stands for a list of lists, (cons (list 'Adam 1) *address-book*) constructs a longer list of the right kind. Hence the **set!** expression just changes the state variable to stand for a different value in the class of (**listof** (list *symbol number*)).

A program that controls a traffic light should have a state variable for the current color of the traffic light. This variable should assume one of three values: 'red, 'green, or 'yellow, which suggests a data definition:

A *TL-color* is either 'green, 'yellow, or 'red.

Here is the variable definition with a contract and purpose statement:

;; *current-color* : TL-color
;; to keep track of the current color of the traffic light
(**define** *current-color* 'red)

As before, the expression

(**set!** *current-color* 5)

is nonsensical because 5 is not one of the three legitimate symbols mentioned in the contract. In contrast,

(**set!** *current-color* 'green)

is perfectly okay.

The right-hand side of an assignment does not have to consist of a value or an expression that almost instantaneously produces a value. In many cases it makes sense to use a function to compute the new value. Here is a function that computes the next color for our traffic light:

```
;; next-color : TL-color → TL-color
;; to compute the next color for a traffic light
(define (next-color c)
  (cond
    [(symbol=? 'red c) 'green]
    [(symbol=? 'green c) 'yellow]
    [(symbol=? 'yellow c) 'red]))
```

Using this function, we can now write an assignment that switches the state of *current-color* appropriately:

```
(set! current-color (next-color current-color))
```

Because *current-color* is one of the three legitimate symbols, we can apply *next-color* to the value of *current-color*. The function also produces one of these three symbols, so that the next state of *current-color* is again proper.

## 36.3   Functions that Initialize Memory

After we have developed contracts and purpose statements for the state variables of a program, we immediately define a function that sets the state variables to proper values. We call this function an INITIALIZATION FUNC-TION or an INITIALIZER. A program's *initializer* is the first function that is used during an execution; a program may also provide other means to invoke the initializer.

For our current examples, the initializers are straightforward. Here is one for the address-book example:

```
;; init-address-book : → void
(define (init-address-book)
  (set! address-book empty))
```

The one for traffic-light is equally trivial:

```
;; init-traffic-light : → void
(define (init-traffic-light)
  (set! current-color 'red))
```

In setting *current-color* to 'red, we follow a conventional rule of engineering to put devices into their least harmful state when starting it up.[70]

At first glance, these initializers don't seem to add much to our programs. Both set the respective state variables to the values that are their defined values. For both cases, however, it is easy to see that the initializer could do some additional useful work. The first one, for example, could create and display the graphical user interface for an address book; the second one could create and display a canvas that displays the current state of the traffic light.

## 36.4 Functions that Change Memory

Once we have the state variables and their initializers in place, we turn our attention to the design of functions that modify a program's memory. Unlike the functions in the preceding parts of the book, the memory-changing functions not only consume and produce data, they also affect the definitions of the state variables. We therefore speak of the EFFECT that functions have on the state variables.

Let us now take a look at the stages of our most basic design recipe and how we can accommodate effects on state variables:

**Data Analysis:** Even functions that affect the state of variables consume and (possibly) produce data. Thus we still need to analyze how to represent information and, if necessary, introduce structure and data definitions.

For example, the traffic-light example benefits from the data definition for *TL-color* (see above).

**Contract, Purpose, and Effect:** The first major change concerns the second step. In addition to specifying what a function consumes and produces, we must also write down which variables it affects and how it affects those state variables. The effect of a function on state variables must be consistent with the purpose statement of a variable.

Consider the traffic-light example again. It requires a function that switches the color of the traffic light in accordance with the traffic laws. The function checks the variable *current-color* and affects its state. Here is how we should specify this function:

---

[70] A device should also go into the least harmful state when it detects an internal failure. Unfortunately, many software engineers don't follow this rule.

```
;; Data Def.: A TL-color is either 'green, 'yellow, or 'red.

;; State Variable:
;; current-color : TL-color
;; to keep track of the current color of the traffic light
(define current-color 'red)

;; Contract: next : → void

;; Purpose: the function always produces (void)

;; Effect: to change current-color from 'green to 'yellow,
;; 'yellow to 'red, and 'red to 'green

;; Header: omitted for this particular example

;; Examples:
;; if current-color is 'green and we evaluate (next), then current-color is 'yellow
;; if current-color is 'yellow and we evaluate (next), then current-color is 'red
;; if current-color is 'red and we evaluate (next), then current-color is 'green

;; Template: data-directed on state-variable that is to be mutated
;; (define (f)
;;   (cond
;;     [(symbol=? 'green current-color) (set! current-color ...)]
;;     [(symbol=? 'yellow current-color) (set! current-color ...)]
;;     [(symbol=? 'red current-color) (set! current-color ...)]))

;; Definition:
(define (next)
  (cond
    [(symbol=? 'green current-color) (set! current-color 'yellow)]
    [(symbol=? 'yellow current-color) (set! current-color 'red)]
    [(symbol=? 'red current-color) (set! current-color 'green)]))

;; Tests:
(begin (set! current-color 'green) (next) (symbol=? current-color 'yellow))
(begin (set! current-color 'yellow) (next) (symbol=? current-color 'red))
(begin (set! current-color 'red) (next) (symbol=? current-color 'green))
```

Figure 100: The design recipe for state variables: A complete example

```
;; next : → void
;; effect: to change current-color from 'green to 'yellow,
;; 'yellow to 'red, and 'red to 'green
(define (next) ...)
```

The function consumes no data and always produces the invisible value; in Scheme this value is called *void*. Because the function has no purpose in the traditional sense, it is accompanied by an effect statement only.

Here is the specification for *add-to-address-book*:

```
;; add-to-address-book : symbol number → void
;; effect: to add (list name phone) to the front of address-book
(define (add-to-address-book name phone) ...)
```

We can tell from the effect statement that the definition of *address-book* is modified in a fashion that's coherent with its purpose statement and contract.

**Program Examples:** Examples are as important as ever, but formulating them has become more difficult. As before, we must develop examples that illustrate the relationship between inputs and outputs, but, because functions now have effects, we also need examples that illustrate those.

Let us return to our first running example, the *next* function for traffic lights. It affects one state-variable: *current-color*. Because this variable can stand for one of three symbols, we can actually characterize all of its possible effects with examples:

```
;; if current-color is 'green and we evaluate (next),
;; then current-color is 'yellow afterwards
```

```
;; if current-color is 'yellow and we evaluate (next),
;; then current-color is 'red afterwards
```

```
;; if current-color is 'red and we evaluate (next),
;; then current-color is 'green afterwards
```

In contrast, the state variable *address-book* can stand for an infinite number of values, so it is impossible to make up a comprehensive series of examples. But it is still important to state a few, because examples make it easier to develop the function body later:

```
;; if address-book is empty and
;; we evaluate (add-to-address-book 'Adam 1),
;; then address-book is (list (list 'Adam 1)) afterwards.

;; if address-book is (list (list 'Eve 2)) and
;; we evaluate (add-to-address-book 'Adam 1),
;; then address-book is (list (list 'Adam 1) (list 'Eve 2)) afterwards.

;; if address-book is (list E-1 ... E-2) and
;; we evaluate (add-to-address-book 'Adam 1),
;; then address-book is (list (list 'Adam 1) E-1 ... E-2) afterwards.
```

Not surprisingly, the language of examples involves words of a temporal nature. After all, assignments emphasize the notion of time in programming.

**Warning**: The state variable is never a parameter of a function. ∎

**The Template:** The template for state-changing functions is like that of an ordinary function, but the body should also contain **set!** expressions to specify the state variables that are to be modified:

```
(define (fun-for-state-change x y z)
  (set! a-state-variable ...))
```

The computation of the next value for *a-state-variable* can be left to an auxiliary function, which consumes *x*, *y*, and *z*. Our two examples fit this pattern.

On occasion, we should add selector and **cond**-expressions, based on the data definitions for the function's inputs. Consider *next* again. The data definition for its input suggests a **cond**-expression:

```
(define (next)
  (cond
    [(symbol=? 'green current-color) (set! current-color ...)]
    [(symbol=? 'yellow current-color) (set! current-color ...)]
    [(symbol=? 'red current-color) (set! current-color ...)]))
```

In this simple case, we can indeed go with either alternative and design a proper program.

**The Body:** As always, the development of the full function requires a solid understanding of the examples, of how they are computed, and of the template. For functions with effects, the completion of the **set!** expression is the most demanding step. In some cases, the right-hand side involves nothing but primitive operations, the function's parameters, and the state variable (or several of them). In others, it is best to develop an auxiliary function (without effect) that consumes the current value of the state variable and the function's parameters and that produces the new value of the state variable.

The function *add-to-address-book* is an example of the first kind. The right-hand side of the **set!**-expression consists of *address-book*, **cons**, **list**, and nothing else.

The traffic-light example, in contrast, is an example for both choices. Here is a definition that is based on the template:

```
(define (next)
  (cond
    [(symbol=? 'green current-color) (set! current-color 'yellow)]
    [(symbol=? 'yellow current-color) (set! current-color 'red)]
    [(symbol=? 'red current-color) (set! current-color 'green)]))
```

Writing one based on an auxiliary function is also straightforward:

```
(define (next)
  (set! current-color (next-color current-color)))
```

For the definition of *next-color*, see page 512.

**Testing:** In the past, we have tested functions by translating the examples into boolean-valued expressions and by adding them to the bottom of the `Definitions` window. For functions with effects, we use a similar approach, but to verify that functions have the desired effect on state variables is a complex task.

There are two ways to test functions with effects. First, we can set the state variable into a desired state, apply the function, and then check whether the function has the desired result and effect. The *next* function is a particularly good one for this approach. We characterized its

complete behavior with three examples. All three can be translated
into **begin**-expressions that test as suggested. Here is one example:

> (**begin** (**set!** *current-color* 'green)
>        (*next*)
>        (symbol=? *current-color* 'yellow))

Each line sets the state variable *current-color* to the desired color, evaluates (*next*), and then checks whether the effect is appropriate. We
can also do this for the *add-to-address-book* function, though the tests
are less comprehensive than those for *next*:

> (**begin** (**set!** *address-book* empty)
>        (*add-to-address-book* 'Adam 1)
>        (equal? '((Adam 1)) *address-book*))

In this test, we check only that *Adam* and 1 are properly added to the
initially empty list.

Second, we can capture the value of a state variable before it is tested,
apply the memory-changing function, and then conduct appropriate
tests. Consider the following expression:

> (**local** ([**define** *current-value-of address-book*])
>   (**begin**
>     (*add-to-address-book* 'Adam 1)
>     (equal? (cons (list 'Adam 1) *current-value-of*) *address-book*)))

It defines *current-value-of* to be the value of *address-book* at the beginning of the evaluation, and at the end checks that the appropriate
entry was added at the front and that nothing changed for the rest of
the value.

To conduct tests for functions with effects, especially tests of the second kind, it is useful to abstract the test expression into a function:

```
;; test-for-address-book : symbol number → boolean
;; to determine whether add-to-address-book has the appropriate
;; effect on address-book and no more than that
;; effect: same as (add-to-address-book name number)
(define (test-for-address-book name number)
  (local ([define current-value-of address-book])
    (begin
      (add-to-address-book name number)
      (equal? (cons (list name number) current-value-of)
              address-book))))
```

Using this function, we can now easily test *add-to-address-book* several times and ensure for each test that its effects are appropriate:

```
(and (test-for-address-book 'Adam 1)
     (test-for-address-book 'Eve 2)
     (test-for-address-book 'Chris 6145384))
```

The **and**-expression guarantees that the test expressions are evaluated in order and that all of them produce true.

**Future Reuse:** Once we have a complete, tested program, we should remember its existence, *what* it computes, and what its *effects* are. We do not, however, need to remember *how* it computes. If we encounter a situation that calls for the same computation and the same effects, we can reuse the program as if it were a primitive operation. **Warning**: In the presence of effects, it is much more difficult to reuse a function than in the world of algebraic programs.

Figures 100 and 101 summarize our two running examples; the header in the first one is omitted because it is useless for the purpose and effect statements in this particular case.

---

## Exercises

**Exercise 36.4.1** Modify the traffic light program in figure 100 to draw the current state of the traffic light onto a canvas. Start by adding the initializer. Use the solutions for section 6.2. ∎

;; <u>Data Def.</u>: lists of arbitrary length: (**listof** *X*), lists of two items: (list *Y Z*)

;; <u>State Variable</u>:
;; *address-book* : (**listof** (list *symbol number*))
;; to keep track of pairs of names and phone numbers
(**define** *address-book* empty)

;; <u>Contract</u>: *add-to-address-book : symbol number → void*

;; <u>Purpose</u>: the function always produces (void)

;; <u>Effect</u>: to add (list *name phone*) to the front of *address-book*

;; <u>Header</u>:
;; (**define** (*add-to-address-book name phone*) . . . )

;; <u>Examples</u>:
;; if *address-book* is empty and we evaluate
;; (*add-to-address-book* 'Adam 1), *address-book* is (list (list 'Adam 1)).
;; if *address-book* is (list (list 'Eve 2)) and we evaluate
;; (*add-to-address-book* 'Adam 1), *address-book* is (list (list 'Adam 1) (list 'Eve 2)).
;; if *address-book* is (list *E-1* . . . *E-2*) and we evaluate
;; (*add-to-address-book* 'Adam 1), *address-book* is (list (list 'Adam 1) *E-1* . . . *E-2*).

;; <u>Template</u>: omitted

;; <u>Definition</u>:
(**define** (*add-to-address-book name phone*)
    (**set!** *address-book* (cons (list *name phone*) *address-book*)))

;; <u>Tests</u>:
(**begin** (**set!** *address-book* empty)
          (*add-to-address-book* 'Adam 1)
          (equal? '((Adam 1)) *address-book*))

Figure 101: The design recipe for state variables: A second example

**Exercise 36.4.2** Modify the phone book program in figure 101 so that it offers a graphical user interface. Start by adding the initializer. Use the solution of exercise 35.4.2. ∎

# 37   Examples of Memory Usage

Designing programs with memory requires experience and practice, which, in turn, come from studying examples. In this section we study three more examples of programs that use memory. The first one illustrates the importance of initializers; the second one demonstrates how to design programs whose effects depend on conditions; and the last one shows how effects can be useful in recursive functions. The last two subsections provide opportunities for practicing what we've learned.

## 37.1   Initializing State

Recall the color-guessing game from exercise 5.1.5. One player picks two colors for two squares; we call those "targets." The other one tries to guess which color is assigned to which square; they are guesses. The first player's response to a guess is to compare the colors and to produce one of the following answers:

1. 'perfect!, if the first target is equal to the first guess and the second target is equal to the second guess;

2. 'OneColorAtCorrectPosition, if the first guess is equal to the first target or the second guess is equal to the second target;

3. 'OneColorOccurs, if either of the guesses is one of the two targets;

4. and 'NothingCorrect, otherwise.

These four answers are the only answers that the first player gives. The second player is to guess the two chosen target colors in as few guesses as possible.

To simplify the game, the choice of colors is limited: see the top of figure 102. Our goal is to develop a program that plays the role of the master player. That is, we want a program that picks the colors and checks the guesses of the second player.

The game description suggests that the program must offer two services: one for setting up two target colors and another one for checking the guesses. Naturally, each service corresponds to a function. Let's call the first *master* and the second one *master-check*. Here is a possible dialogue, based on the two functions:

---

;; <u>Constants</u>:

;; the legitimate colors
(**define** *COLORS*
   (list 'black 'white 'red 'blue 'green 'gold 'pink 'orange 'purple 'navy))

;; the number of colors
(**define** *COL#* (length *COLORS*))

;; <u>Data Definition</u>:
;; A *color* is a symbol on COLORS.

Figure 102: Guessing colors

---

> (*master*)
> (*master-check* 'red 'red)
'NothingCorrect
> (*master-check* 'black 'pink)
'OneColorOccurs

. . .

> (*master*)
> (*master-check* 'red 'red)
'perfect!

The *master* function consumes nothing and produces the invisible value; its effect is to initialize the two targets. Depending on what the chosen colors are, checking the same two guesses may produce 'perfect! or 'NothingCorrect. In other words, *master* sets up some memory that *master-check* uses.

Let us now study how the design recipe applies to the development of the program. The first step is to define the state variables and to specify the purpose of each variable. Our analysis suggests that we need two state variables, one per target:

;; *target1, target2 : color*
;; the variables represent the two colors that the first player chooses
(**define** *target1* (first *COLORS*))
(**define** *target2* (first *COLORS*))

Both variables are set to the first item from *COLORS*, so that they stand for some color.

The second step is to develop an initializer for the two state variables. A single initializer is enough because the two variables go together. Indeed, the initializer is the desired *master* function:

```
;; master : → void
;; effect: set target1 and target2 to randomly chosen items in COLORS
(define (master)
  (begin
    (set! target1 (list-ref COLORS (random COL#)))
    (set! target2 (list-ref COLORS (random COL#)))))
```

The effect comment explains how *master* changes the two state variables by picking an item from *COLORS* based on a random number between 0 and the length of *COLORS*.

Finally, we can turn to the functions that modify and utilize the program's memory. As it turns out, the memory isn't modified after the two target variables are initialized; it is only used to compare to the two guesses of the player. The only other service we need is *master-check*. It uses *check-color*, the solution of exercise 5.1.5, to conduct the comparison. For a summary, see figure 103, which contains the variable and function definitions that we just discussed.

---

```
;; target1, target2 : color
;; the two variables represent the two colors that the first player chose
(define target1 (first COLORS))
(define target2 (first COLORS))

;; master : → void
;; effect: set target1 and target2 to two randomly chosen items from COLORS
(define (master)
  (begin
    (set! target1 (list-ref COLORS (random COL#)))
    (set! target2 (list-ref COLORS (random COL#)))))

;; master-check : color color → symbol
;; to determine how many colors at how many positions are guessed correctly
;; The function defers to check-color, the solution of exercise 5.1.5.
(define (master-check guess1 guess2)
  (check-color guess1 guess2 target1 target2))
```

Figure 103: Guessing colors (Part 2)

---

---

## Exercises

**Exercise 37.1.1** Draw a diagram that shows how *master* and *master-check* interact with memory. ∎

**Exercise 37.1.2** Abstract the repeated expressions in *master* into the function *random-pick*. It consumes a list and chooses a random item from that list. Then use the function to eliminate the repeated expressions in *master*. ∎

**Exercise 37.1.3** Modify the color guessing program so that its final answer isn't just 'perfect! but a list of two items: the symbol *perfect!* and the number of guesses that the second player made. Start by modifying the diagram of exercise 37.1.1. ∎

**Exercise 37.1.4** Modify the color guessing program so that it automatically restarts the game when a player has guessed the correct target colors. ∎

**Exercise 37.1.5** Develop a graphical user interface, similar to that of the teachpack **master.ss**. Instead of colored buttons, use buttons labeled with the color. Show the current selection in message fields. ∎

---

## 37.2   State Changes from User Interactions

Recall the hangman game from 6.7. The goal of the game is to test a person's active vocabulary. One player thinks of a word and draws the noose of a gallows; the other player tries to guess the word, one letter at a time. For every wrong guess, the first player adds another part to the drawing (see figure 15): first the head, then the body, the arms, and the legs. If, however, the player's guess reveals new knowledge about the chosen word, the first player indicates where the the letter occurs in the word. The game is over when the second player guesses the complete word or when the first player has completed the stick figure.

Figure 104 contains the data definitions for letters, words, and body-parts. In particular, *PARTS* not only specifies the body parts that are drawn, but also the order in which they are drawn. The figure also defines an incomplete list of words so that the hangman program can randomly pick a word for us to guess.

```
;; Data Analysis and Definitions:

;; A letter is a symbol in: 'a ... 'z plus '_

;; A word is a (listof letter).

;; A body-part is one of the following symbols:
(define PARTS '(head body right-arm left-arm right-leg left-leg))

;; Constants:
;; some guessing words:
(define WORDS
  '((h e l l o)
    (w o r l d)
    (i s)
    (a)
    (s t u p i d)
    (p r o g r a m)
    (a n d)
    (s h o u l d)
    (n e v e r)
    (b e)
    (u s e d)
    (o k a y)
    ...
    ))

;; the number of words we can choose from
(define WORDS# (length WORDS))
```

Figure 104: Hangman Basics

The random picking of words occurs at the beginning of the game, which suggests a random initialization function, similar to that of the color-guessing program in the preceding section. In contrast to the latter, the hangman program must also remember the number of guesses that a player made, because there is only a limited number of them. After 'left-leg is drawn, the game is over. Counting down the number of body parts also implies that as the program checks each guess, it must inform the player not only what the guess revealed but also which body part, if any, was lost.

Let us capture this thought in a data definition that specifies the legitimate class of responses:

---

A *response* is either

1. "You won"

2. (list "The End" *word*)

3. (list "Good guess!" *word*)

4. (list "Sorry" *body-part word*)

---

Three of the responses are lists so that the program can provide several pieces of information at once. Specifically, the first response says that filling in the guess turns the status word into the chosen word and that the player survived the game. The second response indicates the opposite; the list of available body parts is exhausted and the game is over because the player did not guess all the letters in the word. In the third case, the player's guess was successful and the second item in the list shows how much the player knows about the word. Finally, the fourth response represents a bad guess, in which case the response is a list of three items: a greeting, the lost body part, and a reminder of what the player has found about the word.

We can now imagine the role of the two services in the hangman program. The first, called *hangman*, picks a new word; the second, called *hangman-guess*, consumes a letter and produces one of the four possible responses. Here is a feasible dialogue:

```
> (hangman)
> (hangman-guess 'a)
(list "Sorry" 'head (list '_ '_ '_ '_ '_ '_))
> (hangman-guess 'i)
(list "Good guess!" (list '_ '_ '_ '_ 'i '_))
> (hangman-guess 's)
(list "Good guess!" (list 's '_ '_ '_ 'i '_))
> (hangman-guess 'i)
(list "Sorry" 'body (list 's '_ '_ '_ 'i '_))
...
> (hangman)
> (hangman-guess 'a)
"You won"
```

The dialogue consists of two rounds of hangman. They show that the results of *hangman-guess* depend on the prior use of *hangman*. Furthermore, the first round illustrates how *hangman-guess* applied to the same guess twice produces two different answers. This again means that *hangman-guess* modifies and uses memory, specifically, it counts down the body parts as the player makes useless guesses.

---

```
;; chosen-word : word
;; the word that the player is to guess
(define chosen-word (first WORDS))

;; status-word : word
;; represents which letters the player has and hasn't guessed
(define status-word (first WORDS))

;; body-parts-left : (listof body-part)
;; represents the list of body parts that are still "available"
(define body-parts-left PARTS)

;; hangman : → void
;; effect: initialize chosen-word, status-word, and body-parts-left
(define (hangman)
  (begin
    (set! chosen-word (list-ref WORDS (random (length WORDS))))
    (set! status-word ...)
    (set! body-parts-left PARTS)))
```

Figure 105: Hangman Basics (Part 2)

---

In addition, the dialogue shows that the player loses a body part whenever a guess doesn't contribute any new knowledge. Consider the second guess: 'i. It occurs in the penultimate position of the word and the response of *hangman-guess* says so. When the player enters 'i again as the fourth guess, *hangman-guess* detects no progress because the positions of 'i have already been revealed. In the informal description of the game, this aspect had been left open. By putting together an example, we become aware of this ambiguity and can make a decision.

Thus far, our reasoning has revealed the need for two services and three state variables:

*chosen-word*, which is the word to be guessed;

*status-word*, which records how much of the word has been guessed;

and *body-parts-left*, which remembers how many and which imaginary body parts the player can still lose.

The first two variables always stand for *words*, as their name says. A natural value for the last one is a list of body parts; indeed, the list should always be a suffix of *PARTS*.

Figure 105 contains the definitions of the state variables and their purpose statements. The first two, *chosen-word* and *status-word*, are set to the first items of WORDS, so that they represent some word. The third one is set to *PARTS* because this list represents the entire collection of available body parts.

Next we must develop an initializer for the state variables. As in the preceding section, a single initializer suffices. It is the *hangman* function, and its purpose is to set up the program's memory. Specifically, it picks a word for *chosen-word*, and it sets *status-word* and *body-parts-left* to values that reflect that the game has just begun. The last one is easy because *PARTS* is the appropriate list. The initial value for *status-word* requires a short analysis. First, the value must be a word. Second, it must consist of as many letters as *chosen-word*. Finally, each of the letters is unknown, because the player hasn't made any guesses yet. Thus, the matching action is to build a word as long as *chosen-word* from '_.

---

### Exercises

**Exercise 37.2.1** Develop the function *make-status-word*, which consumes a word and produces an equally long word consisting of just '_. Use the function to complete the definition of *hangman* in figure 105. ∎

**Exercise 37.2.2** Use build-list to create the status word in a single expression. Complete the definition of *hangman* in figure 105. ∎

---

Now we are ready to deal with the most difficult part: the design of *hangman-guess*, a function that uses and modifies the memory. It consumes a letter and produces an answer, specifically a *response*, which depends on how the current value of *status-word*, *chosen-word*, and *guess* compare. At the same time, the function must affect the state variable *status-word* if the player's guess added new knowledge. If not, the function must shorten *body-parts-left*, the list of available body parts. The matching contract, purpose, and effect statements are as follows:

```
;; hangman-guess : letter → response
;; to determine whether the player has won, lost, or may continue to
;; play and, if no progress was made, which body part was lost
;; effect:
;; (1) if the guess represents progress, update status-word
;; (2) if not, shorten the body-parts-left by one
```

We have already considered a sample dialogue that illustrates the workings of *hangman-guess*. By dissecting this dialogue, we can develop specific examples for *hangman-guess*.

The sample dialogue and the purpose/effect statements imply that the result of *hangman-guess* depends on whether or not the guess constitutes progress and, if not, whether or not the guess was the last one. Let's use these distinctions for the development of examples:

1. If *status-word* is (list 'b '_ '_ '_) and *chosen-word* is (list 'b 'a 'l 'l), then evaluating

   (*hangman-guess* 'l)

   produces (list "Good guess!" (list 'b '_ 'l 'l)) and *status-word* becomes (list 'b '_ 'l 'l).

2. If *status-word* is (list 'b '_ 'l 'l) and *chosen-word* is (list 'b 'a 'l 'l), then evaluating

   (*hangman-guess* 'a)

   produces "You won". The evaluation has no effect in this case.

3. If *status-word* is (list 'b '_ 'l 'l), *chosen-word* is (list 'b 'a 'l 'l), and *body-parts-left* is (list 'right-leg 'left-leg), then evaluating

   (*hangman-guess* 'l)

   produces (list "Sorry" 'right-leg (list 'b '_ 'l 'l)) and *body-parts-left* becomes (list 'left-leg).

4. Finally, if *status-word* is (list 'b '_ 'l 'l), *chosen-word* is (list 'b 'a 'l 'l), and *body-parts-left* is (list 'left-leg), then evaluating

   (*hangman-guess* 'l)

   produces (list "The End" (list 'b 'a 'l 'l)) and *body-parts-left* becomes empty.

The first two examples illustrate what happens when the player enters a guess that reveals new information; the last two focus on those cases where the guess contributes nothing.

The case split naturally suggests a basic template based on a distinction between the possible situations:

```
(define (hangman-guess guess)
  (cond
    [... ;; guess did reveal new information:
     (cond
       [... ;; guess completed the search for the word
        ...]
       [... ;; guess did not complete the search for the word
        (begin
          (set! status-word ...)
          ...)])]
    [... ;; guess did not reveal any new information:
     (begin
       (set! body-parts-left ...)
       ... )]))
```

The location of the **set!**-expressions in the template's nested **cond**s specify exactly under which conditions effects happen. First, the outermost conditional distinguishes whether or not *guess* produces new knowledge about the hidden word; if it doesn't, the function must modify *body-parts-left*. Second, if *guess* reveals new knowledge, the function updates the *status-word* variable unless the player has just finished the entire word.

Because we haven't considered yet how to express these tests, we use comments to indicate what the conditions are. Let us turn to this problem first, so that we can start the function-definition step with a full-fledged template. The first missing condition concerns the question whether *guess* reveals new information. To this end, we must compare *guess* with the letters in *chosen-word*. This comparison should produce the new status word.

Here is the specification for the auxiliary function that conducts this computation:

;; *reveal-list : word word letter → word*
;; to compute the new status word from *chosen-word,*
;; *status-word*, and *guess*
(**define** (*reveal-list chosen-word status-word guess*) ...)

Fortunately, we have discussed this auxiliary function twice before (see sections 6.7 and exercise 17.6.2) and know how to define it; figure 106 contains a suitable definition. Using *reveal-list*, we can now formulate a condition that determines whether *guess* reveals new knowledge:

(equal? *status-word* (*reveal-list status-word chosen-word guess*))

The condition uses equal? to compare the current value of *status-word* with its new value, as computed by *reveal-list*. If the two lists are equal, *guess* doesn't produce new knowledge; otherwise it does.

The second missing condition concerns the question whether the given *guess* completes the search for the word. If *guess* is equal to all missing letters in *status-word*, then the player has found the complete word. Here is the corresponding condition:

(equal? *chosen-word* (*reveal-list status-word chosen-word guess*))

That is, the game is over if *chosen-word* is equal to the result of *reveal-list*.

Let's put everything together in a single template:

```
(define (hangman-guess guess)
  (local ((define new-status (reveal-list status-word chosen-word guess)))
    (cond
      [(equal? new-status status-word)
       (begin
         (set! body-parts-left ...)
         ... )]
      [else
       (cond
         [(equal? new-status chosen-word)
          ...]
         [else
          (begin
            (set! status-word ...)
            ...)])])))
```

The template uses a **local**-expression because the result of *reveal-list* is used twice. Also, the two outer **cond**-clauses are swapped because it is more natural to write (equal? *new-status status-word*) than its negation. We can now turn to the function-design step.

Because the template is conditional, we develop each clause separately:

1. Assume that (equal? *new-status status-word*) evaluates to true, that is, the player made no progress. This implies that the player loses an imaginary body part. To capture this effect, the **set!**-expression must change the value of *body-parts-left*. Specifically, it must set the state variable to the rest of its current value:

   (**set!** *body-parts-left* (rest *body-parts-left*))

   The answer depends on the new value of *body-parts-left*. If it is empty, the game is over; the appropriate response is (list "The End" *chosen-word*) so that the player finds out what the chosen word was. If *body-parts-left* is not empty, the response is (list "Sorry" *??? status-word*). The response says that *guess* is useless. Its last part is the current value of *status-word* so that the player sees what he has discovered. The *???* indicates a problem. To understand the problem, take a look at what we have:

   (**begin**
     (**set!** *body-parts-left* (rest *body-parts-left*))
     (**cond**
       [(empty? *body-parts-left*) (list "The End" *chosen-word*)]
       [**else** (list "Sorry" *??? status-word*)]))

   In principle, the question marks should be the body part that the player just lost to the gallows. But, because **set!** modifies *body-parts-left*, we can no longer just say (first *body-parts-left*). As mentioned in section 35.2, when programming with **set!** timing matters. We can solve the problem with a **local**-expression that names the first item on *body-parts-left* before the state variable is modified.

2. The second case is much simpler than the first. We distinguish two subcases:

   (a) If *new-status* is equal to *chosen-word*, the player has won. The response is "You won"; there is no effect.

(b) If the two are not equal, the player made some progress and must be told. Furthermore, the function must keep track of the progress; a (**set!** *status-word new-status*) accomplishes this effect. The response consists of an encouragement and the new status.

Figure 106 contains the complete definition of *hangman-guess*.

---

```
;; hangman-guess : letter → response
;; to determine whether the player has won, lost, or may continue to play
;; and, if so, which body part was lost, if no progress was made
;; effects: (1) if the guess represents progress, update status-word
;; (2) if not, shorten the body-parts-left by one
(define (hangman-guess guess)
  (local ((define new-status (reveal-list chosen-word status-word guess)))
    (cond
      [(equal? new-status status-word)
       (local ((define next-part (first body-parts-left)))
         (begin
           (set! body-parts-left (rest body-parts-left))
           (cond
             [(empty? body-parts-left) (list "The End" chosen-word)]
             [else (list "Sorry" next-part status-word)])))]
      [else
       (cond
         [(equal? new-status chosen-word) "You won"]
         [else
          (begin
            (set! status-word new-status)
            (list "Good guess!" status-word))])])))

;; reveal-list : word word letter → word
;; to compute the new status word
(define (reveal-list chosen-word status-word guess)
  (local ((define (reveal-one chosen-letter status-letter)
            (cond
              [(symbol=? chosen-letter guess) guess]
              [else status-letter])))
    (map reveal-one chosen-word status-word)))
```

Figure 106: Hangman Basics (Part 3)

---

**Exercises**

**Exercise 37.2.3** Draw a diagram that shows how *hangman* and *hangman-guess* interact with the state variables. ∎

**Exercise 37.2.4** Formulate the four examples for *hangman-guess* as boolean-valued expressions that produce true if *hangman-guess* is correct. Develop an additional example for each case; turn these new examples into additional tests. ∎

**Exercise 37.2.5** Develop a graphical user interface, similar to that of the teachpack **hangman.ss**. Connect the functions in this section as call-backs. ∎

**Exercise 37.2.6** Modify the program so that it keeps track of all the guesses. Then, if a player enters the same guess twice for the same round of a hangman game, the response of *hangman-guess* is "You have used this guess before." ∎

**Exercise 37.2.7** Consider the following variant of *reveal-list!*:

```
;; reveal-list! : letter → void
;; effect: to modify status-word based on a comparison of chosen-word,
;; the status-word, and the player's guess
(define (reveal-list! cw sw guess)
  (local ((define (reveal-one chosen-letter status-letter)
            (cond
              [(symbol=? chosen-letter guess) guess]
              [else status-letter])))
    (set! status-word (map reveal-one cw sw))))
```

It changes the state variable *status-word* to a value that is computed from the old value of *status-word*, *chosen-word*, and the guess.

Modify *hangman-guess* so that it works properly with the *reveal-list!* function. ∎

## 37.3  State Changes from Recursion

Functions that affect the memory of a program may not only process simple forms of data but also arbitrarily large pieces of data. To understand how this works, let us take a closer look at the purpose of *reveal-list* from the hangman game program.

As we have just seen, the function compares *guess* with each letter in *chosen-word*. If it is the same, *guess* may uncover new knowledge and is included at the appropriate position in the word; otherwise, the corresponding letter from *status-word* represents what the player knows.

The *hangman-guess* function then compares the result of *reveal-list* with the old value of *status-word* to find out whether the player uncovered new knowledge. Furthermore, the result is compared with *chosen-word* again if the player found new knowledge, because *guess* might have matched all remaining unknown letters. Clearly, both of these comparisons repeat the computations of *reveal-one*. The problem is that the result of *reveal-one* is useful to *reveal-list* and that the result of its individual comparisons are useful in the conditionals of *hangman-guess*.

We can solve the first part of the problem with the use of an additional piece of memory: a state variable that records whether *reveal-one* uncovers a letter. The state variable, let's call it *new-knowledge*, is modified by *reveal-one* if it determines that *guess* uncovers a currently hidden letter in *chosen-word*. The *hangman-guess* function can use *new-knowledge* to find out what *reveal-one* discovered.

Let us now translate our idea into new program definitions systematically. First, we need to specify the state variable and its meaning:

```
;; new-knowledge : boolean
;; the variable represents whether the most recent application of
;; reveal-list has provided the player with new knowledge
(define new-knowledge false)
```

Second, we must consider what it means to initialize the new state variable. From what we know, the state variable is used every time *reveal-list* is applied to *guess*. When the application starts, the state variable should be false; it should change to true if *guess* is useful. This suggests that *new-knowledge* is to be initialized to false every time *reveal-list* is applied. We can achieve this reinitialization by changing *reveal-list* so that it sets the state variable before it computes anything else:

```
;; reveal-list : word word letter → word
;; to compute the new status word
;; effect: to set new-knowledge to false first
(define (reveal-list chosen-word status-word guess)
  (local ((define (reveal-one chosen-letter status-letter) ...))
    (begin
      (set! new-knowledge false)
      (map reveal-one chosen-word status-word))))
```

The underlined expression is the essential modification. The **local** expression defines the auxiliary function *reveal-one* and then evaluates the **local**'s body. The first step of the body is to initialize *new-knowledge*.

Third, we must develop the program that modifies *new-knowledge*. Here the program already exists: *reveal-list*, so our task is to modify it in such a way that it changes the state variable appropriately. Let's describe the idea with a modified effect statement:

```
;; reveal-list : word word letter → word
;; to compute the new status word
;; effect:
;; (1) to set new-knowledge to false first
;; (2) to set new-knowledge to true if guess reveals new knowledge
```

The first part of the effect is necessary for the second one; an experienced programmer may drop it.

Next we should modify the examples for the function to illustrate what kind of effects happen. The purpose of the function is to compute the new status word by checking whether *guess* occurs in the *chosen-word*. There are two basic situations depending on whether *guess* reveals new knowledge or not:

1. If *status-word* is (list 'b '_ 'l 'l) and *chosen-word* is (list 'b 'a 'l 'l), then evaluating

   *(reveal-one chosen-word status-word* 'a)

   produces (list 'b 'a 'l 'l) and *new-knowledge* is true.

2. If *status-word* is (list 'b '_ '_ '_) and *chosen-word* is (list 'b 'a 'l 'l), then evaluating

   *(reveal-one chosen-word status-word* 'x)

produces (list 'b '_ '_ '_) and *new-knowledge* is false.

3. If *status-word* is (list 'b '_ '_ '_) and *chosen-word* is (list 'b 'a 'l 'l), then evaluating

   (*reveal-one chosen-word status-word* 'l)

   produces (list 'b '_ 'l 'l) and *new-knowledge* is true.

4. Finally, if *status-word* is (list 'b '_ 'l 'l) and *chosen-word* is (list 'b 'a 'l 'l), then evaluating

   (*reveal-one chosen-word status-word* 'l)

   produces (list 'b '_ 'l 'l) and *new-knowledge* is false.

The first two examples cover the basic situations; the third one shows that if *guess* reveals several new positions in the word, *new-knowledge* also becomes true; and the last shows how guessing a letter that has been uncovered before means no new knowledge has been added.

---

```
;; reveal-list : word word letter → word
;; to compute the new status word
;; effect: to set new-knowledge to true if guess reveals new knowledge
(define (reveal-list chosen-word status-word guess)
  (local ((define (reveal-one chosen-letter status-letter)
            (cond
              [(and (symbol=? chosen-letter guess)
                    (symbol=? status-letter '_))
               (begin
                 (set! new-knowledge true)
                 guess)]
              [else status-letter])))
    (begin
      (set! new-knowledge false)
      (map reveal-one chosen-word status-word))))
```

Figure 107: The *reveal-list* function

---

Given that we already have a function, we can skip the template step and instead focus on the question of what we need to change in the existing function. The given version of *reveal-list* maps *reveal-one* over the two words, which are lists of letters. It is *reveal-one* that compares *guess* with the letters in *chosen-word* and that determines whether the player has uncovered new knowledge. Hence we must modify the auxiliary function so that it recognizes when *guess* represents new knowledge and to set *new-knowledge* to true in that case.

As it is currently defined, *reveal-one* merely compares *guess* with the letters in *chosen-word*. It does not check whether the player discovers truly new knowledge if *guess* and *chosen-letter* are the same. The letter *guess*, however, represents new knowledge only if the matching letter in the status word is still '_. This suggests the two modifications shown in figure 107. That is, *reveal-one* changes the value of *new-knowledge* if, and only if, both (symbol=? *chosen-letter guess*) and (symbol=? *status-letter* '_) are true.

In summary, we can use state variables if we wish to communicate several results from one computation to distant places. For such cases, the interface of a function is under our control but we choose to design it such that the function has both a result and an effect. The proper way to achieve these combinations is to develop the computations separately and to merge them later, if necessary.

## Exercises

**Exercise 37.3.1** Draw a diagram that shows how *hangman*, *hangman-guess*, and *reveal-list* interact with the state variables. ∎

**Exercise 37.3.2** Turn the three examples into tests, that is, boolean-valued expressions, and test the new version of *reveal-list*. How many times does *reveal-one* modify *new-knowledge* for the third test case? ∎

**Exercise 37.3.3** Modify *hangman-guess* in the hangman program to take advantage of the additional information that *reveal-list* provides through *new-knowledge*. ∎

**Exercise 37.3.4** Modify the hangman program a second time to eliminate the second equal? in *hangman-guess*. **Hint:** Introduce a state variable that counts how many letters the player doesn't know yet. ∎

Let us study a second example of a function that consumes an arbitrarily large piece of data and modifies the program's memory. The example is a natural extension of the traffic light simulator in section 36. We developed two functions:

;; *init-traffic-light :* → *void*
;; effects: (1) to initialize *current-color*; (2) to draw traffic light

and

;; *next :* → *void*
;; effects: (1) to change *current-color* from 'green to 'yellow,
;; 'yellow to 'red, and 'red to 'green
;; (2) to redraw the traffic light appropriately

The first one starts the process; with the second one, we can repeatedly switch the state of the light by evaluating (*next*) in the Interactions window.

Typing in (*next*) over and over again is tiring, so it is natural to wonder how to write a program that switches the state of the traffic light 100 or 1000 or 10000 times. In other words, we should develop a program—let's call it *switch*—that consumes a natural number and that switches the light from one color to another that many times.

The function consumes a natural number and produces (void), after it succeeds in switching the traffic light a sufficient number of times. By now we can immediately write down all the basics, including the template, for a function that consumes a natural number:

;; *switch :* **N** → *void*
;; purpose: it computes nothing of interest
;; effect: switch the traffic light *n* times,
;; holding each color for three seconds
(**define** (*switch n*)
  (**cond**
    [(zero? *n*) ... ]
    [**else** ... (*switch* (− *n* 1)) ... ]))

The template is that of a conventional, structurally recursive function.

Making up an example is also straightforward. If we evaluate (*switch* 4), we wish to see a change from 'red to 'yellow, 'green, and 'red again, with each stage visible for three seconds.

Defining the full function based on the template is straightforward. We proceed by cases. If *n* is 0, the answer is (void). Otherwise, we know that

(*switch* (− *n* 1))

simulates all the necessary switching actions but one. To accomplish this
one additional switch, the function must use (*next*) to perform all the state
changes and the change of canvas and must wait three seconds. If we put
everything together in a **begin**-expression, things happen in the right order:

```
(begin (sleep-for-a-while 3)
       (next)
       (switch (− n 1)))
```

The top of figure 108 is the complete definition for *switch*.

```
;; switch : N → void
;; effect: switch the traffic light n times, holding each color for 3 seconds
;; structural recursion
(define (switch n)
  (cond
    [(= n 0) (void)]
    [else (begin (sleep-for-a-while 3)
                 (next)
                 (switch (− n 1)))]))

;; switch-forever : → void
;; effect: switch the traffic light forever, holding each color for 3 seconds
;; generative recursion
(define (switch-forever)
  (begin (sleep-for-a-while 3)
         (next)
         (switch-forever)))
```

Figure 108: Two ways of switching traffic lights

An alternative is to switch the traffic light forever or at least until it
breaks because of some external event. In this case, the simulator does
not consume any argument and, when applied, runs forever. This is the
simplest form of generative recursion we can possibly encounter:

```
;; switch-forever : → void
;; effect: switch the traffic light forever,
;; holding each color for 3 seconds
(define (switch-forever)

   ...

   (switch-forever))
```

Because the program does not terminate under any conditions, the template contains only one recursive call. This suffices to construct an eternally looping function.

Using this template, we can define the complete function as before. Before recurring, the function must sleep and switch the light with *next*. We can accomplish this with a **begin**-expression, as shown in the bottom definition of figure 108.

In summary, when we must develop recursive functions that modify the program's memory, we choose the design recipe that best matches our situation and proceed accordingly. In particular, if the function has both an interesting purpose and an effect, as for example *reveal-list*, we should first develop the pure function and then add the effects later.

## Exercises

**Exercise 37.3.5** In section 30.2, we discussed how to search for routes in simple graphs. The Scheme representation of a simple graph is a list of pairs (of symbols). The pairs specify the direct connections between the nodes in the graph. Each node is the beginning of exactly one connection, but may be the end of several such connections or none. Given two nodes in a simple graph, the problem is to find out whether one can go from the first to the second.

Recall our first attempt at a function that determines whether the route exists (see also figure 86):

```
;; route-exists? : node node simple-graph → boolean
;; to determine whether there is a route from orig to dest in sg
;; generative recursion
(define (route-exists? orig dest sg)
  (cond
    [(symbol=? orig dest) true]
    [else (route-exists? (neighbor orig sg) dest sg)]))
```

The function checks whether the origination and destination nodes are the same. If not, it generates a new problem by looking up the neighbor of the origination node in the graph.

On occasion, *route-exists?* fails to produce an answer if the graph contains a cycle. In section 30.2 we solved the problem with an accumulator. It is also possible to solve it with a state variable that keeps track of the origination nodes that *route-exists?* has visited for one particular attempt. Modify the function appropriately. ∎

**Exercise 37.3.6** In section 16.2, we developed several simple models of a computer's file system. Develop the function *dir-listing*, which consumes a directory and produces a list of all file names in the directory and all of its subdirectories. The function also sets the state variable *how-many-directories* to the number of subdirectories it encounters during the process. ∎

## 37.4    Finger Exercises on State Changes

**Exercise 37.4.1** Modify *check-guess-for-list* from exercise 9.5.5 so that it also counts how many times the player has clicked on the "Check" button of the interface. **Hint:** The call-back function for the button uses *check-guess-for-list* once per click. ∎

**Exercise 37.4.2** Develop a program that manages a task queue. The program should support at least four services:

1. *enter*, which adds a task to end of the queue;

2. *next*, which determines the next task in the queue, if any;

3. *remove*, which removes the first task from the queue, if any;

4. and *count*, which computes the number of items in the queue.

A user should start the task manager with *start-task-manager*.

After the program is developed and tested, use **gui.ss** to develop a graphical user interface to the task manager. The interface should start up with a friendly message and should always display the first task in the queue and the number of items in the queue:

Unless the queue is empty, clicking the "Next" button should remove an item from the queue and display the first item in the remainder of the queue. If the queue is empty, clicking the "Next" button should have no effect.

**Hint:** The greeting and the year are two separate message items. ∎

**Exercise 37.4.3** In section 10.3, we developed a program that moves pictures across a canvas. A picture is a list of shapes; the program consists of functions that draws, erases, and translates pictures. The main function is *move* (exercise 10.3.6). It consumes a picture and a number *n*. It produces a new picture, moved by *n* pixels; it also erases the original picture and draws the new one.

Develop the program *drive*. It draws a (fixed) picture on a canvas and permits players to move the picture left or right by a player-specified number of pixels.

Modify *drive* so that it also keeps track of some given amount of fuel. A move by one pixel should consume a fixed amount of fuel. ∎

**Exercise 37.4.4** Modify the two functions that control the state of a single traffic light so that they control the state of the two traffic lights at an ordinary intersection. Each light can assume one of three states: 'red, 'green, and 'yellow. When one is 'green or 'yellow, the other one must be 'red.

Recall the basics about the two functions for a single traffic light:

;; *init-traffic-light* : → *void*
;; effects: (1) to initialize *current-color*; (2) to draw traffic light

and

;; *next* : → *void*
;; effects: (1) to change *current-color* from 'green to 'yellow,
;; 'yellow to 'red, and 'red to 'green
;; (2) to redraw the traffic light appropriately

Modify the basics first.

When the program is developed and tested, develop a graphical display like the following:

Use the functions *init-traffic-light* and *next* to drive the display, but keep the functions that display information separate from these two functions. ∎

**Exercise 37.4.5** In sections 14.4 and 17.7 we developed an evaluator for a portion of Scheme. A typical Scheme implementation also provides an INTERACTIVE user interface. In DrScheme, the `Interactions` window plays this role.

An interactive system prompts the reader for definitions and expressions, evaluates them appropriately, and possibly produces some result. Definitions are added to some repository; to confirm the addition, the interactive system may produce a value like true. Expressions are evaluated relative to the definition repository. The function *interpret-with-defs* from section 17.7 performs this role.

Develop an interaction system around *interpret-with-defs*. The system should provide at least two services:

1. *add-definition*, which adds (the representation of) some function definition to the system's repository;

2. *evaluate*, which consumes (the representation of) some expression and evaluates it relative to the current repository.

If a user adds two (or more) definitions for some function $f$, the last addition is the one that matters. The previous ones can be ignored. ∎

## 37.5 Extended Exercise: Exploring Places

Early computer games asked players to find their way through dangerous mazes and caves. The player wanders from cave to cave, finds treasures, encounters creatures of all kinds, fights, kisses, picks up energy, and eventually reaches paradise. This section lays out the basics of such a game, using our iterative approach to program design.

Our tour takes place at one of the scariest places of all: campus. A campus consists of buildings, some more dangerous than others. Each building has a name and is connected to a group of other buildings.

The player is always in a building. We refer to this building as the *current location*. To find out more about the location, the player can ask for a picture of the building and for the list of connections. The player can also move to one of the connected buildings by issuing a *go* command.

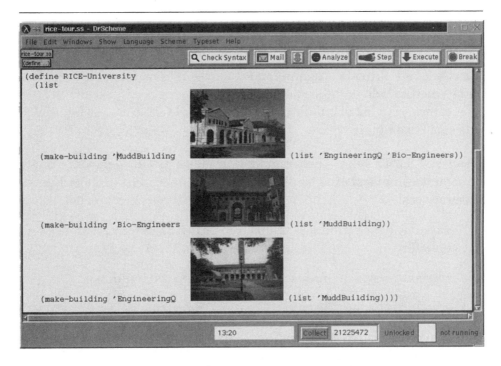

Figure 109: A tour of a university

Figure 110: Take the tour

---

**Exercises**

**Exercise 37.5.1** Provide structure and data definitions for buildings. Include a picture field in the structure.

A campus is a list of buildings. Define a sample campus. See figure 109 for a small example. ∎

**Exercise 37.5.2** Develop a program that permits a player to move through the sample campus of exercise 37.5.1. The program should support at least three services:

1. *show-me*, which produces the picture of the current location: see figure 110;

2. *where-to-go*, which produces the list of connected buildings;

3. *go*, which changes the current location of the player.

If the player issues the command (*go s*) and *s* is not connected to the current location, the function must report an error. Develop other functions as necessary or as desired. ∎

---

Players of early maze games could also gather objects and trade objects at the various sites. Specifically, the player had a bag for carrying objects, and each site contained objects that the player could trade for things in the bag.

---

**Exercises**

**Exercise 37.5.3** Modify the tour program so that each building contains one object. Furthermore, the player should have a *bag* that contains (at most) one object. At each location, the player can pick up an object, if the bag is empty, or swap the object in the bag for the object in the building otherwise.

Modify the program further so that the player can carry an arbitrary number of objects in the bag. ∎

---

The three exercises in this section illustrate how maze games work. From here it is easy to experiment with various flavors of the game. Taking a walk from one building to another may take some energy, and the player may have only a finite amount of energy. Creatures may fight or kiss the player, which consumes or replenishes the player's energy level. Use your imagination to extend the game and have friends take the tour.

# Intermezzo 7: The Final Syntax and Semantics

With the introduction of **set!**-expressions and **begin**-expressions we have covered most of Scheme's kernel language. In DrScheme, this portion is called `Advanced Student Scheme`. Considering the complexity of **set!**, this is a good place to summarize our programming language in the spirit of intermezzo 1. Following the organization of that intermezzo, we discuss the vocabulary, the grammar, and the meaning of `Advanced Student` Scheme. The last subsection explains what kind of errors we may encounter in `Advanced Student` Scheme.

## The Vocabulary of Advanced Scheme

The foundation of any language is its vocabulary. In `Beginning Student` Scheme, we distinguish four categories of words: variables, constants, primitive functions, and keywords. The classification ignores parentheses but we know that every compound phrase is surrounded by a pair of parentheses, and that every atomic phrase stands on its own.

   `Advanced Student` Scheme respects this basic classification, though it contains four important new keywords: **local**, **lambda**, **set!**, and **begin**. The first two are important for organizing and abstracting programs; the last two are important for the computation of effects. Still, keywords per se have no meaning. They are road signs that tell us what is ahead so that we can orient ourselves. It is the grammar and the meaning of a language that explains the role of the keywords.

## The Grammar of Advanced Scheme

Even though Scheme is a full-fledged language with as much power as any other programming language, its designers have kept its grammar simple. The grammar of `Advanced Student` Scheme, which is most of Scheme, is only a few lines longer than that of `Beginning Student` Scheme.

   Figure 111 contains the essential grammar of the `Advanced Student` Scheme language.[71] It extends `Intermediate Student` Scheme with three new forms of expressions: **lambda**-expressions, **set!**-expressions, and **begin**-expressions. The specification of **local**-expressions refers to the category of definitions, which refers back to the category of expressions. A

---

[71]The grammar misses **and**-expression and **or**-expression, and a few other short-cuts.

$$
\begin{aligned}
\langle def \rangle \;=\; & (\textbf{define}\; (\langle var \rangle\; \langle var \rangle \ldots \langle var \rangle)\; \langle exp \rangle) \\
\mid\; & (\textbf{define}\; \langle var \rangle\; \langle exp \rangle) \\
\mid\; & (\textbf{define-struct}\; \langle var0 \rangle\; (\langle var\text{-}1 \rangle \ldots \langle var\text{-}n \rangle))
\end{aligned}
$$

$$
\begin{aligned}
\langle exp \rangle \;=\; & \langle var \rangle \\
\mid\; & \langle con \rangle \\
\mid\; & \langle prm \rangle \\
\mid\; & (\langle exp \rangle\; \langle exp \rangle \ldots \langle exp \rangle) \\
\mid\; & (\textbf{cond}\; (\langle exp \rangle\; \langle exp \rangle)) \ldots ((\langle exp \rangle\; \langle exp \rangle)) \\
\mid\; & (\textbf{cond}\; (\langle exp \rangle\; \langle exp \rangle)) \ldots (\textbf{else}\; \langle exp \rangle))) \\
\mid\; & (\textbf{local}\; (\langle def \rangle \ldots \langle def \rangle)\; \langle exp \rangle) \\
\mid\; & (\textbf{lambda}\; (\langle var \rangle \ldots \langle var \rangle)\; \langle exp \rangle) \\
\mid\; & (\textbf{set!}\; \langle var \rangle\; \langle exp \rangle) \\
\mid\; & (\textbf{begin}\; \langle exp \rangle \ldots \langle exp \rangle)
\end{aligned}
$$

Figure 111: Advanced Student Scheme: The core grammar

---

**lambda**-expression consists of a sequence of variables, enclosed in parentheses, and an expression. Similarly, a **set!**-expression consists of a variable and an expression. Finally, a **begin**-expression is just a sequence of expressions prefixed with the keyword **begin** to distinguish it from an application.

Since functions are values now, the grammar of Advanced Student Scheme is also simpler than that of Beginning Student Scheme in one regard. Specifically, it merges the lines for primitive and function application into a single line. The new line specifies applications, which are now sequences of expressions enclosed in parentheses. Owing to the inclusion of primitive operations into the set of expressions,

   (+ 1 2)

is still an expression. After all, + is now an expression, and so are 1 and 2. The application of **define**d functions works similarly:

   (*f* 1 2)

The first expression is a variable, and the others are numbers. The application is thus a legal expression.

Unfortunately, a language grammar can only specify the large contours of what is a legal sentence construction. It cannot express restrictions that require some knowledge about the context of a phrase. `Advanced Student` Scheme requires a few such restrictions:

1. In a **lambda**-expression no variable may occur twice in the parameter sequence.

2. In a **local**-expression no definition may introduce the same variable as any other definition in the same sequence.

3. A **set!**-expression must occur in the lexical scope of a **define** that introduces the **set!**-expression's left-hand side.

In addition, the old restriction applies that keywords cannot be used as variables.

Consider the following definition, which uses the new constructs:

```
(define switch
  (local ((define-struct hide (it))
          (define state (make-hide 1)))
    (lambda ()
      (begin
        (set! state (make-hide (- 1 (hide-it state))))
        state))))
```

The definition introduces the variable *switch*. The right-hand side of the definition is a **local**-expression. It in turn defines the structure *hide* and the variable *state*, which stands for an instance of *hide*. The body of the **local**-expression is a **lambda**-expression, whose parameter sequence is empty. The function's body consists of a **begin**-expression with two expressions: a **set!**-expression and an expression that consists of just the variable *state*.

All expressions in our program satisfy the necessary restrictions. First, the **local**-expression introduces four names that are distinct: `make-hide`, `hide?`, `hide-it`, and *state*. Second, the parameter list of the **lambda**-expression is empty, so there is no possible conflict. Finally, the **set!**-expression's variable is the **local**ly defined variable *state*, so it is legal, too.

## Exercises

**Exercise 38.2.1** Determine whether the following phrases are syntactically legal or illegal programs:

1. (**define** (*f* *x*)
    (**begin**
      (**set!** *y* *x*)
      *x*))

2. (**define** (*f* *x*)
    (**begin**
      (**set!** *f* *x*)
      *x*))

3. (**local** ((**define-struct** *hide* (*it*))
            (**define** make-hide 10))
      (hide? 10))

4. (**local** ((**define-struct** *loc* (*con*))
            (**define** *loc* 10))
      (loc? 10))

5. (**define** *f*
    (**lambda** (*x* *y* *x*)
      (∗ *x* *y* *z*)))

   (**define** *z* 3.14)

Explain why a phrase is legal or illegal. ∎

## The Meaning of Advanced Scheme

When we first used Advanced Student Scheme, we did so because we wanted to deal with functions as ordinary values. The evaluation rules barely changed. We just agreed to allow expressions in the first position of an application and to deal with the names of functions as values.

The extension of the language with **set!**-expressions required another change to our rules. Now definitions that associate variables and values can change over the course of an evaluation. The informal rules we've used so far deal with changes to the definition of state variables, because they matter the most. But the rules are informal and imprecise, so a precise description of how the addition of **set!** changes the meaning of the language must be our primary concern.

Let's recall how we determine the meaning of a program. A program consists of two parts: a collection of definitions and an expression. The goal is to evaluate the expression, which means to determine the expression's value.[72] In Beginning Student Scheme, the collection of values consists of all the constants plus lists. Only one list has a concise representation: the empty one. All other lists are written down as a series of constructed lists.

The evaluation of an expression consists of a series of steps. At each step we use the laws of arithmetic and algebra to simplify a subexpression. This yields another expression. We also say that we REWRITE the first expression into the second. If the second expression is a value, we are finished.

The introduction of **set!**-expressions into our programming language requires a few small adjustments and extensions to this process:

1. Instead of rewriting just an expression, we must now rewrite definitions and expressions. More precisely, each step changes the expression and possibly the definition of a state variable. To make these effects as obvious as possible, each stage in an evaluation displays the definitions of state variables and the current expression.

2. Furthermore, it is no longer possible to apply the laws of arithmetic and algebra whenever or wherever we want. Instead, we must determine the subexpression that we must evaluate if we wish to make progress. This rule still leaves us with choices. For example, when we rewrite an expression such as

   (+ (∗ 3 3) (∗ 4 4))

   we may choose to evaluate (∗ 3 3) and then (∗ 4 4) or vice versa. Fortunately, for such simple expressions, the choice doesn't affect the final outcome, so we don't have to supply a complete unambigous rule. In general, though, we rewrite subexpressions in a left-to-right and top-to-bottom order. At each stage in the evaluation, we best start by underlining the subexpression that must be evaluated next.

3. Suppose the underlined subexpression is a **set!**-expression. By the restrictions on **set!**-expressions, we know that there is a **define** for the left-hand side of the subexpression. That is, we face the following situation:

---

[72]We also evaluate the right-hand side of definitions if they are not values, but we can safely ignore this minor issue here.

$$
\begin{array}{l}
(\textbf{define } x \; aValue) \\
\quad \ldots \\
\ldots \; \underline{(\textbf{set! } x \; anotherValue)} \ldots \\
= (\textbf{define } x \; anotherValue) \\
\quad \ldots \\
\ldots \; (\textsf{void}) \ldots
\end{array}
$$

The equation indicates that the program changes in two ways. First, the variable definition is modified. Second, the underlined **set!**-expression is replaced by (void), the invisible value.

4. The next change concerns the replacement of variables in expressions with the value in their definition. Until now, we could replace a variable with its value wherever we thought it was convenient or necessary. Indeed, we just thought of the variable as a shorthand for the value. With **set!**-expressions in the language, this is no longer possible. After all, the evaluation of a **set!**-expression modifies the definition of a state variable, and if we replace a variable with its value at the wrong time, we get the wrong value.

   Suppoe that the underlined expression is a (state) variable. Then we know that we can't make any progress in our evaluation until we have replaced the variable with the current value in its definition. This suggests the following revised law for variable evaluation:

$$
\begin{array}{l}
(\textbf{define } x \; aValue) \\
\quad \ldots \\
\ldots \; \underline{x} \ldots \\
= (\textbf{define } x \; aValue) \\
\quad \ldots \\
\ldots \; aValue \ldots
\end{array}
$$

   In short, substitute the value in a state variable definition for the state variable only when the value is needed for this particular occurrence of the state variable.

5. Last, but not least, we also need a rule for **begin**-expressions. The simplest one says to drop the first subexpression if it is a value:

$$
\begin{array}{l}
(\textbf{begin } v \; exp\text{-}1 \ldots exp\text{-}n) \\
= (\textbf{begin } exp\text{-}1 \ldots exp\text{-}n)
\end{array}
$$

That means we also need a rule for dropping **begin** completely:

> (**begin** exp)
> = exp

In addition, we use a rule for dropping several values at once:

> (**begin** *v-1 ... v-m exp-1 ... exp-n*)
> = (**begin** *exp-1 ... exp-n*)

But this is only a convenience.

Although the laws are more complicated than those of Beginning Student Scheme, they are still manageable.

Let's consider some examples. The first one demonstrates how the order of evaluation of subexpressions makes a difference:

> (**define** *x* 5)
> (+ (**begin** (**set!** *x* 11) *x*) *x*)
>
> = (**define** *x* 11)
> (+ (**begin** (void) *x*) *x*)
>
> = ...
>
> = (**define** *x* 11)
> (+ 11 *x*)
>
> = (**define** *x* 11)
> (+ 11 11)

The program consists of one definition and one addition, which is to be evaluated. One of the addition's arguments is a **set!**-expression that mutates *x*; the other is just *x*. By evaluating the subexpressions of the addition from left to right, the mutation takes place before we replace the second subexpression with its value. As a result, the outcome is 22. If we had evaluated the addition from right to left, the result would have been 16. To avoid such problems, we use the fixed ordering but give ourselves more freedom when no state variables are involved.

The second example illustrates how a **set!**-expression that occurs in a **local**-expression actually affects a top-level definition:

```
(define (make-counter x0)
  (local ((define counter x0)
          (define (increment)
            (begin
              (set! counter (+ counter 1))
              counter)))
    increment))
((make-counter 0))
```

The program again consists of a single definition and an expression that is to be evaluated. The latter, however, is an application nested in an application. The inner application is underlined, because we must evaluate it to make progress. Here are the first few steps:

```
= (define (make-counter x0)
    (local ((define counter x0)
            (define (increment)
              (begin
                (set! counter (+ counter 1))
                counter)))
      increment))
  ((local ((define counter 0)
           (define (increment)
             (begin
               (set! counter (+ counter 1))
               counter)))
     increment))
= (define (make-counter x0)
    (local ((define counter x0)
            (define (increment)
              (begin
                (set! counter (+ counter 1))
                counter)))
      increment))
  (define counter1 0)
  (define (increment1)
    (begin
      (set! counter1 (+ counter1 1))
      counter1))
  (increment1)
```

The evaluation of the **local**-expression created additional top-level expressions. One of them introduces a state variable; the others define functions.

The second part of the evaluation determines what (*increment1*) accomplishes:

>     (**define** *counter1* 0)
>     (*increment1*)
>
> = (**define** *counter1* 0)
>     (**begin**
>       (**set!** *counter1* (+ *counter1* 1))
>       *counter1*)
>
> = (**define** *counter1* 0)
>     (**begin**
>       (**set!** *counter1* (+ 0 1))
>       *counter1*)
>
> = (**define** *counter1* 0)
>     (**begin**
>       (**set!** *counter1* 1)
>       *counter1*)
>
> = (**define** *counter1* 1)
>     (**begin**
>       (void)
>       *counter1*)
>
> = (**define** *counter1* 1)
>     1

During the evaluation, we replace *counter1* with its value twice. First, the second step replaces *counter1* with 0, its value at that point. Second, we substitute 1 for *counter1* during the last step, which is its new value.

## Exercises

**Exercise 38.3.1** Underline the subexpression that must be evaluated next in the following expressions:

1. (**define** *x* 11)
   (**begin**
     (**set!** *x* (* *x* *x*))
     *x*)

2. (**define** *x* 11)
   (**begin**
     (**set!** *x*
       (**cond**
         [(zero? 0) 22]
         [**else** (/ 1 *x*)]))
     'done)

3. (**define** (*run x*)
       (*run x*))
   (*run* 10)

4. (**define** (*f x*) (* *pi x x*))
   (**define** *a1* (*f* 10))
   (**begin**
     (**set!** *a1* (− *a1* (*f* 5)))
     'done)

5. (**define** (*f x*)
       (**set!** *state* (− 1 *state*)))
   (**define** *state* 1)
   (*f* (*f* (*f*)))

Explain why the expression must be evaluated. ∎

**Exercise 38.3.2** Confirm that the underlined expressions must be evaluated
next:

1. (**define** *x* 0)
   (**define** *y* 1)
   (**begin**
     <u>(**set!** *x* 3)</u>
     (**set!** *y* 4)
     (+ (* *x x*) (* *y y*)))

2. (**define** *x* 0)
   (**set!** *x*
     (**cond**
       [(zero? <u>*x*</u>) 1]
       [**else** 0]))

3. (**define** (*f x*)
  (**cond**
    [(zero? *x*) 1]
    [**else** 0]))
  (**begin**
    (**set!** *f* 11)
    *f*)

Rewrite the three programs to show the next state. ∎

**Exercise 38.3.3** Evaluate the following programs:

1. (**define** *x* 0)
  (**define** (*bump delta*)
    (**begin**
      (**set!** *x* (+ *x delta*))
      *x*))
  (+ (*bump* 2) (*bump* 3))

2. (**define** *x* 10)
  (**set!** *x* (**cond**
        [(*zeor? x*) 13]
        [**else** (/ 1 *x*)]))

3. (**define** (*make-box x*)
    (**local** ((**define** *contents x*)
          (**define** (*new y*)
            (**set!** *contents y*))
          (**define** (*peek*)
            *contents*))
      (list *new peek*)))

  (**define** *B* (*make-box* 55))
  (**define** *C* (*make-box* 'a))

  (**begin**
    ((first *B*) 33)
    ((second *C*)))

Underline for each step the subexpression that must be evaluated next.
Show only those steps that involve a **local**-expression or a **set!**-expression. ∎

In principle, we could work with the rules we just discussed. They cover the common cases, and they explain the behavior of the programs we have encountered. They do not explain, however, how an assignment works when the left-hand side refers to a **defined** function. Consider the following example, for which the rules still work:

    (**define** (*f x*) *x*)

    (**begin**
      $\underline{(\textbf{set!}\ f\ 10)}$
      *f*)

= (**define** *f* 10)

    (**begin**
      (void)
      *f*)

Here *f* is a state variable. The **set!**-expression changes the definition so *f* stands for a number. The next step in an evaluation substitutes 10 for the occurrence of *f*.

Under ordinary circumstances, an assignment would replace a function definition with a different function definition. Take a look at this program:

    (**define** (*f x*) *x*)
    (**define** *g f*)
    (+ $\underline{(\textbf{begin}\ (\textbf{set!}\ f\ (\textbf{lambda}\ (x)\ 22))\ 5)}$ (*g* 1))

The purpose of the underlined **set!**-expression is to modify the definition of *f* so that it becomes a function that always produces 22. But *g* stands for *f* initially. Since *f* is a the name of a function, we can think of (**define** *g f*) as a value definition. The problem is that our current rules change the definition of *f* and, by implication, the definition of *g*, because it stands for *f*:

= (**define** *f* (**lambda** (*x*) 22))
    (**define** *g f*)
    (+ $\underline{(\textbf{begin}\ (\text{void})\ 5)}$ (*g* 1))

= (**define** *f* (**lambda** (*x*) 22))
    (**define** *g f*)
    (+ 5 $\underline{(g\ 1)}$)

$=$ (**define** $f$ (**lambda** $(x)$ 22))
   (**define** $g$ $f$)
   (+ 5 22)

Scheme, however, does not behave this way. A **set!**-expression can modify
only one definition at a time. Here it modifies two: $f$'s, which is intended,
and $g$'s, which happens through the indirection from $g$ to $f$. In short, our
rules do not explain the behavior of all programs with **set!**-expressions; we
need better rules if we wish to understand Scheme fully.

---

| $\langle vdf \rangle$ | $=$ | (**define** $\langle var \rangle$ $\langle val \rangle$)) |
|---|---|---|
| | | \| (**define-struct** $\langle var \rangle$ $(\langle var \rangle \ldots \langle var \rangle))$) |
| $\langle val \rangle$ | $=$ | $\langle con \rangle$ \| $\langle lst \rangle$ \| $\langle prm \rangle$ \| $\langle fun \rangle$ \| $\langle void \rangle$ |
| $\langle lst \rangle$ | $=$ | empty \| (cons $\langle val \rangle$ $\langle lst \rangle$)) |
| $\langle fun \rangle$ | $=$ | (**lambda** $(\langle var \rangle \ldots \langle var \rangle)$ $\langle exp \rangle$) |

Figure 112: Advanced Student Scheme: The values

---

The problem concerns the definitions of functions, which suggests that
we take a second look at the representation of functions and function definitions. So far, we used the names of functions as values. As we have just
seen, this choice may cause trouble in case the state variable is a function.
The solution is to use a concrete representation of functions. Fortunately,
we already have one in Scheme: **lambda**-expressions. Furthermore, we
rewrite function definitions so that they turn into variable definitions with
a **lambda**-expression on the right-hand side:

   (**define** $(f\ x)$ $x$)

$=$ (**define** $f$ (**lambda** $(x)$ $x$))

Even recursive definitions are evaluated in this manner:

   (**define** $(g\ x)$
     (**cond**
       [(zero? $x$) 1]
       [**else** $(g$ (sub1 $x$))]))

```
= (define g
    (lambda (x)
      (cond
        [(zero? x) 1]
        [else (g (sub1 x))])))
```

All other rules, including the rule for replacing variables with their values, remain the same.

Figure 112 specifies the set of values,[73] as a subset of the set of expressions, and the set of value definitions, as a subset of the definitions. Using these definitions and the modified rules, we can take a second look at at the above example:

```
(define (f x) x)
(define g f)
(+ (begin (set! f (lambda (x) 22)) 5) (g 1))
```

```
= (define f (lambda (x) x))
  (define g f)
  (+ (begin (set! f (lambda (x) 22)) 5) (g 1))
```

```
= (define f (lambda (x) x))
  (define g (lambda (x) x))
  (+ (begin (set! f (lambda (x) 22)) 5) (g 1))
```

```
= (define f (lambda (x) 22))
  (define g (lambda (x) x))
  (+ (begin (void) 5) (g 1))
```

```
= (define f (lambda (x) 22))
  (define g (lambda (x) x))
  (+ 5 (g 1))
```

```
= (define f (lambda (x) 22))
  (define g (lambda (x) x))
  (+ 5 1)
```

The key difference is that the definition of *g* directly associates the variable with a function representation, not just a name for a function.

The following program shows the effects of **set!**-expressions on functions with an extreme example:

---

[73]It lacks a specification of structural values, but they play no role in this discussion.

```
(define (f x)
  (cond
    [(zero? x) 'done]
    [else (f (sub1 x))]))
```

```
(define g f)
```

```
(begin
  (set! f (lambda (x) 'ouch))
  (symbol=? (g 1) 'ouch))
```

The function $f$ is recursive on natural numbers and always produces 'done.
Initially, $g$ is defined to be $f$. The final **begin**-expression first modifies $f$ and
then uses $g$.

At first, we must rewrite the function definitions according to our modified rules:

```
= (define f
    (lambda (x)
      (cond
        [(zero? x) 'done]
        [else (f (sub1 x))])))
  (define g f̲)
  (begin
    (set! f (lambda (x) 'ouch))
    (symbol=? (g 1) 'ouch))
```

```
= (define f
    (lambda (x)
      (cond
        [(zero? x) 'done]
        [else (f (sub1 x))])))
  (define g
    (lambda (x)
      (cond
        [(zero? x) 'done]
        [else (f (sub1 x))])))
  (begin
    (set! f (lambda (x) 'ouch))
    ‾‾‾‾‾‾‾‾‾‾‾‾‾‾‾‾‾‾‾‾‾‾‾‾‾
    (set! f (lambda (x) 'ouch))
    (symbol=? (g 1) 'ouch))
```

Rewriting the definition of *f* is straightforward. The major change concerns the definition of *g*. Instead of *f* it now contains a copy of the value for which *f* currently stands. This value contains a reference to *f*, but that is not unusual.

Next, the **set!**-expression modifies the definition of *f*:

```
    . . .
= (define f
    (lambda (x)
      'ouch))

  (define g
    (lambda (x)
      (cond
        [(zero? x) 'done]
        [else (f (sub1 x))])))

  (begin
    (void)
    (symbol=? (g 1) 'ouch))
```

No other definition, however, is affected. In particular, the definition of *g* remains the same, though the *f* inside of *g*'s value now refers to a new value. But we have seen this phenomenon before. The next two steps follow the basic rules of intermezzo 1:

```
    . . .
= (define f
    (lambda (x)
      'ouch))

  (define g
    (lambda (x)
      (cond
        [(zero? x) 'done]
        [else (f (sub1 x))])))

  (begin
    (void)
    (symbol=? (f 0) 'ouch))
```

```
= (define f
     (lambda (x)
        'ouch))

  (define g
     (lambda (x)
        (cond
           [(zero? x) 'done]
           [else (f (sub1 x))])))

  (begin
     (void)
     (symbol=? 'ouch 'ouch))
```

That is, the application of *g* eventually applies *f* to 0, which yields 'ouch. Hence the final result is true.

## Exercises

**Exercise 38.3.4** Validate that the following program evaluates to true:

```
(define (make-box x)
   (local ((define contents x)
           (define (new y) (set! contents y))
           (define (peek) contents))
      (list new peek)))

(define B (make-box 55))

(define C B)

(and
   (begin
      ((first B) 33)
      true)
   (= (second C) 33)
   (begin
      (set! B (make-box 44))
      (= (second C) 33)))
```

Underline for each step the subexpression that must be evaluated next. Show only those steps that involve a **local**-expression or a **set!**-expression. ∎

While we decided to rewrite function definitions so that their right-hand side are always **lambda**-expressions, we stuck with a function application rule that assumes function definitions in the style of Beginning Student Scheme. More concretely, if the definition context contains a definition such as

(**define** *f* (**lambda** (*x y*) (+ *x y*)))

and the expression is

(∗ (*f* 1 2) 5)

then the next step in the evaluation is

(∗ (+ 1 2) 5)

For other occasions, however, we just replace variables with the values in the respective definitions. If we followed that rule, we would rewrite

(∗ (*f* 1 2) 5)

to

(∗ ((**lambda** (*x y*) (+ *x y*))
    1 2)
  5)

At first glance, this exploration route ends here, because there are no laws for this application.

We can reconcile the two ideas with a new law, suggested by the last expression:

((**lambda** (*x-1* ... *x-n*) exp)
  *v-1* ... *v-n*)
= exp with all *x-1* ... *x-n* replaced by *v-1* ... *v-n*

The law serves as a replacement of the law of application from algebra in the study of the foundations of computing. By convention, this law is called the $\beta_v$ (pronounced "beta value") axiom.

**Beta and the Lambda Calculus:** The orginal $\beta$ axiom was formulated by Alonzo Church in the late 1920s as follows:

> ((**lambda** ($x$) exp)
>   *exp-1*)
> = exp with $x$ replaced by *exp-1*

It does not restrict the argument in a function application to be a value. The interest of Church and other logicians[74] was to explore the principles of computation, what computation could achieve, and what it couldn't. They confirmed that the axiom and a small sublanguage of Scheme, namely,

$$\langle exp \rangle \quad = \quad \langle var \rangle \ | \ (\textbf{lambda} \ (\langle var \rangle) \ \langle exp \rangle) \ | \ (\langle exp \rangle \ \langle exp \rangle)$$

are enough to define all computable functions on a (simulation of) the natural numbers. Functions that cannot be formulated in this language are not computable.

The language and the $\beta$ axiom became known as the $\lambda$ (pronounced: "lambda") calculus. Gerald Sussman and Guy L. Steele Jr. later based Scheme on the $\lambda$ calculus. In the mid-1970s, Gordon Plotkin suggested the $\beta_v$ axiom as a better method for understanding function applications in programming languages such as Scheme. ∎

## Errors in Advanced Scheme

The extension of our language with functions as values introduces not only new powers for the programmer but also new possibilities for errors. Recall that there are three kinds of errors: syntax errors, run-time (or semantics) errors, and logical errors. Advanced Student Scheme turns a class of syntactic errors of Beginning Student Scheme into run-time errors. It also introduces a new form of logical error.

Consider the following program:

```
;; how-many-in-list : (listof X) → N
;; to count how many items alist contains
(define (how-many-in-list alist)
  (cond
    [empty? (alist)]
    [else (+ (how-many-in-list (rest alist)) 1)]))
```

In Beginning Student Scheme or Intermediate Student Scheme, DrScheme would have signaled a syntax error because *alist* is the parameter to a function but is also used as a function. Because functions are

---

[74]Logic is to computing what mathematics is to physics.

values in Advanced Student Scheme, DrScheme must now accept this function definition as syntactially correct. When the function is applied to empty or any other list value, however, DrScheme soon applies empty to no arguments, which is a run-time error. After all, lists are not functions. DrScheme signals immediately with an error message any attempt to apply a non-function and stops the evaluation.

The second form of error is logical. That is, a program that suffers from this form of error doesn't produce a syntax or a run-time error message. Instead, it produces wrong answers. Take a look at the following two definitions:

```
(define flip1                     (define flip2
  (local ((define state 1))         (lambda ()
    (lambda ()                        (local ((define state 1))
      (begin                            (begin
        (set! state (− 1 state))          (set! state (− 1 state))
        state))))                         state))))
```

They differ in the order of two lines. One introduces a **local** definition whose body evaluates to a function. The other defines a function whose body contains a **local**-expression. According to our rules, the definition on the left rewrites to

```
(define state1 1)                 (define flip2
                                    (lambda ()
(define flip1                         (local ((define state 1))
  (lambda ()                            (begin
    (begin                                (set! state (− 1 state))
      (set! state1 (− 1 state1))          state))))
      state1)))
```

The one on the right already associates a name with a function.

Let us now see how the two functions have radically different behaviors. To do so, we evaluate the expressions

```
(and (= (flip1) 0)                (and (= (flip2) 0)
     (= (flip1) 1)                     (= (flip2) 1)
     (= (flip1) 0))                    (= (flip2) 0))
```

in the context of the respective definitions.

Here are the first four steps of the evaluation for the expression on the left-hand side:

```
    (define state1 1)
    (and (= (flip1) 0)
         (= (flip1) 1)
         (= (flip1) 0))

=  (define state1 1)
   (and (= (begin
               (set! state1 (− 1 state1))
               state1)
            0)
        (= (flip1) 1)
        (= (flip1) 0))

=  (define state1 1)
   (and (= (begin
               (set! state1 0)
               state1)
            0)
        (= (flip1) 1)
        (= (flip1) 0))

=  (define state1 0)
   (and (= (begin
               (void)
               state1)
            0)
        (= (flip1) 1)
        (= (flip1) 0))

=  (define state1 0)
   (and (= 0 0)
        (= (flip1) 1)
        (= (flip1) 0))
```

The relevant definition context is the definition of *state1*, which we see changing from 1 to 0 during the third step. From this point, it is not difficult to validate that the expression produces true and that *state1* ends up being 0.

Compare this with the first three steps in the evaluation of the right-hand expression:

```
       (and (= (flip2) 0)
            (= (flip2) 1)
            (= (flip2) 0))


 = (and (= (local ((define state 1))
                (begin
                   (set! state (− 1 state))
                   state))
             0)
          (= (flip2) 1)
          (= (flip2) 0))


 = (define state1 1)
   (and (= (begin
                (set! state1 (− 1 state1))
                state1)
             0)
          (= (flip2) 1)
          (= (flip2) 0))


 = (define state1 0)
   (and (= 0 0)
          (= (flip2) 1)
          (= (flip2) 0))
```

The only definition that matters here is the one for *flip2*. Superficially, the two evaluations are alike. But a closer look shows that the second one differs from the first in crucial way. It creates the definition for *state1* while the first evaluation started with such a definition.

Here is the continuation of the second evaluation:

```
   . . .
 = (define state1 0)
   (and true
          (= (local ((define state 1))
                (begin
                   (set! state (− 1 state))
                   state))
             1)
          (= (flip2) 0))
```

```
= (define state1 0)
  (define state2 1)
  (and true
       (= (begin
             (set! state2 (- 1 state2))
             state2)
          1)
       (= (flip2) 0))

= (define state1 0)
  (define state2 0)
  (and true
       (= (begin
             (void)
             state2)
          1)
       (= (flip2) 0))

= (define state1 0)
  (define state2 0)
  (and true
       (= 0 1)
       (= (flip2) 0))
```

It shows that *flip2* creates a new definition every time it is applied and that it always produces 0. Contrary to its name, it does not flip the value of *state* upon every application. As a result, the evaluation ends now with two new top-level definitions and the value false.

The general moral is that a function defined in a **local**-expression is different from a function whose body contains a **local**-expression. The first ensures that some definitions are accessible only to a function. The definition exists once and only once for this function. In contrast, the second creates a new (top-level) definition for every evaluation of the function body. In the next part of the book, we exploit both ideas to create new kinds of programs.

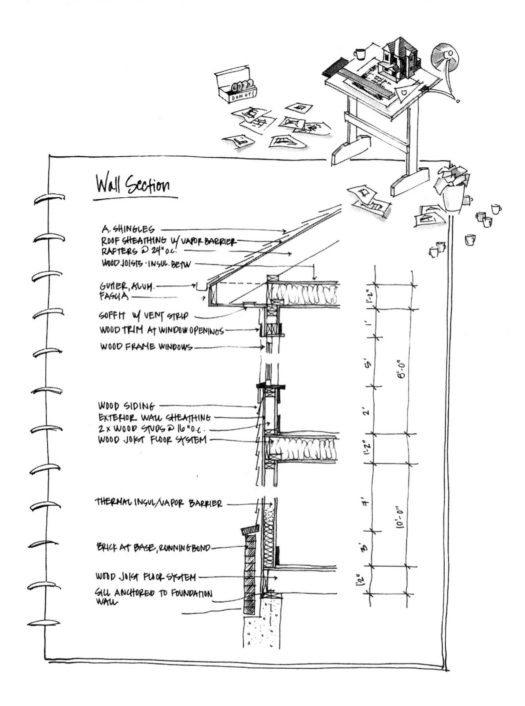

## Wall Section

A. SHINGLES
ROOF SHEATHING W/ VAPOR BARRIER
RAFTERS @ 24" O.C.
WOOD JOISTS · INSUL. BETW

GUTTER, ALUM.
FASCIA

SOFFIT W/ VENT STRIP
WOOD TRIM AT WINDOW OPENINGS
WOOD FRAME WINDOWS

WOOD SIDING
EXTERIOR WALL SHEATHING
2 x WOOD STUDS @ 16" O.C.
WOOD JOIST FLOOR SYSTEM

THERMAL INSUL/VAPOR BARRIER

BRICK AT BASE, RUNNING BOND

WOOD JOIST FLOOR SYSTEM

SILL ANCHORED TO FOUNDATION
WALL

## 39 Encapsulation

When we design a program to control a traffic light, we probably don't want to control just one traffic light, but several. Similarly, when we design a program to manage names and phone numbers, we might wish to manage several address books, not just one. Of course, we could copy the code for a traffic light controller (or an address book manager) and rename the state variables, but copying code is bad. Furthermore, we might wish to create so many traffic lights that copying code is plain impractical.

The proper solution is to use the power of abstraction. Here we abstract over several instances of the address book program and the traffic light program and so on. This differs from the notion of abstraction in part IV because it involves state variables, but the idea and even the technique is the same. We encapsulate the state variables and the functions in a **local**-expression and thus give ourselves the power to create as many versions as necessary. We learn how to encapsulate state variables in the first subsection, and practice it in the second one.

### 39.1 Abstracting with State Variables

Suppose we wish to turn the program in figure 100 (page 514) into a program for managing (simulated) traffic lights. An operator of the simulation should be able to control each traffic light independently of the others. Indeed, the operator should be able to add or shut down traffic lights while the rest of the system remains unchanged and running.

Based on our experience, we know that each traffic light in the simulation requires two definitions:

1. a state variable, *current-color*, which keeps track of the light's current color; and

2. a service function, *next*, which switches the traffic light to the next color according to the traffic laws.

For a graphical simulation, the service function would also redraw the traffic light so that users can view the current color. Finally, each traffic light has a unique location on the canvas:

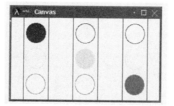

The sample program of figure 100 deals with a single traffic light and lacks the drawing operation. The problem now is to turn this into a program that can create as many traffic lights as needed, each with its own state variables and switching functions and at its own location. If we were to copy the definitions in figure 100 and add definitions for dealing with the canvas, the various instances would differ in only one aspect: the data concerning the location of the traffic light. This thought experiment suggests that we should develop an abstract function that creates and manages traffic lights at various locations.

Because the original program consists of several top-level definitions, we use the recipe of section 22.2, which suggests wrapping the definitions in a **local**-expression inside a function. When local definitions include state variables, as in this example, we prefer to say that we ENCAPSULATE definitions. This terminology emphasizes that the abstract function hides the state variables from other parts of the program. In particular, it implies that by putting a state variable in a **local**-expression we guarantee that it can change only according to the managed services, not by arbitrary assignments. Still, the definition encapsulates and abstracts at the same time, and a programmer must keep this in mind.

The next step is to consider what this function should do, that is, what it should consume, what it should produce, and what effects it should have, if any. Let's start with the name. We call the new function *make-traffic-light*; after all, making a simulated traffic light is the purpose of the abstracted program. Furthermore, according to our abstraction recipes, an abstraction must consume values that represent the unique aspects of an instance. The unique aspect of a traffic light is its position on the canvas; for clarity, let's add a physical address, too.

```
;; View:
;; draw-light : TL-color number → true
;; to (re)draw the traffic light on the canvas
(define (draw-light current-color x-posn) ... ))


;; Model:
;; make-traffic-light : symbol number → (→ true)
;; to create a red light with (make-posn x-posn 0) as the upper-left corner
;; effect: draw the traffic light on the canvas
(define (make-traffic-light street x-posn)
  (local (;; current-color : TL-color
          ;; to keep track of the current color of the traffic light
          (define current-color 'red)

          ;; init-traffic-light : → true
          ;; to (re)set current-color to red and to (re)create the view
          (define (init-traffic-light)
            (begin
              (set! current-color 'red)
              (draw-light current-color x-posn)))

          ;; next : → true
          ;; effect: to change current-color from 'green to 'yellow,
          ;; 'yellow to 'red, and 'red to 'green
          (define (next)
            (begin
              (set! current-color (next-color current-color))
              (draw-light current-color x-posn)))

          ;; next-color : TL-color → TL-color
          ;; to compute the successor of current-color based on the traffic laws
          (define (next-color current-color)
            (cond
              [(symbol=? 'green current-color) 'yellow]
              [(symbol=? 'yellow current-color) 'red]
              [(symbol=? 'red current-color) 'green])))
    (begin
      ;; Initialize and produce next
      (init-traffic-light)
      next)))
```

Figure 113: Managing multiple traffic lights

Every use of *make-traffic-light* should create a traffic light and enable the operator to switch it from one state to the next. The first part suggests an effect. Specifically, the function should initialize the state variable and draw the initial state of the traffic light at the designated position on the canvas. The second part of the statement suggests a result: a function for switching the state of the traffic light.

Figure 113 contains the outline of the traffic simulator, including the complete definition of *make-traffic-light*. The simulator consists of a model and a view. The model is *make-traffic-light*. The view is called *draw-light* and is only sketched; the full definition of the view is left as an exercise.

The definition of *make-traffic-light* is an ordinary function definition. It uses a **local** definition to set up the single state variable, the initializer, and the state-changing function. The body of the **local**-expression uses the initializer and then produces *next* as the function's value.

Using *make-traffic-light* we can create several individual traffic lights or entire collections of them. We could also add lights as time goes by. First, we create a sufficiently large canvas:

```
;; create the canvas first
(start 300 160)
```

Second, we apply *make-traffic-light* as often as needed:

```
;; lights : (listof traffic-light)
;; to manage the lights along Sunrise
(define lights
   (list (make-traffic-light 'sunrise@rice 50)
         (make-traffic-light 'sunrise@cmu 150)))
```

Here we define *lights* to be a list of two traffic lights. Each traffic light is a function, so *lights* stands for a list of two functions.

After creating the traffic lights, we can change their states as desired. To do so, we must keep in mind that each traffic light is represented by a function that consumes nothing and produces true. Its effect is to change the hidden state variable and the drawing on the canvas. In our running example, we could use the Interactions window as follows:

```
> ((second lights))
true
> (andmap (lambda (a-light) (a-light)) lights)
true
```

The first interaction extracts the second item from *lights* and applies it. This sets the light at 'sunrise@cmu to green. The second one switches the state of all items on *lights*.

Each application of *make-traffic-light* turns variants of the **local** definitions into top-level definitions, after renaming them. Because the above **define** contains two applications of *make-traffic-light*, it creates two copies of each **locally** defined function and state variable during an evaluation:

```
;; definitions for 'sunrise@rice
(define current-color@rice 'red)

(define (init-traffic-light@rice)
  (begin
    (set! current-color@rice 'red)
    (draw-light current-color@rice 50)))

(define (next@rice) ...)

(define (next-color@rice current-color) ...)
```

---

```
;; definitions for 'sunrise@cmu
(define current-color@cmu 'red)

(define (init-traffic-light@cmu)
  (begin
    (set! current-color@cmu 'red)
    (draw-light current-color@cmu 150)))

(define (next@cmu) ...)

(define (next-color@cmu current-color) ...)

(define lights
  (list next@rice
        next@cmu))
```

The new top-level definitions of *init-traffic-light* show how the renaming ensures that one of them takes care of 'sunrise@rice and the other one of 'sunrise@cmu.

**Exercises**

**Exercise 39.1.1** What is the effect of the second interaction above? ∎

**Exercise 39.1.2** Fill in the bodies of *next@rice* and *next@cmu* in the hand-evaluated program. Then evaluate ((second *lights*)) in the context of these definitions. ∎

**Exercise 39.1.3** Develop the function *draw-light*. It realizes the view part of the traffic light simulation in figure 113. Each traffic light should be as tall as the canvas, delineated by solid lines on the left and right. The suggested dimensions of a single light are

    (**define** *WIDTH* 50)
    (**define** *RADIUS* 20)
    (**define** *DISTANCE-BETWEEN-BULBS* 10)
    ;; the minimum canvas height
    (**define** *HEIGHT*
      (+ *DISTANCE-BETWEEN-BULBS*
        (* 2 *RADIUS*)
        *DISTANCE-BETWEEN-BULBS*
        (* 2 *RADIUS*)
        *DISTANCE-BETWEEN-BULBS*
        (* 2 *RADIUS*)
        *DISTANCE-BETWEEN-BULBS*))

Develop the necessary definitons separate from the rest of the traffic light program, then create a single function definition using **local**. ∎

    Now suppose we wish to provide the additional service of resetting an individual traffic light. That is, in addition to switching from the current color to the next, an operator should be able to set a traffic light to red. The function for doing so already exists: *init-traffic-light*. It sets *current-color* to 'red and redraws the image on the canvas. But, *init-traffic-light* is inaccessible because it is defined within the **local**-expression of *make-traffic-light*. If we wish the function to be visible, it must be the result of *make-traffic-light* just like *next*.

    To make both *next* and *init-traffic-light* a result of *make-traffic-light* requires some way of combining the two functions into a single value. Since

```
;; make-traffic-light : symbol number → (symbol → true)
;; to create a red light with (make-posn x-posn 0) as the upper-left corner
;; effect: draw the traffic light on the canvas
(define (make-traffic-light street x-posn)
  (local (;; Model:
          ;; current-color : TL-color
          ;; to keep track of the current color of the traffic light
          (define current-color 'red)

          ;; init-traffic-light : → true
          ;; to (re)set current-color to red and to (re)create the view
          (define (init-traffic-light) ...)

          ;; next : → true
          ;; effect: to change current-color from 'green to 'yellow,
          ;; 'yellow to 'red, and 'red to 'green
          (define (next) ...)

          ;; next-color : TL-color → TL-color
          ;; to compute the successor of current-color based on the traffic laws
          (define (next-color current-color) ...)
          ;; service-manager : (symbol → true)
          ;; to apply either next or init-traffic-light
          (define (service-manager msg)
            (cond
              [(symbol=? msg 'next) (next)]
              [(symbol=? msg 'reset) (init-traffic-light)]
              [else (error 'traffic-light "message not understood")])))
    (begin
      ;; Initialize and produce service-manager
      (init-traffic-light)
      service-manager)))
```

Figure 114: Managing multiple traffic lights with a reset service

functions are values in Scheme, we could combine the two functions in a list, a structure, or even a vector. Another possibility is to combine the two functions in a third function. Here we discuss this third possibility because it is an important technique in the context of managing state variables and services.

We call the new kind of function *service-manager*, because it hides and manages functions that implement services. The function accepts two symbols:

1. 'next, which indicates that (*next*) should be evaluated, and

2. 'reset, which indicates that (*reset*) should be evaluated.

Furthermore, the function is the result of the revised version of *make-traffic-light*.

Figure 114 contains the modified definition of *make-traffic-light*. Since an operator may mistakenly apply functions to inappropriate arguments, *service-manager* is a checked function in the sense of section 7.5. It signals an error if the input is a symbol other than 'next or 'reset.

We use the new *make-traffic-light* function exactly like the old one:

```
;; create the canvas first
(start 300 160)
```

```
;; lights : (listof traffic-light)
;; to manage the lights along Sunrise
(define lights
   (list (make-traffic-light 'sunrise@rice 50)
         (make-traffic-light 'sunrise@cmu 150)))
```

The result, however, is that now every traffic light is represented as a function on symbols:

```
> ((second lights) 'next)
true
> (andmap (lambda (a-light) (a-light 'reset)) lights)
true
```

The first interaction switches the initially red light labeled 'sunrise@cmu to 'green. The second one changes the state of every light back to 'red skipping the 'yellow stage for the light at 'sunrise@cmu.

## Exercises

**Exercise 39.1.4** Complete the definition of the program in figure 114, using the function from exercise 39.1.3. Then use DrScheme's Interactions window to switch and reset traffic lights. ∎

Exercise 39.1.5 Evaluate the above program by hand and confirm that the light labeled 'sunrise@rice switches from 'green directly back to 'red. ∎

For the address-book example from part VII, the need for managing two services is even more apparent. After all, the motivating idea behind the example is that users can access one state variable with two different services: *add-to-address-book* for adding new entries and *lookup* for looking up the phone number for a given name. Following our encapsulation recipe, we must

1. define a function *make-address-book* whose body is a **local**-expression;

2. place the definitions in this **local**-expression; and

3. introduce a function called *service-manager* to manage the two services.

By now, we have the first two steps firmly under control; the last one, however, is complex here, because unlike in the previous case, the two functions that implement the services consume different numbers of arguments and produce different kinds of results.

Let's first agree on the inputs for *service-manager*. Two good mnemonic symbols are 'add for adding phone numbers and 'search for looking up the number for some given name. This suggests the following template:

```
(define (service-manager msg)
  (cond
    [(symbol=? msg 'add) ... A ...]
    [(symbol=? msg 'search) ... B ...]
    [else (error 'address-book "message not understood")]))
```

The problem is that it is not clear how to replace *A* and *B* with valid Scheme expressions that compute the appropriate value and effect. For *A*, we need not only *msg* but also a name and a phone number. For *B*, we need the name.

One solution is to produce functions that consume the additional arguments and then perform the appropriate computation. In other words, *service-manager* is now a function that produces a function for two symbols. Since we have not encountered this kind of result before, we introduce a new form of data definition:

> An *address-book* is an interface:
>
> 1. 'add :: *symbol number* → *void*
>
> 2. 'search :: *symbol* → *number*

The data definition refers to the concept of INTERFACE, which is a function that consumes a finite number of symbols and produces functions with different types in return. Because this kind of function is radically different from what we have seen before, we use a different name.

Now it is possible to write a contract and a purpose statement:

```
;; service-manager : address-book
;; to manage addition to, and searches in, the address book
(define (service-manager msg) ... )
```

To define the function, we distinguish the two cases. In the case of 'add, it is obvious what we produce: *add-to-address-book*.

In the case of 'search, we need a function that consumes a symbol and then applies *lookup* to this symbol and the **locally** defined *address-book*. Using **lambda**, we can create such a function on the fly:

```
(lambda (name)
  (lookup name address-book))
```

Since the function is a value, it is the natural answer to 'search.

Figure 115 shows the complete definition of *make-address-book*. The definition is standard by now. It consists of a **local**-expression, which in turn produces the **locally** defined *service-manager* as the result. There is no need for an initializer because the only state variable is immediately initialized and there is no graphical view.

To use an address book, we first create it with *make-address-book*:

```
;; friends : an address book
;; to maintain an address book for friends
(define friends
  (make-address-book "Friends of Charles"))
```

```
;; business : an address book
;; to maintain an address book for business colleagues
(define business
  (make-address-book "Colleagues @ Rice, Inc."))
```

---

```
;; make-address-book : string → address-book
;; to create a function that manages all the services for a hidden address book
(define (make-address-book title)
  (local ((define-struct entry (name number))
          ;; address-book : (listof (list name number))
          ;; to maintain a list of name-phone number associations
          (define address-book empty)

          ;; add-to-address-book : symbol number void
          ;; effect: to add a name-phone number association to address-book
          (define (add-to-address-book name phone)
            (set! address-book (cons (make-entry name phone) address-book)))

          ;; lookup : symbol (listof (list symbol number)) → number or false
          ;; to lookup the phone number for name in address-book
          (define (lookup name ab)
            (cond
              [(empty? ab) false]
              [else (cond
                      [(symbol=? (entry-name (first ab)) name)
                       (entry-number (first ab))]
                      [else (lookup name (rest ab))])]))

          ;; service-manager : address-book object
          ;; to manage addition to, and searches in, the address book
          (define (service-manager msg)
            (cond
              [(symbol=? msg 'add)
               add-to-address-book]
              [(symbol=? msg 'search)
               (lambda (name)
                 (lookup name address-book))]
              [else (error 'address-book "message not understood")])))
    service-manager))
```

Figure 115: Managing multiple address books

---

The two definitions create two distinct address books, one for a collection of friends and a second one for business acquaintances.

Second, we add names and phone numbers to the address book, or we retrieve numbers as desired:

> *((friends* 'add) 'Bill 2)
> *((friends* 'add) 'Sally 3)
> *((friends* 'add) 'Dave 4)
> *((business* 'add) 'Emil 5)
> *((business* 'add) 'Faye 18)

In this case, we added three entries to the address book named *friends* and two to the one called *business*.

An addition to, say, *friends* works in two steps. The first step is to apply *friends* to 'add. This yields the (hidden) function *add-to-address-book*. The second step is to apply this resulting function to a name and a number. In a similar vein, looking up a phone number also works in two steps. The application of, say, *friends* to 'search yields a function that consumes a name. This function is then applied to a symbol:

> *((friends* 'search) 'Bill)
2
> *((business* 'search) 'Bill)
false

The two applications show that the number for 'Bill in *friends* is 2 and that there is no number for 'Bill in colleagues. According to the above additions, that's exactly what we should expect. Of course, we could also co-mingle the two actions in the Interactions window, adding and searching for phone numbers at will.

---

## Exercises

**Exercise 39.1.6** Develop an interface definition for the results of the revised version of *make-traffic-light* (see figure 114). ∎

**Exercise 39.1.7** Show the top-level definitions that the evaluation of *friends* and *colleagues* creates.

What is the state of these definitions after the five 'add expressions have been evaluated? Evaluate *((friends* 'search) 'Bill) in this context. ∎

**Exercise 39.1.8** Design *gui-for-address-book*. The function consumes a list of strings and creates a new address book for each one of them. It also creates and displays a graphical user interface for an address book with a choice menu that lets users choose to which address book they want to add an entry and in which address book the program should search for a number. ∎

## 39.2 Practice with Encapsulation

**Exercise 39.2.1** Develop the program *make-city*. It manages a collection of traffic lights. The program should provide four services:

1. adding a traffic light with a label (string);

2. removing a traffic light by label;

3. switching the state of a traffic light with some given label; and

4. resetting a traffic light to red with some given label.

**Hint:** The first two services are provided directly; the last two are implemented by the simulated traffic lights.

After the development of the program is completed, develop a graphical user interface. ∎

**Exercise 39.2.2** Develop *make-master*. The program consumes nothing, creates an instance of the color-guessing game of section 37.1, and produces the *master-check* function as the only result. After the player has guessed the answer, the function should simply respond with "game over." A typical dialog would proceed as follows:

```
> (define master1 (make-master))
> (master-check 'red 'red)
'NothingCorrect
> (master-check 'black 'pink)
'OneColorOccurs
...
```

Compare this with the first dialogue in section 37.1.

Add a service to *make-master* that reveals the hidden colors. That way a player who is tired of playing the game can find out the answer. ∎

**Exercise 39.2.3** Develop *make-hangman*. The program consumes a list of words, creates a hangman game using the list, and produces the *hangman-guess* function as a result. A player would use the dialogue as follows:

```
> (define hangman-easy (make-hangman (list 'a 'an 'and 'able 'adler)))
> (define hangman-difficult (make-hangman (list 'ardvark . . . )))
> (hangman-easy 'a)
"You won"
> (hangman-difficult 'a)
(list 'head (list '_ '_ '_ '_ '_ '_))
> . . .
```

Compare this with the first dialogue in section 37.2.

Add a service to *make-master* that reveals the chosen word.

An optional extension is to equip the program with a graphical user interface and a graphical view of the stick figure. Reuse existing solutions as much as possible. ∎

**Exercise 39.2.4** Develop *make-player*. The program abstracts over the functions of section 37.5. Using the program, we can create several players that wander through the campus:

```
(define player1 (make-player 'BioEngineering))
(define player2 (make-player 'MuddBuilding))
   . . .
```

The argument to *make-player* specifies the initial position of the player.

Each instance should be able to produce

1. a picture of the current surroundings;

2. a list of the available building connections; and

3. a move from one place to another through an available connection.

**Extension:** Two players may be in the same building at the same time, but they cannot interact. Extend the game so that two players in the same building can interact in some form. ∎

**Exercise 39.2.5** Develop the program *moving-pictures*. It consumes a position and a picture, that is, a list of shapes as defined in sections 6.6, and 7.4, and 10.3. (Also see 21.4 for functions on moving pictures.) It supports two services. First, it can place the shape at a specific position. Second, it can reset the picture to the initially given position. ∎

# 40 Mutable Structures

Encapsulating and managing state variables is similar to forming and managing structures. When we first apply a function that abstracts over state variables we provide initial values for some of the variables. The service manager serves the (current) value of these variables, which is similar to extracting the values of fields in structures. Not surprisingly then, the technique can simulate the constructors and selectors of a **define-struct** definition. This simulation naturally suggests the introduction of functions that modify the value in a structure's field. The following subsections spell out the details behind this idea; the last subsection generalizes it to vectors.

## 40.1 Structures from Functions

---

(**define-struct** *posn* (*x y*))

```
(define (f-make-posn x0 y0)
  (local ((define x y0)
          (define y y0)
          (define (service-manager msg)
            (cond
              [(symbol=? msg 'x) x]
              [(symbol=? msg 'y) y]
              [else (error 'posn "...")])))
    service-manager))

(define (f-posn-x p)
  (p 'x))

(define (f-posn-y p)
  (p 'y))
```

Figure 116: A functional analog of *posn*

---

Take a look at figure 116. The left-hand side is the one-line definition of a *posn* structure. The right-hand side is a functional definition that provides almost all the same services. In particular, the definition provides a constructor that consumes two values and constructs a compound value, and two selectors for extracting the values that went into the construction of a compound value.

To understand why *f-make-posn* is a constructor and why *f-posn-x* and *f-posn-y* are selectors, we can discuss how they work, and we can confirm that they validate the expected equations. Here we do both, because the definitions are unusual.

The definition of *f-make-posn* encapsulates two variable definitions and one function definition. The two variables stand for the arguments of *f-make-posn* and the function is a service manager; it produces the value of *x* when given 'x and the value of *y* when given 'y. In the preceding section, we might have written something like

(**define** *a-posn* (*f-make-posn* **3** 4))

(+ (*a-posn* 'x) (*a-posn* 'y))

to define and to compute with *f-make-posn*. Since selecting values is such a frequent operation, figure 116 introduces the functions *f-posn-x* and *f-posn-y*, which perform these computations.

When we first introduced structures rigorously in intermezzo 1, we said that the selectors and constructors can be described with equations. For a definition such as that for *posn*, the two relevant equations are:

```
(posn-x (make-posn V-1 V-2))
= V-1
```

and

```
(posn-y (make-posn V-1 V-2))
= V-2
```

where *V-1* and *V-2* are arbitrary values.

To confirm that *f-posn-x* and *f-make-posn* are in the same relationship as posn-x and make-posn, we can validate that they satisfy the first equation:

```
(f-posn-x (f-make-posn 3 4))
= (f-posn-x (local ((define x 3)
                    (define y 4)
                    (define (service-manager msg)
                      (cond
                        [(symbol=? msg 'x) x]
                        [(symbol=? msg 'y) y]
                        [else (error 'posn "...")])))
            service-manager))
```

```
= (f-posn-x service-manager)
  ;; add to top-level definitions:
  (define x 3)
  (define y 4)
  (define (service-manager msg)
    (cond
      [(symbol=? msg 'x) x]
      [(symbol=? msg 'y) y]
      [else (error 'posn "...")]))
```

```
= (service-manager 'x)
```

```
= (cond
    [(symbol=? 'x 'x) x]
    [(symbol=? 'x 'y) y]
    [else (error 'posn "...")])
```

```
= x
```

```
= 3
```

It is an exercise to show that *f-posn-y* and *f-make-posn* satisfy the analogous equation.

## Exercises

**Exercise 40.1.1** Which function does the simulation of structures not provide? Why not? ∎

**Exercise 40.1.2** Here is yet another implementation of *posn* structures:

```
(define (ff-make-posn x y)
  (lambda (select)
    (select x y)))

(define (ff-posn-x a-ff-posn)
  (a-ff-posn (lambda (x y) x)))

(define (ff-posn-y a-ff-posn)
  (a-ff-posn (lambda (x y) y)))
```

Evaluate (*ff-posn-x* (*ff-make-posn* V-1 V2)) in this context. What does the calculation demonstrate? ∎

**Exercise 40.1.3** Show how to implement the following structure definitions as functions:

1. (**define-struct** *movie* (*title producer*))

2. (**define-struct** *boyfriend* (*name hair eyes phone*))

3. (**define-struct** *cheerleader* (*name number*))

4. (**define-struct** *CD* (*artist title price*))

5. (**define-struct** *sweater* (*material size producer*))

Pick one and demonstrate that the expected laws hold. ∎

## 40.2   Mutable Functional Structures

Together, sections 39 and 40.1 suggest that structures are mutable. That is, we should be able to change the values of some field in a structure. After all, we introduced the service managers in section 39 to hide state variables, not just ordinary variable definitions.

Figure 117 shows how a small change to the definitions of figure 116 turns the **loca**lly hidden variables into state variables. The modified service manager offers two services per state variable: one for looking up the current value and one for changing it.

Consider the following definition and expression:

(**define** *a-posn* (*fm-make-posn* 3 4))

(**begin**
    (*fm-set-posn-x!* *a-posn* 5)
    (+ (posn-x *a-posn*) 8))

Evaluating them by hand shows how structures change. Here is the first step:

```
(define (fm-make-posn x0 y0)
  (local ((define x y0)
          (define y y0)
          (define (service-manager msg)
            (cond
              [(symbol=? msg 'x) x]
              [(symbol=? msg 'y) y]
              [(symbol=? msg 'set-x) (lambda (x-new) (set! x x-new))]
              [(symbol=? msg 'set-y) (lambda (y-new) (set! y y-new))]
              [else (error 'posn "...")])))
    service-manager))

(define (fm-posn-x p)
  (p 'x))

(define (fm-posn-y p)
  (p 'y))

(define (fm-set-posn-x! p new-value)
  ((p 'set-x) new-value))

(define (fm-set-posn-y! p new-value)
  ((p 'set-y) new-value))
```

Figure 117: An implementation of *posn*s with mutators

```
...
=
  (define x-for-a-posn 3)
  (define y-for-a-posn 4)
  (define (service-manager-for-a-posn msg)
    (cond
      [(symbol=? msg 'x) x-for-a-posn]
      [(symbol=? msg 'y) y-for-a-posn]
      [(symbol=? msg 'set-x)
       (lambda (x-new) (set! x-for-a-posn x-new))]
      [(symbol=? msg 'set-y)
       (lambda (y-new) (set! y-for-a-posn y-new))]
      [else (error 'posn "...")]))
  (define a-posn service-manager-for-a-posn)
```

```
(begin
  (fm-set-posn-x! a-posn 5)
  (+ (posn-x a-posn) 8))
```

It renames and lifts the local definitions from inside of *fm-make-posn*. Because the function definition doesn't change for the rest of the evaluation, we focus on just the variable definitions:

```
(define x-for-a-posn 3)
(define y-for-a-posn 4)
(begin
  (fm-set-posn-x! a-posn 5)
  (+ (posn-x a-posn) 8))
```

= ```
(define x-for-a-posn 3)
(define y-for-a-posn 4)
(begin
  (fm-set-posn-x! service-manager-for-a-posn 5)
  (+ (posn-x a-posn) 8))
```

= ```
(define x-for-a-posn 3)
(define y-for-a-posn 4)
(begin
  ((service-manager-for-a-posn 'set-x) 5)
  (+ (posn-x a-posn) 8))
```

= ```
(define x-for-a-posn 3)
(define y-for-a-posn 4)
(begin
  (set! x-for-a-posn 5)
  (+ (posn-x a-posn) 8))
```

= ```
(define x-for-a-posn 5)
(define y-for-a-posn 4)
(+ (posn-x a-posn) 8)
```

At this point, the definition of *x-for-a-posn* has been modified in the expected manner. From now on every reference to this state variable, which represents the (simulated) *x* field *a-posn*, stands for 5. Every further reference to *x-for-a-posn* produces 5.

## Exercises

**Exercise 40.2.1** Develop a functional representation for the following structure definition:

> (**define-struct** *boyfriend* (*name hair eyes phone*))

such that the fields of the simulated structure can be changed. ∎

**Exercise 40.2.2** Here is a modification of the function-based implementation of *posn* structures in exercise 40.1.2:

```
(define (ffm-make-posn x0 y0)
  (local ((define x x0)
          (define (set-x new-x) (set! x new-x))
          (define y y0)
          (define (set-y new-y) (set! y new-y)))
    (lambda (select)
      (select x y set-x set-y))))


(define (ffm-posn-x a-ffm-posn)
  (a-ffm-posn (lambda (x y sx sy) x)))


(define (ffm-posn-y a-ffm-posn)
  (a-ffm-posn (lambda (x y sx sy) y)))


(define (ffm-set-posn-x! a-ffm-posn new-value)
  (a-ffm-posn (lambda (x y sx sy) (sx new-value))))


(define (ffm-set-posn-y! a-ffm-posn new-value)
  (a-ffm-posn (lambda (x y sx sy) (sy new-value))))
```

Demonstrate how to modify a structure like (*ffm-make-posn* 3 4) so that its *y* field contains 5. ∎

## 40.3  Mutable Structures

Scheme structures are mutable. In `Advanced Student` Scheme, a structure definition such as

>   (**define-struct** *posn* (*x y*))

introduces six primitives, not just four:

1. make-posn, the constructor;

2. posn-x and posn-y, the selectors;

3. posn?, the predicate; and

4. set-posn-x! and set-posn-y!, the MUTATORS.

The mutators are operations that change the contents of a structure.

Recall that we think of a structure as a box with compartments. For example, the structure

>   (make-posn 3 4)

should be visualized as a box with two compartments:

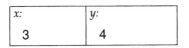

A constructor creates a box; a selector extracts the value from a particular compartment; the predicate recognizes it; and the mutator changes the content of a compartment. That is, a mutator has an effect on its arguments; its result is the invisible value. Pictorially, we should imagine an evaluation step for an expression such as

>   (**define** *p* (make-posn 3 4))
>   (set-posn-x! *p* 5)

as a box with the old *x* value deleted and a new one inserted into the same box:

Consider the following definitions:

>   (**define-struct** *star* (*name instrument*))

    (**define** *p* (make-star 'PhilCollins 'drums))

Let's consider the effect and computation of the following expression:

    (**begin**
      (*set-star-instrument!* *p* 'vocals)
      (list (star-instrument *p*)))

According to our explanation, the first subexpression modifies the *instrument* field of the *star* structure named *p*; the second one produces a list of one item, the current value the *instrument* field in the structure named *p*. By analogy to section 40.2, the evaluation proceeds as follows:

    (**define-struct** *star* (*name instrument*))
    (**define** *p* (make-star 'PhilCollins 'drums))
    (**begin**
      (*set-star-instrument!* *p* 'vocals)
      (list (star-instrument *p*)))

= (**define-struct** *star* (*name instrument*))
    (**define** *p* (make-star 'PhilCollins 'vocals))
    (**begin**
      (void)
      (list (star-instrument *p*)))

= (**define-struct** *star* (*name instrument*))
    (**define** *p* (make-star 'PhilCollins 'vocals))
    (list 'vocals)

The first step changes one part of the value in the definition of *p*, but not the entire value. The second one extracts the current value of the *instrument* field and places it in a list.

    The introduction of mutators for structures requires two changes to our system of evaluation rules:

1. Every constructor expression adds a definition with a new, unique name to the top level, unless it already occurs in a definition.[75]

2. A name that stands for a structure is a value.

---

[75]For simplicity, we use this simple approximation. When a program also uses **set!**-expression, we must rely on the refinement of intermezzo 8.3 to understand its behavior completely. Also see the note on this topic on page 606.

We can understand these changes if we think of each structure as a function that manages services such as looking up the current value of a field and modifying the field. After all, **local** function definitions also create top-level definitions with unique names. And the names of functions are values, too.

Using these two new rules we can study the unusual behavior of mutators in more depth. Here is a first example:

(**define-struct** *star* (*name instrument*))

(**define** *p* (make-star 'PhilCollins 'drums))

(**define** *q p*)

(**begin**
  (*set-star-instrument! p* 'vocals)
  (list (star-instrument *q*)))

It differs from the first in two ways. First, it defines *q* to be *p*. Second, the second subexpression of the **begin**-expression refers to *q*, not *p*. Let's check our understanding of the evaluation process:

    (**define-struct** *star* (*name instrument*))
    (**define** *p* (make-star 'PhilCollins 'drums))
    (**define** *q p*)
    (**begin**
      (*set-star-instrument! p* 'vocals)
      (list (star-instrument *q*)))

= (**define-struct** *star* (*name instrument*))
    (**define** *p* (make-star 'PhilCollins 'vocals))
    (**define** *q p*)
    (**begin**
      (void)
      (list (star-instrument *q*)))

As before, the first step changes one part of the definition of *p*. The second step is to look up *q*'s current value:

    . . .

= (**define-struct** *star* (*name instrument*))
    (**define** *p* (make-star 'PhilCollins 'vocals))
    (**define** *q p*)
    (list (star-instrument *p*))

```
= (define-struct star (name instrument))
  (define p (make-star 'PhilCollins 'vocals))
  (define q p)
  (list 'vocals)
```

Because *q* is *p* and the current value of the *instrument* field of *p* instrument is 'vocals, the result is again (list 'vocals).

What we have just seen is the effect of SHARING (the effects of mutators), which means that a modification of a struture affects the program in more than one place. Sharing is also visible inside lists as our second example shows:

```
(define-struct star (name instrument))


(define q (list (make-star 'PhilCollins 'drums)))


(begin
  (set-star-instrument! (first q) 'vocals)
  (list (star-instrument (first q))))
```

Here, the right-hand side of the definition of *q* is an expression whose only subexpression isn't a value. More precisely, it is a structure expression that must be evaluated:

. . .

```
= (define-struct star (name instrument))
  (define p (make-star 'PhilCollins 'drums))
  (define q (list p))
  (begin
    (set-star-instrument! (first q) 'vocals)
    (list (star-instrument (first q))))
```

```
= (define-struct star (name instrument))
  (define p (make-star 'PhilCollins 'drums))
  (define q (list p))
  (begin
    (set-star-instrument! p 'vocals)
    (list (star-instrument (first q))))
```

Thus the first step is to introduce a new definition, for which we choose *p* as the name. The second step replaces (first *q*) by *p*, because *q* is a list of one item: *p*. The rest proceeds almost as above:

```
    . . .
=   (define-struct star (name instrument))
    (define p (make-star 'PhilCollins 'vocals))
    (define q (list p))
    (begin
      (void)
      (list (star-instrument (first q))))

=   (define-struct star (name instrument))
    (define p (make-star 'PhilCollins 'vocals))
    (define q (list p))
    (list (star-instrument p))

=   (define-struct star (name instrument))
    (define p (make-star 'PhilCollins 'vocals))
    (define q (list p))
    (list 'vocals)
```

Finally, effects can be shared among items in different lists. Take a look at this third variant of our program:

```
(define-struct star (name instrument))

(define q (list (make-star 'PhilCollins 'drums)))

(define r (list (first q) (star-instrument (first q))))

(begin
  (set-star-instrument! (first q) 'vocals)
  (list (star-instrument (first r))))
```

The new definition introduces the variable $r$, which stands for a list that contains two items. Let's use our new rules to determine the values and the effects of this program:

```
    . . .
=   (define-struct star (name instrument))
    (define p (make-star 'PhilCollins 'drums))
    (define q (list p))
    (define r (list (first q) (star-instrument (first q))))
    (begin
      (set-star-instrument! (first q) 'vocals)
      (list (star-instrument (first r))))
```

```
= (define-struct star (name instrument))
  (define p (make-star 'PhilCollins 'drums))
  (define q (list p))
  (define r (list p (star-instrument p)))
  (begin
     (set-star-instrument! (first q) 'vocals)
     (list (star-instrument (first r))))

= (define-struct star (name instrument))
  (define p (make-star 'PhilCollins 'drums))
  (define q (list p))
  (define r (list p 'drums))
  (begin
     (set-star-instrument! (first q) 'vocals)
     (list (star-instrument (first r))))
```

As above, the first step introduces a definition for the new *star* structure. The second and third step create the list named *r*, which contains *p*, the newly created structure, and 'vocals, its current *instrument* value.

The next step selects the first item from *q* and modifies its *instrument* field:

   ...

```
= (define-struct star (name instrument))
  (define p (make-star 'PhilCollins 'vocals))
  (define q (list p))
  (define r (list p 'drums))
  (begin
     (void)
     (list (star-instrument (first r))))

= (define-struct star (name instrument))
  (define p (make-star 'PhilCollins 'vocals))
  (define q (list p))
  (define r (list p 'drums))
  (list (star-instrument p))

= (define-struct star (name instrument))
  (define p (make-star 'PhilCollins 'vocals))
  (define q (list p))
  (define r (list p 'drums))
  (list 'vocals)
```

Because *r* contains *p* as the first item and because the instrument field of *p* is still 'vocals, the result is (list 'vocals) here, too. But, this program still has some knowledge of 'drums, the original value of the *star* structure.

In summary, mutators give us more power than constructors and selectors. Instead of just creating new structures and revealing their contents, we can now change their contents, while the structures remain the same. Next we must contemplate what this means for the design of programs.

## Exercises

**Exercise 40.3.1** Name the mutators that the following structure definitions introduce:

1. (**define-struct** *movie (title producer)*)

2. (**define-struct** *boyfriend (name hair eyes phone)*)

3. (**define-struct** *cheerleader (name number)*)

4. (**define-struct** *CD (artist title price)*)

5. (**define-struct** *sweater (material size producer)*) ∎

**Exercise 40.3.2** Develop the function *swap-posn*, which consumes a *posn* structure and swaps the values in the two fields. Its result is (void). ∎

**Exercise 40.3.3** Develop the function *one-more-date*, which consumes a *girl-friends* structure and increases the contents of the *number-past-dates* field by 1. The structure definition is

  (**define-struct** *girlfriends (name hair eyes number-past-dates)*)

The result of *one-more-date* is (void). ∎

**Exercise 40.3.4** Evaluate the following program, step by step:

  (**define-struct** *cheerleader (name number)*)

  (**define** *A* (make-cheerleader 'JoAnn 2))

  (**define** *B* (make-cheerleader 'Belle 1))

```
(define C (make-cheerleader 'Krissy 1))

(define all (list A B C))

(list
  (cheerleader-number (second all))
  (begin
    (set-cheerleader-number! (second all) 17)
    (cheerleader-number (second all))))
```

Underline in the last program where definitions differ from the initial program. ∎

**Exercise 40.3.5** Evaluate the following program:

```
(define-struct CD (artist title price))

(define in-stock
  (list
    ((make-CD 'R.E.M "New Adventures in Hi-fi" 0)
     (make-CD 'France "simple je" 0)
     (make-CD 'Cranberries "no need to argue" 0))))

(begin
  (set-CD-price! (first in-stock) 12)
  (set-CD-price! (second in-stock) 19)
  (set-CD-price! (third in-stock) 11)
  (+ (CD-price (first in-stock))
     (CD-price (second in-stock))
     (CD-price (third in-stock))))
```

Show every step. ∎

## 40.4 Mutable Vectors

Recall from intermezzo 29 that vectors, like structures, are compound values. To extract a value from a structure, programs use selector operations. To extract a value from a vector, programs use natural numbers as indices.

Hence functions that process vectors defer to auxiliary functions that process vectors and natural numbers.

Not surprisingly, vectors, like structures, are mutable compound values. The only mutator for vectors is **vector-set!**, a function that consumes a vector, an index, and a value. Thus, for example, the following program evaluates to 'blank:

(**define** $X$ (vector 'a 'b 'c 'd))

(**begin**
   (vector-set! $X$ 0 'blank)
   (vector-set! $X$ 1 'blank)
   (vector-set! $X$ 2 'blank)
   (vector-set! $X$ 3 'blank)
   (vector-ref $X$ 2))

The four **vector-set!** expressions change $X$ so that all of its four fields contain 'blank. The last expression extracts the value of one of the fields.

In general, an evaluation concerning mutable vectors proceeds just like an evaluation for mutable structures. In particular, a **vector** expression introduces a new definition:

   (list (vector 1 2 3))
= (list $v$)
   ;; add to top-level definitions:
   (**define** $v$ (vector 1 2 3))

The variable name $v$ is new and unique. Similarly, a **vector-set!** expression modifies a part of a vector definition:

   (*set-vector!* (vector 1 2 3) 0 'a)

= (**define** $v$ (vector 1 2 3))
   (*set-vector!* $v$ 0 'a)

= (**define** $v$ (vector 'a 2 3))
   (void)

Finally, effects to vectors are shared just like effects to structures.

## Exercises

**Exercise 40.4.1** Evaluate the following program:

   (**define** $X$ (vector 0 0 0 0))

(**define** *Y X*)

(**begin**
  (vector-set! *X* 0 2)
  (vector-set! *Y* 1 (+ (vector-ref *Y* 0) (vector-ref *Y* 1)))
  (vector-ref *Y* 1))

Show all steps. ∎

**Exercise 40.4.2** Develop the function *clear*, which consumes a vector with three slots and sets them to 0. ∎

**Exercise 40.4.3** Develop the function *swap*, which consumes a vector with two slots and swaps the values in these slots. ∎

**Exercise 40.4.4** Extend the board representation of exercise 29.3.14 with the function

  ;; *board-flip! : board* **N N** → *boolean*
  ;; to negate the board position with indices *i, j* on *a-board*
  (**define** (*board-flip! a-board i j*) . . . )

Don't forget to develop examples and tests for the function. ∎

## 40.5 Changing Variables, Changing Structures

Structure mutators and **set!**-expressions are related. Indeed, in section 40.2 we explained the effects of the first with the second. Still, there are also important differences that a programmer must understand. Let's start with the syntax:

(**set!** ⟨*variable*⟩ ⟨*expression*⟩)                 set–⟨*structure-tag*⟩–⟨*field*⟩!

A **set!**-expression is an expression that consists of two pieces: a variable and an expression. The variable is fixed; it is never evaluated. The expression is evaluated. In contrast, a structure mutator is a function. As such, it is a value that the program can apply (to two arguments), pass to other functions, store inside of structures, and so on. Structure mutators are created in response to structure definitions, just as structure constructors and selectors.

Next we must consider lexical scope issues (see section 18.2). A **set!**-expression contains a variable. For the **set!**-expression to be valid, this variable must be bound. The connection between a **set!**-expression's variable and its binding occurrence is static and can never be changed.

The scope of a mutator is that of its corresponding **define-struct**. Thus, in the following program

(**define-struct** *aaa* (*xx yy*))

(**define** *UNIQUE*
  (**local** ((**define-struct** <u>*aaa* (*xx yy*)</u>))
    (make-aaa 'my 'world)))

   · · ·

the underlined occurrence of **define-struct** has a limited lexical scope, and its scope is a hole in the scope of the top-level **define-struct**. A result of this scoping is that the mutator for the top-level **define-struct** cannot mutate the structure called *UNIQUE*. The two mutators are unrelated functions that coincidentally have the same name; the rules for the evaluation of **local**-expression dictate that we rename one consistently.

To highlight the differences in syntax and lexical scope, take a look at the following two, apparently similar programs:

(**define** *the-point* (make-posn 3 4))      (**define** *the-point* (make-posn 3 4))


(**set!** *x* 17)                  (set-posn-x! *the-point* 17)

The one on the left is illegal, because the *x* in the **set!**-expression is an unbound variable. The program on the right is perfectly legal; it refers to the field *x* of a *posn* structure.

The largest difference between **set!**-expressions and mutators concerns their semantics. Let's study two examples to understand the differences once and for all. The first illustrates how similar looking expressions evaluate in a radically different manner:

(**define** *the-point* (make-posn 3 4))      (**define** *the-point* (make-posn 3 4))


(**set!** *the-point* 17)             (set-posn-x! *the-point* 17)

The program on the left consists of a definition for *the-point* and an assignment to *the-point*; the one on the right starts with the same definition for *the-point* followed by an application of the mutator. The evaluation of both affects the variable definition but in different ways:

(**define** *the-point* 17)                    (**define** *the-point* (make-posn 17 4))

(void)                                         (void)

On the left, *the-point* now stands for a number; on the right, it is still a *posn* structure but with a new value in the *x*-field. More generally, a **set!**-expression changes the value on the right-hand side of a definition, and the application of a mutator changes the value of just one field in a structure that occurs on the right-hand side of a definition.

The second example shows how an application of mutator evaluates the arguments, which is not the case for **set!**-expressions:

(**define** *the-point* (make-posn 3 4))       (**define** *the-point* (make-posn 3 4))
(**define** *an-other* (make-posn 12 5))       (**define** *an-other* (make-posn 12 5))

```
(set! (cond                                    (set-posn-x!
      [(zero? (point-x the-point))                   (cond
       the-point]                                        [(zero? (point-x the-point))
      [else                                              the-point]
       an-other])                                        [else
  1)                                                      an-other])
                                                   1)
```

Whereas the program on the left is illegal, because a **set!**-expression must contain a fixed variable in the second position, the one on the right is legitimate. The evaluation of the program on the right changes the *x*-field in *an-other* to 1.

Finally, *mutators* are values, which means a function can consume a mutator and apply it:

```
;; set-to-2 : S-mutator S-structure → void
;; to change a field in s to 2 via mutator
(define (set-to-2 mutator s)
  (mutator s 2))

(define-struct bbb (zz ww))

(local ((define s (make-posn 3 4))
        (define t (make-bbb 'a 'b)))
  (begin
    (set-to-2 set-posn-x! s)
    (set-to-2 set-bbb-ww! t)))
```

The function *set-to-2* consumes a mutator and a structure that the mutator can modify. The program uses it to change the *x*-field in a *posn* structure and the *ww*-field in a *bbb* structure. In contrast, if we were to apply a function to a **set!**-expression, it would receive (void) and nothing else.

**Mixing set! and Structure Mutators**: When a program uses both **set!**-expressions and structure mutators, our evaluation rules fail for some cases. Specifically, they don't explain sharing properly. Consider this program fragment:

> (**define** *the-point* (make-posn 3 4))

> (**define** *another-point the-point*)

> (**begin**
>   (**set!** *the-point* 17)
>   (= (posn-x *another-point*) 3))

According to our rules, the two definitions refer to the same structure. The second one does so by indirection. The **set!**-expression changes what *the-point* stands for, but it shouldn't affect the second definition. In particular, the program should produce true. If we were to use our rules in a naive manner, we would not be able to validate this point.

A proper explanation of structures must introduce a new definition for every application of a structure constructor, including those on the right-hand side of definitions in the original program. We will place the new definitions at the beginning of the sequence of definitions. Furthermore, the variable in the new definition must be unique so that it cannot occur in a **set!**-expression. We will use variables such as *struct-1*, *struct-2*, and so on, and agree to use them for this purpose only. These names, and only these names, are values.

Using the minor changes to our rules, we can evaluate the program fragment properly:

> (**define** *the-point* (make-posn 3 4))

> (**define** *another-point the-point*)

> (**begin**
>   (**set!** *the-point* 17)
>   (= (posn-x *another-point*) 3))

```
= (define struct-1 (make-posn 3 4))
  (define the-point struct-1)
  ;; evaluate from here:
  (define another-point the-point)
  (begin
    (set! the-point 17)
    (= (posn-x another-point) 3))

= (define struct-1 (make-posn 3 4))
  (define the-point struct-1)
  (define another-point struct-1)
  ;; evaluate from here:
  (begin
    (set! the-point 17)
    (= (posn-x another-point) 3))
```

At this point, the structure is created, and both of the original variables refer to the new structure. The rest of the evaluation changes the definition of *the-point* but not *another-point*:

```
  . . .
= (define struct-1 (make-posn 3 4))
  (define the-point 17)
  (define another-point struct-1)
  ;; evaluate from here:
  (begin
    (void)
    (= (posn-x another-point) 3))

= (define struct-1 (make-posn 3 4))
  (define the-point 17)
  (define another-point struct-1)
  ;; evaluate from here:
  (= (posn-x another-point) 3)

= (define struct-1 (make-posn 3 4))
  (define the-point 17)
  (define another-point struct-1)
  ;; evaluate from here:
  (= 3 3)
```

The final result is true, as expected.

The modified evaluation rules are a bit more cumbersome than the old ones. But they fully explain the difference between the effects of **set!**-expressions and those of structure mutation, which, for programming in modern languages, is an essential concept. ∎

# 41  Designing Functions that Change Structures

Sections 39 and 40 gradually introduced the idea of mutable structures. In the first of the two sections we studied the idea of changing a **locally** defined variable through a function. In the second one, we discussed how structures could be modified, too.

Now we need to learn when and how to use this new power. The first subsection concerns the question of why a program should modify a structure. The second reviews how the existing design recipes apply when we wish to use mutators. The third one discusses some difficult cases. The last one is dedicated to the differences between **set!** and structure mutators.

## 41.1  Why Mutate Structures

Whenever we apply a structure constructor, we create a new structure. On some occasions, this is truly what we want. Consider a function that consumes a list of personnel records and produces a list of phone book entries. The personnel records may contain information about a person's address, including the phone number, date of birth, marital status, closest relatives, and salary level. The entry for the phone book should contain the name and the phone number and nothing else. This kind of program should definitely generate a new structure from each structure in the given list.

On other occasions, though, creating a new structure doesn't correspond to our intuition. Suppose we wish to give someone a raise. The only way of accomplishing this at the moment is to create a new personnel record that contains all the old information and the new salary information. Or, suppose someone has moved and received a new phone number, and we wish to update the phone book on our PDA. Just like the program that changes a person's salary level, the program that updates the phone book would create a new phone book entry. In reality, however, we would not create a new personnel record or a new entry in the phone book. We would instead correct the existing personnel record and the existing entry in our phone book. A program should be able to perform the same kind of corrective action and, with mutators, we can indeed develop such programs.

Roughly speaking, the examples suggest two cases. First, if a structure corresponds to a physical object and the computation corresponds to a corrective action, the program may mutate the structure. Second, if a structure does not correspond to a physical object or if the computation creates a new kind of value from existing information, the program should create a new structure. These two rules are not clear-cut. We will often encounter situations where both solutions are feasible. In that case, we must consider an ease-of-programming argument. If one of the two solutions is easier to design—often the creation of a new structure, choose it. If the decision leads to a performance bottleneck—and only then, restructure it.

## 41.2 Structural Design Recipes and Mutation, Part 1

Surprisingly, programming with mutators does not require any new design recipes—as long as the mutated fields always contain atomic values. Our receipes work perfectly fine. While the design of non-mutating programs requires the combination of values, programming with mutators requires the combination of effects. Hence the key is to add a well-formulated effect statement to a function's contract and to make up examples that illustrate the effects. We practiced both of these activities for **set!** expressions already in section 36. In this section we learn to adapt the design recipes and effect statements to structural mutations. To do that, we consider a short series of examples. Each illustrates how an applicable design recipe helps with the design of structure-modifying or vector-modifying functions.

The first example concerns the mutation of plain structures. Suppose we are given a structure and a data definition for personnel records:

> (**define-struct** *personnel* (*name address salary*))
> ;; A personnel record (*PR*) is a structure:
> ;; (*make-personnel n a s*)
> ;; where *n* is a symbol, *a* is a string, and *s* is a number.

A function that consumes such a record is based on the following template:

> (**define** (*fun-for-personnel pr*)
>    ... (*personnel-name pr*) ...
>    ... (*personnel-address pr*) ...
>    ... (*personnel-salary pr*) ...)

Consider a function for increasing the salary field:

*;; increase-salary : PR number → void*
*;; effect:* to modify the salary field of *a-pr* by adding *a-raise*
(**define** (*increase-salary a-pr a-raise*) ... )

The contract specifies that the function consumes a *PR* and a number. The purpose statement is an effect statement, which explains how the argument of *increase-salary* is modified.

Developing examples for *increase-salary* requires the techniques of section 36. Specifcially, we must be able to compare the before and after state of some *PR* structure:

(**local** ((**define** *pr1* (*make-personnel* 'Bob 'Pittsburgh 70000)))
  (**begin**
    (*increase-salary pr1* 10000)
    (= (*personnel-salary pr1*) 80000)))

The result of the expression is true if, and only if, *increase-salary* works properly for this example.

We can now use the template and the example to define the function:

*;; increase-salary : PR number → void*
*;; effect:* to modify the salary field of *a-pr* by adding in *a-raise*
(**define** (*increase-salary a-pr a-raise*)
  (*set-personnel-salary! a-pr* (+ (*personnel-salary a-pr*) *a-raise*)))

As usual, the full definition uses only one of several subexpressions from the template, but the template reminds us of what information we can use: the arguments and their pieces; and what parts we can modify: the fields for which we have selectors.

---

## Exercises

**Exercise 41.2.1** Make up examples for *increase-salary* and test the function. Formulate the tests as boolean-valued expressions. ∎

**Exercise 41.2.2** Adapt *increase-salary* such that it accepts only values for *a-raise* between 3% and 7% of the salary. It calls error otherwise. ∎

**Exercise 41.2.3** Develop *increase-percentage*. The function consumes a *PR* and a percentage between 3% and 7%. It increases the value in the salary field of the *PR* by the lesser of the percentage increase or 7000. ∎

**Exercise 41.2.4** Develop the function *new-date*. It consumes a *cheerleader* record and adds a date to the beginning of a list. Here are the relevant definitions:

> (**define-struct** *cheerleader* (*name dates*))
> ;; A *cheerleader* is a structure:
> ;; (make-cheerleader *n d*)
> ;; where *n* is a symbol and *d* is a list of symbols.

For example, (make-cheerleader 'JoAnn '(Carl Bob Dude Adam Emil)) is a valid *cheerleader* record. Develop an example that shows what it means to add 'Frank as a date. ∎

**Exercise 41.2.5** Recall the structure definitions for *square*s:

> (**define-struct** *square* (*nw length*))

The matching data definition specifies that the *nw* field is always a *posn* structure and that *length* is a number:

> A *square* is a structure:
> $$\text{(make-square } p \ s)$$
> where *p* is a *posn* and *s* is a number.

Develop the function *move-square!*. It consumes a square, called *sq*, and a number, called *delta*. It modifies *sq* by adding *delta* to its $x$ coordinate.

Look up the structure and data definition for circles and develop the function *move-circle*, which is analogous to *move-square*. ∎

The second example recalls the design recipe for functions that work on unions of classes. One of our first examples of this kind concerned the class of geometric shapes. Here is the relevant data definition:

> A *shape* is either
>
> 1. a *circle*, or
>
> 2. a *square*.

See exercise 41.2.5 or part I for the definitions of *circle* and *square*.

Following our recipe, a template for *shape*-processing functions consists of a two-clause **cond**-expression:

(**define** (*fun-for-shape a-shape*)
  (**cond**
    [(circle? *a-shape*) ... (*fun-for-circle a-shape*) ...]
    [(square? *a-shape*) ... (*fun-for-square a-shape*) ...]))

Each **cond**-clause refers to a function with the same purpose for the matching kind of shape.

So, suppose we wish to move a *shape* in the $x$ direction by a fixed number of pixels. In part I, we created a new structure for this purpose. Now we can use the mutators for *circle* and *square* structures instead—that is, the function can have an effect:

;; *move-shape! : shape number $\rightarrow$ void*
;; effect: to move *a-shape* in the $x$ direction by *delta* pixels
(**define** (*move-shape! a-shape*)
  (**cond**
    [(circle? *a-shape*) (*move-circle a-shape delta*)]
    [(square? *a-shape*) (*move-square a-shape delta*)]))

The functions *move-circle* and *move-square* are the subject of execise 41.2.5 because they consume and affect plain structures.

---

## Exercises

**Exercise 41.2.6** Make up examples for *move-shape!* and test the function. Formulate the tests as boolean-valued expressions! ∎

**Exercise 41.2.7** The following structure definitions are to represent items that a music store sells:

(**define-struct** *CD* (*price title artist*))
(**define-struct** *record* (*price antique title artist*))
(**define-struct** *DVD* (*price title artist to-appear*))
(**define-struct** *tape* (*price title artist*))

Provide a data definition for the class of *music items*, which comprises *cd*s, *record*s, *dvd*s, and *tape*s. The price must be a number in each case.

Develop the program *inflate!*, which consumes a *music-item* and a percentage. Its effect is to increase the price in the given structure according to the percentage. ∎

**Exercise 41.2.8** Develop a program that keeps track of the feeding of zoo animals. Our zoo has three kinds of animals: elephants, monkeys, and spiders. Each animal has a name and two feeding times per day: morning and evening. Initially a structure that represents an animal (structure) contains false in the fields for feeding times. The program *feed-animal* should consume a structure that represents an animal and the name of a feeding time. It should switch the corresponding field in the animal structure to true. ∎

The next two examples are about mutations when the underlying data definitions involve self-references. Self-references are needed if we wish to deal with data that has no size limit. Lists were the first class of such data we encountered and natural numbers the second one.

Let's first take a look at mutation of lists of structures, using the running data example of this part: the address book. An address book is a list of entries; for completeness, here are the structure and data definitions:

(**define-struct** *entry* (*name number*))

> An *entry* is a structure:
> $$(\text{make-entry } n \ p)$$
> where *n* is a symbol and *p* is a number.

> An *address-book* is
>
> 1. the empty list, empty, or
>
> 2. (cons *an-e an-ab*) where *an-e* is an entry and *an-ab* is an address book.

Only the second one is self-referential, so we focus on the template for it:

```
;; fun-for-ab : address-book → XYZ
(define (fun-for-ab ab)
  (cond
    [(empty? ab) ...]
    [else ... (fun-for-entry (first ab)) ... (fun-for-ab (rest ab)) ...]))
```

If we needed an auxiliary function for processing an *entry*, we might also wish to write out the template for structure-processing functions.

So suppose we want a function that updates an existing entry. The function consumes an *address-book*, a name, and a phone number. The first *entry* that contains the name is modified to contain the new phone number:

*;; change-number! : symbol number address-book → void*
*;; effect: to modify the first entry for name in ab so that its*
*;; number field is phone*
(**define** (*change-number! name phone ab*) ... )

It is justified to develop this function with mutators because just as in reality, most of the address book stays the same while one entry is changed.

Here is an example:

```
(define ab
  (list
    (make-entry 'Adam 1)
    (make-entry 'Chris 3)
    (make-entry 'Eve 2)))
```

(**begin**
  (*change-number!* 'Chris 17 *ab*)
  (= (entry-number (second *ab*)) 17))

The definition introduces *ab*, an *address-book* with three items. The **begin**-expression first changes *ab* by associating 'Chris with 17; then it compares the phone number of the second item on *ab* with 17. If *change-number!* functions properly, the result of the **begin**-expression is true. An even better test would ensure that nothing else in *ab* changes.

The next step is to develop the function definition, using the template and the examples. Let's consider each case separately:

1. If *ab* is empty, *name* doesn't occur in it. Unfortunately, the purpose statement doesn't specify what the function should compute in this case, and there is indeed nothing sensible the function can do. To be safe, we use error to signal that no matching entry was found.

2. If *ab* contains a first *entry*, it might or might not contain *name*. To find out, the function must distinguish the two cases with a **cond**-expression:

    (**cond**
      [(symbol=? (entry-name (first *ab*)) *name*) ... ]
      [**else** ... ])

In the first subcase, the function must modify the structure. In the second, *name* can occur only in (rest *ab*), which means the function must mutate some *entry* in the rest of the list. Fortunately, the natural recursion accomplishes just that.

Putting everything together, we get the following definition:

(**define** (*change-number! name phone ab*)
  (**cond**
    [(empty? *ab*) (error 'change-number! "name not in list")]
    [**else** (**cond**
        [(symbol=? (entry-name (first *ab*)) *name*)
        (set-entry-number! (first *ab*) *phone*)]
       [**else**
        (*change-number! name phone* (rest *ab*))])])))

The only unique aspect of this function is that it uses a structure mutator in one of the cases. Otherwise it has the familiar recursive shape: a **cond** with two clauses and a natural recursion. It is especially instructive to compare the function with *contains-doll?* from section 9.3 and *contains?* from exercise 9.3.3.

---

## Exercises

**Exercise 41.2.9** Define *test-change-number*. The function consumes a name, a phone number, and an address book. It uses *change-number!* to update the address book, and then ensures that it was changed properly. If so, it produces true; if not, it produces an error message. Use this new function to test *change-number!* with at least three different examples. ∎

**Exercise 41.2.10** Develop *move-squares*. It consumes a list of *squares*, as defined above, and a number *delta*. The function modifies each on the list by adding *delta* to the *x*-component of its position. ∎

**Exercise 41.2.11** Develop the function *all-fed*. It consumes a list of *animals*, as defined in exercise 41.2.8, and modifies them so that their field for morning feedings is switched to true. ∎

**Exercise 41.2.12** Develop the function *for-all*, which abstracts *move-squares* and *all-fed* from exercises 41.2.10 and 41.2.11. It consumes two values: a function that consumes structures and produces (void); and a list of structures. Its result is (void). ∎

**Exercise 41.2.13** Develop the function *ft-descendants*. It consumes a descendant family tree (see section 15.1) based on the following structure definition:

(**define-struct** *parent* (*children name date eyes no-descendants*))

The last field in a *parent* structure is originally 0. The function *ft-descendants* traverses the tree and modifies these slots so that they contain the total number of descendants of the corresponding family member. Its result is the number of total descendants of the given tree. ∎

Natural numbers make up another class of values that requires a self-referential description. Recursion on natural numbers per se isn't useful in conjunction with mutation, but recursion on natural numbers as indices into vectors is useful when a problem's data representation involves vectors.

Let's start with a snippet of an elevator control program. An elevator control program must know at which floor people have pressed the call buttons. We assume that the elevator hardware can mutate some status vector of booleans. That is, we assume that the program contains a vector, call it *call-status*, and that a field in *call-status* is true if someone has pushed the call button at the corresponding floor.

One important elevator operation is to *reset* all the buttons. For example, an operator may have to restart the elevator after it has been out of service for a while. We start the development of *reset* by restating the known facts in a Scheme outline:[76]

;; *call-status* : (**vectorof** *boolean*)
;; to keep track of the floors from which calls have been issued
(**define** *call-status* (vector true true true false true true true false))

;; *reset* : → *void*
;; effect: to set all fields in *call-status* to false
(**define** (*reset*) ...)

The first definition specifies *call-status* as a state variable, but of course we use each slot in the vector as a state value, not the entire variable. The second part consists of three pieces: a contract, an effect statement, and a header for the function *reset*, which implements the informally specified service.

---

[76]The notation (**vectorof** *X*) is analogous to (**listof** *X*).

While it is possible to implement the service as

(**define** (*reset*)
  (**set!** *call-status*
    (build-vector (vector-length *call-status*) (**lambda** (*i*) false))))

this trivial solution is clearly not what we want because it creates a new vector. Instead, we want a function that modifies each field of the existing vector. Following the suggestions of intermezzo 5, we develop an auxiliary function with the following template:

;; *reset-aux* : (**vectorof** *boolean*) **N** → *void*
;; effect: to set the fields of *v* with index in [0, *i*) to false
(**define** (*reset-aux v i*)
  (**cond**
    [(zero? *i*) ... ]
    [**else** ... (*reset-aux v* (sub1 *i*)) ... ]))

That is, the auxiliary function consumes not only the vector but also an interval bound. The shape of the template is based on the data definition of the latter.

The effect statement suggests the following examples:

1. (*reset-aux call-status* 0) leaves *call-status* unchanged, because the purpose statement says to change all indices in [0,0) and there are none;

2. (*reset-aux* 1) changes *call-status* so that (vector-ref *call-status* 0) is false, because 0 is the only natural number in [0, 1);

3. (*reset-aux call-status* (vector-length *call-status*)) sets all fields of *call-status* to false.

The last example implies that we can define *reset* with (*reset-aux call-status* (vector-length *call-status*)).

Equipped with examples, we can turn our attention to the definition. The key is to remember that the additional argument must be interpreted as an index into the vector. Keeping the example and the guideline in mind, let's look at each of the two cases separately:

1. If (zero? *i*) holds, the function has no effect and produces (void).

2. Otherwise *i* is positive. In that case, the natural recursion sets all fields in *call-status* with an index in [0,(sub1 *i*)) to false. Furthermore, to complete the task, the function must set the vector field with index

(sub1 *i*) to false. The combination of the two effects is achieved with a **begin**-expression that sequences the natural recursion and the additional vector-set!.

Figure 118 puts everything together. The second clause in the definition of *reset-aux* changes the vector at index (sub1 *i*) and then uses the natural recursion. Its result is the result of the **begin**-expression.

---

```
;; call-status : (vectorof boolean)
;; to keep track of the floors from which calls have been issued
(define call-status (vector true true true false true true true false))

;; reset : → void
;; effect: to set all fields in call-status to false
(define (reset)
  (reset-aux call-status (vector-length call-status)))

;; reset-aux : (vectorof boolean) N → void
;; effect: to set the fields of v with index in [0, i) to false
(define (reset-aux v i)
  (cond
    [(zero? i) (void)]
    [else (begin
            (vector-set! v (sub1 i) false)
            (reset-aux v (sub1 i)))]))
```

Figure 118: Resetting call-buttons for an elevator

---

## Exercises

**Exercise 41.2.14** Use the examples to develop tests for *reset-aux*. Formulate the tests as boolean-valued expressions. ∎

**Exercise 41.2.15** Develop the following variant of *reset*:

```
;; reset-interval : N N → void
;; effect: to set all fields in [from, to] to false
;; assume: (<= from to) holds
(define (reset-interval from to) ...)
```

Use *reset-interval* to define *reset*. ∎

**Exercise 41.2.16** Suppose we represent the position of an object with a vector and the velocity of an object with a second vector. Develop the function *move!*, which consumes a position vector and an equally long velocity vector. It modifies the position vector by adding in the numbers of the speed vector, field by field:

;; *move!* : (**vectorof** *number*) (**vectorof** *number*) → *void*
;; effect: to add the fields of *v* to the corresponding fields of *pos*
;;
;; assumption: *pos* and *v* have equal length
(**define** (*move! pos v*) ...)

Justify why the use of a vector-modifying function is appropriate to model the movement of an object. ∎

**Exercise 41.2.17** Develop the function *vec-for-all*, which abstracts *reset-aux* and the auxiliary vector-processing function for *move!* from exercise 41.2.16. It consumes two values: a function *f* and a vector *vec*. The function *f* consumes indices (**N**) and vector items. The result of *vec-for-all* is (**void**); its effect is to apply *f* to each index and corresponding value in *vec*:

;; *vec-for-all* : (**N** *X* → *void*) (**vectorof** *X*) → *void*
;; effect: to apply *f* to all indices and values in *vec*
;; equation:
;; (*vec-for-all f* (**vector** *v-0* ... *v-N*))
;; =
;; (**begin** (*f N v-N*) ... (*f 0 v-0*) (**void**))
(**define** (*vec-for-all f vec*) ...)

Use *vec-for-all* to define *vector∗!*, which consumes a number *s* and a vector of numbers and modifies the vector by multiplying each field's value with *s*. ∎

The last example covers the common situation when we wish to compute several numeric values at once and place them in a vector. In section 37 we saw that the use of effects is on occasion useful to communicate several results. In the same manner, it is sometimes best to create a vector and to modify it within the same function. Consider the problem of counting how many times each vowel occurs in a list of letters:

;; *count-vowels* : (**listof** *letter*)
;;        → (**vector** *number number number number number*)
;; where a *letter* is a symbol in ′a … ′z
;; to determine how many times the five vowels occur in *chars*
;; the resulting vector lists the counts in the lexicographic order
(**define** (*count-vowels chars*) … )

The choice of vector as a result is appropriate because the function must combine five values into one and each of the values is equally interesting.

Using the purpose statement, we can also come up with examples:

(*count-vowels* ′(a b c d e f g h i))
= (vector 1 1 1 0 0)

(*count-vowels* ′(a a i u u))
= (vector 2 0 1 0 2)

Given that the input is a list, the natural choice for the template is that for a list-processing function:

(**define** (*count-vowels chars*)
  (**cond**
    [(empty? *chars*) … ]
    [**else** … (first *chars*) … (*count-vowels* (rest *chars*)) … ]))

To fill the gaps in the template, we consider each of the two clauses:

1. If (empty? *chars*) is true, the result is a vector of five 0's. After all, there are no vowels in an empty list.

2. If *chars* isn't empty, the natural recursion counts how many vowels and which ones occur in (rest *chars*). To get the correct result, we also have to check whether (first *chars*) is a vowel, and depending on the outcome, increase one of the vector fields. Since this kind of task is a separate, repeated task, we leave it to an auxiliary function:

   ;; *count-a-vowel* : *letter*
   ;;        (**vector** *number number number number number*) → *void*
   ;; effect: to modify *counts* at the appropriate place if *l* is a vowel,
   (**define** (*count-a-vowel l counts*)
       … )

In other words, the second clause first counts the vowels in the rest of the list. This computation is guaranteed to yield a vector according

```
;; count-vowels : (listof letter)
;;        → (vector number number number number number)
;; where a letter is a symbol in 'a ... 'z
;; to determine how many times the five vowels occur in chars
;; the resulting vector lists the counts in the lexicographic order
(define (count-vowels chars)
  (cond
    [(empty? chars) (vector 0 0 0 0 0)]
    [else
     (local ((define count-rest (count-vowels (rest chars))))
       (begin
         (count-a-vowel (first chars) count-rest)
         count-rest))]))

;; count-a-vowel : letter (vector number number number number number) → void
;; effect: to modify counts at the appropriate place if l is a vowel,
;; none otherwise
(define (count-a-vowel l counts)
  ...)
```

Figure 119: Counting vowels

to the purpose statement. Let's call this vector *counts*. Then, it uses *count-a-vowel* to increase the appropriate field in *counts*, if any. The result is *counts*, after the first letter on the list has been counted.

Figure 119 contains the complete definition of the main function. Defining the auxiliary function follows the recipe for non-recursive structure mutations.

## Exercises

**Exercise 41.2.18** Develop the function *count-a-vowel*. Then test the complete *count-vowels* program. ∎

**Exercise 41.2.19** At the end of intermezzo 5, we could have defined *count-vowels* as shown in figure 120. This version does not use vector-set!, but constructs the vector directly using build-vector.

Measure the performance difference between *count-vowels-bv* and *count-vowels*. **Hint:** Define a function that generates a large list of random letters (with, say, 5,000 or 10,000 items).

```
(define (count-vowels-bv chars)
  (local ((define (count-vowel x chars)
            (cond
              [(empty? chars) 0]
              [else (cond
                      [(symbol=? x (first chars))
                       (+ (count-vowel x (rest chars)) 1)]
                      [else (count-vowel x (rest chars))])])))
    (build-vector 5 (lambda (i)
                      (cond
                        [(= i 0) (count-vowel 'a chars)]
                        [(= i 1) (count-vowel 'e chars)]
                        [(= i 2) (count-vowel 'i chars)]
                        [(= i 3) (count-vowel 'o chars)]
                        [(= i 4) (count-vowel 'u chars)])))))
```

Figure 120: Another way of counting vowels

Explain the performance difference between *count-vowels-bv* and *count-vowels*. Does the explanation reflect the measured difference? What does this suggest concerning the vector-set! operation? ∎

**Exercise 41.2.20** Develop *histogram*. The function consumes a list of grades between 0 and 100; it produces a vector of size 101 where each slot contains the number of grades at that level. ∎

**Exercise 41.2.21** Develop *count-children*. The function consumes a descendant family tree, which is a family tree that leads from a family member to the descendants. It produces a vector with six fields. The first five slots contain the number of family members that have that many children; the sixth field contains the number of family members that have five or more children. ∎

## 41.3  Structural Design Recipes and Mutation, Part 2

In the preceding sections, we studied structure mutation for fields that contain atomic data. We know, however, that structures can contain structures. Starting in section 14.1, we even encountered self-referential data definitions involving structures in structures. On occasion, processing such classes of data may also require mutations of structure fields that contain structures. In this section, we work through one such example.

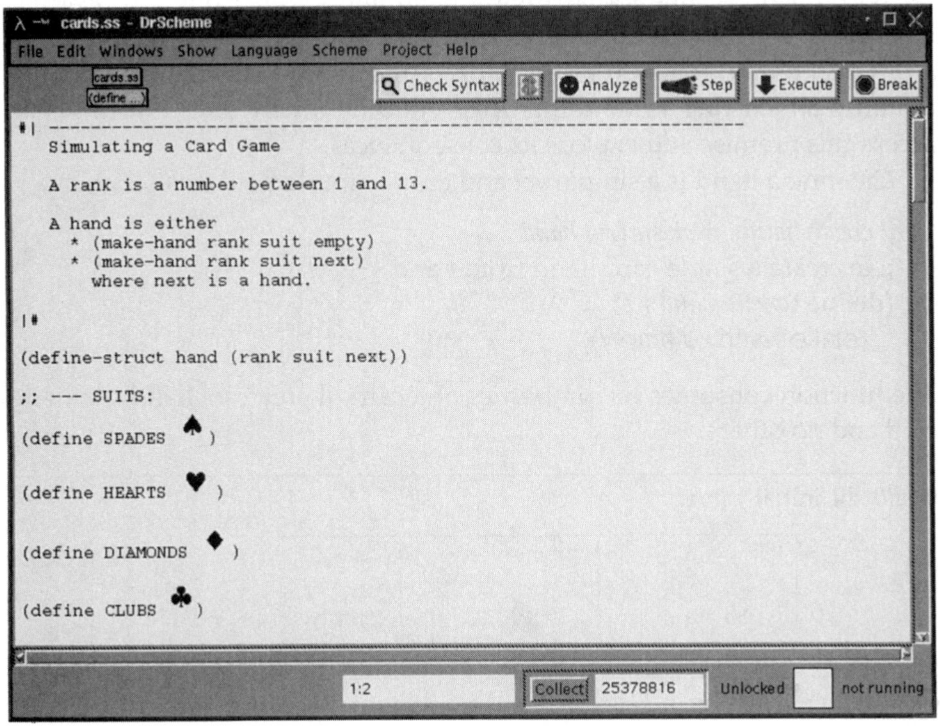

Figure 121: Playing with cards

Suppose we wish to simulate a card game as a program. Each card has two important characteristics: its *suit* and its *rank*. A player's collection of cards is called a *hand*. For now we also assume that every player has at least one card, that is, a hand is never empty.

Figure 121 contains a screen shot of DrScheme with structure and data definitions for manipulating cards and hands. The program fragment does not introduce separate classes of cards and hands, but a single structure and a single data definition for hands. A hand consists of a *hand* structure, which contains a *rank*, a *suit*, and a *next* field. The data definition shows that the next field may contain two kinds of values: empty, which means that there are no other cards, and a *hand* structure, which contains the remainder of the cards. From a global perspective, a *hand* forms a chain of cards; only the last one contains empty in the *next* field.[77]

At first, a player has no cards. Picking up the first card creates a hand. Others cards are then inserted into the existing hand as needed. This calls for two functions: one for creating a hand and another one for inserting a card into a hand. Because a hand exists only once and corresponds to a physical object, it is natural to think of the second function as one that modifies an existing value rather than building a new one. For now, we accept this premise and explore its consequences.

Creating a hand is a simple act and easy to implement as a function:

```
;; create-hand : rank suit → hand
;; to create a single-card hand from r and s
(define (create-hand r s)
  (make-hand r s empty))
```

The function consumes the properties of a card; it creates a hand with one card and no others.

---

*hand0*, the initial value:

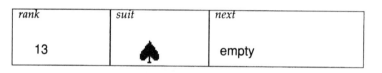

*hand0* after evaluating

    (*add-at-end!* 1 *DIAMONDS hand0*)

Figure 122: Building a hand

---

Adding a card to the end of a hand is a more difficult task. To simplify our life a bit, let's say that a player always adds new cards to the end of the hand. In this case we must process an arbitrarily large value, which means

---

[77]Scheme proper provides list mutators, and a Scheme programmer would use them to represent a hand as a list of cards.

we need a recursive function. Here are the contract, effect statement, and header:

;; *add-at-end! : rank suit hand* → *void*
;; effect : to add a card with *r* as rank and *s* as suit at the end
(**define** (*add-at-end! rank suit a-hand*) . . . )

These specifications say that the function has the invisible value as the result and that it communicates with the rest of the program exclusively through its effects.

Let's start with examples:

(**define** *hand0* (*create-hand* 13 *SPADES*))

If we were to evaluate the following expression

(*add-at-end!* 1 *DIAMONDS hand0*)

in the context of this definition, *hand0* becomes a hand with two cards: a spades-13 followed by a diamonds-1. Figure 122 depicts the change of hand0; the top half displays the initial state of *hand0*, the lower half displays the state after *add-at-end!* has added a card. If we furthermore evaluate

(*add-at-end!* 2 *CLUBS hand0*))

in this context, *hand0* becomes a hand with three cards. The last one is a clubs-2. In terms of an evaluation, the definition of *hand0* should change to

```
(define hand0
  (make-hand 13 SPADES
    (make-hand 1 DIAMONDS
      (make-hand 2 CLUBS empty))))
```

after both additions have been carried out.

Given that the *rank* and *suit* argument to *add-at-end!* are atomic values, the template must be based on the data definition for *hand*s:

```
(define (add-at-end! rank suit a-hand)
  (cond
    [(empty? (hand-next a-hand))
     ... (hand-rank a-hand) ... (hand-suit a-hand) ...]
    [else ... (hand-rank a-hand) ... (hand-suit a-hand) ...
     ... (add-at-end! rank suit (hand-next a-hand)) ...]))
```

The template consists of two clauses, which check the content of the *next* field of *a-hand*. It is recursive in the second clause, because the data definition for *hand*s is self-referential in that clause. In short, the template is completely conventional.

The next step is to consider how the function should affect *a-hand* in each clause:

1. In the first case, *a-hand*'s *next* field is empty. In that case, we can modify the *next* field so that it contains the new card:

   (*set-next-hand! a-hand* (make-hand *rank suit* empty))

   The newly created *hand* structure is now the one that contains empty in its next field, that is, it is the new end of the *a-hand* value.

2. In the second case, the natural recursion adds a new card to the end of *a-hand*. Indeed, because the given *a-hand* isn't the last one in the chain, the natural recursion does everything that needs to be done.

Here is the complete definition of *add-at-end!*:

;; *add-at-end! : rank suit hand → void*
;; effect: to add a card with *v* as rank and *s* as suit at the end of *a-hand*
(**define** (*add-at-end! rank suit a-hand*)
  (**cond**
    [(empty? (hand-next *a-hand*))
     (set-hand-next! *a-hand* (make-hand *rank suit* empty))]
    [**else** (*add-at-end! rank suit* (hand-next *a-hand*))]))

It closely resembles the list-processing functions we designed in part II. This should come as no surprise, because *add-at-end!* processes values from a class that closely resembles the data definition of lists and the design recipes are formulated in a general manner.

## Exercises

**Exercise 41.3.1** Evaluate the following program by hand:

   (**define** *hand0* (*create-hand* 13 *SPADES*))

   (**begin**
     (*add-at-end!* 1 *DIAMONDS hand0*)
     (*add-at-end!* 2 *CLUBS hand0*)
     *hand0*)

Test the function with this example.

Make up two other examples. Recall that each example consists of an initial hand, cards to be added, and a prediction of what the result should be. Then test the function with the additional examples. Formulate the tests as boolean-valued expressions. ∎

**Exercise 41.3.2** Develop the function *last-card*. It consumes a *hand* and produces a list with the last card's rank and suit. How can we use this function to test the *add-at-end!* function? ∎

**Exercise 41.3.3** Suppose a family tree consists of structures that record the name, social security number, and parents of a person. Describing such a tree requires a structure definition:

(**define-struct** *child* (*name social father mother*))

and a data definition:

> A *family-tree-node* (short: *ftn*) is either
>
> 1. false, or
>
> 2. (make-child *name socsec f m*) where *name* is a symbol, *socsec* is a number, and *f* and *m* are *ftn*s.

For now, we assume that everyone has a social security number and that social security numbers are unique.

Following our convention from part III, false represents a lack of knowledge about someone's father or mother. As we find out more information, though, we can add nodes to our family tree.

Develop the function *add-ftn!*. It consumes a family tree *a-ft*, a social security number *ssc*, a symbol *anc*, and a *child* structure. Its effect is to modify that structure in *a-ft* whose social security number is *ssc*. If *anc* is 'father, it modifies the *father* field to contain the given *child* structure; otherwise, *anc* is the symbol 'mother and *add-ftn!* mutates the *mother* field. If the respective fields already contain a *child* structure, *add-ftn!* signals an error.

**Using Functions as Arguments**: Instead of accepting 'father and 'mother for *anc*, the function could also accept one of the two structure mutators: *set-child-father!* or *set-child-mother!*. Modify *add-ftn!* accordingly. ∎

**Exercise 41.3.4** Develop an implementation of a hand with *create-hand* and *add-at-end!* services using encapsulated state variables and function definitions. Use **set!** expression but no structure mutators. ∎

Not all mutator functions are as easily designed as the *add-at-end!* function. Indeed, in some cases things don't even work out at all. Let's consider two additional services. The first one removes the last card in a hand. Its contract and effect statement are variations on those for *add-at-end!*:

;; *remove-last! : hand → void*

;; effect : to remove the last card in *a-hand*, unless it is the only one
(**define** (*remove-last! a-hand*) ... )

The effect is restricted because a hand must always contain one card.

We can also adapt the example for *add-at-end!* without difficulty:

(**define** *hand0* (*create-hand* 13 *SPADES*))

(**begin**
  (*add-at-end!* 1 *DIAMONDS hand0*)
  (*add-at-end!* 2 *CLUBS hand0*)
  (*remove-last! hand0*)
  (*remove-last! hand0*))

The resulting value is *void*. The effect of the computation is to return *hand0* in its initial state.

The template for *remove-last!* is the same as that for *add-at-end!* because both functions process the same class of values. So the next step is to analyze what effects the function must compute for each case in the template:

1. Recall that the first clause represents the case when *a-hand*'s *next* field is **empty**. In contrast to the situation with *add-at-end!*, it is not clear what we need to do now. According to the effect statement, we must do one of two things:

   (a) If *a-hand* is the last item in a chain that consists of more than one *hand* structure, it must be removed.

   (b) If *a-hand* is the only structure that *remove-last!* consumed, the function should have no effect.

   But we can't know whether *a-hand* is the last item in a long chain of *hand*s or the only one. We have lost knowledge that was available at the beginning of the evaluation!

The analysis of the first clause suggests the use of an accumulator. We tried the natural route and discovered that knowledge is lost during an evaluation, which is the criterion for considering a switch to an accumulator-based design recipe.

Once we have recognized the need for an accumulator-style function, we encapsulate the template in a **local**-expression and add an accumulator argument to its definition and applications:

```
(define (remove-last! a-hand0)
  (local (;; accumulator ...
          (define (rem! a-hand accumulator)
            (cond
              [(empty? (hand-next a-hand))
               ... (hand-rank a-hand) ... (hand-suit a-hand) ...]
              [else ... (hand-rank a-hand) ... (hand-suit a-hand) ...
               ... (rem! (hand-next a-hand) ... accumulator ...) ...])))
    ... (rem! a-hand0 ...) ...))
```

The questions to ask now are what the accumulator represents and what its first value is.

The best way to understand the nature of accumulators is to study why the plain structural design of *remove-last!* failed. Hence we return to the analysis of our first clause in the template. When *rem!* reaches that clause, two things should have been accomplished. First, *rem!* should know that *a-hand* is not the only *hand* structure in *a-hand0*. Second, *rem!* must be enabled to remove *a-hand* from *a-hand0*. For the first goal, *rem!*'s first application should be in a context where we know that *a-hand0* contains more than one card. This argument suggests a **cond**-expression for the body of the **local**-expression:

```
(cond
  [(empty? (hand-next a-hand)) (void)]
  [else (rem! a-hand0 ...)])
```

For the second goal, *rem!*'s accumulator argument should always represent the *hand* structure that precedes *a-hand* in *a-hand0*. Then *rem!* can remove *a-hand* by modifying the predecessor's *next* field:

```
(set-hand-next! accumulator empty)
```

Now the pieces of the design puzzle fall into place. The complete definition of the function is in figure 123. The *accumulator* parameter is renamed to *predecessor-of:a-hand* to emphasize the relationship to the parameter proper. The first application of *rem!* in the body of the **local**-expression hands it the second *hand* structure in *a-hand0*. The second argument is *a-hand0*, which establishes the desired relationship.

---

```
;; remove-last! : hand → void
;; effect : to remove the last card in a-hand0, unless it is the only one
(define (remove-last! a-hand0)
   (local (;; predecessor-of:a-hand represents the predecessor of
           ;; a-hand in the a-hand0 chain
           (define (rem! a-hand predecessor-of:a-hand)
              (cond
                 [(empty? (hand-next a-hand))
                  (set-hand-next! predecessor-of:a-hand empty)]
                 [else (rem! (hand-next a-hand) a-hand)])))
      (cond
         [(empty? (hand-next a-hand0)) (void)]
         [else (rem! (hand-next a-hand0) a-hand0)])))
```

Both applications of *rem!* have the shape

(*rem!* (hand-next *a-hand*) *a-hand*)

Figure 123: Removing the last card

---

It is now time to revisit the basic assumption about the card game that the cards are added to the end of a hand. When human players pick up cards, they hardly ever just add them to the end. Instead, many use some special arrangement and maintain it over the course of a game. Some arrange hands according to suits, others according to rank, and yet others according to both criteria.

Let's consider an operation for inserting a card into a *hand* based on its rank:

```
;; sorted-insert! : rank suit hand → void
;; assume: a-hand is sorted by rank, in descending order
;; effect: to add a card with r as rank and s as suit at the proper place
(define (sorted-insert! r s a-hand) ... )
```

The function assumes that the given *hand* is already sorted. The assumption naturally holds if we always use *create-hand* to create a hand and *sorted-insert!* to insert cards.

Suppose we start with the same hand as above for *add-at-end!*:

(**define** *hand0* (*create-hand* 13 *SPADES*))

If we evaluate (*sorted-insert!* 1 *DIAMONDS hand0*) in this context, *hands0* becomes

```
(make-hand 13 SPADES
  (make-hand 1 DIAMONDS empty))
```

If we now evaluate (*sorted-insert!* 2 *CLUBS hand0*) in addition, we get

```
(make-hand 13 SPADES
  (make-hand 2 CLUBS
    (make-hand 1 DIAMONDS empty)))
```

for *hand0*. This value shows what it means for a chain to be sorted in descending order. As we traverse the chain, the ranks get smaller and smaller independent of what the suits are.

Our next step is to analyze the template. Here is the template, adapted to our present purpose:

```
(define (sorted-insert! r s a-hand)
  (cond
    [(empty? (hand-next a-hand))
     ... (hand-rank a-hand) ... (hand-suit a-hand) ...]
    [else ... (hand-rank a-hand) ... (hand-suit a-hand) ...
     ... (sorted-insert! r s (hand-next a-hand)) ...]))
```

The key step of the function is to insert the new card between two cards such that first card's rank is larger than, or equal to, *r* and *r* is larger than, or equal to, the rank of the second. Because we only have two cards in the second clause, we start by formulating the answer for the second clause. The condition we just specified implies that we need a nested **cond**-expression:

```
(cond
  [(>= (hand-rank a-hand) r (hand-rank (hand-next a-hand))) ...]
  [else ...])
```

The first condition expresses in Scheme what we just discussed. In particular, (hand-rank *a-hand*) picks the rank of the first card in *a-hand* and (hand-rank (hand-next *a-hand*)) picks the rank of the second one. The comparison determines whether the three ranks are properly ordered.

Each case of this new **cond**-expression deserves its own analysis:

1. If (>= (hand-rank *a-hand*) *r* (hand-rank (hand-next *a-hand*))) is true,
   then the new card must go between the two cards that are currently
   linked. That is, the *next* field of *a-hand* must be changed to contain a
   new *hand* structure. The new structure consists of *r*, *s*, and the original
   value of *a-hand*'s *next* field. This yields the following elaboration of
   the **cond**-expression:

   > (**cond**
   >   [(>= (hand-rank *a-hand*) *r* (hand-rank (hand-next *a-hand*)))
   >    (set-hand-next! *a-hand* (make-hand *r s* (hand-next *a-hand*)))]
   >   [**else** ... ])

2. If (>= (hand-rank *a-hand*) *r* (hand-rank (hand-next *a-hand*))) is false,
   the new card must be inserted at some place in the rest of the chain.
   Of course, the natural recursion accomplishes just that, which finishes
   the analysis of the second clause of *sorted-insert!*.

Putting all the pieces together yields a partial function definition:

> (**define** (*sorted-insert! r s a-hand*)
>   (**cond**
>     [(empty? (hand-next *a-hand*))
>      ... (hand-rank *a-hand*) ... (hand-suit *a-hand*) ... ]
>     [**else**
>       (**cond**
>         [(>= (hand-rank *a-hand*) *r* (hand-rank (hand-next *a-hand*)))
>          (set-hand-next! *a-hand* (make-hand *r s* (hand-next *a-hand*)))]
>         [**else** (*sorted-insert! r s* (hand-next *a-hand*))])]))

The only remaining gaps are now in the first clause.

The difference between the first and the second **cond**-clause is that there
is no second *hand* structure in the first clause so we cannot compare ranks.
Still, we can compare *r* and (hand-rank *a-hand*) and compute something
based on the outcome of this comparison:

> (**cond**
>   [(>= (hand-rank *a-hand*) *r*) ... ]
>   [**else** ... ])

Clearly, if the comparison expression evaluates to true, the function must
mutate the *next* field of *a-hand* and add a new *hand* structure:

```
(cond
  [(>= (hand-rank a-hand) r)
   (set-hand-next! a-hand (make-hand r s empty))]
  [else ... ])
```

The problem is that we have nothing to mutate in the second clause. If $r$ is larger than the rank of *a-hand*, the new card should be inserted between the predecessor of *a-hand* and *a-hand*. But that kind of situation would have been discovered by the second clause. The seeming contradiction suggests that the dots in the second clause are a response to a singular case:

> The dots are evaluated only if *sorted-insert!* consumes a rank $r$
> that is larger than all the values in the *rank* fields of *a-hand*.

In that singular case, *a-hand* shouldn't change at all. After all, there is no way to create a descending chain of cards by mutating *a-hand* or any of its embedded *hand* structures.

At first glance, we can overcome the problem with a **set!** expression that changes the definition of *hand0*:

```
(set! hand0 (make-hand r s hand0))
```

This fix doesn't work in general though, because we can't assume that we know which variable definition must be modified. Since expressions can be abstracted over values but not variables, there is also no way to abstract over *hand0* in this **set!**-expression.

We're stuck. It is impossible to define *sorted-insert!*, at least as specified above. The analysis suggests a remedy, however. If we introduce a single variable that always stands for the current *hand* structure, we can use a combination of assignments and structure mutators to insert a new card. The trick is not to let any other part of the program refer to this variable or even change it. Otherwise a simple **set!** won't work, as argued before. In other words, we need a state variable for each *hand* structure, and we need to encapsulate it in a **local**-expression.

Figure 124 displays the complete function definition. It follows the pattern of section 39. The function itself corresponds to *create-hand*, though instead of producing a structure the new *create-hand* function produces a manager function. At this point, the manager can deal with only one message: 'insert; all other messages are rejected. An 'insert message first checks whether the new rank is larger than the first one in *the-hand*, the hidden state variable. If so, the manager just changes *the-hand*; if not, it uses *insert-*

A *hand* is an interface:

    1. 'insert :: *rank suit* → *void*

*;; create-hand : rank suit → hand*
*;; to create a *hand* from the *rank* and *suit* of a single card
(**define** (*create-hand rank suit*)
  (**local** ((**define-struct** *hand* (*rank suit next*))

    (**define** *the-hand* (make-hand *rank suit* empty))

    *;; insert-aux! : rank suit hand → void*
    *;; assume: hand is sorted by rank in descending order*
    *;; effect: to add a card with *r* as rank and *s* as suit*
    *;; at the proper place*
    (**define** (*insert-aux! r s a-hand*)
      (**cond**
        [(empty? (hand-next *a-hand*))
        (set-hand-next! *a-hand* (make-hand *r s* empty))]
        [**else** (**cond**
            [(>= (hand-rank *a-hand*)
                 *r*
                (hand-rank (hand-next *a-hand*)))
           (set-hand-next! *a-hand*
             (make-hand *r s* (hand-next *a-hand*)))]
           [**else** (*insert-aux! r s* (hand-next *a-hand*))])])))

    ... *;; other services as needed*

    (**define** (*service-manager msg*)
      (**cond**
        [(symbol=? *msg* 'insert!)
        (**lambda** (*r s*)
          (**cond**
            [(> *r* (hand-rank *the-hand*))
            (set! *the-hand* (make-hand *r s the-hand*))]
            [**else** (*insert-aux! r s the-hand*)])))]
        [**else** (error 'managed-hand "message not understood")])))
  *service-manager*))

Figure 124: Encapsulation and structure mutation for hands of cards

*aux!*, which may now assume that the new card belongs into the middle of the chain.

---

### Exercises

**Exercise 41.3.5** Extend the definition in figure 124 with a service for removing the first card of a given rank, even if it is the only card. ∎

**Exercise 41.3.6** Extend the definition in figure 124 with a service for determining the suits of those cards in *the-hand* that have a given rank. The function should produce a list of suits. ∎

**Exercise 41.3.7** Reformulate *create-hand* in figure 124 such that the manager uses a single **set!**-expression and *sorted-insert* does not use any structure mutation. ∎

**Exercise 41.3.8** Recall the definition of a binary tree from section 14.2:

> A *binary-tree* (short: *BT*) is either
>
> 1. false or
>
> 2. (make-node *soc pn lft rgt*)
>    where *soc* is a number, *pn* is a symbol, and *lft* and *rgt* are *BTs*.

The required structure definition is

    (**define-struct** *node* (*ssn name left right*))

A binary tree is a *binary-search-tree* if every *node* structure contains a social security number that is larger than all those in the left subtree and smaller than all those in the right subtree.

    Develop the function *insert-bst!*. The function consumes a name *n*, a social security number *s*, and a bst. It modifies the bst so that it contains a new node with *n* and *s* while maintaining it as a search tree.

    Also develop the function *remove-bst!*, which removes a node with a given social security number. It combines the two subtrees of the removed node by inserting all the nodes from the right tree into the left one. ∎

The discussion in this subsection and the exercises suggest that adding or removing items from linked structures is a messy task. Dealing with an item in the middle of the linked structures is best done with accumulator-style functions. Dealing with the first structure requires encapsulation and management functions. In contrast, as exercise 41.3.7 shows, a solution without mutators is much easier to produce than a solution based on structure mutation. And the case of cards and hands, which deals with at most 52 structures, is equally efficient. To decide which of the two approaches to use requires a better understanding of algorithmic analysis (see intermezzo 5) and of the language mechanisms and program design recipes for encapsulating state variables.

## 41.4 Extended Exercise: Moving Pictures, a Last Time

In sections 6.6, 7.4, 10.3, and 21.4 we studied how to move pictures across a canvas. A picture is a list of shapes; a shape is one of several basic geometric shapes: circles, rectangles, etc. Following our most basic design principle—one function per concept—we first defined functions for moving basic geometric shapes, then for mixed classes of shapes, and finally for lists of shapes. Eventually we abstracted over related functions.

The functions for moving basic shapes create a new shape from an existing shape. For example, the function for moving a circle consumes a *circle* structure and produces a new *circle* structure. If we think of the *circle* as a painting with a round frame and the canvas as a wall, however, creating a new shape for each move is inappropriate. Instead, we should change the shape's current position.

---

### Exercises

**Exercise 41.4.1** Turn the functions *translate-circle* and *translate-rectangle* of exercises 6.6.2 and 6.6.8, respectively, into structure-mutating functions. Adapt *move-circle* from section 6.6 and *move-rectangle* from exercise 6.6.12 so that they use these new functions. ∎

**Exercise 41.4.2** Adapt the function *move-picture* from exercise 10.3.6 to use the structure-mutating functions from exercise 41.4.1. ∎

**Exercise 41.4.3** Use Scheme's for-each function (see Help Desk) to abstract where possible in the functions of exercise 41.4.2. ∎

# 42  Equality

As we mutate structures or vectors, we use words such as "the vector now contains false in its first field" to describe what happens. Behind those words is the idea that the vector itself stays the same—even though its properties change. What this observation suggests is that there are really two notions of equality: the one we have used so far and a new one based on effects on a structure or vector. Understanding these two notions of equality is critically important for a programmer. We therefore discuss them in detail in the following two subsections.

## 42.1  Extensional Equality

Recall the class of *posn* structures from part I. A *posn* combines two numbers; its fields are called $x$ and $y$. Here are two examples:

(make-posn 3 4)  (make-posn 8 6)

They are obviously distinct. In contrast, the following two

(make-posn 12 1)  (make-posn 12 1)

are equal. They both contain 12 in the $x$-field and 1 in the $y$-field.

More generally, we consider two structures to be equal if they contain equal components. This assumes that we know how to compare the components, but that's not surprising. It just reminds us that processing structures follows the data definition that comes with the structure definition. Philosophers refer to this notion of equality as EXTENSIONAL EQUALITY.

Section 17.8 introduced extensional equality and discussed its use for building tests. As a reminder, let's consider a function for determining the extensional equality of *posn* structures:

```
;; equal-posn : posn posn → boolean
;; to determine whether two posns are extensionally equal
(define (equal-posn p1 p2)
  (and (= (posn-x p1) (posn-x p2))
       (= (posn-y p1) (posn-y p2)))))
```

The function consumes two *posn* structures, extracts their field values, and then compares the corresponding field values using =, the predicate for comparing numbers. Its organization matches that of the data definition for *posn* structures; its design is standard. This implies that for recursive classes of data, we naturally need recursive equality functions.

## Exercises

**Exercise 42.1.1** Develop an extensional equality function for the class of *child* structures from exercise 41.3.3. If *ft1* and *ft2* are family tree nodes, how long is the maximal abstract running time of the function? ∎

**Exercise 42.1.2** Use exercise 42.1.1 to abstract *equal-posn* so that its instances can test the extensional equality of any given class of structures. ∎

## 42.2  Intensional Equality

Consider the following toy program:

```
(define a (make-posn 12 1))
(define b (make-posn 12 1))

(begin
  (set-posn-x! a 1)
  (equal-posn a b))
```

It defines two *posn* structures. The two structures are initially equal in the sense of the preceding subsection. Yet when we evaluate the **begin**-expression, the result is false.

Even though the two structures initially consist of the same values, they are different because the structure mutation in the **begin**-expression changes the *x*-field of the first structure and leaves the second one alone. More generally, the expression has an effect on one structure but not the other. Now take a look at a slightly different program:

```
(define a (make-posn 12 1))
(define b a)

(begin
  (set-posn-x! a 1)
  (equal-posn a b))
```

Here *a* and *b* are two different names for the same structure. Therefore, the evaluation of (set-posn-x! *a* 1) affects both *a* and *b*, which means that (*equal-posn a b*) is going to yield true this time.

The two observations have a general moral. If the evaluation of an expression affects one structure and simultaneously some other structure, the two structures are equal in a deeper sense than *equal-posn* can determine. Philosophers refer to this notion of equality as INTENSIONAL EQUALITY. In contrast to extensional equality, this notion of equality requires not only that two structures consist of equal parts, but that they also simultaneously react to structure mutations. It is a direct consequence that two intensionally equal structures are also extensionally equal.

Designing a function for determining the intensional equality of structures is more work than designing one for determining their extensional equality. We start with a precise description:

```
;; eq-posn : posn posn → boolean
;; to determine whether two posn structures
;; are affected by the same mutation
(define (eq-posn p1 p2) ...)
```

We already have an example, so we move on to a discussion of the template:

```
(define (eq-posn p1 p2)
  ... (posn-x p1) ... (posn-x p2) ...
  ... (posn-y p1) ... (posn-y p2) ... )
```

The template contains four expressions, each one reminding us of the available information and which structure fields we can mutate.

Translating the above observations into a full definition yields the following draft:

```
(define (eq-posn p1 p2)
  (begin
    (set-posn-x! p1 5)
    (= (posn-x p2) 5)))
```

This function sets *p1*'s *x*-field to 5 and then checks whether *p2*'s *x*-field also became 5. If so, both structures reacted to the mutation and are, by definition, intensionally equal.

Unfortunately, our reasoning has a problem. Consider the following application:

```
(eq-posn (make-posn 1 2) (make-posn 5 6))
```

The two *posn*'s aren't even extensionally equivalent, so they should not be intensionally equivalent. But our first version of *eq-posn* would produce true, and that is a problem.

We can improve the first version with a second mutation:

```
(define (eq-posn p1 p2)
  (begin
    (set-posn-x! p1 5)
    (set-posn-x! p2 6)
    (= (posn-x p1) 6)))
```

This function changes *p1* and then *p2*. If the structures are intensionally equal, then the mutation of *p2* must affect *p1*. Furthermore, we know that *p1*'s *x*-field can't coincidentally contain 6, because we first changed it to 5. Thus, when (*eq-posn a b*) produces true, *a* changes when *b* changes and vice versa, and the structures are intensionally equal.

The only problem left now is that *eq-posn* has effects on the two structures that it consumes but has no effect statement. Indeed, it should not have a visible effect because its only purpose is to determine whether two structures are intensionally equal. We can avoid this effect by first saving the old values in *p1*'s and *p2*'s *x* fields, mutating the fields, and then restoring the old values. Figure 125 contains a function definition that performs an intensional equality check without any visible effects.

```
;; eq-posn : posn posn → boolean
;; to determine whether two posn structures
;; are affected by the same mutation
(define (eq-posn p1 p2)
  (local (;; save old x values of p1 and p2
          (define old-x1 (posn-x p1))
          (define old-x2 (posn-x p2))
          ;; modify both x fields of p1 and p2
          (define effect1 (set-posn-x! p1 5))
          (define effect2 (set-posn-x! p2 6))
          ;; now compare the two fields
          (define same (= (posn-x p1) (posn-x p2)))
          ;; restore old values
          (define effect3 (set-posn-x! p1 old-x1))
          (define effect4 (set-posn-x! p2 old-x2)))
    same))
```

Figure 125: Determining the intensional equality of two structures

The existence of *eq-posn* says that all structures have a unique "finger-print." We can inspect two structures (of the same class) for this fingerprint if we have access to the mutators. Scheme and many other languages typically provide built-in functions for comparing two structural values extensionally and intensionally. The corresponding Scheme functions are **equal?** and **eq?**. In Scheme, both functions are applicable to all values, whether mutators and selectors are accessible or hidden. The existence of **eq?** suggests a revision for our guideline on testing.

---

GUIDELINE ON TESTING

Use **eq?** for testing when comparing the identity of objects matters. Use **equal?** for testing otherwise.

---

The guideline is general. Still, programmers should use equality functions that indicate what kind of values they expect to compare, such as **symbol=?**, **boolean?**, or **=**, because the additional information helps readers understand the purpose of the program more easily.

## Exercises

**Exercise 42.2.1** Evaluate the following expressions by hand:

1. (*eq-posn* (make-posn 1 2) (make-posn 1 2))

2. (**local** ((**define** *p* (make-posn 1 2)))
     (*eq-posn* *p* *p*))

3. (**local** ((**define** *p* (make-posn 1 2))
       (**define** *a* (list *p*)))
     (*eq-posn* (first *a*) *p*))

Check the answers with DrScheme. ∎

**Exercise 42.2.2** Develop an intensional equality function for the class of *child* structures from exercise 41.3.3. If *ft1* and *ft2* are family tree nodes, how long is the maximal abstract running time of the function? ∎

**Exercise 42.2.3** Use exercise 42.2.2 to abstract *eq-posn* so that its instances can test the intensional equality of any given class of structures. ∎

# 43   Changing Structures, Vectors, and Objects

This section introduces several small projects on programming with mutable structures. The ordering of the subsections roughly matches the outline of the book, proceeding from simple classes of data to complicated ones and from structural recursion to generative recursion with backtracking and accumulators.

## 43.1   More Practice with Vectors

Programming with mutable vectors is hardly ever needed in the kinds of programs that we encountered. Still, because it is far more prevalent in conventional languages, it is an important skill and deserves more practice than section 41.2 suggests. This section covers sorting with vectors, but its goal is to practice reasoning about intervals when processing vectors.

We encountered the idea of sorting as early as section 12.2, where we designed the *sort* function. It consumes a list of numbers and produces a list of numbers with the same items in sorted (ascending or descending) order. An analogous function for vectors consumes a vector and produces a new vector. But, using vector mutation, we can also design a function that changes the vector so that it contains the same items as before, in a sorted order. Such a function is called an IN-PLACE SORT because it leaves all the items inside the existing vector.

An in-place-sort function relies exclusively on effects on its input vector to accomplish its task:

;; *in-place-sort* : (**vectorof** *number*) → *void*
;; effect: to modify *V* such that it contains the same items
;; as before but in ascending order
(**define** (*in-place-sort V*) ...)

Examples must demonstrate the effect:

(**local** ((**define** *v1* (vector 7 3 0 4 1)))
   (**begin**
      (*in-place-sort v1*)
      (equal? *v1* (vector 0 1 3 4 7)))))

Of course, given that *in-place-sort* consumes a vector, the true problem is to design the auxiliary function that works on specific segments of the vector.

The standard template for a vector-processing function uses an auxiliary function:

```
(define (in-place-sort V)
  (local ((define (sort-aux V i)
            (cond
              [(zero? i) ... ]
              [else
                ... (vector-ref V (sub1 i)) ...
                ... (sort-aux V (sub1 i)) ... ])))
    (sort-aux V (vector-length V))))
```

Following the design ideas of intermezzo 5, the auxiliary function consumes a natural number and uses it as an index into the vector. Because the initial argument is (vector-length $V$), the accessible index is always (sub1 $i$).

Recall that the key to designing functions such as *sort-aux* is to formulate a rigorous purpose and/or effect statement. The statement must clarify on which interval of the possible vector indices the function works and what exactly it accomplishes. One natural effect statement follows:

```
;; sort-aux : (vectorof number) N → void
;; effect: to sort the interval [0,i) of V in place
(define (sort-aux V i) ... )
```

To understand this effect statement in the larger context, let's adapt our original example:

```
(local ((define v1 (vector 7 3 0 4 1)))
  (begin
    (sort-aux v1 5)
    (equal? v1 (vector 0 1 3 4 7))))
```

If *sort-aux* is applied to a vector's length, it should sort the entire vector. This statement implies that if the first argument is less than the vector's length only some initial segment of the vector is sorted:

```
(local ((define v1 (vector 7 3 0 4 1)))
  (begin
    (sort-aux v1 4)
    (equal? v1 (vector 0 3 4 7 1))))
```

In this particular example, the last number remains in its original place, and only the first four vector items are sorted.

Now we can analyze each case in the template of *sort-aux*:

1. If $i$ is 0, the interval of the effect statement is [0,0). This means that the interval is empty and that the function has nothing to do.

```
;; in-place-sort : (vectorof number) → void
;; effect: to modify V such that it contains the same items
;; as before but in ascending order
(define (in-place-sort V)
  (local (;; sort-aux : (vectorof number) N → void
          ;; effect: to sort the interval [0,i) of V in place
          (define (sort-aux V i)
            (cond
              [(zero? i) (void)]
              [else (begin
                      ;; sort the segment [0,(sub1 i)):
                      (sort-aux V (sub1 i))
                      ;; insert (vector-ref V (sub1 i)) into the segment
                      ;; [0,i) so that it becomes sorted"
                      (insert (sub1 i) V))])))

          ;; insert : N (vectorof number) → void
          ;; to place the value in the i-th into its proper place
          ;; in the segement [0,i] of V
          ;; assume: the segment [0,i) of V is sorted
          (define (insert i V)
            ...))
    (sort-aux V (vector-length V))))
```

Figure 126: An in-place sort function: First part

2. The second clause in the template contains two expressions:

   (vector-ref $V$ (sub1 $i$))

   and

   (*sort-aux* $V$ (sub1 $i$))

The first reminds us that we can use the $i - 1$-st field of $V$; the second one reminds us of the natural recursion. In this case, the natural recursion sorts the interval [0,(sub1 $i$)). To finish the task, we must insert the value of the $i - 1$-st field into its proper place in the interval [0,$i$).

The above examples make this case concrete. When we evaluate (*sort-aux v1* 4), the number in the last field of *v1* remains at its place. The first four items in the vectors are: 0, 3, 4, and 7. To sort the entire interval [0,5), we must insert 1, which is (vector-ref $V$ (sub1 5)), between 0 and 3.

In short, the design of *in-place-sort* follows the same pattern as that of the function *sort* in section 12.2 up to this point. For *sort*, we also designed the main function only to find out that we needed to design an auxiliary function for inserting one more item into its proper place.

Figure 126 gathers what we have discussed about *in-place-sort* so far. It also includes a specification of *insert*, the second auxiliary function. To understand its effect statement, we reformulate the example for the second clause of *sort-aux*:

```
(local ((define v1 (vector 0 3 4 7 1)))
  (begin
    (insert 4 v1)
    (equal? v1 (vector 0 1 3 4 7))))
```

In this case, *insert* moves 1 over three numbers: first 7, then 4, and finally 3. It stops when the next number in the leftwards direction, that is, 0, is smaller than the number that is being inserted.

Let's look at a second example for *insert*:

```
(local ((define v1 (vector 7 3 0 4 1)))
  (begin
    (insert 1 v1)
    (equal? v1 (vector 3 7 0 4 1))))
```

Here the problem is to insert 3 into a segment that contains only one number: 7. This means that insert must swap the values in the first two fields and must stop then, because 3 can't move any further to the left.

Now take a look at the template for *insert*:

```
(define (insert i V)
  (cond
    [(zero? i) ...]
    [else
      ... (vector-ref V (sub1 i)) ...
      ... (insert (sub1 i) V) ... ]))
```

It is the standard template for a vector-processing auxiliary function. As usual we distinguish two cases:

```
(define (in-place-sort V)
  (local (;; sort-aux : (vectorof number) N → void
          ;; effect: to sort the interval [0,i) of V in place
          (define (sort-aux V i)
            ...)

          ;; insert : N (vectorof number) → void
          ;; to place the value in the i-th into its proper place
          ;; in the [0,i] segement of V
          (define (insert i V)
            (cond
              [(zero? i) (void)]
              [else (cond
                      [(> (vector-ref V (sub1 i)) (vector-ref V i))
                       (begin
                         (swap V (- i 1) i)
                         (insert (sub1 i) V))]
                      [else (void)])])))

          ;; swap : (vectorof X) N N void
          (define (swap V i j)
            (local ((define temp (vector-ref V i)))
              (begin
                (vector-set! V i (vector-ref V j))
                (vector-set! V j temp)))))
    (sort-aux V (vector-length V))))
```

Figure 127: An in-place sort function: Second part

1. If $i$ is 0, the goal is to insert (vector-ref V 0) into the segment [0,0].
   Since this interval contains only one number, *insert* has accomplished
   its task.

2. If $i$ is positive, the template implies that we may consider another
   item in $V$, namely (vector-ref V (sub1 i)), and that we can perform a
   natural recursion. The immediate question is whether (vector-ref V
   (sub1 i)) is smaller or larger than (vector-ref V i), the item that is to be
   moved around. If so, $V$ is sorted on the entire interval [0,i], because
   $V$ is sorted on [0,i) by assumption. If not, the item at $i$ is out of order
   still.

The **cond**-expression that employs the necessary conditions is

```
(cond
  [(> (vector-ref V (sub1 i)) (vector-ref V i)) ... ]
  [(<= (vector-ref V (sub1 i)) (vector-ref V i)) (void)])
```

The second clause contains (void) because there is nothing left to do. In the first clause, *insert* must—at a minimum—swap the values in the two fields. That is, *insert* must place (vector-ref $V$ $i$) into field (sub1 $i$) and (vector-ref $V$ (sub1 $i$)) into field $i$. But even that may not be enough. After all, the value in the $i$-th field may have to wander over several fields as the first example demonstrated. Fortunately, we can easily solve this problem with the natural recursion, which inserts the (vector-ref $V$ (sub1 $i$)) into its proper place in [0,(sub1 $i$)] after the swapping has taken place.

Figure 127 contains the complete definition of *insert* and *swap*. This second function is responsible for swapping the value of two fields.

---

## Exercises

**Exercise 43.1.1** Test the auxiliary functions for *in-place-sort* from figures 126 and 127. Formulate the tests as boolean-valued expressions.

Develop and test more examples for *in-place-sort*.

Integrate the pieces. Test the integrated function. Eliminate superflous arguments from the auxiliary programs in the integrated definition, step by step, testing the complete function after each step. Finally, change *in-place-sort* so that its result is the modified vector. ∎

**Exercise 43.1.2** The *insert* function of figure 127 performs two vector mutations for each time the function recurs. Each of these mutations pushes (vector-ref $V$ $i$), for the original value of $i$, to the left in $V$ until its proper place is found.

Figure 128 illustrates a slightly better solution. The situation in the top row assumes that the values $a$, $b$, and $c$ are properly arranged, that is,

$(< a\ b\ ...\ c)$

holds. Furthermore, $d$ is to be inserted and its place is between $a$ and $b$, that is,

$(< a\ d\ b)$

$V$ is sorted on [0,i], insert $i + 1$:

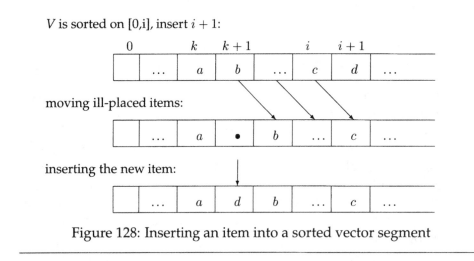

Figure 128: Inserting an item into a sorted vector segment

holds, too. The solution is to compare $d$ with all the items in $k + 1$ through $i$ and to shift the items to the right if they are larger than $d$. Eventually, we find $a$ (or the left end of the vector) and have a "hole" in the vector, where $d$ must be inserted. (The hole actually contains $b$.) This situation is illustrated in the middle row. The last one shows how $d$ is placed between $a$ and $b$.

Develop a function *insert* that implements its desired effect according to this description. **Hint:** The new function must consume $d$ as an additional argument. ∎

**Exercise 43.1.3** For many other programs, we could swap the order of the subexpressions in **begin**-expressions and still get a working program. Let's consider this idea for *sort-aux*:

```
;; sort2-aux : (vectorof number) N → void
(define (sort2-aux V i)
  (cond
    [(zero? i) (void)]
    [else (begin
            (insert2 (sub1 i) V)
            (sort2-aux V (sub1 i)))]))
```

The order implies that *sort2-aux* first inserts the item from (sub1 $i$) into some already sorted part of $V$ and then sorts the remainder of $V$. Here is a picture that illustrates the situation graphically:

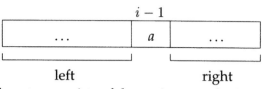

left                          right

The depicted vector consists of three pieces: $a$, the item in field (sub1 $i$), the left fragment, and the right fragment. The questions are which of the two fragments is sorted and into which fragment $a$ should be inserted.

Considering that *sort2-aux* decreases its first argument and thus sweeps over the vector from right to left, the answers are that the right fragment is initially empty and thus sorted in ascending order by default; the left fragment is still unordered; and $a$ must be inserted into its proper place in the right fragment.

Develop a precise effect statement for *sort-aux* based on these observations. Then develop the function *insert2* so that *sort2-aux* sorts vectors properly. ∎

---

In section 25.2, we got to know *qsort*, a function based on generative recursion. Given a list, *qsort* constructs a sorted version in three steps:

1. choose an item from the list, call it *pivot*;

2. create two sublists: one with all those items strictly smaller than *pivot*, another one with all those items strictly larger than *pivot*;

3. sort each of the two sublists, using the same steps, and then append the two lists with the pivot item in the middle.

It isn't difficult to see why the result is sorted, why it contains all the items from the original list, and why the process stops. After all, at every stage, the function removes at least one item from the list so that the two sublists are shorter than the given one; eventually the list must be empty.

Figure 129 illustrates how this idea can be adapted for an in-place version that works on vectors. At each stage, the algorithm works on a specific fragment of the vector. It picks the first item as the *pivot* item and rearranges the fragment so that all items smaller than the pivot appear to the left of *pivot* and all items larger than *pivot* appear to its right. Then *qsort* is used twice: once for the fragment between *left1* and *right1* and again for the fragment between *left2* and *right2*. Because each of these two intervals is shorter than the originally given interval, *qsort* eventually encounters the empty interval and stops. After *qsort* has sorted each fragment, there is a vector fragment with pivot item *p*:

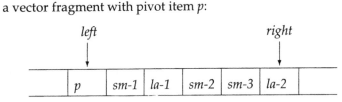

partitioning the vector fragment into two regions, separated by *p*:

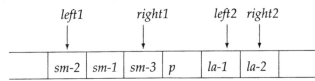

Figure 129: The partitioning step for in-place quick-sort

nothing left to do; the partitioning process has arranged the vector into fragments of ascending order.

Here is the definition of *qsort*, an in-place sorting algorithm for vectors:

```
;; qsort : (vectorof number) → (vectorof number)
;; effect: to modify V such that it contains the same items as before,
;; in ascending order
(define (qsort V)
  (qsort-aux V 0 (sub1 (vector-length V))))
```

```
;; qsort-aux : (vectorof number) N N → (vectorof number)
;; effect: sort the interval [left,right] of vector V
;; generative recursion
(define (qsort-aux V left right)
  (cond
    [(>= left right) V]
    [else (local ((define new-pivot-position (partition V left right)))
            (begin (qsort-aux V left (sub1 new-pivot-position))
                   (qsort-aux V (add1 new-pivot-position) right)))]))
```

The main function's input is a vector, so it uses an auxiliary function to do its job. As suggested above, the auxiliary function consumes the vector and two boundaries. Each boundary is an index into the vector. Initially, the boundaries are 0 and (sub1 (vector-length V)), which means that *qsort-aux* is to sort the entire vector.

The definition of *qsort-aux* closely follows the algoritm's description. If *left* and *right* describe a boundary of size 1 or less, its task is done. Otherwise, it partitions the vector. Because the partitioning step is a separate complex process, it requires a separate function. It must have both an effect and a result proper, the new index for the pivot item, which is now at its proper place. Given this index, *qsort-aux* continues to sort V on the intervals [*left*,(sub1 *new-pivot-position*)] and [(add1 *new-pivot-position*), *right*]. Both intervals are at least one item shorter than the original, which is the termination argument for *qsort-aux*.

Naturally, the key problem here is the partitioning step, which is implemented by *partition*:

;; *partition* : (**vectorof** *number*) **N N** → **N**
;; to determine the proper position *p* of the pivot-item
;; effect: rearrange the vector *V* so that
;; – all items in *V* in [*left*,*p*) are smaller than the pivot item
;; – all items of *V* in (*p*,*right*] are larger than the pivot item
(**define** (*partition V left right*) ... )

For simplicity, we choose the left-most item in the given interval as the pivot item. The question is how *partition* can accomplish its task, for example, whether it is a function based on structural recursion or whether it is based on generative recursion. Furthermore, if it is based on generative recursion, the question is what the generative step accomplishes.

The best strategy is to consider an example and to see how the partitioning step could be accomplished. The first example is a small vector with six numbers:

(vector 1.1 0.75 1.9 0.35 0.58 2.2)

The pivot's position is 0; the pivot item is 1.1. The boundaries are 0 and 5. One item, 1.9, is obviously out of place. If we swap it with 0.58, then the vector is almost perfectly partitioned:

(vector 1.1 0.75 0.58 0.35 1.9 2.2)

In this modified vector, the only item out of place is the pivot item itself.

Figure 130 illustrates the swapping process that we just described. First, we must find two items to swap. To do that, we search V for the first item

finding the swapping points for *partition*:

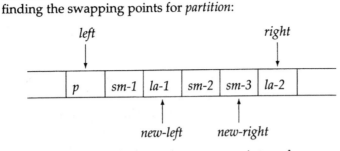

swapping the items and recuring on a new interval:

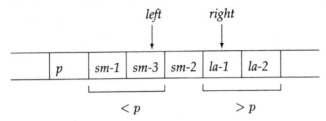

stopping the generative recursion and clean-up:

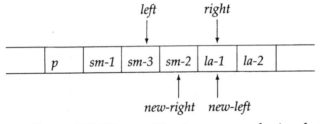

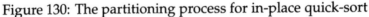

Figure 130: The partitioning process for in-place quick-sort

to the right of *left* that is larger than the pivot item. Analogously, we search *V* for the first item to the left of *right* that is smaller than the pivot item. These searches yield two indices: *new-left* and *new-right*. Second, we swap the items in fields *new-left* and *new-right*. The result is that the item at *new-left* is now smaller than the pivot item and the one at *new-right* is larger. Finally, we can continue the swapping process with the new, smaller interval. When the first step yields values for *new-left* and *new-right* that are out of order, as in the bottom row of figure 130, then we have a mostly partitioned vector (fragment).

Working through this first example suggests that *partition* is an algorithm, that is, a function based on generative recursion. Following our recipe, we must ask and answer four questions:

1. What is a trivially solvable problem?

2. What is a corresponding solution?

3. How do we generate new problems that are more easily solvable than the original problem? Is there one new problem that we generate or are there several?

4. Is the solution of the given problem the same as the solution of (one of) the new problems? Or, do we need to perform an additional computation to combine these solutions before we have a final solution? And, if so, do we need anything from the original problem data?

The example addressed issues 1, 3, and 4. The first step is to determine the *new-left* and *new-right* indices. If *new-left* is smaller than *new-right*, the generative work is to swap items in the two fields. Then the process recurs with the two new boundaries. If *new-left* is larger than *new-right*, the partitioning process is finished except for the placement of the pivot item; placing the pivot item answers question 2. Assuming we can solve this "trivially solvable" problem, we also know that the overall problem is solved.

Let's study question 2 with some examples. We stopped working on the first example when the vector had been changed to

(vector 1.1 0.75 0.58 0.35 1.9 2.2)

and the interval had been narrowed down to [2,4]. The search for *new-left* and *new-right* now yields 4 and 3, respectively. That is,

(<= *new-right new-left*)

holds. Switching the item in field *new-right* with the original left-most boundary places the pivot item in the proper spot:

(vector 0.35 0.75 0.58 1.1 1.9 2.2)

because *new-right* points to the right-most item in the vector that is smaller than the pivot item.

Before we accept this seemingly simple solution, let's check it with some additional examples, especially vector fragments where the pivot item is the largest or smallest item. Here is one such example:

(vector 1.1 0.1 0.5 0.4)

Assuming the initial interval is [0,3], the pivot item is 1.1. Thus, all other items in the vector are smaller than the pivot item, which means that it should end up in the right-most position.

Our process clearly yields 3 for *new-right*. After all, 0.4 is smaller than pivot. The search for *new-left*, though, works differently. Since none of the items in the vector is larger than the pivot item, it eventually generates 3 as an index, which is the largest legal index for this vector. At this point the search must stop. Fortunately, *new-left* and *new-right* are equal at this point, which implies that the partitioning process can stop and means that we can still swap the pivot item with the one in field *new-right*. If we do that, we get a perfectly well-partitioned vector:

(vector 0.4 0.1 0.5 0.4 1.1)

The third sample vector's items are all larger than the pivot item:

(vector 1.1 1.2 3.3 2.4)

In this case, the search for *new-left* and *new-right* must discover that the pivot item is already in the proper spot. And indeed, it does. The search for *new-left* ends at field 1, which is the first field that contains an item larger than the pivot item. The search for *new-right* ends with 0, because it is the smallest legal index and the search must stop there. As a result, *new-right* once again points to that field in the vector that must contain the pivot item for the vector (fragment) to be properly partitioned.

In short, the examples suggest several things:

1. The termination condition for *partition* is ($<=$ *new-right new-left*).

2. The value of *new-right* is the final position of the pivot item, which is in the original left-most point of the interval of interest. It is always acceptable to swap the contents of the two fields.

3. The search for *new-right* starts at the right-most boundary and continues until it either finds an item that is smaller than the pivot item or until it hits the left-most boundary.

4. Dually, the search for *new-left* starts at the left-most boundary and continues until it either finds an item that is larger than the pivot item or until it hits the right-most boundary.

And, the two searches are complex tasks that deserve their own function.

We can now gradually translate our discussion into Scheme. First, the partitioning process is a function of not just the vector and some interval, but also of the original left-most position of the vector and its content. This suggests the use of **locally** defined functions and variables:

```
(define (partition V left right)
  (local ((define pivot-position left)
          (define the-pivot (vector-ref V left))
          (define (partition-aux left right)
            ...))
    (partition-aux left right)))
```

The alternative is to use an auxiliary function that consumes the pivot's original position in addition to the vector and the current interval.

Second, the auxiliary function consumes an interval's boundaries. It immediately generates a new pair of indices from these boundaries: *new-left* and *new-right*. As mentioned, the searches for the two new boundaries are complex tasks and deserve their own functions:

```
;; find-new-right : (vectorof number) number N N [>= left] → N
;; to determine an index i between left and right (inclusive)
;; such that (< (vector-ref V i) the-pivot) holds
(define (find-new-right V the-pivot left right) ...)
```

```
;; find-new-left : (vectorof number) number N N [>= left] → N
;; to determine an index i between left and right (inclusive)
;; such that (> (vector-ref V i) the-pivot) holds
(define (find-new-left V the-pivot left right) ...)
```

Using these two functions, *partition-aux* can generate the new boundaries:

```
(define (partition V left right)
  (local ((define pivot-position left)
          (define the-pivot (vector-ref V left))
          (define (partition-aux left right)
            (local ((define new-right (find-new-right V the-pivot left right))
                    (define new-left (find-new-left V the-pivot left right)))
              ... )))
    (partition-aux left right)))
```

From here the rest of the definition is a plain transliteration of our discussion into Scheme.

```
;; partition : (vectorof number) N N → N
;; to determine the proper position p of the pivot-item
;; effect: rearrange the vector V so that
;; – all items in V in [left,p) are smaller than the pivot item
;; – all items of V in (p,right] are larger than the pivot item
;; generative recursion
(define (partition V left right)
  (local ((define pivot-position left)
          (define the-pivot (vector-ref V left))
          (define (partition-aux left right)
            (local ((define new-right (find-new-right V the-pivot left right))
                    (define new-left (find-new-left V the-pivot left right)))
              (cond
                [(>= new-left new-right)
                 (begin
                   (swap V pivot-position new-right)
                   new-right)]
                [else ; (< new-left new-right)
                 (begin
                   (swap V new-left new-right)
                   (partition-aux new-left new-right))]))))
    (partition-aux left right)))

;; find-new-right : (vectorof number) number N N [>= left] → N
;; to determine an index i between left and right (inclusive)
;; such that (< (vector-ref V i) the-pivot) holds
;; structural recursion: see text
(define (find-new-right V the-pivot left right)
  (cond
    [(= right left) right]
    [else (cond
            [(< (vector-ref V right) the-pivot) right]
            [else (find-new-right V the-pivot left (sub1 right))])]))
```

Figure 131: Rearranging a vector fragment into two partitions

Figure 131 contains the complete definition of *partition*, *partition-aux*, and *find-new-right*; the function *swap* is defined in figure 127. The definition of the search function uses an unusual structural recursion based on subclasses of natural numbers whose limits are parameters of the function.

Because the search functions are based on a rarely used design recipe, it is best to design them separately. Still, they are useful only in the context of *partition*, which means that they should be integrated into its definition when their design is completed.

## Exercises

**Exercise 43.1.4** Complete the definition of *find-new-left*. The two definitions have the same structure; develop the common abstraction.

Use the definitions of *find-new-right* and *find-new-left* to provide a termination argument for *partition-aux*.

Use the examples to develop tests for *partition*. Recall that the function computes the proper place for the pivot item and rearranges a fragment of the vector. Formulate the tests as boolean-valued expressions.

When the functions are properly tested, integrate *find-new-right* and *find-new-left* into *partition* and eliminate superfluous parameters.

Finally, test *qsort* and produce a single function definition for the in-place quick-sort algorithm. ∎

**Exercise 43.1.5** Develop the function *vector-reverse!*. It inverts the contents of a vector; its result is the modified vector.
**Hint:** Swap items from both ends until there are no more items to swap. ∎

**Exercise 43.1.6** Economists, meteorologists, and many others consistently measure various things and obtain time series. All of them need to understand the idea of "n-item averages" or "smoothing." Suppose we have weekly prices for some basket of groceries:

$$1.10 \quad 1.12 \quad 1.08 \quad 1.09 \quad 1.11$$

Computing the corresponding three-item average time series proceeds as follows:

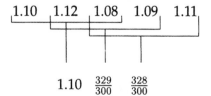

There are no averages for the end points, which means a series with $k$ items turns into $k - 2$ averages.

Develop the function *list-3-average*, which computes the 3-item sliding averages of a list of numbers. That is, we represent a series of grocery prices with lists, and *list-3-averages* consumes a list such as

```
(list 1.10 1.12 1.08 1.09 1.11)
```

and produces

```
(list 1.10 329/300 82/75)
```

in return.

Develop the function *vector-3-averages*, which computes the 3-item sliding averages of a vector of numbers. Since vectors are mutable, this gives us the alternative of producing a new vector or mutating the existing one.

Develop both versions of the function: one that produces a new vector and another one that mutates the vector it is handed.

**Warning:** This is a difficult exercise. Compare all three versions and the complexity of designing them. ∎

**Exercise 43.1.7** All the examples in this section deal with vector fragments, that is, intervals of natural numbers. Processing an interval requires a starting point for an interval, an end point, and, as the definitions of *find-new-right* and *find-new-left* show, a direction of traversal. In addition, processing means applying some function to each point in the interval.

Here is a function for processing intervals:

```
;; for-interval : N (N → N) (N → N) (N → X) → X
;; to evaluate (action i (vector-ref V i)) for i, (step i), ...
;; until (end? i) holds (inclusive)
;; generative recursion: step generates new value, end? detects end
;; termination is not guaranteed
(define (for-interval i end? step action)
  (cond
    [(end? i) (action i)]
    [else (begin
            (action i)
            (for-interval (step i) end? step action))])))
```

It consumes a starting index, called *i*, a function for determining whether the end of the interval has been reached, a function that generates the next index, and a function that is applied to each point in between. Assuming (*end?* (*step* (*step* ... (*step i*) ...)))) holds, *for-interval* satisfies the following equation:

(*for-interval i end? step action*)
= (**begin** (*action i*)
         (*action* (*step i*))
         ...
         (*action* (*step* (*step* ... (*step i*) ...)))))

Compare the function definition and the equation with those for map.

   With *for-interval* we can develop (some) functions on vectors without the traditional detour through an auxiliary function. Instead, we use *for-interval* the way we used map for processing each item on a list. Here is a function that adds 1 to each vector field:

```
;; increment-vec-rl : (vector number) → void
;; effect: to increment each item in V by 1
(define (increment-vec-rl V)
  (for-interval (sub1 (vector-length V)) zero? sub1
        (lambda (i)
          (vector-set! V i (+ (vector-ref V i) 1))))))
```

It processes the interval [0,(sub1 (vector-length *V*))], where the left boundary is determined by zero?, the termination test. The starting point, however, is (sub1 (vector-length *V*)), which is the right-most legal vector index. The third argument to *for-interval*, sub1, determines the traversal direction, which is from right to left, until the index is 0. Finally, the action is to mutate the contents of the *i*-th field by adding 1.

   Here is a function with the same visible effect on vectors but a different processing order:

```
;; increment-vec-lr : (vector number) → void
;; effect: to increment each item in V by 1
(define (increment-vec-lr V)
  (for-interval 0 (lambda (i) (= (sub1 (vector-length V)) i)) add1
        (lambda (i)
          (vector-set! V i (+ (vector-ref V i) 1))))))
```

Its starting point is 0 and the end point is the right-most legal index of *V*. The add1 function determines that the vector is processed from left to right.

Develop the following functions, using *for-interval*:

1. *rotate-left*, which moves all items in vector into the adjacent field to the left, except for the first item, which moves to the last field;

2. *insert-i-j*, which moves all items between two indices *i* and *j* to the right, except for the right-most one, which gets inserted into the *i*-th field (cmp. figure 128);

3. *vector-reverse!*, which swaps the left half of a vector with its right half;

4. *find-new-right*, that is, an alternative to the definition in figure 131;

5. *vector-sum!*, which computes the sum of the numbers in a vector using set! (**Hint:** see section 37.3).

The last two tasks show that *for-interval* is useful for computations that have no visible effects. Of course, exercise 29.3 shows that there is no need for a clumsy formulation such as *vector-sum!*.

Which of these functions can be defined in terms of *vec-for-all* from exercise 41.2.17?

**Looping Constructs:** Many programming languages (must) provide functions like *for-interval* as built-in constructs, and force programmers to use them for processing vectors. As a result, many more programs than necessary use set! and require complex temporal reasoning. ∎

## 43.2  Collections of Structures with Cycles

Many objects in our world are related to each other in a circular manner. We have parents; our parents have children. A computer may connect to another computer, which in turn may connect to the first. And we have seen data definitions that refer to each other.

Since data represents information about real-world objects, we will encounter situations that call for the design of a class of structures with a circular relationship. In the past, we have skirted the issue, or we used a trick to represent such collections. The trick is to use an indirection. For example, in section 28.1, we associated each structure with a symbol, kept a table of symbols and structures around, and placed symbols into structures. Then, when we needed to find out whether some structure refers to another, we extracted the relevant symbol and looked in the table to find the structure for the symbol. While this use of indirection allows us to represent structures with mutual references or structures in a cyclic relationship, it also leads to awkward data representations and programs. This section demonstrates that we can simplify the representation of collections with structure mutation.

To make this idea concrete, we discuss two examples: family trees and simple graphs. Consider the case of family trees. Thus far, we have used two kinds of family trees to record family relationships. The first is the ancestor tree; it relates people to their parents, grandparents, and so on. The second is the descendant tree; it relates people to their children, grandchildren, and so on. In other words, we have avoided the step of combining the two family trees into one, the way it is done in the real world. The reason for skirting the joint representation is also clear. Translated into our data language, a joint tree requires that a structure for a father should contain the structures for his children, and each of the child structures should contain the father structure. In the past, we couldn't create such collections of structures. With structure mutations, we can now create them.

Here is structure definition that makes this discussion concrete:

**(define-struct** *person* (*name social father mother children*)**)**

The goal is to create family trees that consist of *person* structures. A person structure has five fields. The content of each is specified by the following data definition:

---

An *family-tree-node* (short: *ftn*) is either

1. false or

2. a *person*.

A *person* is a structure:

(make-person *n s f m c*)

where *n* is a symbol, *s* is number, *f* and *m* are *ftn*s, and *c* is a (**listof** *person*).

---

As usual, the false in the definition of *family tree node*s represents missing information about a portion of the family tree.

Using make-person alone, we cannot establish the mutual reference between a family tree node for a father and his child. Suppose we follow an ancestral tree strategy, that is, we create the structure for the father first. Then we can't add any child to the *children* field, because, by assumption, the corresponding structure doesn't exist yet. Conversely, if we follow a descendant tree strategy, we first create a structure for all of a father's children, but those structures can't contain any information about the father yet.

---

The (relevant) tree after the creation of the structure for 'Ludwig:

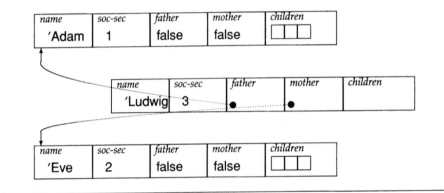

---

...and after the mutation of the structure for 'Adam and 'Eve:

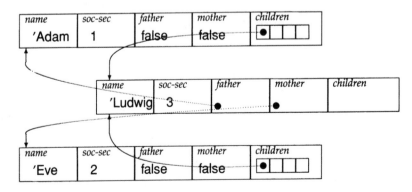

Figure 132: Adding a child

What this suggests is that a simple constructor for this kind of data isn't really enough. Instead, we should define a GENERALIZED CONSTRUCTOR that not only creates a *person* structure but also initializes it properly when possible. To develop this function, it is best to follow the real world, where upon the birth of a child, we create a new entry in the family tree, record the child's parents, and record in the existing parents' entries that they have a newborn. Here is the specification for just such a function:

;; *add-child!* : *symbol number person person* → *person*
;; to construct a *person* structure for a newborn
;; effect: to add the new structure to the children of *father* and *mother*
(**define** (*add-child! name soc-sec father mother*) ...)

Its task is to create a new structure for a newborn child and to add the structure to an existing family tree. The function consumes the child's name, social security number, and the structures representing the father and the mother.

The first step of the design of *add-child!* is to create the new structure for the child:

(**define** (*add-child! name soc-sec father mother*)
  (**local** ((**define** *the-child*
        (make-person *name soc-sec father mother* empty)))
    ...))

This covers the first part of the contract. By naming the structure in a **local**-expression we can mutate it in the body of the expression.

The second step of the design of *add-child!* is to add a body to the **local**-expression that performs the desired effects:

(**define** (*add-child! name soc-sec father mother*)
  (**local** ((**define** *the-child*
        (make-person *name soc-sec father mother* empty)))
    (**begin**
      (set-person-children! *father*
                  (cons *the-child* (person-children *father*)))
      (set-person-children! *mother*
                  (cons *the-child* (person-children *mother*)))
      *the-child*)))

Since there are two specified effects and since the purpose statement also specifies a result, the body of the **local**-expression is a **begin**-expression with three subexpressions. The first mutates *father*, adding *the-child* to the list of children. The second mutates *mother* in an analogous manner. The last one produces the desired result.

Figure 132 illustrates the evaluation of an application of *add-child!*:

```
(add-child! 'Ludwig 3
            (make-person 'Adam ... ... ...)
            (make-person 'Eve ... ... ...))
```

The top-half shows the new structure for 'Ludwig and how it refers to the *father* and *mother* structures. Just as in section 14.1, the picture uses arrows to relate the nodes of a family tree. But now this choice isn't just a convenience, it is dictated by necessity. As the bottom half of the figure shows, the structure mutation of *add-child!* modify the *children* fields of the *father* and *mother* structure. They add an additional item to the list in this field, and this new item is the structure for 'Ludwig. Without arrows, we wouldn't be able to draw this constellation of structures because it is impossible to draw the two structures as nested in each other.

With *add-child!* we can create family trees, one child at a time. What we need to learn is how to design functions that process this new class of family trees. In this case, we can almost always pick one of the two views that we used before: the ancestor family tree or the descendant family tree. Either view just ignores certain fields in the structures. Once we have chosen a view, we design the desired functions following the known recipes. Even if we decide to use the bi-directional relations in the new family tree representation, designing a function is usually simply a matter of formulating those auxiliary functions that correspond to the real-world family relationships and to compose them properly. The following few exercises demonstrate these principles.

## Exercises

**Exercise 43.2.1** Modify *add-child!* so that it has the following contract:

;; *add-child! : symbol number ftn ftn → person*

The function otherwise behaves just like the original version.

Once we have the modified function, there is no need for make-person any more. We can create all forms of *person* structures with *add-child!* directly.

Transliterate the family tree in figure 35 into the new representation; use the new modified *add-child!* function exclusively. ∎

**Exercise 43.2.2** Develop the function *how-many-ancestors*, which consumes a family tree node and determines how many ancestors there are. The node itself counts as an ancestor. ∎

**Exercise 43.2.3** Develop *how-many-descendants*, which consumes a family tree node and determines how many descendants there are. The node itself counts as a descendant. ∎

**Exercise 43.2.4** Develop *names-of-cousins*. The function consumes a *person* and produces the names of the cousins.
**Hints:** (1) Don't forget to use Scheme's built-in functions for processing lists. (2) Use a sufficiently large portion of your own family tree to test the functions. (3) For the testing step, compare the names of the results of the auxiliary functions with the expected results. Because the structures are mutually referential, it is difficult to compare them automatically. Alternatively, use eq?, Scheme's intensional equality predicate, to compare two structures. Why does this work? ∎

In sections 28.1 and 30.2, we encountered the problem of representing and traversing graphs. Recall that a graph is a collection of nodes and connections between nodes. The graph traversal problem is to determine whether there is a route from a node labeled *orig* to one called *dest*. In a simple graph, each node has exactly one one-way connection to another node.

Originally, we represented a graph as a list of named nodes. If one node was connected to another, the corresponding structure for the first node contained the name of the second node, not the node itself. Exercise 30.2.3 introduced a vector-based representation. Still, all of our representations used the indirection trick, so that if we wanted to move from one node to another, we first had to look up the connection in a table.

Using structure mutation, we can eliminate this indirection and create structures for nodes that contain each other, even if the graph contains a cycle. To understand how this works in a concrete manner, let's discuss how to model simple graphs such as those in figure 85 and how to design programs that find routes through such graphs. First, we need a structure definition for nodes:

```
(define-struct node (name to))
```

The *name* field records the name of the node, and the *to* field specifies to which other node it is connected. Second, we need a data definition:

---

A *simple-graph-node* (node) is a structure:
                        (make-node *n* *t*)
where *n* is a symbol and *t* is a *node*.

---

The data definition is unusual in that it is self-referential, but it doesn't consist of several clauses. This immediately raises the question of how we can construct a node that complies with this definition. Clearly, applying make-node doesn't work; instead, we need to define a generalized constructor that immediately sets the *to* field of a node.

The generalized constructor consumes the atomic data for a *node* structure and constructs a legal node structure from there:

```
;; create-node : symbol → node
;; to create a simple legal graph node with a-name in the name field
(define (create-node a-name)
  (local ((define the-node (make-node a-name false))) ... ))
```

The natural candidate to place into the *to* field is the node itself. In other words, the generalized constructor creates a node that contains itself:

```
;; create-node : symbol → node
;; to create a simple graph node that contains a-name and itself
(define (create-node a-name)
  (local ((define the-node (make-node a-name false)))
    (begin
      (set-node-to! the-node the-node)
      the-node)))
```

The generalized constructor makes the node using the ordinary constructor, initializing the *name* field properly and putting false into the *to* field. Although the latter is an improper action according to our data definition, it is acceptable because it is immediately corrected in the **local**-expression's body. Hence an application of *create-node* produces a *node* as promised.

With *create-node* we can create the nodes in a graph, but we can't establish the connections between them. To connect two nodes, we must modify the *to* field of one of the structures so that it contains the other. While this suggestion is generally on target, it raises the problem of how to identify the nodes. The family tree example suggests one solution, namely, to introduce one variable definition per node. Another comes from our orginal work with graphs, where we represented graphs as lists of symbolic pairs of connections or lists of nodes or vectors of nodes. Here we pursue the second option:

> A *simple-graph* is a (**listof** *node*).

Assuming we have a list of all nodes, say *the-graph,* and a function for looking up the node with a given name, say *lookup-node,* we can create a connection from one node to the other with a structure mutation:

(set-node-to! (*lookup-node from-name the-graph*)
              (*lookup-node to-name the-graph*))

We can make connecting two nodes more convenient than that with an auxiliary function:

;; *connect-nodes : symbol symbol graph → void*
;; effect: to mutate the *to* field in the structure with
;; *from-name* in the *name* field so that it contains
;; the structure with *to-name* in the *name* field
(**define** (*connect-nodes from-name to-name a-graph*)
  (set-node-to! (*lookup-node from-name a-graph*)
                (*lookup-node to-name a-graph*)))

Defining *lookup-node* is an exercise in structural function design, though it is best done using Scheme's **assf** function, which abstracts this situation.

Now we can transliterate simple graphs into a Scheme representation. Suppose we start with the graph in figure 85, which is reproduced here in a tabular format:

| *from* | A | B | C | D | E | F |
|---|---|---|---|---|---|---|
| *to* | B | C | E | E | B | F |

The first step is to create a list of all the nodes and to name it. The second step is to establish the connections according to this table. Figure 133 shows the corresponding Scheme expressions. They are straight transliterations of the columns in the tabular representation of the graph. There is no need to reconnect the 'F node because it is already connected to itself.

```
;; create-node : symbol → node
;; to create a simple graph node that contains itself
(define (create-node name)
   (local ((define the-node (make-node name false)))
      (begin
         (set-node-to! the-node the-node)
         the-node)))

;; connect-nodes : symbol symbol graph → void
;; effect: to mutate the to field in the structure named
;; from-name so that it contains the structure named to-name
(define (connect-nodes from-name to-name a-graph)
   (set-node-to! (lookup-node from-name a-graph)
                 (lookup-node to-name a-graph)))

;; lookup-node : symbol graph → node or false
;; to lookup up the node named x in a-graph
(define (lookup-node x a-graph)
   ...)

;; the-graph : graph
;; the list of all available nodes
(define the-graph
   (list (create-node 'A)
         (create-node 'B)
         (create-node 'C)
         (create-node 'D)
         (create-node 'E)
         (create-node 'F)))

;; setting up the graph:
(begin
   (connect-nodes 'A 'B the-graph)
   (connect-nodes 'B 'C the-graph)
   (connect-nodes 'C 'E the-graph)
   (connect-nodes 'D 'E the-graph)
   (connect-nodes 'E 'B the-graph))
```

Figure 133: Creating a simple graph via mutation

## Exercises

**Exercise 43.2.5** Draw a picture of (*create-node* 'A) using the boxes-in-boxes approach from part II and the boxes-and-arrow approach from part III. ∎

**Exercise 43.2.6** Transliterate the given simple graph without creating a list of all nodes. ∎

**Exercise 43.2.7** Develop the function *symbolic-graph-to-structures*. It consumes a list of pairs and creates a *graph*.
Example:

> (**define** *the-graph*
> (*symbolic-graph-to-structures* '((A B) (B C) (C E) (D E) (E B) (F F))))

Evaluating this definition is equivalent to evaluating the definitions in figure 133. ∎

Once we have a method for representing simple graphs, we can turn our attention to the problem of finding a route from one node in the graph to another. Recall the original specification from section 30.2:

> ;; *route-exists?* : *node node simple-graph* → *boolean*
> ;; to determine whether there is a route from *orig* to *dest* in *sg*
> (**define** (*route-exists? orig dest sg*) ...)

Of course, we must reinterpret the names for our data classes in the new context, but otherwise the specification is perfectly fine.

The development of the original function demonstrated two new ideas. First, the function uses generative recursion. Once it is known that *orig* and *dest* are distinct nodes, the search resumes from the node to which *orig* is connected. Second, the function requires an accumulator to remember which nodes have been visited. Without the accumulator, the function may revisit the same node over and over again.

So, let's start from the template for generative recursion:

> (**define** (*route-exists? orig dest sg*)
> (**cond**
> [(*eq-node? orig dest*) true]
> [**else**
> (*route-exists?* ... the node to which *orig* is connected ... *dest sg*)]))

The function *eq-node?* determines whether the two nodes are the same; this may just use eq?, Scheme's intentional equality predicate, or it may compare the names of the nodes, assuming they are unique. If the nodes are the same, a route exists. If not, we can generate a new, potentially useful problem by moving to the node to which *orig* is connected. In the graph representation of section 30.2, this requires looking in *sg*. In our new graph representation, the connection is a part of the *node* representation. Hence we can use node-to instead of looking in *sg*:

```
(define (route-exists? orig dest sg)
  (cond
    [(eq-node? orig dest) true]
    [else (route-exists? (node-to orig) dest sg)]))
```

The function definition shows that, so far, *sg* is useless. Because a node in the new graph representation contains its neighbors, and the neighbor contains its neighbor, and so on, there is no need to use the table.

The termination argument for this function fails, just as for the original one in section 30.2. To see why our new function may fail to terminate, take a look at its definition. It doesn't contain false, and the function cannot possibly produce false—even though we know that our sample graph, for example, doesn't contain a path from 'F to 'A or anywhere else. If we inspect what happens with

```
(route-exists? (lookup-node the-graph 'F)
               (lookup-node the-graph 'A))
```

we see that *route-exists?* repeatedly visits the node 'F. In short, it forgets what it has processed so far.

We know that equipping *route-exists?* with an accumulator overcomes this lack of knowledge, but that requires another table lookup. We can do better than that with a structure mutation that records a visit by the *route-exists?* function. To do that, the *node* structures need an addtional field; we call it *visited*:

```
(define-struct node (name visited to))
```

Initially the field contains false. As *route-exists?* visits a node, it puts true into the field:

```
(define (route-exists? orig dest sg)
  (cond
    [(eq-node? orig dest) true]
    [(node-visited orig) false]
    [else
      (begin
        (set-node-visited! orig true)
        (route-exists? (node-to orig) dest sg))]))
```

To exploit this new knowledge, the function checks the new structure field as one of the new termination conditions. If *orig* has been visited before, there is no route because the function has discovered a cycle in the graph.

The second structure mutation of this example illustrates two ideas. First, structure mutation can replace a table-based accumulator. In general, though, it is best to study a table-based version and to add structure mutations based on a solid understanding of the accumulated knowledge. Second, structure mutations can play a role in termination tests for generative recursion. After all, state change is motivated by the desire to remember things across function applications, and termination tests must discover whether things have changed. While the combination is rare, it is useful, and it appears time and again in the study of algorithms.

## Exercises

**Exercise 43.2.8** The function *route-exists?* assumes that the *visited* fields of all the nodes are initially false. A single use of the function, however, sets some of the fields in a graph to true. This implies that the function cannot be used twice in a row.

Develop a revised version of *route-exists?*, with the same specification, that sets all *visited* fields to false before it searches for a route between the given nodes.

Determine the abstract running time of the new function, assuming the graph has $N$ nodes. ∎

**Exercise 43.2.9** Develop the function *reachable*. It consumes a node in a simple graph. Its effect is to place true into the *visited* fields of all those nodes that are reachable from the given node and to ensure that the *visited* fields of all other nodes are false. ∎

**Exercise 43.2.10** Develop *make-simple-graph,* a function that manages the
state of a **locally** defined graph. The function accepts a simple graph in
the form of lists of pairs of symbols: (**listof** (list *symbol symbol*)). It supports
four services:

1. adding nodes that are connected to already existing nodes (by name);

2. changing the connection of a node (by name);

3. determining whether a route between two nodes exists;

4. and removing nodes that are not reachable from some given node.

**Hint:** Instead of using a list, the manager should use a node sequence,
which is analogous to the *hand* structure from section 41.3. A node sequence relies on the following structure:

   (**define-struct** *sequence* (*node next*))

A sequence is similar to a list, but it supports structure mutations. ∎

The discussion of this section confirms the usefulness of the design
recipes, even for collections of structures that refer to each other. The most
important lesson is that such situations call for a generalized constructor, a
function that creates a structure and immediately establishes the necessary
connections. Generalized constructors correspond to the initializers of section 35; we have also seen the idea in section 41.3 where we created a hand
from a single card. In some cases, such as the one for simple graphs, we
may also want to introduce auxiliary functions for mutating the structures
a second time. Once we have those functions, we can use the standard
recipes, including those for introducing additional structure fields.

## 43.3 Backtracking with State

Section 28 introduced algorithms that backtrack. An algorithm is a recursive function that generates new problems for the recursive step rather than
using the pieces of its input data. On occasion, an algorithm may have to
make choices among several branches on the path to a solution. Some of
them may lead nowhere. In such cases, an algorithm can backtrack. That
is, it can restart the search for a solution with a different branch to check if
it succeeds.

When the data representation for a problem uses structures or vectors, a backtracking algorithm can use structure mutation to test different approaches to a solution. The key is to design a pair of functions that change the state of the problem representation and that undo such a change in case the attempt fails. In this section, we discuss two examples of this kind: the Queens puzzle and the Peg Solitaire problem.

Recall the Queens puzzle from section 28.2. The goal of the puzzle is to place $n$ queens on some board of arbitrary size $m$-by-$m$ such that the queens do not threaten each other. A queen in chess threatens all places on the row, the column, and the two diagonals going through her own position. Figure 79 illustrates the notion with a single queen on an 8-by-8 board.

In section 28.2, we represented chessboards with lists. When we got to know vectors, we also developed a vector-based representation in exercise 29.3.14, as follows:

```
;; A chess-board CB is a (vectorof (vectorof boolean))
;; such that all vectors have the same size.
```

```
;; make-chess-board : N → CB
(define (make-chess-board m)
  (build-vector m (lambda (i) (build-vector m (lambda (j) true)))))
```

The initial value of true indicates that it is still legitimate to place a queen on the corresponding field.

The queen-placement algorithm places a queen on one of the available fields on the given board and creates a new board that reflects the addition of the queen. This step is repeated until there are no more queens to be placed, in which case the puzzle is solved, or until there are no more places to choose from. In the second case, the algorithm backtracks. That is, the algorithm removes the last queen that was added and chooses some other available field. If there are no more fields, it backtracks further. The algorithm signals a complete failure when it becomes impossible to backtrack.

On one hand, creating a new board at each stage is acceptable because the chosen field may turn out to be the wrong one in which case the old board is the starting point for the next step. On the other hand, a human player is more likely to place the queen on the board and to remove it if the position turns out to be a bad choice. Thus the Queens problem is an example of where the ability of computer programs to create many alternative "worlds" clashes with the human world, which offers extremely limited possibilities of this kind[78] and thus restricts human imagination. Still, it is worth exploring how the addition of vector mutation to our vocablulary enables us to mimic the actions of a human player more closely than before.

## Exercises

**Exercise 43.3.1** Placing an additional queen on a chessboard means that some of the fields on the chessboard have to be set to false because they are now threatened and no longer available for future placements of queens. The placement of a queen is a function of the given chessboard and the indices of the new queen:

;; *place-queen : CB* **N N** → *void*
;; effect: to set those fields in *CB* to false that are threatened by
;; a queen on row *i*, column *j*
(**define** (*place-queen CB i j*) ... ))

**Hints:** (1) Recall *threatened?* from exercise 28.2.3. (2) Consider developing an abstract function for processing all items on a board. The function is analogous to *vec-for-all* from exercise 41.2.17. ∎

**Exercise 43.3.2** Develop *unplace-queen*. The function removes a queen and its threats from a chessboard:

;; *unplace-queen : CB* **N N** → *void*
;; effect: to set those fields in *CB* to false that were threatened by
;; a queen on row *i*, column *j*
(**define** (*unplace-queen CB i j*) ... ))

Given any chessboard *CB*, the following equation holds:

$$
\begin{aligned}
&(\textbf{begin} \\
&\quad (place\text{-}queen\ CB\ i\ j) \\
&\quad (unplace\text{-}queen\ CB\ i\ j) \\
&\quad CB) \\
&= CB
\end{aligned}
$$

for all legal positios *i* and *j*. Why is this not true if we swap the first two subexpressions? ∎

---

[78] A program could set up an entirely new board for every new stage in the algorithm and search for solutions in parallel. The additional work is, however, prohibitive for a human being, which is why humans shy away from such simulations.

**Exercise 43.3.3** Modify the solution of the Queens problem in section 28.2 to use the vector-based representation of chessboards and the functions *place-queen* and *unplace-queen* from exercises 43.3.1 and 43.3.2. ∎

**Exercise 43.3.4** Use the **draw.ss** teachpack to develop a view for the Queens problem. Recall that a view is a function that illustrates certain aspects of a problem in a graphical manner. The natural solution here is to display the intermediate stages of the solution process according to the algorithm of exercise 43.3.3, including the backtracking steps. ∎

In section 32.3 we discussed the Peg Solitaire problem. The goal of the game is to eliminate the pegs one by one, until only one peg is left. A player can eliminate a peg if one of the neighboring holes is unoccupied and if there is a peg in the hole in the opposite direction. In that case, the second peg can jump over the first one and the first one is eliminated.

Just as with the Queens puzzle, we can represent the problem state with vectors and indicators for pegs and holes. In the real world, moving a peg corresponds to a physical action that changes the state of the board. When a player backtracks, the two pegs are placed back in their original positions.

## Exercises

**Exercise 43.3.5** Design a vector representation for the triangular peg solitaire board. Develop a function for creating a board with a single hole. ∎

**Exercise 43.3.6** Design a data representation for a move in the Peg Solitaire problem. Develop a function for making a move. Develop a function for undoing a move. The two functions should rely exclusively on effects. Do the functions satisfy an equation analogous to *place-queen* and *unplace-queen* in exercise 43.3.2? ∎

**Exercise 43.3.7** Develop a backtracking algorithm for solving a Peg Solitaire problem whose hole is placed randomly. ∎

**Exercise 43.3.8** Use the **draw.ss** teachpack to develop a view for the Peg Solitaire problem. Recall that a view is a function that illustrates certain aspects of a problem in a graphical manner. The natural solution here is to display the intermediate stages of the solution process according to the algorithm of exercise 43.3.7, including the backtracking steps. ∎

# Epilogue

ROS: *I mean, what exactly do you* do?
PLAYER: *We keep to our usual stuff, more or less, only inside out. We do on stage things that are supposed to happen off. Which is a kind of integrity, if you look on every exit as being an entrance somewhere else.*

—Tom Stoppard, *Rosencrantz and Guildenstern are Dead*

We have reached the end of this introduction to computing and program design. While there is more to learn about both subjects, this is a good point to stop, to summarize, and to look ahead.

## Computing

From elementary school to high school we learn to compute with one form of data: numbers. Our first use of numbers is to count real things, say, three apples, five friends, twelve bagels. Later we use numbers without any appeal to concrete objects, but we have learned that numbers represent information in the real world.

Computing with software is *algebra for all kinds of data*, not just numbers. Nowadays, computer programs process representations of music, molecules, law cases, electrical diagrams, architectures of houses, and poems. Fortunately, we have learned to represent information with other forms of data than just numbers. Otherwise, computing and programming would become extremely tedious tasks.

Above all, we shouldn't forget that computing means manipulating data through proper basic operations. Some operations create new values. Others extract values from values. Yet others modify values. Finally, there are also basic operations for determining to which class a piece of data belongs. Built-in operations and functions are of course just another class of data. Definition is value creation; application is a form of value extraction.[79]

When we define a function, we combine basic data operations. There are two fundamental mechanisms for combining functions: function composition and conditional expressions. The former means that the result of one function becomes the argument of another one. The latter represents a choice among several possibilities. When we eventually apply a function, we trigger a computation.

In this book we have studied the laws of basic operations and the laws of operation combination. Using these laws we can understand, in principle, how any function processes its input data and how it produces its results and effects. Because the computer is extremely fast and good at using these laws, it can perform such evaluations for more data and for larger programs than we can do with paper and pencil.

## Programming

Programs consist of definitions and expressions. Large programs consist of hundreds and thousands of definitions and expressions. Programmers design functions, use other programmer's functions, leave, start on the project. Without a strong discipline we cannot hope to produce software of high quality. The key to programming discipline is to understand the design of programs as a means to describe computations, which, in turn, is to manipulate data through combinations of basic operations.

For that reason, the design of every program—whether it is small and for personal use or large and for business use—must start with an analysis of the surrounding world of information and a description of the classes of data that represent the relevant information. If the classes are unusual or new, we make up examples so we understand the structure of the class description. After we understand the world of information surrounding our project and its data representation, we make a plan.

A project plan identifies what data we wish to produce from the data that the program will be given. In many cases, though, a program doesn't process data in just one way but in many ways. For example, a program for managing bank accounts must handle deposits, withdrawals, interest calculations, tax form generation, and many other tasks. In other cases, a

---

[79] An object in a language such as Java is a function with many different bodies. Each method represents a different way of extracting data from an object.

program may have to compute complex relationships. For example, a program for simulating a ping-pong game must compute the movement of the ball, bounces on the table, bounces from the paddle, paddle movements, etc. In either case, we need to describe what the various ways of processing data are and how they relate to each other. Then we rank them and start with the most important one. We develop a working product, make sure that it meets our specifications, and refine the product by adding more functions or taking care of more cases or both.

Designing a function requires a rigorous understanding of what it computes. Unless we can describe its purpose and its effect with concise statements, we can't produce the function. In almost all cases, it helps to make up examples and work through the function's computation by hand. For complicated functions or for functions that use generative recursion, we should include some examples with the purpose statements. The examples illustrate the purpose and effect statements for others who may have to read or modify the program.

Studying examples tends to suggest the basic design recipe. In most cases, the design of a function is structural, even if it uses an accumulator or structure mutation. In a few others, we must use generative recursion. For these cases, it is important to explain the method for generating new problems and to sketch why the computation terminates.

When the definition is complete, we must test the function. Testing discovers mistakes, which we are bound to make due to all kinds of reasons. The best testing process turns independently developed examples into test suites, that is, a bunch of expressions that apply the function to select input examples and compare its results and effects with expected results and effects (mostly) automatically. If a mismatch is discovered, the test suite reports a problem. The test suite should never be discarded, only commented out. Every time we modify the function, we must use the test suite to check that we didn't introduce mistakes. If we changed the underlying process, we may have to adapt the test suite mutatis mutandis.

No matter how hard we work, a function (or program) isn't done the first time it works for our test suite. We must consider whether the development of the function revealed new interesting examples and turn such examples into additional tests. And we must edit the program. In particular, we must use abstraction properly to eliminate all patterns wherever possible.

If we respect these guidelines, we will produce decent software. It will work because we understand why and how it works. Others who must modify or enhance this software will understand it, because we include sufficient information on its development process. Still, to produce great software, we must practice following these guidelines and also learn a lot more about computing and programming than a first book can teach.

## Moving On

The knowledge and design skills from this book are a good foundation for learning more about programming, computing, and even practical work on software. First, the skills are good for learning the currently fashionable collection of object-oriented languages, especially Java. The two languages share a philosophy of programming. In both settings, computing means dealing with data, and programming means describing classes of values and functions on them. Unlike Scheme, however, Java requires programmers to spell out the class descriptions in Java, not just in English, and to place function definitions with class descriptions. As a result, Java requires programmers to learn a lot of syntactic conventions and is unsuitable as a first language.

Second, a programmer must study the fundamental ideas of computing. Thus far, our studies have focused on the laws of computing for data-oriented programming languages. Using the programming skills from this book, we can design and implement a simulation of how the hardware computes. By doing so we see the laws of computing from a radically different perspective. The contrast points to a number of interesting questions:

1. The two mechanisms of computing are rather different. Can one mechanism compute what the other one can compute and vice versa?

2. The laws we have used are mathematical and abstract. They do not take into account any real-world limitations. Does this mean that we can compute whatever we wish?

3. The (simulated) hardware shows that computers have limitations. How do these limitations affect what we can compute?

**Full Scheme**

Research on these questions created the discipline of computing and still guides the design of most computing curricula.

Finally, the design knowledge of this book is enough to build some real-world programs in Scheme. DrScheme with its built-in Web browser and email capabilities is such a program. Building large real-world programs, however, requires some more knowledge about the functions that Scheme uses to create GUIs, to connect computers on a network, to script things such as shells, common gateway interfaces (CGI), COM objects, and so on.

Material on all three topics is available from this book's Web site in a form that extends the coverage and the style of the book. The book's Web site is

```
http://www.htdp.org/
```

Check in with this site on a regular basis and continue to study computing and programming.

# Index